AF352727

The Trinity in History
A Theology of the Divine Missions

ROBERT M. DORAN

The Trinity in History

A Theology of the Divine Missions

VOLUME 1: MISSIONS AND PROCESSIONS

UNIVERSITY OF TORONTO PRESS
Toronto Buffalo London

© University of Toronto Press Incorporated 2012
 Toronto Buffalo London
 www.utppublishing.com
 ISBN 978-1-4426-4594-3

Lonergan Studies

Library and Archives Canada Cataloguing in Publication

Doran, Robert M., 1939–
The Trinity in history. Volume 1: missions and processions
/ Robert M. Doran

Includes bibliographical references and index.
ISBN 978-1-4426-4594-3
1. Theology, Doctrinal. 2. Trinity. 3. Lonergan, Bernard J.F. (Bernard
Joseph Francis), 1904–1984. I. Title. II. Series: Lonergan studies.

BT75.3.D668 2012   230   C2012-903073-2

This book has been published with the help of a grant from the Canadian
Federation for the Humanities and Social Sciences, through the Aid to
Scholarly Publications Program, using funds provided by the Social Sciences
and Humanities Research Council of Canada.

University of Toronto Press acknowledges the financial assistance to its publishing program of the Canada Council for the Arts and the Ontario Arts
Council.

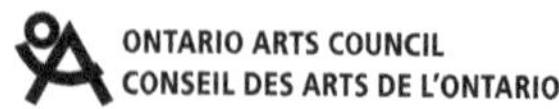

University of Toronto Press acknowledges the financial support for its publishing activities of the Government of Canada through the Book Publishing
Industry Development Program (BPIDP).

Contents

Introduction / ix

PART ONE:
CONSTRUCTING A NEW CATHOLIC SYSTEMATIC THEOLOGY:
A VISION AND AN INVITATION

1 A Catholic Systematic Theology on the Level of Our Time / 5
  1 Interiority, History, and Religion / 6
  2 The Dogmatic-Theological Context / 11
  3 The Role of History / 14

2 The Immanent Constitution of Life in God / 17
  1 The Specifically Theological Dimension of the
    Starting Point / 17
    1.1 The Basic Hypothesis / 18
    1.2 1951–52 Notes on Sanctifying Grace / 19
      1.2.1 The Biblical Basis for the Notion of
           Sanctifying Grace / 20
      1.2.2 The Father Loves Us as He Loves the Son / 24
      1.2.3 The Gift of the Holy Spirit / 29
      1.2.4 Gift and Mission / 30
      1.2.5 Created and Uncreated Grace / 30
    1.3 Grace and the Invisible Mission of the Son / 32
  2 The Analogy of Grace / 33
    2.1 Contrast with Lonergan's Later Trinitarian Analogy / 35

3 Contingent Predication and the Divine Missions / 40
   1 Contingent Predication / 41
   2 The Notion of Formal Effects / 57

4 The Order of the Divine Missions / 65
   1 Lonergan's Early Position / 67
   2 Frederick Crowe's Interpretation of Lonergan's
      Later Position / 71
   3 Theological Doctrines regarding the Divine Missions / 77

5 Social Grace and the Mission of the Word / 83
   1 Transposing the Reign of God / 83
   2 The Invisible and Visible Missions of the Divine Word / 86
      2.1 The Invisible Mission of the Word and the Notion of
           Social Grace / 87
           2.1.1 The Peculiarity of History / 88
           2.1.2 Articulate Cultural Values and Social Grace / 89
      2.2 The Visible Mission of the Word and the Notion of
           Social Grace / 92
           2.2.1 Revelation and the Visible Mission of the Word / 93
           2.2.2 The Reign of God and the Visible Mission of
                  the Word / 96
   3 Filling Out the Social Dimensions of Grace / 98

6 Functional Specialties for a World Theology / 108
   1 The Methodological Meaning of "System" / 108
   2 Nine Functional or Operational Specialties / 111
   3 Expanding the Reach of Theological Functional
      Specialties / 123
   4 Levels of Consciousness / 125

PART TWO: MISSIONS AND PROCESSIONS

7 The Starting Point / 135
   1 The Four-point Hypothesis: Its Significance and
      Limitations / 135
      1.1 The Hypothesis / 135
      1.2 The Place of the Four-point Hypothesis in a
           Unified Field Structure for Systematics / 138
   2 Two Requirements / 142
      2.1 Interiorly and Religiously Differentiated
           Consciousness / 142

2.1.1 Intentional and Nonintentional Components to
Theological Foundations / 143
2.1.2 The Psychological Analogy / 145
2.1.3 Religiously Differentiated Consciousness / 150
2.1.4 Lonergan's Earlier and Later Analogies and
the Times of Election / 153
2.2 History / 162
3 The Character of the Starting Point / 165
4 Theological Development / 168
5 Conclusion / 175

8 **Autonomous Spiritual Processions** / 176
1 Introduction / 176
2 The Fundamental Issue of a Systematics of the Trinity / 178
2.1 Lonergan's Statement / 178
2.2 Comment / 180
2.3 Further on Lonergan's Statement / 180
2.4 Comment / 181
2.5 Lonergan's Position Resumed / 182
2.6 Comment / 183
3 Autonomous Spiritual Processions / 183
4 Insight and Language / 187
5 What Is Autonomous Spiritual Procession? / 190

9 **The Dialectic of Desire** / 196
1 Desire and the Varieties of Procession / 196
2 Varieties of Imitation / 211
3 *Imago Dei* / 218

10 **Sacralization and Desacralization in History** / 227
1 Introduction / 227
2 The Law of the Cross / 231
2.1 A New Community / 231
2.2 The Evils to Be Transformed / 234
2.3 The Structure of the Law of the Cross / 236
3 Terms, Issue, Criteria / 240
4 The Context of Lonergan's Discussion / 245
5 Girard's Contribution to Clarifying the Context / 248
6 A Debate / 248
7 Complementary Solutions / 251
7.1 Progressive Biblical Revelation / 251
8 Summary / 257

11 **Lonergan's Early Analogy** / 259
  1 *Per Modum Operati* and Theological Understanding / 263
  2 The Hypothesis / 278
  3 The Only Hypothesis? / 286
  4 Two Processions / 291
    4.1 Terminology / 292
    4.2 Lonergan's Argument for the Second Assertion / 299
    4.3 Generation and Spiration / 300
      4.3.1 Generation / 300
      4.3.2 The Divine Nature as Intellectual / 301
      4.3.3 Emanation of Word and Emanation of Love / 304
      4.3.4 The Argument / 307
      4.3.5 Resolving a Problem / 307

12 **Enriching the Context** / 310
  1 The Rule of the Kingdom and the Emergence of
     Genuine Autonomy / 310
  2 Returning to Lonergan's Text: Four Questions / 316
    2.1 Understanding and Word / 316
    2.2 Can We Demonstrate That There Is a Word in God? / 328
    2.3 Does the Word Proceed from the Father's Understanding
         of Creatures? / 336
    2.4 The Presence of the Beloved within the Lover:
         Is It Constituted or Produced by Love? / 340
      2.4.1 The Treatment in *De Deo Trino* / 340
      2.4.2 "Nihil Amatum Nisi Praecognitum":
             Is This True? / 344

Index / 403

Introduction

This is the first book-length installment on my part to contribute to constructing a contemporary systematic theology. For a number of years I have been attempting in articles and lectures to retrieve from Bernard Lonergan's trinitarian systematics a four-point hypothesis linking four created realities in the order of grace with the four divine relations, to unpack the meaning of this hypothesis, and to transpose that meaning into the categories of a methodical systematic theology, enabling it to take a place at the very beginning of such a theology.

Up to 1990, when *Theology and the Dialectics of History* was published,[1] I was engaged principally in what Lonergan calls the functional specialty of Foundations. My first venture into systematics properly so-called was the article "Consciousness and Grace," published in METHOD: *Journal of Lonergan Studies* in 1993.[2] I revised this essay in 2009 by adding new footnotes, and uploaded it to the website www.loneranresource.com, and in footnote 3 of the revised essay indicated that the four-point hypothesis was "only barely contemplated" as a starting point for systematic theology at the time this article was written. But the hypothesis came into prominence for me fairly quickly after that article, as is evident from its appearance at the very beginning of the second article that I wrote in systematics, notably entitled "Revisiting 'Consciousness and Grace.'"[3] It is safe to say that the hypothesis has remained the center of my efforts to do systematics ever since, and so from 1994 to the present, even as my understanding both of what it meant for Lonergan himself and of its implications and potentialities for transposition continue to develop.

The hypothesis is presented in the chapter on the divine missions in *The Triune God: Systematics*, which is the Collected Works version of the 1964 *De Deo Trino: Pars Systematica*.[4] It had appeared in a 1957 publication, *Divinarum*

Personarum,[5] Lonergan's earlier rendition of his trinitarian systematics, and even earlier in an unpublished form in his 1951–52 notes on sanctifying grace, which are being published for the first time in volume 19 of the Collected Works, *Early Latin Theology*.[6] The hypothesis links four created supernatural realities with the four divine relations that were subjected to systematic understanding in the earlier chapters of the trinitarian systematics. And so it articulates a hypothesis about how it can be that the very life of the triune God is communicated to human beings.

The text that follows includes the most substantial account of the hypothesis that I have been able to produce to date. My own original work in the area of the hypothesis has centered on two parts of it, namely, that "sanctifying grace is a created participation of active spiration, and so has a special relation to the Holy Spirit; and the habit of charity is a created participation of passive spiration, and so has a special relation to the Father and the Son." What has been called sanctifying grace is thus the created base of a created relation to the uncreated Holy Spirit, and as the base of a relation to the Holy Spirit it shares in the eternal divine relation to the Holy Spirit, which is the Father and the Son breathing the Holy Spirit in active spiration. Again, charity is spirated by sanctifying grace and as such is the created base of a created relation to the uncreated Father and Son, and as such shares in the eternal uncreated relation to the Father and the Son that is the Holy Spirit, passive spiration.

Elaboration of this set of connections is the very heart of the theology that is offered here. I argue in the second chapter that to understand these two statements is to provide the immanent constitution of life in God. Further chapters in this book argue that unpacking these two statements provides another version of the basic psychological analogy for understanding the trinitarian processions, in the same line and tradition as the versions provided by Augustine, Aquinas, and the early and later Lonergan. I then develop the implications in terms of a universal mission of the Holy Spirit, with all the possibilities of interreligious dialogue and cooperation that this opens up for Christians. I suggest several refinements on Lonergan's notion of functional specialties, in order to promote the possibility that Christians will expand their horizons to a world theology that takes into consideration, in the limit, all the data of human religious living in every time and place. I spend a good deal of time linking Lonergan's philosophical and theological developments to the mimetic theory of René Girard, whose significance for theology, in my estimation, is enormous.

The starting point in the analogy that I am proposing is also what Augustine called *memoria*, understood in Heideggerian terms as the *Befindlichkeit*, the state of mind, the disposition that accumulates in a subject appropriating his or her entire life, the summation of that life as being on the receiving end of unqualified love, with all of this grasped in a reflective act of evaluative insight that grounds the emergence of an ineffable judgment of value. These two together – *memoria* providing the data for a supernatural evaluative insight, and the "yes" that flows from that grasp and that *is* the faith that Lonergan describes as the knowledge born of religious love – constitute our participation in active spiration. They name in categories that appeal to consciously locatable realities what a metaphysical theology calls sanctifying grace. From *memoria* and faith thus understood there emanates, proceeds, charity, as the love of God in return. And so, as in the Trinity from active spiration there emanates the passively spirated proceeding Love that is the Holy Spirit, so in the graced analogue, from the participation in active spiration there emanates the charity that constitutes our participation in the Holy Spirit and that relates us back, as it were, to the Son in companionship if we know the revelation of God in Christ Jesus and to the divine Word in love of wisdom even if we do not know that revelation, and also to the Father in hope of eternal life and beatific knowing and loving.

All of this is worked out over some 400 pages in a theology of the divine missions, and especially of the mission of the Holy Spirit, and applied to a number of contemporary philosophical and theological issues. That theology also emphasizes that the knowledge born of religious love, the faith that constitutes the word emanating from the gift of God's love, the ineffable judgment of value that proceeds from the gift, is a created participation in the eternal Word, and so represents the external term of the invisible mission of the divine Word. I make a number of suggestions concerning the word that proceeds once one has accepted, either explicitly or implicitly, being gifted with a share in that invisible mission. The *visible* mission of the divine Word is also treated in the book. My emphasis, though, is on the mission and gift of the Holy Spirit, and I insist that the gift of the Holy Spirit is universal. Here I follow Frederick E. Crowe's great paper "Son of God, Holy Spirit, and World Religions,"[7] which I think should ground the work of Lonergan scholars in systematic theology well into the twenty-first century. If Crowe is right, his thesis changes the parameters of systematic theology in a radical fashion, so that systematics begins with that portion of the four-point hypothesis that speaks of participations in active and passive spiration as universally accessible realities. And so the mission of the divine Word is understood as the definitive revelation of God's love that already has been poured into human hearts everywhere and from the beginning.

The four-point hypothesis constitutes what I am calling the contemporary dogmatic-theological context for doing systematic theology. And the same hypothesis is one of two parts in what I am calling the unified field structure for systematics. Systematics has to start somewhere, and following Lonergan it has to follow the order of teaching, as opposed to the order of discovery. In the order of teaching its starting point, on a macro level, would treat the Trinity, the gift of the Holy Spirit, the Incarnation, and the promise of beatific knowing and loving in eternal life, and, I propose, would do so in that order. These are the absolutely supernatural realities in which God is attained as God is in God's own triune being. They have already received firm and clear doctrinal status in the church's own development of its constitutive meaning: the Trinity with the "consubstantial" of Nicea, the Incarnation with the "one and the same" of Chalcedon, the gift of the Holy Spirit with the medieval theorem of the supernatural, and the promise of eternal life with the original message itself, located by Lonergan in 1 Corinthians 15.3–5, with its proclamation of the resurrection and the promise of eternal life. The elaboration of these four central Christian mysteries constitutes, in my view, the dogmatic-theological context for the future development of systematics, whose task it is, in its attempts to understand the church's constitutive meaning, to inch the church toward an equally firm dogmatic-theological framework for such matters as revelation, original sin, redemption, creation, the church, and the very large category of praxis, which includes not only the reorientation of commonsense living in harmony with an integral scale of values but also the interdisciplinary collaboration that would head toward reoriented human science and a new formulation of philosophy's contribution to the articulation of foundational reality. In other words, the dogmatic-theological context will expand as systematics does its work.

The four-point hypothesis is systematic in that it integrates the doctrines about absolutely supernatural reality and the self-communication of the triune God that constitute the dogmatic-theological context – the Trinity, Christology, grace, and beatific knowing and loving – in one systematic formulation. It is as such, as doing this, that it provides the dogmatic-theological context for the rest of systematics. But in addition to the dogmatic-theological context there is what I have called the unified field structure. I borrow the term from Daniel Monsour, my long-term colleague in editing Lonergan's Collected Works, but I have developed my own suggestion for precisely what such a structure would be.

What do I mean by the unified field structure? Aquinas's master edifice was the result not only of his biblical commentaries and Philip the Chancellor's theorem of the supernatural – these gave him only the special categories in his theology – but also of his appropriation of Aristotle's metaphysics and by extension of Aristotle's psychology, ethics, and even physics. Because he brought these general categories into systematic integration with the transformative realities expressed in the special categories, he transformed Aristotle into the systematic *Begrifflichkeit* that could provide the integration that made his own theology systematic. His unified field structure, if you will, was a function of the combined power of the theorem of the supernatural and his appropriation of Aristotle. I am suggesting that it is entirely continuous with Aquinas that a contemporary unified field structure for systematics be composed of the four-point hypothesis, which differentiates the theorem of the supernatural, and what Lonergan calls the *Grund- und Gesamtwissenschaft*, the total and basic science, which represents the culmination to date of the effective history of Thomas's Aristotelianism: namely, Lonergan's own cognitional theory, epistemology, metaphysics, and existential ethics. I have also suggested that this general-categorial component to the unified field structure be further specified by bringing Lonergan's total and basic science to bear on the construction of a theory of history, so that systematics may take as its mediated object precisely what Lonergan at the time of his breakthrough to functional specialization said it should take as its mediated object, namely, *Geschichte*, the history that is lived and written about. So the four-point hypothesis and a theory of history based in Lonergan's fundamental achievement would constitute the unified field structure for a contemporary systematic theology.

This unified field structure is not fixed for all time any more than Aquinas's corresponding structure was fixed. Both components will develop. The special-categorial domain in the realm of the supernatural will unfold as secure achievements in understanding revelation, sin, redemption, creation, the church, praxis, and so on, go forward. And the general-categorial domain in the realm of history will unfold as the human sciences, including economics, are reoriented and incorporated into that part of the unified field structure of systematics that constitutes a theory of history. The scale of values frames that theory of history, and the four-point hypothesis, especially insofar as it names the immanent constitution of life in God, constitutes the realm of "religious values" in that understanding of history. Fidelity to the work of participating in the invisible mission of the divine Word will enable the systematics of history to develop its understanding of the other levels of value – personal, cultural, social, and vital – in an ongoing mediation between an increasingly global cultural matrix and the significance and role of religious living in that matrix.

Such is the overall vision. The present volume, which focuses on divine mission and procession, only begins to articulate its contours, focusing almost exclusively on the relation between religious and personal values. A second volume, which will treat divine mission in connection with the divine relations and persons, will expand the consideration of the Trinity in history, social grace, with the realms of cultural and social values. The present volume is centered on the universal mission of the Holy Spirit. Far more consideration will be given in the second volume to the mission of the Word, visible and invisible.

A final concern that should be mentioned in this introduction is my hope that this volume will encourage readers to tackle the magnificent trinitarian theology of Bernard Lonergan, both in its doctrinal and in its systematic portions.[8] It is my belief and hope that Lonergan will someday be named a Doctor of the Church. Be that as it may, without his work on the Trinity, which brings forward the trinitarian theology of Aquinas but on the basis of a far more detailed appropriation than appears in Thomas of the analogue in human rational consciousness for the divine processions, not a page of the present book could have been written.

I must say a word about the form of presentation, namely, the use of theses. I am retrieving a certain kind of systematic theological form, which I think works and is needed. The theology presented here is obviously not neo-Scholastic, but the book does retrieve an important form of exposition from that tradition, a form which, when properly employed, assists a work in being strictly systematic. I am not presenting narrative theology, nor am I offering a history of theological viewpoints or a review of the important literature on the topics I am treating. All of these are valuable tasks. They are not systematic theology. Systematic theology is explanatory exposition in direct discourse on the level of one's own time. It is a distinct functional specialty. The thesis format, in my view, helps maintain the distinct focus of systematics. I did not start the book with that format in mind. It emerged as I was writing, and I slowly became convinced that it was an efficient manner of providing a systematic organization to what I was attempting to say.

Readers will no doubt want more explicit connections than I have provided to other figures in the contemporary systematic-theological scene. But I have found that students with different interests are quite capable of providing these on their own. As Lonergan begged his readers at the beginning of *Method in Theology* "not to be scandalized because I quote scripture, the ecumenical councils, papal encyclicals, other theologians so rarely and sparingly," because he was doing method, not theology, so I have to ask that readers allow the systematic task to stand on its own and that they make their own connections to other theologians and theological emphases.

Thanks are owed to many people. I can mention only a few. I tested this manuscript on a doctoral seminar at Marquette University during the spring semester of 2011, and the superb students in that seminar encouraged me to believe that it was just about ready to see the light of day: Juliana Vazquez, Chris Hadley, s.j., Rick Barry, Raymond Foyer, Jeremy Blackwood, John Volk, and Ben Suriano. I thank them for their encouragement and suggestions for the final version.

Since 2001, first at the Lonergan Research Institute in Toronto and then under the auspices of Marquette University, Greg Lauzon has provided me not only with very supportive friendship but also with an enormous amount of technical assistance in every aspect of my efforts to keep the Lonergan legacy alive, thriving, and growing. The best decision I ever made in the Lonergan portion of my work and life has been to hire Greg, and I got to do it twice!

Dr John D. Dadosky of Regis College, Toronto, is a superb colleague and friend and a very creative theologian whose mind moves along many of the same tracks as my own and who has been present as friend and interlocutor through thick and thin over a substantial number of years.

I wish to conclude by thanking the Rev. Robert A. Wild, s.j., president of Marquette University from 1996 to 2011, for the help that he provided me and Greg Lauzon in funding the establishment of a Marquette Lonergan Project. Due to Fr Wild's help and support, we have been provided with everything we need to get our work done.

The Trinity in History

A Theology of the Divine Missions

Constructing a New Catholic Systematic Theology: A Vision and an Invitation

1

A Catholic Systematic Theology on the Level of Our Time[1]

The subtitle of the first part of this book speaks of "a vision and an invitation." I speak of a vision, and I will present in this first part some of the principal emphases to be developed in the work that follows both in this book and in hoped-for subsequent volumes, where I attempt to contribute to a new Catholic systematic theology for our time. But I speak as well of an invitation, because, in the last analysis, such a theology must be a collaborative enterprise, the work of a community of people building on common or complementary foundations, employing common or complementary methods, and sharing common or complementary presuppositions as to what systematic theology is and what is needed to move it forward. Within those parameters there must be acknowledged what Bernard Lonergan has called a legitimate and permanent pluralism of theologies.[2] The chapters of this book are envisioned as the beginning of one particular line of contemporary systematic theology that, while it is in continuity with permanent dogmatic and theological achievements in the tradition of Western Catholic thought, also moves beyond them on selected points.

These chapters are also an invitation to others to join in the collaboration that alone will carry that tradition forward, advance it in response to the exigencies of our time, and bring it into dialogical contact with other theological trajectories. Like any other contemporary science, systematic theology resides, not in an individual mind, but in a community.

As far as the vision is concerned, this part of the book develops areas in which the present work builds on my previous work, and especially on the two books *Theology and the Dialectics of History* and *What Is Systematic Theology?*[3] These books developed the notion of psychic conversion that was the focus of my earliest work and made clear its relevance to theology. Items taken from these works will be clear to anyone who has read them, but the theological implications of some of the items are expanded and refined in the present work.

1   Interiority, History, and Religion

Thesis 1: *A Catholic systematic theology on the level of our time will be*
(a) like all systematic theologies, an attempt to understand the mysteries
of Christian faith and the other meanings constitutive of the Christian
community;
(b) grounded in interiorly and religiously differentiated consciousness
expressive of four dimensions of conversion: religious, moral, intellec-
tual, and psychic;
(c) a theological theory of history; and
(d) expressed in the context of the multi-religious and interreligious world
in which we live.

With Bernard Lonergan, I take as my first clue for what a Catholic systematic theology would be the statement of the First Vatican Council to the effect that reason illumined by faith, when it inquires diligently, reverently, soberly, reaches with God's help (*Deo dante*) an imperfect but extremely fruitful understanding of the mysteries of faith (DS 3016). Those mysteries constitute, ground, and express the "something more," the dimension of the supernatural, whose heuristic structure is set forth in thirty-one points in the final chapter of Lonergan's *Insight: A Study of Human Understanding*.[4] That "something more" is grace, and especially both the uncreated gift of the life of the Trinity and the created gifts that are the consequent conditions that this uncreated grace be given. These gifts, as we will see, themselves have a Trinitarian form. At its core, that "something more" was systematically isolated in the medieval theorem of the "supernatural," which gave theology its special realm of study and speculation. According to Vatican I, the understanding of this "something more," which is the principal task of that dimension of theology called systematics, rests on analogies with what we know naturally and on the interconnection of the dimensions of the mystery of grace with one another and with our last, supernatural end, the direct vision of God. This understanding never becomes capable of grasping the mysteries of faith in the way we understand what lies within the proper range of our intellectual capacities, for the divine mysteries by their very nature so exceed created intellect that, even when given in revelation and accepted by faith, they remain wrapped in the veil of faith.[5] As Karl Rahner wrote, theological reason is "the capacity of the incomprehensible, ... the capacity of being seized by what is always insurmountable, not ... the power of comprehending, of gaining the mastery and subjugating."[6] Whatever a systematic theologian's basic options may be – transcendental, hermeneutical, phenomenological, dramatic, aesthetic, narrative, etc. – that capacity of theological reason may not be lost or eclipsed, nor may it be exaggerated beyond its very limited competence.

The principal function of systematic theology is to present on the level of our time such an imperfect, obscure, analogical, but fruitful understanding of the mysteries of Christian faith. The title of this first part speaks, though, not simply of a Catholic systematic theology, but of a *new* Catholic systematic theology. Similarly, I have referred to a theology "on the level of our time." These qualifications reflect an attitude that was quite in vogue in the immediate aftermath of the Second Vatican Council, one that we can now retrieve with perhaps greater responsibility than was shown by many at that time.[7] What do they add to the notion of an imperfect and analogical understanding of the mysteries of faith?

First, drawing again on the First Vatican Council, Lonergan stresses that, while it is the same mysteries that are being understood, the understanding grows and advances down the ages.[8] I have tried to capture part of what this conciliar statement entails by speaking of the genetic sequence of systematic theologies.[9] No matter how comprehensive an integrated understanding of the mysteries of faith may be at any given time, questions will arise either from within the system of thought itself or from human cultural development that cannot be answered on the basis of the resources already contained even in a perfectly coherent system, including the system's doctrinal sources. The sum of questions always exceeds, either actually or potentially, the sum of the resources presently available to answer them.[10]

Our age is no exception, and to the question of what is needed to bring systematic theology into our time and then to move it forward, Lonergan's basic answer was twofold.

First, systematic theology must be grounded in a thorough exploration of religious, moral, intellectual, and affective interiority. More precisely, it must be grounded in an exploration and appropriation of the various conversions that occur in each of these dimensions of interiority, conversions that propel the subject to self-transcendence in these diverse realms. Lonergan stressed intellectual, moral, and religious conversion,[11] all of which are the work of a lifetime in that they involve constant withdrawals from inauthenticity. But he also expressed agreement with me on the need for, and foundational position of, a psychic conversion that would connect spiritual intentionality with the energic resources, the primordial intersubjectivity, the tidal movement, the passionateness of being, within which intentional operations function: that would, in Heidegger's terms, establish the link of *Verstehen* and *Befindlichkeit* as equiprimordial constitutive ways of being *Dasein*.[12] I will refer to this ground, that is, to interiority in its twofold constitution, as a concrete universal that may be called "the normative subject,"[13] and I will suggest that we acknowledge a ninth functional specialty both in general methodology and in theological methodology, a specialty devoted exclusively to the ongoing exploration and clarification of this ground.

Regarding psychic conversion, we may say that just as what Lonergan describes as intellectual, moral, and religious conversion overcome and heal the effects of what he calls general, group, and individual bias, so what I am calling psychic conversion negotiates and corrects what he calls the "dramatic bias" that is located in the subject's repressive censorship. This censorship is exercised primarily over images that would give rise to unwanted insights, but also over the affects concomitant with these images, over the vagaries, subterfuges, and traumas of intersubjective encounters, and over the demand of human consciousness itself to preserve a taut equilibrium of spiritual intentionality with the sensitive psyche. Psychic development occurs, in my view, as one moves from what René Girard calls the interdividuality of an immature interiority through what Carl Jung calls individuation to what Lonergan calls the interpersonal dynamic state of being in love, or again from a primordially intersubjective *Mitsein*, open to all the pitfalls of mimetic struggle emphasized by Girard, to a deliberate commitment to love in intimate partnerships, in the civic community, and with the triune God.[14] Psychic conversion aids the appropriation of that development.

The foundational role of psychic conversion is most fully articulated to date in my *Theology and the Dialectics of History*, where the general categories of a theological theory of history depend on *both* Lonergan's intentionality analysis and a reoriented depth psychology. As I argued in chapter 2 of that book, the key to the notion of psychic conversion lies in the recognition of the duality of human consciousness, something that, as we will see, Lonergan expressly acknowledges. As Heidegger would affirm that *Dasein* is both *Befindlichkeit* and *Verstehen*, so for Lonergan consciousness is both psyche and intentional spirit. For each of these thinkers the two dimensions are equiprimordial and constitutive. If there is a difference between them on this point – and there is – it would lie in Lonergan's notion of the vertical finality of the sensitive psyche to participate in the cognitional and existential adventure of intentionality. This difference probably cuts through *all* the major lines of the philosophical orientations of these two great thinkers. It determines their relation to one another in a radical fashion. The lack of such vertical finality in Heidegger's fundamental ontology of *Dasein* – precisely the vertical finality of *Befindlichkeit* to *Verstehen* – may ultimately close the door to transcendence; at least it is, I believe, the source of Heidegger's immanentizing of most or all of the basic categories of Christian existence. "Being" for Heidegger lies within, and is conditioned by, time, while time for Lonergan time is "within" being: time *is*. The difference is radical, and it depends on respective views regarding the relations between *Verstehen* and *Befindlichkeit*, intentionality and psyche. Negotiation of the difference is dependent on what Lonergan calls intellectual conversion, without which my insistence on psychic conversion cannot be correctly understood. I tried in chapter 2 of *Theology and the Dialectics of History* to capture something of what the vertical finality of the psychic to the intentional might mean, though without attention to Heidegger. The relation of the two dimensions articulated there determines the rest of that book.

Lonergan stresses that interiorly differentiated consciousness is the basis of the general theological categories that theology will share with other disciplines. If this is the case, then each of these dimensions of interiority must be subjected to a process of self-appropriation and conversion. If Carl Jung, whose work I studied and immersed myself in as I worked out the notion of psychic conversion, did not have a clear handle on the intentional dimension of consciousness, many students of Lonergan have been reluctant to acknowledge the contribution of the psychic dimension. The articulation not only of psychic conversion but also of what Lonergan calls intellectual conversion in particular is addressed to "our time." Advances in scientific method have made that articulation not only necessary but also incrementally possible in a new and more thorough fashion. As for intellectual conversion, the critical realism that appears in Lonergan's *Insight* and that is developed in his treatment of the methods of history in *Method in Theology* and reflected in the work, for example, of the late Ben F. Meyer in biblical exegesis is crucial to a contemporary theology.[15] When critical realism is applied not to exegesis or history but to systematics, it will distinguish sharply between description and explanation, and it will insist that the goal of systematics is an approximation to a hypothetical explanatory understanding of the mysteries of Christian faith. But those foundations must also include an appropriation of the second "way of being conscious," the sensitive psyche that precedes, accompanies, and extends beyond the operations of the intentional spirit and that changes as these operations are either performed or not performed. This should become increasingly clear as we proceed, and especially as we attempt to make the most of Girard's contributions to systematic theological articulations of some of the most important dimensions of Christian constitutive meaning. It should also be clear from the theory of history presented in *Theology and the Dialectics of History*, where the three dialectical processes constitutive of personal, cultural, and social values have psychic as well as intentional poles.

And this brings us to the second emphasis, namely, that a contemporary systematic theology must be a theological theory of history.[16] A new systematic theology, one that addresses the meaning of the mysteries of Christian faith in our time, will attempt the task of understanding God's redemptive work in human history. Other emphases – the dramatic-aesthetic insistence of Hans Urs von Balthasar, the liberation emphasis on the option for the poor, and the groundbreaking insight into the structure of evil contained in the mimetic theory of René Girard – have helped me think through this option for systematic theology. *Theology and the Dialectics of History* is the initial fruit of appropriating that option, laying the groundwork for the general structure of a theology of history, but I have incrementally added to the vision of a theology of history since the publication of that book, and the present volume will see three major advances beyond anything that has appeared to this date: a clearer articulation of the structure of "religious values," a position on the structure of social grace, and a theological appropriation of Girard's mimetic theory.

To these two emphases from Lonergan – interiority and history – I wish to add a third: a contemporary Catholic systematic theology must articulate its understanding of the mysteries of Christian faith in the context of the multi-religious and interreligious world in which we live. Concretely, this means that the central emphases in a contemporary and foreseeable Catholic systematic theology will be Trinitarian and Pneumatological, without any sacrifice of the central doctrinal thrust of the Christological dogmas, of the New Testament basis of those dogmatic developments, or of the understanding of those dogmas that can be found in the systematic theologies of Thomas Aquinas and Lonergan. If anything, the significance of the mission of the divine Word becomes more pronounced in our understanding of revelation once we acknowledge the universality of the mission of the Holy Spirit, for clarification on the latter mission will open up new possibilities for understanding the invisible mission of the Word and for appropriating the significance of the Word's incarnation in Jesus of Nazareth. But it is the mission of the Holy Spirit that accounts for the radical move beyond the permanent achievements of past systematic theology, a move that in no way goes back on those achievements but rather propels them forward. That move will be articulated here in the form of a suggestion regarding the functional specialties of a world theology, a theology that would sublate Catholic dogmatics and systematics into the context of interreligious dialogue and understanding, so that a new "world systematic theology" may eventually (probably later rather than sooner) emerge.

This project on *The Trinity in History* finds here, then, its first installment, in the form of an attempt to relate the theology of the Trinitarian processions to the historical missions of the Word and the Holy Spirit. God willing, it will be followed in due time by further volumes. The present work attempts to meet three exigencies of systematic theology in our time: groundedness in the affective, intentional, and religious interiority of the concrete universal that is the normative subject; expression in terms of a theological theory of history; and sensitivity to the interreligious context in which we are living.

In this introductory chapter I wish to discuss as well the notions of the dogmatic-theological context (§2) and the role of history in elaborating systematic positions (§3). Subsequent chapters in this first part will treat the starting point in the mission of the Holy Spirit, a new instantiation of the psychological analogy for understanding the Trinitarian processions, the intricacies of contingent predication about God, the notion of formal effects, the order of the divine missions, social grace, the application of a functionally specialized method to the universal religious situation, and the question of the levels of consciousness from which the basic terms and relations of a systematic theology are derived. I will include a suggestion regarding a further differentiation regarding the notion of functional specialization, so as to open the possibility of a ninth functional specialty, one whose task is the ongoing articulation and appropriation of the normative subject.

2   The Dogmatic-Theological Context

Thesis 2: *A contemporary Catholic systematic theology will begin by rearticulating the theology of the divine missions in the contemporary context defined by thesis 1. Thus, renewed Trinitarian, Pneumatological, and Christological articulations will form the dogmatic-theological context for the development of theological doctrines and systematic positions regarding revelation, original sin, redemption, church, sacraments, eternal life, creation, and other emergent elements of Christian constitutive meaning.*

If I say to someone, "You are taking my remarks out of context," what is meant by the word "context?" "Context" here refers to everything else that you would have to take into consideration if you were properly to understand my remarks. If I say to someone, "You are taking my remarks out of context," I mean that you are neglecting to consider factors that are relevant to understanding precisely what I mean, and so in effect you are misunderstanding what I mean.

In a set of lectures on "The Method of Theology" delivered in 1962 at Regis College in Toronto, Lonergan introduced the notion of the dogmatic-theological context, where "context" means precisely this remainder of other factors that need to be taken into consideration if given theological statements are to be properly understood.[17] In these same lectures Lonergan suggested that statements within systematic theology regarding church and sacraments must be set in a context of Trinitarian, Pneumatological, and Christological presuppositions.[18] My point in recalling these comments is that a Christian systematic theology begins with the triune God and proceeds to a Christology and to a doctrine of grace, or perhaps (as will be my option) to a doctrine of grace first and then to a Christology,[19] and that these form the contemporary dogmatic-theological context for the remainder of the issues to be treated in systematics.[20] So, on Lonergan's account in these 1962 lectures, it is within the dogmatic-theological context of Trinitarian theology, Pneumatology, and Christology that one would develop an ecclesiology, and it is within the context of statements about the church that one would proceed to a sacramental theology. It is in this sense that we may speak of a dogmatic-theological context of other theological statements.

This context figures, not in the way of discovery, but in the order of teaching, the *ordo doctrinae*, where the emphasis is on the relations of things not to us but to one another.[21] From the standpoint of the way of discovery, the original context is found in the kerygmatic message of the apostles and the church's confession of faith in the risen Lord and in the redemption wrought in his passion, death, and resurrection.[22] It was from that original context that the church's formulation of its Trinitarian, Christological, and Pneumatological faith slowly emerged, and it was to that context that the church continued to return in settling disputes and proclaiming the faith. Moreover, continual return to this original font will prevent the Trinitarian and Pneumatological emphases of a contemporary Catholic systematics from losing sight of the revelation of God in Christ Jesus that makes all talk of the Trinity and the Holy Spirit possible in the first place.

If it is the case that certain areas of theological discourse presuppose a context set by other areas, it would seem legitimate to assume that the parameters regarding the presuppositions that form the context will be more secure than those regarding the implications of or developments upon these presuppositions. Thus, in the example under consideration, the dogmatic-theological context set by Trinitarian, Christological, and even Pneumatological doctrine is more sharply defined than are the ecclesiological and sacramental matters that depend on these presuppositions.[23] For Lonergan and for me, these parameters are, respectively, in Trinitarian theology the *homoousion* introduced at Nicea, subsequently clarified by Athanasius and extended to the doctrine of the Holy Spirit at Constantinople I, in Christology the doctrine "one and the same" of Chalcedon, and in the doctrine of grace the medieval theorem of the supernatural as applied in the thought of Thomas Aquinas to both habits and acts and as reconciled eventually by Aquinas with earlier insights on grace as healing.[24] The other areas that I have mentioned call for similar developments even with respect to basic doctrinal commitments. Thus, there is not yet in the church's dogmatic-theological context anything that would function in ecclesiology in the same way as the *homoousion* functions in Trinitarian theology. This is very clear in contemporary discussions about the church. No satisfactory position has yet been reached, for instance, on the relation of *communio* ecclesiology to "people of God" ecclesiology, on conflicting interpretations of the ecclesiology of the Second Vatican Council, or on conflicting views concerning the relation of local churches to the universal church. Part of the reason for this is that there has yet to emerge the category that will do for ecclesiology what *homoousion* does for Trinitarian theology. Not only are these issues currently caught up in the neuralgia of the internecine politics of the solid right and the scattered left. The basic problem in the ecclesiological debates is the lack of an adequate dogmatic-theological context for the discussion. In a question-and-answer session at the 1962 Institute on "The Method of Theology," Lonergan singled out church and sacraments as areas calling for further *doctrinal* determination before an adequate systematic theology can be done in their regard,[25] and it seems to me that we may extend this call to other areas: revelation, creation, redemption, original sin, the last things, and so on.

The position to be taken here is that these tasks demand first an updating of the basic Trinitarian, Pneumatological, and Christological parameters, in the light of the three determinants of the contemporary context: interiority, history, and the world religions. The shift to interiority, history, and the interreligious setting means that even within Christology there is a great deal of new work to be done on such matters as the historical causality of Jesus, the relation of the divine and human consciousnesses and the divine and human knowledge of Jesus, the relation of the mission of the Word to the mission of the Holy Spirit, and the historical meaning of the redemption wrought in Christ Jesus. Similarly, within Pneumatology there is the urgent question regarding the universal mission of the Holy Spirit and its meaning for the dialogue of Christians with representatives of the other world religions. The answers to these sets of questions, answers that we have not yet reached, will decisively alter the dogmatic-theological context for future systematic theologies, but if these answers are worked out in fidelity to the parameters already set in Trinitarian theology, Pneumatology, and Christology, and in fidelity to the functionally differentiated method proposed by Lonergan, they will alter this context, not by jettisoning previous dogmatic achievements but by expanding them. In much of the theology that has been done in recent decades there has been evident the supposition that renewing the parameters in Trinitarian, Christological, and Pneumatological areas entails jettisoning parts of the doctrinal heritage. I will not entertain such an option even for a moment. In fact, I hope that the efforts recorded here will discourage the call for such an option.

It would seem reasonable, then, to begin a systematic theology by attempting to understand and appropriate the dogmatic pronouncements that set clear parameters, and to update them in light of the exigencies imposed by interiority, history, and the interreligious situation. The first three areas to be submitted to the process of systematic articulation, then, are the Trinity, the Incarnation, and the mission of the Holy Spirit in grace. For these areas of dogmatic commitment and of systematic elaboration would seem to set the dogmatic-theological context required for a balanced presentation of all other theological topics, many of which will never receive adequate doctrinal and systematic expression until the Trinitarian, Pneumatological, and Christological context is renewed and brought up to date.

At the same time, there is no need to repeat secure achievements in these areas. I rely, for instance, on Lonergan's Trinitarian systematics, on his original contributions to Christology in the form of a position on the human and divine consciousnesses and knowledge of Christ (one divine subject with two – divine and human – subjectivities), and on his elaboration of a systematics of grace. I intend to build on these and develop them, not simply rehearse them. The present work builds in particular on his position on the relation between the divine processions and the missions of the Son and the Holy Spirit, insisting that we can move on in systematic theology, effecting a genetic advance, if we begin from Lonergan's position on the divine missions as setting the very context for our attempts to understand the processions. The last step in Lonergan's systematics of the Trinity thus in a way becomes the first step in the systematics proposed here, since it is a position that synthesizes the theologies of the divine processions, the divine relations, and the divine persons that preceded the treatment of the divine missions in Lonergan's systematics of the Trinity. Thus in the present efforts, returns will be made *from* the position on the missions to review what has already been established in Lonergan's work concerning the processions, relations, and persons. But I see no need to begin where Lonergan began; I prefer to integrate his beginning point into my own; my wager is that it will be much more fruitful to begin where he ended in Trinitarian theology, and to call on the resources of his earlier steps as they are needed to help us move forward.

3   The Role of History

Thesis 3: *Theological doctrines and systematic positions regarding revelation, original sin, redemption, church, sacraments, eternal life, and* *creation will catalyze the development of the dogmatic-theological context for yet further understanding. But these doctrinal and systematic positions require a theological theory of history grounded in the Trinitarian, Pneumatological, and Christological context and employing and developing basic categories of history expressed by Lonergan in terms of progress, decline, and redemption, and developed by the present writer in terms of the scale of values and the dialectical structure of personal, cultural, and social values.*

If what I have been saying is true, then once the basic elements of the context (the Trinitarian, Pneumatological, and Christological components) have been updated, the development of theological doctrines and doctrinal parameters in the areas that are still calling for clarity – not only ecclesiology and sacramental theology, but also the theologies of revelation, original sin, redemption, creation, and the last things – would be one way, perhaps the principal way, in which the church's dogmatic-theological context will expand and provide the ground for yet further development. That context will be freed to develop by the advances in Trinitarian theology, Pneumatology, and Christology, and catalyzed by the exigencies of interiority, history, and the interreligious situation. The dogmatic-theological context will move forward as the theology of revelation, the theology of original sin, soteriology, ecclesiology, sacramental theology, the theology of creation, and eschatology undergo development. Moreover, if it is through work in these areas that the church's dogmatic-theological context will develop, it is also here that systematic theology will take its next step forward, but only after the renewal and updating of the basic contextual parameters.

Now if we turn to these areas – revelation, original sin, soteriology, ecclesiology, sacramental theology, creation, and an eschatology built on the creedal affirmation of the resurrection of Jesus – we will find that the issues all have to do, in one way or another, with *God's action in history.* In notes that he wrote in 1965 just after he made his major breakthrough to the structure of the whole of theology in terms of the functional specialization of theological operations, Lonergan assigned as the "mediated object" of developing work on "Doctrines" what he called "redemption in history," and as the "mediated object" of a future "Systematics" *Geschichte*, history, the history that is lived.[26] In other words, as the church in its doctrinal development, and theology in its systematic development, build upon but also move beyond the fundamental areas of Trinitarian doctrine, the doctrine of grace, and Christological doctrine and into these other areas, it will increasingly be the case that the doctrines, ecclesial and theological, that the theologian affirms will not be an unorganized list of affirmations but will already be organized into some kind of integrated pattern governed by the doctrinal affirmation that God works in a redemptive fashion in human history. Today that action will be acknowledged as bringing the religions of the world into convergence and thus overcoming the history of violence that has all too often marked their relations. The attempt to understand these doctrines will take the form of a theological theory of history, of the history that is lived and written about, the history that throughout his career Lonergan understood in terms of the three approximations of progress, decline, and redemption and that I have attempted to understand also in terms of the scale of values and the dialectical structure of personal, cultural, and social values. In order to elevate the theology of revelation, the theology of original sin, soteriology, ecclesiology, sacramental theology, the theology of creation, and an eschatology based in the resurrection of Jesus to a status in a contemporary or future dogmatic-theological context that enjoys the clear parameters already given to the doctrines of Trinity, Incarnation, and grace, there is required in theology and in the teaching of the church itself the development of a position on the immanent intelligibility of human history. The systematic theology of the future will be a theological theory of history.

Thus it may be claimed that the dogmatic-theological context required for this future development both of Christian doctrine and of systematic appropriation of Christian doctrine will be joined with a developing philosophical and theological theory of history to yield a unified field structure constituted by the integration of renewed Trinitarian, Pneumatological, and Christological commitments with the heuristics of history. Against that background and in the context of statements regarding the Trinity in history, these other areas of systematic consideration – revelation, original sin, redemption, church, sacraments, creation, and eschatology – will have room to develop. The contemporary unified field structure for further development in systematic theology will be found, then, in as thorough a treatment as possible of what we may call "The Trinity in History." The renewal and updating of Trinitarian theology, Pneumatology, and Christology will themselves launch the whole of systematic theology on the path of a theological theory of history. For (1) the primary locus for the renewal and updating of Trinitarian theology has to do with our understanding of the divine missions in history, (2) the primary locus for the renewal and updating of Pneumatology has to do with the role of the Holy Spirit in the whole of human history both within and outside the context of Judeo-Christian revelation, and (3) the primary locus for the renewal and updating of Christology has to do with the historical efficacy of Jesus, and in fact with a developing theology of both the invisible and the visible missions of the eternal divine Word.

2

The Immanent Constitution of Life in God

1   The Specifically Theological Dimension of the Starting Point

Thesis 4: *The key to the* nexus mysteriorum *that is the concern of systematics lies in the links that Lonergan has drawn between the four divine relations and four created participations in and imitations of these relations. The starting point in unpacking that four-point hypothesis is the link between sanctifying grace and charity as created participations in, respectively, active spiration and passive spiration. From the standpoint of religiously and interiorly differentiated consciousness, these created participations are (1) the recalled reception (memoria) of the gift of God's love (that is, of sanctifying grace as it affects consciousness) grounding a subsequent set of judgments of value (faith), as these together participate in active spiration and so set up a special relation to the indwelling Holy Spirit, and (2) a return of love (charity) participating in the Proceeding Love that is the Holy Spirit, which establishes a special relation to the indwelling Father and Son. Memory and faith combine to imitate and participate in active spiration, and charity imitates and participates in passive spiration.*

It is within the context set by chapter 1 that I would situate this book entitled *The Trinity in History: Missions and Processions*. In very brief compass, I am attempting to begin renewing the basic dogmatic-theological context, the Trinitarian, Pneumatological, and Christological parameters for all other systematic-theological statements, and to do so with explicit attention to the already mentioned demands regarding interiority, history, and the world's religions. Within those renewed doctrinal parameters, the rest of systematic theology would be constructed, on solid Trinitarian, Pneumatological, and Christological grounds. The renewal of the parameters will be in terms of the categories provided by interiority for understanding the religious phenomenon, for adjudicating authentic and deviated transcendence in history, and for affirming and exploring Christian doctrinal commitments within the interreligious situation of our time.

1.1 The Basic Hypothesis

It will come as no surprise to any who have followed my work even remotely over the past decade or so that I regard the key to the renewal of the basic dogmatic-theological parameters to lie in Lonergan's statement concerning created participations in and imitations of the four divine relations. These participations and imitations will give us the basic meaning of the phrase "the Trinity in history," and this in turn will enable us to develop a Catholic systematic theology, a systematics that at its core is Trinitarian and Pneumatological, a theology that relies on the insights of Trinitarian theology, of a developed Pneumatology, and of a renewed Christology to state the meaning of Christian faith in the interreligious situation of our time.

The dogmatic-theological context that we have inherited from the tradition specifies that there are four real divine relations: paternity, filiation, active spiration, and passive spiration. It affirms that three of these – paternity, filiation, and passive spiration – are really distinct by opposed relations of origin and are identical with the three divine persons: respectively, the Father, the Son, and the Holy Spirit. The fourth divine relation, active spiration, is really identical with and only conceptually distinct from the Father and the Son as together they "breathe," "spirate" the Holy Spirit.[1] The hypothesis that we are proposing asserts that memory and faith together imitate and participate in paternity and filiation, Father and Son, together as they breathe the Holy Spirit, and that charity imitates and participates in passive spiration, the Holy Spirit, as proceeding from the active loving, the *notionaliter diligere*, that is Father and Son spirating.

Lonergan's original hypothetical systematic development regarding the divine missions affirms that to each of the divine relations there corresponds a created participation in and imitation of divine life. Through that development he has managed to link Trinitarian theology with Christology and the theology of grace in a manner that is potentially more systematic, in my view, than anything else that has been achieved in the long history of Christian theology, and thus to find at perhaps its most profound level that *nexus mysteriorum* of which the First Vatican Council spoke in its pronouncements on the ecclesial vocation of theology.

I will claim that these participations in and imitations of the divine relations find their effectiveness in history as they influence the integral functioning of the scale of values that provides the immanent intelligibility of human history. Together, the four-point hypothesis and the theory of history unite to constitute what I mean by speaking of the Trinity in history. And the Trinity in history, thus understood, is identical to what in a more methodological context I called the unified field structure of systematic theology.[2]

Lonergan's hypothesis appeared in print in his 1957 *Divinarum personarum*, and reappeared in *De Deo Trino: Pars Systematica* in 1964.[3] As translated in *The Triune God: Systematics* it reads:

> ... there are four real divine relations, really identical with the divine substance, and therefore there are four very special modes that ground the external imitation of the divine substance. Next, there are four absolutely supernatural realities, which are never found uninformed,[4] namely, the secondary act of existence of the incarnation, sanctifying grace, the habit of charity, and the light of glory. It would not be inappropriate, therefore, to say that the secondary act of existence of the incarnation is a created participation of paternity, and so has a special relation to the Son; that sanctifying grace is a participation of active spiration, and so has a special relation to the Holy Spirit; that the habit of charity is a participation of passive spiration, and so has a special relation to the Father and the Son; and that the light of glory is a participation of sonship, and so in a most perfect way brings the children of adoption back to the Father.[5]

1.2 1951–52 Notes on Sanctifying Grace

This 1957 statement of the hypothesis was not the first appearance of this systematic synthesis in Lonergan's work, though it was the first published instance of it. The hypothesis makes an earlier appearance in notes Lonergan composed for a course on sanctifying grace at the Jesuit Seminary in Toronto in 1951–52. Here it is explained more fully than in the Trinitarian systematics.[6] There follows here, then, a summary statement of some of the relevant features of those notes, particularly as they bear upon the relation of sanctifying grace and charity.

The notes are divided into three sections: (1) a set of historical points, (2) treatment of the biblical basis of the doctrine of sanctifying grace, and (3) a systematic synthesis of that doctrine.

I treat the historical position only very briefly. In this portion Lonergan is concerned (though this is not a central concern of the entire set of notes) with connecting the steps that led to the Lutheran and Reformed positions on justification. He roots these positions in Scotus, and so in confrontationalism and conceptualism, and in subsequent nominalist and voluntarist doctrine. His concern in the section seems to be almost exclusively to set up a context that calls for a review of what the scriptures say about justification and salvation, which, he claims, cannot support the Lutheran and Reformed positions. That review follows immediately, and it heads him into the systematic treatment of the issue. Whether the far more ecumenical Lonergan of *Method in Theology* would present the same historical analysis is an open question; there are probably not enough data to answer it, though it surely is true that his negative view of Scotus is a constant throughout his work.

1.2.1 The Biblical Basis for the Notion of Sanctifying Grace

The extremely rich scriptural notes begin with an important synthetic statement of the biblical basis for the notion of habitual or sanctifying grace, a notion which as such does not appear in scripture. The point to the biblical section in the context of these course notes is to present a scriptural basis for the Catholic understanding of justification, over against the Lutheran and Reformed traditions as Lonergan understands them. His synthetic statement of biblical doctrine reads as follows, in translation.

> To those whom God the Father loves [1] as he loves Jesus, his only-begotten Son, (2) he gives the uncreated gift of the Holy Spirit, so that (3) into a new life they may be (4) born again and (5) become living members of Christ; therefore as (6) justified, (7) friends of God, (8) adopted children of God, and (9) heirs in hope of eternal life, (10) they enter into a sharing in the divine nature.[7]

Every one of these ten points, Lonergan maintains, has a firm biblical basis. He supports that claim with abundant references from the New Testament. Taken together these ten points and the texts that support them provide the scriptural warrant for the later doctrine of habitual or sanctifying grace. "Sanctifying grace" or "habitual grace," then, is a synthetic category that unites these ten features of biblical doctrine. The systematic part of the treatise will then show how the biblical doctrine that Lonergan has expressed in this synthetic statement can be true. Each of these ten features of biblical doctrine will be seen in the systematic portion of the notes to represent a "formal effect" of sanctifying grace, where the issue of formal effects has to do with the question, What true judgments can be made once one knows a formal cause – judgments whose truth is founded in that formal cause?

Already in the biblical notes, though, Lonergan makes systematic statements. These statements relate directly to the biblical data the Aristotelian framework in which the notion of sanctifying grace emerged. Thus, not only is the specific character of habitual or sanctifying grace found in its unifying capacity with respect to the ten features of the biblical synthesis, but also Lonergan draws a parallel to Aristotle's notion of the unifying capacity of "anima" vis-à-vis habits and operations of various kinds, and so he links the notion of sanctifying grace as an entitative habit *rooted in the essence of the soul (anima)* to the biblical texts he is synthesizing. As for Aristotle and Aquinas the soul is to the potencies of the soul and the habits rooted in them and the operations that flow from the habits, so sanctifying grace is to the various features synthesized in the statement of biblical doctrine, all of which are formal effects of sanctifying grace and constitute an elevation of the natural life of the human soul into participation in divine life. These various features will later, in the systematic part of the treatise, be organized in a way that parallels, at least roughly, the Aristotelian relations of soul to potencies, potencies to habits, and habits to operations. The analogy holds up because these features name characteristics of new and transformed operations, or of new and transformed habits or states, and so of new and transformed or elevated faculties or potencies of an elevated soul. The systematic part of the notes will show how this is the case, treating each of the features of the biblical synthesis in terms of the metaphysical category of formal effects.

The treatment is breathtaking in its systematic coherence and elegant brevity. Still, these terms will seem foreign to many contemporary readers. Their theoretical context belongs to what Lonergan calls the second stage of meaning, where meaning is controlled by theory governed by logic, and is expressed in metaphysical terms. In the third stage of meaning, such metaphysical terms must find their grounding in categories derived from interiorly and religiously differentiated consciousness.[8] As I have argued rather strenuously elsewhere, the metaphysical terms and relations provide a necessary control of meaning vis-à-vis all attempts to rely on interiority and religious experience, and must be appropriated on their own by any theologian who wishes to construct a contemporary systematics that is a genetic outgrowth of the best in the Catholic tradition.[9] There is no third stage of meaning without passing through the second and sublating it into interiorly differentiated consciousness, where for every term and relation there will be, in one way or another, a grounding in intentional consciousness. Any appeal to interiority that bypasses metaphysics is a regression to commonsense controls, which in effect means a regression to a lack of control, at least of the control needed in systematic theology. Commonsense interiority may be abundant, rich, and fruitful, as is clear in the writings of Augustine, Pascal, and Newman. But it is not systematic theology.

Nonetheless, a contemporary systematics cannot be first and foremost a metaphysical theology.

It is important also to attend to Lonergan's basic statement on such transposition *in its entirety*, in order to avoid fruitless efforts never intended in his prescriptions. The statement is as follows: "For every term and relation there will exist a corresponding element in intentional consciousness. Accordingly, empty or misleading terms and relations can be eliminated, while *valid ones can be elucidated by the conscious intention from which they are derived.*"[10] The emphasized portion is too often neglected, with the result of attempting to provide an interior equivalent to every metaphysical term. This is valid for some terms: thus what in a metaphysical context is called "agent intellect" can be transposed into an interiority context as the pure, unrestricted desire to know. However, Lonergan's basic statement on transposition does not insist on such equivalence in every instance, simply on an isomorphism of knowing and known and so an ability to locate for every known the corresponding intentional operation in which it is known. At times it is sufficient to name the intentional operation or state from which the metaphysical term or relation is derived. This will prove to be very important, I believe, in the discussion of the meaning of the term "secondary act of existence," for which we would have a difficult time finding a conscious equivalent but for which we may and indeed must name the intentional operation from which that category was derived. On the other hand, I will be claiming that the transposition of "sanctifying grace" and "the habit of charity" may indeed appeal to equivalent realities in conscious experience itself, however much finding those equivalences depends on the cultivation of a spiritual life.

The same Aristotelian framework demands that sanctifying grace be distinct from the virtue or habit of charity, which is a more proximate principle of operations rooted not in "anima" but in the will, that is, in one of the faculties or potencies of the soul. In the Aristotelian framework, this renders sanctifying grace somehow "entitative" (rooted in the essence of the soul) and charity somehow "accidental" (rooted in a potency or faculty of the soul), a terminology that demands a real distinction of the two. Thus, the distinction between sanctifying grace and charity that is so important in the four-point hypothesis arose within and was required by the Aristotelian metaphysical framework within which Lonergan was working. A question that abides to this day is whether the replacement of the Aristotelian framework with a methodical analysis of religious interiority will demand or even support this distinction. A problem has been raised over my continuing appeal to the four-point hypothesis,[11] and the problem has to do precisely with this distinction of sanctifying grace and charity. In effect, the question is being asked whether the distinction survives the transition from a metaphysical to a methodical theology. I have affirmed and will continue to affirm the permanent validity of the distinction, not of course as a matter of church doctrine but as an aid to systematic understanding.

As far as the history of Lonergan's position on the issue is concerned, we may say the following. He made it very clear as early as 1946 that the doctrine affirming an absolutely supernatural communication of the divine nature can be maintained whether or not one's systematic understanding of the doctrine includes a distinction between sanctifying grace and charity – a distinction that Aquinas makes, that Lonergan repeats from Aquinas, and that Scotus denies.[12] The distinction remains clear in his theological writings in a Scholastic mode, and is very much to the fore in the notes under investigation. The distinction perhaps survives briefly in the transposition to a methodical theology, since in his 1968 lectures on *Method in Theology* at Boston College, it is charity, not sanctifying grace, that is transposed into "the dynamic state of being in love with God."[13] However, in a question-and-answer session at the 1974 Lonergan Workshop, and so after the publication of *Method in Theology*, Lonergan admits that his later methodical transposition of the category of sanctifying grace into the expression "the dynamic state of being in love with God" represents an "amalgam" of sanctifying grace and charity.[14] I have long regarded this as a regressive step in the effort to achieve religiously differentiated consciousness, and I will suggest that the methodical transposition of the distinction can be refined so as to preserve it, and that it is desirable to do so. I want to preserve the distinction for a number of reasons, including my respect for the metaphysical context that demanded it. Preserving that context, I am convinced, will prevent our later methodical language from retreating to undifferentiated common sense about interiority. But also, as we will see, the distinction also provides a hypothetical understanding of how it can be true that we do indeed enjoy distinct created relations to each of the three uncreated divine persons as terms of these relations. The amalgamation of the two terms does not preserve an explanation of these distinct relations; at least no such explanation can be found in Lonergan's writings once he conflated these two realities.

But we are getting ahead of ourselves. Let us return to the biblical notes.

The points in the biblical synthesis that are most relevant to my present concerns are the first two, and so I will concentrate on those: To those whom God the Father loves (1) as he loves Jesus, his only-begotten Son, (2) he gives the uncreated gift of the Holy Spirit.

Even with respect to these two points I will not be able to cover all the rich detail in Lonergan's notes, which must be studied on their own, representing as they do his most complete systematic statement on sanctifying grace.

1.2.2 The Father Loves Us as He Loves the Son

The key texts are from John, and they read: "… I in them and you in me, that they may be perfectly one, so that the world may know that you have sent me and have loved them even as you have loved me" (17.23);[15] and "… that the love with which you have loved me may be in them, and I in them" (17.26). Pauline texts are cited as well, but between the Johannine and Pauline texts, Lonergan introduces systematic categories from Aquinas to elucidate the point, and even more to set up his later systematic discussion.

Thus, in commenting on these texts Lonergan presents Thomas's distinction between essential and notional divine love, and a corresponding distinction between divine efficient causality and the entire question of immanent constitution. These distinctions are crucial to his position on these issues. The created gift by which God draws us into participation in the divine life, that is, the created grace by which it is true that the Holy Spirit is given to us and dwells in us – in Lonergan's ontology of grace, the created base of a created relation to the uncreated Holy Spirit – is to be conceived as *effected* by essential divine love, that is, by the love that is common to the three divine persons; but the same gift is also to be conceived in its full complexity as *immanently constituted* in terms of the notional acts proper to each of the divine persons. The word "notional" refers to the personal properties of the divine persons, precisely as that by which we *know* each of them as distinct from the others.[16] The one love common to the three divine persons is exercised in a distinct manner by each of the divine persons. That distinct manner is a function of that person's "notional act." The "notional acts" are a function of the relations of opposition that *are* the divine persons. The love common to the three, not *finding* us good in the special way that a theology of grace is seeking, *makes* us good by the gift of elevation to participation in divine life. But that gift establishes in us distinct relations to the distinct persons. Thus the gift of a created base of the created relation to the indwelling uncreated Holy Spirit is called "gratia *gratum faciens*," the grace that *makes us pleasing* to God. That grace, as caused by God, is the result or effect of the love common to the three divine persons, but at the same time it establishes in us distinct relations to each of the divine persons and a distinct participation in the divine life of each of them, in keeping with the distinct fashion in which each of them exercises the divine creative love. Thus the Holy Spirit is proceeding love, *Amor procedens* (*Summa theologiae*, 1, q. 37, a. 1 c. and ad 4m), and the Father and the Son love themselves and each other and us (*notionaliter diligere*) by the Holy Spirit, that is, by proceeding Love (q. 37, a. 2 c. ad fin. and ad 2m). Therein is contained the distinction of active (*notionaliter diligere*) and passive (*Amor procedens*) spiration. Sanctifying grace, as *effected, caused,* by the essential divine love common to the three persons, is a participation in active spiration and so establishes a created relation to the Holy Spirit, but as breathing charity, it establishes in us distinct relations to the Father and the Son. The gift, while effected by the three, is immanently constituted in terms of the distinct divine relations and is to be understood as establishing a created imitation of and participation in those divine relations. More precisely, it is the base of a created relation to the uncreated Holy Spirit, who is an uncreated relation to the Father and the Son; by our relation to the Holy Spirit, there is created in us a base of a created relation to the Father and the Son, a participation in the Spirit, namely, what a metaphysical theology calls the habit of charity and what a methodical theology would call the state of loving God in return and the operations that flow from that state. Charity is the grace-enabled assent to the gift of God's love. Thus the gift of God's love, sanctifying grace, becomes the love with which we love. But with a certain ontological priority it is the origin of a faith that is the knowledge born of love, which participates in an invisible mission of the divine Word, the *Verbum spirans Amorem*; from the love recollected in memory and the knowledge born of that love, an ultimately ineffable assent, there flows the love of God in return, the charity that participates in the passively spirated Holy Spirit. The relation is to Father and Son as breathing love: distinctly to the Father in eschatological hope, and to the Son in companionship, whether thematically through Christian conversion or non-thematically by fidelity to the universalist faith that emerges from the gift of God's love. This is the immanent constitution of our life in God.[17]

A bit of history might help locate the significance of the issue. At the beginning of his 1947–48 course on sanctifying grace, Lonergan distributed to the students a list of theses that he would be propounding during the course. But when he came to teaching thesis 22, which dealt with the issue of the relation of sanctifying grace and the indwelling of the Holy Spirit, created and uncreated grace, he told the class that he had come to realize that his formulation was wrong but that he had not yet thought through an acceptable alternative. So there was a break in the course until he had figured it out to his satisfaction. He called them back two weeks later.

The formulation that he had come to see was wrong was: "*Through this same finite effect* [that is, created sanctifying grace] there is *constituted* not only the indwelling of the Holy Spirit but also the vivification of the justified through the same Spirit" (emphasis added). This formulation of the relation between created and uncreated grace contains a difficulty remarkably similar to that which Karl Rahner at almost the same time recognized in the mainline Scholastic tradition. For Rahner, the mainline Scholastic theology of grace had made created grace the *basis* of the divine self-communication, whereas the scriptures and the Fathers acknowledge created grace as a *consequence* of this self-communication.[18] Rahner's solution applies to the divine self-communication the Scholastic ontology of the beatific vision, so that "God communicates himself to the [person] to whom grace has been shown in the mode of *formal* [later in the same paper, quasi-formal] causality,"[19] as distinct from efficient causality, which is given short shrift in Rahner's treatment of the issue. Lonergan, on the other hand, reformulated the problematic thesis 22 as follows: "The uncreated gift, as uncreated, is constituted by God alone, and by it God stands to the state of the justified person not only as an efficient principle but also as a constitutive principle; but this constitutive principle is not present in the justified person as an inherent form but is present to the justified person as the term of a relation." It is interesting that two of the great Catholic theologians of the twentieth century spotted the same problem at roughly the same time, probably without being aware of each other's work, but proposed quite distinct solutions. Moreover, I would maintain that it is possible that something approaching Rahner's solution might obtain for the highest regions of mystical union. I do not think Lonergan's position would be against that possibility. But short of something like Teresa of Avila's spiritual marriage, which surely is a taste of heaven on earth, an appeal to the ontology of the beatific vision and so to formal causality is explicitly ruled out.[20]

By 1951–52, that is, four years later, Lonergan was quite prepared to speak of distinct relations to the three divine persons, and so of the three divine persons as distinct terms of distinct relations. This is a problem that he had acknowledged in 1947–48 but nearly passed over in that course, perhaps because he had just reformulated his position and was still working out its consequences, and perhaps because he was concerned not to violate Pius XII's strictures regarding the question. Pius had warned that all things must be held to be common to the Trinity inasmuch as they relate to God as their supreme efficient cause (see DB 2290, DS 3814, ND 1996). This statement made many theologians reluctant to speak of distinct relations to the three divine persons in any other way than by appropriation. Even in 1947–48, however, Lonergan is on to what will become his response, for he writes, "This statement perhaps leaves a certain latitude when God is not considered as an efficient principle but as a constitutive principle." But he adds, "We shall leave this question to the treatise on the triune God, both on account of its difficulty and also in order not to deal with distinct questions at the same time." By 1951–52, Lonergan was quite prepared in the course on grace itself to speak of distinct relations to the three divine persons, and proposes a way to do so. Moreover, he writes that arguments to the contrary do no more than prove that grace not as a term but as an effect is related to the essential divine love common to the three persons. So there is a distinction that already was introduced into the 1947–48 revised thesis 22 between divine love considered as an efficient cause and divine love considered constitutively, and that distinction will by 1951–52 lead to a remarkably rich theology of the divine indwelling.

Thus I am visiting here the 1951–52 notes with the specific intention of presenting Lonergan's solution to the question of how the divine self-communication, constituted by God alone, allows each of the persons of the Trinity to be present to those to whom the created grace of God's favor (*gratia gratum faciens*) has been given, and to be present precisely as distinct terms of created relations. I am also asking how we can preserve this solution in a methodical transposition of these issues. Preserving it will entail a methodical transposition of Aquinas's distinction of sanctifying grace and charity, not a jettisoning of the distinction or an amalgamation of the distinct realities. It is precisely the appearance of the four-point hypothesis in the notes of 1951–52, with its distinction of sanctifying grace and charity as created participations in and imitations of, respectively, the divine relations of active and passive spiration, that enables Lonergan to speak of distinct relations to each of the divine persons. For this reason above all, I maintain that the distinction should be maintained as a legitimate and fruitful systematic hypothesis.

The main point, again, of Lonergan's theological commentary on this section, drawing on Aquinas, is that the special love by which God draws us into participation in the divine life is to be understood as *effected* by essential divine love but as immanently *constituted* in terms of the notional divine acts. Divine love does not find us good until it has made us good, and this it does through "gratia gratum faciens," the grace that makes us pleasing to God. That grace, as caused by God, is the effect of the essential divine love common to the three divine persons, but it establishes in us distinct relations to each of the divine persons and a distinct participation in the divine life of each of them.

The issue has to do with what can be said of God contingently in the order of sanctifying grace. What can be said of God contingently will be said in terms of transcendent formal effects of sanctifying grace: judgments that can truly be said of God, judgments whose truth is grounded in what Lonergan would soon call the "created consequent condition" called sanctifying grace.[21]

These transcendent formal effects are of two kinds. For sanctifying grace can be considered as an effect of divine love, since it is out of love that God produces grace in a person, and it can also be considered as a term of divine love, for God loves the person made pleasing. The transcendent formal effects of sanctifying grace as an effect of divine love regard essential divine love, and so all three divine persons without distinction. All three persons are equally one effective principle of every creature whatsoever.

Thus this effective divine love is predicated equally of all three persons; and love that is predicated equally of all three is essential love. But the transcendent formal effects of sanctifying grace as term are related to notional divine love, that is, to the distinct manner in which each person is subject of the one divine intelligent and loving consciousness and the distinct manner in which each person is the term of a created relation. This assertion is proposed as probable with an intrinsic probability; for what scripture and the Fathers say about the various relations of the divine persons to the just seems to postulate that grace, while an effect of essential divine love, also be immanently constituted as a term of notional divine love, once such a theoretical framework has been established to deal with the issues.

So for our present purposes, it is sufficient to say that Lonergan uses the first of the biblical elements, "God the Father loves us as he loves his only-begotten Son Jesus," to introduce the distinction between the essential divine love common to the three divine persons and the specific manner in which each of the divine persons is subject of that love. Anything further about the dynamics of that specific manner is dependent on the way in which Lonergan elucidates the next point, namely, that the Father gifts those whom he loves in this special way with the uncreated gift of the Holy Spirit.

To summarize Lonergan's commentary on the first point, then, we may say the following. The love that the first of the biblical elements affirms is the love proper to the Father, that is, it is the Father's proper way of exercising divine love: "*God the Father* loves us," with an active loving that corresponds to Aquinas's "notionaliter diligere" and to the Father's role in active spiration. That loving is similar to the Father's love for his only-begotten Son become incarnate, Jesus of Nazareth, a love manifest at the baptism of Jesus in the Father's words, "This is my beloved Son." This means as well that, as the Father in his love communicates to the eternal Word the divine nature that the Word manifests in becoming incarnate, so the Father communicates to us some participation in that same divine nature. Sanctifying grace will be that created communication of the divine nature, to use the language of the first thesis in "De ente supernaturali."[22] In commenting on what is affirmed in the first element in the synthetic statement of biblical doctrine, Lonergan introduces the distinction of essential and notional divine love. When he comes to talk about sanctifying grace, it will be essential divine love that effects sanctifying grace, but that grace itself, as a created communication of the divine nature, will ground a created relation to the uncreated Holy Spirit, in a manner analogous to the way in which the Father's eternal love for the Son and the Son's eternal reciprocal love for the Father ground the procession of the uncreated relation that *is* the Holy Spirit; they love each other in the Holy Spirit; the Father loves us in an analogous manner to the way in which he loves the Son in the Holy Spirit; this in turn will establish the possibility of distinct relations to the other two divine persons. This is the next point in the biblical synthesis. (The role of the Son in active spiration and the specific identification of the participation in the Son's role through sanctifying grace will be addressed after we have summarized Lonergan's position on this next point.)

1.2.3 The Gift of the Holy Spirit

The second affirmation contained in the general synthetic statement of scriptural teaching tells us just why and how this is the case. The affirmation is to the effect that the Father gifts those whom he loves in this way with the uncreated gift of the Holy Spirit. Again, both John and Paul are cited in support, with numerous texts from each, including Romans 5.5, which became Lonergan's principal text on the issue.

How can a divine person be given? Lonergan refers to the following text from Aquinas:

> The word "gift" conveys the idea of being givable. Something given has a relation both to the donor and to the recipient. The donor would not give unless a gift were his to give; and it is given to the recipient for it to belong to her. A divine person is said to belong to someone ("esse alicuius") either because of origin, as the Son is the Son of the Father, or because the divine person is possessed by someone. Now, "to possess" means to have something at one's disposal to use or enjoy as one wishes, and a divine person can be possessed in this sense only by a rational creature joined to God. Other creatures can be acted upon by a divine person, but not in such a way that they have it in their power to enjoy the divine person or to use his effect. In some cases the rational creature, however, does reach that state, wherein she becomes *a sharer in the divine Word and in the proceeding Love*, so that she has at her disposal a power to know God and to love God rightly. Only a rational creature, then, has the capacity to possess a divine person. She cannot, however, come to this by her own resources; it must be given to her from above; for we say that something is given to us that we have from someone else. This is the way that to be "given" and to be "Gift" are terms applicable to a divine person.[23]

Aquinas is appealed to again in Lonergan's theological interpretation. From *Summa theologiae*, 1, q. 38, aa. 1 and 2, Lonergan draws the following. A divine person can be given if the person belongs to another divine person by origin; and a divine person can be had by a rational creature joined to God, provided the divine person has been given to the rational creature by the person or persons to whom that person belongs by origin. It is only then that the rational creature "becomes *a sharer in the divine Word and in the proceeding Love*, so that she has at her disposal a power to know God and to love God rightly."[24] The divine person that is properly called "Gift" is the Holy Spirit, since the first gift responsible for all other gifts is love, and the Holy Spirit proceeds in God precisely as Love.

The fundamental divine gift is the gift of the Holy Spirit, because "Gift" is a personal name proper to the Holy Spirit. As Aquinas writes, "… what we give first to anyone is the love with which we love him. Clearly, then, love has the quality of being our first gift; through love we give all other gratuitous gifts. Since, then …, the Holy Spirit comes forth as Love, the Spirit proceeds as the first Gift." If the other persons are given or give themselves, it will somehow be a function of the gift of the Holy Spirit.

1.2.4 Gift and Mission

This gift is also a mission of the Holy Spirit. Again, the scriptural quotations are explained by referring to Aquinas: "A divine person is said to be sent if that person exists in a new way in someone, and is said to be given if that person is possessed by someone. And neither of these occurs except in accord with [*secundum*] the grace that makes one pleasing to God."[25] And "… the very notion of mission means that the one who is sent either begins to be where previously he or she had not been, as happens in creaturely affairs, or begins to be where the one who is sent had previously been, but now in a new way, as is the case when mission is attributed to divine persons. Thus, *two things must be considered in the one to whom the mission happens: indwelling by grace and something new brought through grace.* There is, then, an invisible mission to all in whom these two features are found."[26]

How are these two "things" or features related to one another? That is the key question.

1.2.5 Created and Uncreated Grace

The relation between these two "things" that "must be considered" has been a matter of dispute. We have already seen how Lonergan and Rahner identified the same problem in the mainline Scholastic tradition at roughly the same time, but arrived at different alternatives. As Lonergan drew upon the intricacies of contingent predication about God to explain his revised thesis in 1947–48, so four years later he appeals to the same rules of predication to explain the second element in the synthetic statement of biblical doctrine. Thus, the Holy Spirit is given to us insofar as the Spirit is had by us, and this posits a change, not in the Holy Spirit or in God but in us. For whatever is predicated contingently of God is true through extrinsic denomination, and requires a created consequent condition if the predication itself is to be true. In our present instance, the change in us is denoted by the term *gratia gratum faciens*, and it is understood in terms of something being given to us, created in us, that renders us pleasing to God in a special, supernatural way, that is, in a way that correlates with our being somehow participants in Trinitarian life. The statement that the Father and the Son send the Holy Spirit could not be true were it not for this change in us. For anything predicated contingently of God, while constituted by the divine perfection, demands, if it is truly predicated, that there be a created consequent condition of the truth of the statement that contains the predication. In this case, the created consequent condition of the truth of the statement that affirms the gift and mission of the Holy Spirit is *gratia gratum faciens*. And *gratia gratum faciens* makes us pleasing to God in this special way precisely because – and here again we see the difference between Lonergan and Rahner on the issue – it elevates the created subject to become the subject of a created relation to the uncreated Holy Spirit as term of the created relation. The Holy Spirit is given to us precisely as the uncreated term of a created relation grounded in a created gift, a gift that elevates the central form of the person to participation in divine life through this created relation to an uncreated divine person. The elevation entails precisely the created base of the created relation to the uncreated Holy Spirit, a relation that imitates and participates in the relation called active spiration, which is the relation of the Father and the Son themselves to the Holy Spirit.

Thus the created relation to the uncreated Holy Spirit shares in the uncreated relation to the Holy Spirit that is Father and Son, that is, in paternity and filiation breathing the Spirit, in active spiration. And so *gratia gratum faciens*, as grounding such a relation, can with some theological fittingness be thought of as some kind of created participation in and imitation of active spiration, the eternal relation of the Father and the Son together to the Holy Spirit. Here we see the reasoning behind the statement in the four-point hypothesis that sanctifying grace is a created participation in and imitation of active spiration; it is so precisely because it grounds a created relation to the Holy Spirit, in a manner analogous to the way in which active spiration is an uncreated relation to the same Holy Spirit. What makes us pleasing to God, then, in this special way that we call grace is that we have been given a share in the relation that in God is called active spiration, the Father and the Son "breathing" the Holy Spirit, where the Son is precisely *Verbum spirans Amorem*, a Judgment of Value that breathes eternal Love. That change in us, which may fittingly be conceived as involving a created supernatural set of judgments of value, is simultaneously the created base of a created relation to the uncreated Holy Spirit, a relation that makes it possible for us to say truly that the Holy Spirit is sent to us by the Father and the Son and dwells in us as the other term, the uncreated term, of that created relation. It is the elevation of the created subject of a created relation to the uncreated Holy Spirit that is the habitual grace that unifies or integrates the various elements contained in Lonergan's ten-point statement of biblical doctrine on grace. This is an elevation of "central form," and the ten elements in the biblical doctrine represent, reflect, and manifest elevations of operations, habits, states, and potencies to the supernatural order: "so that (3) into a new life they may be (4) born again and (5) become living members of Christ; therefore as (6) just, (7) friends of God, (8) adopted children of God, and (9) heirs in hope of eternal life, (10) they enter into a sharing in the divine nature."

Moreover, active spiration is the "notional love" of the Father and the Son from which the Holy Spirit proceeds, and so sanctifying grace, as a share in that "notional love" entailing a created supernatural set of judgments of value, sets up a relation that is precisely a relation of active loving. Furthermore, the Holy Spirit, to whom we are related anew and in this special way, is a Proceeding Love in God that is an uncreated relation to the Father and the Son, a passive spiration that in its proper character is nothing but Love, the mutual Love of Father and Son. And so if the Holy Spirit abides in us, is present to us, as the uncreated term of a created supernatural relation, it is appropriate to say that there takes place in us some further created change that is the base of a created inverse relation to the Father and the Son. Our created share in active spiration obviously does not spirate the Holy Spirit, but if it is a share in active spiration, it must spirate something. It spirates charity. The further created change is charity. Charity is our created participation in the Holy Spirit, a change in us that proceeds from sanctifying grace in a manner that is analogous to the procession of the Holy Spirit from the Father and the Son and that grounds a created relation to the uncreated Father in hope and to the uncreated Son in companionship. Sanctifying grace, then, stands to charity in the created supernatural order as active spiration stands to passive spiration in the uncreated immanent Trinitarian life, and all three persons are present to us precisely as the uncreated terms of distinct but intimately connected created relations of love. They are all our beloved, and the presence of the beloved in the lover is constituted by and identical with love.[27]

1.3 Faith and the Invisible Mission of the Son

Thesis 5: *Sanctifying grace as participation in active spiration includes also a judgment of value, an ineffable "Yes" that constitutes the universalist faith that is the knowledge born of religious love. As a participation* *in active spiration, this faith reflects the invisible mission of the Son, the divine Word, the Trinitarian* Verbum spirans Amorem.

I conclude this treatment of Lonergan's 1951–52 notes with a suggestion of my own, already mentioned briefly. We have seen that the created change called charity proceeds from the unification that is *gratia gratum faciens*. But that unification participates in active spiration, and so it includes something in the order of a created supernatural *judgment of value* as a ground from which the proceeding created love emanates. As the Holy Spirit proceeds from the Father and the Son, where the Son is *Verbum spirans Amorem*, the Judgment of Value that spirates Proceeding Love, so *gratia gratum faciens* includes a judgment of value that, like the eternal Son of the Father, is *verbum spirans amorem*. In this case the proceeding *amor* is the charity that grounds a created relation of love to the Father and the Son. I wish now to suggest that this judgment of value constitutes the universalist "faith," the knowledge born of religious love, that the later Lonergan distinguishes from the beliefs of particular religious traditions, and that faith so conceived is the created external term of an invisible mission of the Son. That knowledge is an ultimately ineffable "Yes," a global judgment of value, that sometimes gets articulated in formulated statements of value. These articulated judgments of value are an outer word that is partly constitutive of the human world, thus representing the fruit of the Word's invisible mission in the silence of our hearts, the word born of our reception of the divine Word in the gift of God's love. As Charles Hefling has emphasized, the faith that flows from the gift of God's love is an ultimately ineffable knowledge. "The *inexpressibility* of faith is the cognitional counterpart of the *unrestrictedness* of the love from which it is 'born.'"[28] We will return to the effect of the outer articulations of the ineffable "yes" later, in our discussion of social grace. At the moment I wish only to establish the point that, as I am developing these materials, Lonergan's universalist faith, the knowledge born of religious love, represents the invisible mission of the Son, the divine Word.

2   The Analogy of Grace

Thesis 6: *The trinitarian structure of created grace provides a psychological analogy for understanding Trinitarian life, an analogy whose structure is isomorphic with the analogies suggested by Augustine, Aquinas, and Lonergan. Thus there is established an analogy for understanding Trinitarian processions that obtains in the supernatural order itself. This analogy joins Augustine in positing* memoria *as the first step, where* memoria *is the retrospective appropriation of the condition in which one finds oneself gifted by unconditional love.* Memoria *and*

> *the judgment of value (faith) that follows from it as* verbum spirans
> amorem *participate in active spiration. The charity that flows from
> them participates in passive spiration. Together, these form the special
> basic relations of a systematic theology.*

With the last point of the preceding section, I moved from reporting on and interpreting Lonergan to my own direct discourse. Moreover, I have suggested even in previous writings the possibility of developing a Trinitarian analogy in the order of grace.[29] But reflection on what we have just seen provides a sharper formulation of such an analogy than I have been able to come up with previously. The analogy in the order of grace begins with the gift of God's love, retrospectively interpreted as a gift of being on the receiving end of a love that is without qualification and that has about it something that seems to emanate from the foundation of the universe. I suggest that this retrospective interpretation may be linked to Augustine's *memoria*, which was the starting point of the first great psychological analogy. The various modalities that such experience can take are as varied as are the individual lives of men and women gifted with this love. This experience is the conscious manifestation of "gratia *gratum* faciens," of the grace that makes one pleasing to God in the special way that elevates one into participation in the divine life. It is the gift of God's love precisely as both received and as retrospectively acknowledged as a fundamental and permanent undertow in one's life and development, and in that acknowledgment grasped as sufficient evidence for the judgment of value that follows in the form of the assent of faith.

This initial step, then, is composed of two elements: the gift itself recollected and acknowledged in *memoria* and the inner word of a judgment of value that proceeds from the evidence of *memoria* and acknowledges the goodness of the gift. These together are the conscious manifestation of a created participation in active spiration, in divine *notionaliter diligere*, in the loving of the Father and the Son from which divine *Amor procedens*, passive spiration, the Holy Spirit, originates. My response to the question, In what does sanctifying grace, the created supernatural communication of the divine nature, consist *consciously?* is that what is metaphysically conceived as the base of a created relation to the uncreated Holy Spirit is represented in human consciousness as *memoria* and its emanating *verbum spirans amorem*, the conscious self-possession of being on the receiving end of an unrestricted love and the ineffable judgment of value that is the knowledge born of that gift of love.

The gift and its confirming word of faith, as a created participation in active spiration, ground a created relation to the Holy Spirit, who dwells in the innermost being of the person thus gifted, precisely as the uncreated term of this created relation. But the confirming word that is an element in this created participation in active spiration is a *verbum spirans amorem,* a word that breathes love, just as the uncreated reality of active spiration includes the eternal *Verbum spirans Amorem,* from whom and the Father who utters this Word there proceeds the mutual Love that is the Holy Spirit. The created love that issues from the gift and its word is the disposition of charity, the antecedent universal willingness that is a created participation in and imitation of the Holy Spirit. The relation between the love acknowledged in *memoria* and its word, on the one hand, and charity on the other is analogous to the relation between active and passive spiration in God. Moreover, the disposition of charity grounds a reverse created relation of love as its uncreated term, a relation to the Father in hope and to the Son in companionship. Thus it may be said that the three divine persons dwell in us and among us, are present to us, precisely as the uncreated terms of created supernatural relations: supernatural, because their subjects are created participations in divine life, namely, sanctifying grace (gift and word, *notionaliter diligere*) and charity (*amor procedens*). Sanctifying grace and charity, thus conceived, are the special basic relations that ground the derivation of special categories in theology.

That is the basic analogy that I want to appropriate and develop. Many further elements stand in need of clarification, including the relation of this analogy to the later analogy suggested by Lonergan, the distinction of faith and beliefs found in *Method in Theology,* the universalist faith that Lonergan proposes in the same book, distinguishing it from the beliefs proper to different religious communities and traditions, even from beliefs that themselves come from divine revelation, and Lonergan's reversal of the adage *Nihil amatum nisi praecognitum,* Nothing is loved unless it has first been known. At the moment I will treat only the first of these. The others will be taken up later.

2.1 Contrast with Lonergan's Later Trinitarian Analogy

Lonergan has given us a very succinct presentation of the analogy that he suggests in his later work. It appears in "Christology Today: Methodological Reflections."

> The psychological analogy ... has its starting point in that higher synthesis of intellectual, rational, and moral consciousness that is the dynamic state of being in love. Such love manifests itself in its judgments of value. And the judgments are carried out in decisions that are acts of loving. Such is the analogy found in the creature.
>
> Now in God the origin is the Father, in the New Testament named *ho Theos,* who is identified with *agapē* (1 John 4.8, 16). Such love

expresses itself in its Word, its Logos, its *verbum spirans amorem*, which is a judgment of value. The judgment of value is sincere, and so it grounds the Proceeding Love that is identified with the Holy Spirit.

There are then two processions that may be conceived in God; they are not unconscious processes but intellectually, rationally, morally conscious, as are judgments of value based on the evidence perceived by a lover, and the acts of loving grounded on judgments of value. The two processions ground four real relations of which three are really distinct from one another; and these three are not just relations as relations, and so modes of being, but also subsistent, and so not just paternity and filiation [and passive spiration] but also Father and Son [and Holy Spirit]. Finally, Father and Son and Spirit are eternal; their consciousness is not in time but timeless; their subjectivity is not becoming but ever itself; and each in his own distinct manner is subject of the infinite act that God is, the Father as originating love, the Son as judgment of value expressing that love, and the Spirit as originated loving.[30]

As Lonergan remarks in a question-and-answer session in the 1974 Lonergan Workshop, the only difference between this proposed analogy and the one that he develops in his earlier Trinitarian systematics has to do with the first element in the analogy. "My systematics on the Trinity is in terms of *Ipsum Intelligere*, and then the word and proceeding love. You can now start off from *Agapē*. 1 John 4.4–9 and 4.20: God is love, where God is *ho theos*. *Ho theos* in the New Testament is God the Father, unless there is contradictory evidence, and there's no contradictory evidence in 1 John. So it is the Father that is *Agapē*, and the *Agapē* is being in love, Absolute Being in Love; and the Logos is the Eternal Judgment of Value; and the Spirit is the Gift; and the person gives his loving, the act of loving; the Spirit is proceeding love from the Judgment of Value. A minor change: the structure remains the same, but we shift from orthodoxy to ortho-praxy."[31]

The difference between the analogy that I am proposing here and Lonergan's later analogy is also a difference that affects only the first element in the analogy. As Lonergan went from *Ipsum Intelligere* to *Agapē* as the dynamic state of being in love, so I am suggesting a shift from the dynamic state of being in love, which for me in the supernatural order is charity and not sanctifying grace, to a principle of love understood precisely as lovableness recollected in something like Augustine's *memoria*.

This proposed shift is not without support in Lonergan's work. In his 1951–52 notes on sanctifying grace, Lonergan lists participation in active spiration as one of the primary immanent formal effects of sanctifying grace. Primary immanent formal effects include anything that can truly be said of a subject because of what is intrinsically constitutive of that subject. What is intrinsically constitutive of the recipient of sanctifying grace is that, because this grace founds a created relation to the Holy Spirit, it can fittingly be conceived to be a created participation in active spiration. But, Lonergan goes on to say, since uncreated active spiration is the principle of the Holy Spirit, it is also the principle of proceeding divine Love itself. And the principle of proceeding love is lovableness. Love proceeds in God because the Father and the Son acknowledge each other as lovable. And so active spiration is God as lovable. Therefore, because sanctifying grace imitates active spiration, it imitates God insofar as God is lovable, and so it makes the one who possesses it lovable with a special divine love, prompting in us the judgment of value "*This* is very good," "It is very good to be loved in this way," which becomes a *verbum spirans amorem*, a word that grounds the created procession of charity.

Perhaps, as I have suggested, we are rejoining Augustine at this point, for whom "memoria," understood precisely as the condition under which the mind is present to itself, functions as the analogue for the divine Father. The condition under which the mind is present to itself, of course, can be lovableness or it can be just the opposite, and ultimately it is self-presence that has known "gratia gratum faciens" that is "memoria" as the mind present to itself in a manner that can function as the supernatural analogue for the divine Father. Augustine's "memoria" thus understood, we might say, is at least roughly similar to Heidegger's "Befindlichkeit," when the latter is graced in the same way. As "memoria" and "mens" are equiprimordial for Augustine's understanding of self-consciousness, and as "Befindlichkeit" and "Verstehen" are equiprimordial ways of being "Dasein" for Heidegger, so perhaps lovableness recollected in *memoria* and *intelligere* as *dicere*, where what are uttered are supernatural judgments of value, are equiprimordial constituents of the originating element in a psychological analogue for the Trinity in the order of grace. All of this is marked, notice, by a massive "perhaps." Systematic theology is irretrievably hypothetical. Nonetheless, I think the argument is compelling.

Even in his comments on the synthetic statement of biblical doctrine, then, Lonergan is setting up the need for a twofold terminology, entailing both sanctifying grace and charity, for the reality of the divine indwelling when that indwelling comes to be explained systematically. And he is doing so in a context that is at least in principle independent of the Aristotelian metaphysical framework.

What is the new framework that could support that continued distinction? The richness of Lonergan's reflections on scripture in the notes that he wrote in 1951–52 leads me to ask, as I asked in an earlier article entitled "Consciousness and Grace,"[32] whether to speak of the methodical transposition of the category of sanctifying grace in terms of "being in love with God," or more precisely, in terms of an otherworldly being-in-love that is without conditions or qualifications or restrictions or reservations, as Lonergan does,[33] is perhaps too compact. As I have already indicated, Lonergan later admitted that this transposition represents an amalgam of the categories of sanctifying grace and charity. To me Lonergan's later expressions connote our participation through charity in the relation to the Father and the Son that is the Holy Spirit, but do not satisfactorily convey the participation in the created relation that makes it be true that the Holy Spirit is precisely *given* to us as a term of a relation; that is, it does not convey "gratia *gratum faciens*"; it does not adequately convey the "making pleasing" that for me is better articulated biblically in 1 John 4.10 and 4.19 than in Romans 5.5, which leaves itself open to an interpretation that misses the point:[34] "This is the love I mean: not our love for God, but God's love for us when he sent his Son ... We are to love, then, because he loved us first." More needs to be done to articulate the experiential emphasis relevant to sanctifying grace, an element that will have something to do with the literal meaning of "gratum faciens," with being on the receiving end of a divine love that makes us pleasing to God by giving us a created participation in divine life in the form of a created relation to the Holy Spirit that shares in the uncreated relation of active spiration and that releases in us the love for God in return, the charity that is a created relation to the Father and the Son and a created participation in and imitation of the Holy Spirit, who is their mutual love for each other. The gift element is shortchanged when the distinction of sanctifying grace and charity, or of their conscious representations, is neglected. The gift can be increasingly differentiated, and this represents one of the fruits of religious development. I am attempting here a theoretical interior differentiation of the gift.

This corroborates the genius of some of the best directors of the Ignatian *Spiritual Exercises,* who begin by asking the exercitant to meditate on scriptural passages that could enkindle in one's memory the sense of being on the receiving end of divine love, just as Ignatius himself ends the *Exercises* with a contemplation for obtaining the love of God in return. And in another aside let me add that, while I was first composing this material in an earlier version, I came across the following from Diadochus of Photice in the Divine Office for Friday of the Second Week in Ordinary Time: "Anyone who loves God in the depths of his heart has already been loved by God. In fact, the measure of a man's love for God depends upon how deeply aware he is of God's love for him. When this awareness is keen, it makes whoever possesses it long to be enlightened by the divine light, and this longing is so intense that it seems to penetrate his very bones. He loses all consciousness of himself and is entirely transformed by the love of God."

That passage reflects a mystical intensification of the set of relations offered in grace to all men and women at every time and place. These relations would constitute the "special basic relations" that for some reason are left out of the following central methodological passage in *Method in Theology*: "[G]eneral basic terms name conscious and intentional operations. General basic relations name elements in the dynamic structure linking operations and generating states. Special basic terms name God's gift of his love and Christian witness. Derived terms and relations name the objects known in operations and correlative to states."[35] The special basic relations are the created participations in the divine relations of active and passive spiration, through being on the receiving end of God's love in *gratia gratum faciens* and loving God in return in charity.

3

Contingent Predication and the Divine Missions

Thesis 7: *The divine missions are constituted by God alone as consequent upon the relations of opposition that are the Trinity, but the judgments that affirm the missions require a created term external to God as a consequent condition of the truth of the judgments. In the case of the mission of the Son, that external term is the secondary act of existence that is the base of a real relation of the human nature of Jesus to the eternal Word which, precisely as a divinely constituted relation to the Word, participates in the eternal relation to the Word that is paternity. In the case of the mission of the Holy Spirit, the external term is twofold. "Sanctifying grace" has been the name given the created base of a real relation to the Holy Spirit; that base thus participates in active spiration, the divinely constituted relation to the Holy Spirit, and so in the Father and the Son as together they breathe the Holy Spirit. The disposition of charity flows from that participation in active spiration, and so is the base of a real relation to the Father and the Son that participates in passive spiration, the divinely constituted eternal relation to the Father and the Son, and so in the Holy Spirit. In terms of religiously differentiated consciousness, these may be characterized, respectively, as the reception of the unqualified love of the Father and of the eternal judgment of value that is the Son, both of these in the Holy Spirit, and as the return of love to the Father and the Son, again in the Holy Spirit. These missions are extended in the mission of the church, in part to catalyze non-violent responses to evil. This is part of the grounding statement of a theology of social grace. Finally, the light of glory as the created consequent condition of beatific knowledge is the created supernatural participation in and imitation of filiation, as in the Holy Spirit the Son brings us, his brothers and sisters, children by adoption, perfectly back to the Father.*

The disposition of hope that flows from the gift of God's love is our present historical participation in this ultimately eschatological relation.

1   Contingent Predication

I have already mentioned the requirements of contingent predication about God. Before we go any further, it would be best to explain more fully what this means. Lonergan states the basic principle very succinctly: "The principle in all of this is that contingent truths, whether predicated of the divine persons commonly or properly, have their constitution in God but their term in creatures. Therefore, although the external works of God are necessarily common to the three persons, the missions in the strict sense are necessarily proper, since a divine person operates by reason of the divine essence but is not really and truly sent except by reason of a relation of origin."[1] The issue has to do with the proper way to consider the "term in creatures" of a divine mission. On Lonergan's understanding, the created external term is a "consequent condition" of the truth of the contingent predication.

Thus, his fifteenth assertion in *The Triune God: Systematics* reads as follows: "What is truly predicated contingently of the divine persons is constituted by the divine perfection itself, but it has a consequent condition in an appropriate external term."[2] The assertion is demonstrated quickly in three points. First, "any constitutive formality other than the divine perfection itself is superfluous for constituting whatever is truly predicated contingently of the divine persons," since "each divine person as well as all together are infinite in perfection" and "where there is present a formality constitutive of infinite perfection, any other formality is superfluous."[3] Second, the inquiry is about contingent truths, what can be or not be but in fact is, but the infinite divine perfection is necessary; and "the correspondence of truth is lacking where a truth is contingent but the corresponding reality is absolutely necessary."[4] Thus there must be some appropriate term external to God if what is truly predicated contingently of the divine persons is to have the correspondence of truth. And third, that "necessary external term is not a constitutive cause [of divine operation] but only a condition [of the truth of the contingent predication], and indeed a condition that is not prior or simultaneous [with respect to the contingently predicated operation] but consequent [upon it],"[5] since it neither precedes nor accompanies the constitution or production of something else but follows it. "[T]he divine persons are absolutely independent with respect to all created things."[6]

Assertion 16 goes on to speak of the application of this principle to what we saw an instance of in the last chapter, namely, what is attributed to the three divine persons together – for instance, essential divine love. "Whatever is truly predicated contingently of the divine persons as regards divine cognitive, volitional, and productive operation is constituted by the divine perfection common to the three persons as both the principle-by-which and the principle-which, and therefore is attributed distinctly and equally to each divine person."[7] Lonergan appeals precisely to the statement of Pius XII that had perhaps left him hesitant in 1947 to affirm the possibility of distinct relations on our part to each of the divine persons: "[T]his most certain truth must be firmly borne in mind, that in these matters all things are to be held as being common to the Holy Trinity, inasmuch as these same things are related to God as their supreme efficient cause" (DB 2290, DS 3814, ND 1996).

Again, the argument is straightforward. "Whatever a divine person knows, wills, and produces, that person knows, wills, and produces by that person's own knowledge, will, and power." But "the knowledge, will, and power of a divine person is the same in reality as the divine essence itself," which as subsistent is not only a principle-by-which but also a principle-which. And this divine essence is identical with the divine perfection common to the three persons, and so "whatever a divine person knows, wills, and produces, that person knows, wills, and produces by the divine perfection common to the three persons equally as both the principle-by-which and the principle-which."[8] Still, the three persons have the same knowledge, the same will, the same power according to an order that is in keeping with the divine relations, and so they exercise the divine knowledge, will, power not in a confused fashion but distinctly, each as the person that person is according to the order of the divine relations.

Let us take the statement, "God knows, wills, and makes the universe to exist." The truth of that statement is a contingent truth. It does not have to be true; it simply is true. What is required for that statement to be true? The existence of the universe affirmed in the statement "God knows, wills, and makes the universe to exist" is *constituted* by the divine intelligent intention to create the universe, and by that alone, and yet there is also required a created consequent condition if the statement under consideration is to be true, namely, the existence of the universe. But the divine essence *is* the three divine persons, each in the order to the other two determined by the infinite divine relations; and so each exercises the divine cognitional, volitional, and productive essence in a manner consonant with the person's exercise of the divine nature: the Father as *Dicens*, the Son as *Verbum*, and the Holy Spirit as *Amor procedens*.

An analogous structure of constitution and condition is required if we are to understand the divine missions, the sending of the Son and the Holy Spirit, the missions that in effect are the Trinity in history. Thus Lonergan's assertion 17 reads, "The mission of a divine person is constituted by a divine relation of origin in such a way that it still demands an appropriate external term as a consequent condition."[9] But we are no longer speaking of what is attributed to the three divine persons together as regards divine cognitive, volitional, and productive operation, but of what is predicated distinctly of each person. So before he proceeds to this assertion, Lonergan first must pause to consider four questions.

The first is, "Did God the Father send the Son to redeem the human race?"[10] The second is, "Do the Father and the Son send the Holy Spirit?"[11] The third is, "Is a divine person sent by the person or persons from whom that person proceeds?"[12] And the fourth is, "Is it by appropriation that the Father and the Son are said to send the Holy Spirit?"[13] As questions that can be answered either yes or no, these are doctrinal questions, not systematic questions. Thus the first is answered in the statement that "sacred scripture most clearly teaches that God the Father sent his Son to redeem the human race."[14] It is well to quote Lonergan's substantiation of this affirmation.

> Galatians 4.4: "But when the fullness of time had come, God sent his Son, born of a woman, born under the law, in order to redeem those who were under the law, so that we might receive adoption as children."
>
> St John has more fully expounded this same teaching. For the one who sends is God the Father (John 3.16–17, 5.23, 8.16, 14.24, 20.21), the living Father (6.57), the Father testifying (5.37), the Father drawing [people to Jesus] (6.44), the Father giving a command [to Jesus] (12.49), the only true God (17.3), whom the persecutors do not know (15.21).
>
> The Son who was sent teaches not a doctrine of his own but that of the one who sent him (John 7.16, 7.18, 8.28, 12.49, 14.24); similarly, the Son who was sent seeks not a will of his own but the will of the one who sent him (4.24, 5.30, 6.38, 8.29); indeed, the Son can do nothing by himself (5.19, 5.30).
>
> The Son was not sent to be alone (John 8.16, 8.29, 10.30, 38), nor did he come on his own (7.28, 8.42); but he knows the one from whom he is and who has sent him (7.29), and he can say, "Whoever sees me sees him who sent me" (12.45), and finally, he goes to him "who sent me" (7.33, 16.5).
>
> The Son was sent out of the Father's love (1 John 4.9; John 3.16; Romans 8.32), was sent in the likeness of sinful flesh (Romans 8.3), for the salvation of the world (John 3.17), that we might live through him (1 John 4.9), that the world might believe and know the Father

who sends and the Son who is sent (John 5.24, 6.29, 11.42, 17.8, 21, 23, 25) and have eternal life (John 5.24, 17.3).

This mission has its extension. For just as the Father sends the Son, so the Son sends the apostles (John 17.18, 20.21). "Just as the living Father sent me, and I live because of the Father, so whoever eats me will live because of me" (John 6.57; see 5.26). "Whoever receives one whom I send receives me; and whoever receives me receives him who sent me" (John 13.20; see Matthew 10.40, Luke 10.16); conversely, "Anyone who does not honor the Son does not honor the Father who sent him" (John 5:23).

The conclusion is equally clear. "It is clear, therefore, (1) that a divine person is the one sending, (2) that another divine person is sent, (3) that the divine person who is sent lives because of the one sending, teaches the doctrine of the one sending, wills the aim of the one sending, and performs the works of the one sending, (4) that the divine person is sent to human persons in order that they may live, believe, know, love, and perform greater works (John 14.12; see 9.3–4, 10.32, 10.37, 14.10–11, 15.24, 17.4), and (5) that through the mediation of others this mission extends to other human persons."[15]

Again, the second question is answered in the affirmative, and on the same basis. "[S]acred scripture clearly and with certitude teaches the sending of the Holy Spirit by the Father and the Son." Thus:

Galatians 4.6: "And because you are children, God has sent the Spirit of his Son into your hearts, crying, 'Abba, Father.'"

John 14.26: "But the Advocate, the Holy Spirit, whom the Father will send in my name, will teach you everything, and remind you of all that I have said to you." See John 14.16–17.

John 15.26: "When the Advocate comes, whom I will send to you from the Father, the Spirit of truth who comes from the Father, he will testify on my behalf." See John 16.7 and 1 Peter 1.12.

Hence, the Holy Spirit who is sent is said to be given (John 14.15; Romans 5.5; 1 Thessalonians 4.8; 1 John 3.24, 4.13), to be received (Romans 8.15; 1 Corinthians 3.2; Galatians 3.2; John 20.22; see 2 Corinthians 11.4), to be had (Romans 8.9; 1 Corinthians 7.40; see Hebrews 6.4; Jude 19), indwelling (Romans 8.9, 11; 1 Corinthians 3.16, 6.19; 2 Timothy 1.14), to be poured out (Titus 3.5; Acts 2.33), to be supplied (Galatians 3.5), to be the pledge of our inheritance (Ephesians 1.14; see 2 Corinthians 1.22; Romans 8.23), to be a seal (Ephesians 1.13, 4.30).

Besides, as the doctrine of the Son who is sent is not his own but that of the Father, so also the Spirit who is sent does not teach his own doctrine; John 16.13: "When the Spirit of truth comes, he will guide you into all the truth; for he will not speak on his own, but will speak whatever he hears …"

Furthermore, as the Son who is sent is not alone (John 8.16, 29), so also the Spirit who is sent and indwelling is not alone. For after John tells about the Advocate who is to be sent "to be with you forever" and says that "he abides with you, and he will be in you" (John 14.16–17), he soon adds, "We will come to them and make our home with them" (John 14.23). St Paul likewise very easily goes from the Spirit to Christ: "since the Spirit of God dwells in you" (Romans 8.9), and "if Christ is in you" (Romans 8.10). Thus, both John and Paul sometimes speak of God abiding (1 John 4.12, 13, 16), and of the temple of God (1 Corinthians 3.16, 6.16).[16]

While the third question is also doctrinal, the answer, after responding by citing biblical doctrine, moves into systematic-theological considerations.

Thus, when "mission" is understood in the sense meant by the New Testament, "it is clear that a divine person himself is sent and indeed is sent by that person or by those persons from whom he proceeds."[17]

> [I]n the New Testament (1) the Father alone among the divine persons is not sent; (2) the Son is sent to the world by the Father to teach not his own doctrine but that of the Father, to seek not his own will but that of the Father, to perform not his own works but those of the Father; (3) the Holy Spirit is sent by the Father and the Son, not to speak on his own but to teach what he has heard; (4) St Paul in the very same text (Galatians 4.4–6) uses the word *exapostellō* twice, first to designate the mission of the Son and then to designate the mission of the Spirit of the Son; and (5) in the New Testament the words *apostellō, apostolos, exapostellō,* and *pempō* generally have a somewhat technical meaning, namely, that the person sent receives authority from the one sending to fulfil some duty towards others.[18]

From the standpoint of systematic understanding, then, "the relation of origin of the person sent is included in the formality of mission,[19] and accordingly … the Holy Spirit proceeds from the Son because he is sent by the Son."[20] Thus, "When the sense is that a divine person is really and truly sent by a divine person, as is the case in the New Testament, a real relation "*who from another*" is included in the very formality of mission; and since this sort of real relation in God is not really distinct from the relation of origin, it necessarily follows that a divine person is not sent except by the one or by those from whom that person proceeds."[21] Lonergan refers to this scriptural usage as the "technical" meaning of the term "mission."[22]

The importance of this precision shows up in the response to the fourth question, for that the Holy Spirit is sent might mean simply that a finite spiritual effect is produced in a creature, and then the statement is true by appropriation, since all works of God ad extra are common to the three divine persons. Or it may mean that the Holy Spirit "comes into" a creature, and then again the meaning is by appropriation, for "to come into" does not imply a relation of origin, and distinct predications regarding divine persons are proper only when distinction is by relational opposition. But "if the Holy Spirit is really and truly sent by the others, there is in the Holy Spirit himself a true and real relation according to which he is ordered to the ones who send as to those from whom. This real relation of the Holy Spirit can only be passive spiration, which is wholly proper to the Holy Spirit." And so in this sense of New Testament mission it is not true to say that it is by appropriation that the Holy Spirit is said to be sent by the Father and the Son.

These doctrinal considerations have allowed Lonergan to proceed to his assertion 17, which we have quoted above. What is the ontological constitution that establishes the truth of the affirmations that God the Father sends the Son and that the Father and the Son send the Holy Spirit? To ask such a question is to ask "what is required and is sufficient for it to be true that the Son is sent by the Father, and that the Holy Spirit is sent by the Father and the Son?"[23] Lonergan responds: "We answer this question with two assertions: first, that the mission of a divine person is constituted by a divine relation of origin itself; second, that although such a mission is constituted by a relation of origin alone, nevertheless an appropriate external term is required."[24] The position, then, distinguishes between what is added to the infinite, that is, nothing, and what is constituted by the infinite, namely, what is not finite. Next, the analogy that the position uses in order to understand the affirmation that it is making is taken from divinity itself as expounded in the previous two assertions: "[J]ust as God knows that contingent things exist through his own knowledge, and not through an external term, which is nevertheless required, and just as God wills that contingent things exist through his own volition, and not through an external term, which is nevertheless required, and just as God makes contingent things exist through his own omnipotence and not through an external term, which is nevertheless required, so also the [incarnate] Son *is* all that he is through his own proper divine act of existence and not through an external term, which is nevertheless absolutely required, and the Holy Spirit is sent through that which the Holy Spirit is and not through an external term, which is nevertheless absolutely required."[25] Further with respect to the Holy Spirit,

"[I]f the Holy Spirit is really and truly sent by the Father and the Son, there is present in the Holy Spirit himself a real relation, '*who from others.*' This real relation [*which constitutes the mission*] is really identical with passive spiration but conceptually distinguished from it. It is really identical, because nothing real and intrinsic can be added to the infinite perfection of a divine person; it is conceptually distinct, because passive spiration is eternal and necessary and needs no created term, whereas a mission is temporal and contingent and requires a created consequent term as a condition."[26]

The first step in the argument regarding proper contingent predication is that a divine mission is not constituted without an eternal divine relation of origin. "Inasmuch as it is true that the Father sends the Son, it is true that the Father is the one sending, that the Father is not the one sent, that the Son is not the one sending, and that the Son is the one sent. Now, opposites are not really and truly predicated of the divine persons except according to relations of origin; but "to be sending" and "to be sent" are opposites that are really and truly predicated of divine persons; therefore they are predicated according to relations of origin ... Similarly, inasmuch as it is true that the Father and the Son send the Holy Spirit, it is true that the Father and the Son are the ones who send and not the ones sent, and that the Holy Spirit is the one sent and not the one sending."[27] The second part of the argument adds that, since the eternal relations of origin are identical with the divine essence and so are infinite in perfection, no other cause or constitutive reason is required for the constitution of the divine missions: "just as a divine person is and knows and wills and operates by the divine essence, and is distinguished as generating or generated, or as spirating or spirated, by a divine relation of origin, so also a divine person is constituted as sending or as sent by a divine relation of origin."[28] And the third part states that the fact that a divine person is sent is contingently true, and because what is contingently true cannot have the correspondence of truth through what is necessary alone, there must be an appropriate term external to God if the propositions regarding the divine missions are to be true, and this external term cannot be either a prior or a simultaneous condition but only a consequent condition. The person sending and the person sent in no way depend on the creature, and so, although the term is a condition, because it is required, it cannot be a previous or simultaneous condition.

What does it mean to say that the appropriate external term is consequent upon the constituted mission? How can this be?

God is *ens per intellectum* and *agens per intellectum,* being by understanding and agent by understanding. That is, God *is* through understanding, in that God's act of existing is God's act of understanding and of willing; and God acts through understanding, in that God's act of producing is God's act of understanding and of willing. Thus, by the very fact that the Father and the

Son and the Holy Spirit conceive and will that one of the divine persons be sent, already there are had the constituted mission and the produced appropriate external term. There is had the constitution because God *is* through understanding, and so whatever God understands about God is God. There is had the production because God acts through understanding, and so whatever God understands to be external to God *is* external to God. The external term is consequent upon the divine intention to constitute a divine mission.

To explain this further, Lonergan distinguishes (1) constitution in an active sense, (2) constitution in a passive sense, (3) production in an active sense, and (4) production in a passive sense. Then: (1) constitution in an active sense is common to the three persons, since the three conceive and will (active) that the Father sends the Son and that the Father and the Son send the Holy Spirit; (2) constitution in a passive sense is proper to the sender and the sent, in that each is a distinct recipient of the common understanding, knowledge, and will of the three: the three conceive and will, not that the three send and are sent, but that the Father sends the Son, and that the Father and the Son send the Holy Spirit; each of them, understood and willed to be either sending or sent, is on the "receiving" end of the common divine intention, and this is what is meant by constitution in the passive sense; the senders and the sent are truly and really respectively constituted as sender and sent; (3) production in an active sense is common to the three persons, since the three conceive and will that an appropriate external term be produced, and since the very conceiving joined to willing *is* the very omnipotent act of producing; (4) although constitution in an active sense and production in an active sense are common to the three persons, they are common not in a confused way but in a way distinct to each: that the Son understands and wills that he himself is sent by the Father is something the Son has from the Father just as the Son has substance from the Father; that the Holy Spirit understands and wills that she is sent by the Father and the Son is something the Holy Spirit has from the Father and the Son just as the Spirit has substance from the Father and the Son; and similarly for production in an active sense; each is subject of constitution in an active sense and subject of production in an active sense in a distinct fashion; (5) production in a passive sense *is* the appropriate external term itself, as dependent upon its first efficient cause; (6) to the intrinsically immutable divine persons nothing real and intrinsic is added whether by constitution in an active sense or by constitution in a passive sense or by production in an active sense; (7) nevertheless, through the infinite and unlimited divine perfection, common or proper as the case may demand, the three persons truly and really do constitute, the senders and the sent are truly and really respectively constituted as senders and sent, and the three persons truly and really equally produce the appropriate terms; (8) just as the divine immutability makes a real and intrinsic addition to God impossible, so also the divine infinity makes it superfluous.[29]

The incarnation of the Son and the giving of the Holy Spirit are similar in their mode of constitution and production, in that the eight items just listed are found in each. But they differ altogether in many respects with regard to what is constituted and produced. First, in the incarnation the material external term of the mission (the external term considered in abstraction from the formality that makes it precisely the external term of a *mission*)[30] is a non-subsistent human nature, non-subsistent because the hypostatic union is in and on the basis of the divine person, not a human person; but in the gift of the Spirit the material external term is a subsistent human nature, since the union of grace is between persons. Thus, while the subsistent nature that is the material external term of the gift of the Holy Spirit subsists through its own proper and proportionate act of existence, the non-subsistent nature that is the material external term of the incarnation does not subsist, since it lacks a proper and proportionate act of existence: the proper act of existence of the incarnate Word is the act of existence of the divine Word.

Moreover, in the incarnation the Son is both God and a human being through a proper divine act of existence; but this contingent truth qua contingent is true because there is an external created term that Thomas calls the *esse secundarium*. Since this assumption exceeds the proportion of human nature, which has only an obediential potency to it, the *esse secundarium* also exceeds the proportion of the assumed nature. Thus it is supernatural. But in the giving of the Holy Spirit the Holy Spirit by the Spirit's own proper perfection is both the gift and given to us; this contingent truth qua contingent is true because there is the external created term that we know as sanctifying grace, by which a subsistent nature (material external term) is graced (*gratum*) and rendered holy to God; as we have seen this term is a created supernatural base of a created relation to the uncreated Holy Spirit, which is precisely the manner in which the Holy Spirit is given to us; and since the uncreated gift and the created holiness exceed the proportion of this nature, which has only an obediential potency to them, so also sanctifying grace exceeds the proportion of nature, and so is supernatural. Moreover, there is a difference in the manner in which the one sent is not alone. In recounting the scriptural data earlier in the chapter, Lonergan had stated that in either mission, the one sent is not alone. "Whoever sees me sees the one who sent me." "*We* will come to that one and make our home there." Now he adds, "Although in the incarnation the Son as God is not alone, it is the Son alone who becomes incarnate. But in giving the Spirit, although the Spirit alone according to his proper perfection is gift, still, since to give one's entire love is the same as to give oneself, and since the Father and the Son give their entire proceeding Love, they also give themselves and therefore are said to come and dwell in the just."[31] Thus Lonergan concludes that "the Father, the Son, and the Holy Spirit understand, will, constitute, and accomplish different things in the incarnation and in the giving of the Spirit."[32]

It is precisely at this point that Lonergan introduces the four-point hypothesis, and he does so in response to a question regarding the *supernatural* character of the formal terms of the missions. These terms are supernatural because they are respective created imitations of and participations in the four divine relations. Through them we become participants in the divine nature. We live with the life of God. They name the immanent constitution of our life in God.

Let us review what we have said about contingent predication and the divine missions. We begin with the mission of the Word. The divine Word, the Son sent by the Father, is incarnate in the human being Jesus of Nazareth. What is required for that affirmation to be true?

First, sending and being sent are opposites: the Father sends while the Son is sent. Now the inherited tradition of theological doctrines informs us that the only way in which opposites can be predicated of the divine persons is in terms of the relations of origin immanent in the triune God. And so the statements that the Father sends the Son and that the Son is sent by the Father cannot be true unless they are a function of the eternal relations of origin by which the Father generates the Son and the Son is born of the Father. What is required for our affirmation to be true, what is required for the mission that the statement affirms, is first, then, the eternal divine procession of the Son from the Father.

Second, nothing else is required to *constitute* the mission affirmed in the statement that the divine Word, the Son sent by the Father, is incarnate in the human being Jesus of Nazareth. We are talking about a relation that is immanent in the infinite God, and surely nothing more is required beyond God's own infinite perfection as constitutive reason of anything that is a function of that relation. Aquinas, Lonergan, and Hans Urs von Balthasar agree that there is a very definite sense in which the mission of the divine Word *is* the procession of the divine Word.[33]

Third, the affirmation "The divine Word, the Son sent by the Father, is incarnate in the human being Jesus of Nazareth" expresses also something that cannot be accounted for by the eternal procession of the Word alone, even though the truth affirmed is constituted by that procession alone. That something else is not constitutive of the mission affirmed in the statement. But it is a created consequent condition required for the affirmation of the mission to be true. There is an incarnation, the incarnation is in the human nature received from Mary, and the incarnation is the incarnation of the divine Word, of the Son, alone. These three statements are true. We hold their truth in faith. But their truth is contingent: it did not have to be this way. The procession of the divine Word immanent in the Godhead is not contingent. It is a dimension of God's necessary being. It alone is constitutive of the mission affirmed in the statement, a mission which in a very definite sense is identical with the procession. But the mission of that Word in history is thoroughly contingent, and the procession cannot be contingent in history without a created condition consequent upon the divine disposition constitutive of the mission. An affirmation of the contingent mission requires such a created condition. Just as the statement "God knows, wills, and makes the universe to exist" requires nothing more to constitute its truth than the divine intelligent intention, and yet the truth of the statement requires as a created consequent condition the existence of the universe, so the affirmation that the divine Word is incarnate in Jesus requires nothing more to constitute its truth than the eternal relation of origin of the Son from the Father, and yet the truth of the statement requires a created consequent condition.

That created condition is not simply the created humanity of Jesus. My humanity and yours are created by God, and yet it is not true that the divine Word, the Son sent by the Father, is incarnate in us. Created humanity is nature. That the divine Word is incarnate in a created human being expresses a truth in the supernatural order. There must be some created supernatural reality in that human being that makes it possible that there be a created relation to the uncreated divine Word. In the 1951–52 expression of the four-point hypothesis, that created condition is called by Lonergan *gratia unionis*, the grace of union; but in *The Triune God: Systematics*, Lonergan revives a Thomist notion and calls the condition the *esse secundarium incarnationis*, the secondary act of existence of the Incarnation. Moreover, in *The Ontological and Psychological Constitution of Christ*, that created grace is spoken of in terms of or in reference to the real *relation* of the created humanity of Jesus to the divine Son alone. There Lonergan speaks of a created act in the substantial and not accidental order that is related to the person of the Son of God, an act that both perfects the obediential potency of the human nature of Jesus so that it is actually assumed by the Son of God, and constitutes the external term whereby this contingent fact is true, namely, that the Son of God has actually assumed this human nature. It is not enough, however, to speak of a real created relation. In the order of creation, relation is always the relation of some term to another term, or if you will of a base to a term. The external, created, contingent, appropriate condition must be the created base of a real relation of the assumed nature to the Son alone, a base that guarantees three contingent truths:

(1) there is an incarnation; (2) the incarnation occurs in the nature received from Mary; (3) it is the incarnation of the eternal Word of God. A real relation is possible only when a real foundation or base for that relation exists. That foundation has to be a supernatural substantial act that is received in a complete individual human nature in such a way that that nature *cannot* receive the substantial act of existence to which it is naturally proportionate: it receives a "secondary" act to which it is not naturally proportionate, one that is absolutely supernatural, the actuation of an obediential potency. The Word did not assume a human person but a human nature. Hence there must be ruled out from the assumed human nature that substantial act of existence to which that essence is naturally ordered and proportionate. In metaphysical terms, the human nature of Christ is not actuated as a natural potency, and so, although by its essence there is potentially here a subsistent finite being, that subsistent finite being never actually came to be, since the subsistent being that is Jesus of Nazareth is the eternal Son of the Father. As obediential potency the human nature is indeed actuated, but as the nature assumed by the Word. There is a substantial supernatural act received in Christ's human nature that is the base of the real relation of the assumed nature to the Word alone. This "secondary act of existence" is required, not for the human essence of Christ to be real, not for the existence of that essence, not as the constitutive cause whereby Christ the man exists, not as some intermediary linking and uniting the divinity and humanity, not as the grace of union constituting the union, but only as the grace of union required by and consequent upon the constitutive cause of the union. "In the hypostatic union there is present besides the infinite act of existence of the Word a secondary substantial act of existence as a term received in Christ's human essence, just as in the justification of a sinner besides the uncreated gift of the Holy Spirit there is also present as a term sanctifying grace received in the soul as an accident, and in the beatific vision in addition to the divine essence, which in a way fulfills the function of an intelligible species, there is just such a term in the light of glory."[34] Without the real created relation of the assumed humanity to the eternal Word, a relation founded in that secondary act of existence of the assumed humanity, it would not be true that there is an incarnation of the divine Word in Jesus, that the complete humanity of Jesus is the complete humanity of the divine Word.[35] Thomas Aquinas, and Lonergan following him, expressed the created base of that created real relation in the metaphysical term *esse secundarium*, the secondary act of existence of the assumed human nature.

However, that expression, while accurate, should not distract us from the real *relation* that the *esse secundarium* makes possible, the created relation of the humanity of Jesus to the eternal Word of God, making it be true that the complete humanity of Jesus is the complete humanity of the divine Word. Without that created relation the affirmation with which we began would not be true.

Now in the four-point hypothesis that appears in Lonergan's Trinitarian theology and earlier in the 1951–52 notes, this real relation of the assumed humanity to the Son alone is conceived as a created participation in and imitation of a *divine* relation. Perhaps counter-intuitively at first, that real divine relation is the relation of paternity.[36] The base of the created relation of the humanity of Jesus to the eternal Son is a participation in and imitation of the Father. That hypothesis – and as a statement proper to systematic theology it is nothing more than a hypothesis – expresses the kind of Christology that from a scriptural standpoint is most apparent in the Gospel of John but that is not absent from the synoptic Gospels, and in fact could even be argued to provide a kind of theological context for the more elemental narrative-dramatic portrayal of Jesus in the synoptic Gospels. "The Son can do nothing by himself; he can do only what he sees the Father doing; and whatever the Father does the Son does too. For the Father loves the Son and shows him everything he does himself" (John 5.19–20). "My teaching is not from myself: it comes from the one who sent me" (John 7.16). "To have seen me is to have seen the Father" (John 14. 9). Etc., etc., etc.

Again, the divine Word immanent in the Godhead does not speak; the immanent divine Word is spoken; in technical theological language, its notional act is not *dicere*, to speak, but *dici*, to be spoken. But the incarnate Word speaks, and he speaks only what he hears from the Father. The relation of the assumed humanity to the person of the divine Word alone is also a created participation in and imitation of the Father's real relation to the Son, a participation in and imitation of the relation to the Son, the *Dicere*, that we call paternity. *The secondary act of existence grounding the relation of the assumed humanity of Jesus to the eternal divine Word is in our history the base of a created participation in and imitation of the Father's eternal relation to the Word that the Father eternally speaks.*

We will see the meaning of this hypothesis more clearly in terms of history if we move on to our next consideration.

Here we consider another affirmation of faith: The Holy Spirit is sent by the Father and the Son. Nothing more is required for the mission to be *constituted* than the relation of origin according to which the Holy Spirit eternally proceeds from the Father and the Son. There is a very definite sense in which the mission of the Holy Spirit is the procession of the Holy Spirit. But as with the mission of the Son sent by the Father, so here too the mission of the Holy Spirit sent by the Father and the Son is contingent and temporal, and so it requires an appropriate created external term, not as constitutive of the mission affirmed in the statement "The Holy Spirit is sent by the Father and the Son" but as a consequent created condition of the truth of that affirmation. Without that created external term the proposition "The Holy Spirit is sent by the Father and the Son" would not be true.

What is the relevant created external term? Again, the relevant created external term is expressed in relational terms, but in this case two created relations are entailed. There are two relevant created external terms of the mission of the Holy Spirit, and they are relational, in the sense of mutually opposed relations of origin.

First, we may presume that the Holy Spirit is sent as what the Holy Spirit is. Just as the Son is sent as the Father's divine Word, so the Holy Spirit is sent as proceeding Love, the Love spirated, breathed, by the Father and the Son in an eternal spiration through which the Father and the Son love themselves and one another and us precisely by the Holy Spirit.[37] The Holy Spirit is thus sent as a special divine Love through which *we* are enabled to love with a love that participates in and imitates God's own love.[38] That created love is what our inherited dogmatic-theological context has called charity. And so the appropriate created external term is charity, a created share in God's own proceeding Love. Charity is a created participation in and imitation of the divine relation of passive spiration, that is, of the Holy Spirit.

But that divine relation is a relation to the Father and the Son, who together are active spiration breathing the Love that proceeds from their mutual interrelation. And so, Lonergan says, "although the Spirit alone according to his proper perfection is gift, still, since to give one's entire love is the same as to give oneself, and since the Father and the Son give their entire proceeding Love, they also give themselves and therefore are said to come and dwell in [us]."[39] And so if charity is created participation in and imitation of the Holy Spirit, it must be grounded in and proceed from a created supernatural participation in and imitation of the Father and the Son as they breathe the Holy Spirit. This divine relation is what the theological tradition calls active spiration. So while charity is the created supernatural participation in and imitation of passive spiration, that is, of the Holy Spirit, the divine Gift, charity proceeds in us from a created supernatural participation in and imitation of active spiration, of the Father and the Son together breathing the Holy Spirit.

The latter participation and imitation is what traditional theology has called sanctifying grace.[40] Sanctifying grace is the created supernatural participation in and imitation of Father and Son, *Agapē* and Word, as together they "breathe," spirate, the proceeding Love that is the Holy Spirit. Father and Son are divine *Agapē* and its Word, its Logos, its Judgment of Value, its *Verbum spirans Amorem.* Sanctifying grace is conceived as a created participation in and imitation of the divine *Agapē* and its Word, as these together constitute an active loving based on a mutual recognition of lovableness, a loving from which a proceeding Love is breathed forth. What is breathed forth from sanctifying grace is charity, the love of God above all things and in all things and the love of neighbor as ourselves, the gift of fidelity to the two greatest commandments. As the Holy Spirit is the *Amor* that proceeds from divine *Agapē* and its *Verbum spirans Amorem,* so charity proceeds from the created participation in and imitation of the Father and the Son together breathing the Holy Spirit. That created participation is *gratia gratum faciens,* the grace that makes us pleasing to God in this special way, the grace that includes us in divine life itself as we receive the infinite love of God and are made lovable in this reception itself.

This mission is further clarified as Lonergan proceeds beyond the four-point hypothesis in *The Triune God: Systematics* to ask whether the Holy Spirit is sent as or on the basis of notional love. Certainly the Holy Spirit *proceeds* as love. But a true and real mission of a divine person is nothing other than the procession of the same person, to which there adheres in a consequent fashion an appropriate external term. Therefore, the Holy Spirit cannot be sent except on the basis of, in accord with, *secundum,* proceeding love, the love that is the characteristic property of the Holy Spirit, in fact that *is* the Holy Spirit.

Essential love and notional love are not really distinguished in God. They are distinguished only conceptually. Essential love is the divine essence itself, and notional love is the same divine essence co-understood with a relation of origin. Therefore the divine love common to the three persons is essential, and with that love Father and Son and Holy Spirit love everything they love. But notional love is the Holy Spirit proceeding, *Amor procedens.* Its principle is the Spirator, that is, the Father and the Son spirating love, lov*ing* (*notionaliter diligere*), and by this spiration Father and Son love both themselves and one another and us by the Holy Spirit (*Summa theologiae,* 1, q. 37, a. 2). Thus active and passive spiration are both notional love, one as actively breathing and the other as proceeding. The Holy Spirit as notional love does have a created analogy: every creature that loves loves, not by its own essence but by an act received in its own will, of which act the creature itself is a principle. Moreover, the first object of divine love is the divine goodness itself common to the three persons, the second is the finite goodness proper to individual creatures, and the third is a certain special object that is a function of God loving certain creatures with a view to communicating to them the infinite good itself (*Summa theologiae,* 1-2, q. 110, a. 1). It is in accord with this third, special love that there is the mission of the Holy Spirit on which follows as consequent condition the gift of sanctifying grace. The constitution of a divine mission is through divine conception and volition. Insofar as "constitution" is meant actively, it is common to the three persons, but insofar as it is meant passively it is proper to one or the other. Thus, since the Spirit is sent, insofar as the constitution of this mission is considered actively, there is a special divine love (third kind of love) that is common to the three and essential; and since this love is with a view to communicating the infinite good itself, it exists as a divine gift of self by which the three divine persons give themselves to us (*Summa theologiae*, 1, q. 43, a. 4, ad 1m; q. 38, a. 1, ad 1m). But if the same constitution is considered passively, the Father and the Son are loving and sending and giving, while the Spirit is proceeding love and the person sent and the gift given. And since this love is altogether special, through it Father and Son love us, and give to us, *by* the Holy Spirit (*Summa theologiae*, 1, q. 37, a. 2; q. 38, a. 1, ad 4m; a. 2, ad 3m). Finally, since necessarily there follows on this special love, both essential and notional, an appropriate external term, besides the [uncreated] grace that is the very divine favor toward someone there is also the [created] *gratia gratum faciens* (*Summa theologiae*, 1-2, q. 110, a. 1), which is a quality and accident received in the "soul of the justified."[41]

To round out the exposition of the thesis we may anticipate an implication of a question that we will take up more fully later, namely, Why are the Son and the Holy Spirit sent? Here we come closer to beginning to understand the role of history in the development of a systematic theology. While Lonergan portrays sanctifying grace in the four-point hypothesis as a created participation in and imitation of active spiration, still it is more often understood by Christians mainly as a created participation in and imitation of the incarnate Word, the incarnate *Verbum spirans Amorem*, whose assumed humanity is itself a participation in and imitation of the one Jesus called "Abba, Father." And what is this "Father"? What would it be to participate in the incarnate Son, who himself is an imitation of "Abba"? What would the charity be that proceeds from that participation? The Son incarnate tells us. "Love your enemies and pray for those who persecute you; in this way you will be children of your Father in heaven, for he causes his sun to rise on the bad as well as the good, and his rain to fall on honest and dishonest alike" (Matthew 5.44–45). Again, just a few verses later, "You must therefore be perfect as your heavenly Father is perfect" (Matthew 5.48), where being perfect means this nonviolent response to evil, this return of good for evil. It is in this participation and imitation alone that history is moved beyond the otherwise endless cycle of violence, recrimination, judgment, blame, accusation, murder, hate, and false religion. So this habit of grace, rooted in the essence of the soul (as traditional theology would put it), sets up a state of grace, where the state of grace is a historical and social situation, a set of interpersonal relations where charity prevails.[42] The founding subjects, as it were, are the three divine subjects, and grace prevails because they have come to dwell in us and with us. That state of grace is manifest in charity, the created participation in and imitation of the passive spiration that is the Holy Spirit, but as this participation and imitation becomes the disposition to return good for evil. As recent theologians have developed the notion of social sin, so it is time for contemporary theologians to develop the notion of social grace. The foundation of that notion lies in the interpersonal relations that prevail once the divine Trinity has in fact enabled us to participate in and imitate the very life of God through sharing in the divine relations of active and passive spiration. Those interpersonal relations take their measure, as it were, from the gift of a dialectical attitude that returns good for evil.[43] And as Neil Ormerod has seen in his own reflections on these same matters, this charity that is our created participation in the mission of the Holy Spirit is also the foundation of our own mission to spread the kingdom of God in this world.[44] "As the Father has sent me, so I also send you," says Jesus, and the foundation of that sending is the gift of the Holy Spirit in charity that proceeds from our participation in the Father and the Son who do the sending. It is here, I suggest, that we will find the basic parameters for a doctrine and a theology of the church, once the dogmatic-theological context has been established in a renewed Trinitarian theology, Pneumatology, and Christology.[45] The church's mission is community, grounded in the church's participation in the divine missions and measured by the Law of the Cross.

Finally, in the same hypothesis the light of glory that is the created consequent condition of beatific knowledge is conceived as the created supernatural participation in and imitation of filiation, of the Son, the divine Word, as in the Holy Spirit he brings us, his brothers and sisters, children by adoption, perfectly back to the Father. We may conceive the disposition of hope that flows from the gift of God's love as our present historical participation in this ultimately eschatological relation, although it is likely that there is a more intense and direct participation in some mystical states.

2   The Notion of Formal Effects

> **Thesis 8:** *The notion of sanctifying grace unifies the elements of biblical doctrine by allowing them to be conceived as formal effects.*

We leave Lonergan's chapter on the divine missions for the time being in order to return to his earlier notes. We have reviewed very briefly the historical portion of Lonergan's 1951–52 notes on sanctifying grace, and have examined that part of his biblical reflections that is relevant to our present concern. We have filled out these considerations by appealing to relevant material in the final chapter of *The Triune God: Systematics*. But in the earlier notes the systematic synthesis toward which the historical and biblical considerations are heading shows *how* it can be true that sanctifying grace unifies the various elements mentioned in the synthetic statement of biblical doctrine. Lonergan's answer is in terms of formal effects, and the consideration of formal effects is intimately connected with what we have said about contingent predication.

As I have mentioned already, the notion of formal effects provides a general answer to the question, What true judgments can be made once one knows a formal intelligibility of some sort? In this case, the formal intelligibility is the entitative habit known as sanctifying grace, and the true judgments that can be made once one posits that intelligibility name formal effects that have to do both with the person gifted with sanctifying grace and with the God who gives the gift. The latter judgments concern what is truly said of God as the term of the relations that are established with the gift of *gratia gratum faciens*. In all instances, these judgments about God are contingent predications.

With respect to divine love, these judgments can be concerned either with divine love considered essentially and so as common to the three divine Persons or with divine love properly attributed to one or other divine Person. Divine love insofar as it is an *effective* principle is predicated essentially and so equally of the three divine persons. A corollary of this fundamental theorem is that every grace, insofar as it is related to divine love as its effective principle, is related not to notional but to essential divine love. And if such love is predicated of one divine person, excluding the others, that predication is not proper but by appropriation.

However, as we have just seen, not everything that is predicated contingently of the divine persons is predicated by appropriation; and not everything that is predicated of the divine persons in respect to grace is predicated by appropriation. The mission of a divine person is predicated properly, not by appropriation, for one person sends and another is sent, and the one who sends is not sent and the one who is sent does not send. This applies to the missions of the divine persons with respect to *gratia gratum faciens*.

In the 1951–52 notes what we have come to call the four-point hypothesis makes perhaps its first appearance in Lonergan's work, precisely in the claim that there are four graces to which the word "grace" applies in a pre-eminent way: the grace of union, the light of glory, sanctifying grace, and the habit of charity.

As we have seen, the grace of union is that finite reality received in the humanity of Christ so that it exists through the personal act of existence of the divine Word. This grace is the external term of divine efficient causality in accord with which it is truly said, "The Word became flesh." Lonergan refers to *Summa theologiae*, 3, q. 17, a. 2, and the issue there is settled in terms of relation ("habitudo"). "[B]y the human nature there accrued to Him no new personal being, but only a new relation of the pre-existing personal being to the human nature (nova habitudo esse personalis praeexistentis ad naturam humanam), in such a way that the Person is said to subsist not merely in the divine but also in the human nature."

The light of glory is that finite reality by which a created intellect is disposed to receive the divine essence as intelligible species and so to see God as God is in God's own self.

Sanctifying grace is that finite reality by which a finite substance is reborn and regenerated to participate in divine life itself.

The habit of charity is that finite reality by which a finite regenerated substance habitually possesses true friendship with God.

The ontological foundation of these four is grounded in exemplary causality, a point not mentioned as such in Lonergan's later expression of the four-point hypothesis, even though it is implicit in the references to imitation. The divine essence is the first exemplary cause which every finite being, whether created or "creatable," substantial or accidental, imitates. But the divine essence can be considered in two ways: insofar as it is absolute and common to the three divine persons, and insofar as it is really identical with one of the real divine relations, whether paternity or filiation or active spiration or passive spiration.

Since every finite substance has something of absolute reality about it, every finite substance can be said to imitate the divine essence considered insofar as the divine essence is absolute and common to the three divine persons. But since the four preeminent graces are intimately connected with immanent divine life, they can appropriately be said to imitate the divine essence insofar as the divine essence is identical to one or other divine relation.

Thus the grace of union imitates and in a finite manner participates in divine paternity, the light of glory imitates and in a finite manner participates in filiation, sanctifying grace imitates and in a finite manner participates in active spiration, and the habit of charity imitates and in a finite manner participates in passive spiration. This we have already seen, in the somewhat different language of the later formulation of the hypothesis. But I wish to concentrate on the way in which Lonergan argues that the ten elements presented in the synthetic statement of biblical doctrine are unified by the notion of sanctifying grace. For that is where we are locating our starting point, in the Father's love for us that parallels the Father's love for the incarnate Son.

Sanctifying grace, Lonergan has just stated, is a participation in the divine relation of active spiration. He now proceeds to argue for the synthetic unity of the biblical elements by showing how each of these elements can be understood as a formal effect of that participation in active spiration that is sanctifying grace: first, immanent formal effects and then transcendent formal effects.

There are primary and secondary immanent formal effects and primary and secondary transcendent formal effects. With each of these I will put in parentheses the number in the synthetic statement of biblical doctrine cited above that corresponds to a particular formal effect of sanctifying grace.

Primary immanent formal effects are what can truly be said of a subject because of what is intrinsically constitutive of that subject. There are two intimately related primary immanent formal effects of sanctifying grace, that is, two predications that can truly be said of us because of the gift of a participation in active spiration. First, it makes the one who has it a participant in divine life (10), for it imitates active spiration, and so establishes a special relation to the Holy Spirit (2). Second, simultaneously as it were, it makes one pleasing to God, lovable with a special divine love (1).

We have already anticipated Lonergan's explanation of the second of these primary immanent formal effects. Since active spiration is the principle of the Holy Spirit, it is also the principle of proceeding divine Love itself. But the principle of love, says Lonergan, is lovableness, and therefore active spiration is God as lovable. The divine goodness as the principle of love is the divine goodness as lovable. Therefore, because sanctifying grace imitates active spiration, it imitates God insofar as God is lovable; it imitates the divine goodness in breathing love; and so it makes the one who possesses it lovable with a special divine love (1). Thus there returns the central theme of God's love for us, in connection with sanctifying grace.

Secondary immanent formal effects are what can truly be said of a subject as distinct, necessary consequences of what is intrinsically constitutive of that subject. In this sense the infused virtue of charity, by which one is habitually a friend of God (7), is a secondary immanent formal effect of sanctifying grace. Again I am reminded of 1 John 4.19: We are to love, because God has first loved us. As active spiration stands to passive spiration, so sanctifying grace stands to charity. And as sanctifying grace imitates active spiration, so the virtue of charity imitates passive spiration, love that flows forth because it is the resultant of divine *notionaliter diligere*. Active spiration stands to passive spiration as principle stands to its resultant, and so sanctifying grace, *gratia gratum faciens*, stands to charity as a principle stands to its resultant. Besides, active spiration and passive spiration really are distinct, correlative, inseparable, and equal. Therefore, sanctifying grace and charity are really distinct; they are correlative and inseparable, in that with the infusion of grace, charity is also infused, and when charity is lost, so is grace; and they are equal: the measure of grace in a person is the same as the measure of that person's charity.

Other secondary immanent formal effects of sanctifying grace are relative to one's state in life. For example, in those living on earth, faith and hope (9) would be secondary immanent formal effects of sanctifying grace. These I have already attempted to understand as born of the gift of love itself, with faith being constituted as a participation in the invisible mission of the Word and hope being understood as an anticipation of our being brought home to the Father in the light of glory that shares in the divine relation of filiation.

There are also mixed immanent formal effects of sanctifying grace. They are introduced in the text without explanation of what is meant by "mixed," but that term means, I think, that they include both primary and secondary immanent formal effects. Thus, a first instance of these mixed effects is regeneration or rebirth (3) into a new life (4). Regeneration here means the arrival of a new nature to an existing person, a new first and remote principle of operation and new proximate principles of operation. Through sanctifying grace there comes to an existing rational creature primarily that grace itself which is the first and remote principle of operating supernaturally and meritoriously, the reciprocal relations to the Holy Spirit and to the Father and the Son, but secondarily the infused virtues and gifts which are the proximate principles of a supernatural life.

Another mixed immanent formal effect of sanctifying grace is that a rational creature is justified (6) with that justice of God by which God makes us just. There are several dimensions to that justice of God. Justice is primarily truth (*Summa theologiae*, 1, q. 21, a. 2), not as simply existing in the intellect but as existing in the intellect and directing and moving the will (to call upon the faculty psychology language that Lonergan uses in the 1951–52 notes). Thus the justice of God is the Word spirating love, which of course belongs to active spiration. Participation in and imitation of that Word in sanctifying grace releases the gift of speaking the true word in love, the word that establishes justice in history and in historical relations of human beings to one another, to God, to the environment, and to the entire created universe. Like faith as the knowledge born of religious love, so speaking the true word in love is a participation in the invisible mission of the Word. (We will resume these themes later in speaking of social grace.)

So much for sanctifying grace considered in its immanent formal effects. Another major section considers sanctifying grace in its transcendent formal effects, effects that are truly said of one subject, in this case God or one or other of the divine persons, because of what is intrinsically constitutive of another subject or because of what flows from what is intrinsically constitutive of another subject, that is, us once we have been elevated to participation in divine life. This is where contingent predication becomes essential to the methodological integrity of the discourse.

Whatever is said of God contingently is said not entitatively but "terminatively," that is, of God as the term of a created relation. Many things are said of God contingently in the order of sanctifying grace, and so there exist transcendent formal effects of sanctifying grace.

These transcendent formal effects are of two kinds. For sanctifying grace can be considered as an effect of divine love, since it is out of love that God produces grace in a person, and it can also be considered as a term of divine love, for God loves the person made pleasing.

The transcendent formal effects of sanctifying grace as itself an effect of divine love regard essential divine love. All three persons are equally one effective principle of every creature whatsoever. And so this effective divine love is predicated equally of all three persons. And love that is predicated equally of all three is essential love. But the transcendent formal effects of sanctifying grace as terms are related to notional divine love. Lonergan proposes this assertion as probable with an intrinsic probability; for what scripture and the Fathers say about the various relations of the divine Persons to the just seem to postulate that grace be a term of notional divine love. As we have seen, arguments to the contrary put forth by theologians, in Lonergan's view, do no more than prove that grace as an effect is related to essential divine love but not grace as a term.

Thus, a transcendent formal effect of sanctifying grace in Christ as a human being is that the Father loves the Son as a human being with that notional love that is the Holy Spirit, that is, Gift. The Father eternally and necessarily loves the Son as God by the Holy Spirit. In time and contingently the Father loves the Son as a human being by the Holy Spirit. This fact, being contingent, requires an appropriate external term. This appropriate term is nothing other than sanctifying grace in Christ, for it imitates extrinsically that active spiration whereby the Father loves, and sets up a created relation of the assumed humanity of Jesus to the uncreated Holy Spirit. Eternally and by reason of his procession the Holy Spirit is Gift. In time and contingently the Holy Spirit is given to this particular human being Jesus of Nazareth. This fact, being contingent, requires an appropriate external term; and this appropriate term is sanctifying grace, for it imitates active spiration and therefore establishes a special relation to that passive spiration which is the Holy Spirit. (All of this is background to statement 1 in the biblical synthesis.)

Again, the transcendent formal effects of sanctifying grace in us represent systematic articulations of the elements contained in the synthetic statement of biblical doctrine. God the Father loves us with a love that is similar to that with which he loves Christ the man (1). By sanctifying grace we become adopted children of the Father (8). Therefore we are heirs, with the hope of eternal life (9). One who is truly adopted is made an heir. But our adoption now is incomplete, and will become complete with eternal life; therefore "with hope." Adoptive sonship means being made like God's natural Son. Through sanctifying grace we are made like the Son as the Word spirating love (active spiration). Here we can add our own reflections on faith as the knowledge born of divine love and participation in the invisible mission of the Word. Through the light of glory we are like the Son as Son, the Word begotten by the Father. The list continues: those who have been justified live as members of Christ (5), a point to which Lonergan devotes quite a bit of attention. The relation of Christ the Head to his members is also spelled out in some detail, which we must skip for the moment. These considerations can be resumed in the further context of ecclesiology, where the church itself is understood as mission, and where the mission is understood in terms of formal effects of the divine gift. These are considerations for a later volume.

Another transcendent formal effect of sanctifying grace in the justified is that the Holy Spirit, existing from eternity as uncreated Gift, in time becomes the Gift given to the justified (2). Lonergan repeats his explanation, after commenting on some biblical passages. What is given to someone is possessed by that person. The just possess the Spirit insofar as this uncreated Gift is given to them through grace. Further, grace is the appropriate external term of this donation because it externally imitates active spiration and therefore possesses a proper relation to uncreated passive spiration. But the Spirit is had by participation through infused charity. For the virtue of charity externally imitates passive spiration, which is the Holy Spirit. Finally, in terms of fruition the Spirit is possessed insofar as through grace the just habitually have a true knowledge of God and a proper love for him.

A further transcendent formal effect of sanctifying grace in the justified is that the Father and the Son send and give the Holy Spirit to the justified person (2). Galatians 4.6: "God has sent the Spirit of his Son into our hearts, crying, 'Abba! Father!'" John 14.16: "And I will pray the Father, and he will give you another Counselor, to be with you forever ..." John 14.26: "... the Counselor, the Holy Spirit, whom the Father will send in my name ..." John 15.26: "But when the Counselor comes, whom I shall send to you from the Father ..." John 16.7: "I will send him to you." This mission and giving express both the eternal procession of the Spirit from the Father and the Son and the temporal term that makes it possible for us to say that the Father and the Son send and give the Spirit and that the Spirit is sent and given. Since grace is the term of proceeding Love, it is the appropriate term according to which the Father and the Son are said to be sending and giving. Therefore, the three divine persons dwell in the souls of the justified. Accordingly, the three equally produce grace in the justified. And so they are present according to the same norm as that by which God is present in all things. This means that grace is a term of essential love. And so all give themselves, inasmuch as "to give" means a free communication of oneself.

But grace is also a term of notional love. The Father is present as sending and giving; the Son is present as sent and giving; and the Spirit is present as sent and given. Accordingly, grace is the first intrinsic principle of supernatural life. And so in terms of fruition the divine Persons are possessed insofar as they are truly known and rightly loved. There is friendship in the true sense of the word between God and the justified (7). Friendship is a mutual love of benevolence founded upon an exchange of goods. This friendship is founded upon the communication of the divine nature of God himself. It is benevolent love on the part of God, for grace is the term of both essential and notional divine love. It is also benevolent love on our part, for the love of God has been poured into our hearts by the Holy Spirit who has been given to us (Romans 5.5).

In short, the ten features of the biblical synthesis proposed in the scriptural portion of the notes under scrutiny are explained systematically in terms of formal effects, immanent or transcendent, of the *gratia gratum faciens* that is the created participation in divine active spiration. Such is the import of the methodological doctrine regarding contingent predication.

4

The Order of the Divine Missions

Thesis 9: *The invisible mission of the Holy Spirit is universal. It precedes in time the visible mission of the Son, and is fulfilled by it. Pentecost is the manifestation of that fulfilment.*

In the sixth chapter of *The Triune God: Systematics*, Lonergan moves immediately after the statement of the four-point hypothesis to the question of the order of the divine missions. His later developments in light of the interreligious context of contemporary Catholic theology prompt me to suggest a change in the theological doctrine that he proposes there. The mission of the Holy Spirit is a universal reality, not something limited to the biblical religions. This theological doctrine is part of our starting point in a theology of the divine missions, a theology of the Trinity in history. "A theology mediates between a cultural matrix," writes Lonergan, "and the significance and role of a religion in that matrix."[1] The world-cultural matrix of our day is multi-religious. A universalist systematic theology, one that would mediate Christian faith and the multi-religious cultural matrix, labors to express the meaning of the mysteries of explicitly Christian faith with a view to communication with sincere believers who adhere to other religious traditions, practices, and communities. Robley Edward Whitson, a Quaker author whose book *The Coming Convergence of World Religions,* won Lonergan's admiration, calls specific traditions to identify just what it is that they uniquely bring to the interreligious dialogue, even while they remain ready to hear and engage the unique contributions of the other communities engaging in dialogue.[2] The mediation that Lonergan has in mind is what he calls a mutual self-mediation. It is not a one-way street, from the Christian religion to the cultural matrix, but is rather marked by a readiness to learn from the other participants just as it hopes the other participants will be ready to learn from

Christianity. Nor is it engaged simply in mediating into the present a past that is uniquely Christian. That would be an instance of what Lonergan calls self-mediation. Self-mediation, obviously, is important, and in fact is required if we are to know and articulate what is uniquely ours; but it does not equip the church to be engaged along with others in the contemporary religious quest or to participate in the emerging religious consciousness of our time. For that consciousness will emerge precisely out of what Whitson calls the coming convergence of the world's religions.

The unique contributions that Christianity offers to this world-cultural matrix are three: the incarnation of the eternal Word of God in Jesus of Nazareth, the Trinitarian nature of God, and the resurrection of Jesus from the dead. Closely tied to these are the implications of the passion, death, and resurrection of Jesus for a non-violent response to the scandal of evil in the world. Remove any one of these, and Christianity has been eviscerated of the very marrow of its bones, however much hierarchical structures may continue to function. Without a living commitment to these realities, all magisterial teaching is sounding brass and tinkling cymbal; it signifies nothing, and it has nothing to bring to the interreligious table.

Moreover, the pattern of the paschal mystery, the law of the cross, is found elsewhere than in the Judeo-Christian scriptures, and while the significance of this pattern is a matter of Christian revelation, its presence wherever it is found is the central manifestation of the gift of the Holy Spirit.

The first and most important doctrinal commitment that lies behind the convictions already expressed, then, affirms the universal mission of the Holy Spirit, which means the mission of the Spirit beyond the explicit boundaries of the Christian communions. There is an opening upon this recognition in the very creeds that Christians pronounce, for those creeds acknowledge that the Holy Spirit, the third person of the Blessed Trinity, spoke through the prophets of Israel, who, like some folks in the Acts of the Apostles and many in the other religions of the world, did not have the slightest idea that there was a Holy Spirit in the Trinitarian sense affirmed by the creed. It is especially the doctrine of the universal mission of the Holy Spirit that I wish to begin to try to understand in this work, by providing from the treasure-house of Christian theology certain indications of what that mission would be even when the Holy Spirit is sent to people who do not share our doctrinal convictions and commitments, including the affirmation that there is a Holy Spirit in the fully Trinitarian sense, a third subject of the one divine consciousness, who proceeds from the first two subjects of that same consciousness as their mutual love for each other. It is also incumbent upon us to relate that prior mission to the events narrated in the Acts of the Apostles regarding the outpouring of the Holy Spirit upon the apostles and others gathered in the upper room.

I will begin this chapter with a summary of the position Lonergan expressed in *De Deo Trino* (*The Triune God: Systematics*) and will then turn to the principal paper within the community of Lonergan's students regarding his later position on this issue, namely, Frederick E. Crowe's groundbreaking essay "Son of God, Holy Spirit, and World Religions,"[3] delivered as the Chancellor's Lecture at the Regis College Convocation, University of Toronto, on the day of Bernard Lonergan's death, 26 November 1984.

1   Lonergan's Early Position

Lonergan's systematic text on the Trinity is divided into assertions and related questions. His position on the order of the missions appears not in an assertion but in response to the question, Are the divine missions ordered to each other? He responds that the order in the divine missions corresponds to the order in the divine relations of origin, since the missions are constituted by these relations together with appropriate external terms. More precisely, the order affects both the constitution of the missions and the consequent terms. As to the constitution, in God there is no procession of love except in an order to the procession of the Word who breathes Love, and so "since the missions are constituted by the divine processions and relations, it is clear that as to their constitution the missions have an order to each other,"[4] that is, precisely the order that the processions and relations in God enjoy. As to the terms, Lonergan turns to Galatians 4.4–6: "God sent his Son ... so that we might receive adoption as children. And because you are children, God has sent the Spirit of his Son into your hearts crying, 'Abba, Father!'" Lonergan concludes from these words that "the mission of the Son is to make us children of God by adoption, and that the mission of the Holy Spirit is in accord with this adoption." But, he adds, "precisely what this connection is needs further consideration."[5]

Now, the further consideration contains little more than what we have already seen in commenting on the first two elements in Lonergan's 1951–52 statement of the synthesis of biblical teaching regarding what later came to be called sanctifying grace. Thus, the Holy Spirit is sent as a special notional divine love ordering those who receive it to the divine good. Lonergan makes more explicit here than in 1951–52 the special reason for this love, namely, God's own Son, mediator and redeemer. But the explanation of this remains the same as in 1951–52.[6]

> The Son is mediator because as a divine person he has a human nature.[7] This means that God the Father, as he loves the divine Son and gives to him by the Holy Spirit, so he loves the Son as man and gives to him by the Holy Spirit. This is revealed to us in the baptismal

epiphany. For as the Father was saying, "This is my Son, the Beloved, with whom I am well pleased," the Son coming up out of the water "saw the Spirit of God descending like a dove and alighting on him."[8] Here at the same time the love of the Father, which is the Holy Spirit himself, is affirmed and is manifested as the Holy Spirit himself coming and alighting on Jesus.

In like manner, Christ's baptism is the exemplar of our baptism. For on account of the redemptive work of the mediator, God the Father also loves the just as he loves his own Son; as it is said, "You have loved them even as you have loved me."[9] So then, if the Father loves us as he loves his own Son, the Father loves us as though we were his children; and our adoption as children of God is surely a consequence of this love. Again, if the Father loves us as he loves his own Son, he surely loves us and gives to us by the Holy Spirit. *From all this, we gain some understanding of the order of the divine missions; for the Son was sent so that the Father might be able to love us as he loves his own Son, and the Spirit is sent because the Father does love us as he loves his own Son.* Indeed, this love, which is, as it were, proper to the divine persons, is what implies and grounds the absolutely supernatural order.[10]

We can come as closely as possible to understanding the comprehensive intelligibility of the divine missions only by analogy with human missions. And what is found in a human mission is captured by the following seven points: "(1) the movement from one place to another so that either (2) some particular operation or (3) some new series of operations may be accomplished there, whether (4) solely by the person sent or (5) by the persons to whom he or she is sent, (6) to be carried out according to the mind or command of the sender (7) revealed and entrusted to or imposed upon the person sent."[11]

The first characteristic yields little or no understanding. Even in a human mission this movement can be lacking (even more so with e-mail!). And since the divine persons are not only incorporeal but also omnipresent, movement from place to place has nothing to do with understanding a divine mission. "[A]lthough it is quite devotional and most useful for us to imagine the Son or the Holy Spirit coming down from the heights of heaven, our present quest is for an understanding, not an image, of a divine mission."[12] Regarding the second and third characteristics, "both the mission of the Son and the mission of the Spirit regard not some particular operation but a whole new series of operations. For the Son has been sent to gather up[13] and reconcile[14] all things, that God may be all in all.[15] And the Holy Spirit is sent, not for this or that particular operation, but to preside over the whole of Christian living in every one of the just."[16]

There is a difference, however, in the way the two persons sent are subjects of the operations for which they are responsible in one way or another. One way of formulating the difference would be to say that, while neither the Son nor the Spirit is alone in the mission, they are "not alone" in different ways.

> Since the Son has assumed unto himself a human nature, he is able through this assumed nature to perform works that are proper to himself. Therefore, since the Son has been sent as mediator, redeemer, reconciler, head of the church, king, and judge, incarnation evidently belongs to the mission of the Son, since all these functions are envisaged as requiring works that are proper to the Son. On the other hand, since the Holy Spirit has no nature other than the divine, he does no works that the Father and the Son do not likewise do, and from this we conclude that the Holy Spirit is not sent in such a way as to do anything by himself alone, without the other divine persons.[17]

The works entailed in being mediator, redeemer, reconciler, head of the church, king, judge are not common to all three divine persons. But since the Son assumed a human nature, he can perform these works proper to himself *through this assumed nature.* The incarnation belongs to this mission. But the gift of the Holy Spirit is simultaneously the self-gift of the ones who breathe forth and send the Spirit. In this respect then, the Spirit does not "operate" anything that the Father and the Son do not likewise operate, each of course in their own way; and so it follows that the Holy Spirit is not sent in such a way as to operate anything alone, without the others.

There are further implications regarding community. Any mission, human or divine, entails the cooperation of others and so the initiation and strengthening of personal relations if the mission is to be successful. "Hence, in order to understand a divine mission, one must consider not only the works proper to the person sent but also the personal relations that that person initiates or strengthens in order that the end of the mission may be attained through the cooperation of others."[18] Both missions are marked by intimate friendship with those to whom the persons are sent. "As the Father has loved me, so I have loved you; abide in my love. If you keep my commandments, you will abide in my love, just as I have kept my Father's commandments and abide in his love."[19] "Do you not know that your body is a temple of the Holy Spirit within you … and that you are not your own?"[20] "And do not grieve the Holy Spirit of God, with which you were marked with a seal for the day of redemption."[21]

All anthropomorphism must be removed from our conception of the "mind of the sender and of the one sent." These are to be understood solely in terms of the trinitarian constitution of the divine missions.

Finally, the order that the divine missions have to one another is such that there is one end to the two missions together. The Son is sent "while we were enemies,"[22] to initiate through his work as mediator and redeemer and reconciler new interpersonal relations between God the Father and all human persons. And the Holy Spirit will be sent as "the pledge of our inheritance,"[23] when God has "saved us, not because of any works of righteousness that we had done, but according to his mercy, through the water of rebirth and renewal by the Holy Spirit. This Spirit he poured out on us richly through Jesus Christ our Savior, so that, having been justified by his grace, we might become heirs according to the hope of eternal life."[24] Moreover, the one end to the two missions, which is not attained without the cooperation of human persons, allows Lonergan to relate the distinct terminal points of the missions to distinct stages whereby the end of the mission is accomplished. The material here should be quoted in full, since it reveals Lonergan's early position quite clearly on the order of the divine missions.[25]

> [T]he mission of the Son begins with the incarnation, not because the Son is sent in order to assume a human nature,[26] but because through the incarnation the Son is constituted as the mediator sent to us. The mission of the Son was carried on throughout his mortal life, during which time the Son of Man entered into personal relationships with the children of men. A principal objective of his mission was accomplished when in dying on the cross he became the source of eternal salvation for all who obey him.[27] The mission of the Son is continued through the apostles and their successors: "as the Father has sent me, so I send you";[28] "whoever welcomes you welcomes me, and who welcomes me welcomes the one who sent me";[29] "whoever listens to you listens to me, and whoever rejects you rejects me, and whoever rejects me rejects the one who sent me";[30] "Saul, Saul, why do you persecute me?"[31]
>
> Yet another principal objective of the mission of the Son is accomplished whenever one who is unjust is justified and a just person is further justified; for "I came that they may have life and have it abundantly."[32] The ultimate end of this mission, however, is attained in the beatific vision of the citizens of heaven, "when he hands over the kingdom to God the Father."[33]
>
> Just as the Son has been sent to all people, since he died for all, so is the Holy Spirit sent to each of the just. "And because you are children, God has sent the Spirit of his Son into your hearts crying,

'Abba, Father!' So you are no longer a slave but a child, and if a child then also an heir, through God."[34] "Do you not know that you are God's temple and that God's Spirit dwells in you? If anyone destroys God's temple, God will destroy that person. For God's temple is holy, and you are that temple."[35] "… God's love has been poured into our hearts through the Holy Spirit that has been given to us."[36] "… those who are in the flesh cannot please God. But you are not in the flesh; you are in the Spirit, since the Spirit of God dwells in you."[37] "If the Spirit of him who raised Jesus from the dead dwells in you, he who raised Christ from the dead will give life to your mortal bodies also through his Spirit that dwells in you."[38] For the Spirit, since he is the pledge of our inheritance, is given with an ordination to eternal life, so that the mission of the Spirit tends to the same ultimate end as the mission of the Son.

This being so, there is not one formality of divine mission. For although each mission is the sending of a divine person, the mission of the Son is from the Father while the mission of the Spirit is from the Father and the Son. Also, although each mission has the same ultimate end, which is the heavenly city for the glory of the Father, *the first mission is that of the Son for the reconciliation of all human persons to God the Father, and the consequent mission of the Spirit is to each one of the just, who have been reconciled.* Besides, although the two missions are for the sake of initiating and strengthening new personal relationships between God and human beings, the Son, having assumed another nature besides the divine, not only enters into new personal relationships but also through the nature he assumed, and then through those whom he has sent, performs works that are proper to himself; but the Holy Spirit, not having another nature besides the divine, does not do anything proper to himself, but provides the foundation for cooperation in that it is through the Spirit's self-donation that the new personal relationships are strengthened. Finally, since the divine persons are sent to accomplish such a great task throughout the world by themselves or through others, the [external] term of the missions is assigned not in a brief statement, but rather by distinguishing the successive stages of this, the greatest of all works.[39]

2   Frederick Crowe's Interpretation of Lonergan's Later Position

We turn now to Crowe's paper. It will be my contention in what follows that the shift in Lonergan's thinking on this issue between 1964 and his position in *Method in Theology* and later would (1) retain much of the same basic doctrine but formulate it in Trinitarian terms rather than in terms entirely dependent on the mystery of the Incarnation, and (2) formulate the italicized words in the quotation on p. 71 above as follows: *From all this, we gain some understanding of the order of the divine missions: the Spirit is sent because from eternity the Father loves us as he loves his own Son, and the Son was sent so that the Father might be able to communicate and reveal his love in the most explicit manner possible.*

Crowe's paper consists of an introduction and two numbered sections, the first on "Son and Spirit in the World" and the second entitled "Christianity and World Religions." In the introduction Crowe acknowledges that he is speaking as a Christian to Christians, and is attempting to define an approach to the world religions precisely from the Christian side. That approach, he suggests, will be defined by one basic thesis: "We have simply to reverse the order in which commonly we think of the Son and Spirit in the world. Commonly we think of God first sending the Son, and of the Spirit being sent in that context, to bring to completion the work of the Son. The thesis says that, on the contrary, God first sent the Spirit, and then sent the Son in the context of the Spirit's mission, to bring to completion, perhaps not precisely the work of the Spirit, but the work which God conceived as one work to be executed in the two steps of the twofold mission of first the Spirit and then the Son." This thesis, Crowe says (quite correctly, I believe), is "the tacit supposition permeating all Lonergan's later work on the Son and Spirit." Moreover, a complete theology of the divine self-gift would add to the missions of the Spirit in love and the Son in the outer word the self-gift of the Father in hope.[40]

This basic thesis has a corollary regarding the Christian approach to the world's other religions, namely, that "their positive moment is the fruit of the Spirit present among them, but ... this partial moment calls for its completion: the need of the world religions to hear the gospel message is the same need still that the world had when God sent the only Son to be its way and truth and life."[41] It is this twofold movement that I wish to speak of in this chapter.

Crowe's basic thesis, he says, is nothing more than an instance of the time-honored principle that "what is first in our eyes is not first in itself; on the contrary, what is first in our eyes is last in itself, and what is last in our eyes is first in itself." Thus, he continues, "We speak, with Augustine, Aquinas, and a whole tradition, of the visible mission of the Son and the invisible mission of the Spirit. Obviously, what is visible must be first in the cognitional order of discovery, that is, first for us, and what is invisible must be last for us. But is it altogether fantastic, is it not rather to be expected, that the real order is the exact opposite?"[42]

The affirmation of the Holy Spirit as God's first gift is found in Augustine and Aquinas, and most systematically in the latter's *Summa theologiae*, 1, q. 38, a. 2, a text that we have already visited. The later Lonergan universalized and historicized this affirmation, to "make the gift universally applicable throughout the world, and so come to a theology of the Spirit's worldwide presence among us, a presence from the beginning of human time and to the ends of human space."[43] Here too, his work is not unique, since the doctrine has slowly emerged in the churches that everyone receives sufficient grace for salvation, that is, everyone receives the divine favor and its transforming power. If love is the first gift, then everyone receives the Holy Spirit, and receiving the Holy Spirit is precisely the meaning of the sanctifying grace that the church has taught is required for salvation.

This first affirmation is joined to a second, namely, that "in the fullness of time God sent the Son, not in opposition but in unity, not in subordination but in complementarity."[44] The unity and complementarity are ordered, and the order is understood through the analogy of human love. Crowe quotes Lonergan: "When a man and a woman love each other but do not avow their love, they are not yet in love. Their very silence means that their love has not reached the power of self-surrender and self-donation. It is the love that each freely and fully reveals to the other that brings about the radically new situation of being in love and that begins the unfolding of its life-long implications."[45] More precisely, it is the outer word of avowal that seals the interpersonal component in the relation, the mutual presence of self-donation, and the need for sustained development and growth. The sending of the Spirit is, as it were, God's "falling" in love with us, but God's outer word of avowal of that love is given incrementally in the progressive revelation that culminates in the sending of the one and only Son to be our savior, a sending that occurred in the context of first-century Palestinian Judaism. The love that Paul and John say has been disclosed and revealed to us in Jesus is "the very Love that is a divine person, the *amor donabilis* of God, given to all of us since the world began."[46]

In the second section, Crowe focuses on two questions for the Christian: "How will our understanding of non-Christians as gifted with the Spirit affect our general attitude and relation to them? And how will it affect our particular task of evangelizing them, of preaching Jesus the Lord to all creation?"[47]

The corollary to the basic thesis, Crowe remarks, requires a radical change in our attitude and in our religious relationship to the peoples of the world.[48] He expresses that radical change:

> It is not enough to thank God daily for the blessings bestowed on us in Christ the Lord, blessings that seem to make us a people set apart,

unless we acknowledge also that the infinite generosity of God our savior has included all the peoples of the world in the divine family, has made them all vessels of the divine election, and has blessed them all with the first and foundational gift of God, the divine Love in the person of the Holy Spirit. We ... have to beware lest, by refusing to acknowledge the breadth and depth and height of the divine mercy, we become unfaithful stewards of the very privilege that we do in fact possess ...[49]

We share a religious community, then, with the people of the world religions, one grounded in a common orientation to the mystery of love and awe through what Christians would confess to be the indwelling Holy Spirit, with whom we are placed in relation by the gift of God's love. "We do not ... go to the world religions as to strangers, as to heathens, pagans, enemies of God. For we are one with them in the Spirit, and expect to find in them the fruits of the Spirit," where the fruits of the Spirit are precisely those listed by Paul in Galatians 5.22: "love, joy, peace, patience, kindness, goodness, fidelity, gentleness, and self-control."

The new attitude will force upon us the need to develop, first, a new language for our own self-understanding, in order to express to ourselves our new relation to the world religions, and second, a language in which to communicate across the borders of the religions. Crowe's paper makes significant inroads on that first task. But the second task, as he admits, is far more complex and will take much longer to accomplish. The common language will not be specifically Christian, nor specifically Hindu, Buddhist, or Muslim, or whatever. In his paper "Prolegomena to the Study of the Emerging Religious Consciousness of Our Time," Lonergan distinguished between long-range approaches and present possibilities. He seems particularly attracted, as am I, to Robley Edward Whitson's proposals as far as the long term is concerned, but for the present he acknowledges that we are confined to adopting the formulation of some particular tradition as at least a temporary convention, and he suggests we speak of God's love given to us through the Holy Spirit as the convention that will get us started on expressing the experienced orientation that he believes we have in common.[50] If that will not do, Crowe says, we have other suggestions: an orientation to transcendent mystery that provides "the primary and fundamental meaning of the name, God";[51] the "experience of the holy";[52] an unobjectified experience of the mystery of love and awe that "remains within subjectivity as a vector, an undertow, a fateful call to a dreaded holiness."[53] I would suggest, however, that these are not equivalent expressions. The orientation to transcendent mystery is nature, while the unobjectified experience of the mystery of love and awe connotes the supernatural satisfaction of that natural orientation, its inchoate fulfilment. I would suggest instead that we employ the twofold relation suggested here: the memory of being on the receiving end of an unqualified love and the invitation to love in an unqualified fashion in return.

At any rate, for Crowe as for me it is the language of love that is the Christian contribution to the emerging religious consciousness of our time. Evangelization is no more a secondary matter for theology, even with this new approach, than it was a secondary matter for God that the eternal Word took flesh and was born of the Virgin Mary. Christians in fact have no choice but to preach among the peoples the treasures of wisdom and knowledge hidden in Christ, where the love of God poured out in our hearts is explicitly revealed for what it is. Our approach to the task will be modified if the basic thesis of Crowe's paper is accepted, but once the centrality and universality of the gift of the Holy Spirit is acknowledged, "then, as much as ever, one needs the word – the word of tradition that has accumulated religious wisdom, the word of fellowship that unites those that share the gift of God's love, the word of the gospel that announces that God has loved us first and, in the fullness of time, has revealed that love in Christ crucified, dead, and risen."[54] It is the fulfilment of the universal mission of the Holy Spirit in the outer word of the death and resurrection of Jesus that is celebrated by the triune God in their magnificent outpouring of the Spirit recorded in the Acts of the Apostles.

More precisely, though, Crowe wisely turns to chapter 20 of *Insight* to find the core of Lonergan's proposal as to how to proceed, the strategy of evangelization in a multi-religious world. That is, he would begin by addressing in evangelical terms the problem common to the human race, the problem of evil. "[I]f God is good, then there is not only a problem of evil, but also a solution,"[55] and that solution, while it is offered everywhere and when accepted is operative everywhere, is revealed in the life, passion, death, and resurrection of Jesus of Nazareth. It is what Lonergan calls the Law of the Cross, at the heart of which is the self-sacrificing charity that returns good for evil. That revelation, in fact, articulates what the prior mission of the Holy Spirit was about all along, for grace gives rise to charity, and charity flows from the gift of God's love that is the Holy Spirit and that is revealed in the mission of the Word.

In my own categories, genuine evangelization promotes a soteriological differentiation of consciousness, which, I have wagered and will continue to wager, is more sharply articulated in Christianity than anywhere else, even if what such a differentiation acknowledges is present wherever the gift of the Holy Spirit has been gratefully received, however anonymously.[56] We have already seen how we may account for a universalist faith that follows upon the reception of unqualified love, a faith that Lonergan distinguishes in his later work from the beliefs of particular religious traditions, a faith that can be and undoubtedly is found in diverse traditions, and that for Lonergan is responsible for a hope that the religions of the world will find common ground and common cause in the gift of God's love. I am suggesting that this faith, the knowledge born of the gift of God's love, participates in the invisible mission of the divine Word. But chapter 20 of *Insight* was explicitly oriented to providing the heuristic structure to the divine solution to the problem of evil. Evil is intimately and recognizably bound up with the deviated transcendence of inauthentic religion, which results in violence that reaches at times the scale of mass destruction but that continues in less drastic fashion in the denigration of women and sexual minorities, in the alignment of religious authority with authoritarian secular powers, and in many other ways. Let me make clear that I am speaking of certain strands in *all three* so-called Abrahamic traditions, of Hindu fundamentalism, and of other manifestations of a failure to acknowledge the gift of God's love that constitutes authentic religion. The situation that Lonergan addressed in the 1950s was the standoff of East and West, coming as it did toward the end of what he calls the longer cycle of decline, with its potential for nuclear devastation. While the nuclear threat remains and may indeed be even more ominous than earlier, our situation today takes on an *explicitly* religious significance, so that the discussion among interlocutors in the dialogue in pursuit of what constitutes authentic and inauthentic religion is not simply a conversation of theologians seeking religious understanding, but a conversation of citizens of the world seeking religious peace. It is in that concrete context that the problem of evil must be addressed in our time, especially in the dialogue among practitioners and theologians from the diverse religious traditions of humankind. And it is in that concrete context that the gift of the Holy Spirit will be most notably discerned in our time.

What makes chapter 20 of *Insight* pertinent to our discussion of the foundations in sanctifying grace and charity is that in this chapter Lonergan suggests a heuristic structure for identifying the divine solution to the problem of evil before suggesting that this structure points to the explicit revelation of God in Israel and Christianity. In fact, the solution begins, not with faith (which at that time was for Lonergan identical with explicit Christian beliefs) but with charity, the charity that enables one to return good for evil. "[I]t is only inasmuch as [people] are willing to meet evil with good, to love their enemies, to pray for those that persecute and calumniate them, that the social surd is a potential good. It follows that love of God above all and in all so embraces the order of the universe as to love all [people] with a self-sacrificing love."[57] It is, I suggest, in this context, that all genuine evangelization, all proclamation of the other divine mission, that of the eternal

Word of God, is to be carried out. And if this is the case, then the visible mission of the Word is intimately linked with the social objectification of the gift of the Holy Spirit.

3   Theological Doctrines regarding the Divine Missions

I wish now to state my own theological position on the matters discussed thus far in this chapter.

First, then, the Holy Spirit is God's first gift, and so a theology of the divine missions should begin with the mission of the Holy Spirit and continue to the mission of the Incarnate Word. I believe this order of things is reflected in the structure of Thomas Aquinas's *Summa theologiae*, where grace is treated before the explicit treatment of the Incarnation. At any rate, Thomas argues in question 38 of the first part of the *Summa theologiae* that "Gift" is a personal name for the Holy Spirit (article 1) and a proper and not appropriated name for the Holy Spirit (article 2). If that is the case, all supernatural divine gifts, including the mission of the divine Word, are somehow "in" the Holy Spirit.

The Holy Spirit is, first and foremost, the gift that the Father and the Son eternally give to each other as together they communicate the divine nature to the relation of love that unites them. But if the divine missions are the divine processions linked to a created, contingent, and consequent term, then the mission of the Holy Spirit historicizes and universalizes the eternal gift mutually uniting the Father and the Son. That eternal gift is present in human history.

Second, wherever there has been or is or will be human attentiveness, intelligence, rationality, and moral responsibility pursuing the transcendental objectives of the intelligible, the true and the real, the good, with these pursuits encased, as it were, in a tidal movement that includes aesthetic and dramatic intentions of the transcendental objective of the beautiful, there has been the offer of the gift of God's love, that is, the gift of the Holy Spirit, as the inchoate supernatural fulfilment of a natural desire for union with God, and as a pledge of the beatific knowing and loving that is our supernatural destiny. The gift of the Holy Spirit is thus universal.

Third, the visible mission of the Word is to be conceived as occurring "in" the Holy Spirit and in relation to the Holy Spirit's universal mission. In the fullness of the Holy Spirit's time, the Father sent the Son, who was conceived by the Holy Spirit in the womb of the Virgin Mary, baptized in the power of the Spirit by John the Baptist, driven by the same Spirit into the desert for forty days, led back by the Spirit to preach the coming of God's reign, and raised to life from death by the Father in the power of the Holy Spirit. The mission of the Holy Spirit, that is, the gift of divine love, is not only intensified but also revealed, made thematic, in the visible mission of the Son, where it plays a constitutive role. That same Holy Spirit was then sent by the Father and the Son on the apostles and the other women and men gathered in the upper room on Pentecost, in what may be called a visible mission of the Holy Spirit, to fulfill the twofold mission of the Son and the Spirit, and to enable a public acknowledgment that what happened in Jesus was indeed the revelation of the triune God in history. Pentecost began the ongoing fifth act in the drama of the salvation wrought by Jesus as the latter is conceived by Raymund Schwager, an act in which we are all among the principal protagonists, the act in which the mutual interplay of divine and human freedom can now be carried on in explicit recognition of what, prior to the revelation that occurs in the mission of the incarnate Word, necessarily remained *vécu* but not *thématique*, implicit but not recognized, conscious but not known, or to employ a Scholastic designation, present *in actu exercito* but not *in actu signato*.[58] The mission of the Word is among other things the explicit revelation through linguistic and incarnate meaning of what God has always been doing and continues to do in the inner word of the invisible mission of the Holy Spirit, namely, pour out divine love upon human beings.[59] That invisible mission becomes visible at Pentecost, in confirmation of the revelation that occurs in the visible mission of the Word.

Fourth, we Christians share a religious community with all human beings, including the people of the world's other religions, because of this universal gift of what we call the Holy Spirit. The community in which we participate is grounded both in the common orientation of human nature as obediential potency through intentional consciousness to the mystery of love and awe that in fact is the transcendent triune God, and in the universal gift of the transcendent God's triune life through what Christians would confess to be the indwelling Holy Spirit. In methodological terms, it is grounded in the bases of both general and special theological categories.[60]

Fifth, to a large extent, however, that community is only potential. Community is an achievement of common meaning, and common meaning is a matter not only of common experience, but also of compatible understandings, mutually agreed upon judgments or affirmations of fact and of value, common decisions, and solidarity in action. The work of interreligious dialogue is to promote as much as possible the emergence of a community that is not only potential through shared experience, but also formal through shared meanings, actual through shared affirmations of fact and value, and constitutive of our human world through common decisions and actions. Needless to say, we, the members of the world's religions, have a long, long way to go before we move beyond merely potential community.

Sixth, a Christian and Catholic theology of the immanent constitution of life in God will help Christians participate in establishing such a community.

We have already seen my theology of the immanent constitution of life in God due to the gift of the Holy Spirit, but I review it here in eight points.

(1) There is an uncreated gift given to us by the Father, a gift whom Christians name the Holy Spirit. The gift, as uncreated, is constituted by God alone. By the gift the triune God assumes a constitutive role in our living, not as an inherent form or quasi-form, but as the term of a set of created relations. The human subject of the first of those relations, the relation to the Holy Spirit, is the person elevated by an entitative habit bestowed at the core of his or her identity, at the level of central form, of the soul: elevated to participation in the inner trinitarian life of God. The term of that created relation of the created central form through the created gift of elevation is the uncreated Holy Spirit. In terms of the scale of values that we will see in some detail shortly, this begins the theological explication of the relation between religious and personal values.

(2) This divine self-communication, constituted by God alone, allows not only the Holy Spirit but each of the persons of the Trinity to be present to those to whom the created grace of God's favor (*gratia gratum faciens*) has been given. The gift of the Holy Spirit as the uncreated term of a created relation also allows the other persons of the Trinity to be present as distinct terms of distinct created relations, for the Holy Spirit is an uncreated relation to the Father and the Son, and so to be related to the Holy Spirit must entail being related to the Father and the Son as terms of a distinct relation.

(3) The created gift by which God gives us this participation in divine life is *effected*, created, by the love that is common to the three divine persons; but it is *immanently constituted* in terms of created participations in what Aquinas calls the "notional acts" proper to each of the divine persons. The divine gift establishes relations to each of the divine persons. It is not simply by appropriation that the Christian prays, "Our Father," "Lord Jesus Christ," "Come, Holy Spirit." Those three prayers express distinct relations to three distinct persons. Those relations share in and imitate the trinitarian relations, and so bestow on us a distinct participation in the divine life of each person, in keeping with the distinct fashion in which each of them exercises the divine creative love. The question for systematics is, How can this be?

(4) The created consequent condition by which it is possible to affirm a created *relation* to the uncreated Holy Spirit, that is, what has been known as sanctifying grace, imitates and participates in the uncreated relation to the Holy Spirit that the Father and the Son together are. That is, it imitates and participates in what the psychological analogy has traditionally called active spiration. The created gift called sanctifying grace is the reception of actively spirating love as it elevates central form to a created supernatural relation to the uncreated Holy Spirit. As such, it is a created participation

in the Father and the Son as, acknowledging their respective lovableness, together they actively "breathe" the Holy Spirit. It is experienced, at least as recollected and made thematic in memory, as being on the receiving end of unconditional love and loving. We have been given a share in the relation to the Holy Spirit that in God is the Father and the Son actively loving each other and in that loving "breathing," "spirating," the Holy Spirit. In this active loving, the Father communicates divine love to the Son, who responds precisely as *Verbum spirans Amorem*, an eternal Judgment of Value that breathes eternal love, the proceeding love that is the Holy Spirit issuing as the mutual love of the Father and the Son.

(5) Participation in the *Verbum spirans Amorem* thus takes place through a created supernatural judgment of value or, better, set of judgments of value, from which there proceeds the created love that we call charity. The gift of God's love thus includes a participation in an invisible mission of the divine Word. The charity that proceeds from the participation in the Word breathing love shares in the Proceeding Love that is the Holy Spirit. Charity relates us back to the Father and the Son in a created participation in the passive spiration of the Holy Spirit, setting up an inverse created relation to the uncreated Father and Son, who thus also dwell in us as terms of a distinct created relation.

(6) The set of judgments of value that participates in the Word's role in breathing the Holy Spirit, our participation in the invisible mission of the Word, constitutes a universalist "faith" that is common to all who have assented to the reception of unqualified love. Accordingly, the mission of the Son is just as universal as is the mission of the Holy Spirit. This knowledge called faith grounds the proceeding charity that a Christian theology acknowledges as a created participation in the passive spiration that is the Holy Spirit. This universalist faith Lonergan distinguishes in his later work from the beliefs of particular religious traditions. The faith reflected in such judgments of value can be and is found in diverse traditions, and is responsible, it would seem, for Lonergan's hope that the religions of the world will find common ground and common cause in the gift of God's love. Such faith is "the knowledge born of religious love,"[61] a knowledge contained in judgments of value consequent upon the reception of the gift of unqualified love. Articulating those common judgments of value represents, I believe, the locus of interreligious dialogue today, which, as it engages in such articulation, will in fact be making explicit the invisible mission of the divine Word. For Christians that locus will be a share explicitly in that invisible mission. The articulation of those common judgments of value will raise our community with the people of the world's religions from the potential community constituted by a shared experience to the formal and actual state generated by shared understanding and affirmation, and

because the judgments in question are judgments of value, also to the status of a community that can act in solidarity in the collaborative constitution of the human world.

(7) An analogy for understanding the divine processions can be suggested from this structure of the divine gift. The analogy starts with the reception of the gift of God's love, recollected in memory, from which, when this is grasped as evidence, there proceeds a set of judgments of value; from these two together (the gift and the word) there flows the charity that is the love of God in return. The recollection in memory of the divine favor is an analogue for the divine Father, the set of judgments of value that proceeds from this *memoria* is an analogue for the divine Son, and the charity that is the love of God in return is an analogue for the proceeding Love that is the Holy Spirit. Created grace thus has a Trinitarian form. The analogy in the order of grace begins with the gift of God's love, retrospectively interpreted as a gift of being on the receiving end of a love and a loving that are without qualification. The initial step in the analogy is composed of the gift of God's love recollected in memory and acknowledged as evidence for a particular existential orientation. This step issues in the inner word of a judgment of value proceeding from memory and grasp, and acknowledging the goodness of the gift. This judgment of value is the foundation of a universalist faith that is present in all authentic religion. The recollection and judgment of value together constitute a created share in, participation in, imitation of, divine active spiration, the active loving of the Father and the Son for each other from which divine *Amor procedens*, passive spiration, the Holy Spirit, originates. *Memoria* and its *verbum spirans amorem* give rise to the disposition of charity, the antecedent universal willingness that is a created participation in and imitation of the Holy Spirit, a disposition that establishes a reverse relation of love for the Father and the Son. The reverse relation to the Son becomes companionship, as the revelation of the Son in the visible mission is accepted. The reverse relation to the Father is an eschatological hope. Thus it may be said that not only is there a universalist faith; there are also universalist hope and charity. The relation between the love acknowledged in *memoria* and its word, on the one hand, and charity on the other is analogous to the relation between active and passive spiration in the triune God. The three divine persons dwell in us and among us, are present to us, precisely as the uncreated terms of created supernatural relations: supernatural, because their term is God as God is in God's threefold conscious self, which is beyond the proportion of any created nature and so absolutely supernatural.

(8) This theology constitutes a twofold transposition – theoretical and methodological – of the movement of the *Spiritual Exercises* of St Ignatius: from the reception of divine love at the beginning to the "Contemplation

for Attaining Love of God" in return at the very end. That contemplation contains the basic structure that I am suggesting: memory recollecting and making thematic the gift that one has received, the judgment of value that this is indeed very good, and the awakening of love for the One who has first loved us. Memory and judgment of value together are a created share in active spiration, and the awakening of love in return is a created participation in passive spiration.

5

Social Grace and the
Mission of the Word

1   Transposing the Reign of God

> **Thesis 10:** *The preaching of the reign of God by the incarnate Word can be integrated into a systematic theology by complicating the structure of the scale of values. Thus there emerges the social character of grace.*

The conclusion of the previous chapter brings us back to the social dimensions of grace. These would be fleshed out, as it were, in a theology that would articulate the constitution of what, in the second divine mission, Jesus preached and inaugurated as the reign or kingdom of God. In order to spell this out in a bit of detail, I will discuss the other major component of the unified field structure that I am suggesting, the notion of history, and particularly mission in history. My notion of history can be found in the theory of history expressed in *Theology and the Dialectics of History*. I want here only to point out the way in which the matters that I have been speaking about thus far relate to the components of historical process discussed there.

In *Method in Theology* Lonergan presents an ascending scale of values, where the scale itself is based on the degree of self-transcendence to which we are carried in our responses to different kinds of values. Lonergan writes:

> [W]e may distinguish vital, social, cultural, personal, and religious values in an ascending order. Vital values, such as health and strength, grace and vigor, normally are preferred to avoiding the work, privations, pains involved in acquiring, maintaining, restoring them. Social values, such as the good of order which conditions the vital values of the whole community, have to be preferred to the

> vital values of individual members of the community. Cultural values
> do not exist without the underpinning of vital and social values, but
> none the less they rank higher. Not on bread alone doth man live.
> Over and above mere living and operating, men have to find a mean-
> ing and value in their living and operating. It is the function of cul-
> ture to discover, express, validate, criticize, correct, develop, improve
> such meaning and value. Personal value is the person in his self-
> transcendence, as loving and being loved, as originator of values in
> himself and in his milieu, as an inspiration and invitation to others
> to do likewise. Religious values, finally, are at the heart of the mean-
> ing and value of man's living and man's world ...[1]

In my own work, I have posited two sets of relations among the various
levels of value, one "from below" as it were and the other "from above."
Obviously, functioning schemes of recurrence at the more basic levels are
required if sustained activity at the more complex levels is to be possible.
But more important is the issue of what happens when things go wrong at
the more basic levels. For if it is true that the sustained activity of the more
complex levels depends on the functioning vitality of the more basic levels,
then there is raised a problem that can be met only by the introduction of
transcendent love and the truth that is born of such love. Very briefly and
schematically we may say that problems at the more basic levels give rise
to questions that can prompt transformations at the more complex levels,
and that these transformations are required in order to meet the problems
that arose at the more basic levels. Thus, problems regarding the equitable
distribution of vital goods will be met by adjustments at the level of social
values: technological, economic, and political adjustments, or changes in
peoples' spontaneous intersubjectivity, or both. But where are these adjustments to come from? They may well call for conditioning adjustments in
the sets of meanings and values informing peoples' ways of living, that is to
say, at the level of cultural values. The transformation of cultural values, in
turn, depends on people striving for self-transcendence in all they do, and
such consistent self-transcendence is not possible without God's grace, in
fact without the grace that enables the return of good for evil. Conversely,
then, it is the gift of God's grace that alone can meet the underlying difficulties. Grace is the condition of sustained personal value, which itself
conditions the emergence of the genuine cultural values that in turn are
required for a just social order assuring the equitable distribution of vital
goods to the entire community. The gift of God's grace that is the ultimate
base is understood in terms of the created participations in and imitation
of the triune God that occur in sanctifying grace and the charity that flows

from it, that is, in terms of the mission and gift of the Holy Spirit, both in and beyond the boundaries of the Christian communions.

We have to this point in effect been suggesting the contours of what is called the level of religious values in the scale of values. But the incarnate Word's preaching of the reign of God is the announcement of that gift in the articulate speech that at some point, sooner or later, will call for reflection that relates that gift to the other dimensions of human living: to personal integrity, to refined cultural pursuit of the intelligible, the true, the good, the beautiful, to renewed social structures and healed intersubjectivity, and to justice for all in the distribution of the earth's resources. In the immanent Trinity, the divine Word does not speak (*dicere*) but is spoken (*dici*). The incarnate Word speaks because his assumed nature enjoys a created relation to the eternal Word, a relation that participates in the Father's eternal relation to the same Word. In this sense, the assumed humanity of the incarnate Word shares in a created participation in the relation of paternity that is identical with the Father's uttering the eternal judgment of value that is the Word. That Word in history, that Word incarnate, announces the reign of God in history, in an announcement that anticipates the fulfilment of the integral relations of the various dimensions of value expressed in the objective and normative scale of values. To spell out those integral relations is to provide in terms of interiorly and religiously differentiated consciousness and in the context of a theology of history precisely the invariant contours of what the reign of God would be. And to speak words at the level of cultural values that would call the community to fidelity to the scale of values is in fact to participate in the invisible mission of the Word.

Lonergan has spoken of the structure of history in terms of the simultaneous interplay of the forces that make for progress, those that head to decline, and those that redeem from decline. In a very schematic articulation he writes: "[The] first approximation [to the structure of history] was that [people] always do what is intelligent and reasonable, and its implication was an ever increasing progress. The second approximation was the radical inverse insight that [people] can be biased, and so unintelligent and unreasonable in their choices and decisions. The third approximation was the redemptive process resulting from God's gift of grace to individuals and from the manifestation of his love in Christ Jesus."[2] My own position complicates that structure, to argue that being intelligent and reasonable on a communal or collective level means the integral functioning of the scale of values, that the spread of bias leads to a breakdown in the relations among the various levels of the scale, and that the gift of God's grace affects not only the individual in his or her intelligent, reasonable, and responsible living but, through the scale of values, the entire community in its collective responsibility for a good of order that is truly good for all and not only for some. That gift will stretch people to the self-sacrificing charity that refuses to return evil for evil, to the nonviolent love that returns good for evil, that prays for enemies, that prays for the gift to be able to forgive, that seeks the truth that alone can lead to reconciliation, and that fosters discernment and understanding of what God is doing in our midst. This is something of what constitutes charity and distinguishes it from the natural love that we have for one another and even for God. Such charity is not only a function of the gift of God's grace but a created participation in and imitation of the Holy Spirit, a participation and imitation breathed forth in us by the Father's and the Son's giving of their own love that elevates us to participation in Trinitarian life, precisely as we respond to being sent, to being on mission, as Jesus responded to his own being sent by the Father. But the gift itself includes as well participation in the invisible mission of the Word, which includes explicit attention to the human community's fidelity to the integral scale of values. It is in these terms that I would begin to transpose into a contemporary systematic-theological context the meaning of that reign of God that Jesus himself both preached and inaugurated.

2   The Invisible and Visible Missions of the Divine Word

The scale of values is obviously the key to the notion of social grace that I would like to suggest here. Briefly, the gift of God's love, that is, the gift of the Holy Spirit (religious values) is the condition of the possibility of sustained personal integrity (personal value); persons of integrity represent the condition of possibility of genuine meanings and values informing ways of living (cultural values); the pursuit of genuine cultural values is a constitutive dimension in the establishment of social structures and intersubjective habits (social values) that would render more probable something approaching an equitable distribution of vital values to the human community (vital values).

Now the link between cultural and social values as thus expressed concentrates exclusively on meaning as the controlling factor in human affairs, and there is a complex surd that at times escapes personal and communal control that prevents the scale from functioning in a seamless manner precisely by preventing integral meaning from becoming operative in the constitution of the good of social order, the social mediation of the good. That complex surd is precisely what is meant by social sin. Lonergan addresses this surd in his treatment of individual, group, and general bias. I have attempted to address it further by speaking of the need for a psychic conversion that would join Lonergan's intellectual, moral, and religious conversions in a united front against the destructive force of bias in human affairs. But for my present purposes, it is enough to state that the integral functioning of the full scale of values is constitutive of what I mean here by the "social grace" that I would set over against social sin.

My purpose in the present chapter is to flesh out the notion of social grace precisely in relation to this connection between cultural and social values and to relate social grace, and with it the scale of values that is its principal constituent, to the other divine mission, that of the Incarnate Word. I will emphasize that the invisible mission of the Word has something to do with the connection between cultural values and social values. But if it is true that the notion of social grace is a contemporary transposition of the biblical category "the reign of God," then as such it is inextricably linked also to an adequate theology of the visible mission of the divine Word in Jesus of Nazareth.

I have reviewed my theological doctrines regarding the divine missions, and so regarding what in the scale of values is summed up in the brief expression "religious values." Here I will begin to add to these preliminary positions by speaking again of an *invisible* mission of the divine Word flowing from the structure expressed in the first part, and I will relate that invisible mission to the scale of values and so to social grace. And I will continue with a discussion of some of the parameters of the theology of the *visible* mission of the Word in Jesus of Nazareth, again in relation to the same scale of values constitutive of what I am calling social grace, but now under the rubric of the reign or kingdom of God as announced by Jesus, and with reference to the revelation of God in Jesus that comes to expression precisely in that announcement.

2.1 The Invisible Mission of the Word and the Notion of Social Grace

I have said something about the invisible mission of the divine Word in speaking of the set of judgments of value in which we share in the divine life of the Word. I have also mentioned the visible mission of the divine Word, as it occurs in relation to the invisible mission of the Holy Spirit and even gives rise to a visible mission of the Holy Spirit at Pentecost. My point now is twofold: first, to link the universalist faith that articulates a share in the invisible mission of the Word to the social grace that constitutes the integral functioning of the scale of values (2.1), and second, to open upon the specifically Christian faith that emerges as we confess the entrance of divine meaning and value, the divine Logos, into human history in the visible mission of the Word (2.2).

I will elaborate on the notion of social grace in two steps. The first has to do with the peculiarity of history as a field of investigation. The second has to do with the role of articulate cultural values in that peculiar field.

2.1.1 The Peculiarity of History

Taking my cue from Lonergan, I speak of the peculiarity of history by contrasting history with autobiography and biography. As we move from autobiography to biography, there is a transition from "life," that is, my life, to "the life and times" of another human being. And as we move from biography to history, the "times" are no longer a subordinate clarification of an individual "life." Rather, attention is centered on the *common* field that only in part is explored in each of the biographies or autobiographies that are or might be written. That common field "is not just an area in which biographies might overlap. There is social and cultural process. It is not just a sum of individual words and deeds. There exists a developing and/or deteriorating unity constituted by cooperations, by institutions, by personal relations, by a functioning and/or malfunctioning good of order, by a communal realization of originating and terminal values and disvalues," and, I might add, by the vicissitudes of meaning struggling to become common or falling apart on the shoals of human waywardness and bias. "Within such processes," continues Lonergan, "we live out our lives. About them each of us ordinarily is content to learn enough to attend to his own affairs and perform his public duties. To seek a view of the actual functioning of the whole or of a notable part over a significant period of time is the task of the historian."[3] My first approximation to the notion of social grace is to indicate that grace as a social reality would be the gift of God's love considered not so much as affecting individual biographies and establishing within them created relations to each of the uncreated divine Persons, though of course it is not unrelated to grace so understood, but as transforming the "functioning and/or malfunctioning good of order," the "communal realization of originating and terminal values and disvalues," and the ongoing genesis or deterioration of meaning as affecting that social and historical reality that is more than "just a sum of individual words and deeds." We have developed in the past several decades a fairly sophisticated theology of social sin, a theology that explains how sin is not simply a reality that affects, indeed infects, individual biographies but that distorts the entire functioning of the good of order and replaces terminal values with terminal disvalues. I continue to maintain that Lonergan's diagnosis of bias is the single most powerful ingredient in the theology of social sin. The notion of social grace, when developed, would speak of grace not only as it affects individual biographies but as it makes a difference in the actual development of common meanings, in the functioning of the good of order, and in the delivery of vital goods to the entire community.

2.1.2 Articulate Cultural Values and Social Grace

Now, in order to develop the notion of social grace in terms of the scale of values, I want to double back to the notion of the judgments of value that proceed from the gift of divine love, and to suggest that social grace can be understood as grounded in a participation in the shared or universalist faith that flows from that gift, and so in the invisible mission of the Word. These judgments of value constitute human graced participation in the procession of the Son from the Father, in the actively spirating Word breathing Love from which or through which ("Filioque" or "per Filium") the Holy Spirit originates. Thus, that participation through judgments of value born of the gift of God's love is the invisible mission of the Son. These judgments of value constitute the universalist faith that is a knowledge born of religious love. The gift of God's love releases an inner word that God speaks in our hearts, a word that relates us to the Holy Spirit. The knowledge born of that gift, the invisible mission of the Word, is an ultimately ineffable "Yes," a global judgment of value, that sometimes gets articulated in formulated statements of value. And these articulated judgments of value to which the gift gives rise are an outer word that is constitutive of the human world, precisely at the level of cultural values in the scale of values. These cultural values are responsible for making the human world different from what it would be were we not empowered by the invisible missions of the Spirit and the Word to utter them. That outer word not only flows from a participation in the invisible mission of the Word through the ultimately ineffable Yes that flows from the gift of divine love. It also begins a participation in the visible mission of the eternal Word, the eternal Judgment of Value, by calling for and entering into the collaboration that generates publicly shared understandings and publicly shared affirmations. In other words, at the heart of what I am calling the social reality of grace is an articulate set of cultural values that arise from the collective discovery, expression, validation, criticism, correction, development, improvement of the formulations of the judgments of meaning and value that flow from the gift of God's love that Christians call the gift of the Holy Spirit.

Lonergan would express that universalist faith in something like the following terms (and this is not a direct quotation, but is based on the section "Faith" in his chapter on religion in *Method in Theology* at 116–18). As you read this set of statements, I invite you to insert these meanings and values into the locus of cultural values in the scale of values, and to sense what a difference they make in the human world mediated and constituted by meaning as they come to be shared by many.

> All other values are placed in the light and the shadow of transcendent value, which is supreme and incomparable and which links itself to all other values to transform, magnify, glorify them. Thus the originating value is not human intelligence and responsibility but divine light and love, and the terminal value is not the human good we can bring about but the whole universe. Human development is not limited to skills and virtues but extends to holiness. The power of God's love brings forth a new energy and efficacy in all goodness. The limit of human expectation ceases to be the grave. The world is the fruit of God's self-transcendence, the expression and manifestation of God's benevolence and beneficence, God's glory. God made us in the divine image, and so our authenticity consists in being like God, origins of value in true love. In particular, God calls us to the higher authenticity that overcomes evil with good. We can do this only because faith, the knowledge born of religious love, places human efforts in a friendly universe, revealing an ultimate significance in human achievement and strengthening new undertakings with confidence. That higher authenticity that overcomes evil with good enters with religious faith, unwavering hope, and self-sacrificing charity into a world that inflicts on individuals the social, economic, and psychological pressures that for human frailty amount to determinism; a world that multiplies and heaps up the abuses and absurdities that breed resentment, hatred, anger, violence; a world that houses people in ideological prisons; a world that dooms people to the vast pressures of social decay. The gift of God's love awakens a knowledge of our sinfulness and of our real guilt, a firm purpose of amendment of our ways, and a confidence that the one who bestowed the gift of love is, despite our sinfulness and unworthiness, everlasting mercy and forgiveness.

That is the closest Lonergan comes to expressing what this universalist faith, this participation in the invisible mission of the Word, might be. It cannot be denied that he is employing terminology that he learned from his Christian heritage, but he is using that terminology to frame a set of affirmations that he hopes could be agreed upon by others who have consciously been on the receiving end of divine love, once they recognize that gift for what it is. And now I must, following Charles Hefling, insist that even these expressions are not that faith itself, but beliefs, articulations that flow from that faith. I have already quoted Hefling to the effect that the faith itself that flows from the gift of God's love is an ineffable knowledge, a global "Yes" that will never be adequately formulated, a knowledge that can be expressed only by formulating statements that, as statements, would have to be classified as statements, not of faith but of belief.[4] Again, "The *inexpressibility* of faith is the cognitional counterpart of the *unrestrictedness* of the love from which it is "born.""[5] To articulate one's faith, even if that articulation is intended to express something that could be agreed upon universally, is to effect a transition from ineffable to effable knowledge. That transition is not unimportant. The outer word is not a mere addendum to the inner word of the gift of God's love. It is constitutive of the religious situation, in a manner remotely analogous to the way in which the outer avowal of love between two persons is not a mere addendum to their love but is constitutive of their being in love.

At this point, I should say something more about the validity of this notion of the scale of values.

In Avery Dulles's notes on Lonergan's 1964 Institute at Georgetown University on the issues of theological method, it is recorded that Lonergan referred to the normative subject disclosed in his generalized empirical method as a concrete universal. The subject that is a compound of empirical, intelligent, rational, and moral consciousness is normative because that subject gives the law to himself or herself, a law that Lonergan summarizes in the transcendental precepts, Be attentive, Be intelligent, Be reasonable, Be responsible. These imperatives are for Lonergan the basis of natural law. But that this normative subject is a concrete universal means, among other things, that the results in history of being attentive, intelligent, reasonable, and responsible, as well as the results in history of being inattentive, stupid, silly, and irresponsible represent an objectification of the human spirit, somewhat along the lines of the Hegelian objectification of *Geist*, except that Lonergan's conception is not worked out in an idealist vein but in the critical realist conviction that genuine objectivity does indeed issue from authentic or normative subjectivity, and particularly in the *judgments* of fact and value that are not explicitly acknowledged in Hegelian philosophy as constitutive of human knowing. That objectification is precisely the field of historical investigation that is more than an overlapping of individual biographies.

The structure of that historical objectification is captured in Lonergan's scale of values, for this scale represents human attentiveness, intelligence, reasonableness, and responsibility writ large in the social and cultural structures of historical living. That is to say, the scale of vital, social, cultural, personal, and religious values is isomorphic with the levels of consciousness: vital values with experience, social values with understanding, cultural values with judgment of fact and of value, personal values with decision, and religious values with the gift of God's love. The structure of the gift of the Holy Spirit constitutes a dimension of the fifth level, a dimension which, to borrow and perhaps adapt a term from Karl Rahner, could be called a supernatural existential inchoately fulfilling the natural yearning for union with God that unfolds through human empirical, intelligent, reasonable, and morally responsible operations. The integral functioning of the scale of values thus may be regarded as a social embodiment or objectification of the grace that is the communication of divine life to men and women in the gift of the Holy Spirit, a communication that moves from above downwards not only in human consciousness but also in the social objectification of that consciousness in the scale of values. The knowledge born of that love becomes articulate in judgments of value that reflect a universalist faith that shares in the invisible mission of the Word. Those judgments enter into the scale of values primarily at the level of cultural values, to transform the meanings and values by which entire groups of people are constituted and thus to effect a more integral functioning of the entire scale. All who are engaged in such transformative efforts based on self-transcendence are participating in the invisible mission of the Word, whether explicitly or not.

Ultimately, it is the integral functioning of the scale of values that is the expression of the social dimension of grace or of what I am calling, in a kind of shorthand, social grace, a social grace that is established by the knowledge born of religious love that is faith. As I argued at some length in *Theology and the Dialectics of History*, the articulation of the scale also represents, in my view, a transcendental validation of what has come to be known as the preferential option for the poor, since it is the global maldistribution of vital goods that sets the question regarding the entire scale. At any rate, all of these convictions are belief statements that express what ultimately is an ineffable assent to the communication of divine life in the gift of God's love, an ineffable assent that participates in the invisible mission of the divine Word, but that becomes articulate as one relates the gift of love to the set of meanings and values that constitutes the cultural values of one's milieu. That articulation is constitutive of the functioning of grace precisely as a social reality.

2.2 *The Visible Mission of the Word and the Notion of Social Grace*

What happens theologically to the notion of the visible mission of the divine Word, and so to our theology of the Incarnation and our soteriology, in the context that we have been expressing? The implications, I believe, are twofold. The first has to do with the notion of revelation, and the second with the notion of the kingdom or reign of God. The Word became flesh and dwelt among us; the very Word in whom all who assent to the gift of God's love participate in that very assent has pitched his tent among us as one of us.

2.2.1 Revelation and the Visible Mission of the Word

In spelling out the implications for the notion of revelation, I wish to stress two points. The first is that the visible mission of the Word is to be understood at least in part as a revelation in linguistic and incarnate meaning of the more elemental meanings, often inarticulate and at times ineffable, contained in the universal and invisible missions of the Holy Spirit and of the Word. The revelation is analogous to the avowal of love between two human beings, but it is an avowal in which the first to say "I love you" is God. Like the avowal of love, it is no mere addendum to the inner gift but is constitutive of the religious situation. Christians would go even further and add that the word, like the inner gift, is from God, and indeed in one instance *is* God.

The second point is that the structure of revelation itself must be understood in terms of a theological position on the human consciousness and the human knowledge of the incarnate Word, Jesus of Nazareth, which is the principal site of revelation itself.[6] As such, the revelation that comes with the visible mission of the Word goes far beyond an explicit revelation of what is elementally contained in the invisible missions of the Holy Spirit and of the Word. It conveys a knowledge beyond the universalist faith that is the knowledge born of religious love, a knowledge beyond both the ineffable "yes" that flows from that love and such articulations of that "yes" as the beliefs that are present in what I have already developed from Lonergan, and so a knowledge beyond our participation through a universalist faith in the invisible mission of the Word. The knowledge that revelation conveys has something to do with *other* beliefs, namely, the beliefs that can be discovered by studying the history of Christian doctrine, the specific and unique beliefs that Christians would bring to the table of interreligious dialogue. For the content of at least those doctrines that are of prime importance, doctrines that go beyond the beliefs that flow proximately from a universalist faith, is a content that itself has been divinely revealed.[7] And the primary locus of that revelation is the human knowledge of the incarnate Word of God, Jesus of Nazareth. My effort here is to tease out how that is possible, how that statement can be maintained.

To say that the primary locus of such revelation of the divine mysteries is given in the human knowledge of Jesus of Nazareth, the incarnate Word of God, is to view revelation as a matter of Jesus moving from *his* ineffable knowledge, which is different from ours, to an expression of that knowledge in human language. His ineffable knowledge is not the same as our "faith as the knowledge born of divine love," nor is the effable knowledge through which he learned to articulate the mystery of his person and of God the same as the generic beliefs that flow from the universalist faith that is the "Yes" born of religious love. It is the source of those beliefs that express contents of mysteries that, had they not been revealed, we could never know, even from the gift of God's love in the invisible mission of the Spirit. What makes the difference between the ineffable knowledge of Jesus and the faith that is the ineffable knowledge born of religious love is the beatific knowing that in Jesus takes the place of what in us is the faith that flows from the gift of God's love.

The ontological constitution of Christ, as Lonergan understands it, may be set forth in four points, which I take from Charles Hefling's masterful interpretation of Lonergan's Christology.

First, "Whatever Christ may be inasmuch as he is a [human being], it is not what he is inasmuch as he is God. Humanity and divinity remain 'unconfused, unmixed,' as Chalcedon insists."[8] The reason is that God is unrestricted and necessary, and no restricted, finite, and contingent being, no finite creature, including Christ's human nature, is God; all are related to God in the same way, as one intelligible part of the contingent whole that is the emergently probable universe. God remains the same whether or not God brings about the existence of anything else, including the humanity of Jesus.

Second, however, Christ's humanity is not related to God *only* as creature to Creator. *This* humanity is the humanity of the Word who is God. Just as God is intrinsically the same whether or not he brings about the existence of anything else, so also the Word is intrinsically the same whether or not he *becomes* anything else. The Word retains his own identity whether or not he has in fact become a human being. But because the Word did become a human being, that human being's humanity is not only created: it is assumed, and consequently that human being has his identity in the Word.[9]

Third, "the one divine person who subsists in two natures is also one divine subject of two consciousnesses ... [A]s the subject of humanly conscious operations Christ is like us in all things ... [and so] his human consciousness is precisely *not* divine, and the fact that it is a divine subject's human consciousness does not make it so."[10]

And fourth, "there exists one human consciousness by which a divine subject is present to himself, namely, the human consciousness that is a constituent of the incarnate Word. Through conscious acts that are altogether human, the eternal Word was made aware of the selfsame eternal Word."[11] But because consciousness is only self-presence, and because it is not knowing in the fully human sense, and in particular not self-knowing, this awareness does not entail his conscious operations being either an act of understanding what it is to be the incarnate Word, or an act of judging that the one who is performing the operations is the incarnate Word. That knowledge is given to him not by the hypostatic union but by revelation. The Incarnation as such gives Christ no human knowledge of himself, because it gives him no knowledge of anything at all. Consciousness is not knowledge. Consciousness is being at a certain level of perfection. Simply *being* the incarnate Word did not provide Christ with access to knowledge that other men and women cannot achieve. Unless something further can be stated, something that goes beyond the ontological constitution of Christ and its translation into psychological terms and relations, we would be left with the anomaly that "although Christ's words *were* the words of the Word, he did not *know* they were."[12]

But Christ as human did know by immediate vision or beatific knowing both God and the mysteries hidden in God. This doctrine, which Lonergan shares with Aquinas, is "the key to understanding the Incarnation as the definitive 'site' of revelation."[13] Jesus of Nazareth, Christ the man, God the Word precisely as subsisting in a human nature, the divine subject of human consciousness precisely as humanly conscious – and those four expressions designate the same reality – enjoyed immediate knowledge of God. This knowledge is not divine knowledge but human knowledge. It is beatific human knowing. It is finite, created, but also disproportionate to the knowing that is the fruit of natural human attentiveness, inquiry, understanding, reflection, and judgment; it was not gained through those operations. It is knowledge, not consciousness. It is a knowledge that is always in act. To know realities by beatific knowledge is to know them, not severally or sequentially, but all at once and all together. The intelligibility that such knowledge grasps is not mediated by anything sensible. Its content is inexpressible or ineffable. "As our ordinary acts of understanding grasp intelligibility in some presentation or representation, some 'phantasm' so, too, they express themselves in concepts, inner words, objects of thought that retain an imaginative component. Similarly, the outer words that convey what we have understood and conceived require some vehicle such as articulate sound or discrete markings. No such multiplicity, succession, or imaginability can pertain to the expression of an intelligibility that was never so mediated in the first place. Neither concepts nor language, therefore, are capable of expressing what is known by 'seeing' God."[14] The knowledge is literally ineffable.

By this ineffable knowledge, Christ is more than the divine subject of human consciousness, because knowledge is more than consciousness. By it he *understands* what it is to be God – that is what beatific knowledge is, after all – and what it is to be eternally begotten of the Father, and he *judges* that what he *experiences* in a humanly conscious way *is* what he *understands* through beatific knowledge. As Lonergan puts it in a very carefully phrased sentence, "Christ as man, through his human consciousness *and* his beatific knowledge, clearly understands, and with certainty judges, himself to be the natural Son of God and true God." Christ did not need beatific knowledge to *be* Word and Son, but without it he could not have known, humanly, the mystery of his own identity.[15]

This knowledge, however, is ineffable, and so the clarity and certainty with which he grasps his own identity cannot be expressed humanly, even to himself. "Not only eternal Sonship, but everything else that Christ knows by beatific knowledge, he knows not through the mediation of sensible data, but through the mediation of the divine essence. It seems, then, that the character of the knowledge that is his to share prevents him from sharing it. What he knows, he cannot think about; and what he cannot think about, he cannot deliberately communicate."[16] To say that his humanly constituted thinking does or did express the inexpressible is to introduce a development on the notion of revelation. The inexpressible intelligibility of divine mystery became expressible in the single human consciousness of Jesus of Nazareth as subject of his earthly life. He learned how to express it. His earthly life *was* the expression of his grasp of the divine mystery. It was that expression not only in intersubjective and symbolic carriers of meaning such as smiles and gestures, but also in linguistic carriers of meaning, in outer words. He knew *both* the transcendent intelligibility that cannot be expressed in language that emerges out of the normal way of human learning *and* the meaningful language in which to express this otherwise inexpressible mystery. He knew the former by beatific knowing and the latter by human insights that are themselves the fruit of revelation. We proceed from the unrestricted *intention* of being to the acquisition of our effable knowledge. Christ the human being proceeded from his ineffable *knowing* of the unrestricted act to the formation of his effable supernatural knowledge. He needed both ineffable and effable knowledge: the former in order to know divine mysteries, and the latter in order to express them. His effable knowledge is the fruit of the ongoing process of insight in his own development, but in his case this is not only the insight that proceeds from sensible data imaginatively construed so as to yield understanding, from below as it were, as with us, but also from the ongoing and self-correcting process of learning that enabled him to form in human language the ineffable knowledge that he had through beatific knowing.

2.2.2 The Reign of God and the Visible Mission of the Word

The mystery is deepened if we take from Lonergan the affirmation that, as sanctifying grace and charity are, respectively, the created consequent conditions of human participation in and imitation of Trinitarian active and passive spiration, Trinitarian active loving and proceeding love, so there is a created consequent condition without which the statement "The eternal Word of God is incarnate in Jesus of Nazareth" would not be true. As we have seen, that created consequent condition is not sanctifying grace or charity, though Jesus did enjoy both, but, following Aquinas, what Thomas calls the "esse secundarium" of the Incarnation, the secondary act of existence by which it is true that the assumed humanity of the incarnate Word shares in the eternal relation of the uncreated Word to the Father. Now, in the same sentence in which he conceives sanctifying grace and charity as participations in active and passive spiration, Lonergan calls the "esse secundarium" of the Incarnation, the grace of union, a created imitation of and participation in the divine relation of paternity. "Whoever sees me sees the Father." For our present purposes, the most significant point to this affirmation is the following: in the eternal Godhead, the Word does not speak; the Word is spoken; the Word's notional act is not *dicere*, to speak, but *dici*, to be spoken. The Incarnate Word, however, speaks, and he speaks because the grace of union is a participation in the eternal "speaking" that is the divine Father. He speaks, but he speaks only what he has heard from the Father in the Holy Spirit through his beatific knowing and his learning to articulate that knowing in human language, and that "hearing from the Father in the Holy Spirit" is precisely the principal site in human history of the divine revelation that not only allows him ineffably to know who he is but makes it possible for him through created human insights and language to communicate to us the ineffable knowing that he enjoyed by beatific vision, and to communicate it word by word, step by step, in the definitive entrance of divine meaning and value into human history through not only intersubjective and symbolic carriers of meaning but also in human language. That definitive entrance of divine meaning and value is precisely what is meant by the reign of God. Here, as in so many other ways, Lonergan's thought can join with a theological transformation of Martin Heidegger's: Language is the house of being, and care for language at the level of cultural values is central to the social grace that mediates the divine love expressed in religious values to the social structures that make it possible that human beings live in harmony and peace with one another – a goal that is shared by all who have said "yes" to the uncreated gift of the Holy Spirit in the invisible mission of the Word, and a goal that is communicated in the visible mission of the Word as Jesus learns the language in which to express what he knows ineffably through his beatific knowledge.

What precisely was it that he learned to communicate? Let us visit for a moment René Girard's sobering reminder of what a divine Word spoken in and entering into a sinful human world entails, a world in which the scale of values has been distorted, and in fact Girard's reminder of a dimension of the revelation that Jesus enjoyed from his beatific knowing. I note with interest that Girard relies on Heidegger for this reminder, even as he moves decisively beyond him. The Johannine Logos that was in the beginning with God and that was God and that became flesh and that revealed God, the Logos of love, is a Word that puts up no resistance, that always allows itself to be expelled by the logos of violence, but at the same time it is a Logos that reveals its own expulsion and in so doing reveals also the logos of violence for what it is. The logos of violence is a word that can exist only by expelling the true Logos even while feeding upon it in one way or another. "[T]he Word of truth [is] the true knowledge of the victim, continually eluded and rejected by [humankind]."[17] This ultimate meaning of history in the Law of the Cross is at the heart of the revelation that is gradually communicated by God throughout the history of biblical literature, a revelation that finds its principal site in the beatific knowledge of Jesus of Nazareth.

3   Filling Out the Social Dimensions of Grace

Thesis 11: *As elevation by grace affects every level of consciousness, so it influences also each of the levels of value isomorphic with the levels of consciousness.*

More needs to be said about the social objectification of grace, of the lived presence of the undertow of God's gift that is made thematic in the announcement of the reign of God. We may do this by commenting further on the place that my earlier work *Theology and the Dialectics of History* plays in the emerging systematics that is being expressed here.

Lonergan's 1977 address to the American Catholic Philosophical Association, "Natural Right and Historical Mindedness" links us back to chapter 7 of *Insight*, in that, like that chapter, it attempts the articulation of the intelligibility of "a single object that can gain collective attention,"[18] an intelligibility that can be articulated even though the situations that embody it are as a whole "commonly … neither foreseen nor intended" by most people affected by them.[19] In chapter 7 of *Insight* this single object is, in the words of the title of the chapter, "Common Sense as Object," while in "Natural Right and Historical Mindedness" it is "collective responsibility," the coalescence of "the manifold of isolated responsibilities" into the unfolding of a history that flows from a total and dialectical source of meaning.[20] In each case the issue is the relation between a subjective field and at least a portion of what would play in Lonergan's thought something of the role that objective *Geist* plays in Hegel's. Thus chapter 6 of *Insight* is called "Common Sense and Its Subject" and chapter 7 "Common Sense as Object," but "common sense as object" means at least partly the objectification in culture and society of the subjective field introduced in chapter 6; again, in "Natural Right and Historical Mindedness," the question is how "the issues that individuals have to deal with in their own minds and hearts" become "writ large" in the dialectic of history.[21] These are essentially the same topics. They are major topics. They must be addressed, and Lonergan has given us some of the tools to do just that.

Chapter 7 of *Insight* gains further precision from the presentation in "Natural Right and Historical Mindedness" of the plateaus on which the "single object" of objective *Geist* unfolds.[22] In some manner whose details can probably never be traced, these two works became the inspiration behind much of what I tried to do in *Theology and the Dialectics of History*. In that book, the groundwork is laid so that "collective responsibility," in the concrete dispensation that is ours, may be elevated into something like "social and cultural grace." By this term I mean the objectification, the being writ large in the overarching dialectic of history, of God's entry into human affairs in the two divine missions: in the divine love that floods our inmost hearts through the Holy Spirit that has been given to us and in the revelation of that love in Christ Jesus. What is at stake here, then, is the historical effects of the divine missions. What difference does it make not simply to individuals but to the dialectical processes of human history that there is a universal offer of what Christians call the Holy Spirit? What difference does it make to the same dialectic that the mission of the Son is among other things a revelation in incarnate and linguistic meaning of that universal offer? Here again, there are a subjective and an objective obverse and reverse. It is as though there are several manners in which to express the correlative subjective fields and their objectifications: in one version they are "Common Sense and Its Subject" and "Common Sense as Object"; in another they are "the issues that individuals have to deal with in their own minds and hearts" and the coalescence of their negotiations of those issues into collective responsibility for the dialectic of history; and in the present effort they are the reality that is given to many individuals and in fact that is offered to all, a reality that Catholic theology understands as participation in divine, that is, Trinitarian life, and that good Catholic systematic theology differentiates precisely in its Trinitarian form, and the coalescence of those individual gifts into a single object that can gain collective attention, an object that we might call the social objectification of grace, or in shorthand social grace, or in biblical terms the reign of God in human history. In fact, the global implications of the scale of values, as these are articulated in *Theology and the Dialectics of History*, provide an extraordinary litmus test for the major authenticity of the various religious traditions in our world, where "major authenticity" refers not to the authenticity of individuals vis-à-vis their traditions – one can be authentic to an inauthentic tradition – but to the authenticity of the traditions themselves as currently appropriated and implemented or exercised.

The mission of the Word, then, is carried on, participated in, both in and beyond the church, partly through the gifts and vocations of theologians, philosophers, scientists both natural and human, and scholars, all speaking intelligible words of truth, justice, and reconciliation to a broken world. The mission of the Word is in particular exercised in the link between cultural and social values. Of special importance are breakthroughs whose significance could so reorganize the social mediation of the human good that genuine transformation of social structures could take place. It is time for theology to turn its attention explicitly to social grace, in the context of both divine missions. Liberation theologians and others have made us aware of the social objectifications of sin. These objectifications were already captured by Lonergan in chapter 19 of *Insight* where he speaks of the "moral evils" that are the consequences of "basic sin."[23] Most of us have little difficulty today in acknowledging the existence of "sinful social structures," that is, of the social and cultural coalescence into a single object of manifold refusals or failures to do what is right or to reject what is wrong. But we should also attempt to disengage just what would be the structure of the coalescence into a single object of manifold instances, first, of fidelity to the transcendental precepts, and second, of the elevating and healing divine grace that not only maintains one as consistently faithful to these precepts, but also stretches one to the love that returns good for evil.

The transcendental imperatives themselves are nature, in fact precisely part of the nature that is the immanent principle of movement and rest in "Natural Right and Historical Mindedness."[24] Refusal or failure to observe the imperatives, though, is sin, and recovery or redemption occurs through a grace that elevates the nature whose law is expressed in the imperatives to participation in a radically other nature, a Trinitarian nature that is absolutely supernatural in that it cannot be attained in any immediate fashion by any created nature whatsoever, except and only insofar as it gives itself, bestows itself in gratuitous and extravagant generosity, even wastefulness, upon an obediential potency that is capable only of receiving it. This is the upshot of Lonergan's brilliant treatment of moral impotence in chapter 18 of *Insight*, an analysis that is permanently valid despite his own disclaimer regarding his approach to the dynamics of decision in that work.[25] This treatment was, of course, foreshadowed by his studies of operative and co-operative grace in Aquinas and by his doctrinal supplement on the supernatural order.[26]

However, by the time of "Natural Right and Historical Mindedness" if not before, the source of progress, the normative source of meaning in history, resides not simply in the transcendental precepts but in the coalescence of individual responsibilities, in the communities that are faithful to the demands of ongoing self-transcendence, communities toward which the levels of consciousness themselves are oriented precisely because of their function in a "tidal movement that begins before consciousness, unfolds through sensitivity, intelligence, rational reflection, responsible deliberation, only to find its rest beyond all of these" in "being-in-love."[27] And the source of decline now resides in collective infidelity to these demands, while the source of redemption or recovery in history lies, we may surmise (though this is not mentioned as such in the paper), in the coalescence into common living of the individual gifts of participation in Trinitarian life that God has bestowed, whether explicitly or anonymously. The self that God bestows on a nature that is obediential potency to receive it is Trinitarian and so interpersonal, and the bestowal itself has a Trinitarian and so interpersonal structure. What John Dadosky has called the fourth stage of meaning begins, I submit, with this movement to recognizing that beyond the individual interiority of intentional consciousness there is an interpersonal level of consciousness, where, as Lonergan said as early as his Latin work on the Trinity, the presence of the beloved in the lover is constituted by love itself.[28] This interpersonal dimension coalesces into communities faithful to what the turn to interiority revealed in the first place.[29] If this fidelity is itself a function ultimately of grace, then the expression "social grace" assumes some valid significance, at least as much significance as the expression "social sin."

Theology and the Dialectics of History makes a contribution to the question of just precisely what is the structure of the social objectifications of divine grace. The basic move comes with the recognition that the scale of values articulated in *Method in Theology* and spelled out in greater detail in *Theology and the Dialectics of History* is an objectification of the structure of individual consciousness, just as "Common Sense as Object" is an objectification of "The Subjective Field of Common Sense," and just as negotiation of the issues that individuals have to deal with in their own minds and hearts coalesces into the situations that emerge from the dialectic of history. The normative subject is a concrete universal.[30] The scale of values is the structure of intentional consciousness writ large, and its unfolding is the unfolding of the coalescence of individual authenticity and inauthenticity into a single object that can gain collective attention. The relationship between the structure of consciousness and the scale of values, then, is analogous to that between the same structure and functional specialization, in that in each case we are speaking of a communal objectification of a subjective structure.

All of this is already clear in part 1 of *Theology and the Dialectics of History*, "Basic Terms and Relations." The first set of such terms and relations consists of those found in Lonergan's analysis of conscious intentionality. These are traced in chapter 1 in accord with their chronological emergence in Lonergan's thought: the self-affirmation of the knower, the emergence of a distinct fourth level, the post-*Method* focus on love and the possibility of an affirmation of a fifth level, the two vectors in consciousness – the creative vector moving from below upward and the healing vector moving from above downward. These together I conceive now as constituting some of the dynamics of the normative source of meaning that becomes a central category in "Natural Right and Historical Mindedness."

But first, that normative source of meaning must be filled out by acknowledging another dimension of consciousness. This insistence is present in "Natural Right and Historical Mindedness" itself, where the dynamics of intentional consciousness are swept up in the tidal movement that I have just mentioned. This movement precisely as movement assumes conscious form in the dispositional or aesthetic-dramatic participation of the sensitive psyche in the adventure of conscious intentionality, an adventure that Eric Voegelin has called the search for direction in the movement of life.[31] Second, the total source of meaning in history includes bias and its effects, as well as conversion in the movement from above downward. The sensitive psyche is left to chapter 2, but the dialectical functioning of bias and the healing through conversion are included in chapter 1's presentation of Lonergan's development.

I found it essential even twenty years ago to relate this discussion to the notion of "patterned experience" that appears toward the end of chapter 1. This notion already situates this structure in the dialectic of history, in the context, if you want, of the relative dominance of the dialectic of community vis-à-vis a plurality of individual dialectics of subjects. The notion of patterned experience became for me later what I call "received meaning" as partly constitutive of empirical consciousness itself. All empirical consciousness, except for surprising events, is *patterned* experience. Presentations – sensations, memories, images, emotions, conations, bodily movements, associations, spontaneous intersubjective responses, free images, utterances[32] – are patterned presentations. Some of these patterns are governed by interests that we have made our own, and then we enter a given pattern because it is something we have chosen or accepted or perhaps been chosen for, whether the pattern be artistic or intellectual or practical or dramatic or mystical, to name the principal possibilities. But the pattern can be a function not only of my own self-determined interests, but also of psychological, social, economic, political, linguistic conditioning and seeming determinisms, conditioning operating "from above" in one's development to establish schemes of recurrence that are inimical to development, and so not a function of autonomous artistic, intellectual, practical, interpersonal, or mystical orientations, but of psychological and social pressures. The person *governed* by negative patterns may also tend to believe that this is the way it has to be, that there is no alternative. Then the patterning is under the control of a bias, but in this case a bias that is not of one's own doing. What is required is a recognition that can initiate a reinterpretation; the reinterpretation makes possible new patterns and the appropriation of the power to establish patterns of experience on the basis of new interests. Such a recognition occurs through a set of *insights,* including the "inverse insights" that interrupt the very flow of one's conscious intentionality with the recognition that one is on the wrong track. But such insights occur *outside* the normal patterns, outside the box, if you want, and launch a possibility of a new interpretation of experience, including the acknowledgment that insight itself is what begins to break these patterns. Next is the further owning not just of a spirit of inquiry but also of the ability for critical reflection on one's own insights. What is the guarantee that the new insight or set of insights is not just the function of a new arbitrary and falsifying way of patterning experience? And we rise above the conditioned patterns of our experience not only by insight and judgment but also and primarily by decision, in which we select what it is worthwhile to do, what kind of world we want, what kind of people we want to be, and how we are going to move toward that. Finally, chapter 8 of *Theology and the Dialectics of History* argues that only being on the receiving end of a love that is unconditional and so graced, however that love may be mediated by human community, is the ultimate condition of possibility of such recovery and redemption.

Already by the end of chapter 1 of *Theology and the Dialectics of History,* then, the structure of intentional consciousness is coalescing into a single object that can command collective attention. A crucial second step in determining the basic terms and relations comes with the acknowledgment that consciousness is twofold, and so that the relatively dominant dialectic of community as it issues in received meaning, meaning that Eugene Gendlin argues becomes stored in the body for better or for worse,[33] can affect either or both of its dimensions, and can do so either positively or negatively. I now make capital of the following quotation from *The Triune God: Systematics*: "[W]e are conscious in two ways: in one way, through our sensibility, we undergo rather passively what we sense and imagine, our desires and fears, our delights and sorrows, our joys and sadness; in another way, through our intellectuality, we are more active when we consciously inquire in order to understand, understand in order to utter a word, weigh evidence in order to judge, deliberate in order to choose, and exercise our will in order to act."[34] The entire argument of *Theology and the Dialectics of History* from chapter 2 forward depends on what is affirmed in that sentence. As chapter 2 of *Method in Theology* speaks of operational development and a distinct affective development, so the self-appropriation that constitutes the "total and basic science"[35] has to include the vagaries of the dispositional, aesthetic-dramatic dimension of the sensitive psyche that precedes, accompanies, and overarches the operations of conscious intentionality, influences those operations, and is influenced by them. Self-appropriation without this dimension runs the risk of fostering the basic form of alienation, alienation from one's very self. As Heidegger affirmed *Verstehen* and *Befindlichkeit* to be equiprimordial but distinct ways of being *Dasein*,[36] so I am affirming that the aesthetic-dramatic dimension is always co-constitutive of consciousness along with our intentional operations. And perhaps beyond Heidegger, I maintain that this dimension includes its own set of aesthetic-dramatic operators of human development that orient this dimension in vertical finality to participation in the adventure of understanding, judgment, and decision. In like manner, if consciousness is a search for direction in the movement of life, the search is a function of intentional inquiry, while the movement is experienced in the pulsing flow of the aesthetic dimension. The two together are essential ingredients of the notion of dialectic that, along with the scale of values, functions as the key category in the entire work.

That notion of dialectic constitutes the next installment on basic terms and relations. From the addition of the psychic, dispositional, aesthetic-dramatic dimension to the structure of the normative and total sources of meaning in history, there comes a refinement on Lonergan's notion of dialectic. For Lonergan "dialectic" refers to the concrete, the dynamic, and the contradictory. The refinement is to the effect that "dialectic" is a notion that refers to the concrete, the dynamic, and the *opposed*, but that opposition can take two quite distinct forms. I believe this complex notion is already operative in chapters 6 and 7 of *Insight*, though it is not articulate there precisely as a complication of the basic notion. We are conscious in two ways, one being more passive than active, the other more active than passive. These two ways are not contradictory to one another, unless they become so when one of them is neglected in favor of the other. Their opposition I call, for better or for worse, that of contraries rather than of contradictories. To confuse contradictories and contraries or mix them up with one another can be quite disastrous, not only theoretically but also existentially.

This distinction has been a bone of contention among some, but I continue to hold to it, and for very serious reasons. I first came upon the distinction by negotiating the Jungian tendency to reduce all oppositions to what I am calling contraries and so to attempt to achieve a position beyond good and evil: a tendency that I regard as self-destructive and perhaps even demonic. But there is the other tendency, all too prevalent in Christian spirituality and moral teaching, and, may I add, in some of the "effective history" of Lonergan's own work, to regard the contrariness of sense and spirituality, neural demands and the censorship, intersubjectivity and practical intelligence, as a matter of contradictories and so, practically, to neglect or even suppress the sensitive psyche and intersubjectivity as if they were evil, and, theoretically, to interpret all the limitation that is imposed on intentional operations by their dependence on sense as itself, if not as evil at least as concupiscent. I was dismayed to find Lonergan himself doing this when, in a response to a question asked him at a Lonergan Workshop regarding the notion of limitation that he sets in tension with transcendence in some brilliant paragraphs in chapter 15 of *Insight,* he limited his response to the discussion of the limitation imposed by moral impotence and sin.[37] That is not at all what he is talking about when he first introduces the notion of limitation. Of course, to regard the criteria of the world of immediacy as though they were the criteria of human knowing in a world mediated by meaning does set up something contradictory. The remedy for that philosophical blunder is, in Lonergan's terms, to break the duality of our knowing and to affirm that fully human knowing unfolds through the three dimensions of experience, understanding, and judgment. But breaking the duality of knowing does not mean breaking the duality of consciousness. It means rather affirming that duality in the series of sublations of empirical consciousness by the intelligent, rational, and existentially world-constitutive and self-constitutive operations of human conscious intentionality. To break the duality of the unity-in-tension of consciousness in favor of either sense or intellect is to invite either empiricism or idealism, whereas to affirm their unity-in-tension is to affirm at least implicitly a critical realism, where insights are into imagined data, where verification almost always entails a rational return to concrete sensible data, and where apprehensions of possible values are given in insights laden with feeling. The dialectical structure of the aesthetic-dramatic and intentional ways of being conscious is then writ large in the dialectic of community between intersubjectivity and practical intelligence and in what I would like to promote as an emerging dialectic of culture between cosmological and anthropological sets of constitutive meaning. Contradictory dialectical relations obtain not internally to these distinct but related processes, but with regard to requisite higher syntheses: the higher synthesis of the dialectic of the subject in the acceptance or rejection of grace; that of the dialectic of culture in the acceptance or rejection of personal authenticity; and that of the dialectic of community in the pursuit or refusal of cultural values.

Lonergan's scale of values is complicated to yield an explanatory account of the relations of these three sets of dialectical processes. The dialectic of the subject is correlated with personal values, the dialectic of culture with cultural values, and the dialectic of the community with social values. The scale is also expanded to present a basic optic on the global situation of our time, yielding a sympathetic impetus to the best of liberation theology in its insistence on a preferential option for the poor and the marginalized.

Finally, the section on "Basic Terms and Relations" concludes with a chapter that begins to express some of the dynamics of the church's mission in the world. "As the Father has sent me, so I send you." Those dynamics would now be swept into a more heuristic view of the church understood in reliance on the category of mission, where ecclesial mission becomes a participation in the missions of both the Son and the Spirit in the world, just as the character of "servant" that was highlighted in the chapter on the church in *Theology and the Dialectics of History* understood the church as participating in Jesus's embodiment and fulfilment of the Deutero-Isaian vision of the servant of God.

Thus, just as there is a graced elevation of the various levels of consciousness (the relation of religious and personal values), so the presence of grace can be acknowledged also at the levels of cultural and social values with an impact on vital values. The establishment of a category of social grace will depend on arguing that the objectification of the subjective structure of intentional consciousness that is found in the complete scale of values can, like intentional consciousness itself, receive a graced elevation to the participation of society in divine life, in divine meaning, and in the divine community of the three persons of the Trinity. The state of grace, as Lonergan begins to argue in the still neglected sixth chapter of his Trinitarian systematics, is a social, interpersonal situation.[38] It is likely that we will be able to locate in communal living an objectification at the level of social values of the kind of elevation of the level of understanding that grace brings to individual consciousness, and that we will be able to locate in the same communal living an objectification at the level of cultural values of the kind of elevation of the level of judgment that accrues from elevating grace. Moreover, further work on the relation of religious to personal values will disclose an elevation of the operations of deliberation, evaluation, and decision, and this will no doubt find objectification in the communal sphere of policies and planning. The central move is the objectification in culture and society of the individual structure of consciousness gifted by God with the grace of an unconditional and unqualified love.

There is a great deal more that could and should be said to fill out these last few paragraphs, but I must move on. What needs to be done in a theology of the Trinity in history is to present at least a heuristic structure for identifying the healing and elevating effects of grace at the various levels of value beyond the personal: at the levels of cultural, social, and vital values. "The Trinity in history" is coterminous with a social doctrine of grace. It is toward such a social doctrine of grace that the foundational work of *Theology and the Dialectics of History* was heading. Here I have added to that heuristic structure the basic contours of the gift of grace itself. This delineation of religious values should be added to the structure of history presented in the earlier work, complementing and filling out what is said there about the servant church, soteriological constitutive meaning, anagogic symbolization, and other anticipations of this realm of transcendent mystery that conditions the possibility of historical integrity.

6

Functional Specialties for a World Theology

1   The Methodological Meaning of "System"

Thesis 12: *We can identify two meanings of the word "system" as this word is used with reference to theology. There is a methodological meaning that is applied to the "system" of the whole of theology, and there is a strictly theological meaning that refers to the strictly systematic component within that whole.*

The only way in which anything that is done in theology can be intelligibly related to anything else that is done in theology is through understanding the *operations* that are performed by all members of the community of theologians and the *horizons* within which those operations are performed. Then there is a sense in which it is valid to speak of the entire discipline as in some sense a system, since a system is precisely what emerges as various elements in a given domain of data are intelligibly related to other elements in that domain. From the standpoint of operations or tasks, then, the whole of theology can be said to have a systematic meaning, where "system" is understood in the sense of intelligible relations among the operations that are performed by all in the community and among the horizons in which the operations are performed. Lonergan's notion of the functional specialties means that this system, like the scale of values, is an objectification of the concrete universal that is the normative subject.

The various theological tasks include preparing critical texts, doing exegesis, writing history, addressing conflicts, stating the grounds of one's own resolution of the conflicts, deriving one's categories from those grounds, transposing and formulating one's doctrines, pursuing an ordered understanding of these doctrines, communicating the meaning emergent in these various tasks. If it can be shown how these various tasks are intelligibly interconnected, then the entire discipline of theology will take on a meaning that is systematic, in the sense of the intelligible interconnection of various elements, where the elements are precisely the operations and horizons. We can call this system "methodological." It is not a matter of the systematic interrelation of theological *content* or *objects*, but rather of the systematic interrelation of theological *operations* and *horizons*: doing research, doing exegesis, doing history, etc., from the standpoint of religious, moral, intellectual, and affective integrity or inauthenticity. Insofar as methodological system also interrelates theological objects, it does so only insofar as these objects are the objects of different related sets of operations. This methodological meaning of the word "system" as applied to theology emerges in reading Lonergan's *Method in Theology*.

When Lonergan began to focus his attention explicitly on the development of a method for theology, one of the major problems he faced was what he called the chasm that existed between, on the one hand, the religious life of people and the symbolic, intersubjective, and commonsense manner of communicating something of that religious life in the scriptures and in most Patristic literature and, on the other hand, the incipient technical language of many of the dogmas and the deliberately technical language of systematics. In his first document on the problems of method, he frankly admits that he does not yet have an answer to the problem of the chasm.[1] *Method in Theology* aims to provide that response, by showing how the various sets of theological operations are interrelated in a community of inquiry, and by differentiating the various carriers and expressions of meaning and showing how these too are interrelated.

But already we can see another, more limited meaning of the word "system" as used in theology, a meaning that has to do not with the operations that theologians perform but with the content of what theologians know through these operations. For in listing the various tasks performed by theologians as we have just done, we spoke of one of them as "pursuing an ordered understanding of doctrines." There is a sense, then, in which we may speak of the "system" of the whole of theology, and then there is another sense in which we may speak of the strictly systematic component within that overall "system." The "system" of the whole of theology is a methodological or operational position, and so we approach it with the help of Lonergan's book *Method in Theology*. Again, we might speak of the "system" of the whole of theology – the methodological system – as *a generalized theory of theological operations or tasks*. On the other hand, once some theological meanings have been affirmed to be true (doctrines), there emerges the strictly theological meaning of "system," which has to do with organizing these dogmatic affirmations in a systematic manner by striving for some imperfect and analogical understanding of precisely how they can be true. The first of these meanings of "system" we will refer to as "method," and the second as "systematics" or "systematic theology." While this book is by and large an exercise in the second meaning of "system," this chapter comments on the first meaning, precisely in the context of the interreligious situation that is part of our present context.

We can move, then, to a preliminary notion of each of these meanings of "system" in theology.

As we discuss the "system" of the whole of theology, the generalized theory of theological operations or tasks, the reader should think not of any one individual doing all of them, for that does not happen, but rather of the entire theological community throughout the world and in fact throughout history, each member of which is involved in doing some one or several of the following operations.

First, then, there are the operations involved in doing the kind of research that establishes critical texts, performs archeological digs, deciphers monuments, statues, coins, etc., relevant to the religious life of humankind. These operations can be referred to as Research.

Second, there are other operations involved in interpreting these texts and other artifacts to discover what they mean. These operations constitute Interpretation.

Third, there are further operations involved in narrating the history of what was going forward in the development of the meanings determined by Interpretation. This set of operations yields History.

Fourth, there are still further operations involved in discerning the roots of the differences and conflicts that emerge in the content of that history as well as the roots of the conflicts that occur today among interpreters and historians. These operations sort out differences and conflicts that are complementary from those that are genetically related, and also distinguish both of these from differences and conflicts that are dialectically related. These operations can be referred to as Dialectic.

Fifth, there is an entirely different set of operations involved when theologians turn from stating what others have said and done to providing the grounds for their own positions. I call this operational specialty Horizons.

Sixth, as one then attempts to state what one holds to be true, one has the task of deriving the categories in which one is going to state what one holds to be the case. Those categories will be grounded in the position on the normative subject that one has presented in Horizons. The work of deriving categories we can refer to simply as Categories.

Seventh, the work of deriving categories is for the sake, first, of stating in contemporary terms our own positions. The work involved in these operations we can refer to operationally as Doctrines, which includes transpositions of previous positions, and new positions articulated by theologians in response to new situations.

Eighth, we also have the responsibility of articulating how we understand what we hold to be true, and how the various elements that we hold to be true are related to one another. This is the operational specialty known as Systematics. It is the specialty that we are principally concerned with in the present book.

Finally, there is the work of determining how to communicate what we hold to be true to contemporary women and men. This is the work of Communications.

It is my position that all theological operations are embraced in this list of the sets of tasks.

2 Nine Functional or Operational Specialties

How do these operations relate to one another? How do the meanings intended in these operations relate to one another? Do they constitute just a sequential list or is their interconnection more intelligible than that? I propose the following scheme, which alters somewhat the organization proposed by Lonergan, but only by differentiating it a bit further.

Thesis 13: *The relations among the sets of operations may be schematized as follows.*

5 Horizons

4 Dialectic	Categories 6
3 History	Doctrines 7
2 Interpretation	Systematics 8
1 Research	Communications 9

Understanding the methodological "system" of the whole of theology is a matter of grasping the relations between such tasks or operations as textual criticism, interpretation of scripture and hermeneutics, the history of dogma and of theology, the conflicts to be found within that history and within contemporary interpretations and evaluations of it, the horizons responsible for the different positions, the derivation of the categories one will employ in taking one's own stance, doctrinal theology, systematic theology, and communications or pastoral theology. The methodological key to the "system" of the whole of theology, to the generalized theory of theological operations and meanings, lies in the "system" that is our own conscious intentionality within a mutually self-mediating historical community of intentionally conscious theological subjects. This is what gets objectified in the work of "Horizons." It is the singular merit of *Method in Theology* that it begins to provide us with a consistent understanding of these various interrelations that together constitute the concrete universal that is the normative subject.

> **Thesis 14:** *The functional specialty that Lonergan calls Foundations should thus be divided into two functional specialties. The specialty called "Horizons" stands outside the other eight and objectifies the concrete universal, the normative subject, that effects the transition from the first phase to the second phase. The first specialty in the second phase is called Categories.*

Lonergan writes:

> The functional specialty, foundations, will derive its first set of categories from religious experience. That experience is something exceedingly simple and, in time, also exceedingly simplifying, but it also is something exceedingly rich and enriching. There are needed studies of religious interiority: historical, phenomenological, psychological, sociological. There is needed in the theologian the spiritual development that will enable him both to enter into the experience of others and to frame the terms and relations that will express that experience.[2]

The point of the chapters in this first part is to offer a set of heuristic guidelines not only for the studies that Lonergan recommends in the passage just cited, but also for a broader range of activity that would include "studies of religious interiority" as but one of its responsibilities. But first there is required a slight but important modification of that passage. I wish to suggest that we need to divide what currently is the functional specialty "foundations" into two specialties, "horizons" and "categories." These two would fulfill the tasks currently assigned to the specialty "foundations," but dividing these tasks into two specialties would have several advantages.

First, it would acknowledge that these are two quite distinct tasks.

Second, it would respond to the difficulties raised by Lonergan's recognition of a fifth level of consciousness, which we will visit in detail shortly, in that the specialty "horizons" would occur outside the other eight and would have as its objective the ongoing and cumulative thematization of the normative subject responsible for mediating from the specialties of the first phase to those of the second. That subject would be thematized in all its concrete dimensions, no matter how many so-called "levels" of conscious states and operations that might eventually entail. "Horizons" in effect becomes a ninth functional specialty in generalized empirical method and in theological method in particular, a specialty whose sole task is the ongoing articulation of the structure of the concrete universal that is the normative subject. The ninth specialty stands outside the other eight, and as theological objectifies the source of the movement from the functional specialties of the first phase to the functional specialties of the second.

From the beginning of Lonergan's articulation of the structure of functional specialization, the normative subject was acknowledged as responsible for the movement from the specialties of the first phase – research, interpretation, history, and dialectic – to those of the second phase – categories, doctrines, systematics, and communications. A space for the tasks of what I am calling the specialty "horizons" was, of course, provided in Lonergan's notion of the functional specialty "foundations," as the latter was conceived and presented in *Method in Theology*. But that space is too crowded. "Foundations" in *Method in Theology* is assigned two quite distinct tasks. It seems to me that the articulation of the first set of both general and special categories, both of which are involved in the specialties of both the first and the second phase, should be assigned to a distinct specialty outside, and responsible for, the other eight. The ninth functional specialty as I conceive it would articulate the base of the general categories in generalized empirical method or interiorly differentiated consciousness and the base of the special categories in religiously differentiated consciousness. The major (though by no means complete) contribution to this ninth specialty is, and perhaps always will be, a little book called *Insight*. This specialty belongs neither to the first nor to the second phase, since it objectifies what is responsible for authentic performance in either phase and for moving from the first phase to the second, namely, religious, moral, intellectual, and psychic conversion. The responsibility of the normative subject for moving from the first phase to the second has always been acknowledged in Lonergan's presentation of the specialties, from the very first draft of the specialties written in his hand, where it is called the "mediating subject,"[3] to the articulation in *Method in Theology* itself, where it is "foundational reality," providing "the added foundation needed to move from the indirect discourse that sets forth the convictions and opinions of others to the direct discourse that states what is so."[4] The language of *Method* obviously places the objectification of the normative subject within the functional specialty "foundations" itself. I am suggesting simply that such objectification constitutes a distinct functional specialty outside the eight differentiated by Lonergan. I would call this specialty "horizons." Its sole task would be the objectification of "the mediating subject," "the normative subject," "foundational reality." The specialty that begins the second phase I would call "categories." This specialty would continue to fulfill the second task currently assigned in the chapter on foundations, namely, deriving the general and special categories that are employed not only in doctrines, systematics, and communications but also in interpretation and history. In other words, I am suggesting that the present specialty "foundations" be differentiated into two specialties, "horizons" and "categories" and that "horizons" be placed outside the other eight.

The need for the distinction of the present specialty "foundations" into the two specialties "horizons" and "categories" is at least remotely analogous to the need for an expansion of the levels of consciousness beyond the three articulated in *Insight* to Lonergan's acknowledgment of a distinct fourth level soon after the publication of *Insight.* This need is experienced by most readers of *Insight*'s chapter 18, who find the framework provided by cognitional theory, epistemology, and metaphysics too small, too restricted, for the content of a chapter on ethics. In similar manner, much of the talk that has transpired (sparked by Lonergan himself) over the question of a fifth level of consciousness acknowledges a similar straightjacket imposed by the four-level structure, this time on love, whether the love be the human love of family and community or the divine love that introduces us to a new and vibrant communion with the three divine subjects and that overflows into the self-sacrificing charity of the suffering servant in the world. There results the acknowledgment of a distinct, interpersonal level of personal consciousness. On this level, as I hope to argue later, the primordial intersubjectivity or "interdividuality"[5] of psychic *Mitsein* has passed through the individuation made possible by fidelity to the transcendental precepts in their call for the autonomy by which one gives the law to oneself. The law is precisely to be attentive, intelligent, reasonable, and responsible. At the distinct level beyond what this law calls for, one has entered an interpersonal community of love, where the beloved ones are in the consciousness of the lover by reason of love alone. That love always begins as a gift from others, human or divine. The subject in whom all of this has occurred passes in his or her development from interdividuality, through individuation resulting from the transcendental precepts, to communion. The objectification of this subject expresses an approximation to the normative subject, the concrete universal capable of effecting the movement from the phase of study that reports on what others have said and done, thus mediating from the past to the present, to the phase of creativity where one says and does what one knows is true and right, and so mediates from the present to the future. That normative subject is the focus of the ninth functional specialty, horizons. The remote objective of the ninth specialty is the objectification of normative subjectivity in all its dimensions.

At one point in a question-and-answer session Lonergan envisioned the possibility of such a specialty, but named it "spirituality."[6] I think this word as it is presently used connotes less than what is to be objectified when one objectifies the concrete universal that is the normative subject. The "spirit" that perhaps could be intended in the word "spirituality" is closer to the *Geist* of Hegel's *Phenomenology* than it is to narrow, descriptive, and parochially confined notions of "spirituality." It is true, as we will see, that I have employed the word "spiritual" in rendering the meaning of *emanatio intelligibilis* as "autonomous spiritual procession," so we might risk at least provisionally using the word "spirituality" for the ninth functional specialty, as long as we acknowledge that the specialty extends beyond the articulation of religiously differentiated consciousness to the objectification of intellectual, moral, and affective integrity as well. But I think the risk too great. The heuristic structure of the studies that Lonergan mentions in the citation with which I began this chapter envisions what in one place he calls the *Grund- und Gesamtwissenschaft*, the *scienza nuova* composed of cognitional theory, epistemology, metaphysics, existential ethics, and the phenomenology of authentic religion.[7] All of these are topics to be articulated in the ninth functional specialty. The normative subject articulated in that specialty propels the movement from the first phase of theology to the second. "Spirituality" as this word is currently employed simply has too narrow a connotation to fulfill the task of objectifying the normative subject. "Horizons" fills the bill perfectly.

> **Thesis 15:** *The first column in the structure of the functional specialties names the operations involved in the mediating phase of theology, the phase that mediates from the past into the present by interpreting, narrating, and evaluating what others have said and done. The second column names the operations entailed in a second phase, when the theologian takes his or her own stand on the issues raised in the mediating phase and in the cultural matrix within which the theologian is operating and states in contemporary terms the positions that have been mediated from the past into the present. Thus, this phase may be referred to as the mediated phase. But taking a stance also entails a further mediation from the present into the future, which renders this phase also constitutive, at least in intention. Moreover, each set of operations has its own set of objects.*

This thesis has to do with the notion of mediation. It will help us explain the structure just diagrammed in terms of "up" and "down" movements, and mediating and mediated objects as well as the mediating subject.

The first set of tasks, again, mediates meaning from the past into the present. Who is involved in this mediating phase? Or, better, when would I be involved in this phase? All whose principal operations involve establishing critical texts, biblical exegesis, interpretation of historical texts, composition of historical narratives, etc., are involved in this *mediating* phase of theology. Whenever one is involved in reporting on what others have said and done, one is engaged in the first phase of the theological enterprise.

The second phase expresses a meaning largely continuous with that *mediated* meaning in the contemporary situation and with an eye to *further mediation from the present into the future.* That further mediation into the future is also constitutive, at least in intention. That is, theologians are mediating into the future the meanings and values that they believe should constitute the Christian community. Those whose principal operations are in the realms of categories, doctrines, systematics, and communications are involved in this second kind of mediation. "Horizons" determines the grounds of the second mediation.

But obviously, each of these sets of operations has objects, for operations and objects are intelligible only in terms of each other. So if the first phase is correctly referred to as a "mediating" phase, then the objects of each set of tasks in that phase can be called "mediating" objects; and if the second phase is correctly referred to as a "mediated" phase, then the objects of each set of tasks in that phase can be called "mediated" objects. And if the specialty called Horizons is a mediation of the mediating subject, of the subject who mediates between the first phase and the second, then the object of the tasks of Horizons can be called the "mediating subject." Horizons mediates the mediating subject.

The mediating object of Research is "data." The mediating object of Interpretation is "meaning," i.e., the meaning of the data. The mediating object of History is "what really happened," and in that sense "truth." In theology, the "truth" of the functional specialty history refers also to the true doctrinal judgments toward which development heads. The mediating object of Dialectic is "encounter."

The mediated object of Horizons is "the mediating subject," that is, the subject who mediates between the tasks of indirect discourse and those of direct discourse. So "mediating" and "mediated" come together in Horizons.

The mediated object of Categories consists in the general and special categories that will be employed in the other specialties. The mediated object of Doctrines is the truth of the tradition transposed into contemporary terms. Lonergan articulated those contemporary terms in the language of redemption. The mediated object of Systematics will be the history in which redemption occurs. And the mediated object of Communications will be the world itself as the arena in which the reign of God is to be established, and more precisely, the reign of God itself that theology would help establish in that world.

Method in Theology, then, is a generalized theory of theological operations and meanings, of meaning and meant, of acts of meaning and terms of meaning. Acts and terms are concomitant and isomorphic. Thus, there is no seeing without a seen, no hearing without a heard, no touching without a touched, no inquiry without something that is inquired about, no understanding without an understood, no affirming without an affirmed, etc. And so the structure of the operations is isomorphic with the structure of the concomitant terms.

Operations (acts) and concomitant meanings (terms) within any discipline, at least in the human sciences, philosophy, and theology, that is, in any discipline that draws on the past to guide our transition into the future, have these two phases. The "functional specialties," as far as their structure is involved, are not peculiar to theology.

> **Thesis 16:** *In the first phase – research, interpretation, history, dialectic – theology is hermeneutical in the broad sense of understanding what others have said and done; and it is historical in the sense of narrating what was going forward as a result of what others have said and done. The results of this phase, the results of mediating the past into the present, comprise at least the following three aspects: (1) the history of what is regarded in the community as the very action of God in history; thus we speak of "salvation history"; (2) the history of the community's struggles to articulate its salvation history in doctrines and dogma; and finally (3) the history of the discipline of theology itself, which reflects on salvation history and doctrine. All three aspects entail the emergence of meanings and value within specific cultural contexts.*

So we have (1) religion, (2) doctrine, and (3) theology. Each of these has a history, and the history of each of these is contained in the first phase.

Moreover, in the contemporary scene there has arisen the question of religious traditions other than our own, and the related question of the relation of Christian theology to the religious studies that perform the tasks of research, interpretation, and history with regard to these other traditions. I am going to propose that we are entering a phase in theology in which all the data on the religious life of humankind become data for Christian theology itself, and so where the functional specialties must determine the relation of their operations to a far wider expanse of data than before.

But we can come back to that later. What I want to tease out in this statement and the next thesis is the difference between the two phases.

First, then, there is the mediating phase, the phase that mediates from the past into the present. Here the discipline is hermeneutical in the broad sense of this term, that is, it mediates an understanding of what others have said and done; and it is historical, since it is concerned with what was really going forward as a result of what others have said and done.

In a methodology for this phase of "indirect discourse," heuristic directives are presented for understanding and evaluating (1) the history of the founding events, (2) the history of the subsequent doctrines of the community that takes its origins from those founding events, and (3) the history of the discipline (the history of theology).

In theology, this first phase interprets the previous history of the discipline – biblical, patristic, medieval, Reformation and counter-Reformation, modern, contemporary – but it also narrates the previous history of what the discipline itself is all about. Without the narration of the history of God's action (salvation history) and of the community's attempts to capture that in doctrine (all of which has a soteriological significance), the history of the discipline is meaningless, for the discipline is concerned with the religion that acknowledges God's action and with the doctrines that attempt to articulate that action. With respect to the issue of the other religions, if there is any possibility that God's presence and action extend beyond what the previous history of the discipline was prepared to acknowledge, then the narration of the history of God's action must include that broader range of data. What the discipline is all about is the action of God in history and the community's attempts to articulate that action. And we have already affirmed universal invisible missions of the Holy Spirit and of the Word that breathes love.

Lonergan's approach understands the action of God in history, the community's attempts to capture that action in doctrine, and theology's attempts to understand both the religious events and the doctrinal attempts, in terms of the interrelation of various cultural matrices with the significance and role of the grace that informs the actions and words of living religious people and communities within those matrices. This is the meaning of the statement that "a theology mediates between a cultural matrix and the significance and role of a religion within that matrix."[8] All three dimensions of the first phase have to do with particular cultural matrices: (1) God's action in history occurs in and with relation to particular cultural matrices; (2) the community's attempts to articulate God's action in history occur in and with relation to particular cultural matrices; (3) theology's attempt to articulate salvation history and the community's articulation of salvation history occurs in and with relation to particular cultural matrices. This first phase tells what was going forward, then, in the discipline itself (3), but more radically it tells what was going forward in the religious community on whose life the discipline reflects (2), and in the founding events of that religious community (1).[9]

> **Thesis 17:** *In the second phase, theologians state not what others have said and done but what they hold to be the case. In Lonergan's words, the second phase is "direct discourse," "oratio recta," while the first is "indirect discourse," "oratio obliqua." If the first phase mediates the tradition into the present, theologians in the second phase state in their own words what they hold to be the mediated tradition. Thus the first phase is "mediating" and the second "mediated." But the second phase also mediates from the present into the future, and in this sense is constitutive, at least in intent.*

Thus, theologians not only mediate what others have said and done, whether these others be strictly religious figures like Jesus (1) or church teachers like the framers of dogmas (2) or theologians reflecting on dogma and doctrine and interrelating their various meanings (3). Theologians also stand on their own two feet and say and do what they think is true and good. Lonergan calls the second phase, not "mediating," but "mediated," because in the second phase theologians are concerned not so much with the history of, e.g., Christological doctrine (2) or of systematic Christologies (3) as they are with what they maintain to be the *correct* Christological doctrine or the best or most adequate systematic Christology. So here one is concerned, not with the conciliar history of Christological dogma (2), not with the disputes over Christological dogma (2), but with affirming what one holds to be the correct Christological dogma; and one is concerned not with the Christology of Aquinas or Calvin or Schleiermacher or Barth or Tillich or Rahner or Lonergan or anyone else other than oneself (3), but with one's own Christology. "You have heard it said … but I say to you."

As we have seen, however, this second phase is also a "mediating" phase in a certain sense, in that it lays the groundwork for mediating from the present into the future, a groundwork that will be picked up on by subsequent inquiry studying what we and our contemporaries have said and done and making that into the data for the ongoing first phase of theology. In stating what one holds to be true and good, one is inviting the community to accept one's statements, and in this sense is offering constitutive meaning to guide the development of the community.

In this sense, the second phase is also constitutive. It not only articulates and affirms meanings and values mediated from the past. It also articulates meanings and values that one would have be constitutive of the Christian community and perhaps of a cultural matrix with an eye to the future. Thus, theologians in the second phase state their own theological doctrines, and some of these may eventually be worked into the official teaching of their respective ecclesial communions. John Courtney Murray's work on religious liberty would be a clear example of this. While Murray backed up his position by taking his stand on certain strands in the Catholic tradition, and so did his homework in the first phase, still his own position was a transformation of the official position, and in that sense it is more than a matter of stating meanings and values mediated from the past. It is creating a new line of thought and praxis in the church, to be studied by future generations working in the first phase.

Again, Lonergan refers to this second phase not as mediating but as mediated. I will begin with this designation for the second phase, but I regard it as only partly accurate. I will go on to a further set of terms that I think is consonant with his intentions but that also expresses more clearly what the second phase is all about. The second phase, precisely as mediated in Lonergan's sense, is the result of the critical appropriation and evaluation of the first phase on the basis of certain basic considerations that can be called foundational for this second phase. Those considerations are articulated in Horizons. But normally the second phase will also go on from there; it will not be content simply with meaning mediated from the past, but will prescribe what the constitutive meaning of the ecclesial community today and in the future ought to be, how it ought to function, and what the interrelations of this community with other communities ought to be. That is more than stating meaning mediated from the past. It is also articulating meaning that one would have be constitutive of the future.

A clear example of what I'm talking about here lies in the questions that arise when Christians reflect on the religiously pluralistic world in which many find themselves. Questions for systematics can arise from communications, Lonergan says.[10] This would be a clear instance of the interplay between the phases, with the clear possibility of new doctrinal meanings being articulated and a new systematic understanding of previously determined meanings as these meanings are illuminated and expanded by facing the questions presented by a new situation.

In theology, the second phase is mediated, in that it selects options from the interpretation and history that constituted the first phase, presents these options as the correct ones, and attempts to understand these various options in relation to one another. It will state what is true from the meanings mediated into the present from the past (transposed doctrines) and it will attempt to understand these doctrinal affirmations in a coherent manner (systematics). But the second phase is more than mediated, in this sense of the word "mediated." That expresses only part of what the second phase is and does. The second phase is also a constructive enterprise. It offers not only meaning mediated from the past through the filter of horizons, but also the constitutive meaning that the theologian judges ought to be formative of specific religious communities and of the specific cultural bodies with which it is theology's task to mediate the meanings affirmed by the religious communities. And so I want to refer to the second phase, not only as the mediated phase of theology but also as the constitutive phase, the constructive phase. Thus, in this second phase one (1) states one's agreement or disagreement with the positions of past theologians, (2) transposes the categories of these theologians into contemporary idioms, (3) states new positions, (4) works out a systematically coherent understanding of what one holds to be true, and (5) applies all of this to concrete situations and to dialogue with other disciplines and other religions. These tasks, all of which Lonergan recognizes as part of his second phase, are more than a matter of stating meaning mediated from the past into the present.

Again, the two phases can be understood in terms of the mediating (first phase) and mediated (second phase) *objects* of each of the specialties. Operations and objects, as we have seen, are correlative and isomorphic. Thus, in the first phase the mediating objects are: data (Research), meaning (Interpretation), truth (History), encounter (Dialectic). In the second phase the mediated objects are categories (Categories), redemption in history (Doctrines), history itself (Systematics), and the reign of God in the world as this is catalyzed by (Communications). Catalyzing the movement from the first to the second phase is Horizons, whose mediated object is the normative and mediating subject.

In the first phase, one is understanding already embodied meaning and evaluating it. The meaning is embodied principally in texts but also in other cultural and religious artifacts, in the various carriers of meaning. In the second phase, one is accepting some of the embodied meaning from the past, but also promoting meaning, advancing its ever fuller being. The term "mediated" for the second phase adequately reflects the acceptance of embodied meaning from the past, but does not adequately reflect the promotion and advancing of meaning that occurs in this second phase. Thus, in the second phase, one's activity is in part praxis, the praxis of meaning, the ongoing advance of meaning, the creation of the meaning of the community as this community moves into its future. Specifically for theology, one's activity is oriented to the constitution by meaning of the Christian community and of one's cultural situation. And as we shall see in greater detail, it is oriented in an ulterior way to the promotion of the human good in history, since promoting what one holds to be true meaning is an essential aspect in promoting the human good.

Thesis 18: *Not only does a theology mediate between a cultural matrix and the significance and role of a religion in that matrix, but the* *mediation in question is a mutual self-mediation. It is for this reason that the second phase in theology not only states the assimilated or mediated tradition but also is at least potentially constitutive of the ongoing tradition.*

"Questions for systematics can arise from communications." But perhaps not only questions but also elements of an answer can arise from communications. Not only is it the case that the operations and meanings of the second phase are only partly a matter of what has been assimilated and mediated from the past, and not only is it the case that these operations and meanings are primarily concerned with the articulation, affirmation, and implementation of constitutive meaning, of the meaning that the theologian judges should be constitutive of the Christian community and of the particular cultural matrix or matrices with which one is mediating Christian theological meaning, but also we must say that these cultural matrices have a decisive influence upon the formulation of theological meaning in the second phase. Problems for the second phase can arise from communication with the cultural matrix, but the elements of answers can also come from the cultural matrix and not from the Christian tradition itself conceived in a narrow sense.

The novelty or innovation that we are insisting is part of the second phase of theology is not a function simply of the genius or temperament of the theologian working in this phase. It is a matter of his or her (or the community's) appropriation of the cultural matrix within which one is doing theology. De facto, this has always been the case. The first great truly systematic theologian in the history of Christian theology was Thomas Aquinas, and Thomas was a tremendous innovator. But the innovations that he introduced into theology were largely a function of his appropriation of the Aristotelian culture in which he was involved while teaching at the University of Paris. That culture provided not only questions for systematic integration but also elements of answers to those questions. Systematic understanding is technical and explanatory. That is, it moves beyond the commonsense communication regarding "things in their relation to us" to the scientific communication regarding "things in their relations to one another." And Aristotelian metaphysics was a particularly apt tool for such systematic understanding in the thirteenth century, since it supplied a way of integrating on the level of its time the fruits of various scientific, that is, systematic, technical, explanatory meanings. Thomas's systematic theology is in part a function of his appropriation of Aristotelian metaphysics, which provided Thomas with what Lonergan would call the general categories of Thomist thought. In the very appropriation of Aristotle, however, Thomas was also profoundly developing

Aristotelian philosophy itself. And so he was engaged in a mutual self-mediation between the *doctrina Christiana* and Aristotelian philosophy. Both were changed as a result of this mediation.

A major question for systematic theology today, now that Aristotle has gone out of vogue at least in the manner in which he was employed in the thirteenth century, is, What takes the place in a contemporary systematic theology of Aristotelian thought in the theology of Thomas Aquinas? As we have seen, Lonergan stipulates the answer to this question in terms of the *Grund- und Gesamtwissenschaft* that comprises cognitional theory, epistemology, critical metaphysics, existential ethics, and the phenomenology of religion, particularly as together these yield the general categories of a theory of history.

3   Expanding the Reach of Theological Functional Specialties

> **Thesis 19:** *The theological and methodological options expressed thus far entail a vast expansion of the range of Catholic theology. The functional specialties of such a theology are now applied to the movement from data to results in the worldwide religious community of humankind.*

The next piece in the vision being presented here entails a vast expansion of the range of Catholic theology. The proposal is at once theological and methodological. Its theological ground is the doctrine of the universal mission of the Holy Spirit. Its methodological component is Lonergan's notion of functional specialization. I wish to propose a vision of Catholic theology in which the nine functional specialties are applied to the universal religious situation of humankind.

More radically, the methodological component in this proposal is the invariant structure of intentional consciousness that, when complicated, becomes, among other things, functional specialization.[11] This methodological component meets the theological ground when it is acknowledged that the gift of God's love is the supernatural fulfilment of the obediential potency of nature, that is, of intentional consciousness as a principle of movement and rest in quest of true meanings and a normative and nuanced scale of values.[12] When the two meet, there is achieved an integration of religious studies and theology, a major fruit of what Lonergan called the ongoing genesis of methods.[13]

I presume familiarity with the methodological component. Elsewhere, I have offered clarifications regarding intentional consciousness,[14] but the judgment that the structure is not subject to radical revision is common currency among Lonergan students. Still, the debate surrounding the theological component rages on.

My views regarding the theological component have already been indicated, in two steps. First, I rely on Crowe's position on the mission of the Holy Spirit; in fact, if Crowe's position is not correct, then what I am proposing regarding functional specialties for a world theology is not viable. The position proposed here depends on Crowe's theological doctrine regarding the mission of the Holy Spirit in relation to that of the Son. The second step is the position on the structure of the gift of the Holy Spirit that I suggested in the second chapter. The issue in this section regards the implications of these positions for a methodical theology, that is, for a collaborative effort structured by functional specialization.

Lonergan says in *Method in Theology* that the correct answer to the question, What data are relevant to Christian theology? occurs, not in the functional specialty concerned with the data themselves, that is, not in research, but in the functional specialty concerned with doctrines. But, he goes on to ask, "how can [this] specialty be reached, if one does not know which are the areas relevant to theological research, and how each area is to be weighted?" His answer is typical: "[L]et Christian theologians begin from where they already stand. Each will consider one or more areas relevant to theological research. Let him work there. He will find that the method is designed to take care of the matter."[15]

Now, my question is, What happens if a Christian theologian stands on Crowe's theological doctrine regarding the relation of the mission of the Holy Spirit to the mission of the Son? What happens if such a theologian affirms that we Christians share a religious community with all human beings, including the people of the world's religions, precisely because the divine person whom we call the Holy Spirit has been sent to all of them, that is, precisely because the created participations in Trinitarian active and passive spiration that Christian theologians are enabled to make thematic are in fact a universal offer on the part of the triune God to all women and men at every time and place in human history, whether that offer be *vécu* or *thématique*?

What happens is that the relevant data for Christian theology are magnified exponentially; and the consequences for the other functional specialties in the first phase of theology are enormous in their implications. For all the data on human religious living, whether that living be explicit or compact, are now to be made available for Christian theology itself; they are to be interpreted in accord with the hermeneutic theory presented in both chapter 17 of *Insight* and chapter 7 of *Method*; and the relevant history for Christian theology itself expands to include the religious history of all humanity. That such a proposal does not mean the collapse of theology into positivist religious studies is guaranteed by accepting the functional specialization of theological tasks; for then, beyond research, interpretation, and history, which is where religious studies would stop, there remains, in the first phase, the dialectic that would mediate the differences, and then there is the normative subject, the concrete universal that moves the whole of theology to a second phase. In that second phase, there will emerge vastly expanded functional specialties of categories, doctrines, systematics, and communications. The result will be a vast collaboration constructing what we may call a world theology, a theology that takes its stand on the theological and ecclesial doctrine of the universal mission and gift of the Holy Spirit, and applies the methodological doctrine of functional specialization to the task of mediating from data to results an entire worldwide community of men and women receiving and responding to what Christians know as the third divine Person, the Holy Spirit of God, proceeding Love in the Trinity poured out in the hearts of all by the gift of the triune God to all. The content of all nine functional specialties is expanded vastly if we take our stand on Crowe's theological doctrine.

4   Levels of Consciousness

Thesis 20: *The social dimensions of grace are rooted in a level of consciousness that is beyond the four levels of experience, understanding, judgment, and decision and that sublates them. This unitive and inclusive level of consciousness is interpersonal, and when self-transcendent it is marked by love in intimacy, in devotion to the human community, and in the reception of God's love and the return of love for God in charity. The functional specialty Horizons will include this dimension in its mediated object.*

The final installment in this introductory presentation of the vision has to do with the question of whether there are levels of consciousness beyond the four that figure so centrally in Lonergan's work.

In a paper entitled "Consciousness and Grace" published in METHOD: *Journal of Lonergan Studies* in 1993, I defended the following position:

The gift of God's love for us poured fourth into our hearts is an uncreated grace that effects in us, as a relational disposition to receive it, the created grace of a fifth level of consciousness, at which we experience ourselves as loved unconditionally by God and invited to love God in return. This experience of being loved unconditionally and of being invited to love in return is the conscious basis of (1) our share in the inner life of God, (2) our consequent falling in love with God, and (3) the dynamic state of our being in love with God. The dynamic state of being in love with God, in turn, as equivalent to what the Scholastic tradition called the infused virtue of charity, is the proximate principle of the operations of charity whereby God is attained as God is in God's own self. The created, remote, and proportionate principle of these operations – what Scholastic theology called the entitative habit or sanctifying grace of a created communication of the divine nature – is the fifth level of consciousness, the experience of resting in God's unconditional love for us and of being invited to love in return, the real relation *to* and *constituted by* the indwelling God as term of the relation.[16]

Responses to the paper appeared quickly, and for the most part they were critical of my position. Particular attention was drawn to my affirmation of a fifth level of consciousness; in fact, most of the rest of what I had to say was not addressed at all. The most helpful criticism came not in print but in a conversation with Joseph Komonchak, who did not address the issue of a fifth level at all, but indicated that I needed to refine my expression in a way that was more sensitive to the distinction between consciousness and knowledge, and that I needed to relate what I was saying to the history of Lonergan's own attempt to treat these problems.

Regarding the first of Komonchak's points, then, to say that "we experience ourselves as loved unconditionally by God and invited to love God in return" is not quite accurate. To affirm that we have conscious experiences that *subsequently may be interpreted in this way* is a far more acceptable way of speaking. This is what I am now attempting by linking my position to an interpretation of Augustine's meaning of *memoria*. Komonchak also advised that I turn more in depth to unpublished works of the early Lonergan on the question of sanctifying grace to see whether these support or modify my position, again not on the issue of a fifth level, about which these early works say nothing, but rather regarding the basic thrust of my article. Obviously, that investigation is what much of chapter 2 was about. It is in this spirit that I have reported on an item in the Lonergan archives, the notes on sanctifying grace from 1951 to 1952, that I find remarkably relevant to the discussion that followed my 1993 article.

That discussion has subsequently expanded to include the question of the validity, permanent or temporary, of the so-called four-point hypothesis contained in the sixth chapter of Lonergan's Trinitarian systematics, in which the four divine relations are linked, respectively, to four created participations and imitations. The major issue in that portion of the discussion prompted by my suggestions is whether Lonergan's later three-point statements regarding the divine self-communication – the Incarnation, the gift of grace, and the beatific vision – are sufficient, and whether the four-point statement that results from distinguishing sanctifying grace and charity is little more than the fruit of the Aristotelian metaphysical framework within which the four-point hypothesis originally appeared. The archival document that I have reported on is pertinent to the discussion of this hypothesis. In these notes, the significance of the hypothesis approaches the importance that I granted it, since it is explicitly called the foundational statement in a systematic theology of sanctifying grace.

But I believe the emphases of these notes also support the basic thrust of the position I offered in "Consciousness and Grace," namely, that the gift of God's love effects in us a relational disposition to receive it, the disposition consequent upon being on the receiving end of God's love, a disposition that relates us to the Gift itself, the Holy Spirit. This disposition is the created basis of the relation to the Holy Spirit that gives us our share in divine life. That share, as participating in active spiration, is the foundation of our loving God in return in charity, which participates in passive spiration. I also think the 1951–52 notes lend support to our continuing to try to mine the riches of the four-point hypothesis. The alternative, I fear, is that we will leave the theology of grace in a metaphysical halfway house between the commonsense affirmations of scripture and the methodical affirmations of a theology that takes its stand on interiorly and religiously differentiated consciousness. I do not believe a methodical theology can take its stand in a genuine third-stage-of-meaning fashion without transposing and sublating Lonergan's earlier metaphysical analyses of these matters. If the new systematics that is emerging does not work with the metaphysics, it will revert to a first-stage-of-meaning affair, a commonsense elucidation of religious interiority. This might be all right in some exercises in the functional specialty "Communications," but it will not do in Systematics. In a sense, the issue reduces to the question, What are we to do with Lonergan's metaphysical theology as we attempt to construct the new theology grounded in basic method? As I have argued elsewhere, the metaphysics should not be dropped – it is too rich, and it provides a needed control of meaning – but rather carried over and sublated into interiority.[17] I stand by that affirmation. In this case, the metaphysical distinction of sanctifying grace and the habit of charity is transposed into the categories of being on the receiving end of God's unqualified and unconditional love and loving God in return with all our hearts and minds and souls and strength and loving our neighbors as ourselves.

What, then, of the suggestion of a fifth level of consciousness? The history of the responses to the suggestion of a fifth level that I took from Lonergan and tried to develop has been very accurately summarized by Jeremy Blackwood in a paper that he first wrote for a course at Marquette University and then shortened for presentation at the West Coast Methods Institute at Loyola Marymount University in April 2009. The paper is entitled

"Sanctifying Grace, Elevation, and the Fifth Level of Consciousness: Further Developments within Lonergan Scholarship." It is a major contribution to an ongoing conversation among some of Lonergan's students. I will conclude the present portion of this book by summarizing Blackwood's paper, which is the most complete treatment to date of this issue and by suggesting several other possible connections. Page numbers in Blackwood's WCMI paper are given in parentheses.

Blackwood indicates that Christiaan Jacobs-Vandegeer's article in *Theological Studies* in 2007, "Sanctifying Grace in a Methodical Theology," correctly suggests that sanctifying grace should be understood in a methodical theology as an intrinsic qualification of the *unity* of consciousness.[18] The moment I saw Jacobs-Vandegeer's statement to this effect, I knew it was correct. However, Blackwood also points out that "further development of his position is required on two points: the precise meaning of 'elevation' needs clarification, and recently-noticed materials in the Lonergan archives suggest that the notion of a fifth level needs re-evaluation" (1). The first point is further articulated in two sub-points: "First, just what occurs in this elevation of central form and consequent enlargement of horizon is not fully explained, and a deeper appropriation of Jacobs-Vandegeer's solution requires a fuller articulation of the meaning of 'elevation.' Second, elevation of central form pertains to all the levels of consciousness [a point I also made in 'Consciousness and Grace' but that escaped subsequent discussion], and a significant element in the discussion has been the possible relevance of a fifth level. If the whole subject is elevated in virtue of the elevation of central form, a fuller grasp of the number of levels in consciousness is required" (2–3), or (and here I'm speaking in my own voice), if you don't want to talk about levels and numbers of levels, then we might say that a fuller grasp of the full range of sublating and sublated operations and states is required. In my view, restriction of self-appropriation to four levels of intentional consciousness will result in the appropriation of a severely truncated self, a self where openness as fact, openness as achievement, and openness as gift are all neglected.[19] Moreover, whether "level" language is kept or not, an indication must be provided of what elevation would mean for what we have up to now referred to as the levels of experience, understanding, judgment, and decision, for the feelings that accompany these levels, and for the vital, social, cultural, and personal levels of value that are respectively isomorphic with these levels of consciousness. In any event, the basic four levels of intentional consciousness are not enough, and to say that they are is to place on our consciousness a similar kind of straightjacket to the one that for at least some of us was experienced when we tried to bunch our existential decision-making into the confines of chapter 18 of *Insight*. While that chapter remains a valid account of one mode of making decisions, a mode that St Ignatius Loyola formulated in his third "time of election," this is not the only mode, and other accounts are required.[20] So too with elements of consciousness that lie beyond the levels of intentional consciousness, on either end.

Blackwood finds an indication of an elevation of cognitional levels of consciousness in Lonergan's papers "The Natural Desire to See God"[21] and "Openness and Religious Experience," while the Latin "Analysis Fidei" offers a detailed account of such elevation with respect to the level of judgment.[22] In "The Natural Desire to See God," Lonergan points to philosophy, theology, and the beatific vision as three successive ways in which the human intellect knows the intelligible unity of the existing world order. Blackwood relates these successive ways, respectively, to the three Scholastic epistemological principles of the light of intellect (philosophy), the light of faith (theology), and the light of glory (the beatific vision). The movement from the lower to the higher involves an elevation of knowing, and so "it is to knowing, and specifically to the horizons of knowing constituted by the light of intellect, the light of faith, and the light of glory, that we ought to attend in order to begin to grasp Lonergan's notion of elevation in consciousness" (3). "[W]hether or not a given object is supernatural to a particular knower is not determined by the object itself, but by the light by which that object is attained" (5). Elevation pertains to judgment, as is emphasized especially in "Analysis Fidei," but it can be extended beyond judgment. It is the addition of absolutely supernatural formal objects of judgment, but that definition too "can be extended to other levels of consciousness, such that at each of the levels of intentional consciousness, an elevated subject has two formal objects – the natural/proportionate and the supernatural/disproportionate" (5–6). The details remain to be worked out for the levels of experience and understanding. The relation of the natural and supernatural objects of any level is one of obediential potency. And the conscious experience of elevation at each level is related to "an act, the content of which is not fully accounted for by the act itself" (6).

In an important piece of research, Blackwood goes on to indicate how records of question-and-answer sessions from Lonergan Workshops, records that had not been appealed to in previous discussion of my suggestion regarding a fifth level, confirm that Lonergan did maintain a fifth level, but that it is not exclusively connected with the supernatural. I believe these sessions make that affirmation unassailable. There is a level of love in its various forms, including the unrestricted being-in-love that he identifies with sanctifying grace. It cannot be reduced to the four levels of experience, understanding, judgment, and decision. The distinguishing characteristic of the fifth level is not the supernatural as opposed to the natural but the interpersonal character of so-called fifth-level experience, the concern with the "other" and especially with *the beloved whose presence in the lover is constituted precisely by love itself.* Fifth-level experience is the conscious relation between the conscious subject in love and the other with whom the subject is in love. One thinks readily of Lonergan's discussion in *The Triune God: Systematics* of the presence of the beloved in the lover, a presence that is *constituted* by love.[23] In Blackwood's words, "[T]he fifth level is constituted insofar as the subject operating is also operated on" (8).[24] Lonergan's own notes for one of his responses reads, "love is subjectivity linked to others." Lonergan explicitly relates the fifth level of love and the fourth level of deliberation in a manner parallel to the relation between other higher and lower levels, a relation of sublation. Moreover, the sensitive psyche is related to the levels of intentional consciousness through vertical finality, which is reaching toward being in love. "[T]he unconscious desire to being in love underlies the first through fourth levels, and it reaches beyond and through the horizontal finalities of those levels as a vertical finality fulfilled in the fifth level" (9).[25] Aside from the expression "unconscious desire," this is a position that I think is supported by "Mission and the Spirit"[26] and "Natural Right and Historical Mindedness."[27] Lonergan explicitly subdivides the so-called fifth level into domestic, civil, and religious loves, and characterizes it as "the level of [total] self-transcendence, self-forgetting, the level at which the subject is no longer thinking of him- or herself" (10). Thus, in "Philosophy and the Religious Phenomenon,"[28] we find that "beyond the moral operator that promotes us from judgments of fact to judgments of value … there is a further realm of interpersonal relations and total commitment," which in a 1980 question-and-answer session he speaks of as "the sublation of deliberation by self-forgetting love" (10).[29]

Blackwood thus characterizes fifth-level operation as constituted by the self-forgetting of love, "the self-possessed handing over of one's central form to the determination of another" in love. He speaks of a fifth-level question in terms of "What would you have me do?" And the fifth-level object is persons as persons, as subjects. As elevated, the fifth level gains the absolutely supernatural personal object of the three divine persons of the Trinity. The advance made by Jacobs-Vandegeer is not negated by this return to fifth-level talk, since the fifth level is the elevation of central form itself in complete self-transcendence in the triune God.[30]

I find Blackwood's discussion convincing. I also find it relevant to John Dadosky's proposal regarding a fourth stage of meaning – a stage that, as I understand Dadosky, has to do with the communal discernment that would lead to the collective responsibility of a community of persons in love.[31] We might also correlate such a discussion with Lonergan's treatment of beauty as a transcendental, as found for example in his response to several questions at the 1971 Dublin Institute on Method. Beauty is a transcendental, he says, but in a different way from the intelligible, the true and the real, and the good, in that it is not the objective of a specific transcendental notion but rather "evokes a response from the whole person." Perhaps in this way we might link the emphases of Hans Urs von Balthasar's theological aesthetics to the still unfolding Lonerganian analysis of the unity and levels of consciousness, and we might include the vertical finality of the passionateness of being or tidal movement that begins before consciousness, permeates each level, and comes to its fulfillment in love: an emphasis that I have explicitly linked to the notions of psychic conversion, of the series of dramatic-aesthetic operators that precede, accompany, and reach beyond intentional consciousness as attentive, intelligent, reasonable, and responsible, and to the role of those operators in partly constituting the normative source of meaning in history.[32] Perhaps that fulfillment in love is also intimately related to our response to the transcendental "beauty," a response that satisfies not a particular transcendental notion but the entire person, central form. Perhaps, then, Balthasar's theological aesthetics are articulating the elevation of that response of the total person to the transcendental "beauty" under the gift of God's divine love orienting us to the glory of God, precisely as the inner word entailed in this response has been articulated and confirmed in or perhaps awakened by the outer revelatory deeds and words that, while articulating a universal reality, are as articulated peculiar to Israel and Christianity.[33]

I close this part of the book with a question. Is it the case that the rejection of the notion of psychic conversion is linked with the rejection of such further notions as the fifth level of consciousness, the affirmation of beauty as a transcendental, the fourth stage of meaning, and the role of aesthetic-dramatic operators in the promotion of authenticity in oneself, one's culture, and one's social milieu? The answer, I think, is clear.

PART TWO

Missions and Processions

7

The Starting Point

1 The Four-point Hypothesis: Its Significance and Limitations

Thesis 21: *While the four-point hypothesis constitutes the specifically theological dimension of the starting point, it must be joined by a theory of history if our systematics is to integrate the realities named in special categories with those named in general categories. Revelation introduces God's meaning into history. The Incarnation is the personal entrance of God's Meaning into history under intersubjective, aesthetic, symbolic, linguistic, and incarnate carriers. The mission of the Holy Spirit is the inner word of God's meaning in history. Together, the four-point hypothesis and the theological theory of history constitute the unified field structure of a contemporary systematics.*

1.1 The Hypothesis

I have appealed to the four-point systematic-theological hypothesis expressed by Lonergan in *Divinarum personarum* and again in the revision of that document that constituted the *pars systematica* of *De Deo trino.*[1] I have also called attention to the earlier appearance of the hypothesis in class notes that Lonergan wrote for a course in 1951–52. Despite its heavy overdose of Scholastic language, which must undergo fairly massive transposition in the contemporary context without the loss of the metaphysics entailed,[2] the hypothesis contains the core systematic conceptions around which other special theological categories can be integrated.[3] Again, as I phrased the matter earlier, the hypothesis names the core elements in the dogmatic-theological context for further theological statements.

Once again, the hypothesis reads:

> [T]here are four real divine relations, really identical with the di-
> vine substance, and therefore there are four very special modes that
> ground the external imitation of the divine substance. Next, there
> are four absolutely supernatural realities, which are never found un-
> informed, namely, the secondary act of existence of the Incarnation,
> sanctifying grace, the habit of charity, and the light of glory. It would
> not be inappropriate, therefore, to say that the secondary act of ex-
> istence of the Incarnation is a created participation of paternity, and
> so has a special relation to the Son; that sanctifying grace is a partici-
> pation of active spiration, and so has a special relation to the Holy
> Spirit; that the habit of charity is a participation of passive spiration,
> and so has a special relation to the Father and the Son; and that the
> light of glory is a participation of sonship, and so in a most perfect
> way brings the children of adoption back to the Father.[4]

The hypothesis thus speaks of four absolutely supernatural ways of imitating God through a created participation in the divine relations. One of
these (the created base[5] of the created relation of the humanity of Jesus to
the eternal Word, a participation in the eternal relation of paternity) is peculiar to Jesus of Nazareth, the incarnate and linguistic revelation of divine
Meaning in history; all others are offered a created participation in divine
paternity only through the participation through sanctifying grace in active spiration, which is grounded in paternity. Two ways of imitating God
(sanctifying grace and charity, participating in active and passive spiration,
respectively, and so in the entire life of the Trinity) are given to us in this
life in the inner word of divine meaning that is the gift and mission of the
Holy Spirit, response to which in charity that flows from a faith that participates in the invisible mission of the Word establishes also the indwelling of
the Father and the Son as terms of the relation of which charity is the base.
I began to transpose the latter position in the second chapter. The final way
of imitating God (the light of glory, participating in filiation) is promised to
us in the life to come. Because there are four real divine relations, because
God *is* four real divine relation, three of which are really distinct, there are
four special ways, graced ways, in which created realities can imitate God:
special, because in each of them the creature attains God as God is in Godself. Each of the four ways is a created participation in one of the four divine
relations, where "participation" must be understood analogously. Thus:

(1)   the secondary act of existence of the incarnate Word, which is
       the created base of a created relation of the assumed human

nature of Jesus to the eternal divine Word, participates in and
imitates the uncreated divine relation of paternity, and so bears
a special relation to the Son;

(2) sanctifying grace, *gratia gratum faciens*, the reception of the Father's love as including us and becoming our love, participates
in and imitates active spiration, that is, the Father and the Son
together as they "breathe" the Holy Spirit, and so bears a special
relation to the uncreated Holy Spirit;

(3) the habit of charity, which in *Insight* is referred to as an antecedent universal willingness,[6] and for which I want to reserve the expression that Lonergan assigns to sanctifying grace, namely, the
dynamic state of being in love without qualifications or restrictions or reservations, proceeds from the reception of divine love
in sanctifying grace and from the assent to that gift in faith, and
participates in and imitates passive spiration, the proceeding Love
"breathed" by and proceeding from the Father and the Son, and
so bears a special inverse relation to the Father and the Son; and

(4) the light of glory participates in and imitates filiation, and so
bears a special relation to the eternal Father.

In terms that are perhaps more accessible,

(1) in the Godhead the Word does not speak but is spoken; the incarnate Word speaks, but only what he hears from the Father;
thus, the relation of the assumed humanity to the eternal divine
Word is a created participation in and imitation of the Father's
eternal relation to the Word, that is, the relation of *Dicens*, of
speaking, which is divine paternity, expressing divine Meaning
under the various carriers of meaning: intersubjective, aesthetic,
symbolic, linguistic, and incarnate; moreover, as Lonergan put it
in his notes on grace in 1951–52, the foundation of the relation is
that, as *Dicens* is paternity generating its Word, the eternal Son,
so the Incarnation is a regeneration in which there proceeds,
not a new person, as in divine generation, but a new nature
joined to the already existing person of the divine Word;[7]

(2) the reception of the Father's love as love for us that becomes
our love as we yield to it and assent to it in a set of judgments of
value is, as the inner word of the received divine love, a created
participation in and imitation of the Father and the Son as together they "breathe" the Holy Spirit;

(3) the disposition that we know as charity, which in the terms of
Lonergan's *Insight* is an antecedent universal willingness that

> embraces the return of good for evil in an abiding friendship
> with God, and to which there should be predicated Lonergan's
> expression regarding unrestricted being in love, is a created
> participation in and imitation of the proceeding Love, the Holy
> Spirit, breathed by the Father and the Son, and so grounds a cre-
> ated relation to the uncreated Father and Son; and
>
> (4) the light of glory is a created participation in and imitation of
> the divine Son as he brings all of us, his brothers and sisters,
> children by adoption, to the Father.

I have already stated that this four-point hypothesis is the beginning of the efforts in systematic theology that will be offered here.

In this work and the work that will follow it, I have chosen to express the hypothesis at the beginning and to fill out its meaning later from positions expressed by Lonergan in chapters 2 through 5 of *The Triune God: Systematics*, positions expressing a systematic understanding of the divine processions, relations, and persons. In the present work, following the *ordo doctrinae*, I will begin that filling out by introducing Lonergan's chapter on the divine processions (chapter 2 of *The Triune God: Systematics*). A subsequent volume will relate the missions to Lonergan's theology of divine relations and divine persons (chapters 3, 4, and 5 of *The Triune God: Systematics*). The review of all the earlier chapters in Lonergan's Trinitarian systematics will be mainly for the purpose of sublating that material into the theology of the divine missions, and so will be punctuated regularly with concerns already raised in the first part of the present work. Chapter 6 of *The Triune God: Systematics* and texts related to it, texts that treat the divine missions, constitute the immediate basis in Lonergan's writings for what I am saying, and we have already seen a great deal of what is contained in that chapter. In particular, I am grounding my work in the hypothesis just mentioned, along with the more detailed treatment of the hypothesis in Lonergan's earlier notes of 1951–52.

1.2 The Place of the Four-point Hypothesis in a Unified Field Structure for Systematics

In *What Is Systematic Theology?* I appealed to the hypothesis in an attempt to articulate what I called a *unified field structure* for systematic theology, that is, a heuristic core around which a systematic theology can be organized. As I said there,

> The unified field structure would be ... an open and heuristic
> set of conceptions that embraces the field of issues presently to

be accounted for and presently foreseeable in that discipline or functional specialty of theology whose task it is to give a synthetic understanding of the realities that are and ought to be providing the meaning constitutive of the community called the Church. The unified field structure would be found in a statement, perhaps a quite lengthy one, perhaps even one taking up several large volumes, capable of guiding for the present and the foreseeable future the ongoing genetic development of the entire synthetic understanding of the mysteries of faith and of the other elements that enter into systematic theology. It would guide all work at bringing these elements into a synthetic unity.[8]

In terms that Lonergan employs elsewhere and that I used above in chapter 1, the unified field structure includes the articulation at any given time of the most fundamental elements in what happens to be the contemporary dogmatic-theological context. But it includes them in a manner that makes systematic development possible. Thus, the four-point hypothesis would constitute only part of the unified field structure, not the whole of it. The unified field structure goes beyond the contemporary articulation of the dogmatic-theological context in that it consists of the four-point systematic-theological hypothesis *integrated with a theological theory of history*, a theory that flows from complicating the basic structure of Lonergan's intentionality analysis.[9] More concretely, the second component of the unified field structure, the component added to the four-point hypothesis, is what Lonergan calls the *Grund- und Gesamtwissenschaft*, the basic and total science, which consists in (1) cognitional theory, (2) epistemology, (3) the metaphysics of proportionate being, and (4) existential ethics.[10] In this sense, it includes the whole of *Insight* and much of *Method in Theology*, in addition to the complementary material on psychic self-appropriation found in my own work, as all of these enter into the constitution of a theory of history. These would play a role in a contemporary systematics analogous to the role played by Aristotle's metaphysics in the systematics of Thomas Aquinas. As Aristotle's metaphysics provided Aquinas with his general categories and Philip the Chancellor's theorem of the supernatural grounded Aquinas's special categories, so Lonergan's "basic and total science" as complemented with the material on psychic conversion would ground today's general categories, and his four-point hypothesis would ground today's special categories. But the general categories will consist in the philosophic contributions of a basic and total science *precisely as they give rise to a theory of history*, the kind of theory of history articulated in *Theology and the Dialectics of History*. As I indicated above, Lonergan says in some notes that he wrote around the time of his breakthrough to the notion of functional specialization that the mediated object of the functional specialty "doctrines" is redemption in history, and the mediated object of the functional specialty "systematics" is *Geschichte*. The theory of history emergent from the cognitional theory, epistemology, metaphysics, and existential ethics proposed by Lonergan, joined with the insistence in chapter 2 of *Theology and the Dialectics of History* on the duality of consciousness and the need for psychic as well as intentional self-appropriation, provides systematics with the structure of its basic general terms and relations, and through these with the structure of the categories that theology shares with other disciplines. The four-point hypothesis, again, contains the structure of the basic special terms and relations, and through these the structure of the categories peculiar to theology. When integrated into a position on redemption in history, the two components together yield a vision of the reign of God that the incarnate Son preached and established. A position on what constitutes the reign of God may thus be said to constitute the unified field structure of systematic theology.[11]

Why is the addition of a theory of history required? Why is the four-point hypothesis not enough to provide a statement of the dogmatic-theological context that can get a contemporary systematics started?[12]

First, if the four-point theological hypothesis were left to stand alone, the theology that would be built around it would be abstract and static. The hypothesis would ground only the use of special categories, that is, of categories peculiar to theology, and not of those general categories that theology shares with other disciplines. This, it seems, is a perennial theological temptation. The theology that would be developed around the hypothesis alone would be like a soul without a body: perhaps something like Bonaventure without Aquinas, or Hans Urs von Balthasar without Bernard Lonergan.[13] On its own the hypothesis is not able to account concretely and historically for the sets of relations between the divine and the human that formed the focus of Jesus's public ministry, that define the meaning of revelation, that are the meaning of Jesus's death and resurrection, that explain the significance of the mission of the Holy Spirit, and that, precisely for all these reasons, constitute the core intelligibility of a systematic theology. In that sense the hypothesis cannot provide on its own an articulation of a unified field structure that would articulate the dynamics that constitute the reign of God. The hypothesis provides categories for speaking about the divine and about created supernatural realities that enable human beings to reach the very being of God in love, but it provides very little to guide our understanding of the human precisely as nature and as history. The theory of history provided in *Theology and the Dialectics of History* attempts to add such guidance, precisely by relating "religious values" (which I am now grounding in the "special basic relations" contained in the four-point hypothesis) to the rest of the scale of values proposed by Lonergan and developed further in that book: personal, cultural, and social values, and the equitable distribution of vital values to the entire community. Together, the hypothesis and the theory of history yield a theological synthesis regarding the kingdom or reign of God in the world.

Since the hypothesis articulates a series of created participations in the divine processions and relations, the integration of the hypothesis with a theory of history would articulate the manner in which historical reality participates in divine life; more precisely, it would articulate the structure of that participation. Such an articulation would constitute what I am looking for, the unified field structure for a systematic theology. Systematic theology, which in its entirety at any one time is always located in a community of inquirers and not in any single individual, is concerned primarily with the participation of historical humankind in divine life. While its principal function is the imperfect and analogical understanding of the mysteries of Christian faith, today that understanding will take the form of a theological theory of history.

Still, the hypothesis does name some of the specifically theological realities or central special categories of the theology that we are here constructing, some of the core categories peculiar to theology. In fact, it names those special categories to which all other special categories must be explicitly related if they are to qualify as special categories in Christian theology.[14] It is for this reason that it forms the dogmatic-theological context for work in all other areas of systematics beyond Trinitarian theology, Christology, and Pneumatology. And so the first task before us is to offer as thorough and systematic a treatment of the realities contained in that hypothesis as we are able to provide. While I will emphasize that the unified field structure in its entirety constitutes the starting point of systematic theology, an elaboration of the four-point hypothesis is essential to such a beginning, constituting as it does the dogmatic-theological context for the rest of a specifically theological system.

Such a statement, of course, is made from a "macro" point of view. The hypothesis explicitly embraces the doctrines of the triune God, the incarnate Word, the inhabitation of the Holy Spirit, and the last things, and it does so in such a way that the mysteries affirmed in these doctrines are related systematically or synthetically to one another. Thus, it presents in a systematic order some of the principal realities named by the special categories that a systematics will employ, indeed (it may be argued) the central or core specifically theological realities affirmed in Christian faith. To unpack the hypothesis is a major enterprise, one to which much of this work entitled *The Trinity in History* is devoted. But the systematics also constantly relates the hypothesis to the structure of history, and only that relation constitutes the unified field structure and the starting point of systematic theology.

2   Two Requirements

If I am to be faithful to my own prescriptions in *What Is Systematic Theology?* and to those of Bernard Lonergan, whose method I am following and amplifying and whose efforts in systematics I am attempting to sweep up into the perspective of a theological theory of history, two requirements must be met: the foundational requirement of interiorly and religiously differentiated consciousness, and the insistence that the general categories of a contemporary systematics will unite to form a theological theory of history. Brief mention was made of these requirements in chapter 1, but a fuller argument is required.

2.1 Interiorly and Religiously Differentiated Consciousness

Thesis 22: *The objects intended in systematic theology must be identified, as far as possible, in categories derived from interiorly and religiously differentiated consciousness.*

The first requirement is that the objects intended in systematics must be identified, as far as possible, in categories that are based in elements in interiorly and religiously differentiated consciousness. The metaphysical terms and relations of an earlier theology, while still helpful and in my view necessary if the turn to interiority is not to be a reversion to commonsense interiority, are nevertheless not enough. For such terms and relations, if they are valid, are derived from and isomorphic with operations and states of the conscious subject in his or her authenticity, and a methodical theology is methodical precisely and only insofar as it grounds such terms and relations in those conscious operations and states.

The significance of this prescription is momentous. The very meaning of the terms used to name the metaphysical elements will be different depending on whether or not this prescription is followed. As Lonergan writes, "Empiricism, idealism, and realism name three totally different horizons with no common identical objects." When it is a matter of the metaphysical elements – potency, form, and act – "realism" in this sentence must be distinguished into naive realism and critical realism, for a Gilsonian Thomist and a student of Lonergan have different meanings for these terms. The difference affects primarily the term "form," but because potency is potency for form, and act is act of form, the difference affects these terms as well. Lonergan is one of very few roughly contemporary thinkers with some basis in the Aristotelian-Thomist tradition to relate the metaphysical elements intimately to modern science. For Lonergan the form corresponding to, say, "tree" is not known by seeing several trees and abstracting "tree." That is

Scotism, not Thomism. It is also philosophically vacuous. The formal intelligibility of a tree is known hypothetically in the science of botany, and that knowledge is expressed, not in the word "tree," but in complex scientific formulae that will differentiate trees from other botanical species and different kinds of trees from one another. Such "trees," as explained, cannot be imagined, let alone seen and pointed to. That difference is rooted in an appropriation of the difference between commonsense and theoretical knowing, that is, in the critical exigency that emerges once the two realms have been distinguished, and in the complementary meanings of "real" in the two domains. In Lonergan's words:

> Is common sense just primitive ignorance to be brushed aside with an acclaim to science as the dawn of intelligence and reason? Or is science of merely pragmatic value, teaching us how to control nature, but failing to reveal what nature is? Or, for that matter, is there any such thing as human knowing? So man is confronted with the three basic questions: What am I doing when I am knowing? Why is doing that knowing? What do I know when I do it? With these questions one turns from the outer realms of common sense and theory to the appropriation of one's own interiority, one's subjectivity, one's operations, their structure, their norms, their potentialities. Such appropriation, in its technical expression, resembles theory. But in itself it is a heightening of intentional consciousness, an attending not merely to objects but also to the intending subject and his acts. And as this heightened consciousness constitutes the evidence for one's account of knowledge, such an account by the proximity of the evidence differs from all other expression.[15]

It is this withdrawal into interiority that is required if we are to make the necessary distinction of common sense from science and to provide the general basic terms and relations of both philosophy and theology. Again, "For every term and relation there will exist a corresponding element in intentional consciousness. Accordingly, empty or misleading terms and relations can be eliminated, while valid ones can be elucidated by the conscious intention from which they are derived."[16]

2.1.1 Intentional and Nonintentional Components to Theological Foundations

Thesis 23: *While the corresponding element is most often found in intentional consciousness, the experience of the gift of God's love, manifest, for example, in what St Ignatius Loyola calls consolation without a*

previous cause, introduces complexities regarding the relation of knowl-
edge and love, and so regarding intentional and nonintentional compo-
nents at the level of theological foundations.

I would qualify somewhat the statement of Lonergan's just quoted, though not in the manner that some might prefer, namely, by claiming that Lonergan is exaggerating when he says "every." He is not. Nor am I in following him. Rather, the qualification is twofold.

First, as I indicated above,[17] at times the closest one can come to satisfying this prescription is by naming the cognitional operation in which the designated metaphysical term is known. This is particularly the case with such terms as "the secondary act of existence of the Incarnation." Lonergan's analysis leading to the affirmation of the *esse secundarium* is thoroughly metaphysical, and this in a book where he does not hesitate to raise questions concerning the consciousness and knowledge of Christ.[18] There *are* terms that are strictly metaphysical, reached by analysis that is strictly metaphysical. *Esse secundarium* is an instance. So, in a much more mundane context, is *species intelligibilis*, "intelligible species," a term that is crucial to Thomas Aquinas's cognitional theory and whose importance Lonergan retains even though he provides no corresponding term in intentional consciousness. What *is* provided is a statement of the cognitional act or acts by which such terms come to be formulated and affirmed. And that is enough to satisfy Lonergan's prescription for basic and derived terms and relations in systematics.

The second qualification is to the effect that the corresponding conscious element is most often found in intentional consciousness, but it may also be found in nonintentional conscious states. This is particularly the case with the basic gift of God's love, which, *insofar as it is not a response to an object apprehended by the one who receives the gift,* is in its originating moment nonintentional *in that person's consciousness.* One is first *in* love because one has been loved and has yielded to a love that becomes one's own because it has been given. One is in love before one understands who or what it is that one is in love with. In its originary moment, this gift, as consciously received, is nonintentional, from the human standpoint. The intentionality that it certainly has is God's intentionality, the intentionality of the giver, something not clearly available as such to the human recipient of the gift. If the gift may be related to St Ignatius Loyola's "consolation without previous cause," that is, consolation with a content but without any apprehended object to which it responds, as Karl Rahner proposed and as Lonergan seems to agree, it is pure gift. This is why Lonergan constantly cites Romans 5.5, "God's love has been poured into our hearts through the Holy Spirit that has been given to us." That is why I find 1 John 4.19 just as foundational a scriptural text. "We are to love, then, because God loved us first."

Such a conclusion makes sense only in that we are talking about a consolation that is not a response to an *apprehended* object. And it is in itself an incomplete conclusion. It rings partially true, but not completely true to our religious experience of such consolation. Lonergan provides what we need to solve the conundrum. This consolation comes from God and is the fruit of the outpouring of the Holy Spirit from the Father and the Word, and so at its source it is *God's own response to God as God apprehends God.* In that sense, this consolation without a previous cause *does* proceed from knowledge, but that knowledge is not ours. It is identical with the eternal Father and the Father's only begotten Son, the eternal Word of the Father, the eternal Judgment of Value, the *Verbum spirans Amorem.* But we do not know that simply by experiencing it.

2.1.2 The Psychological Analogy

The theological significance of this first prescription or requirement, that of grounding every term and relation in interiorly and religiously differentiated consciousness, is multiform, but for now we can limit our consideration to two matters of importance. In *Theology and the Dialectics of History* and elsewhere, I have insisted that interiorly differentiated consciousness includes both intentionality and psyche, and that insistence is particularly significant for grounding that part of the unified field structure that presents a theory of history. The two matters of importance that I wish to stress here refer to other issues: the psychological analogy, and the constitution of what Lonergan calls religiously differentiated consciousness. The two are interrelated, since I have already suggested that religiously differentiated consciousness, in the form of an appropriation of the relation of sanctifying grace to charity, would enable the articulation of a new development in the history of the so-called psychological analogy, a development in the range of religious values themselves.

> **Thesis 24:** *Lonergan's work on the psychological analogy is required background for the advances being suggested here. It shows how an understanding of human dynamic consciousness in its immanent terms and relations – an understanding of how act proceeds from act in the autonomous spiritual dimension of human consciousness – provides the basic framework for an analogical understanding of Trinitarian processions and relations. In all forms of the analogy, the inner word that provides the analogue for the procession of the divine Word is a judgment of value.*

We must consider the future of what has been called the psychological analogy under the conditions that I am proposing. The basic point of the psychological analogy, as it has been proposed by Augustine and developed by Aquinas and most completely by Lonergan, is that the divine processions, which are at the core of the four-point hypothesis, are conceived on an analogy with human dynamic consciousness. Such consciousness, then, must be accurately understood in its immanent terms and relations, and the understanding must be presented as thoroughly as possible. For this there is no substitute for a long and repeated struggle with Lonergan's work on *verbum* in Aquinas, his subsequent work in *Insight*, and his unfolding of the analogy in *The Triune God: Systematics*. Lonergan's work enables an articulation of the psychological analogy that is far more detailed than Aquinas's own presentation of *emanatio intelligibilis*, even while it displays clearly what Aquinas meant by that elusive term. There is no excuse for not going to the most highly developed instance of the analogy if we want to understand its potential contribution. Our "macro" perspective assumes the four-point hypothesis into the starting point of a systematic theology. That starting point itself consists in the elaboration of the unified field structure of a theological heuristic of history. But the initial task involved in unpacking the hypothesis is to provide a hypothetical understanding of the four divine relations, and this will entail rehabilitating the psychological analogy. That analogy can be rehabilitated only by engaging in the self-appropriation to which one is invited in *Insight* and then applying that self-appropriation to the construction of an analogy for understanding procession in God. And the rehabilitation will be essential for grasping both Lonergan's later development of the analogy and the movement that I have suggested here to an analogy within the order of grace itself.

The psychological analogy has fallen on hard times in theology.[19] Part of the reason, I believe, is that it has rarely been understood. What has not been understood very well in the history of theology is how *act proceeds from act in the autonomous spiritual dimension of human consciousness*, and in particular how different acts of understanding ground a series of inner words. Nothing has more potential to revive academic and intellectual culture in general than to awaken a sense of this dimension of human spirituality. The transcendental notions of the intelligible, the true, and the good would become the heart of such a culture. I suspect that the opposition to the psychological analogy on the part of both Karl Rahner and Hans Urs von Balthasar, two great theologians otherwise not united on many fronts, is due to their not grasping precisely this procession in consciousness of word from understanding and its significance for a remote analogical understanding of the procession of the divine Word.

Lonergan's later reflections on the analogy make available the possibility of reorienting the analogy in a more existential and religiously significant way. And my further suggestions move even more in this direction. But we can follow these developments only after having grasped the cognitive emphasis that is to the fore in the Trinitarian theologies of Aquinas and the early Lonergan. The traditional emphasis found in Aquinas and made much more explicit in the early work of Lonergan concentrates on how the act of understanding grounds a proceeding inner word, and on how understanding and inner word together ground acts of love.

While it is true that neither of these dimensions of the dynamism of consciousness moving "from below," that is, neither the cognitional nor the existential, has been adequately grasped in the history of theology subsequent to Aquinas, and so that Lonergan's retrieval of these emphases is one of the most welcome features in the whole of twentieth-century thought, still it must also be emphasized that these presentations of the analogy for the Trinity, once they have been understood in their own right, can be supplemented by other versions of the analogy that, while related to the analogy "from below," will be more appealing at least to some students of theology and perhaps more pertinent for the pastoral communication of the gospel message. Lonergan explicitly acknowledged in his late reflections on Trinitarian theology the possibility of another approach to the psychological analogy, one in which love, not knowledge, is the starting point. Love is not simply the end result of spiritual procession, as in the analogy as it was presented by the early Lonergan. Love propels the entire set of autonomous spiritual processions. I have provided further contributions in the second chapter of this work, shifting once again the basic starting point in the analogy.

Perhaps, though, there is something of an internal inconsistency in Lonergan's own presentation of the analogy in his early Trinitarian work, an inconsistency that invites further development. For even in his Trinitarian treatises written at the Gregorian University in the 1950s and 1960s, the inner word that provides an analogue for the divine Word is not a concept, not even a judgment of fact, but a judgment of value; and yet his unpacking of the processions in *Divinarum Personarum* and *De Deo Trino: Pars systematica* is still in terms of the emanation of a purely cognitional judgment, a judgment of fact in which there is formed (in Thomas's words) a *likeness* (*similitudo*) of what is known to be. Lonergan was still working out the difference between judgments of fact and judgments of value while he was writing the systematic treatise on the Trinity. The truth of a judgment of value cannot be expressed in the way one expresses the truth of a judgment of fact, for a true judgment of value may disapprove of what is and approve of what is not, and then there is not formed in the judgment of value a likeness of what is known to be. The work of elaborating in what the truth of a judgment of value consists, even when that judgment is generated in a movement from below, remained to be done while he was writing the Trinitarian material, and in fact much of that task remains to be done even in our time. An overhauling even of the early analogy "from below" is required, once it is acknowledged that the relevant inner word is a judgment of value. What makes for the truth, not of a judgment of fact, but of a judgment of value? The appropriation of the emanation of a word that is a judgment of value is by no means as clear in Lonergan's work as is the appropriation of the procession of a true judgment of fact, which, once one has caught on to what Lonergan is about, is really very clear. In a question-and-answer session following his 1965 lecture at Marquette University, "Dimensions of Meaning," Lonergan states, "The approach in *Insight* is existential in the sense of existential philosophy but it has dimensions that are not acknowledged ordinarily in existential philosophy, namely, this level of judgment and the possibility of judgments of value being true."[20] The process of arriving at a true judgment of value is not articulated in *Insight* or anywhere else by Lonergan in a fashion that is as clear and thorough as his treatment of reflective insight grasping the sufficiency of evidence for a judgment of fact. We must try to shore up what is still inchoate in his writings, even in the later writings, where a new notion of value emerges.[21]

The retrieval of the earlier forms of the analogy, and especially of the emanation of word from understanding, is also made more difficult today by the one-way emphases of much philosophy of language, whether analytic, Heideggerian, or poststructuralist.[22] The linguistic idealism that has neglected the dependence of inner and outer word upon direct and reflective understanding is the culmination of a trajectory of decline in philosophy and theology alike that was initiated by Scotus and Ockham and others and extends in myriad ways into some of the main arteries of twentieth-century philosophy. A rehabilitation of the psychological analogy involves a massive reversal of centuries of philosophic decline in this one area, even as gains were undoubtedly made in others.[23]

There are, then, two psychological analogies in Lonergan's writings, two analogies drawn from the dynamic consciousness of the intelligent creature. One of these, the purely cognitional analogy, is natural, while the other, the one that begins with love, is open to being an analogy in the supernatural order, that is, when the love with which it begins is God's love poured out in our hearts by the Holy Spirit who has been given to us. The cognitional analogy has been worked through by Lonergan, even if with the inconsistency pointed out above, but it is the supernatural analogy, I believe, that is really the one to which a future systematics might want to hitch its star; and this analogy can be pushed further, as I have tried to do in chapter 2.

For all that, though, we must follow Lonergan in articulating first the cognitional analogy. Only on that basis can we take up the challenge that he opened late in life, a challenge to develop an analogy in the supernatural order. By following through on his work in this way, we will locate the inconsistency and the relative deficiency of the earlier analogy, but we will also have the best opportunity we could ask for in a systematic theology to present the extraordinary analysis of cognitive and existential interiority that Lonergan has offered us. Since this analysis grounds all our general categories, it must be featured from the outset in our efforts to construct a systematics. While I cannot repeat the work of *Insight* every time I write something new, I can subsume it into the new work and point to its abiding significance. In a Trinitarian theology, the way to do this is to review the work that Lonergan himself has done in moving toward an acceptable psychological analogy for Trinitarian processions. The next several chapters will develop his work by speaking of *autonomous spiritual processions.*

Perhaps I need to say a bit more about the precise issue at stake here.

As we have seen, the First Vatican Council speaks of theological understanding in the following manner: "Reason illumined by faith, when it inquires diligently, reverently, and judiciously, with God's help attains some understanding of the mysteries, and that a highly fruitful one, both from the analogy of what it naturally knows and from the interconnection of the mysteries with one another and with our last end" (DB 1796, DS 3016, ND 132). Lonergan appeals repeatedly to this statement of the Council in his various attempts to explain what the systematic part of theology is all about. This is the case both before and after he reached the highly differentiated account of theological operations that constitutes his notion of functional specialization. Thus, in his 1954 review article "Theology and Understanding,"[24] in which he engages with both respect and qualifications Johannes Beumer's book *Theologie als Glaubensverständnis,* he finds himself in agreement with the author on the interpretation of the Council but in disagreement with Beumer's interpretation of the texts of St Thomas Aquinas that have to do with theological understanding. On Lonergan's interpretation, Aquinas's position and practice are entirely in keeping with the later teaching of the Council and provide a clear example of what the Council was talking about. Again, in the 1957 *Divinarum Personarum* and its 1964 revision *De Deo Trino: Pars systematica,* the teaching of the Council frames Lonergan's view of what he is doing as he works out a systematic understanding of the church's Trinitarian dogmas. These writings all appeared before Lonergan made the great methodological breakthrough to functional specialization, where systematics becomes but one of eight differentiated sets of theological operations. Despite that breakthrough, the principal task of systematics remains what it was before Lonergan arrived at the notion of functional specialization, namely, the promotion of the kind of understanding of the mysteries that is spoken of in the conciliar document.[25]

Still, as we have seen, in a very late statement regarding the nature of an analogy to assist us in gaining some imperfect but highly fruitful understanding of the mystery of the divine processions, the divine relations, and the divine persons, Lonergan at least potentially opens the possibility of a different kind of analogy from that emphasized by the Council, an analogy not based on natural knowledge, at least not proximately, but grounded in the supernatural life of grace, a certain kind of analogy of faith, if you wish, or better, an analogy of grace. The Council spoke of understanding the mysteries of faith not only by analogy with what reason knows naturally but also through the interconnection of the mysteries with one another. But Lonergan's late statement goes beyond both of these avenues to theological understanding, in that it evokes the possibility of an analogy between various mysteries of faith. It is the possibility of such an analogy that I am emphasizing and developing further. When he writes that "the psychological analogy ... has its starting point in ... the dynamic state of being in love," he is opening the possibility of a new dimension of analogical understanding, one that begins not in the natural but in the supernatural, graced order. In the second chapter, I tried to specify more precisely what the process is within the order of grace from the gift of *gratia gratum faciens* through judgments of value grounded in that gift to acts of loving and a habit of charity. This amounts to the articulation of the relation of sanctifying grace and charity, which themselves are created imitations of and participations in the divine relations of active and passive spiration, and which constitute "special basic relations" for the elaboration of theological categories. It is in this sense that the analogy within the order of grace takes shape. We take up the discussion again in the next thesis.

2.1.3 Religiously Differentiated Consciousness

Thesis 25: *Religiously differentiated consciousness is to be distinguished into the two moments of being on the receiving end of divine love and loving in return in an unrestricted manner.*

The starting point of Lonergan's later analogy is claimed to be "the dynamic state of being in love." How does Lonergan understand that dynamic state? For an answer to this question, I turn to *Method in Theology*, where being in love is affective self-transcendence, as distinguished from intellectual and moral self-transcendence. One is self-transcendent affectively when one falls in love, and that happening is described as follows by Lonergan: "when the isolation of the individual [is] broken and he spontaneously [functions] not just for himself but for others as well."[26]

Now if we return to the analysis presented in our second chapter, there would seem to be grounds for distinguishing this event into two intimately related components, often difficult to distinguish: to use the language of the citation just mentioned, there is the breaking of the isolation of the person, and there is the release of a new way of being, so that one spontaneously functions not just for oneself but for others as well. The two components are causally related. Spontaneous functioning with affective self-transcendence is not possible until something has released one from one's isolation. What releases one from one's isolation is the conscious experience, whether articulate or not, of being on the receiving end of a love that one can trust. It is clear from our second chapter that I wish to stress the twofold character of this event, perhaps more than Lonergan himself does, and that this stress is central to my position and to what I would maintain is the correct appropriation through interiority of the relation between sanctifying grace and charity. There is a two-step process here, and it is essential to grasp it.

This insistence on my part puts me in the awkward position of finding my mentor's late reduction of the four-point hypothesis to a three-point statement to be too compact, in fact to be something of a reversion from theoretically differentiated consciousness to common sense. In my view (and in Lonergan's) that is not what interiorly differentiated consciousness is all about. Such consciousness is *post*-theoretical, sublating theory into a new realm of being. The self-affirmation of the knower in chapter 11 of *Insight* is explanatory, not descriptive, and this sets the standard for all further developments upon this initial step in self-appropriation, including developments in the realm of grace and the supernatural life. This insistence is also entirely continuous with the phenomenology and causal analysis presented in chapter 8 of my *Theology and the Dialectics of History*, where I insist on the need for being released from isolation as the condition of the possibility of habitual loving. This necessity is, of course, like the law of genuineness in *Insight*, conditional and analogous, depending on the previous history of the person.[27] My insistence is also consistent with the emphasis in my paper delivered at the 2008 Lonergan Workshop at Boston College, "Preserving Lonergan's Understanding of Thomist Metaphysics: A Proposal and an Example,"[28] in which I urged that, while metaphysics becomes derivative in the third stage of meaning, it remains essential for the control of meaning. From this standpoint, then, further differentiations will have to be introduced into Lonergan's account of what he calls being in love with God.

Lonergan distinguishes three forms of affective self-transcendence. There is "the love of intimacy, of husband and wife, of parents and children," where in many instances key events with a far larger significance occur. The mother's smile welcoming her infant into the universe can be a medium of communicating a love that prevents isolation. Next, there is "the love of mankind devoted to the pursuit of human welfare locally or nationally or globally." Finally, there is a "love that [is] other-worldly because it [admits] no conditions or qualifications or restrictions or reservations." Lonergan claims that this otherworldly love, when considered "not as this or that act, not as a series of acts, but as a dynamic state whence proceed the acts ... constitutes in a methodical theology what in a theoretical theology is named sanctifying grace."[29] As sanctifying grace is for Thomas Aquinas's metaphysical or theoretical theology an entitative habit rooted in the essence of the soul, so for Lonergan the dynamic state of being in love without qualifications or reservations or conditions is an elevation of "central form," that is, an elevation of that by which a human being is constituted as intelligibly one unity-identity-whole, and so in effect an elevation of the person in his or her conscious and unconscious totality. The elevation is to participation in Trinitarian life. In the refinements that I am suggesting, *gratia gratum faciens* is the communication of the divine love that welcomes one into Trinitarian life, and the dynamic state of being in love is the habitual charity that flows from that gift, mediated by the judgments of value that proceed from the gift itself and that "breathe" such love in return, judgments that participate in the Word's role in active spiration.

Sanctifying grace, then, is a created share in the active spiration that is Father and Son breathing the eternal Spirit of Love, while the habit of charity, the antecedent universal willingness that is disposed to return good for evil, the dynamic state that proceeds from the gift of divine love, is a created share in the passive spiration that is the Holy Spirit. This willingness is itself a gift that discloses itself in the succession of free acts of "originated loving" to which the gift of God's love, the judgments of value born of that gift, and the willing of the end in charity give rise. We have here the entire dramatic scenario for locating in human religious experience *gratia operans* and *gratia cooperans,* in the orders of both habitual and actual grace.

Given these refinements, then, the analogy that Lonergan suggests in "Christology Today" undergoes several modifications. It might be said that it undergoes a reduplication. For there is an analogy from reception of divine *agapē* to judgments of value corresponding to a universalist form of faith, and from these together to the proceeding habitual state of being in love; and there is a further analogy from that habitual state of being in love now constituted as a created relation to Father and Son, through further judgments of value, to acts of loving that proceed from *agapē* and its word of value, its *verbum spirans amorem.* This reflects a complication of the relation expressed in chapter 2 between Lonergan's later analogy and the analogy I am suggesting.

Now it is true that Lonergan's initial sketch in "Christology Today" of a Trinitarian analogy that begins with love does not necessarily imply a supernatural analogy, an analogy within the order of grace, the analogy of created participations in active and passive spiration, since there are other forms of being in love besides the otherworldly love that is my preferred locus. But neither does it exclude the possibility of such an analogy, and this possibility is what I propose to pursue here. Any of the three kinds of love may function in an analogy that starts from love, but it seems antecedently probable that Lonergan would be partial to an analogy that is based on the total self-transcendence that is the gift of God's own love. But my stress is on being on the receiving end of unqualified love as this gives rise to judgments of value that one would not utter were one not gifted in this way. These judgments "spirate" the universal willingness that alone can meet the problem of evil in self-sacrificing love. The first analogy in the supernatural order moves from the state of being on the receiving end of a love that is without conditions, qualifications, restrictions, reservations, to a set of judgments of value that proceed from such giftedness, and from these considered together to the antecedently habitual universal willingness that cumulatively gives rise to acts of loving that coalesce into an ever firmer disposition of charity. The *agapē* received as a love without conditions is the graced analogue for the divine Father, the judgments of value that proceed from that state of being loved without conditions constitute the graced analogue for the divine Word, and these two considered together function in graced consciousness in a manner remotely analogous to the way active spiration functions in divine consciousness, precisely because they are a created participation in the divine Father and Son together breathing the Holy Spirit. As from being gifted with love and consequent judgments of value there proceeds the antecedent willingness that coalesces free acts of loving into an ever firmer disposition of charity, so from divine paternity and filiation together there proceeds the Love that is the Holy Spirit. Such is the analogy of grace I am suggesting, building on Lonergan's shift of the significance of the psychological analogy from what it had been in the tradition to a new level of exposition and relevance.

2.1.4 Lonergan's Earlier and Later Analogies and the Times of Election

Thesis 26: *Lonergan's early analogy corresponds to* Insight's *account of decision and to Ignatius Loyola's third time of election, and his later analogy corresponds to* Method's *account of judgments of value and decision and to Ignatius's second time of election. Our distinct analogy,* *a development upon Lonergan's second analogy, reflects participation in divine active and passive spiration.*

What, then, is the difference between this position and the analogy found in Thomas's *Summa theologiae, Prima pars,* questions 27 through 43, and in a far more expansive form in Lonergan's earlier systematics of the Trinity? The difference between the two analogies is basically the difference between Lonergan's earlier and later accounts of judgments of value and decision: the earlier analogy corresponds to the earlier account of these realities, the account found in *Insight,* while the later analogy corresponds to the later account presented in *Method in Theology.*

There are, then, two quite distinct treatments of judgments of value and decision in Lonergan's writings. In *Insight,* in Lonergan's own words, the good is "the intelligent and reasonable." A good decision is a decision consistent with what one *knows* to be true and good. The decision-making process is very similar to the cognitional process, adding only the further element of free choice. Decision is an extension of intelligence and reason into the realm of action. In the process one assembles the data, one has a practical insight into what is to be done, one grasps that the evidence supports the practical insight, one judges that this is to be done, one freely chooses to do it. Again, the good is the intelligent and reasonable. There is no explicit mention of a fourth level of consciousness, a level beyond the three cognitional levels of experience, understanding, and judgment, but if in fact there is a fourth level latent in this account, it lies only in free choice and the consequent action. Even the judgment is not explicitly called a judgment of value in *Insight*'s treatment of "rational self-consciousness."

In *Method in Theology,* on the other hand, the good is, as Lonergan says, a notion distinct from the intelligent and reasonable. This does not mean, obviously, that the good is the stupid and silly, but that it is intended in a kind of question that is distinct from the question for intelligence, What is it? and from the question for judgment, Is it so? The question that intends the good is rather something like, Is this worthwhile? Is it truly or only apparently good? Is it better than such and such an alternative way of proceeding? The good is aspired to in an intentional response of feeling to values. Possible values are apprehended in the feelings that accompany deliberative insights. The judgment of value that knows the good proceeds from a discernment of these feelings in which possible values are apprehended, in order to determine which are the possible values that are apprehended by love and which are ambiguous or not at all to be acknowledged from the standpoint of performative self-transcendence or personal authenticity.

Such discernment is a very precarious affair. We are easily subject to illusion and deception. Still, when these judgments of value are made by a virtuous or authentic person with a good conscience, or even better by a person in love in an unqualified fashion, by one who is in the dynamic state of being in love with God, what is good is clearly known. There is no other criterion beyond authenticity or integrity. The good is then brought about by deciding and living up to one's decisions.

All of this activity, from the intending of value all the way up to and through fidelity to good decision, belongs now to a fourth level of consciousness, a level whose operations are beyond those that occur at the three levels constitutive of cognitional process, that is, experience, understanding, and judgment of fact.

Thus, there are significant differences between the two presentations of decision. The second account offers a much fuller expansion of consciousness, especially at the fourth level. The difference is found precisely in the following sentences from *Method in Theology*:

> Intermediate between judgments of fact and judgments of value lie apprehensions of value. Such apprehensions are given in feelings. The feelings in question are not ... non-intentional states, trends, urges, that are related to efficient and final causes but not to objects. Again, they are not intentional responses to such objects as the agreeable or disagreeable, the pleasant or painful, the satisfying or dissatisfying. For, while these are objects, still they are ambiguous objects that may prove to be truly good or bad or only apparently good or bad. Apprehensions of value occur in a further category of intentional response which greets either the ontic value of a person or the qualitative value of beauty, of understanding, of truth, of noble deeds, of virtuous acts, of great achievements.[30]

These intermediate apprehensions of possible values in feelings are not mentioned anywhere in the account of decision in *Insight*.

Now it is often thought that the treatment in *Method in Theology* represents an alternative position to the treatment in *Insight*, and that in Lonergan's view the presentation in *Insight* should be discarded in favor of that which appears in *Method*. I have long resisted this position, even if Lonergan himself may have held it (and there is some evidence that he did).[31] In my view each of Lonergan's articulations of the dynamics of decision has its own limited validity. We sometimes do make decisions in the way articulated in *Insight*, and at other times we follow the mode of operation specified in *Method in Theology*. The two articulations complement each other. The first is not overshadowed by the second. Rather, they mark distinct times of making decisions, where the times are a function of the disposition of the existential subject. They are both permeated by love and grace. And the criteria of both accounts must be satisfied in every decision that we make.

The basis for my position is found not in Lonergan, but in St Ignatius Loyola. I have argued elsewhere that Lonergan's two approaches to decision-making present the general form of two of the three times of election presented in the Ignatian *Spiritual Exercises*.[32] The account in *Insight* presents the general form of St Ignatius's third time of election, and the account in *Method in Theology* the general form of the second time. In the second time, "much light and knowledge is obtained by experiencing consolations and desolations, and by experience of the discernment of various spirits," whereas "the third time is one of tranquility: when one considers, first, for what one is born, that is, to praise God our Lord, and to save one's soul; and when, desiring this, one chooses as the means to this end a kind or state of life within the bounds of the church, in order that one may thereby be helped to serve God our Lord, and to save one's soul. I said a time of tranquility; that is, when the soul is not agitated by divers spirits, but enjoys the use of its natural powers freely and quietly."[33] As there is a complementarity between the second and third times in St Ignatius, so there is a complementarity between the two presentations of decision in Lonergan. That is, the judgment of value and the decision that one arrives at in Ignatius's second time, by discerning affective pulls and counterpulls ("divers spirits"), must be able to be adjudicated as well by the criteria of intelligence, reason, and responsibility that are explicitly appealed to in the third time; conversely, the judgments of value and decisions that are arrived at in Ignatius's third time must produce the same "peace of a good conscience" on the part of a virtuous person that would result from the proper discernment of affective pulls and counterpulls in the second time. So too, the decisions that one arrives at by employing intelligence and reason as outlined in *Insight* must be confirmed by the peace of a good conscience, whereas the decisions that one reaches by the discernment of affective pulls and counterpulls, as in the account in *Method in Theology*, must be able to be adjudicated by the criteria of intelligence and reasonableness, however much these may be modified by the life of grace, where what seems foolishness to the wise of this world may be really the wisdom of God.

The account of decision in *Insight* explicitly prescinds from any discussion of affective involvement,[34] and so it at least implicitly presupposes that the person making a decision is not agitated in such a way that one is prevented from employing his or her natural powers of experiencing, understanding, judging, and deciding. In this account one's decisions are good decisions if in fact they are harmonious with what one knows to be true and good. Moral integrity is a matter of generating decisions and consequent actions that are consistent with what one knows, that is, that are consistent with the inner words of judgments of fact and judgments of value that one has sufficient reason to hold to be true. If this is the case, then Lonergan's account in *Insight* would remain as permanently valid as St Ignatius's account of the third time of election. It just is not the only account, because it names only one of the times of making a good decision.

In contrast, in the presentation that is found in *Method in Theology* it is self-transcendent affectivity, affectivity that matches the unrestricted reach of the transcendental notion of value, the affectivity of a person in love, in the limit the affectivity of a person in love in an unqualified fashion, with the charity that participates in God's own love poured out in one's heart through the Holy Spirit that has been given one (Romans 5.5), that provides the criteria for the decision. In the latter case the question becomes, Which course of action reflects, embodies, incarnates the self-transcendent love that matches the reach of the transcendental notion of value, especially as that unrestricted intention reaches fulfilment in God's gift of God's own love as embodied in the incarnate Word of God, in his life, death, and resurrection from the dead? The answer to that question gives the indication as to the direction in which one is to go as one heads toward a judgment of value and a consequent decision. This presentation, again, corresponds to St Ignatius's second time of election.

Now these two accounts of decision provide, respectively, the elements also of Lonergan's two distinct but complementary approaches to a psychological analogy for a systematic understanding of the divine processions and relations. At this point the Trinitarian mysticism of Lonergan joins and – if I may be so bold as to suggest it – advances the Trinitarian mysticism of St Ignatius. If I am right about the correspondence of Lonergan and Ignatius on times of decision, then we can say that Lonergan relates the Trinity to St Ignatius's moments for making decisions that proceed from authentic judgments of value.

In the first psychological analogy found in Lonergan's work, which is presented in intricate detail in the systematic part of his work *De Deo Trino* (*The Triune God: Systematics*), the analogue in the creature is found in those moments of existential self-constitution in which we grasp the sufficiency of evidence regarding what it would be good for one to be, utter the judgment of value, "This is good," and proceed to decisions commensurate with that grasp of evidence and judgment of value. From the act of grasping the evidence there proceeds the act of judging value, and from the two together there proceeds the love that embraces the good and carries it out. The analogy follows completely the account of decision presented in *Insight*: from grasp of evidence to judgment of value, and from grasp of evidence and judgment of value together to good decision.[35] So too in divine self-constitution, from the Father's grasp of the grounds for affirming the goodness of all that the Father is and knows (including the divine economy of our salvation), there proceeds the eternal Word of the Father saying Yes to it all, and from the Father and the Word together there proceeds the eternal mutual Love of Father and Son that is the Holy Spirit. This theology of God's own self-constitution in knowledge, word, and love is informed by an analogy with human rational self-consciousness as Lonergan has understood the latter in *Insight*. One's appropriation of one's rational self-consciousness in the form in which it is presented in *Insight* – and it is such consciousness that functions without technical self-appropriation in St Ignatius's third time of election – will ultimately entail recognizing those processes, those processions, as constituting an *image* of the Trinitarian processions themselves, the *imago Dei*. And of course we must emphasize with the Fourth Lateran Council that "one cannot note any similarity between Creator and creature – however great – that would obviate the need always to note an ever greater dissimilarity." In this instance, the ever greater dissimilarity is shown in part in the fact that the human analogue is constituted by the procession of act from act. The judgment of value is an act distinct from the act of grasping evidence, and the act of loving decision is an act distinct from both the act of grasping evidence and the act of judgment of value. The similarity lies in the fact that all is in the realm of "act." But in God there are not really distinct acts but really distinct relations within the one infinite act that God is. The linking of consubstantiality with emanation or procession is the heart of the Trinitarian mystery. We are not able to penetrate any further than this. We are asked simply to affirm that this is the way it must be and bow before the mystery.

Now in his later work Lonergan proposes or at least suggests the distinct psychological analogy for the Trinity that I have already cited. This analogy is more closely related to the account of decision in *Method in Theology* and to St Ignatius's second time of election. As moral integrity, according to the presentation in *Method in Theology*, entails generating the judgments of value of a person who is in love, and as religious integrity entails generating the judgments of value of a person who is in love in an unqualified way, without reservations or conditions, and as those judgments of value are carried out in decisions that are acts of loving, so the Father now is infinite and eternal being-in-love, *Agapē* that generates a Word, the eternal Yes that is the Son, a Word that breathes love, a Yes that grounds the Proceeding Love that is breathed forth from *Agapē* and from its manifestation in such a Word.

In *De Deo Trino*, where the earlier analogy is developed more extensively perhaps than at any other point in the entire history of theology, Lonergan repeats over and over again the affirmation of the First Vatican Council that we are able to attain an imperfect, analogical, developing, and most fruitful understanding of the divine mysteries by proceeding from analogies with what we know by natural knowledge. It is clear from this constant repetition of the Council's statement that he intends the analogy that he is presenting in *De Deo trino* to be an analogy from nature. It is a commonplace interpretation that, while the earlier analogy proceeds from below upwards in human consciousness, the later analogy proceeds from above downwards. But there is the much more important difference that we have already noticed. Each of the analogies is an analogy found in the creature, but the earlier analogy is found in our natural powers of understanding uttering a word of assent and of love proceeding from understanding and word, while the created analogue in the second analogy allows for the possibility of a basis in the supernatural order, in the experienced gift of God's own love, the felt sense of being on the receiving end of an unqualified love and of being invited to participate in that love wherever such participation will take one. As I said earlier, this is the felt sense, as it were, of "gratia gratum faciens," and so is the conscious manifestation of what theology has traditionally called sanctifying grace. Together with the set of judgments of value that constitute the faith that is the eye opened by the reception of such love, it releases the dynamic state of being in love in an unqualified way, the state that corresponds to what theology has traditionally called the habit of charity. In Lonergan's theology, sanctifying grace is a created participation in, and imitation of, the active spiration of Father and Word lovingly breathing the Holy Spirit, while the habit of charity that flows from sanctifying grace is a created participation in, and imitation of, the passive spiration, the divine Proceeding Love, that is the Holy Spirit. To repeat what I introduced in part 1, more concretely for Christians sanctifying grace is a created participation in, and imitation of, the Incarnate Word, the incarnate *Verbum spirans Amorem*, whose humanity is itself a participation in, and imitation of, the one he called "Abba, Father," the imitation of whom Jesus characterizes in the words, "[L]ove your enemies and pray for those who persecute you; in this way you will be children of your Father in heaven, for he causes his sun to rise on the bad as well as the good, and his rain to fall on honest and dishonest alike" (Matthew 5.44–45). *That* is being in love in an unqualified fashion, supernatural charity. As the Holy Spirit proceeds from the *Agapē* that is the Father and from the Word that the Father utters in saying Yes to God's own goodness, so the habit of charity – a love that extends to enemies and that gives sunshine and rain to all alike – flows from our created participation in, and imitation of, that active spiration, that is, from the entitative change that is the grace that makes us not only pleasing to God, *gratia gratum faciens*, but somehow imitative of the divine goodness because participants in it. "You must therefore be perfect as your heavenly Father is perfect" (Matthew 5.48). Again, it is in this participation and imitation, this mimesis of God, if you will, that we are moved beyond the otherwise endless cycle of violence, recrimination, judgment, blame, accusation, murder, hate, and false religion. Such is the state of grace understood as an interpersonal situation whose founding subjects are the three divine subjects as they have chosen to come and dwell in us and with us.[36]

In the first, natural analogy, the analogy that recognizes in human nature an image of the Trinitarian processions, love flows from knowledge and word, as Lonergan emphasizes over and over again in *De Deo Trino*. In the second, supernatural analogy, the analogy that recognizes that grace makes us not only images of but also participants in the Trinitarian relations, the felt sense of being on the receiving end of unqualified love precedes a knowledge that in Lonergan's late work is explicitly called "faith," where faith is understood as the knowledge born of love. More precisely, this knowledge born of love entails (1) the grasp of evidence that is possible only for one aware of such love and (2) the judgments of value that proceed from that grasp. In its perfection this reflective act of understanding is the grasp of evidence for nonviolent resistance even to hatred and evil rather than for violent return of evil for evil, and faith's judgments of value are judgments that proceed from that grasp. From this felt sense of unqualified love and its *verbum spirans amorem* there flows the dynamic state of being in love that is charity.

More radically, however, it must be said that here too love flows from knowledge. The felt sense of being on the receiving end of unqualified love flows, not from our knowledge but from the eternal *Verbum spirans Amorem*, the Word breathing Love, that is the image of the eternal Father, the Word who himself proceeds from eternity as the Father's judgment of value pronouncing an infinite Yes to God's own goodness, to the goodness of one who makes his sun to rise on the bad as well as the good, and his rain to fall on honest and dishonest alike. And the dynamic state of being in love that is charity proceeds from the faith that is the knowledge born of the felt sense of "gratia gratum faciens."

In this case the psychological analogue for the Trinitarian processions, while it is still a created analogue, is no longer a natural one. For the felt sense of "gratia gratum faciens" that is the analogue for the divine Father is itself the conscious representation of the supernatural created habitual grace that we have known as sanctifying grace. And so the psychological analogy now provides, not simply an image of the Trinitarian processions, but a participation in them and *an imitation, a mimesis, of them*. We can say this even as we remember once again the strictures of the Fourth Lateran Council: "one cannot note any similarity between Creator and creature – however great – that would obviate the need always to note an ever greater dissimilarity." In this instance the dissimilarity is obvious. Who of us can honestly claim that he or she is spontaneously always ready to conform to the evangelical injunction to imitate the divine Father in allowing "sun and rain" to be given to those who hate us as well as to those who love us? But this is a constitutive element in the kingdom of God, the reign of God, whose structure constitutes the unified field structure of our systematic theology.

To return for a moment to St Ignatius's times of election: (1) in the third time, we employ our natural powers of experiencing, understanding, judging, and deciding to arrive at good decisions, and in so doing we are embodying the natural analogue for the divine processions, where we are images of the Trinity; Lonergan's account of decision in *Insight* provides the general form of such a set of operations; (2) in the second time, we are discerning the pulls and counterpulls of affective resonances, so as to arrive at decisions that will promote in us not only an image of the Trinity but participations in the divine lovableness uttering the eternal Yes and with that Yes breathing the eternal Proceeding Love, and so that will enable us to be not only images of but also participants in the divine processions; Lonergan's account in *Method in Theology* presents the general form of this quite distinct process of decision; and (3) in St Ignatius's first time, of which I have not yet spoken, that conscious representation of "gratia gratum faciens" and its word of value judgment are so dominant that the loving decisions and actions flow spontaneously forth from them in a way that admits no doubt as to where they come from or whose life is being reflected in them: "I live, now not I, but Christ lives in me." This corresponds to Lonergan's modification of an Augustinian maxim, "Ama Deum et fac quod vis, Love God and do what you will." In these instances, the apprehension of values in loving affectivity stands to judgments of value, not as direct insight, which may be right or wrong, but rather as reflective insights, grasping the fulfilment of conditions, stand to judgments of fact. Whereas in the second time the apprehension of values in feelings is an apprehension of *possible* values, in the first time there are no further questions, and one knows that this is the case.

The analogy grounded in love, especially when that love is God's love poured out in our hearts through the Holy Spirit who has been given to us, opens onto the second point of significance for the requirement of interiorly and religiously differentiated consciousness. For, since the four-point hypothesis speaks of realities that are named in special categories, the base of these categories in religiously differentiated consciousness must also be specified as carefully as possible. This is particularly true for the second and third points of the hypothesis, those having to do with sanctifying grace and the habit of charity as created participations, respectively, of active and passive spiration. In fact, our understanding of the first and fourth points of the hypothesis (the secondary act of existence of the incarnate Word and the light of glory) can be had only by extrapolation from and modification of our understanding of the second and third points. These created participations in active and passive spiration are precisely the area in which the supernatural creaturely analogy for the Trinitarian relations is developed. Thus such efforts will be providing something of significance, I believe, for the theological treatment of spirituality. What, in terms derived from religiously differentiated consciousness, is such a created participation in divine life? How can we name terms and relations in religious experience that express created participations in active and passive spiration? And, since active spiration is identical with paternity and filiation considered together, the question reflects our participation in Trinitarian life *in toto*. That is the question. That is the task. The first part of this book and what we have written to this point in the present chapter indicate the way in which it can be met.

2.2 History

Thesis 27: *The second component of the unified field structure is provided when the general categories of a contemporary systematic theology are focused around the dialectical process of human history.*

There is a second requirement. I indicated in *What Is Systematic Theology?* and I have repeated here that the systematics that I wish to begin will assume the general form of a theology of history, and this means not only that the realities named in its special categories must be mediated with those named in its general categories – this would be the case no matter what the option regarding the overall form of systematic theology – but also that the general categories will be focused around the complex dialectical process of human history. These categories are at present partly supplied by Lonergan (most subtly but also most completely in his late paper "Natural Right and Historical Mindedness")[37] and partly, I hope, by my book *Theology and the Dialectics of History*. But no doubt there are more categories to be generated on the basis of these still early reachings for a comprehensive heuristic of history. I think in particular of Lonergan's efforts to develop a macroeconomic theory in the context of his notion of the dialectic of history,[38] and of the issue of articulating the effects of grace on the cultural, social, and vital levels in the scale of values.

In *Theology and the Dialectics of History*, relying on Lonergan, I add or develop the following notions: (1) the analogy of the dialectics of the subject, community, and culture, (2) distinct dialectics of contraries and contradictories in each of these realms, and (3) the scale of values as explaining the intelligible ongoing relations in history among these three complex dialectical processes.[39] The mediation of general and special categories in a theology of history would also enable us to generate theological doctrines regarding revelation, original sin, redemption, church, sacraments, creation, and praxis, which are not explicitly included in the core "focal meanings"[40] contained in the four-point hypothesis, and to submit to systematic consideration these doctrines, as well as those that are explicitly mentioned in that core statement. But that mediation itself will primarily be a matter of bringing the supernatural realities affirmed in the four-point hypothesis, realities that constitute the core of religious values, to bear on the other levels of value: personal, cultural, social, and vital. In this book I am primarily concerned with the relationship between religious and personal values. While there is some mention of the other levels of value, the next volume, which treats persons in relation, will be much more to the point regarding the integrity of culture and the justice of the good of social order. All of these mediations will express human participation in Trinitarian life as it is at work in the very heart of the dialectical process of history. They will give a contemporary theological meaning to the expression "reign of God." Such a move, I believe, is essential if in fact the functional specialty "doctrines" is to be organized around the theme of redemption in history and if the mediated object of the functional specialty "systematics" is to be *Geschichte*.[41]

The implications of such a procedure can already be dimly glimpsed. It is one thing to transpose, for example, Trinitarian theology into categories dictated by interiorly and religiously differentiated consciousness. Such a transposition is essential for a contemporary systematic-theological understanding of the mystery we profess in faith. But we are already familiar with the historical precedents of such a transposition. The psychological analogy of Augustine, which begins from *memoria*, seems to move both in the order of nature and in that of grace. Aquinas's analogy and that of the early Lonergan, where the starting point is understanding, provide successive developments of the analogy from nature, culminating in Lonergan's articulation of the analogy in terms of interiorly differentiated consciousness. Lonergan's later analogy begins with being in love. It can be interpreted as an analogy developed from nature or as one developed from religiously differentiated consciousness. But if the latter starting point is desired, this analogy best gives way, I believe, to the further variant on the same structure that I have suggested in chapter 2, where perhaps Augustine's starting point in *memoria* is rejoined. But it is another thing to add to this requirement of self-appropriation, which in one form or another and to a greater or lesser extent is already followed by or rooted in the great Trinitarian theologies of Augustine, Aquinas, and Lonergan, the additional requirement of formulating all this material eventually in terms of a theory of history. This adds a new dimension to the theology of the Trinity. The direct impact, of course, is on that dimension of Trinitarian theology that treats the divine missions. But

(1) when intelligent, reasonable, and responsible emanations in the order of nature and emanations in the order of love in the supernatural order become the source of the making of history, of historical progress, of healing and creating in history,[42]

(2) when these emanations are conceived as the analogue according to which we are to approach some imperfect understanding of the processions within God of Word and Spirit, and

(3) when the missions are identified with the processions linked to an external term as consequent condition of the procession being also a mission, the full implication is something like this:

(a) the emanations of Word and Spirit in God, linked to their appropriate contingent external terms in history (the *esse secundarium* of the Incarnate Word, sanctifying grace, the habit of charity, and – beyond history but proleptically within it in the form of hope – the light of glory), are the ultimate condition of possibility of any consistent and sustained intelligent and responsible emanations in human beings, precisely through the gift of the Holy Spirit which is the eternal emanation of the Spirit in God linked to its external term in history and proceeding not only from the eternal Father and Word but also from the same Word as incarnate and as sent by the Father;[43] and

(b) such a collaboration of autonomous spiritual processions, divine and human, is the condition of the possibility of the consistent authentic performance of that normative source of meaning that, building on Lonergan's analysis in "Natural Right and Historical Mindedness," I have already identified with the taut dialectical tension of psyche and intentionality in human conscious acts – that very normative source that is the origin of progress in history, whether in a creative mode "from below upwards" or a healing mode "from above downwards."[44] In his later work on the dialectic of history, Lonergan emphasizes the two dimensions of the normative source of meaning in history, intentional and psychic. In addition to the precepts of authentic intentional performance there is reference to a dimension whose conscious manifestation can be called "psychic": "a tidal movement that begins before consciousness, unfolds through sensitivity, intelligence, rational reflection, responsible deliberation, only to find its rest beyond all of these" in love.[45] Elsewhere the same dimension is called "the passionateness of being" that "underpins and accompanies and reaches beyond the subject as experientially, intelligently, rationally, morally conscious."[46] The articulation of this psychic dimension and of its integration with the operations of intentional consciousness is the meaning of most of my earliest published work. I now conceive this dimension in terms of three facets of an aesthetic-dramatic operator: the symbolic operator that precedes the emergence of intentional consciousness, the affective operator that accompanies such consciousness, and the communitarian operator that reaches beyond the subject as experientially, intelligently, rationally, and morally conscious.

The starting point for a systematic theology, then, consists in the elaboration of the unified field structure. The first step lies in unfolding the four-point theological hypothesis, with the help of analogies drawn from cognitional and ethical theory and from religious experience. The second step relates that unfolding in greater detail to the complex dialectical process of history, though the first step will itself incorporate a large amount of material relevant to the theological theory of history. The general character of this unified field structure is found in the title of the project, *The Trinity in History*. For the four-point hypothesis presents an analogical understanding of Trinitarian doctrine, where the analogy is twofold, natural and supernatural, and the theory of history completes the unified field structure precisely by locating the realities named in the four-point hypothesis in the dynamic unfolding of human history.

3   The Character of the Starting Point

> **Thesis 28:** *The analogy proposed here differs from those of Aquinas and the early Lonergan on two counts: it is explicitly located in the supernatural order, and it initiates a theology of history.*

If the unified field structure in its entirety is the beginning, then the beginning of the beginning lies in a systematic understanding of the doctrine of the triune God. But this systematic understanding will differ from those of Aquinas and the early Lonergan in two important and far-reaching respects.

Like those theologies, it will proceed by analogy from naturally known realities to an obscure understanding of divine mystery.

Like those theologies, it will follow the way of teaching and learning rather than the way of discovery, and so it will begin with those realities whose understanding does not presuppose the understanding of anything else, but which, once understood, render possible the understanding of everything else. In Trinitarian theology this means starting with the divine processions.

But unlike those theologies, it will, almost from the beginning and not simply at the end of the entire systematic Trinitarian treatise, appeal also to an analogy with created realities in the supernatural order, that is, to an analogy with what we know only by revelation, to an analogy with realities in the order of grace: realities that enable us consciously to participate in, and so to imitate, the conscious inner life of the very God whose mystery we are attempting to understand. I say "*almost* from the beginning" because even these analogies from created supernatural realities, precisely as humanly constructed analogies, are themselves grounded in analogies from what is naturally known. And it should be emphasized that the imitation of God's life is at first and for a long time in most people's lives not a deliberate mimesis, but a function of the participation in divine life that is given to us in grace, whether we are cognizant of this or not.[47]

The first difference from the classic expositions of the psychological analogy, then, is that there are not only natural analogues for the divine processions and relations but also supernatural analogues in the realm of created grace, and that both of these sets of analogues can and should be drawn upon in the elaboration of a systematic understanding of this central mystery of faith. While we will begin, as we must, with the natural analogues, the introduction of the supernatural analogies encouraged by Lonergan's later remarks on Trinitarian theology and developed in our second chapter opens the possibility for the following developments:

(1) What a metaphysical theology calls the secondary act of existence of the assumed humanity of the incarnate Word, which grounds the relation of that assumed humanity to the eternal divine Word, is a supernatural analogue for the divine relation of paternity, a created participation in and imitation of the Father, of the one who speaks the Word, of "Abba." "Whoever has seen me has seen the Father" (John 14.9). Again, the divine Word as immanent in God does not speak; the divine Word is spoken by the Father; the incarnate Word speaks, but he speaks only what he hears from the Father.

(2) What a metaphysical theology calls sanctifying grace includes the felt sense of being on the receiving end of an unqualified

being in love. It is a supernatural analogue for divine active spiration, a created participation in and imitation of the Father and the Son as the one principle, the "lovableness," from which the Holy Spirit proceeds. As the Father and the Son breathe the Holy Spirit, so sanctifying grace, as elevating central form and as providing an orientation that favors evidence for affirming the goodness of being and that issues in an affirmation of value and an openness to ever greater mystery on the part of one who is in love in an unqualified fashion and so with a participation in God's own love, gives rise to the disposition inspiring loving acts that coalesce into an ever firmer habit of charity.

(3) What a metaphysical theology calls the habit of charity is a supernatural analogue for divine passive spiration, a created participation in and imitation of the Holy Spirit, who proceeds eternally from the Father and the Son. As the Holy Spirit proceeds from the Father and the Son, so the habit of charity proceeds from sanctifying grace, from the created and tacitly experienced participation in the *notionaliter diligere* of Father and Son as they breathe proceeding Love.

And (4) what a metaphysical theology calls the light of glory is a supernatural analogue for divine filiation, a created participation in and imitation of the Son, the Word, whose entire being is a relation to the eternal Father from whom he proceeds and to whom he refers, subjects, and brings home all things.

This is part of the significance of accepting the four-point hypothesis as the special-categorial component of the unified field structure of systematic theology.

Obviously the second and third of these supernatural analogues will be the most prominent, and it is to them that we refer when we develop and modify Lonergan's later analogy. Only by extrapolating from our own participation in divine life can we find some structural understanding of the human Jesus's created participation in divine paternity (first analogue) and of the saints' participation in the divine Son (fourth analogue), even as we remain aware of the differences in the constitution of the various participations.

The second difference in the systematic understanding of the triune God that I am proposing vis-à-vis the classical psychological analogies of Aquinas and the early Lonergan is that this Trinitarian theology initiates a theology of history. It spells out the religious values that are the condition of the possibility of an integral functioning of the entire scale of values, where personal, cultural, social, and vital values are related to one another in such a way as to yield the structure of history. As sustained personal integrity is impossible without divine grace, so sustained social harmony grounded in authentic cultural values that issue in a just social order is itself a function of the same gift of divine life. This vision of history has been spelled out at least inchoately in *Theology and the Dialectics of History* and will be largely assumed here. When placed into the context of a systematic theology, it will yield a doctrine of social grace.

4   Theological Development

> **Thesis 29:** *The proposals being offered here represent an instance of the genetic sequence of systematic theologies. The starting point now becomes a synthetic position that treats together the divine processions and the missions that are identical with the processions joined to a created term as consequent condition of the missions. The missions are the divine processions in history.*

I am proposing here an instance of what in *What Is Systematic Theology?* I called the genetic sequence of systematic theologies.[48] Precisely because of the Trinitarian theologies of Aquinas and the early Lonergan, theologies which begin with the processions, move to the relations, progress to the persons, and end with the missions, we are now able to come full circle and begin a systematics of the Trinity somewhere else: namely, with a synthetic position that treats together both the divine processions and the divine missions. The missions are the processions in history, the processions linked with a created consequent condition that makes it possible that the procession be also a mission.

This "somewhere else" does not depart from the starting point that is to be found in Aquinas and the early Lonergan, but sublates that starting point into a more comprehensive dogmatic-theological context that has emerged partly as a result of their work. The four-point hypothesis itself is part of our starting point, not of our conclusion, and that hypothesis aims at an obscure understanding not only of divine processions but also of divine missions and of the created consequent conditions of divine missions – the secondary act of existence relating the assumed humanity to the eternal divine Word, sanctifying grace, the habit of charity, and the light of glory – as a new set of analogues from which we can gain an obscure understanding of the processions and relations immanent in God's being. Theology is an ongoing enterprise, and what was not possible for Aquinas because of the historical limitations of the dogmatic-theological context of his time, and what Lonergan arrived at only toward the end of his systematics of the Trinity, may well be the starting point for another generation, precisely because of Aquinas's own gains in understanding and Lonergan's firmer rooting of these gains in interiorly and religiously differentiated consciousness.

Thus, as the way of discovery that Lonergan outlines in *De Deo trino: Pars dogmatica*[49] ended with Augustine's psychological analogy, which then became the starting point of the way of teaching and learning, so Lonergan's particular embodiment of the way of teaching and learning ended with a four-point hypothesis that now informs the starting point of a new venture along the same kind of path, the *ordo doctrinae*. If we are beginning our systematics in its entirety where Lonergan ended his systematics of the Trinity, it is only on the basis of the development found in his own Trinitarian theology that we are able to do so. He began with the processions. We begin, on a "macro" level, with the processions and missions together, affirming with Lonergan's assistance that they are the same reality, except that the mission adds a created contingent external term that is the consequent condition of the procession being also a mission. The procession alone constitutes the mission, but the procession is not the mission unless there is the created contingent external term.

As is clear from the foregoing, we must, of course, also relate these supernatural analogues of divine life to operations and states identified in our own interiority and to our participation in the historical dialectic. We are obliged to this

(1) by the core meanings expressed in the passage that we have taken as central to our systematics, the four-point hypothesis,
(2) by the stress on interiorly and religiously differentiated consciousness, and
(3) by the insistence that a systematic theology must be a theology of history.

It will be crucial, then, to pinpoint just what we are talking about by identifying it with operations and states in interiority. And that is not easy, especially in the case of the supernatural analogy. A phenomenology of grace has barely begun to be composed.

In fact, in the case of the secondary act of existence of the incarnate Word, there are available to us no data whatever for such a phenomenology, even if the affirmation of the *esse secundarium* can be shown to be isomorphic with human acts of reasonable judgment, and even if we are able to conclude from dogmatic premises something about the consciousness and knowledge of Jesus.

Nor is there available any material that would enable us to compose a phenomenology of the light of glory and the beatific vision. The closest approximation would be found in the most profound mystical experience.

In the case of both the secondary act of existence and the light of glory, then, we must move by extrapolation from what is available to us, namely, the dynamic state of being on the receiving end of unqualified love and the consequent originated loving that follows habitually from such a felt sense.

Thus, only in the realm of the supernatural analogues of active and passive spiration do we have the data for a phenomenology of grace; and even there, only with great difficulty.

Thus too, Pneumatology will become, in such a systematic theology, the source of much of Christology and eschatology. That too is a function of the evolving dogmatic-theological context. Only today is the theology of the Holy Spirit emerging into its own in systematic theology: only in a day when perhaps the very future of the human race depends on our being able to specify with a precision sophisticated in the way of religious interiority just how we can affirm that the Holy Spirit is poured out on all people and is found in religions other than Christianity as well as in the Christian churches. This will not, may not, entail the kind of "Spirit-Christology" that sets itself up as an alternative to "Logos-Christology," though it will entail a Spirit-Christology that is in harmony with Logos-Christology. It is the relation of the assumed humanity of Jesus to the eternal Word that we will attempt to understand by extrapolating from the gift of the Holy Spirit in sanctifying grace and the habit of charity and then making the necessary adaptations demanded by the dogmatic tradition. In the course of working out such a Christology, the role of the Holy Spirit in the life of the incarnate Word will be stressed.

Lonergan's systematic treatment of Trinitarian doctrine in *The Triune God: Systematics* proceeds according to the same *via systematica* that Aquinas follows in his *Summa theologiae*, questions 27–43, in that, like Aquinas, he begins the systematic treatment with the divine processions, for understanding how processions can be said to exist in God does not presuppose an understanding of the other elements that will be treated in a systematics of the Trinity, but rather grounds our analogous and imperfect understanding of these other elements: relations, persons, notional acts, missions. "For the processions are the basis for the relations, and in accordance with our manner of conceiving, the divine persons are conceived subsequently to conceiving the relations."[50] Thus, like Aquinas, Lonergan moves from processions to relations, from processions and relations to persons in themselves, from the foregoing to persons in relation to one another, and from all of these to the divine missions of Word and Spirit. This order is just the reverse of the order of discovery through which the church arrived at its Trinitarian doctrines: missions, persons, relations, processions. The New Testament begins with the missions of the Son and of the Holy Spirit and moves to the three divine persons. Early theology, and especially the

Cappadocian Fathers, realized that the personal characteristics had to be understood. Augustine understood these in terms of relations, and then Aquinas came to the conclusion that an understanding of procession in God was the key to understanding the divine relations. Aquinas reversed the order of ideas, and began his Trinitarian theology by asking whether there are processions in God and answering how this could be the case.[51]

Our procedure here will also follow the *ordo doctrinae* or *via systematica*, but we take as our fundamental statement the unified field structure presented in chapter 7 of *What Is Systematic Theology?* and developed in the present chapter, namely, the four-point theological hypothesis linked to the theory of history proposed in *Theology and the Dialectics of History*. The four-point hypothesis links the processions and the missions, so that our Trinitarian starting point is the unity of these two. For reasons linked to the limitations of human thought and language, each of these components must be treated separately before they can be united into one *unified* field structure. But the consequence for our procedure here is that if we begin with the natural analogy for understanding divine processions, namely, the intelligent emanation of a word of "yes" from the grasp of sufficient evidence for a judgment of value and the responsible emanation of self-transcendent decision and love from that grasp and judgment considered as one principle of the latter emanation, we also move on from there to identify in the order of grace certain correlates, indeed participations and imitations, that correspond in some way to the divine mystery that we confess and are attempting to understand. This requirement is imposed by the dual standard of grounding everything in interiorly and religiously differentiated consciousness and constructing systematics as a theology of history.

Thus, if there is a divine relation of paternity, we must understand it not only by analogy with the grasp of evidence giving rise to the judgment of value but also from the very participation in and imitation of divine paternity that is found in history, namely, in the secondary act of existence of the incarnate Word, Jesus of Nazareth.

Again, if there is a divine relation of active spiration, which itself is identical with paternity and filiation together "breathing" the Holy Spirit, we must understand it not only by analogy with the combined influence of the grasp of evidence and the word of a judgment of value that proceeds from it, as these are the principle of acts of love and of good decisions; we must also understand this divine relation in the very participation in active spiration, in paternity-filiation, that is found in history, namely, in the entitative habit radicated by "gratia gratum faciens" in the essence of the soul, or rooted in the very core of our being, that initiates our sharing in the very *notionaliter diligere* of God; from this sharing there proceeds in human consciousness "from above," through faith and hope, the originated loving that has been metaphysically conceived as the habit of charity, our historical participation in and imitation of the Holy Spirit, who proceeds as *Amor procedens* from the Father and the Son.

In other words, in the supernatural analogy the grasp of evidence that is not only an analogy for the Father but also the created participation in and imitation of paternity, and the consequent "yes" that is not only an analogy for the Son but also the created participation in and imitation of filiation, are themselves in the supernatural order. They are the grasp of evidence (understanding) and the consequent "yes" (judgment) of a person already on the receiving end of God's own love (tacit, even ineffable, experience). What an earlier theology called sanctifying grace is an elevation of central form, of the unity-identity-whole of the human person, manifest consciously in a habitual orientation to the grasp of evidence and a consequent habitual "yes" on the part of one who is in love with God's love freely given in a gift that makes one pleasing to God in a quite special way. The grasp of evidence and the affirmation that together constitute the conscious dimension of this entitative habit spirate the habitual performance of loving acts. This grasp and affirmation are themselves habitual, the manifestation of what the medievals saw to be an entitative habit rooted at the deepest and most intimate core of our being. The latter is a habit that is a gift from God operating a person's participation in, and imitation of, divine active spiration. This habit is rephrased by Lonergan as the conscious dynamic state of unqualified being-in-love. But if we are going to continue to distinguish sanctifying grace from the habit of charity, as the four-point hypothesis invites us to do, it is important to specify some distinction in consciousness here; and I suggest that the distinction is one between this entitative habit manifesting itself in a felt sense of being on the receiving end of unqualified love, prompting the habitual grasp and affirmation of the lover in a set of value judgments, and, on the other hand, the habitual state of originated loving that flows from the felt sense and the judgments of value. The divine love is the starting point, since it is the gift of divine love that orients us to the habitual grasp of evidence for a global judgment of value that determines our entire life. The grasp of evidence and the judgment of value are the grasp and affirmation of one who already is in love, entitatively, by being loved. And they ground the habitual dynamic state that we call the habit of charity. To repeat, the distinction corresponds to the Trinitarian distinction between the *notionaliter diligere* that is Father-and-Son as one principle and the *amor procedens* that is the Holy Spirit. Because of this correspondence, these distinct terms ground the special basic relations of a systematic theology.

Again, if there is a divine relation of passive spiration, identical with the Holy Spirit who proceeds from Father-and-Son as one principle of divine emanation, we must understand that relation from the beginning not only (a) by analogy with the acts of love that proceed in human consciousness from the combined influence of evidence grasped and consequent judgment of value, but also (b) by analogy with the very participation in and imitation of passive spiration that is the habit of charity and the acts of unqualified love that proceed from the habit in a regular sequence of schemes of recurrence.

Finally, if there is a divine relation of filiation, which itself is identical with the eternally proceeding Word of God, we must understand it from the beginning not only by analogy with the word of a judgment of value that says yes to evidence grasped as conclusive regarding our own existential self-constitution as authentic human persons. We must understand it also by analogy with the very participation in and imitation of divine filiation that is the light of glory that enables the perfect return of all God's children to the divine Father in the inheritance promised to us in the incarnate Son and confirmed by the pledge of the gift of the Holy Spirit.

In other words, the basic hypotheses that will have a profound effect on the remainder of our systematic theology are more complex than those found at the beginning of Aquinas's or Lonergan's Trinitarian systematics. That greater complexity is a function of a theological history decisively influenced by Aquinas and Lonergan themselves. This history now permits us, from the very beginning, to add to the natural analogies employed in understanding the divine processions and relations the graced participations in those relations, and so to begin a Trinitarian systematics with the processions and missions as one piece. In the context of the theory of history constituted internally by the scale of values and the three dialectical processes of subjects, cultures, and social communities (that is, the theory proposed in *Theology and the Dialectics of History*), these graced participations constitute the realm of religious values. The theory of history based on the scale of values displays precisely what the historical significance and influence is of these religious values, these participations in and imitations of divine relations. For from above, grace conditions personal integrity and authenticity, which itself is the condition of possibility of genuine and developing cultural values. The latter, in turn, influence the formation of integrally dialectical communities at the level of social values, and only such communities functioning in recurrent schemes of a good of order guarantee the equitable distribution of vital goods to the entire community. The resultant of such an analysis will be a doctrine of social grace. I am suggesting a way of going about that task, a way that also connects with Lonergan's redefinition of what we have called "the state of grace." As we have seen, for Lonergan the state of grace is not an individual but a social reality. It is the divine-human interpersonal situation that resides in the three divine subjects giving themselves to us. That gift itself, while "intensely personal, utterly intimate," still "is not so private as to be solitary. It can happen to many, and they can form a community to sustain one another in their self-transformation and to help one another in working out the implications and fulfilling the promise of their new life. Finally, what can become communal can become historical. It can pass from generation to generation. It can spread from one cultural milieu to another. It can adapt to changing circumstances, confront new situations, survive into a different age, flourish in another period or epoch."[52]

This position is not a denial of the analogies from nature that provided Aquinas and Lonergan with an initial glimpse of the divine mysteries. Quite the contrary. These analogies are required if we are to have any understanding, however imperfect it may be, of the supernatural life itself that is our participation in the divine relations. For that reason, we will support the analogy we are presenting with a thorough presentation and interpretation of Lonergan's understanding of divine processions. Sanctifying grace, again, orients us to the elemental habitual grasp of evidence (understanding) and the elemental habitual consequent yes (judgment) that flow from being invested with a share in divine love (elemental experience recollected in *memoria*): the horizon of the graced person. Thus, if we are really to understand anything at all about sanctifying grace, we will have to understand what is meant by "elemental or tacit or ineffable experience," by "a grasp of evidence," and by a "consequent yes," and that means understanding the natural analogy.

Still, in his later work Lonergan proposes not only a natural analogy but also the possibility of a supernatural one, where, again, the psychological analogy "has its starting point in that higher synthesis of intellectual, rational, and moral consciousness that is the dynamic state of being in love. Such love manifests itself in its judgments of value. And the judgments are carried out in decisions that are acts of loving. Such is the analogy found in the creature." But that "higher synthesis ... that is the dynamic state of being in love" (enabling the grasping of evidence that only a lover can grasp) and the manifestation of that love in an attitude that is a habitual judgment of value may themselves be created participations in divine paternity-filiation, in active spiration, from which created participation there proceed in a habitual fashion the acts of love of a person who *is* in love. We could not understand these supernatural participations if we did not have the natural analogy that is provided, possibly for all time, in Lonergan's work on insight, *verbum*, and the divine processions themselves. That work will provide the analogy not only for our understanding of the Trinitarian processions but also for the habitual grasp and habitual judgment of value and habitual proceeding love in us that are created participations in the divine relations. These supernatural realities, which provide a psychological analogy for the divine processions, can be understood only by analogy with what we know by nature regarding the spiritual dimensions of the dynamics of human interiority.

5   Conclusion

The starting point of the systematic theology that I envision is the elaboration of the basic set of special and general categories of that theology. The basic set of special systematic categories is found in the four-point hypothesis suggested some fifty-plus years ago by Bernard Lonergan. The basic set of general systematic categories will consist of a theory of history derived from and grounded in Lonergan's cognitional theory, epistemology, metaphysics, and existential ethics, and in the complement to these that I have tried to suggest in speaking of psychic conversion. The basic sets are bound together by the scale of values suggested by Lonergan in *Method in Theology* and worked out in greater detail in my *Theology and the Dialectics of History*. Together these basic sets of categories constitute a unified field structure for systematic theology in its present state of evolution, the basic dogmatic-theological context for a systematic theology on the level of our time, a contemporary theological doctrine of the kingdom or reign of God. Once these sets of categories are elaborated in their integration with one another, they will enable a fuller systematic presentation of the other doctrines that enter into the church's constitutive meaning: revelation, original sin, redemption, church, sacraments, creation, praxis. The elaboration will also consolidate the permanent achievements in the theological tradition to the present time, and the consolidation will be the point of departure for the next advances in the genetic sequence of systematic theologies. For questions will arise out of the elaboration of the unified field structure that cannot be answered on the basis of that elaboration itself. Those questions will be the operators of further systematic-theological development.

8

Autonomous Spiritual Processions

1   Introduction

Thesis 30: *While relations constitute the unifying key to the obscure, analogical understanding of the Trinity considered both immanently and economically, still understanding the divine relations depends on understanding how there can be processions in God.*

The four-point hypothesis begins as follows: "[T]here are four real divine relations, really identical with the divine substance, and therefore there are four very special modes that ground the external imitation of the divine substance."[1]

The four real divine relations, as relations, are paternity, filiation, active spiration, and passive spiration. Active spiration is really distinct from passive spiration, but it is also really identical with paternity and filiation considered together as one principle only conceptually distinct from these two really distinct relations. To say "yes" and to be the "yes" uttered *are* to breathe love. For the Father to beget the Son and for the Son to be begotten *is* for them together to spirate the Spirit of love. To utter the Word and to be uttered by the Father are actively to spirate Proceeding Love. Two really distinct mutually opposed relations (speaker and word, Father and Son) together make up one relation (active spiration) that is mutually opposed to the love that proceeds from them.

In the analogy being suggested here, active spiration is understood by remote analogy to the manner in which a grasp of remembered evidence of having received unqualified love and a consequent assent in an ineffable judgment of value *together* give rise to the disposition of charity grounding acts of love in good decisions. Thus, while there are three really distinct divine relations – paternity (the Father), filiation (the Son), and passive spiration (the Holy Spirit) – the four-point hypothesis includes a strong reliance on the relation of active spiration, Father and Son, paternity and filiation, together spirating the Holy Spirit as their mutual love. Thus, the emphasis here will be on the *four* real relations.

The relations are also identical with the processions, with the persons, and with what have been called the notional acts. Moreover, the four-point hypothesis makes them relevant also to the divine missions. We are in search of a unifying key to the obscure, analogical understanding of the Trinity considered both immanently and economically. There is a distinct advantage to emphasizing relations as the central Trinitarian notion in the elaboration of this unifying key. For, as has been indicated, the methodological category of "special basic relations" was left out of Lonergan's program for the transposition of traditional terms and relations, and it is probably only here, in created imitations of the divine relations, that we will be able to find that category and round off a basic methodological statement. As I have indicated,[2] we can fill out the statement by adding what appears here in italics to Lonergan's own words: "[G]eneral basic terms name conscious and intentional operations. General basic relations name elements in the dynamic structure linking operations and generating states. Special basic terms name God's gift of his love and Christian witness. *Special basic relations name created participations in or imitations of the divine relations that are identical with divine being.*"[3]

Understanding the statement that "there are four real divine relations, really identical with the divine substance, and therefore there are four very special modes that ground the external imitation of the divine substance" entails understanding the principal points of Lonergan's systematics of the Trinity. Part of what follows, then, will consist of an exposition and interpretation of Lonergan on the Trinitarian processions and their connection to the divine missions. I will, however, add my own comments and additions and ultimately provide a new organization to Lonergan's work and new applications of it, in keeping with the program outlined in the previous chapters.

Understanding of the divine relations is grounded in an understanding of divine processions. The relations are identical with the processions, of course, but it has been common currency since Aquinas that in the order of our systematic conceptions the first step is to understand how there can be processions in the utterly simple God. For Lonergan the movement from processions to relations is taken by asking what kind of *reality* is to be accorded to the processions, what kind of *being* divine generation and divine spiration are.[4] The answer is given in terms of relations. It is also in terms of the divine relations that the four-point hypothesis is set forth. Participations in or imitations of divine being are, at their root, ontological determinations of human being, but just as the relations specify the being of the divine processions, so participation in that being is participation in divine relations, as these participations constitute our own relations to the divine persons.

Thus, the systematic treatment follows the *ordo doctrinae,* and the key to the *ordo doctrinae* is to begin with that theorem or hypothesis which, once it has been understood is seen not to presuppose any other theorem or hypothesis in order to be understood, but on the contrary renders possible the understanding of everything else. Lonergan interprets Aquinas as stating that understanding how there can be processions in God does not presuppose understanding any other specifically Trinitarian matters (relations, persons, missions), but rather grounds an analogous and imperfect understanding of these other elements. "[T]he systematic way begins from what can be understood without presupposing the understanding of anything else."[5]

In this chapter, then, we begin presenting, interpreting, and commenting on Lonergan's theology of divine procession, reordering it at times, relating it to his theology of the divine missions, and integrating it with contemporary concerns. That will be the program of the remainder of this book. In this way a treatment of divine processions and divine missions together in Trinitarian theology becomes the first major part of a systematic theology.

2   The Fundamental Issue of a Systematics of the Trinity

> **Thesis 31:** *The fundamental issue in Trinitarian systematics for Lonergan, namely, how it can be true that (1) the Son is both a se and not a se, (2) the Holy Spirit is both a se and not a se, and (3) the way in which the Son is not a se is different from the way in which the Holy Spirit is not a se, is, with the genetic development being suggested here, swept up into the larger question of a Trinitarian systematics that would be the beginning of a theology of history, namely, how the Trinitarian relations are imitated, and participated in, in history.*

2.1 Lonergan's Statement

Lonergan appeals to the church's dogmatic statements to articulate what for systematics, which attempts to understand what is affirmed in those statements, is the fundamental Trinitarian problem. That problem is stated in three propositions. (1) The Son is both *a se* and not *a se.* (2) The Holy Spirit is both *a se* and not *a se.* (3) The way in which the Son is not *a se* differs from the way in which the Holy Spirit is not *a se*.[6] The fundamental trinitarian problem is, How can this be?

The Son and the Holy Spirit can both be said to be *a se*, for each is God and God is *a se*. But the Son is also not *a se*, precisely as "the Son, the only-begotten, born of the Father, from the Father's substance, God from God, light from light, true God from true God."[7] And the Holy Spirit, too, is not *a se*, for the Spirit proceeds from the Father,[8] and is "eternally and at once from the Father and the Son, and has essence and subsistent act of existing at once from the Father and the Son, and eternally proceeds from both as from one principle and by one spiration."[9] Finally, the manner in which the Son is not *a se* differs from the manner in which the Holy Spirit is not *a se*, because the Son is the only-begotten,[10] whereas the Spirit is not begotten but proceeding, *procedens*.[11] The Son proceeds by generation, the Holy Spirit by "spiration."[12] This fundamental complex of assertions, then, is a simple statement of the core Trinitarian mystery. Because it would be contradictory for the manner or aspect in which the Son and the Holy Spirit are *a se* to be the same manner or aspect in which they are not *a se*, the fundamental systematic Trinitarian issue for Lonergan is one of determining (1) how the Son is *a se* and how not, (2) how the Holy Spirit is *a se* and how not, and (3) how the manner in which the Son is not *a se* differs from the manner in which the Holy Spirit is not *a se*. These three doctrinal statements formulate the fundamental question for a Trinitarian systematics, that is, for understanding, however imperfectly, the doctrines articulated by the church concerning the Trinity.

Obviously, then, this statement of the problem means that what is needed is (1) an understanding of how God can be from God, not as one god from another god but as the same God from the same God; (2) a grasp of the difference between the way in which the Son is God from God and the way in which the Spirit is God from God; and (3) an apprehension of the first precisely as generation, as begetting, as a relation of Father and Son, and an apprehension of the reason why the second has to be something different.

The understanding will be not simply conceptual, however, since we affirm in faith something about reality. So the question will move on from conception (note the title of chapter 2 in *The Triune God: Systematics*, "An Analogical *Conception* ...") to the question of the kind of *reality* that could make this conception true, namely, the reality of *relation*. And the third step will lead to the affirmation that the subsistent relations are persons both in the ontological and in the psychological sense. At that point the fundamental trinitarian problem is answered: We will see, with some glimmer of understanding, how it can be true that there are *three really distinct persons* in one and the same divine nature and substance and being.

2.2 Comment

Let me comment on this formulation of the problem. The problem as thus formulated by Lonergan is indeed the fundamental question as long as the systematics of the Trinity remains a systematics purely of the immanent Trinity. We will find as we proceed, however, that Lonergan's own systematics of the Trinity has become now a set of theological doctrines that can themselves be understood in a new ordering that integrates through the four-point hypothesis the theology of the divine processions and the theology of the divine missions, and so the immanent Trinity and the economic Trinity. The "fundamental" character of the issue as formulated by Lonergan is thus somewhat devalued, if you will, to the status of a partial fundamental problem. The real fundamental problem of a systematics of the Trinity that would make a genetic advance on the tradition in which Lonergan stands sweeps up his achievement into the four-point hypothesis. The fundamental issue of a Trinitarian systematics that would be the beginning of a theology of history thus becomes one of understanding how the Trinitarian relations are imitated, or participated in, in history, and in particular how created participation in the uncreated relations of active and passive spiration is related to the uncreated Holy Spirit and how created participation in uncreated paternity is related to the Incarnate Word, the historical figure of Jesus of Nazareth. We still have to follow Lonergan through the resolution of the problem of the aseity of the Son and the Holy Spirit, but that issue will be swept up into the more inclusive theological context of the four-point hypothesis as the hypothesis suggests divine and indeed Trinitarian presence in history.

With that much understood, we may proceed with an exposition of Lonergan's comments on the issue of aseity.

2.3 Further on Lonergan's Statement

Thesis 32: *The link between Lonergan's formulation of the fundamental Trinitarian problem and ours is found in identifying the distinct meanings of "emanation" as this term is applied analogically to divine processions, and in identifying the reality of what is so named in terms of relations that are participated in historically through created emanations in human consciousness.*

Lonergan rules out as insufficient both purely linguistic and purely conceptual resolutions of the question of the aseity of the Son and of the Holy Spirit.

First, it will not be sufficient simply to rearticulate the doctrines so as to express them in a manner that responds to the problem thus formulated. This is just the first step. "It is very easy to say that, as God, the Son is *a se*, from himself, but, as begotten, the Son is not *a se*, not from himself. It is also very easy to say that, as God, the Holy Spirit is *a se*, from himself, but, as spirated, the Holy Spirit is not *a se*, not from himself. Lastly, it is very easy to say that being begotten is different from being spirated."[13] But to leave it at that is to let the solution lie only in words, without any understanding, and even to risk suggesting heresy by leaving the impression that the generation of the Son and the spiration of the Spirit are a mere matter of words.[14] What is needed is (1) some understanding of the *emanation* according to which God is from God, yet not as one god from another god, but as the same God from the same God; (2) some obscure grasp of the difference between the emanation by which the Son is generated and that by which the Spirit is spirated; and (3) some apprehension of why the first emanation is truly called generation and why the second is not. These are the issues to be treated in that step in a systematics of the Trinity that articulates how there can be processions in God.

Second, it is not enough to understand the meaning of the words "generation" and "spiration" and to leave it at that. Lonergan's treatment of the processions remains, on his own admission, in the order of conception. But we can conceive what is meant by "generation" and "spiration" without locating these in reality, and then we are dealing only with concepts (*entia rationis*); and to say that the generation of the Son and the spiration of the Holy Spirit are only conceptual realities is heretical. The reality to be attributed to the processions will be named in terms of relations. The issue of how, in the utterly simple God, the Son and the Spirit *are* in one regard *a se* and in another not *a se*, that is, how the plurality of persons and their seemingly complex relation to the issue of aseity are not in contradiction with divine simplicity, will ultimately be answered in terms of relations. The four-point hypothesis adds to this statement about immanent divine constitution the affirmation that the divine relations are participated in and imitated historically through the divine gift of God's self to us in several distinct manners.

2.4 Comment

Thesis 33: *Lonergan's fundamental Trinitarian problem can be addressed in a manner that links with the present work by understanding his later statement that each of the divine subjects has a unique manner of being subject of the unrestricted act: the Father as originating love, the Son as judgment of value expressing that love, and the Spirit as originated loving.*

It must be noted that for Aquinas, simplicity is the first question to be explored after establishing God's existence. We cannot know what God is, but only what God is not, and so we must proceed by considering the ways in which God does *not* exist. The treatment of divine simplicity in *Summa theologiae*, 1, q. 3, is really, then, a treatment of *non*-composition in God. Lonergan's presentation of divine simplicity, on the other hand, is stated "in the eleventh place" in *Insight*'s treatment of "the notion of God" that precedes his affirmation of the existence of God. The different order seems to be dictated by the fact that for the Lonergan of *Insight* God is to be known primarily as the unrestricted act of understanding. That unrestricted act is first conceived and only then affirmed to exist. The other characteristics of the one act of unrestricted understanding follow upon its conception and are all affirmed once the act itself is affirmed. Thus, that act of understanding is the primary truth (2), the primary being and spiritual (3), perfect (4), the primary good (5), perfect affirming and perfect loving (6), self-explanatory (7), unconditioned (8), necessary (9), one (10). Only then is it said to be simple.[15] In shorter compass and drawing on Lonergan's later emphases, God is the unrestricted act of understanding and loving. That act is *principium totius entis, actus totius entis*. It is conscious, and each of the divine subjects has a unique manner of being subject of the unrestricted act: in Lonergan's later terms, "the Father as originating love, the Son as judgment of value expressing that love, and the Spirit as originated loving."[16] Understanding that affirmation would resolve the fundamental Trinitarian problem as the latter is conceived by Lonergan. And transposing that affirmation into the context of a theology of history would get us started in the direction that we want to take in the present work.[17]

2.5 Lonergan's Position Resumed

For Lonergan, then, the "fundamental Trinitarian problem" is stated thus: Since the Son is God, and since God is utterly simple, and since in what is utterly simple there cannot really be one thing and another, is it not contradictory to maintain that the Son on the basis of the same reality is both *a se* and not *a se*? And does not the same problem arise with respect to the Holy Spirit? What kind of reality are generation and spiration, such that they can figure in non-contradictory assertions of divine being? The question is met by treating the divine relations. We must ask whether there are real relations in God, and if so, how many; we must investigate whether they are really distinct from one another; and we must inquire whether they are really or only conceptually distinct from the divine essence. Treatment of the relations, though, will bring us only to the affirmation that, while there are four real divine relations and while three of them are really distinct from one another, still what we confess in faith is that there are three divine *persons* who are really distinct from one another. So the question arises, Can the distinct subsistent divine relations truly be named persons in both the ontological and the psychological meaning of that word? If so, then without contradiction and with some understanding, three really distinct persons in one and the same divine nature are conceived and truly affirmed; and with that affirmation the fundamental Trinitarian problem has reached resolution at least on an initial plateau. From there systematic theology can proceed to an understanding of the relations of the three divine persons to one another and of the missions of the Word and Spirit in history.

2.6 Comment

While it is true that in Lonergan's systematics of the Trinity it is in the context of that last topic, the missions, that the four-point hypothesis that constitutes one of the dimensions of our unified field structure is established, we are presuming, as a set of theological doctrines to be interpreted and advanced, the totality of Lonergan's achievement in Trinitarian systematics as we proceed here, and so we are bringing the four-point hypothesis forward to join the understanding of the processions and relations *from the beginning*. This is our way of honoring Karl Rahner's Trinitarian *Grundaxiom*, "The immanent Trinity is the economic Trinity, and vice versa."[18] While Lonergan's understanding of the unity of processions and missions is, I believe, far more differentiated and far more satisfactory than Rahner's rather thin Trinitarian theology, it is also closer to Rahner's real intention, I believe, than some of the applications that have been made of the *Grundaxiom* would suggest.[19]

3   Autonomous Spiritual Processions

> **Thesis 34:** *What Aquinas refers to as* emanatio intelligibilis *can be formulated in the language of autonomous spiritual procession, where "autonomous" refers to processions of act from act grounded in an intelligible proportion between what proceeds and the principle from which the procession originates.*

The key to resolving Lonergan's fundamental Trinitarian problem lies precisely in understanding emanation in the order of spirit, that is, in grasping what Thomas Aquinas called *emanatio intelligibilis*. The term is Aquinas's, but a fuller exposition is provided by Lonergan, perhaps the fullest in the entire history of Trinitarian theology. Here I rely almost entirely on the summary statements that he provides in *De Deo trino*, but a more thorough understanding of his position can be achieved by the combined efforts of (1) following his reading of Aquinas in *Verbum* and (2) submitting to the exercises in cognitional and existential self-appropriation that he offers in both *Insight* and, more compendiously, in *Method in Theology*. The second step will help us to transpose the meaning of *emanatio intelligibilis* into a more contemporary idiom, even if we will have to go broader afield to locate the precise problem as it affects the present situation.

The literal translation of *emanatio intelligibilis* is, of course, "intelligible emanation." One problem with this is that the Latin word *intelligibilis*, at least in some medieval Scholastic contexts, means more than the English word "intelligible" means. The Latin word includes more directly in its meaning "intellectual" or "intelligent," that is, it conveys a reference not only to the object that is understood, affirmed, or decided upon but also to the *subject* who understands, judges, and decides; it means both intelligible and intelligent.

In *Insight* Lonergan draws a distinction between the intelligible and the intelligent.

> [I]ntelligibility is intrinsic to being [in the sense that being is the objective of the desire to know, and so whatever is intelligently grasped and reasonably affirmed]. There is in the universe of proportionate being a potential intelligibility that makes experience a necessary component of our knowing, a formal intelligibility that makes understanding a necessary component, and an actual intelligibility that makes judgment a necessary component. But we too are. Besides the potential intelligibility of empirical objects, there is the potential intelligence of the disinterested, detached, unrestricted desire to know. Besides the formal intelligibility of the unity and the laws of things, there is the formal intelligence that consists in insights and grounds conceptions. Besides the actual intelligibility of existences and occurrences, there is the actual intelligence that grasps the unconditioned and posits being as known. Finally, we not only are but also know ourselves. As known to ourselves, we are intelligible, as every other known is. But the intelligibility that is so known is also intelligence and knowing. It has to be distinguished from the intelligibility that can be known but is not intelligent and does not attain to knowledge in the proper human sense of that term. Let us say that intelligibility that is not intelligent is material, and that intelligibility that is intelligent is spiritual. Then, inasmuch as we are material, we are constituted by otherwise coincidental manifolds of conjugate acts that unconsciously and spontaneously are reduced to system by higher conjugate forms. But inasmuch as we are spiritual, we are

orientated towards the universe of being, know ourselves as parts within that universe, and guide our living by that knowledge.[20]

The initial distinction of intelligible and intelligent, once developed along the lines that the passage just cited suggests, becomes a distinction of spiritual intelligibility, which also is intelligent, and material intelligibility, which is not. *Emanatio intelligibilis* is referring to what in *Insight* Lonergan calls spiritual intelligibility, that is, intelligibility that is also intelligent. Moreover, the word "intelligible" in its ordinary English meaning is appropriate in the sense that, as we will see, in the processions that are named "intelligible emanation" what proceeds is *because of* and *in accord with* or *in proportion to* that from which it proceeds. That is, the procession gains its meaning or intelligibility from the fact (1) that what proceeds does so in direct accord with, or in direct proportion to, the principle from which it proceeds, and (2) that this direct accord or proportion is somehow known to the subject. Thus, for example, a sound judgment is sound because it proceeds from a grasp of sufficient evidence known to be sufficient, and in accord with or in proportion to the evidence that has been grasped. In this case the intellectual or intelligent or autonomous spiritual procession of judgment from grasp of evidence is also an *intelligible* emanation. There is an intelligibility in the "because of" and "in accord with" or "in proportion to" that makes the word "intelligible" in its normal English sense quite appropriate.

Still, in order to avoid confusion as much as possible, in order to include explicitly not only cognitional but also moral or existential process, not only knowing but also deciding, and in order to distinguish the autonomous processions that alone provide a remote analogy for Trinitarian life from the spontaneous processions that obtain even in human spiritual living, I have chosen to use the expression "autonomous spiritual procession" as the preferred way of rendering what is meant by *emanatio intelligibilis*. Again, "inasmuch as we are spiritual, we are orientated towards the universe of being, know ourselves as parts within that universe, and guide our living by that knowledge." The word "autonomous" refers precisely to the "because of" and "in accord with" or "in proportion to" aspect of the procession, as that aspect is known to constitute the relation between the principle and what proceeds from it. Thus, what Lonergan writes of the intelligible aspect of such processions in the following passage in *Verbum* defines precisely what I mean by "autonomous"; and by that word I mean nothing more than what is contained in this passage:

> There is ... the intelligible aspect: inner words do not proceed with mere natural spontaneity as any effect does from any cause; they

proceed with reflective rationality; they proceed not merely from a sufficient cause but *from sufficient grounds known to be sufficient and because they are known to be sufficient.* I can imagine a circle, and I can define a circle. In both cases there is efficient causality. But in the second case there is something more. I define the circle because I grasp in imagined data that, if the radii are equal, then the plane curve must be uniformly round. The inner word of defining not only is *caused by* but also is *because of* the act of understanding. In the former aspect the procession is *processio operati.* In the latter aspect the procession is *processio intelligibilis.* Similarly, in us the act of judgment is caused by a reflective act of understanding, and so it is *processio operati.* But that is not all. The procession of judgment cannot be equated with procession from electromotive force or chemical action or biological process or even sensitive act. Judgment is judgment only if it proceeds from intellectual grasp of sufficient evidence as sufficient. Its procession also is *processio intelligibilis.*[21]

Thus, if the key lies in what Aquinas called *emanatio intelligibilis,* it lies in an analogy derived from processions that occur in our own intellectual, rational, and deliberative or existential activity, processions that form the basis of an analogy that gives us a glimpse of what the divine processions might be. But it lies not in all processions that occur in this realm, for there are spiritual processions that are better called spontaneous than autonomous, and these will not provide a fitting analogy for divine procession. As we will see in more detail, the term "spontaneous processions," even in the realm of spirit, refers to processions of act from potency, whereas "autonomous processions" is used exclusively of processions of *act from act.* Formal intelligence, Lonergan writes in the quotation cited a bit back from *Insight,* "consists in insights and grounds conceptions." Actual intelligence "grasps the unconditioned and posits being as known."[22] And in another place he writes that the "development that reaches its goal in the existential decision and in fidelity to that decision is the emergence of the autonomous subject."[23] Here too, the autonomy is constituted by the procession of act from act in existential self-constitution. Much more will be said of this dimension of spiritual autonomy as we proceed, for it is here above all that, even in his early work on these issues, Lonergan finds the appropriate analogy for the divine processions.

More fully, Lonergan offers three assertions regarding the divine processions. They investigate, respectively, (1) how we are to conceive in general "emanation of God from God," (2) how it is, given that understanding, that we can conceive two and only two such emanations, and (3) why the first emanation is properly called generation and the second is not. The presentation of these assertions is preceded by a discussion of the notion of emanation, and specifically of *emanatio intelligibilis*. My own procedure will be to rely on Lonergan's presentation of *emanatio intelligibilis*, but to render this term in English as "autonomous spiritual procession," and to include in it quite explicitly not only cognitional but also existential processes.

The question may be raised, Is such a shift in terminology really helpful? The editors of Lonergan's Trinitarian systematics have already made clear the distinction between "intelligible" and "intelligent" and have related that distinction to the meaning of *emanatio intelligibilis*. Why is yet another shift in terminology recommended? We proceed next to an initial argument for the fittingness on the contemporary scene of such a shift.

4   Insight and Language

> **Thesis 35:** *The meaning of autonomous spiritual procession is illuminated by contrasting the ordinary and original meaningfulness that Lonergan introduces into his discussion of analytic philosophy, and by identifying autonomy with what occurs in the production of original meaningfulness.*

These issues have a far more important significance for contemporary discussion than might at first sight be obvious. First, they are especially germane to contemporary concerns with language and the relation of language to understanding, whether these concerns be analytic, phenomenological, or poststructuralist. Second, the discussion is pertinent to psychological and anthropological suspicions raised over the possibility of autonomous human operations. Clarification of these two issues will help us gain precision on the psychological analogy. I will treat here the first of these contemporary discussions, and the second in the next chapter.[24]

We proceed to some imperfect and obscure understanding of the divine processions by analogy with human cognitional and existential process conceived precisely according to its reality and nature as *human* cognitional and existential process. The key is the act of understanding, or insight, and in that respect the intellectual context of the expression *emanatio intelligibilis* is correct and justified. In Lonergan's judgment on the history of theology, St Thomas Aquinas correctly conceived human cognitional process precisely because he grasped the intelligibility and significance within that process of the act of understanding,[25] the same act that Lonergan studied in intricate contemporary fashion in *Insight*. Others in the theological tradition, and particularly Scotus and his followers (whose negative significance or *Wirkungsgeschichte* in the history of philosophy and theology is a recurrent theme in Lonergan's work),[26] have confused the issue of a "psychological analogy" in Trinitarian theology, because of a mistaken cognitional theory. The mistake is twofold. First, there is a neglect of the act of understanding. Second, human intelligence is conceived on the analogy of sense knowledge. "[T]he human intellect is conceived first as proceeding from external words to universal concepts [the neglect of understanding], then as proceeding from the corporeal act of seeing to some simple spiritual apprehension whereby concepts become known to us [the ocular analogy]."[27] Any such approach overlooks precisely the element that allows some analogy to be developed, and so, for all its labors and efforts at argument, it reaches no clear conclusions.[28] As Lonergan states in *Verbum*: "Scotus ... posits concepts first, then the apprehension of nexus between concepts. His *species intelligibilis* is what is meant immediately by external words ...; it is proved to exist because knowing presupposes its object and indeed its object as present ...; its production by agent intellect and phantasm is the first act of intellect, with knowing it as second act or inner word ...; it is not necessarily an accident inhering in the intellect but necessarily only a sufficiently present agent cooperating with intellect in producing the act of knowing; ordinarily it is the subordinate, but may be the principal, agent ...; sensitive knowledge is merely an occasion for scientific knowledge ...; as our inner word proceeds from the species, so the divine word proceeds from the divine essence ... *The Scotist rejection of insight into phantasm necessarily reduced the act of understanding to seeing a nexus between concepts; hence, while for Aquinas understanding precedes conceptualization which is rational, for Scotus understanding is preceded by conceptualization which is a matter of metaphysical mechanics.*"[29]

Perhaps I may note in passing the residual conceptualism involved in (1) George Lindbeck's "cultural-linguistic" explanation of the nature of doctrine[30] – as Lonergan describes the Scotist position, the "*species intelligibilis* is what is meant immediately by external words"; (2) various proponents of a "method of correlation" – again, Lonergan: "rejection of insight into phantasm necessarily reduce[s] the act of understanding to seeing a nexus between concepts"; and (3) even the non-correlationist suspicion of the significance of *general* categories found in, for example, Karl Barth. Barth's procedures, while frequently doctrinally unobjectionable (as even in his idiosyncratic but ultimately, I believe, orthodox treatment of the dogma of the Trinity), often fail, and this on explicit principle, to make the move from multiple rearticulations of doctrines to systematic understanding of them. The explicit principle is expressed as follows: "It [dogmatics] must try ... not to allow itself to take its problems from anything else but Scripture," for to do so seems *ipso facto* to allow another revelation alongside that attested in scripture.[31] And yet Barth correctly begins his dogmatics (after perhaps the most lengthy prolegomena in the history of theology!) with the doctrine of God, and this for reasons that are not foreign to Lonergan's (and Thomas's) notion of the *ordo doctrinae* to be followed in systematic theology. However – to come to my point – Barth's frequent *modus procedendi* is caught in the following statement: "We need to examine it [the doctrine of the Trinity] at this stage in order to make it clear that the Christian *concept* of revelation already includes within it the problem of the doctrine of the Trinity, that we cannot *analyse the concept* without attempting as our first step to bring the doctrine of the Trinity to expression."[32] Hence, too, there follows his treatment of doctrines, not as a function in part of differentiations of consciousness, nor as answers to historically unfolding questions, but as interpretations, in other concepts, of the concepts that are already "there" in the Bible.[33] The simple fact is that the concept, for example, of *homoousios* is simply not "there" in the Bible, and cannot be drawn from the Bible by analyzing concepts that *are* "there." What can be discerned in the New Testament with respect to the Trinity is a set of elemental meanings that, through differentiation and the questions that emerged in specific cultural contexts, were elevated to the formal, full, and constitutive meaning declared at Nicea and later explained by Athanasius. Again Barth: "We arrive at the doctrine of the Trinity by no other way than that of an *analysis of the concept* of revelation."[34] Not so: not only do *we* not arrive at the doctrine of the Trinity in this way; the *church* did not arrive at it in this manner.

The issue is rendered far more complex in contemporary discussions between students of Lonergan and followers of Wittgenstein and Heidegger. I have treated the issue in some detail elsewhere,[35] and so can be a bit schematic here.

We must distinguish between the ordinary meaningfulness stressed by Wittgenstein and the original meaningfulness delineated by Lonergan, and between Heidegger's stress in speaking of *Verstehen*, which functions in hermeneutic phenomenology for the most part in the realm of ordinary meaningfulness, and Lonergan's stress in speaking of insight, which, as a release to the tension of inquiry, is at the source of original meaningfulness. (We must also distinguish the *Befindlichkeit* associated with these two quite distinct moments of cognition. In fact, this may be the key to the relation between Lonergan and Heidegger.) The psychological analogy for the Trinity appeals to moments of *original* meaningfulness in human consciousness. Every instance of what we are here calling "autonomous spiritual processions" is a moment of original meaningfulness. Lonergan writes:

[T]he ordinary meaningfulness of ordinary language is essentially public and only derivatively private ... [But] what is true of the ordinary meaningfulness of ordinary language is not true of the original meaningfulness of any language, ordinary, literary, or technical. For all language develops and, at any time, any language consists in the sedimentation of the developments that have occurred and have not become obsolete. Now developments consist in discovering new uses for existing words, in inventing new words, and in diffusing the discoveries and inventions. All three are a matter of expressed mental acts ... Unlike ordinary meaningfulness, then, unqualified meaningfulness originates in expressed mental acts, is communicated and perfected through expressed mental acts, and attains ordinariness when the perfected communication is extended to a large enough number of individuals.[36]

In my view, the genuine contributions of both Wittgenstein and Heidegger to a philosophy of ordinary meaningfulness can not only be accommodated in the cognitional and existential theory, and the consequent position on history, based on Lonergan's work; the latter developments need these contributions if they are to approach some sort of completeness on the intricate relations between understanding and language as well as a more rounded notion of the "level" of consciousness that Lonergan calls "experience." And, as I have argued, not only does Lonergan's position need these contributions; it invites them, anticipates them, and explicitly provides the ground for admitting them. All that a student of Lonergan need do in order to realize this is to call into question the very narrow but unfortunately all too common understanding of Lonergan's notion of "experience." For in the realm of human affairs the data that come into consciousness at the level of "experience" are already invested with meaning precisely as they come into consciousness; thus, the level of "experience" already involves something of the level of "understanding." That affirmation is already explicit in Lonergan's work, in fact, throughout that work.[37] But the fact remains that Lonergan's principal contributions, unlike those of both Heidegger and Wittgenstein, are not in the realm of elucidating ordinary meaningfulness, but in that of clarifying original meaningfulness. What he means by *emanatio intelligibilis* will never be understood on any other grounds than this.

5   What Is Autonomous Spiritual Procession?

Thesis 36: *"Autonomous spiritual procession" means the conscious origination of a real, natural, and conscious act from a real, natural, and conscious act, both within the spiritual dimension of consciousness and also by virtue of the spiritual dimension of consciousness itself as determined by the prior act. Such a procession is exhibited in the procession of concepts from understanding, of judgments from reflective grasp*

*of evidence, and of good decision from an authentic judgment of value.
It is only in the procession of act from act that an analogy for the Trinitarian processions can be found.*

The psychological analogy reflects a cognitional and existential theory that was more than implicit in Aquinas and that is worked out by Lonergan in intricate detail. In *Verbum* he locates especially the cognitional aspect in Aquinas's own writings. In *Insight* he develops it – again especially (but not exclusively) the cognitional aspect – in the contexts of (1) modern mathematics and science, (2) a contemporary theory of the dialectic of history that includes an account of common sense, and (3) the turn to the subject in modern philosophy.

For the moment we will be content with the three affirmations that Lonergan repeats from Aquinas at this point in his argument. The key to what Thomas means by *emanatio intelligibilis* is found if we consider together the following three statements. If we attend to our interior intellectual experience, claims Lonergan, we will find these three statements to be true; and he maintains that Thomas must have discovered this by adverting to his own interior intellectual experience.

(1)   "Whenever we understand, *by the mere fact that we do understand, something proceeds within us*, which is the conception of the thing understood, issuing from our intellective power and proceeding from its knowledge."[38]

(2)   "It is of the nature of love not to proceed except from a conception of the intellect."[39]

(3)   "What proceeds internally by an intellectual process does not have to be different [from its source]. Indeed, the more perfectly it proceeds, the more it is one with that from which it proceeds."[40]

If these three statements are understood, Lonergan says, then what for him constituted the fundamental Trinitarian problem is virtually solved: namely, how it can be true that the Son is both *a se* and not *a se*, how it can be true that the Holy Spirit is both *a se* and not *a se*, and how it is that the manner in which the Son is not *a se* differs from the manner in which the Holy Spirit is not *a se*. Other matters demand, not a further understanding to be acquired, but further applications of a quite suitable and flexible grasp of the meaning of these three statements.

To grasp that meaning is to understand *emanatio intelligibilis*, or what we are calling autonomous spiritual procession. The "intellectual process" mentioned in the third of the quotations from Aquinas is the key to

Lonergan's understanding of the divine processions. In the body of the same article (*Summa theologiae*, 1, q. 27, a. 1, *Utrum sit processio in divinis*), Thomas called it an *emanatio intelligibilis* precisely in order to contrast it with processes that occur in nonintellectual or nonspiritual realities. Arius and others considered procession in God along the lines of the coming of an effect from its cause; and Sabellius considered procession in God along the lines of the proceeding of causal influence into an effect by setting the effect in motion or impressing on it the likeness of the cause. In either case procession is conceived (or imagined) as a going forth to something else (*ad aliquid extra*). But the divine processions are *ad intra*; they regard activity that remains within the agent. "Et hoc maxime patet in intellectu, cuius actio, scilicet intelligere, manet in intelligente. Quicumque enim intelligit, ex hoc ipso quod intelligit, procedit aliquid *intra ipsum* quod est conceptio rei intellectae ex vi intellectiva proveniens et ex eius notitia procedens. Quam quidem conceptionem vox significat; et dicitur verbum cordis, significatum verbo vocis." Here "procession" is understood "non ... secundum quod est in corporalibus vel per motum localem vel per actionem alicuius causae in exteriorem effectum, ... sed secundum emanationem intelligibilem, utpote verbi intelligibilis quod manet in ipso."[41]

In itself the matter is fairly simple. At the level of factual judgment, which Lonergan mentions first in this context (although his usual manner of proceeding is to begin with the level of understanding and conceptualization),[42] what is the difference between a rash judgment and a reasonable one? A rash judgment is rash because it is offered without sufficient evidence. A reasonable judgment is one that is so grounded in sufficient evidence that by a kind of intellectual necessity or, perhaps better, exigency – what *Insight* calls an immanent *Anankē*[43] – the judgment inevitably issues forth in a mind that is open to truth. The difference shows precisely what is meant by *emanatio intelligibilis*, by one instance of autonomous spiritual procession, for this is precisely what is lacking in a rash judgment and what is present in a true judgment. Whoever grasps sufficient evidence for a judgment, precisely by so grasping, makes a true judgment with an intellectually conscious exigency.[44] But Lonergan's point is that we all know *from experience* the difference between a rash judgment and a sound judgment.[45] And so we can grasp by reflection on experience what, we will see in more detail, is meant by a procession of *act from act*: in this case, a procession of judgment from grasp of evidence. There is an interior shift to "yes" that precedes any linguistic formulation. It is that relation that Thomas and Lonergan are getting at: grasp of sufficient evidence grounding an inner assent.

Again, on the level of understanding and conceptualization, what is the difference between parroting a definition from memory and proposing one because one has understood something? This difference, too, is something we all know from experience. It is the difference between uttering sounds based on sensitive habit, on the one hand, and, on the other hand, expressing what one has understood and doing so in different ways and by the use of examples, where everything that is said is directed and even, as it were, necessitated by the act of understanding. "[W]hat is lacking in someone repeating things by memory but present in someone who understands and displays that understanding in a variety of ways is again what we are calling an intellectual or intelligible emanation. Indeed, this emanation is nothing other than the fact that, whenever we understand, from the very fact that we understand, by an intellectually conscious necessity we bring forth definitions as well as explications and illustrations."[46] Again, from experience we can know what is meant by a procession of *act from act*: in this case, a procession of conceptualization from direct understanding. At first the inner word may be little more than "I've got it," that is, the inner realization that one has understood. Formulation follows in time, sometimes instantly and at other times with effort.

Finally, we also know from experience the difference between an inordinate act of choice that is repugnant to reason and one that is ordered, correct, obligatory, even holy. When we intelligently grasp and reasonably approve something that is good, we are obliged to it in such a way that, should we choose against the dictates of reason, we would be irrational, and should we follow these dictates, we would be rational. "[W]hat is lacking in a morally evil act but present in a morally good act is that spiritual and moral procession that effectively obligates the will in such a way that we not only ought to love the good, but actually do love it. This procession too is an intellectual or intelligible emanation, for it consists in the fact that a potentially rational appetite becomes actually rational because of a good grasped by the intellect."[47] Again, it is in order to include this procession as well as those that occur at the levels of understanding and judgment that I have decided to employ the generic term "autonomous spiritual procession" rather than some direct translation of the Latin term *emanatio intelligibilis* that would emphasize the cognitional and overlook the moral. "Autonomous spiritual procession" includes all three types of example mentioned here by Lonergan. They are all processions of *act from act*: in this final case, good decision from an authentic judgment of value.

What, then, is the procession in our own consciousness that we experience and that subsequent reflection upon our experience enables us to recognize as the differential between being intelligent and being stupid, being reasonable and being silly, being responsible and being irresponsible? How is it to be defined? What is its generic intelligibility?

It is, says Lonergan, *the conscious origin [that is, procession] of a real, natural, and conscious act from a real, natural, and conscious act, both within intellectual consciousness and also by virtue of intellectual consciousness itself as determined by the prior act.*[48] I will make one change in this definition, but it occurs twice: rather than speaking of "intellectual consciousness," I will speak of "the spiritual dimension of consciousness." Thus, I would define "autonomous spiritual procession" as *the conscious origination of a real, natural, and conscious act from a real, natural, and conscious act, both within the spiritual dimension of consciousness and also by virtue of the spiritual dimension of consciousness itself as determined by the prior act.*

The notion of autonomous spiritual procession on which the psychological analogy is built does not proceed, then, from a grasp of sensitive consciousness or psychic process, but from a grasp of intellectual consciousness or spiritual process. The distinction is crucial to all that I have said in my work regarding psychic conversion and the dialectics of history. Perhaps most clearly, Lonergan articulates the key distinction as follows: "[W]e are conscious in two ways: in one way, through our sensibility, we undergo rather passively what we sense and imagine, our desires and fears, our delights and sorrows, our joys and sadness; in another way, through our intellectuality, we are more active when we consciously inquire in order to understand, understand in order to utter a word, weigh evidence in order to judge, deliberate in order to choose, and exercise our will in order to act."[49] Moreover, within both sensitive and spiritual process, a distinction is to be drawn between the emergence of act from potency and the emergence of act from act. At the level of the spiritual, this becomes a distinction of spontaneous and autonomous processions. Spontaneous procession is exemplified in the procession of understanding from questions; it is a procession of act from potency. Autonomous procession is the procession of act from act such as is exemplified in the three instances that Lonergan presents: concept from understanding, judgment from grasp of evidence, and decision from the judgment of value.

It is important to emphasize the existential and psychological significance both of the distinction of the two dimensions of consciousness and of the distinction within the spiritual dimension of the spontaneous processions of act from potency and the autonomous processions of act from act. Even more, I wish to highlight the theological importance of these distinctions. The second, active dimension, governed as it is not by what we undergo but by transcendental imperatives regarding intelligibility, the unconditioned, and value, is constitutive of human spirituality, of our spiritual *nature*, if you will, whose natural law it is to be attentive, intelligent, reasonable, and responsible. It is in this strictly spiritual dimension of our being that we are images of the triune God, but only as it entails processions from act to act. This transcendental orientation is a participation in uncreated light, and it is this especially as it proceeds *from act to act*, since something remotely analogous to procession from act to act is precisely what constitutes the life of the triune God. I say "remotely analogous" because in God there is not procession from one act to another absolutely distinct act, as in ourselves. Rather, within the one divine act we posit processions based exclusively on mutual relations of origin. But it is the procession from act to distinct act in human consciousness that provides us with the analogy for doing so. So Lonergan distinguishes within this intellectual consciousness a fundamental light of intelligence, which metaphysically he identifies with Aristotle's agent intellect and psychologically with his own "pure desire to know," from its further determinations. First, there is the fundamental light of intelligence. The desire to know is a created and natural participation of the uncreated light that is God. It is the source of our wonder, inquiry, reflection, and deliberation. To it are attributed in Scholastic philosophy such general principles as identity, non-contradiction, and sufficient reason, as well as the precept that good is to be done and evil avoided. It is the dynamism of intellectual consciousness (*vis ipsius conscientiae intellectualis*) mentioned in the definition of intelligible emanation. But that definition specifies that what is intellectually and consciously operative in us lies also in the further determinations that come from our own acts. Our intellectual consciousness is determined, informed, by the prior acts from which, by intellectual emanation, there proceed other acts. The presence and operative character of these prior acts is emphasized in the following: "[W]hen we understand and by the very fact that we understand, from our intellective power, which is the general light of intellectual consciousness, and from the knowledge contained in the act of understanding that adds a determination to the general light, there proceeds within our intellectual consciousness a conception or definition of the reality understood. Similarly, when we grasp that the evidence is sufficient, by the very fact that we grasp it, and from the exigency of intellectual light as determined through that grasp, there proceeds within our intellectual consciousness either a true affirmation or a true negative assertion. Similarly again, when we judge some good as obligatory, by the very fact that we so judge, through our intellectuality, our rationality, we spirate an act of will."[50]

9

The Dialectic of Desire

1   Desire and the Varieties of Procession

Thesis 37: *The procession of act from act in the spiritual dimension of consciousness is to be sharply distinguished from the procession of act from potency in that same dimension, as well as from all processions in the sensitive-psychic dimension of consciousness.*

The transcendental orientation of which we have been speaking participates in uncreated light not only in its movements from act to act but also in its movements from potency to act, but the latter participation does not offer the created analogy for providing us with a glimpse of divine procession. This preliminary created participation in uncreated light is "the source in us that gives rise to all our wonder, all our inquiry, all our reflection";[1] it is our desire to know, the notion of being; it is also the transcendental notion of value. In us those notions are potential. Ultimately, they are obediential potency for a created participation in divine life through the gift of God's love. For the moment, though, let us simply emphasize that they have objectives. Being is the objective of the pure desire to know. Reaching being is thus a task, and the task involves primarily negotiating the vagaries of desires that would interfere with the unfolding of the self-transcendent exigencies of intelligent and rational consciousness. Again, the good is the objective of the transcendental notion of value. Attaining the good in judgments of value and pursuing it in decisions is also a task, and it involves the negotiation of desire that the Christian spiritual tradition has called discernment. But it is not in the movement from potency to act that our participation in uncreated light provides us with an analogy for understanding, however remotely, how there can be procession in God, but rather such cumulative achievements of that potentiality for being and value as are reached when from understanding we speak an inner word, or from grasping sufficient evidence we utter a judgment, or from grasping what it would be good for us to do or to be we consent, decide, and act. These are movements from act to act, not from potency to act. While the originating act and the originated act are in each case absolutely distinct, and while that is not and cannot be the case in God, still it is from here and from here alone that we may draw a remote analogy for understanding the divine processions.

I mentioned in the last chapter that the areas of contemporary discussion to which the present work is relevant include not only contemporary concerns with language and the relation of language to understanding, but also psychological and anthropological suspicions raised over the very possibility of autonomous human operations. It is at this point in commenting on Lonergan's theology of divine procession that we can begin to address the second of these areas, one that will be extremely important to the theology being constructed here.

I have spoken of the vagaries of desire, and especially of desires that would interfere with the unfolding of the transcendental, spiritual, autonomous, active desire for being and value, the pure, unrestricted, detached, disinterested desire for what is, what is true, and what is good. It is especially in the realm of desire that we can distinguish the two dimensions of consciousness that Lonergan is talking about, and locate more firmly that dimension that will help us gain some obscure and imperfect understanding of the mystery we hold in faith.

First, some more or less incidental remarks may prove helpful.

(1) Lonergan's affirmation of two dimensions to human consciousness can be added to other texts from Lonergan to which I have appealed in my efforts to establish the validity of the notion of psychic conversion and its compatibility with Lonergan's own work. The difference between the two dimensions of consciousness also grounds my notion of dialectic.[2]

(2) We should note also the passive or receptive element in understanding itself, precisely in the sense of insight as a release to the tension of inquiry. This passive element is connected with the fact that the emergence of understanding involves what Lonergan, following Thomas, will call a *processio operationis*, a procession from potency to act. We must wait for insight, in patience. The passive character of understanding (*intelligere est pati*) is highlighted in *Verbum* more perhaps than in *Insight*.[3] While Lonergan's affirmation of the two dimensions of human consciousness includes inquiring in order to understand (*processio operationis*)

as an element in the active and transcendental dimension of
spiritual consciousness, the spiritual *autonomy* of that dimension
is found not in the procession of act from potency and so of insight from inquiry, but in the procession of act from act (*processio
operati*). Thus, Lonergan uses the term "spontaneous" to refer to
processiones operationis and the term "autonomous" to refer only to
processiones operati at the spiritual level. This will be important in
our discussion of the work of René Girard, who tends to use the
terms "spontaneous" and "autonomous" almost interchangeably
and to draw suspicion to any claims that our desires are spontaneous and autonomous rather than mimetic and borrowed from
others: in the terms of some traditional Christian theology, it
may be said that for Girard our desires are elicited, not natural.[4]
It is only in the dimension of spiritual processions of act from
act (*processiones operati*) that the psychological analogy for the divine processions is to be found. Here alone is where human consciousness provides instances of autonomous spiritual procession,
here alone is where "the proper principle of intellectual emanation [of the spiritual procession] is not the object [or someone
else's desire mediating the object, as in Girard's mimetic theory]
but the subject … intellectually [spiritually] conscious in act …
Because intellectual consciousness owes it to itself to express to
itself its own understanding, and to express it truly, it follows that
what is being understood ought to be expressed truly. Because
intellectual consciousness owes it to itself to bestow its own love
rightly, it follows that what is judged as truly good ought also to
be loved. And if perchance understanding is deficient or judgment erroneous, an unknown obligation does not prevail in such
a way that one is duty-bound to act against one's conscience;
rather, a known obligation prevails, so that one is duty-bound to
judge in accordance with the evidence one has and to choose in
accordance with one's judgment." And, most importantly, "the
autonomy of human consciousness is indeed subordinate, not
to every object whatsoever, but to the infinite subject in whose
image it has been made and whom it is bound to imitate."[5]

(3) Finally, we should note that the empirical consciousness of an
intelligent subject is itself invested with intelligence, and that
in human affairs there is a reception of meanings and values in
such empirical consciousness that involves a devalued formal
and perhaps even actual intelligibility.[6] This *Verstehen* informing empirical consciousness is a quality of human intelligence

distinct from Lonergan's "insight" as a release to the tension of inquiry. The distinction, again, is in terms of what Lonergan calls ordinary and original meaningfulness. When Lonergan speaks of the fundamental light of consciousness, he is referring in part at least to the active process that gives rise to original meaningfulness. It is in that spiritual process or set of spiritual processions that we find the *imago Dei* that can legitimately function as an appropriate "psychological analogy" for understanding the divine processions, namely, the various instances of *processio operati*, processions of act from act.

This is how we are to understand another of Lonergan's statements, namely, that divine processions are, not *processiones operati*, but *per modum operati*. Processions from potency to act are *processiones operationis*, processions of an operation. Processions from act to act are *processiones operati*, processions of something "operated," where the principle and what proceeds are distinct in an absolute fashion. Divine processions are understood along the lines of *processiones operati*, and in this sense they are called *processiones per modum operati*. The distinction in God of principle and what proceeds is real, but not absolute; rather it is a distinction of opposed relations of origin.[7]

> **Thesis 38:** *The distinction of two ways of being conscious opens us upon the possibility of making a theological contribution to mimetic theory.*

Again, as we have seen, for Lonergan "[W]e are conscious in two ways: in one way, through our sensibility, we undergo rather passively what we sense and imagine, our desires and fears, our delights and sorrows, our joys and sadness; in another way, through our intellectuality, we are more active when we consciously inquire in order to understand, understand in order to utter a word, weigh evidence in order to judge, deliberate in order to choose, and exercise our will in order to act."[8] In actual fact, the discrimination of these two "ways of being conscious" is an extraordinarily sensitive and delicate business. For the first "way of being conscious" permeates the second, and it does so either in support of the transcendental orientation to intelligibility, truth, being, and the good, or in conflict with that orientation. Again and more precisely, it *precedes, accompanies, and overarches* the intentional operations that constitute the second "way of being conscious." In that sense it is partly constitutive of the vertical finality, the "tidal movement" or "passionateness of being" that Lonergan refers to in the following two passages.

[M]ust not the several principles [of intentional consciousness, of the second "way of being conscious'] be but aspects of a deeper and more comprehensive principle? And is not that deeper and more comprehensive principle itself a nature, at once a principle of movement and of rest, a tidal movement that begins before consciousness, unfolds through sensitivity, intelligence, rational reflection, responsible deliberation, only to find its rest beyond all of these? I think so.[9]

… [The] passionateness [of being] has a dimension of its own: it underpins and accompanies and reaches beyond the subject as experientially, rationally, morally conscious.

Its underpinning is the quasi-operator that presides over the transition from the neural to the psychic. It ushers into consciousness not only the demands of unconscious vitality but also the exigences of vertical finality. It obtrudes deficiency needs. In the self-actualizing subject it shapes the images that release insight; it recalls evidence that is being overlooked; it may embarrass wakefulness, as it disturbs sleep, with the spectre, the shock, the shame of misdeeds. As it channels into consciousness the feedback of our aberrations and our unfulfilled strivings, so for the Jungians it manifests its archetypes through symbols to preside over the genesis of the ego and to guide the individuation process from the ego to the self.

As it underpins, so too it accompanies the subject's conscious and intentional operations. There it is the mass and momentum of our lives, the color and tone and power of feeling, that fleshes out and gives substance to what otherwise would be no more than a Shakespearian "pale cast of thought."

As it underpins and accompanies, so too it overarches conscious intentionality. There it is the topmost quasi-operator that by intersubjectivity prepares, by solidarity entices, by falling in love establishes us as members of community. Within each individual vertical finality heads for self-transcendence. In an aggregate of self-transcending individuals there is the significant coincidental manifold in which can emerge a new creation. Possibility yields to fact and fact bears witness to its originality and power in the fidelity that makes families, in the loyalty that makes peoples, in the faith that makes religions.

But here we meet the ambiguity of man's vertical finality. It is natural to man to love with the domestic love that unites parents with each other and with their children, with the civil love that can face death for the sake of one's fellowmen, with the all-embracing love that loves God above all. But in fact man lives under the reign of sin, and his redemption lies not in what is possible to nature but in what is effected by the grace of Christ.[10]

It is because of the ambiguity of our vertical finality that distinguishing intellectually and negotiating existentially the two "ways of being conscious" is such a delicate exercise, in fact, that it is an exercise calling for what the Christian spiritual tradition has called discernment. It is precisely this ambiguity that is missed by Heidegger even as he correctly acknowledges that *Verstehen* and *Befindlichkeit* are equiprimordial ways of being *Dasein.* For the relation between *Verstehen and Befindlichkeit* is precisely the vertical finality that would orient *Befindlichkeit* to participation in the life of *Verstehen.* The presentation of *Being and Time,* I believe, can be interpreted and dialectically reoriented on the basis of this notion of vertical finality. What "we undergo rather passively" in "what we sense and imagine, our desires and fears, our delights and sorrows, our joys and sadness" affects the entire range of vertical finality as it actually unfolds. Under optimal circumstances, this whole dimension bolsters and supports the second "way of being conscious," where "we consciously inquire in order to understand, understand in order to utter a word, weigh evidence in order to judge, deliberate in order to choose, and will in order to act." But those optimal circumstances are rare indeed, and to the extent that they do not obtain, we can speak of a statistical near-inevitability of distortion precisely in the spiritual dimensions of human operation. There *is* a realm in which human desire and human operation are autonomous, not in the sense of a self-asserting effort at what Ernest Becker called the *causa sui* project[11] (the sort of thing Heidegger promoted in his infamous address on the self-assertion of the German university),[12] but in the sense of our operating under transcendental exigencies for the intelligible, the true and the real, and the good. These desires are natural, not elicited, and spiritual, not psychic. There are moments in that transcendental operating in which act flows from act: concept from understanding, judgment from grasp of sufficient evidence, decision from judgment of value. But that realm, as Lonergan says of human authenticity, is ever precarious; it is reached always by withdrawing from inauthenticity. It is the realm of the pure, detached, disinterested desire to know that Lonergan highlights in *Insight* and of the equally pure, detached, disinterested sublation of the desire to know by the transcendental intention of value. No one, not even the greatest saint, lives in that realm untroubled, serene, free of temptation and distortion.

Treating the question now might obviate difficulties that some might bring against an appeal to an "autonomous" dimension of consciousness; and it will also highlight precisely in what consists the created participation in and imitation of the divine and how this is distinguished from elements of consciousness that are more a function of the passive undergoing of "our desires and fears, our delights and sorrows, our joys and sadness," where, as we will see, our desire is again mimetic, but now not of the divine processions. In that sense, taking this approach will help us to fine-tune our portrayal of the psychological analogy. *What is it genuinely and in grace to imitate God, and how does that differ from other forms of mimesis?* That is the question that I wish to introduce at this point, partly in order to get hold of the analogy of *autonomous spiritual procession* and partly to indicate the profound significance of such a Trinitarian theology for the understanding and guidance of historical process.

> **Thesis 39:** *The distinction of the two dimensions of consciousness will enable a clarification of the precise character of the image of God found in the spiritual processions of act from act, whether in the realm of nature or in that of grace.*

I have called attention to the four-point hypothesis that will provide the central special-categorial framework for our systematic theology. That hypothesis speaks of created imitations of the divine relations, through a participation in those relations effected by elevating grace. I have also emphasized that the key to the immanent constitution of these created imitations of the divine relations lies in the field of processions of act from act in the spiritual dimension of consciousness. There are natural processions of act from act that provide the traditional analogy for the Trinitarian processions. One set of these processions entails the emanation of the word of value judgment from the gift of love, and the emanation of loving acts from the gift and its judgment of value. But there also are supernatural processions of act from act. A portion of the hypothesis provides a supernatural psychological analogy for the divine processions, namely, that portion that relates (1) sanctifying grace, which is the gift of God's love, (2) faith as the knowledge born of that gift, and (3) the charity grounding the kind of loving acts that would even return good for evil. These are created participations, respectively, in active and passive spiration. It is here and here alone, in these natural and supernatural processions of act from act, that we may speak of a genuine autonomy in the unfolding of conscious operations and states. In either case we find the procession of a judgment of value from a loving grasp of evidence, and this is the human analogue for the procession of the divine Word. And in either case we find the increasingly habitual procession of acts of love from loving grasp and judgment of value, and this is the human analogue for the procession of the Holy Spirit. Charity gives rise to the relationship of companionship with the Son, for those who know Christ, and of love of wisdom for those who do not. And it gives rise to the supernatural virtue of hope, which is in fact, if not always known as such, a relation to the Father. It must be emphasized that even the supernatural analogue needs to be understood by analogy with the natural analogues that formed the psychological analogies of Aquinas and the early Lonergan.

Among contemporary authors, René Girard in particular has called our attention to the extremely precarious nature of any human claims to autonomous subjectivity. These precautions are salutary for anyone hoping to resurrect the psychological analogy in Trinitarian theology. That analogy speaks of autonomous processions of act from act both in natural process and in the supernatural created participations in active and passive spiration. In each form of the psychological analogy what matters is a procession of judgment of value from grasp of evidence, and a procession of love from the grasp and judgment functioning as one principle of commitment. It is in this sense and this sense alone that the hypothesis speaks of autonomy. Our authenticity lies in the self-transcendence that characterizes these processions. But not only is such authenticity, which is still our most prized possession, ever precarious, ever a withdrawal from unauthenticity, but also "every successful withdrawal only brings to light the need for still further withdrawals."[13] Girard's thought is, in many ways, a stark reminder of the precariousness of all human claims to the autonomous processions that alone guarantee human authenticity.

Lonergan has called attention to authenticity and unauthenticity in the realms of understanding, truth, moral development, and religion:[14] the areas that are positively treated when he speaks of intellectual, moral, and religious conversion. Throughout my own work I have been calling attention to a distinct dimension of the subject, of authenticity, of conversion. This distinct dimension affects primarily the first "way of being conscious" in its relation to the second, and so I have spoken of a *psychic* conversion. Girard's work on the nature of human desire will give us good purchase, I think, on important aspects of this psychic dimension, and being very clear with him about the character of false mimesis and deviated transcendence, which are very common precisely *in* intellectual, moral, and religious discourse, will help us isolate much more clearly just where in consciousness the genuine *imago Dei* really lies. For while the *imago Dei* is implanted in the very nature of human consciousness, it is not some automatic functioning that we need simply locate through introspective analysis or some other technique. Lonergan writes of the end of the age of innocence, in which it was presumed that human authenticity could be taken for granted.[15] Perhaps that illusion infected systematic theology, even very good systematic theology! At any rate, we must be very clear that the precise locating of the *imago Dei* that can function in a psychological analogy for the divine processions is crucial for systematics, and just as crucial for human self-understanding. It will clarify the two dimensions of consciousness, and ultimately it will give us a firmer hold on what does and does not constitute a valid analogy for the divine processions. Does the autonomous, transcendental realm of human operating that Lonergan relies on for this analogy really exist, or is the claim that we are operating from that kind of autonomy the kind of claim that Girard has exposed as illusory? The question cannot be evaded, especially by Lonergan students, who have tended to downplay the role of psychic bias, the need for psychic conversion, and the crucial role of psychic self-appropriation in establishing theological foundations. It is best to raise the question now, not only for the sake of the Trinitarian analogy itself, but also to draw attention to the historical context in which I wish a systematics of the Trinity to unfold. For "The Trinity in History" would presumably have a great deal to do with and to say about the problems of violence and about the collusion of religion in violence. Such problems are at the heart of Girard's work. Relating the four-point hypothesis to Girard's mimetic theory is crucial for unpacking on the level of our time the meaning of the reign of God, and only such unpacking will keep our systematic theology in some sort of continuity with the mission of the incarnate Word in history.

Again, despite his acknowledgment of the two dimensions of consciousness, Lonergan's emphasis is on the distinction within the second dimension, the spiritual or intellectual dimension, between spontaneous and autonomous processions, that is, between what Scholastic language called *processiones operationis* and *processiones operati*, or, again, between processions of act from potency and processions of act from act. This distinction is relatively easy to grasp and to affirm once one has admitted the distinct realm constituted by the second "way of being conscious" (which, in our time particularly, is a much more difficult discovery for very many people). A much larger problem lies in distinguishing the two ways in the first place and in acknowledging that the two ways of being conscious also signal two modalities of human desire – a point that becomes particularly clear when we grasp the distinct character of those spiritual processions that we are calling autonomous, that is, the processions of act from act in the order of the human spirit. I proceed on the assumptions (1) that what Girard has written about mimetic desire concerns desire in the first "way of being conscious," that is, in the sensitive, psychic dimension of consciousness, but also (2) that this dimension penetrates our spiritual orientation to the intelligible, the true and the real, and the good, for better or for worse, and so that distorted mimetic desire can infect human spiritual operations, while positive mimesis can strengthen and enhance them.

Thesis 40: *Lonergan's first "way of being conscious" is interdividual in many of its manifestations. Psychic development entails the negotiation*

*of this interdividual field in the direction of what Jung calls individua-
tion. But this negotiation calls upon the operations of the second "way of
being conscious." Inadequate negotiation of the interdividual field can
and will distort this second way, while authentic negotiation of the same
field will help the second way flourish in the development of the person.
This authentic negotiation is a function of the second way itself, that is,
of insight, judgment, and moral responsibility, including the autonomous spiritual processions of act from act at each level.*

The major component of René Girard's worldview is the notion of mimetic
or triangular desire, and it is acquisitive mimesis in particular that we must
be concerned about, for such mimesis easily becomes conflictual as the
object drops out of sight and the subject becomes concerned with the person who had mediated his or her desire in the first place. When such conflictual mimesis spreads, so that it infects the entire group, its destructive
power can be stemmed only if it is turned onto one individual or group, a
scapegoat whose exclusion through murder or expulsion brings peace and
reconciliation to the community.

Ultimately, this vision will figure centrally in our soteriology, filling out
and enriching enormously Lonergan's theology of the "law of the Cross,"
which provides, as it were, a heuristic structure that to a large extent is given
specific determination by the dynamics that Girard discloses.[16] But for the
moment my concern is exclusively with the assistance Girard gives us in
gaining precision on the notions of desire and imitation, in order to isolate,
as distinct from acquisitive mimetic desire, the authentically autonomous
dimension of human consciousness from which a genuine analogy may be
drawn for an obscure understanding of the divine processions.

The mediation of mimetic desire can be either external or internal, to use
Girard's terminology. While Girard groups mediated desires into these two
fundamental categories, he allows that within this division there "can be an
infinite number of secondary distinctions."[17] There is *external mediation* of
desire when the distance between the subject and the model is "sufficient
to eliminate any contact between the two spheres of possibilities of which
the mediator and the subject occupy the respective centers." There is *internal mediation* when this distance "is sufficiently reduced to allow these two
spheres to penetrate each other more or less profoundly."[18] The "distance"
referred to in either case is, of course, not primarily physical but psychological or symbolic or spiritual. Thus, to cite perhaps Girard's favorite example, Don Quixote and Sancho are physically together, but still there is no
rivalry between them, and their harmony is never seriously troubled, even
as Sancho borrows almost all of his desires from Don Quixote, who himself
is imitating the legendary Amadis of Gaul. "The hero of external mediation

proclaims aloud the true nature of his or her desire."[19] One is proud to be the disciple of so worthy a model, as was Don Quixote with respect to Amadis and as is the Christian with respect to Jesus. The hero of internal mediation, on the other hand, carefully hides his or her efforts to imitate a model. While *all* mimetic desire runs the risk of impairing its victims' perceptions of reality, since the desirability of the object stems not from its own merits but from its designation by the mediator, in internal mediation the result is always conflict, even hatred. That is not the case in external mediation. In internal mediation the rivals can come to resemble each other through the identity of their desires, so that finally they are no more than each other's doubles. The actual source of any desire is so obscured that the subject may even reverse the logical and chronological order of desires in order to hide his or her imitation. That is, one may assert that one's own desire is prior to that of the rival whose desire one is imitating, and that the mediator is responsible for the rivalry. Everything that originates with the mediator is systematically belittled although still secretly desired. The mediator becomes a shrewd and diabolical enemy who tries to rob the subject of his or her most prized possessions and obstinately thwarts his or her most legitimate ambitions. Desiring individuals come to believe in the autonomy of their desires, and so deny the importance of the mediator.

Imitation thus occurs not only in the sphere of representation or knowledge, as Plato had emphasized, but also in the sphere of appropriating objects. We learn what to desire by copying the desires of others. Our desires are rooted not in their objects nor in ourselves but in a third party, the model or mediator, whose desire we imitate in the hope of resembling him or her. Thus, the ground of desire resides, not in any one subject, but *between* subjects. This throws into question the intrinsic desirability of the object, recasting its value as a product of the intersubjective, or in Girard's term "interdividual," relation. It recasts object-relations theories, including Freudian psychoanalysis. My own appropriation of Girard's work will emphasize that what Lonergan calls the first "way of being conscious" is precisely interdividual in many of its manifestations, that psychic development entails the negotiation of this interdividual field in the direction of what Jung calls individuation, that this negotiation calls upon the operations of the second "way of being conscious," that inadequate negotiations of the interdividual field can and will distort this second way, and that authentic negotiation of the same field will allow the second way to flourish in the development of the person. It remains true, however, that this authentic negotiation is a function of the second way itself, that is, of insight, judgment, and moral responsibility.

The notion of mimetic desire was proposed by Girard in the book *Deceit, Desire, and the Novel,* which contains studies of Cervantes, Dante, Stendhal,

Proust, and Dostoyevsky. The book was first published in French in 1961, with the title *Mensonge romantique et vérité romanesque.* Those novels that portray desire as spontaneous and autonomous[20] embody the *mensonge romantique,* the romantic lie. Those novels that acknowledge that desire is triangular convey the *vérité romanesque.* The romantic lie valorizes all instances of originality and spontaneity as indicators of personal superiority. The romantic construal of desire is that of a straight line running between a desiring subject and an intrinsically valuable desired object. The *vérité romanesque,* on the other hand, describes the interdividual situation of desire. The conclusion to such a work may introduce a new mode of interpersonal relations, one that is not predicated on the slavish but largely unwitting imitation of others, one that rather displays an authentic negotiation of this intersubjective field through operations that in fact *are* genuinely autonomous because they entail processions of act from act in the spiritual realm. We cannot attain total independence from others, in some sort of putative heroism that is really self-possessed pride. The latter is still thoroughly entangled with the Other, precisely in an attempt to distinguish oneself. What we can attain is a purified relationality that is not caught up in imitative violence. But we can do this only through recognizing the fact that we have indeed been so caught up and through a decision to allow ourselves to be freed from such contagion. Novels that distinguish these components in human relations are for Girard far more faithful to the true human condition than those that treat desire as spontaneous, autonomous, and directly object-related.

Desire, Deceit, and the Novel begins with the following quotation from *Don Quixote*:

> I want you to know, Sancho, that the famous Amadis of Gaul was one of the most perfect knight errants. But what am I saying, one of the most perfect? I should say the only, the first, the unique, the master and lord of all those who existed in the world ... I think ... that, when a painter wants to become famous for his art he tries to imitate the originals of the best masters he knows; the same rule applies to most important jobs or exercises which contribute to the embellishment of republics; thus the man who wishes to be known as careful and patient should and does imitate Ulysses, in whose person and works Homer paints for us a vivid portrait of carefulness and patience, just as Virgil shows us in the person of Aeneas the valor of a pious son and the wisdom of a valiant captain; and it is understood that they depict them not as they are but as they should be, to provide an example of virtue for centuries to come. In the same way Amadis was the pole, the star, the sun for brave and amorous

> knights, and we others who fight under the banner of love and chivalry should imitate him. Thus, my friend Sancho, I reckon that whoever imitates him best will come closest to perfect chivalry.

For Girard this means that Quixote "has surrendered to Amadis the individual's fundamental prerogative: he no longer chooses the objects of his own desire – Amadis must choose for him. The disciple pursues objects which are determined for him, or at least seem to be determined for him, by the model of all chivalry. We shall call this model the *mediator* of desire."[21] In romantic works of fiction, the characters have desires which are simpler than Don Quixote's. There is no mediator, there is only the subject and the object. But, says Girard, "the great writers apprehend intuitively and concretely, through the medium of their art, if not formally, the system in which they were first imprisoned together with their contemporaries,"[22] the system of triangular desire, of which we are all victims. And we are victims because "from the moment the mediator's influence is felt, the sense of reality is lost and judgment is paralyzed."[23] We "borrow [our] desires from the Other in a movement which is so fundamental and primitive that [we] completely confuse it with the will to be Oneself."[24]

Note that literature portrays two varieties of such imitative desire. The person whom Stendhal refers to as *vaniteux* – the vain person – cannot draw his or her desires from his or her own resources, but must borrow them from others. "A *vaniteux* will desire any object so long as he is convinced that it is already desired by another whom he admires. The mediator here is a *rival*, brought into existence as a rival by vanity, and that same vanity demands his defeat."[25] But this kind of rivalry between the mediator and the one who desires is quite different from the situation of Quixote: "Amadis cannot vie with Don Quixote in the protection of orphans in distress, he cannot slaughter giants in his place."[26] Don Quixote's situation is not one of competing desires; the mediator is not also a rival or obstacle. Obviously, the same is true of the Christian's imitation of Christ, if it is genuine. And the difference is constituted by an "enormous spiritual gap"[27] between, for example, Don Quixote and Stendhal's *vaniteux*, to say nothing of Christ and the Christian.

Relationships of internal mediation can become so complex and impossible that the only way out of the bind is to break the circle of desire. But even this can be a ploy. Renunciation can take place for the sake of the desire itself. The goal can be to discourage further imitation, but if the object desired is another person, this renunciation can actually occur for the sake of secretly opening the road to the desired object by making the desired object desire oneself. One who feigns indifference can seem to the desired object to be so self-possessed that this seeming self-mastery and peace becomes itself an object of desire on the part of the subject's own object of desire. The object now desires the subject who desires the object. Depending on the ontological emptiness of the object and the feigned or even real self-mastery of the subject, the object may want to absorb the very being of the subject into his or her own. The subject who was imitating the model or mediator of desire now becomes imitated by the object, desire for whom was mediated by the model or mediator.

It is here, in these complications, that Girard finds the source of all mimetic desire: "Imitative desire is always a desire to be Another" because of the radical insufficiency of one's own very being.[28] To covet what the other desires is to covet the other's essence. In the first case this was a matter of the subject desiring the person who is also desired by the model or mediator: the subject really wants not only what the mediator wants or perhaps has, but even what the mediator is. In the second case, when the subject feigns being above it all, the object now desires the self-sufficiency that the subject seems to be displaying. In either case, this conception of desire presupposes a radical insufficiency in the very being of the desiring individual. This individual must be painfully conscious of his or her own emptiness to crave so desperately the fullness of being that supposedly lies in others. This attraction to the "putative autarky"[29] of the other Girard calls *metaphysical desire*, because the figures onto whom it is projected mediate being for us; it is via them that we seek to become real, and it is through wanting their very being that we come to imitate them. The wish to absorb, or to be absorbed into, the substance of the Other implies an insuperable revulsion for one's own substance. Metaphysical desire is masochism or pseudo-masochism: a will to self-destruction as one becomes something or someone other than what one is. As the desire to be absorbed "suffers disappointment after disappointment, the metaphysical quest is not abandoned: rather, the masochist merely seeks out more powerful mediators from which to attain real, substantial being ... The masochist ... is a casualty of metaphysical desire; he hopes that realizing the desires that he sees in the Other will bring about the hoped-for self-sufficiency and allow him to participate in his divine being. But since the self-sufficiency, divinity, or plenitude that the masochist attributes to the model is illusory, his project to attain the same is doomed from the outset. The masochist vaguely perceives the fruitlessness of his quest but fails to give it up because to do so would mean that the promise of salvation would have to be given up along with it."[30]

Moreover, the subject who has been rejected can choose to be the tormentor. This is sadism or pseudo-sadism, but it backfires sooner or later. "Pseudo-sadism emerges at the point when the masochist, who has worshipped violence, begins to emulate those who have blocked his access to objects of desire ... The sadist looks for imitators whom he can torture in the same way that he thought he was tortured prior to adopting the role. Indeed, it is the sadist's prior experience as victim that suggests the appropriate course of action. Yet, the emergence of sadism, of this "dialectical reversal," is by no means the simple "opposite" of masochism: it is, rather, the same condition at a different moment. Nor is the movement from masochism to sadism stable or irreversible; both masochism and sadism are subject to the same double-imperative – of wanting to overcome the rival and simultaneously to be overcome *by* the rival."[31]

There is, then, a radical ontological sickness at the core of mimetic desire, and especially internal mimetic desire. For Marcel in *Remembrance of Things Past*, so intense is the sense of his own inadequacy that he feels that everyone else, indeed everything around him, possesses more substance than he does.[32] Under these conditions, the search for the mediator who alone can relieve the individual's anguish becomes a constant and all-consuming obsession. As the mediator changes, so does one's own being. One self replaces another as one mediator replaces another. Mimetic desire moves from one model to another, destroying the unity and continuity of the individual without the individual's even being aware that this is what is happening. The result is the decomposition of the personality. There is no single unified individual any longer, just a succession of selves brought on by successive mediations.

The "depredation of internal mediation" is for Girard most acute in the later works of Dostoyevsky. In his heroes the wish to be absorbed into the substance of the Other implies an insuperable revulsion for one's own substance. In Dostoyevsky there can be no final victory, no fulfilment, in the world of mediated desire. The only triumph possible is the complete renunciation of mimetic desire and of the ontological malady that accompanies it.

These readings of great novelists gave rise to a new psychological theory that Girard calls interdividual. It begins with a critique of Freudian psychoanalysis. Despite Girard's respect for Freud's acuteness of observation, he claims that Freud hovered around the basic insight without ever coming to acknowledge it. "Freud's initial mistake consists in taking the sexual appetite to be 'the sole motor and basis of [the] psychic process.'"[33] The sexual drive is, says Girard, "subordinate to the mimetic process, which plays a much more vital and decisive role in psychic processes and human actions."[34] Next, Girard rejects the Freudian premise that desire is object-oriented. The crucial role is that of the mediator, who stimulates and directs the individual's desires toward the object in question. Third, Girard rejects what he finds to be a fundamental duality in Freudian desire (both Oedipal and narcissistic). There is only one desire, in the realm at least of acquisitive or appropriative wishes, and it is always mimetic.[35]

I have gone into this much detail on Girard's position at this point in the work – and Girard will return later – for several reasons. First, I wish to indicate that there is a much greater complexity to the "two ways of being conscious" than might be obvious from Lonergan's almost facile description. The mimetic model of desire indicates how much more enters into the first way than is indicated in Lonergan's description, or for that matter even in Lonergan's portrayal of dramatic bias in chapter 6 of *Insight*. In this first way, as we have seen, we are by and large the passive recipients of "what we sense and imagine, our desires and fears, our delights and sorrows, our joys and sadness." But that passive reception is not some simple, unidimensional thing. It is extraordinarily complex, and the mimetic model of desire throws more light on that complexity than any other position of which I am aware.

Next, Girard's position shows the interrelations of the two "ways of being conscious." For one thing, it is ultimately a spiritual emptiness that leads to the derailments of mimetic desire, an emptiness reminiscent of Augustine's "You have made us for yourself, and our hearts are restless until they rest in you." The ontological sickness pertains to the second way, but mimetic desire manifests how it contaminates the first. But also, the only resolution of mimetic violence is the complete renunciation of the rivalry to which triangular acquisitive desire leads us, and that renunciation is an intensely spiritual act flowing from a decision that itself proceeds from recognizing the facts of the situation. In other words, the resolution of the problems to which acquisitive mimetic desire gives rise takes place through a series of *autonomous spiritual processions* that are precisely the sort of emanations that Lonergan regards as appropriate for the psychological Trinitarian analogy.

Third, if any contemporary elucidation of the dynamics of sin is possible, it must include the elements that Girard emphasizes. And if the resolution to the problem of sin occurs through those processions in us that are both analogies for and participations in the immanent life of the Trinity, then the significance of Girard's work for a contemporary systematic theology is momentous indeed.

Finally, I have written fairly abundantly on the topic of psychic conversion and on the dramatic bias from which psychic conversion can help set us free. I have come to regard the vagaries of mimetic desire to which Girard gives us entrance as among the principal instances of dramatic bias and of the psychological components of other forms of bias.

2   Varieties of Imitation

Thesis 41: *If grace in history is a matter of created imitations of the divine relations, sin in history is a matter of quite different kinds of*

> *imitations leading to destructive and violent relations. These would be
> the counterfoil, as it were, to a vision of the social and cultural mean-
> ing of grace. The mimetic theory of René Girard helps us identify such
> infected mimesis.*

I have been setting the dogmatic-theological context for theological advance, especially for renewal of the theology of the Trinity, and I have
maintained that this context lies in a set of created supernatural relations
that imitate and participate in the divine relations. I have maintained that
participation in the divine relations is offered to all men and women, ir-
respective of whether or not the invitation and response be thematically
acknowledged. From this context I have already suggested that the basic
parameters for advance in ecclesiology are to be found in the notion of mission, of the church as mission, or more precisely of the church as servant
of God on mission from Jesus. "As the Father has sent me, so I send you – I
send you on mission so that, participating in the divine relations, you may
extend to the ends of the earth the message of a love that enables human
beings to love even their enemies."

In this chapter I have called attention to the mimetic theory of René Girard. If grace in history is a matter of created imitations of the divine relations, then perhaps sin in history is a matter of quite different kinds of
imitations leading to destructive and violent relations. These would be the
counterfoil, as it were, to a vision of the social and cultural meaning of grace.

Lonergan indicates that the root by default, as it were, of decline in
human affairs lies in bias, and I have come to see the intimate relationship
between the mimetic theory of René Girard and Lonergan's notion of bias.
I was originally put onto this relationship by a couple of papers delivered
at Lonergan workshops by Professor John Ranieri of Seton Hall University.[36] Briefly, sensitive desire is not peculiar to the individual but is, to use
Girard's neologism, interdividual; it is a function of the priority of the intersubjective over the individual. For Girard, the dramatic or emotional or
psychic form of bias is a function of the mimetic character of human desire.
What occurs at the level of the passive undergoing of our desires and fears,
our delights and sorrows, our joys and sadness, is mimetic. Many, perhaps
most, of our desires are not autonomous or innate, but copied from others.
"If I desire a particular object, I do not covet it on its own merits but because I 'mimic,' or imitate, the desire of someone I have chosen as a model.
That person – whether real or imaginary, legendary or historical – becomes
the mediator of my desire, and the relationship in which I am involved is
essentially 'triangular.'"[37]

Now mimesis in itself (or in the abstract) is neutral. But *acquisitive* or *appropriative* mimesis leads to violence, whether overt or covert. Acquisitive

mimesis, focused on the object *because of* the model or mediator, becomes conflictual mimesis when the object drops out of sight and the subject becomes concerned only or at least primarily with the model or mediator. What we are calling the "object" can be located at or related to any of the levels of value in the scale of values. Conflictual mimesis is contagious. It can infect a community, an institution, a governing body, a religious establishment, and it can endanger the welfare and even the survival of the groups it affects, at least until the focus turns on one individual or group, namely, the scapegoat, whose immolation, exclusion, or expulsion brings a precarious peace. "It is better for you," said Caiaphas, "to have one man die for the people than to have the whole nation destroyed" (John 11.50). Such is the basic schema that governs much of Girard's thinking.

Moreover, there is a progressive revelation in the biblical texts of precisely this set of mimetic mechanisms, which finally become unveiled for all to see – and so lose their power – in the crucifixion of Jesus. This liberation is one element of the salvation that the cross and resurrection of Jesus effect. Perhaps through Girard's help we will come to see it as the central element in soteriology, and perhaps also we will see appropriative mimetic desire as the basic element in original sin. And so again, perhaps we have a glimpse of how the dogmatic-theological context can go forward as we move into this new age of theology.[38]

Girard's work obviously raises the question of a radical ontological desire that itself is not mimetic but that is involved in all mimetic desire. That is, imitative desire is brought on by a sense of spiritual inadequacy that is endemic to the human condition. Perhaps we might say that the story of imitative desire is a story of the successes and failures of *mutual self-mediation*[39] as we attempt together to find the completion of our being, a completion that is possible only by reason of a supernatural participation in divine life itself. Mimetic violence, which springs from imitative desire, is the fate of mutual self-mediation gone wrong. But there is also healthy mutual self-mediation, and it begins in the mutual self-mediation of the Trinity in history with us through the gift of grace.[40] What enables one to renounce mimetic rivalry, without using this renunciation as a feigned indifference that is just another way to get what one wants, is precisely the gift of love that enables us to want, and to strive, to be perfect in mercy and forgiveness as our heavenly Father is perfect. Perhaps it is precisely here, in the realm of contaminated human relationships and the readiness for truthful forgiveness that alone transcends them, that we have the clearest indication that we are going to find as to whether our love is God's love and so truly without conditions, reservations, restrictions, or qualifications.

There are three steps to such a resolution of human conflict. The first is non-retaliation on the part of the person or group that has been wronged.

The second is forgiveness. And the third is reconciliation. This third step is not possible without the full disclosure of the truth of what has gone wrong. Any attempt at reconciliation without truth simply papers over injuries and injustices.

The theological significance of Girard's work is momentous. The original temptation is represented in the Book of Genesis as awakening a desire to be like God (or like gods). The first murder recorded in the bible is prompted by mimetic rivalry. The Gospels of Mark and Matthew tell us that Pilate knew that the reason the chief priests had handed Jesus over was out of jealousy (Mark 15.10, Matthew 27.18). Even the extraordinarily insightful exegete N.T. Wright, whose work I follow very closely when attempting to understand the public ministry of Jesus, does not emphasize this verse and the dynamics that it reflects as much as I believe he should in his otherwise brilliant discussion of "The Reasons for Jesus' Crucifixion."[41] Raymund Schwager has made what I regard as essential contributions to the same overall project that Wright and the late Ben F. Meyer have so laudably begun, precisely because he does take these emphases more seriously.[42] Lonergan was on the same track, I believe, without having studied Girard's work, and I think this is reflected especially in his recognition of the importance of Max Scheler's book *Ressentiment,* which captures some of the same dynamics without quite the same emphasis on mimesis as the engine that drives them (though I don't think Scheler is ignorant of the power of mimetic desire).[43] I support the efforts of John Ranieri to rearticulate Lonergan's theory of the biases with the help of Girard's mimetic theory. Moreover, those like James Alison who have turned to Girard for an understanding of what the Christian tradition means by "original sin" are also right on the mark.[44] If all these statements are true, then any systematic theology that purports to be a theological theory of history must take Girard's work with utmost seriousness. If the imitation of God that Jesus means when he says, "You must therefore be perfect as your heavenly Father is perfect" (Matthew 5.48), and that Lonergan anticipates when he refers to sanctifying grace and charity as created imitations of the divine relations of active and passive spiration, means what Jesus says it means, then it is set directly over against the deviated transcendence that is rooted in acquisitive mimesis. For being perfect as our heavenly Father is perfect means precisely "Love your enemies and pray for those who persecute you; in this way you will be children of your Father in heaven, for he causes his sun to rise on the bad as well as the good, and his rain to fall on the honest and the dishonest alike" (Matthew 5.44–45). God creates in grace the imitation, the mimesis, that is truly life-giving, and that imitation, that mimesis, is an imitation of, in fact even a created participation in, the divine relations themselves. Grace too is interdividual, and I suspect and hope that one of the principal theological developments of this still very young century will be the understanding of just how this is so.

> **Thesis 42:** *Mimetic violence is the story of mutual self-mediation gone wrong. There is another kind of mutual self-mediation established in grace that overcomes conflictual mimesis. The gift of divine love enables consistent fidelity to the transcendental imperatives attached to the notions of the intelligible, the true and the real, and the good, and such fidelity is the key to individuation. But that gift also has a dimension of its own, a dimension that transcends through forgiveness the contamination of human relations brought on by conflictual mimesis. Our love is God's love and so truly without conditions, reservations, or qualifications, when we love our enemies and pray for them, for God's love makes the Father's sun rise on the evil and the good and rain fall for the just and the unjust alike (Matthew 5.44–45).*

As I said earlier, these considerations lead us to ask whether there is a radical ontological desire that itself is not mimetic but that is involved in all mimetic desire, and also whether it has anything to do with the transcendental notions of the intelligible, the true and the real, and the good that lie at the heart of Lonergan's thinking. Is imitative desire brought on by a frustration of these spiritual desires, by a sense of spiritual inadequacy that is connected with the tremendous gap between aspiration and achievement? Again, we may ask whether the story of imitative desire reflects the successes and failures of mutual self-mediation in the attempt, itself completely legitimate, to find the completion of one's being that these transcendental notions intimate – a completion that can be found only in community? In the theology that will be put forth here, these transcendental notions are themselves obediential potency for the completion that is possible only by reason of a supernatural participation in divine life itself. They are a natural desire ultimately for the vision of God. And that participation in divine life overcomes conflictual mimesis to the extent that it enables an imitation of the divine relations. In the words of the current thesis, Girard's mimetic violence, which springs from imitative desire, is the story of mutual self-mediation gone wrong, and there is another kind of mutual self-mediation established in grace that overcomes conflictual mimesis. The gift of divine love enables consistent fidelity to the transcendental imperatives attached to the notions of the intelligible, the true and the real, and the good. Such fidelity brings in its wake the individuation that Jungian psychology aspires to but ultimately fails to bring about. But that gift also has a dimension of its own, a dimension that transcends through forgiveness the contamination of human relations brought on by conflictual mimesis. Our love is God's love and so truly without conditions, reservations, or qualifications, when we love our enemies and pray for them, for God's love makes the Father's sun rise on the evil and the good and rain fall for the just and the unjust alike (Matthew 5.44–45).

The fact of choosing a model for oneself is the result of a tendency common to all people to compare themselves with others; all jealousy, all ambition, and even an ideal like the imitation of Christ are based on such comparisons.[45] But this tendency is itself rooted in an ontological emptiness that only God can fill, and the ultimate meaning of the complicated vagaries of our tortured and tormented relationships lies in the way in which we negotiate this emptiness itself. There is a way of negotiating it that transcends victimization by the triangular situation that necessarily will be involved in the negotiation. Here lies, I believe, the source of our fascination with the saints, whether they be those whom the Catholic Church has canonized or those whom we acknowledge even without such official recognition as bearing in themselves a certain dignity that we can not only admire and respect but also imitate. Think of Ignatius Loyola asking, "What if I were to do what Saint Francis did, or to do what Saint Dominic did?"[46] The mimetic quality of the question is obvious, but we may trust that it led to something quite other than the tortured quality of internally mediated relations (however much the sons of Ignatius may have to struggle to transcend mimetic rivalry in their own midst!). It led, in fact, to autonomous spiritual processions of word and love that were in fact created participations in triune life, even if not always recognized as such. Think too of the constant appeals being made in our violent time to Gandhi and Martin Luther King and Dorothy Day, whose way of promoting justice for the victims of history is so different from the way of violence and hatred. Think of Ignatius's own prayer in the *Spiritual Exercises*: "… protesting that I wish and desire, and that it is my deliberate determination … to *imitate* Thee in bearing all insults and reproaches, and all poverty, as well actual poverty as poverty of spirit, if Thy Divine Majesty be pleased to choose and receive me to this life and state."[47] The sentiment is like that of Don Quixote vis-à-vis Amadis of Gaul, but in Ignatius's case, at least once he overcame his own tendencies to carry things to an unhealthy extreme, it did not lead to distortion of judgment or misperception of reality.

What makes the difference, as I have been emphasizing, are the transcendental desires of the human spirit, Lonergan's "second way of being conscious," and their ground and fulfilment in the gift of God's love. "All people by nature *desire* to know," says Aristotle at the very beginning of the *Metaphysics*. This becomes Lonergan's leitmotif throughout the book *Insight*, where he unpacks the dynamics of the desire to know in science, in common sense, and in philosophy, as well as some of the devices that we employ in fleeing understanding when the truth is something we do not want to face. In his later work he extends this transcendental desire, as well as the devices we use to escape its consequences, to the notion of the good.

How is all of this related to the mimetic quality of desire emphasized by Girard? Girard insists, correctly, that almost all learning is based on imitation,[48] and so satisfying the desire to know involves mimetic behavior, however natural the desire to know may be, and however elicited mimetic desire always is. In this sense, too, in the realm of representation, mimesis is the essential force of cultural integration, even if in the realm of acquisitive desire it is also the force of destruction and dissolution. The desire to know and the transcendental intention of value are not themselves a function of acquisitive mimesis. Acquisitiveness is a perversion of these desires. There is such a thing as a detached, disinterested desire to know. For Girard himself, integrating isolated discoveries into a rational framework and transforming them into real knowledge is the true vocation of thought, which in the end, after periods in which it appears to have run its course, is always reaffirmed.[49] This true vocation of thought reflects something other than acquisitive mimesis. It can, of course, be infected and derailed by acquisitive mimesis, as anyone who has spent any time in an academic institution knows all too well. But in itself the orientation that can become a vocation is natural, non-acquisitive, and in the last analysis not imitative or elicited. Lonergan may have set out to do for our day what Aquinas did for his, and his journey was to that extent mimetic. But in the actual judgments and decisions that he made along the way, he was on his own, and he knew it. Girard's work assumes a greater historical and theoretical significance to the extent that it can be shown to illuminate both how our true vocations are probably always rooted in imitative behavior and how the deviations from true vocation occur. But the fulfilment of vocation will always lie in the autonomous spiritual processions that at the supernatural level are our created participation in Trinitarian life and at the natural level are analogues of that participation and so of the divine processions themselves.

The significance, then, of imitating the divine relations is not purely inward and spiritual but historical and social. In *Violence and the Sacred*[50] and *Things Hidden since the Foundation of the World*, Girard faces the questions of the origins of mimetic desire and of its impact on cultural and social institutions. It is here that he discovers the scapegoat mechanism, which enables him to reassess the meaning of rites, rituals, and myths. "[N]ot only the prohibition but also ritual and ultimately the whole structure of religion can be traced back to the mechanism of acquisitive mimesis. A complete theory of human culture will be elaborated, beginning with this single principle."[51] At least one of the keys to authentic religion lies precisely in negotiating the "mechanism" that Girard has elaborated.

One further notion should be introduced in this context: the sacrificial crisis. A sacrificial crisis is a crisis in a community that can be resolved only by means of the sacrifice or expulsion of a surrogate victim or scapegoat. A sacrificial crisis entails the collapse of the social hierarchy and the loss of difference within the group. With the effacement of social distinctions the members of the community lose sight of who and what they are. In the chaos other distinctions are lost as well: good and evil, right and wrong, rationality and irrationality. In *Violence and the Sacred* Girard writes: "[C]oherent thinking collapses and rational activities are abandoned … all values, spiritual and material, vanish."[52]

One of Girard's interlocutors in *Things Hidden since the Foundation of the World* maintains that Girard's thesis is not primarily a theory of religion but a theory of human relations and of the role that the victimage mechanism plays in those relations, that the theory of religion is simply a particularly noteworthy aspect of a fundamental theory of mimetic relations, and that religion is one means of misinterpreting mimetic relations. Girard agrees. The sacred, he says, is to our understanding of human relations what phlogiston was to the understanding of combustion, and mimesis is to our understanding of human relations what oxygen is to the understanding of combustion. "Our own oxygen is mimesis and all that accompanies it." Again, Girard is working in and clarifying what Lonergan calls the first way of being conscious. But the influence that distorted mimesis has on the realm of the sacred indicates just how important this theory of human relations, indeed of primordial intersubjectivity, is for theology. In its authenticity the realm of the sacred pertains primarily to the second way of being conscious. The importance of mimetic theory in its regard is displayed already in our systematic theology, in that it helps us get straight just where the genuine *imago Dei*, and so the genuine *imitatio Dei*, lies in human consciousness and where it does not. To place it where it does not reside is precisely a matter of deviated transcendence.

And so we move explicitly to a consideration of the various meanings of the term "image of God" and of the ways in which they all enter into the elaboration of an analogical understanding of the triune God.

3   *Imago Dei*

> **Thesis 43:** *Foundationally the image of God lies in the created participation in active and passive spiration that is the share in divine life given us in grace. The historical mission of the Word reveals precisely in what that imitation lies, namely, in the love that returns good for evil. Derivatively, the image of God lies in fidelity to the transcendental imperatives of human consciousness, and particularly in the way these*

give rise to successive processions of act from act in cognitive and exis-
tential subjectivity. The foundational instance, which is first in itself,
will be understood by analogy with the derived instance, which is first
for us.

Where, then, does the image of God lie? Where is the *imago* that is also an *imitatio?*

Foundationally, it lies in the created participation in active and passive spiration that is the share in divine life given to us here and now. That participation is (1) the gift of unqualified love, which (2) alters the horizon in which evidence regarding one's existential self-constitution is grasped, to ground a radical assent or fundamental option for the good, (3) from which there flows that radical yes to the value of such self-constitution that (4) grounds the habitual performance of loving acts. The movements from evidence grasped to radical assent and then from evidence and assent together to proceeding love are instances of *emanationes intelligibiles* or autonomous spiritual processions, in the order of grace. The first three of these items constitute the created participation in active spiration, and the fourth the created participation in passive spiration. This image, this imitation, is foundational because it is first *quoad se.*

The historical mission of the Word, however, shows us concretely what it is to imitate the *Verbum spirans amorem* and the Father whose Word he is, that is, to imitate the two persons who *are* active spiration. Girard illumines the concrete dynamics of what Lonergan articulates heuristically as follows, precisely in his discussion of the "appropriate willingness" required to transcend the mystery of iniquity:

> [T]he will can contribute to the solution of the problem of the social surd inasmuch as it adopts a dialectical attitude that parallels the dialectical method of intellect. The dialectical method of intellect consists in grasping that the social surd neither is intelligible nor is to be treated as intelligible. The corresponding dialectical attitude of will is to return good for evil. For it is only inasmuch as men are willing to meet evil with good, to love their enemies, to pray for those that persecute and calumniate them, that the social surd is a potential good. It follows that love of God above all and in all so embraces the order of the universe as to love all men with a self-sacrificing love.[53]

What Lonergan here is calling a dialectical attitude of will is expressly called by Jesus an imitation of the divine Father: "You have heard that it was said, 'You shall love your neighbor and hate your enemy.' But I say to you, Love your enemies and pray for those who persecute you, so that you may be children of your Father who is in heaven; for he makes his sun rise on the evil and on the good, and sends rain on the just and on the unjust. For if you love those who love you, what reward have you? Do not even the tax collectors do the same? And if you salute only your brethren, what more are you doing than others? Do not even the Gentiles do the same? You, therefore, must be perfect, as your heavenly Father is perfect."[54] At this point, it seems, our systematic considerations and the integration of these considerations with the mimetic theory of René Girard join in bearing witness to the biblical revelation's unmasking of the principal dynamics of evil in history and to the same revelation's pointing the way to transcending these dynamics. In the order of grace, the supernatural order, the mission of the Holy Spirit is first *quoad se*, but the revelation in the incarnate Word of precisely what constitutes the imitation of God is first *quoad nos*.

If this imitation in the order of grace is the foundational instance of the *imago Dei*, the derived instance in the order of nature lies in the constant fidelity to the natural unfolding of the transcendental exigencies to be attentive, intelligent, reasonable, and responsible, each with their own processions of act from act. This fidelity is made possible by the gift of grace itself. It requires the supernatural solution to the problem of evil, a supernatural solution that, in God's own dispensation, consists in the gift of created participations in the divine relations grounding imitations of the triune God. This natural unfolding of the transcendental aspirations of the human mind and heart are even more first *quoad nos*, as the desire to know functions spontaneously, independently of any divine revelation.

While the supernatural *imitatio* is foundational, it is understood by analogy with the natural *imago*, with the imitation in the very order of nature, an imitation that lies, first, within actively intelligent, actively reasonable, actively deliberative consciousness. We proceed, then, to consider this natural analogue more fully.

Here a distinction is drawn between the fundamental light of human consciousness and the further determinations of that same light. In the context of cognitional process, that fundamental light is what Aristotle and then Aquinas called agent intellect, which Lonergan explicitly identifies with the desire to know. It is what is referred to in Thomas's words "ex vi intellectiva." In that same cognitional context, the further determinations of that same light are referred to in Thomas's "ex eius notitia procedens."[55] The desire to know is a created participation, in the natural order, in the uncreated light that is divine understanding, and it is the source of all our wonder, inquiry, and reflection. In its authentic functioning it is pure, detached, disinterested. Built into its constitution, as it were, are the most general principles that are operative independently of any determination from experience: the principles of identity, non-contradiction, and sufficient reason. But it is also the transcendental notion of value, setting the criterion not only for cognitional process but also for decisions. And the "precept" that is built into it at that level is, in Thomist terms, that good is to be done and evil to be avoided. The entire reality of this fundamental light in its active or intentional dimensions is expressed in the transcendental precepts or imperatives that Lonergan expresses thus: "Be attentive, Be intelligent, Be reasonable, Be responsible." Thus, the "principles" constitutively built into this fundamental light function not deductively but heuristically in actively intelligent and deliberative consciousness. They are not principles in the sense of premises from which conclusions are drawn in a logically consistent manner. While we have to articulate them in premises if we are to talk about them, the premises simply express universal features of intellectual, rational, and existential dynamism that function spontaneously in all genuine inquiry and deliberation.

Our definition of autonomous spiritual procession contains the phrase *by virtue of the spiritual dimension of consciousness itself as determined by the prior act*. The fundamental light of the spiritual dimension of consciousness is the "by virtue of the spiritual dimension of consciousness itself" referred to in this definition, the *vis ipsius conscientiae intellectualis* referred to in Lonergan's definition of *emanatio intelligibilis*. But what is intellectually and consciously operative in us lies not only in this light. It is also further determined by our conscious acts themselves. We are determined as intellectually, rationally, and morally conscious and consciously active and operative: materially or potentially by the objects of sensation, with an incipient and devalued formal and actual intelligibility in the reception of meanings and values, formally by our own acts of understanding as a release to our own inquiry, more formally still as these acts of understanding give rise to the act that is the first inner word (act from act), then actually by our own grasp of evidence and the judgments that proceed from that grasp (again, act from act), and constitutively by our deliberations and decisions flowing from our judgments of value (act from act once more). Thus, if the dynamism of the spiritual dimension of consciousness lies in the light of intelligence, reasonableness, and moral responsibility within us, the further determinations added by our own activities are in part what the definition refers to when it describes this consciousness as determined by the prior acts from which, by *emanatio intelligibilis*, by autonomous spiritual procession, there proceed other acts. Thus, the notion of *emanatio intelligibilis* is what Aquinas is illustrating when he writes, "Whenever we understand, by the mere fact that we do understand, *something proceeds within us*, which is the conception of the thing understood, issuing from our intellective power and proceeding from its knowledge."[56] Lonergan expands: "Accordingly, when we understand and by the very fact that we understand, from our intellective power, which is the general light of intellectual consciousness, and from the knowledge contained in the act of understanding that adds a determination to the general light, *there proceeds within our intellectual consciousness a conception or definition of the reality understood.* Similarly, when we grasp that the evidence is sufficient, by the very fact that we grasp it, and from the exigency of intellectual light as determined through that grasp, *there proceeds within our intellectual consciousness either a true affirmation or a true negative assertion.* Similarly again, when we judge some good as obligatory, by the very fact that we so judge, through our intellectuality, our rationality, *we spirate an act of will.*"[57]

The definition of *emanatio intelligibilis*, then, speaks first of *acts*, operations, that are *real, natural,* and *conscious. Act* here is implicitly defined in relation to form and potency. "act : form : potency :: seeing : eyesight : eye :: hearing something : the faculty of hearing : the ear :: understanding something : the intelligible species : the possible intellect :: willing : willingness : will :: existence : substantial form : prime matter."[58] *Real* acts are acts of which it can reasonably be affirmed, "They are, they occur, they happen." While the acts in question are intentional acts, they are considered here not in their intending of an object but as occurring in their own right, hence as *natural.*[59] To say that they are *conscious* means that the presence of the subject to himself or herself is constitutive of the acts themselves. The subject is present, not as what is intended (the object, which also is rendered psychologically present by the act), but as what intends; and the act is present to the subject as that by which the object is intended. The presence of the subject to himself or herself in these acts is distinct, too, from the presence of the subject through reflection or introspection. Reflection on oneself renders oneself present as an object, but this would not be possible unless the subject were already present to himself or herself as a subject, through consciousness – not as what is intended but as what intends.[60]

The emanation is a procession of one such real, natural, conscious act from another such real, natural, conscious act, *within intellectual consciousness,* or, differently put for our present purposes, within the order of spirit. That is, it is a conscious psychological event *constituted by intelligent and/or existential acts and the conscious nexus between them.* It is in the sustained recurrence of such conscious psychological events that the derived *imago Dei,* the natural *imitatio Dei* that we are, is to be found.

As *within consciousness,* the procession is considered precisely as such a *psychological* event. Its explicitation or objectification belongs to intentionality analysis rather than to metaphysics. True, an authentic metaphysics would articulate it also, as an accident inhering in a substance or as an act received in a potency. The same reality that, metaphysically considered, is correctly thus described is also psychologically an event that occurs within the field of consciousness; and that is the way we are studying it here. Nor,

Lonergan emphasizes, does "conscious" add anything to "being," for being is not a genus, and what is beyond or outside of being is precisely nothing. "Conscious" simply names a certain degree of perfection within being.

As *within intellectual consciousness* (Lonergan's expression), or within the order of spirit (my preferred way of speaking), the procession is constituted by intellectual, rational, and existential acts, not by sensitive acts. The latter are not left behind, of course, but are sublated into the richer context furnished by intelligent, reasonable, responsible acts. "Sublation" is a term that Lonergan adopts from Karl Rahner, where its meaning is not the Hegelian sense of *Aufhebung* but something much more straightforward: "[W]hat sublates goes beyond what is sublated, introduces something new and distinct, puts everything on a new basis, yet so far from interfering with the sublated or destroying it, on the contrary needs it, includes it, preserves all its proper features and properties, and carries them forward to a fuller realization within a richer context."[61] Our one consciousness is not homogeneous, but is diversified in accord with the diverse nature of its acts.

The emanation is not only conscious; it is a conscious procession (*origo*), and it occurs in virtue of the dynamism of consciousness itself. The emergence of one real, natural, and conscious act from another real, natural, and conscious act is itself conscious and occurs in virtue of conscious dynamism itself. Here we need only revert to the examples that Lonergan provides: the difference between a rash judgment and a reasonable one, the difference between repeating a memorized definition and uttering it as something one has understood, and the difference between disordered and responsible choices. In this way consciousness *mediates* the procession. To say that consciousness mediates means (1) that the conscious subject as conscious is the agent principle (*principium quod*) of the procession; (2) a conscious act as conscious is the instrumental principle (*principium quo*) of the procession; (3) the procession itself has an intrinsic element that is lacking in an unconscious procession such as a chemical procession; and (4) the proceeding act is somehow consciously *because of* and consciously *in accordance with* the act from which it proceeds.[62]

But the mediation that renders possible an autonomous *spiritual* procession or emanation is a mediation that occurs in virtue of the dynamism of the spiritual dimension of human consciousness itself, a dynamism in the order of spirit, and not in virtue of the dynamics of sensitive consciousness. One act can proceed from another within sensitive consciousness, but the procession does not possess the characteristics constitutive of an *emanatio intelligibilis*. To cite Lonergan's example, from seeing a large, fierce-looking animal on the loose there *spontaneously* arises in sensitive consciousness a sense of fear, precisely *because* one has seen the animal; and so one conscious act proceeds from another *because of and in accordance with* the first

act. But in sensitive consciousness this occurs by some automatically functioning law of a particular nature. The same may be said of the triangular
nature of mimetic desire, which functions precisely in this sensitive, psychic, and now intersubjective or "interdividual" domain, however much it
may be a function of a spiritual vacuum. But when one real, natural, and
conscious *intelligent* or *reasonable* or *responsible* act proceeds from another
real, natural, and conscious *intelligent* or *reasonable* or *responsible* act, the
link is constituted not by an automatically functioning law but by the *self-*
governing, *autonomous*, and *transcendental* exigencies of intelligence and reasonableness and responsibility, according to which our integrity as human
subjects is a function of our ordered allegiance to complete intelligibility,
truth, being, and goodness. We give the law to ourselves. The transcendental laws of human spirituality commit us to a set of objectives that embrace
everything, the concrete universe of being. Our fidelity to these exigencies
can be violated, for our performance in this realm is not a function of specific and automatically functioning laws but is such that in the relevant acts
the human spirit is determinative of itself and in that sense autonomous.
That performance can be cut off, strangled, rendered impotent, by one's
own existential decisions, by major defaults in one's cultural and social situations, or by the interference of that other type of desire on which Girard
has thrown so much light. That spiritual spontaneity is regulated, not by
being bound to any automatic response, but only insofar as it is actually
constituted by a transcendental desire for being and value. It rules itself,
insofar as under God's agency it determines itself to its own acts according
to the exigencies of its own being as spiritual. But insofar as this is the case,
one conscious act will arise or proceed from another conscious act through
the mediation of intelligent, reasonable, responsible consciousness itself.

It is in the context of talk about the autonomy of these operations that
we have found our first fruitful encounter with the mimetic theory of René
Girard. Girard has introduced a necessary hermeneutics of suspicion into
the project of self-appropriation initiated by Lonergan, a hermeneutics that
is probably the best categorial articulation to date of what my own work has
anticipated heuristically by speaking of psychic conversion. For there is an
interference of acquisitively mimetic desire with the unfolding of the transcendental orientation to the intelligible, the true and the real, the good,
and God, and Girard with ruthless precision has captured some of the dynamics, indeed something of the mechanism, of that interference.

Girard is working in the area of the psychic dimension of consciousness.
But as we have seen, not every spiritual procession is autonomous either.
There is another kind of procession within the spiritual dimension of consciousness, one that does not satisfy the requirements of an analogy for divine procession. For from questions there can spontaneously proceed an

act of understanding, but then the procession is not from act to act but from potency to act: in consciousness from questions to answers, and metaphysically from the "possible intellect" to "intelligible species." This kind of procession Lonergan, following Aquinas, calls a procession of an operation (*processio operationis*). The more autonomous procession that alone qualifies as an analogue for divine procession is the procession of a subsequent act *from* a prior act and *in accordance with* that prior act. "[T]hus, we define *because* we understand and *in accordance with* what we understand; again, we judge *because* we grasp evidence as sufficient and *in accordance with* the evidence we have grasped; finally, we choose *because* we judge and *in accordance with* what we judge to be useful or proper or fitting or obligatory."[63] This type of procession Lonergan, again following Aquinas, calls, not a procession of an operation (*processio operationis*) but a procession of something operated (*processio operati*).[64]

There is, then, an *imago Dei*, an *imitatio Dei* – "image" and "imitatio" are from the same root – that is natural, that resides in our spiritual nature, where "nature" is understood in the Aristotelian sense of an immanent principle of movement and of rest. The *imago* or *imitatio Dei* is not the whole of that spiritual nature, for that nature is "the human spirit as raising and answering questions"[65] and so as potency *in genere intelligibilium*, in the realm of spiritual things. But there are moments in which that nature precisely as nature imitates pure act, however remotely: when from understanding as act there proceeds an inner word of conceptualization as act; when from the grasp of evidence as sufficient there proceeds an inner word of judgment; and when from the judgment of value based on the grasp of evidence there proceeds a decision. That natural image can be used as an analogy from which we may understand the more radical image or imitation that lies in a created participation in the divine relations of active and passive spiration. Between these two analogies lies Lonergan's own later analogy, and I conclude this chapter by quoting him again and expanding briefly again on his words.

> The psychological analogy ... has its starting point in that higher synthesis of intellectual, rational, and moral consciousness that is the dynamic state of being in love. Such love manifests itself in its judgments of value. And the judgments are carried out in decisions that are acts of loving. Such is the analogy found in the creature.[66]

I have placed the starting point in the remembered reception of unqualified love that provides evidence for the judgment of value and with it constitutes a created participation in divine active spiration. From the remembered reception of love there flows evidence perceived by a lover, from which one's judgments of value proceed as act from act. What proceeds from this created participation in active spiration are the decisions that are acts of loving, and as such created participations in passive spiration. The supernatural analogy found in the creature imitates by participation the entire life of the triune God, and it is only by the grace of this created imitation that the natural transcendental unfolding of our spiritual aspirations remains consistently authentic.

10

Sacralization and Desacralization in History

1   Introduction

> **Thesis 44:** *Lonergan's heuristic anticipation in history of (1) a sacralization to be dropped, (2) a sacralization to be fostered, (3) a secularization to be welcomed, and (4) a secularization to be resisted can be specified in terms of his notions of the Law of the Cross and of the transcendental exigencies of the human spirit, and in terms of Girard's notion of the scapegoat.*

In my interpretation of Lonergan's Trinitarian systematics I am slowly introducing as well some developments upon the theory of history that I first presented in *Theology and the Dialectics of History.* In this chapter I continue along those lines before returning explicitly to Lonergan's chapter on the divine processions and to linking that work with his theology of the divine missions within the context of a theology of history.

In a posthumously published paper entitled "Sacralization and Secularization" Lonergan offers a set of suggestions for discriminating "(1) a sacralization to be dropped and (2) a sacralization to be fostered; (3) a secularization to be welcomed and (4) a secularization to be resisted."[1] The point of the present chapter is to develop these suggestions with the help of René Girard. But before the suggestions can be developed, they have to be specified more precisely, and that is not a particularly easy task. I believe Lonergan never completed to his satisfaction the paper "Sacralization and Secularization," and for this reason he did not publish it in his lifetime. Moreover, the suggestions that can be deciphered in "Sacralization and Secularization" must be complemented by considerations that appear in other works of Lonergan.

The conclusions at which I have arrived can be stated at the outset. Before stating them, however, let me indicate that the question as it is addressed here and in Lonergan's paper has to do with the sacred *in human history*, as contrasted with its manifestations in nature. I have no doubt that creation is a reflection of the glory of God and a source of legitimate sacralizations in worship and prayer, song and dance, liturgy and art, and that exploits despoiling the natural environment are a desecration of God's creation. But I am for the moment prescinding from the sacred in nature except insofar as history itself is located within the universe created by God. It is in human history that I wish to locate the fourfold set of realities anticipated by Lonergan's distinctions. In other words, which *historical arrangements of human affairs* should be sacralized, and which desacralized; which should be secularized, and which desecularized? It is within the context of providing answers to these questions that ecological concerns can be fruitfully addressed in theology. But for our present purposes in this book, the answers to these questions will have something to display regarding the effective presence through grace and nature of the Trinity and its supernatural and natural *imitationes* in history. It is for this reason that the material is introduced at this point.

My conclusions, then, are the following.

(1) Setting the standard of sacralizations to be dropped in the conduct of human affairs are any and all attempts to employ the name or word of God or any other sacral trappings to justify not only natural evils but also persecution, exclusion, and scapegoating both of carriers of the genuine religious word and, given the character of that word itself, of anyone else. While an astute philosophy of God will speak of physical evils in terms of emergent probability, God is not the cause of basic sin and moral evils in any way whatsoever. The divine presence is offered as consolation and strength to those affected by both natural disaster and human sinfulness.

(2) The standard of sacralizations to be fostered in the conduct of human affairs can be spoken of in Christian terms as adherence to what Lonergan calls the just and mysterious Law of the Cross. This standard entails recognizing and celebrating the transformation of evil into a greater good, indeed a supreme good, precisely through the absorption of evil in love, an absorption that imitates the attitude of the Incarnate Word of God, to see whom is to see the Father. The reality of the Law of the Cross, which is revealed progressively in the Israelite scriptures and embodied in the Incarnate Word, is itself a specification of a genuine or authentic

religious component that can be found in other religious traditions as well, even if it is more clearly differentiated progressively in the Hebrew Bible and definitively in the New Testament. What is specific to Christianity are the mysteries of the Incarnate Word and the Trinity, but part of what is specific to the Incarnate Word himself as embodying a Trinitarian mission is that in him there is revealed a law of utmost generality affecting the very constitution of history. It seems clear from the study of other religions that this law is present there as well, even if not as clearly instantiated as in the anticipations to be found in the Hebrew Bible's suffering servant of God and in the realization of those anticipations in the Passion, death, and Resurrection of the Incarnate Word. It was, after all, the Hindu Gandhi who quotes from the Gujarati didactic stanza, "And return with gladness good for evil done."[2] That *is* the Law of the Cross. This reality, wherever it is found, is determinative of what in my first point I called the genuine religious word, as that word affects historical action or praxis; any word that would purport to be religious but that runs counter to this dimension is fraudulent, a manifestation of deviated transcendence.

(3) Setting the standard of secularizations to be welcomed in the conduct and organization of human affairs are, first, the realities that Lonergan formulates in his transcendental precepts: Be attentive, Be intelligent, Be reasonable, Be responsible – realities that his work enables us to make our own through what he calls self-appropriation; and second, the *Befindlichkeit* dimensions of mood or disposition or concomitant affect that precede, accompany, and go beyond these realities and that determine the nature of what the Christian tradition has called discernment.[3] The natural orientation of the human spirit to intelligibility, the true and the real, and the good, and to beauty as the splendor of these transcendental objectives, and the concomitant affective dispositions that match this orientation will disclose over time and over the development of human culture which cultural and social arrangements can and should be granted their own autonomy from the mantle of sacral authority, while still encouraging the influence of religious and personal values in the cultural and social spheres. But it should be noted at once that, as Lonergan makes abundantly clear, sustained fidelity to such integrity is possible only by the gift of God's love, and so only by some lived participation in the genuine sacred, in the participations in active and passive spiration that we have already seen, and so in the love embodied in the Law of the Cross.

(4) Setting the standard of secularizations to be resisted in the conduct and organization of human affairs are any and all attempts, whether or not grounded in a false sacralization, to condemn or scapegoat carriers of the genuine religious word in whatever tradition, and any consequent efforts to locate human "coming of age" as a perfection to be attained exclusively in this life and exclusively on the basis of human resources.

A number of points are clear already. The first is that the issue of sacralization, secularization, and desacralization in history is an expansion into the social and cultural fabric of human history of the classical problem of the relation of human nature to the supernatural, a relation that Lonergan unfolded in terms of a precise understanding of the category of obediential potency. In the terms of the present work, this relation is manifest in the relation between the carriers of the supernatural analogy and those of the natural analogy.

Second, the reader will no doubt have noticed the similarity between sacralizations to be dropped and secularizations to be resisted. The Gospel narrative exposes this similarity, indeed this identity, since we see that sacral authorities turned to secular power to execute Jesus, thereby negating the sacrality of their entire project. But contemporary secularism has removed the sacral trappings from what the Gospel narrative reveals to be a false sacralization of a genuinely profane event, namely, murder. Thus today, in societies where religion and the state are distinguished, these secularizations appear more honestly, in that they are not sanctioned by any appeal to divine authority; but, as Girard has pointed out over and over again, the danger of violence getting out of hand is far greater when religion can no longer be appealed to, however inauthentically, to limit the effects of violence. Religion has limited violence precisely by resorting to violence, through what Girard calls the single victim mechanism of scapegoating. Now that this mechanism has been exposed by the Gospel, the danger is even greater that violence will wreak total, indeed apocalyptic, destruction.

Third, perhaps the reader familiar with Lonergan and Girard will also have noticed that Lonergan has provided the positive and Girard the negative marks of identification. Both sacralizations to be fostered and secularizations to be welcomed are understood in terms drawn from Lonergan. Both sacralizations to be dropped and secularizations to be resisted are understood in terms drawn from Girard.

Finally, perhaps the reader will agree with me that this is no accident. It is Lonergan's notion of the subject, and through that notion his understanding and affirmation of human nature and of its relation to the supernatural order of divine grace, that enables him to retrieve a primary meaning for such realities as culture, religion, the sacred, and sacrifice, while it is Girard's trenchant analysis of these realities gone wrong that exposes at least some cultural and religious aberrations more profoundly than does any other writer whom I have studied. Still, as we proceed further, we will discover that the two authors complement one another in each of these areas. It must be obvious to any student of current affairs that the issue of sacralization, secularization, and desacralization is crucial for all religious identity at this time in world history, and, precisely because of the importance of religious identity for that history itself, it is crucial for the future of humanity. Lonergan and Girard can help first the Christian churches but then other traditions as well to discriminate the relevant factors, and especially to distinguish the mythic consciousness that sets up theocracies from the genuinely sacred that at times will go so far as to dismantle what mythic consciousness erected. The issue is not unrelated to "enlightenment," and the responsibility of the churches is not to oppose enlightenment but to ensure that it not be simply a matter of secularist rejection of the genuine sacred.

2   The Law of the Cross

2.1 A New Community

Thesis 45: *The supreme good into which fidelity to the Law of the Cross, which enjoins the return of good for evil done, transforms the evils that afflict the human race is the emergence of a new community in history and in the life to come, a community that in theological terms can be understood as the whole Christ, Head and members, whether explicitly Christian or not, in all the concrete determinations and relations constitutive of this community.*

Because of the centrality of the Law of the Cross in the conclusions that I have stated at the outset of this chapter, I find that I can best proceed by examining first the extent to which Lonergan and Girard are at one in their understanding of this redemptive constituent of history and the extent, if any, to which they differ.[4]

Perhaps we may proceed most expeditiously by reflecting on the following statements of each author and asking whether and to what extent they are saying the same thing. The Lonergan statement is Thesis 17 of *De Verbo incarnato*: "This is why the Son of God became man, suffered, died, and was raised again: because divine wisdom has ordained and divine goodness has willed, not to do away with the evils of the human race through power, but to convert those evils into a supreme good according to the just and mysterious Law of the Cross."[5] The Girard statement reads as follows: "If God allowed Satan to reign for a certain period over humankind, it is because God knew beforehand that at the right time Christ would overcome his adversary by dying on the Cross. God in his wisdom had foreseen since the beginning that the victim mechanism would be reversed like a glove, exposed, placed in the open, stripped naked, and dismantled in the Gospel Passion texts, and he knew that neither Satan nor the powers could prevent this revelation ... The divine wisdom knew that thanks to this death the victim mechanism would be neutralized."[6]

The key to answering these questions lies in identifying what Lonergan means by the "supreme good" into which the evils of the human race are transformed according to the Law of the Cross. Locating this supreme good is very important for three reasons. First, it concretizes what otherwise would be left indeterminate. Second, it names something that is not explicit in Girard's account as here reported, though it may be claimed to be implicit in all that he says about the matter. And third, despite its importance it tends to be overlooked in studies of the soteriology expressed in Lonergan's thesis on the Law of the Cross.

It would seem that this "supreme good," as defined by Lonergan, is more than a reversal or neutralization of the victim mechanism, however much these elements from the Girardian model may help in articulating elements, even the central elements, in the process of transformation. The supreme good is "the whole Christ, Head and members, in this life as well as in the life to come, *in all their concrete determinations and relations* [including] (1) communicated goods [the grace of the Incarnation, of sanctifying grace, of the habit of charity, and of the light of glory], (2) a good of order in that quasi-organic unity which is Christ and the church, and (3) particular goods both of Christ the Head and of the members." Through what Lonergan calls "the just and mysterious Law of the Cross," then, the "evils of the human race" are transformed into "the whole Christ, Head and members, in this life as well as in the life to come," in all the concrete determinations and relations of that community. The evils of the human race are transformed into a new community, a community that has a new set of concrete determinations and relations. How does this occur? Through the Law of the Cross. What is the Law of the Cross? A precept of utmost generality that enjoins not overcoming these evils by power but absorbing them in a loving surrender that returns good for evil done.

Again, the Law of the Cross is itself a developmental process. The process begins, in many instances, with a simple refusal to retaliate. That refusal may itself precede forgiveness, precede loving absorption, precede return of good for evil, but it marks the beginning of the process toward these characteristic elements of a response. Beyond these is reconciliation, which, as Archbishop Desmond Tutu has taught us in our time, demands the recognition by all of the truth of what has occurred.

Later in the thesis (in the Preliminary Note) this "supreme good" that is "the whole Christ, Head and members" is referred to as the *form* of the economy of salvation, a form that is introduced into the "matter" that is the human race infected with original sin, burdened with actual sins, entangled in the penalties of sin, alienated from God, and divided both within individuals and between them, or socially. The emergence of that form, that "supreme good," that "solution to the problem of evil," in the terms of *Insight*, "will be in accord with the probabilities ... that regard the occurrence of [our] intelligent and rational apprehension of the solution and [our] free and responsible consent to it." Lonergan continues: "[T]here are stages in human development when there is no probability that men will apprehend and consent to a universally accessible and permanent solution that meets the basic problem of human nature. Moreover, all human development has been seen to be compounded with decline, and so it fails to prepare men directly and positively to apprehend and consent to the solution. Accordingly, it seems necessary to distinguish between the realization of the full solution and, on the other hand, the emergent trend in which the full solution becomes effectively probable."[7] The "form" that is the "supreme good" consists not of a hierarchically ordered group of people, a "good of order" in the formal sense of an organized institution, but radically of a threefold (or, as I have argued here, fourfold) communication of God to us (in the hypostatic union, in the uncreated gift of the Holy Spirit,[8] and in the beatific vision), and a consequent order of personal relations brought about through both wise apprehension of the divine self-communication and the habit of charity flowing from sanctifying grace. The "form" of this new community obtains both in this life and in the life to come, which is why the community itself in its entirety is called the communion of saints. The supreme good into which the evils of the human race are transformed by the cross of Christ is the communion of saints, a community of friendship with the three divine persons and among ourselves.

This emphasis in *De Verbo incarnato* on a new community, a new social reality, as the supreme good into which the evils of the human race are transformed corresponds to one of the most startling statements in Lonergan's treatment of the divine missions in *De Deo trino: Pars systematica*. The "state of grace" for Lonergan is a social, intersubjective situation – in Girardian terms a transformed "interdividuation" – grounded in the three divine subjects of the one consciousness of God. The threefold (or fourfold) communication of God is explicitly referred to in the Trinitarian systematics as an *imitatio* of the divine relations, which under Girardian emphases we could see as a mimesis that runs counter to the infected mimesis that constitutes or at least affects the evils of the human race from which we are freed by the Law of the Cross. It may be presumed, then, that Lonergan's explicit statement of the supreme good that results from the reversal wrought by the Cross does not run counter to Girardian expectations, even though the latter are not expressed in the same overtly theological terms. In fact, there is no reason to doubt that Girard has named something constitutive of the "evils of the human race" that are transformed into this new community of human and divine subjects, and perhaps the central element of those evils.

2.2 The Evils to Be Transformed

Thesis 46: *The evils transformed by the Law of the Cross are the distortions of relations that hinder genuine community from ever being realized. These are understood in terms of basic sin and moral evil, both of which are traced ultimately to original sin. With minor qualifications, these realities may be conceptualized more concretely in terms of the failure to reject the mimetic cycle and the consequences of such failure. The new community embodies a new kind of "interdividuation," one that is constituted by the imitation of the four divine relations in grace.*

This brings us to our next question. What precisely are the "evils of the human race" that are transformed into this community that Lonergan calls the whole Christ? In line with Lonergan's definition of the "supreme good," it might be best to speak of the evils of the human race as *all defects of the good in the concrete determinations and relations of human life.* If the supreme good into which the evils are transformed is a new community, then it is reasonable to suppose that the evils that are transformed into this new community are precisely the distortions of relations that hinder genuine community from ever being realized. These defects of the good are understood by Lonergan in terms of basic sin and moral evil. Basic sin, which is the category employed in *Insight,* is in *De Verbo incarnato* called "the evil of fault" (*malum culpae*). And the moral evil (again, the category employed in *Insight*) that follows from basic sin is in *De Verbo incarnato* called "the evil of punishment" (*malum poenae*). I greatly prefer the terminology of *Insight,* especially since I wish to steer completely away from any connotations of a darkly sacrificial, penal substitution notion of redemption.

Moral evil is the consequence of basic sin. It includes such things as deteriorating relations, systemic injustices, and bias of several kinds. All of these are "the evils of the human race" that in Christ are converted into a new community. According to Catholic teaching, these evils of the human race (basic sin and moral evil, including bias) are traced ultimately to what has been called original sin.

Perhaps it is time to indicate some questions that would foster integration with the work of Girard.

(1) To what extent may we associate what the Catholic tradition calls "original sin" with the mimetic cycle precisely as a "mechanism"? More fully: To what extent may we fruitfully regard "peccatum originale originans (originating original sin)" as an original and originating failure to reject a mimetic cycle ("You shall be like God" – Genesis 3.5), and "peccatum originale originatum (originated original sin)" as the mechanism unleashed by that original failing to reject this primordial mimetic cycle?

(2) To what extent would what Lonergan calls "basic sin" or "the evil of fault" be fruitfully understood as a matter of failing to reject the mimetic cycle? Is that failure one instance of basic sin, or is it more than that, perhaps the core of this basic root of irrationality in human rational consciousness?

(3) To what extent are the moral evils that follow upon basic sin (the deterioration of human relations, the systematizing of injustice, and the elevation of various forms of bias to the determining principles of human affairs) the consequences of failing to reject the mimetic cycle?

Let me rephrase the last two questions. To what extent is failing to reject the mimetic cycle the contraction of consciousness that constitutes basic sin, and to what extent is the satanic sequence of events that follows from failing to reject the mimetic cycle coincident with the "consequences of basic sins" that constitute moral evil? And to what extent do the biases that are structural elements in these consequences predispose us to further failures to reject the mimetic cycle?

It is obvious that I am inclined to find a great deal of complementarity between Lonergan and Girard on these issues. Where I would tend to find the two respective statements not entirely able to be mapped onto one another, at least as explicit statements, lies in the respective identifications of the result of the divinely ordained transformation. With Lonergan, I would have to say that that result is more than a textual revelation that exposes what was hidden. It is that, of course, but only as one constitutive element in the formation of a new set of concrete relations and determinations, a new social situation called "the state of grace," a new community in history, a new community that also extends beyond history into the state we call eternal life. But Girard enables us to affirm that this community is genuinely new only to the extent that it has been freed from the mimetic cycle, or, if you want, only to the extent that it embodies a new kind of "interdividuation," one that is constituted by the *imitatio* of the four divine relations in grace. And of course, we are well aware of the extent to which this is ever precarious, ever a withdrawal from mimetic rivalry (to paraphrase Lonergan's statements about authenticity as ever a withdrawal from unauthenticity).

To this point, then, I want to suggest that Girard, by filling in a heuristic structure provided by Lonergan, helps us specify the evils of the human race that are transformed, and that Lonergan is clearer on the reality into which these evils are transformed. Again, there should be no surprise here: Girard is proceeding anthropologically, and so can be expected to help us gain concrete precision on the human condition; and Lonergan is speaking theologically, and so can be expected to illuminate us as to God's ultimate intention and plan. I see no fundamental contradiction, at least to this point, between their respective positions on the Passion and Resurrection of Jesus, simply a difference of emphasis that can be turned into a mutual complementarity. The complementarity corresponds to the acknowledgment that, while Lonergan helps identify positive sacralizations and secularizations of human living, Girard enables us to specify deviated sacralizations and inhumane secularizations.

2.3 The Structure of the Law of the Cross

> **Thesis 47:** *The Law of the Cross as embodied in Jesus has a threefold structure: the massive mimesis in which the failure of will that is basic sin is displayed, the transformation of the evil of his suffering and death into a new community, and the resurrection of Jesus as first-born from the dead. This structure, which determines the direction of soteriology, is to be embodied in Christ's members as they lovingly absorb the consequences of basic sin and transform these into new life for the world by returning good for evil.*

What, then, is the Law of the Cross, precisely as a determinant not primarily of texts but of events, a reversal not only in meaning but also in the reality meant?

Lonergan answers this question in three steps, corresponding to the way in which the law is embodied in Jesus as an individual human being, the way in which it is embodied in him as the last Adam and Head of the Church, and the way in which it is embodied in his members.

As embodied in Jesus as an individual human being, the Law of the Cross entails three steps. First, from the "basic sin" responsible for his death (which, we may accept from Girard, was a matter of mob failure to reject the mimetic cycle), there follow the moral evils, the consequences of basic sin, that is, principally that death itself. Second, there is a transformation of these moral evils, these consequences of basic sin, into good, precisely by his freely submitting to them. Third, God the Father blesses this transformation in the Resurrection. Thus, Jesus (1) suffered and died because of the basic sin, the failure of will, that brought him to this point (again, in Girardian terms, massive mimesis). He (2) transformed the evil of suffering and death, accepted in love and obedience, into a supreme moral good, a new community emergent from these events, the whole Christ, Head and members, in all their concrete relations and determinations, which were entirely different from the relations and determinations that preceded this event. And God the Father (3) raised him from the dead as the first-born into this new community of "the whole Christ, Head and members."

The manner in which the Law of the Cross is embodied in Jesus as the last Adam, the Head of the Church, the first-born into the new and supreme good, is expressed by Lonergan in terms of his subtle but extensive reorientation of the theological tradition regarding satisfaction. I have had to refrain from extensive commentary here on this issue, since it entails a far more thorough study than is necessary at this point. I refer the reader, however, to a very fine paper by Charles Hefling on this matter.[9] Suffice it to say that I believe that Lonergan transcends what Neil Ormerod[10] has called a darkly sacrificial interpretation of the Passion, and that I believe it is possible to integrate with Lonergan's thesis the Girardian insistence that (1) Jesus suffered and died because of the single-victim mechanism of the mimetic cycle that affects the entire human race; and (2) his death exposed, placed in the open, revealed once for all at the level of elemental meaning this single-victim mechanism, and in so doing neutralized it. Certainly from Lonergan's standpoint, this revelation could be considered a constituent feature of the transformation of evil into good, in terms of the concrete determinations and relations of the new community reality that we call "the whole Christ, Head and members." And the Girardian perspective would agree with Lonergan that God the Father raised Jesus from the dead precisely as a manifestation of the "victory" of the cross. Note, however, that I am attempting to incorporate the Girardian emphases into a theological account of *events*, namely, Jesus's actual death and actual resurrection, and so into a position that transcends the primacy accorded by Girard to the texts in which these events are narrated.

Finally, there is an embodiment of the Law of the Cross in the members as well as in the Head. The members are those "whom [God] foreknew, and predestined to be conformed to the image of his Son" (Romans 8.29), "provided we suffer with him in order that we may also be glorified with him" (Romans 8.17). Lonergan says that "the Law of the Cross teaches us through both precept and example, by its complete generality, (1) that *every* evil in human, volitional realities is to be regarded as sin's penalty ... and (2) that *each* person should 'daily take up his cross' (Matthew 16.24) and 'complete what is lacking in Christ's afflictions' (Colossians 1.24), so that (3) '*all* things work together for good to those who love God' (Romans 8.28)." The way the Law of the Cross is observed in Christ is different from the way it is observed in the members. It appears in Christ as in the redeeming principle, and in the members as in what is to be redeemed; we have to *learn and believe*, and come *freely to consent* to Christ, living in him, operating through him, being associated with him, so that we may be assimilated and conformed to him in his dying and rising.

This is precisely part of the set of formal effects of the gift of participation in and imitation of divine active and passive spiration. If I may quote something that I wrote years ago, "The church's participation in the specifically paschal dimension of 'what Jesus did' is twofold. First – and this is what distinguishes the church's 'place' in the economy of redemption from that of Jesus himself – the Christian is invited to acknowledge Jesus' suffering and death as *his or her own* redemption. But, second, the Christian is *then* invited as well to have some share in the historical catalytic agency of *that* suffering and death as its power mediates the transition from a prevailing situation to an alternative one, and to do so precisely by allowing there to become incarnate in his or her own person, as minister of the new covenant in the blood of Jesus, the very pattern or immanent intelligibility of Jesus' own redemptive self-offering: '... in my own body to do what I can to make up all that has still to be undergone by Christ for the sake of his body, the church' (Colossians 1.24)."[11]

Girardian complements and correspondences to this vision of the members would specify the statement that every evil in human volitional realities is to be regarded as sin's penalty, by saying that every defect in the concrete determinations and relationships of human life is due to mimesis gone awry, which is basically Girard's meaning of sin. Thus, the two statements are complementary. Consequently, that each person should "daily take up his cross" (Matthew 16.24) and "complete what is lacking in Christ's afflictions" (Colossians 1.24), so that "all things work together for good to those who love God" (Romans 8.28), would mean learning the epistemology of love that Girard finds in the New Testament, that is, living from the same stance that enabled Jesus once and for all to expose the victimage mechanism and in exposing it to overcome it. Certainly it is true that for Lonergan the kingdom of God is precisely what Girard says it is: being merciful as

Abba is merciful, love of enemies, offering no resistance to injury. The "intelligibility of redemption" is "the victory of suffering, of accepting the consequences of sin, the evils of this world, in the spirit that animated Christ. It is the transformation of the world that arises when evil is transformed into good by the Christian spirit. Christ refused the strict justice of an eye for an eye and a tooth for a tooth. He imposed upon his followers a command of patience and submission under wrong, because impatience usually creates only more wrong. And the meaning of his own words is fundamentally the transformation of evil into good ... What was Christ doing dying and rising again? He was overcoming in himself, and also through his followers, all the evils in the world, and overcoming them to rise again, that by his resurrection we might know and realize and act upon those words of St Paul in Romans, chapter 8, verse 28, 'To those that love God, all things conspire unto the good.'"[12]

The only point at issue, then, is the tension between events and texts that seems to mark the relation of Lonergan and Girard in these matters. In chapter 9 of *I See Satan Fall Like Lightning* Girard says that the transformation from the mimetic cycle to what, following Lonergan, we may call the Law of the Cross is like the reversal of a glove, due to the fact that the Law of the Cross is the positive *revelation* of the mimetic cycle, destroying its power precisely by revealing it. I believe that this revelation is only part of the real reversal that took place, that as it stands – and here I draw from Charles Hefling[13] – Girard's theological contribution is to a theology of the Christian *word*, but that this word tells us something about what *is*. In the order of what is, loving absorption of the evils that flow from basic sin, loving suffering of the effects of the failure to reject the mimetic cycle, and most important of all loving return of good for evil, is part of the transformation of that cycle itself into a new set of imitative relationships in which, de facto if not often explicitly, the four divine relations are imitated through a set of receptions of their created consequent conditions: divine paternity is imitated in the "secondary act of existence" of the Incarnate Word that is the consequent condition of that Word being substantially a human being; divine active spiration is imitated in the reception of unqualified love that is sanctifying grace; divine passive spiration is imitated in the charity that loves in return; and divine filiation is imitated in the light of glory allowing us all to be led back as adopted children to the eternal Father.

I conclude this section by emphasizing the adjective "new." The Law of the Cross is misinterpreted in destructive ways if it is taken to mean simply submission to the old law of mimetic violence. In simple terms, the alternative is not simply "Fight or Flight." *Datur tertium*; there is a third possibility. The third possibility, however, is primarily God's work in founding something far beyond human expectations for community. The church emerged precisely from Jesus' submission to the Law of the Cross. The reign of God moved on to a new covenant that did not abrogate the old but sublated it into a new set of human relationships that could not be envisioned as long as people remained within the parameters set by the earlier dispensation. Something similar must occur in other instances. Out of the suffering of submission to the evils of the mimetic cycle, a new community, a new set of possibilities, a new set of relationships emerges. The submission is a step, and only a step, in a far larger process that God is guiding according to the hidden counsels of the divine mystery. This qualification, I believe, is of crucial importance. And meeting it calls on the resources and ingenuity of human creativity and collaboration. But the primary collaboration must be with divine creativity itself.

3   Terms, Issue, Criteria

> **Thesis 48:** *The transition from sacral and secular to really sacred and really profane is catalyzed by the emergence of soteriologically differentiated consciousness. This is what provides a key to discriminating which sacralizations are to be dropped and which to be fostered, and which secularizations are to be welcomed and which to be resisted. This statement is compatible with Lonergan's specification of personal, communal, and historical criteria for this transition.*

On this reading, then, (1) what constitutes the genuine sacred in history is the transformation of the evils that affect the human race into a new community of human beings with the three divine subjects and with one another through the very absorption of those evils themselves; and (2) Girard helps us concretize those evils in terms of his mimetic model. With this clarification, let us return to Lonergan's paper "Sacralization and Secularization." The paper can be properly understood, I think, only from some such perspective as Lonergan's development of the Law of the Cross. And interpreting the paper will open us onto further complementarities of Lonergan's thought with Girard's.

We begin with the meaning of the principal *terms* in the paper. The words "secular," "secularize," "secularization," "secularist," and the words "sacral," "sacralize," "sacralization," "desacralize," "desacralization" are value-neutral terms describing attitudes of persons and communities. Roles, places, times, and objects are sacral when the activity involved is regarded as religious by the participants, and secular when the activity involved is not so regarded. These terms do not refer to what really is sacred and what really is profane, but only to what the participants regard as sacred and what they regard as profane. Similarly, "desacralize" and "desacralization" denote a withdrawal of sacrality from what previously had been regarded as religious.[14] Thus, for example, "one may say that meat sacralized by pagans was desacralized by Christians."[15]

The real issue, then, has to do with the transition from "sacral" to "really sacred," from "secular" to "really profane," and, in the case of desacralization, from "sacral" first to "secular" and then to "profane" – that is, from what participants regard as such and such to a true judgment about what really is so. Only by meeting the issue thus defined can we determine which sacralizations are to be dropped and which to be fostered, and which secularizations are to be welcomed and which to be resisted.

It is in terms of what I am calling the genuine religious word, wherever that word is found, that this determination can be made. And because of Girard's contribution to the theology of the Christian word, he has offered an essential element in this discrimination. In my view, with which I presume both Lonergan and Girard would agree, the Hebrew and Christian scriptures manifest the most articulate process of development toward the formation of the genuine religious word. It is in part a development toward what I have called soteriologically differentiated consciousness.[16] But it is this only because more radically it is a progressive revelation on the part of God. I have wagered that this authentic or genuine religious word is more clearly differentiated in the Hebrew and Christian trajectory than anywhere else, even though I would insist that what it means is present outside this trajectory. And in this particular revelatory trajectory, this word is most apparent first in the Deutero-Isaian vision of the suffering servant, and then in the Paschal narratives of the four Gospels. But we must assume that parallels to this soteriological differentiation effected by divine revelation can be found in other traditions, and we must actively search them out, since it is those parallels more than anything else that will disclose what is from God in those traditions, just as the suffering servant and the Paschal narratives disclose what God was revealing progressively in Israelite history and definitively in the Incarnation, life, death, and Resurrection of the Word made flesh.

The real issue, then, the transition from the sacral to the sacred and from the secular to the profane, from what people regard as sacred to what is really sacred and from what they regard as profane to what is really profane, may be reminiscent of the words of Jesus, "You have heard it said to you …, But I say to you …" (see Matthew 5.21–48). In these sayings of Jesus, what his listeners had heard said to them from their tradition was what spokespersons for the tradition had purported to be truly sacred, but what Jesus was saying to them was what he claimed to be truly sacred. As we know, there was a vast difference in the respective identifications of the sacred, and that difference led to the murder of Jesus and to the beginning of a new "way" in the very tradition in which he stood, a way which, he himself made clear, was completely continuous with the Israelite revelation as the latter came to its fulfilment in the vision of the suffering servant.

So much for the terms and the issue. There are, Lonergan says, three *criteria* for the transition from what is sacral, that is, regarded as sacred, to what is really sacred, for the transition from what is secular, that is, regarded as profane, to what is really profane, and for the transition from what has been inappropriately or even incorrectly sacralized to what is first secularized and then truly judged to be profane. One criterion is personal, one communal, and one historical.

The personal criterion is the authenticity of the subject, an authenticity that results cumulatively from one's attentiveness, one's intelligence, one's reasonableness, one's responsibility, and one's affective development. This authenticity, generically defined, is a matter of consistent self-transcendence. While it reflects the basic natural law of the human spirit, it receives concretely whatever consistency it may have only from the gift of God's love in grace. This is due to the compound reality that Lonergan summarizes under the term "moral impotence," a term whose meaning can be understood ultimately only in theological terms having to do with such realities as original sin, basic sin, and moral evil. Complementing this statement of the first criterion with emphases from Girard, we may say that the personal criterion involves a good deal of liberation from mimetic contagion, rivalry, and violence, for, as John Ranieri in particular has argued, these dynamics exposed by Girard are involved in and perhaps even constitutive of what Lonergan calls dramatic, individual, group, and general bias,[17] and the biases may be regarded as prominent among the moral evils that are consequent upon what Lonergan calls basic sin and that set up the likelihood of further basic sin. Moral impotence is at least partly constituted by the dynamics of what Girard has exposed in his mimetic theory or model.

If the personal criterion is the authenticity of the individual, the communal criterion is the authenticity of the subject's tradition. We may appeal to Girard for help in specifying the communal criterion. For in Girardian terms, the same communal criterion of the tradition might be specified by appeal to the Gospel's meaning of "the kingdom of God" as opposed to the kingdom of the "principalities and powers." In Girard's understanding of both of these kingdoms, we are dealing once again with a radical liberation from mimetic determinants of human relationships.[18]

The historical criterion arises inasmuch as religion and culture themselves develop. Within firm parameters set by the natural law of human interiority, by its supernatural fulfilment, and by the Law of the Cross as constituting the reality of what is genuinely sacred in human history, it may be said that what is perhaps most intelligently regarded as a sacral domain at one stage of religious development can be secularized. There may, for instance, be a quite legitimate point to surrounding economies, polities, family arrangements, and even legal institutions with some sacral trappings when civilizations are in decline or when new civilizations are just beginning to emerge. But such a sacralization will be challenged as people grow and develop. Sacral domains can also be desacralized, and one wonders whether Jesus himself did not foster that process in many of the things he is reported to have said about the religious priorities of some of the teachers of Israel. Again, what seems to be secular activity can be given a genuine religious significance. "As often as you did it for the least of these, you did it for me" (Matthew 25.40). Finally, one style of religious development may be defective in comparison with another style. "When you pray, do not imitate the hypocrites, for they love to say their prayers standing up in the synagogues and at the street corners for people to see them … But when you pray, go to your private room and, when you have shut your door, pray to your Father who is in that secret place" (Matthew 6.5–6). That statement itself may be reflective of religious development, particularly if there is some truth, however much it would be amplified in a Christian context, to Whitehead's definition of religion as "what the individual does with his [or her] own solitariness," involving "the transition from God the void to God the enemy, and from God the enemy to God the companion."[19]

The criteria, in other words, whether personal, communal, or historical, have to do with issues of development and retardation. Moreover, the key to the second and the third criteria for Lonergan, that is, to the communal and the historical, would be found in the first, the personal, for no matter what the dominance of the dialectic of community over the dialectical emergence of the subject, still, the authenticity of self-transcendence, measured by the standards of cumulative attentiveness, intelligence, reasonableness, and responsibility, with all of these preceded, accompanied, and transcended by a movement of life promoted and sustained by the grace that is the gift of God's love, is the key to the authenticity of traditions, to collective as well as individual responsibility, and to both healing and creating in history. These social and cultural realities are objectifications of the concrete universal that is the normative subject. Again, since the gift of God's grace is required for sustained fidelity to these standards, the truly sacred is the source of all genuine development, even when genuine development entails a secularization of a domain of life that had previously been sacralized. The relations among the various levels in the scale of values are such that religious values condition personal authenticity, personal authenticity provokes cultural development, cultural development enhances the social good of order, and the social good of order promotes the equitable distribution of vital goods.[20] Thus, no genuine secularization is an abandonment, only a refinement, of authentic religion.

Let us get our bearings. We began by discriminating with Lonergan the categories of a sacralization to be dropped, a sacralization to be fostered, a secularization to be welcomed, and a secularization to be resisted. We formulated the position that the discriminant of these four processes will have something to do with the Law of the Cross, and we outlined what that Law entails, drawing not only on Lonergan but also on Girard. Then we returned to the paper in which Lonergan discriminated these four categories, and we commented on his definition of terms, his statement of the issue, and his understanding of the criteria for adjudicating the issue.

Obviously the issue is very complex. But already we may say, in Christian terms, that a sacralization to be fostered would be grounded in fidelity to, and appropriation and implementation of, the radical turnabout that Jesus identified in our understanding of God (outer word) and in our conviction of the truth of that revelation as it is confirmed in the gift of God's love (inner word). The revelation itself is present in the earlier tradition in which Jesus stands, and especially in the Deutero-Isaian vision of the suffering servant. And, as I stated above, if we believe in the universal mission of the Holy Spirit, we must assume that some corresponding truth is found in other religious traditions as well.

We may also say that a secularization to be welcomed, that is, any legitimate freeing of a domain of life from the realm of sacrality, would be rooted in fidelity to, appropriation of, and graced implementation of, the operations according to which subjects, singly and in community, are faithful to what Lonergan calls the transcendental precepts – Be attentive, Be intelligent, Be reasonable, Be responsible – and to the dispositional *Befindlichkeit* that constitutes the mood of genuine discernment. That secularization would itself be a fruit of grace, since consistent fidelity to the transcendental precepts is impossible without divine grace. Even as a fruit of grace it may entail "the liberation of a secular domain from the once but no longer appropriate extension of the sacral." If it does, the extension of exclusively or dominantly religious feeling over the domain will be acknowledged as no longer appropriate. On the other hand, if that acknowledgment has not occurred, then what is really a legitimate secularization will be regarded and mourned as nothing but a desacralization of what, it is claimed, should be allowed to remain sacral.[21]

From the same standpoint, both sacralizations to be dropped and secularizations to be resisted – which, we have seen, Girard helps us understand as perhaps more intimately connected than Lonergan may have acknowledged – are a function of the failure of individuals and groups to be faithful first to what, in Christian terms, we may call the Gospel's radical reversal of the meaning of religion (which, again, we may assume can be found in other traditions as well), and second to the imperatives of authenticity and the grace that sustains such fidelity.

Governing all this is the conviction that, in Lonergan's terms, the sacralization to be fostered will be found precisely in the dynamics of the redemptive process that is a constitutive feature of the structure of history, that is, in the Law of the Cross. The Law of the Cross, I have argued in *Theology and the Dialectics of History*, characterizes all genuine and sustained fidelity to the integral scale of values, which provides the ultimate grid or litmus test for genuine progress in history, whereas all historical retardation is a function of more or less extensive breakdowns of that same scale of values.[22] Here Girard contributes a great deal, for his model of mimetic desire, contagion, and rivalry contributes to our understanding of the concrete dynamics entailed in the Law of the Cross as well as to our understanding of the breakdown of the scale of values.

4   The Context of Lonergan's Discussion

Thesis 49: *The same prescription specifies the context of religious development and retardation, both individual and social, within which Lonergan raises these issues.*

With some such clarification of terms, it is possible to return to the beginning of Lonergan's paper and to situate the issue in the context that he finds most appropriate. It is in a discussion of Paul Ricoeur's work on Freudian psychoanalysis that Lonergan finds the appropriate context for giving the terms "sacralization" and "secularization" the more precise meaning that he eventually provides. That context, again, is one of development and retardation: personal, cultural, and social. Freud would regard all religion, and so all sacralization, in the course of personal, cultural, and social unfolding as the product of a movement of consciousness that is the source of an illusion, and so of at best a pause and at worst a retardation in development. He would restore to human beings what had been alienated in a false transcendence, and that restoration would amount to a fairly wholesale secularization of everything in life. Ricoeur, on the other hand, would distinguish religious maturity and religious retardation, and would thank Freud for helping him make the distinction. Lonergan applauds Ricoeur's discernment, and relies on it to draw his own correlations: religious maturity is growth in love beyond "the terrors of guilt," and growth in hope as confidence in the goodness of God beyond "the law," which was perhaps a necessary but definitely a temporary pedagogue. In this way he agrees with Ricoeur that "as in the past Freud has reinforced the faith of unbelievers, so in the future he may be used to reinforce the faith of believers."[23] But he will do so by challenging believers to avoid, in Lonergan's terms, "mistaking retardation for development and mistaking development for retardation and, most disastrous of all, … triumphantly living out a mistake as though it were the truth, or living out a truth in the agony of fearing it to be a mistake."[24]

Lonergan has his own way of expressing this context of development and retardation, and it influences the appropriation he makes of Ricoeur's notion of a hermeneutics of recovery that would advance genuine developments and a hermeneutics of suspicion that would discern and reverse the sources of retardation. We find Lonergan's treatment expressed most clearly in his statements in other writings regarding minor and major authenticity and unauthenticity, and in the question he asks in one of his most mature papers about how we can gain legitimate assurance regarding the genuineness of our religious convictions.

Thus, in a much-quoted passage repeated with minor variations in several of his works, Lonergan writes the following:

> [E]xisting may be authentic or unauthentic, and this may occur in two different ways. There is the minor authenticity or unauthenticity of the subject with respect to the tradition that nourishes him. There is the major authenticity that justifies or condemns the tradition itself. In the first case there is passed a human judgment on subjects. In the second case history and, ultimately, divine providence pass judgment on traditions.

Lonergan goes on to say the following about minor authenticity and unauthenticity:

> As Kierkegaard asked whether he was a Christian, so divers men can ask themselves whether or not they are genuine Catholics or Protestants, Muslims or Buddhists, Platonists or Aristotelians, Kantians or Hegelians, artists or scientists, and so forth. Now they may answer that they are, and their answers may be correct. But they can also answer affirmatively and still be mistaken. In that case there will exist a series of points in which they are what the ideals of the tradition demand, but there will be another series in which there is a greater or less divergence. These points of divergence are overlooked from a selective inattention, or from a failure to understand, or from an undetected

rationalization. What I am is one thing, what a genuine Christian or Buddhist is, is another, and I am unaware of the difference. My unawareness is unexpressed. I have no language to express what I am, so I use the language of the tradition I unauthentically appropriate, and thereby I devaluate, distort, water down, corrupt that language.

Finally, Lonergan relates minor and major authenticity and unauthenticity to one another.

> Such devaluation, distortion, corruption may occur only in scattered individuals. But it may occur on a more massive scale, and then the words are repeated, but the meaning is gone. The chair was still the chair of Moses, but it was occupied by the scribes and Pharisees. The theology was still scholastic, but the scholasticism was decadent. The religious order still read out the rules, but one wonders whether the home fires were still burning. The sacred name of science may still be invoked but, as Edmund Husserl has argued, all significant scientific ideals can vanish to be replaced by the conventions of a clique. So the unauthenticity of individuals becomes the unauthenticity of a tradition. Then, in the measure a subject takes the tradition, as it exists, for his standard, in that measure he can do no more than authentically realize unauthenticity.[25]

In a later paper, Lonergan asks about the source of genuine religious conviction. More precisely, he asks, How can one tell whether one's appropriation of religion is genuine or unauthentic and, more radically, how can one tell one is not appropriating a religious tradition that has become unauthentic?[26] His answer to that question, and by extension to the dilemma offered by the possibility that one may be participating in major unauthenticity, or may be mistaking development for retardation and retardation for development, appeals to his position on the subject. Ultimately, then, one's recourse must be to the inner conviction of authenticity generated by the self-transcendence that is promoted and sustained by the gift of divine love; and so the intentionality analysis that differentiates precisely what self-transcendence is, in operations and in correlative affective states, assumes paramount importance. Thus, in the total context of Lonergan's work, the position on the subject elevated to participation in Trinitarian life mediates the resolution of the questions raised by Freud and further refined by Ricoeur, questions that have to do with religious development and retardation.

We turn now to Girard's contribution to the development of our understanding of the same context of retardation and development.

5   Girard's Contribution to Clarifying the Context

> **Thesis 50:** *Girard establishes a more thoroughgoing hermeneutic of suspicion regarding the false sacred than does Freud. His understanding of psychic aberration or of what Lonergan calls dramatic bias is easily joined with Lonergan's understanding of other biases, and can be put in aid of Lonergan's hermeneutics of the recovery of individual and communal authenticity.*

Girard provides, in my view, a far more convincing maieutic of the dramatic bias that is associated with psychogenic disease than did Freud, and on that basis he is an exponent of a ruthless hermeneutic of suspicion regarding what people revere as genuinely sacred. His understanding of the dynamics of what, following Lonergan, we may call dramatic bias, the bias of unacknowledged motivation, exposes its mechanism in a manner that is almost epochal in its cultural implications. In *Insight*, Lonergan relied on a modified Freudianism to expound what he meant by dramatic bias. But Girard goes far more directly to the source and root of a specifically psychogenic religious aberration and departure from coherence. And he also helps us understand why it is that liberation from psychic bias is given only through the grace that enables one to live by what Lonergan calls the Law of the Cross. Not only is that grace what frees human intelligence, reasonableness, and responsibility for their tasks precisely in this world, through what I am affirming to be participation in the invisible mission of the divine Word: that is, for the advance of scientific knowledge, for gaining intelligent control over what otherwise would approximate various forms of historical determinism, for conducting human affairs on the basis of what Jürgen Habermas calls communicative competence, and in so doing for secularizing domains of human living that previous ages had sacralized. That grace also liberates the intersubjective psyche from mimetic violence and rivalry, and that liberation is itself, among other things, freedom for development in attentiveness, intelligence, reasonableness, and responsibility, that is, for development precisely in the habits and operations that Lonergan regards as crucial to the determination of the genuineness of cultural and religious traditions and convictions. Girard's hermeneutic of suspicion can be put in aid of Lonergan's hermeneutic of recovery, analogously to the manner in which Ricoeur sublated the Freudian hermeneutic of suspicion into his own hermeneutic of recovery.

6   A Debate

> **Thesis 51:** *The legitimate domain of sacralization, the genuine sacred, in history lies in the redemptive religion that overcomes bias and*

restores progress. The legitimate domain of secularization, the genuine profane, in history lies in the progress that results from human beings being consistently attentive, intelligent, reasonable, and responsible. The appropriate symbolizations will be found primarily in the incarnate meaning of persons and of communities that, gathering in the name of Jesus, radiate peace and joy. But that symbolization is no substitute for the hard work of understanding, judgment, and decision, indeed of collective responsibility, sharing in the invisible mission of the divine Word.

After setting a context of development and retardation by appealing to Ricoeur's work on Freud, Lonergan turned in "Sacralization and Secularization" to a debate current at the time that he wrote the paper, and implicitly locates the debate within the context of development and retardation. The particular debate that Lonergan summarizes was between Marie-Dominique Chenu, o.p., and Jean Daniélou, s.j., on "the tension between the inner life of prayer and the secular, desacralized world in which we live."[27] It is easy to see how little the debate has been settled several decades later. It is still very much alive in the Catholic church.

Chenu and Daniélou both

> want faith to penetrate social and political life and … both reject an oversimplified separation of the spiritual and the temporal, the sacred and the profane, the Christian and the political element. Again, both are haunted by the evangelization of the world, by a realistic presence of the church in the world. Where they differ is in their view of man in his concrete situation. Chenu would have progress in Christian life promote the natural processes and inherent freedom of this world. Daniélou, while he has abandoned the dream of a Christendom as it existed in the Middle Ages, wants the faith to have other securities than God's word alone. He wants some kind of sociological preparation for the faith, certain zones where sacred and religious elements are preserved so that the faith of the poor is not left without cultural and social foundations.[28]

These summaries by Lonergan are purely descriptive of the debate, and they display little more than contrasting judgments on the mental and institutional complex known as Christendom. Chenu expects the church to abandon this complex, while Daniélou begs the church to reconsider and to come up with something that would replace the medieval form of Christendom. Daniélou is quoted as saying such things as, "There can be no Christianity for the masses without a Christendom," and "in a world threatened by atheism, we must defend the substance of the sacred wherever it is found."[29]

If we may move to a more explanatory analysis of the debate, it would seem that for Lonergan the debate reduces to a contemporary variation on the theme that was played out in the Aristotelian-Augustinian debates in the Middle Ages. Chenu is "a Thomist, … a disciple of the thinker who broke with the symbolic thought of his medieval predecessors and contemporaries, who acknowledged the reality of human nature and the legitimacy of its proper sphere of activity." It is from this basis that Chenu "'gladly supports the progress of natural and profane forces all through history, and he is of the opinion that this support, far from jeopardizing the domain of grace, ensures its transcendence and richness.'"[30] Lonergan expresses a basic agreement, but with an important proviso. "I wholeheatedly share Chenu's acceptance of progress in all its forms; but I would refer back to chapter 7 of my little book *Insight* for an account of the many ways in which progress is corrupted by bias and turned into decline; and I would refer to chapter 20 of the same book for an indication of the redemptive role of religion in overcoming bias and restoring progress."[31] The quotation is important, as it provides perhaps the first key in the paper "Sacralization and Secularization" to what Lonergan would regard as the genuine domains of both sacralization and secularization. The legitimate domain of sacralization, the genuine sacred, in history lies in the redemptive religion that overcomes bias and restores progress. The legitimate domain of secularization, the genuine profane, in history lies in the progress that results from human beings being consistently attentive, intelligent, reasonable, and responsible.

Daniélou, on the other hand, represents a contemporary variant of the symbolic mentality from which Aquinas broke free. Still, Lonergan expresses a basic but qualified agreement with him as well. "[W]hile all sane men need symbols, only a small minority ever seriously get beyond the limitations of symbolic thinking. Hence, in a developed culture, religion has to be pluralist: it needs some measure of symbolization for all; it needs only a limited measure for the few that get beyond symbolic thinking; and it needs a bounteous dose for the many that do not."[32] Education in the genuine sacred is required even if people are to respond in a balanced manner to processes of secularization, and appropriate symbolization is crucial in that education. But there are no easy solutions as to what constitutes such appropriate symbolization, and it is important that in the last analysis Lonergan rejects as inadequate what he calls "lines of solution … [only] in terms of intersubjectivity … [that] seem to offer no more than a sacralization of an infrastructure."[33] For not only is there a false sacred; there is also religious development, and this development indicates that much secularization is long overdue. For example, Daniélou speaks of providing cultural and social foundations for the faith of the poor, but, writes Lonergan, "the basic step in aiding [the poor] in a notable manner is a matter of spending one's nights and days in a deep and prolonged study of economic analysis."[34] In the midst of this and other secularizations, the appropriate symbolization will be found for Lonergan primarily in the incarnate meaning of persons and of communities that, gathering in the name of Jesus, radiate peace and joy. But that symbolization is no substitute for the hard work of understanding, judgment, and decision, indeed of collective responsibility.[35] Grace, in fact, sustains such secular undertakings aimed at human betterment. They are, after all, when engaged in under grace, at least lived if not thematic participations in the invisible mission of the divine Word.

7   Complementary Solutions

7.1 Progressive Biblical Revelation

Thesis 52: *The word of Hebrew revelation provides progressively clearer indications of precisely what does and does not qualify as the "genuine sacred" in history. The high point of that progressive revelation in the history of Israel is in the Deutero-Isaian vision of the suffering servant. For Christians the clearest revelation of the genuine sacred is in the mind and heart, the human consciousness and knowledge, of Jesus of Nazareth, where revelation itself finds its central locus and primary meaning. And there, in that revelation, we are told that the kingdom of God is a mimesis of the one Jesus called Abba, who "causes his sun to rise on the bad as well as the good, and his rain to fall on the honest and dishonest alike." Imitating Abba means: "love your enemies, and pray for those who persecute you; in this way you will be children of your Father in Heaven." This orientation is central to the very revelation itself that comes through God's word and that is progressively disclosed through the course of the biblical writings. The same orientation is moved into an explicitly systematic-theological framework in the four-point hypothesis regarding the divine missions, where sanctifying grace and charity are created external imitations, mimetic, respectively, of the active spiration of Father and Son breathing the Spirit of Love and of the passive spiration of the Holy Spirit being breathed.*

We are now in a position to examine the contributions that Lonergan would present to a more complete diagnostic of sacralizations and secularizations to be accepted and rejected, and as well to complement these contributions with Girardian reflections.

First, we must address Daniélou's support of "the substance of the sacred," for this remark would set off alarms in anyone coming from a Girardian perspective, and rightly so. Although Lonergan was not writing with Girard's work in mind, I find that his efforts are helpful especially in determining what meanings can be given to the expression "the substance of the sacred" and in distinguishing a "genuine sacred" from a "false and mendacious, indeed satanic, sacred." That distinction, in turn, will be crucial to the discernment of which sacralizations are to be dropped and which fostered, and of which secularizations are to be welcomed and which resisted.

Lonergan first makes a distinction that I find, precisely as it is here expressed, only in this paper, between religions of the infrastructure and religions of the suprastructure, or, what amounts to the same thing, between religions governed by primordial intersubjectivity and religions whose directive principles are found in what may be called the word, and principally in an outer word that claims, rightly or wrongly, to name the inner word that God speaks in our hearts, and so that claims, again rightly or wrongly, to be directly or indirectly from God and to support and sustain genuine interpersonal relations with the persons of the Trinity and with one's fellow men and women. While it is primarily the inner word that constitutes the authentic religious disposition, nonetheless the advantages that accrue to the religious community from having an outer word that articulates and to a certain extent codifies the inner word should not be underestimated, especially if that outer word is itself not simply a product of human ingenuity.[36]

Thus to the social infrastructure that at its most basic intersubjective level is a matter of simple prolongations of prehuman achievement – and both Lonergan and Girard would so identify primordial intersubjectivity or "interdividuality" – there corresponds a religious infrastructure that clings to the world of immediacy and fixates on sacred objects, acknowledges sacred places, hallows sacred times, celebrates sacred rites, wears sacred clothes, consecrates sacred persons. Lonergan is, by and large, a generous if cautious observer of human social constructions, just as he is of texts – more generous, I would hazard to say, than Girard. And so of such religions of the infrastructure he writes that they "can, in principle, be as authentic and genuine as any, for I do not suppose that the grace of God is refused to certain stages in the unfolding of human culture yet granted to other stages." Still, they are human, and not only are they subject to the dialectic of progress and decline like all things human, but also, precisely because they have as yet no guiding and directing outer word, the statistical probabilities of aberration are even higher than they would be in religions of the word when the word comes from God. "More than other religions, the religions of the infrastructure are open to palpable idolatry and superstition, to orgiastic and cruel cults, even to the ritual murder of human sacrifice."[37] Or, in terms of the issue that Lonergan is addressing in his paper and that we are addressing here, the probability is far greater that religions of the infrastructure will misplace, misidentify, misconstrue precisely what constitutes "the substance of the sacred." We may presume that it is for this reason, or something like it, that Lonergan regards as inadequate to the present crisis intersubjective solutions that would simply resacralize some infrastructure of human living.

This presumes, of course, that there is some primary meaning of "the sacred" that in principle can be found in religions of the infrastructure but that is distorted by the aberrations to which cultures of the infrastructure are particularly prone. For Lonergan it is this primary meaning of the sacred that comes progressively to light in the biblical revelation. This understanding of progressive revelation corresponds very closely to Girard's understanding, even while the language concerning "the sacred" is different.[38] Thus Lonergan writes:

> So it was with reason that Abraham was called to leave the land of his fathers and to sojourn in a strange land, that Moses was ordered to lead the people of Israel away from the fleshpots of Egypt and into the desert, that the book of Deuteronomy in its most solemn manner commanded: "Hear, O Israel: The Lord our God is one Lord, and you shall love the Lord your God with all your heart and with all your soul and with all your might" ... It was a momentous command, spelt out positively in the many ways in which the Old Testament makes known the transcendence of God and, more practically, negatively by the prohibition of any sharing in the cults of neighboring peoples. It was a difficult command, as witnessed by the repeated backsliding of the people of God; and, if one would understand that difficulty today, I can only suggest that one think of it as an epochal transition in which religious experience of transcendence began to express itself in the style, not of the infrastructure but of the suprastructure. For if Hebrew religion had its sacred objects, its sacred places and times, its sacred recitals and rituals, still its God was hidden, powerful above all, creator of heaven and earth, one sole Lord God brooking no strange gods before him despite all the diversity of creation and despite the contradictions in which man implicated himself.[39]

The word of Hebrew revelation, then, provides progressively clearer indications of precisely what does and does not qualify as the "genuine sacred" in history. As Girard has argued, that progressive revelation discloses that God is not in the least bit interested, except negatively, not only in human sacrifice but also in animal sacrifices (which, by the way, even Mary and Joseph offered in the temple at the time of the presentation of Jesus), and that what God wants is a humble heart ready to come to the need of the poor and the oppressed, of victims everywhere. For Girard, as for Eric Voegelin, the high point of that progressive revelation in the history of Israel is in the Deutero-Isaian vision of the suffering servant. Christians would move on from here. For them the clearest revelation of the genuine sacred is in the mind and heart, the human consciousness and knowledge, of Jesus of Nazareth, where, as Charles Hefling has argued, with firm backing in Lonergan's own writings, revelation itself finds its central locus and primary meaning.[40] And there, in that revelation, we are told, as Girard insists, that the kingdom of God is a mimesis of the one Jesus called Abba, who "causes his sun to rise on the bad as well as the good, and his rain to fall on the honest and dishonest alike." Imitating Abba means: "love your enemies, and pray for those who persecute you; in this way you will be children of your Father in Heaven."[41] This orientation is correctly regarded by Girard as central to the very revelation itself that comes through God's word and that is progressively disclosed through the course of the biblical writings.

The same orientation is moved by Lonergan into an explicitly theological framework in the four-point hypothesis regarding the divine missions, where, among other things, sanctifying grace and the habit of charity are created external imitations, mimetic, respectively, of the active spiration of Father and Son breathing the Spirit of Love and of the passive spiration of the Holy Spirit being breathed. These emphases of Lonergan transcend the principal weakness in the Girardian account, namely, the almost exclusive attention to texts. Revelation takes place not primarily in texts but in minds and hearts engaged in deeds in history. And it takes place first and foremost in the human consciousness of the Incarnate Word himself. "[T]he Son can do nothing by himself; he can do only what he sees the Father doing; and whatever the Father does the Son does too" (John 5.19).

Thus, again, if there are any conflicts or tensions to be identified and negotiated between Girard and Lonergan, they would seem to be rooted in the relative priority given to texts in Girard and to events in Lonergan. It is on this basis that we can understand (1) Lonergan's perhaps more generous acknowledgment of the possibility of authenticity in religions of the infrastructure, which do not have the advantage of the progressive biblical revelation of both false and genuine transcendence, and where there is a minimum of the revealing word in general – the possibility of authenticity there, despite the high probability of precisely those acts of savage violence that Girard has identified with "the primitive sacred,"[42] and (2) the related and implicit claim in Lonergan's analysis that there is a primary meaning of "the sacred" that is progressively revealed in the history of Israel, that has nothing to do with violence, and that is to be preserved.

A firm Girardian might respond that at least to this point no critical stand-point has been identified in Lonergan's paper from which to adjudicate the authenticity of religions of the suprastructure, that is, of their outer word, and that it is precisely the texts of the Hebrew and especially Gospel scriptures that provide this set of criteria. For religions of the word are guilty of much violence in history as well. To this I would respond, first, that for Lonergan the original meaningfulness of one's own insights, judgments, and decisions is always at play in the acceptance, rejection, or qualification of the ordinary meaningfulness of any tradition, religious or cultural or both, and second that Lonergan's presentation of the Law of the Cross represents his understanding of the culmination of the progressive revelation in outer word that has made religions of the suprastructure, or at least Israel and Christianity, possible in the first place.

Girard's positive contribution to the discussion of sacralization, secularization, and desacralization would lie (1) in the model he provides for exposing the dynamics of religious infrastructures, (2) in the help he provides, precisely because of his awareness of these dynamics, in disengaging the anthropological moment in the stages of development of the outer word that articulates and interprets the inner word that is the gift of God's love, and (3) in the concrete specification in terms of mimetic rivalry of the embodiment of the "evils of the human race" that resulted in the murder of Jesus and that through the Law of the Cross are transformed or converted into a new social reality, a new interdividuation, in the supreme good of the whole Christ, Head and members, in all their concrete determinations and relations. I would submit that the relationship between Lonergan and Girard on this issue, then, is basically complementary, with Lonergan providing a heuristic structure that Girard enriches and fills in, and with very little if any serious dispute between the two. In fact, I think ultimately that Lonergan could ask of Girard only that he transcend the emphasis on texts to focus on the events that the texts narrate and the history in which those events occurred.

We should make a more complete application of these considerations to our theme of sacralization and desacralization. On the basis of the foregoing analysis Lonergan concludes his discussion of religious infrastructure and religious suprastructure with some hints from Christian revelation itself regarding what would constitute a sacralization that is to be accepted and fostered and a secularization that is to be resisted, and so regarding two of the four sets of anticipatory categories that we have adopted to guide our inquiry. For, he says, "it was sacralization for Christ according to the flesh to be esteemed, revered, listened to, followed," and "it was a new and far superior sacralization for him to rise again according to the flesh, to sit at the right hand of the Father, to rule in a kingdom that has no end." And "it was secularization for the secular power to condemn him to suffering and death."[43]

Thus, if there is a sacralization that is to be fostered in history, then on this account it lies in adherence to the mystery of the Incarnate Word in his life, passion, death, and resurrection, that is, in what Lonergan calls "the Law of the Cross." This sacralization, this adherence to the mystery of the Incarnate Word, extends for us, as it did for Jesus, beyond the confines of this earthly life. "[A]s Christ attained his full stature when he entered into the glory of his Father, so too for Christian hope 'coming of age' is not some human perfection attained in this life but being received by Christ in the kingdom of his Father."[44]

Again, if there is a secularization that is to be resisted in history, it would consist at its base in any and all attempts to condemn or scapegoat carriers of the genuine religious word, of whom Jesus as revealing the Law of the Cross is, as it were, the prime analogate: every genuine religious word would be compatible with the revelation that comes through him. By implication from this base, secularizations to be resisted would consist in attempts whether explicit or implicit to locate human "coming of age" as a human perfection to be attained exclusively in this life.

Now it is precisely at this point, I would suggest, that Girard adds something very important that is not to be found as clearly in Lonergan, namely, that at least the basic instance of a "secularization to be resisted," as it is portrayed in the Passion narrative, is itself tied to a false sacralization, a sacralization to be dropped, perhaps the prime instance of such a reality. For the murder of Jesus in which religious authorities appealed to the secular power to complete a scapegoating mechanism that they did not themselves have the wherewithal to bring off is the revelation of the satanic sacralization that drives out violence by violence. In this case at least, Lonergan's "secularization to be resisted" is also a result of a "sacralization to be dropped" or desacralized. From a Girardian perspective, this is precisely what happened. As this false sacralization is disclosed for what it is, it is also desacralized.

Today, of course, precisely because the Christian revelation has unveiled the religious subterfuges that often enough are involved in the justification of violence, the sacral base of such scapegoating will often not be prominent, unless the scapegoating is being done by so-called "religious" people for so-called religious reasons; but the dynamic remains the same. A sacralization that would condemn *in God's name* the carriers of a genuine religious word in a scapegoating fashion is very close to what Jesus called the "blasphemy against the Holy Spirit." Certainly it is the case that Jesus's own remark about the sin against the Holy Spirit occurs precisely in the context of the accusation that he casts out devils by Beelzebul.[45] But the secular identification of "coming of age" as a purely this-worldly development is a natural evolution of this false transcendence. This is what it means to call all purely secular humanism a form of idolatry. This is what happens to false transcendence when it is exposed by the Law of the Cross but refuses to acknowledge the truth. It becomes a form of mimetic violence that is without the overt sacral trappings of earlier religious forms of scapegoating. It is perhaps even closer to the primordial temptation, "You shall be like God," than are the overtly sacrificial religions. Arguments may be made in this direction, I believe, and they expose the element of truth in the Daniélou position, with its horror of secularist exaggerations. They also confirm the observations that Girard makes at the very end of *I See Satan Fall Like Lightning*, where secularism is seen to be "the most powerful mimetic force," "the most powerful anti-Christian movement."[46] In secular societies human sacrifice is now engaged in without appealing to any sacral justification. It can only be said that the church's insistence on the inviolable dignity of every human being from conception to and beyond death acknowledges the spiritual antidote to such secularized sacrality. But this insistence must extend in church teaching far beyond the cases of abortion and euthanasia to the issues of war and peace, capital punishment, the human dignity of women and sexual minorities, and overcoming the abuses of clerical privilege in all its forms.

8   Summary

Our analysis has brought us to the statements that were listed at the very beginning of the paper as my first, second, and fourth conclusions. What I listed there as my first conclusion is that what sets the standard for sacralizations to be dropped in history are any and all attempts to employ the name or the word of God or any other sacral trappings to justify persecution, exclusion, and scapegoating, first, of carriers of the genuine religious word and, second, precisely because that word itself exposes all scapegoating and replaces it with the Law of the Cross, of anyone else. What I indicated as my second conclusion is that what sets the standard for sacralizations to be fostered in history is adherence to and symbolic celebration of what Lonergan calls the Law of the Cross. And what I listed as my fourth conclusion is that what sets the standard for secularizations to be resisted in history are any and all attempts, whether or not grounded in a false sacralization, to condemn or scapegoat carriers of the genuine religious word, and any consequent efforts to locate human "coming of age" as a human perfection to be attained exclusively in this life and exclusively on the basis of human resources. Prominent among the latter efforts would be any and all instrumentalizations of human life in the pursuit of an illusory "coming of age" in this life.

What remains to be determined is the nature or quality of the prime or basic instance of the third category specified by Lonergan, namely, a secularization to be welcomed. On this we must be brief, and indicate that Lonergan eventually returns to the merits of Ricoeur's work on Freud as providing an example of an answer to this problem. "There do arise new developments that cast a searching light on human affairs but present their findings in an unsatisfactory manner. They are not to be rejected outright. They are not to be swallowed whole. They are to be met with a distinction ... that presupposes a basis in long and patient study and that can be formulated only when the ... oversight has been pinpointed and the relevant insight has uncovered the appropriate correction."[47] Thus Ricoeur, after much work, was able to announce that if, in the past, Freud had reinforced the unbelief of many, he now could be used to reinforce the belief of many. Ricoeur sets an example, one that illustrates that when secularization becomes secularism, the secularism can be overcome by an analysis that includes the genuine secularization of what can be understood by the natural and human sciences and a concomitant resacralization of what should never have been secularized. Growth in fidelity to the transcendental precepts would seem to be the key to, or set the standard for, secularizations to be welcomed. And such fidelity is possible only as a result of the grace that, explicitly or anonymously, elevates us to participation in the divine relations, and in particular of the faith that is a participation in the invisible mission of the divine Word. But Lonergan's words regarding such a solution in the paper that has been our primary source to this point in the argument may be complemented with his more famous words at the end of "Dimensions of Meaning": "There is bound to be formed a solid right that is determined to live in a world that no longer exists. There is bound to be formed a scattered left, captivated by now this, now that new development, exploring now this and now that new possibility. But what will count is a perhaps not numerous center, big enough to be at home in both the old and the new, painstaking enough to work out one by one the transitions to be made, strong enough to refuse half measures and insist on complete solutions even though it has to wait."[48]

11

Lonergan's Early Analogy

Thesis 53: *The psychological analogy that proceeds from nature is help-ful if we are to appreciate and understand the psychological analogy in the order of grace that has been proposed here. Firm possession of both analogies also helps to establish the link between religious and personal values in the scale of values. The relevant processions in the order of nature have to do with our existential autonomy, where the procession of a judgment of value from existential-ethical grasp of sufficient evidence for the judgment regarding what it would be good for the existential subject to do and to be provides the analogue for the procession of the Son. From that grasp and that judgment operating together as a single principle there proceeds loving decision to do and to be precisely what has been affirmed, and this is the natural analogue for the procession of the Holy Spirit.*

The context has been set for a more thorough exploration of Lonergan's theology of divine procession and divine mission, not simply on their own, but within a theology of history. The movement to Lonergan's own text in these last two chapters may seem abrupt to some readers, but the point of it is primarily to link what we have said about "religious values" in terms of participations in active and passive spiration with the "personal values" that constitute the authenticity of the subject and decisively affect the develop-ment of genuine cultural values, the social values of a just good of order, and the equitable distribution of vital goods to the whole human commu-nity. Only in a later volume will we be able explicitly to extend our analysis to the point of stating the contours of social grace in any detail. We will have to be content in the present volume to show the link between religious and personal values in the integral scale of values. For that purpose, and to il-luminate the structure of personal authenticity, we turn to Lonergan's early psychological analogy.

The autonomous spiritual processions that are most pertinent to an analogical theological understanding of Trinitarian mystery are processions of act from act within the expanded horizon of consciousness cleared by the gift of God's love: the procession of a set of judgments of value that bear upon one's self-constitution in gratitude for the gift – judgments flowing from the evidence grasped by a person consciously on the receiving end of unqualified love – and the acts of love that habitually flow from the cooperation with that gift that makes for a habitually converted mentality. But another analogy is required to unpack the structure of the self-transcendent subject in his or her knowing and doing. While that structure works consistently only under the influence of grace, in itself it is nature. But even as nature it provides a remote analogy for understanding the divine processions, and this analogy may be helpful in fixing our understanding of the contours of the supernatural order itself. It is doubtful that our analogy in the order of grace would ever have been developed had we not already immersed ourselves in the natural analogy as Lonergan understands it. This analogy from nature, possibly more fully articulated in Lonergan's *The Triune God: Systematics* than anywhere else in the theological tradition, appeals to processions of act from act in the spiritual operations that are natural to us, that is, in the dimensions of understanding, judgment, and decision. This is still a very generic statement, however: as we have already mentioned and as we will see in greater detail, there are *specific* processions of act from act that are more relevant or pertinent than others. While it is true that the notable examples of procession of act from act in human consciousness are the procession of a hypothesis from an act of direct understanding, the procession of a judgment of fact from a reflective act of understanding, the procession of a judgment of value from an act of existential ethical insight, and the procession of a decision from the combined principle of existential ethical insight and judgment of value, still we must find greater specificity than this if we are to present an acceptable remote analogical hypothesis that will help us understand the link between created participations in the divine relations and processions, on the one hand, and authentic human performance in knowing and doing, on the other.

With this as our agenda, we propose in this chapter first to follow Lonergan through the first assertion in *The Triune God: Systematics*.

Lonergan's first assertion in Trinitarian systematics reads: "The divine processions, which are processions according to the mode of a *processio operati*, are understood in some measure on the basis of a likeness to intellectual emanation; and there does not seem to be another analogy for forming a systematic conception of a divine procession."[1]

To anticipate what is a difficult technical discussion, we may say (1) that we profess in faith that *God proceeds from God* (Son from Father, Holy Spirit from Father and Son); (2) that these processions, as processions of God from God, are, metaphysically speaking, along the lines of processions of *act from act*; (3) that the act that is principle and the act that proceeds *cannot be absolutely distinct acts*, for then there would be three gods, and the fundamental Trinitarian problem would not be solved, that is, to understand how it is that the Son and the Holy Spirit are both *a se* and not *a se*, and that they differ in the respective ways in which they are not *a se*; (4) that the distinction must be a *distinction of opposed relations* in the one act that is the absolute reality of God; and (5) that we can reach an analogical, mediated, and imperfect understanding of how this can be by *likening it to certain processions* within our own consciousness, namely, those processions that are processions of act from act; but since these analogues are all examples in which the act that is principle and the act that proceeds are absolutely distinct acts (*processiones operati*), we must qualify the analogy in some way so as to indicate the difference of the divine processions. They are, if you will, "along the lines of" a *processio operati* in human consciousness, but they also differ, in that the distinction of the act that is principle and the act that proceeds must not be a distinction of absolutely distinct acts but of opposed relations. This is the meaning of Lonergan's phrase *per modum operati*. Furthermore, there are several processions of act from act in human consciousness, and they are not all equally relevant; the relevant processions have to do with our *existential self-constitution*, where the procession of a judgment of value from existential-ethical grasp of sufficient evidence for the judgment, *precisely with regard to what it would be good for the existential subject to do and especially to be*, is the best analogue from nature for the procession of the Son, and the procession, from that grasp and that judgment operating together as a single principle, of loving decision to do and to be precisely that, is the analogue for the procession of the Holy Spirit. In other words, while he does not use the language explicitly at this point, Lonergan is taking his analogy from the "existential moment" in which "the individual ... comes to find out for himself that he has to decide for himself what to make of himself."[2] Again, the analogy is taken from "the point where we discover that it is up to ourselves to decide for ourselves what we are to make of ourselves, where we decisively meet the challenge of that discovery, where we set ourselves apart from the drifters."[3] We are speaking, then, of a process of "existential autonomy" (a term that is used explicitly in this context in *De Deo Trino: Pars systematica*),[4] where act proceeds from act precisely in the realm of that rational self-consciousness which Lonergan began to unpack in chapter 18 of *Insight*.

Some terminological issues are worth mentioning at this point. Subsequently to *Insight*, which was basically completed in 1953, the context for the discussion of the existential autonomy of rational self-consciousness gradually (very gradually) expanded. This is reflected partly in the development of Lonergan's vocabulary for speaking about the relevant operations, and especially about that operation that would become the analogue for the divine Word, namely, the judgment of value.[5] By the time he proposed the first extended version of the analogy, in the text *Divinarum personarum* of 1957, that operation had become something called (in one brief spot in the text) *iudicium practicum seu iudicium valoris*, a practical judgment or judgment of value. That language does not appear in this context in *Insight*. The first mention in *Insight* of judgments of value occurs in chapter 20, in the context of the discussion of belief, where the expression "judgment of value" arises in such a way that, unless one did the necessary research, one would think he had spoken of judgments of value in so many words earlier in the book.[6] He had not. The judgment that is part of the source or originating act of a decision is not given any special name in the discussion of these matters in chapter 18. It is not even called a practical judgment, much less a judgment of value. Mention is made of "the practical insight" and of "practical reflection," but the latter leads to a "practical" knowing in which "one can grasp the virtually unconditioned and thereby attain certitude on the possibility of a proposed course of action, on its agreeableness, on its utility, on its obligatoriness." The word "judgment" is not used to speak of this "practical knowing," for the point that Lonergan is making is that there is no "internal term" to the practical reflection; its term is external to the process, lying as it does in the decision itself. More precisely, "Insofar as it is a knowing, it can reach an internal term," but "insofar as this knowing is practical, insofar as its concern is with something to be done and with the reasons for doing it, the reflection has not an internal but an external term; for the reflection is just knowing, but the term is an ulterior deciding and doing."[7] By the time of *Divinarum personarum* in 1957, the internal term of the practical reflection is called *iudicium practicum seu iudicium valoris*, which in *De Deo Trino: Pars systematica* (1964) becomes simply *iudicium valoris*.[8] But even then, the expression is used only once, in the definition of "spirans" ("spirating") in assertion 2: "the principle of intellectual emanation inasmuch as that principle is determined by both the act of understanding and the consequent word, *when that word is a judgment of value*."[9] The expression does not occur in the earlier, and key, section on "existential autonomy" (which did not appear at all in *Divinarum personarum*): "[Autonomy] is exercised in the existential sphere insofar as one asks about oneself, understands what kind of person one ought to be, judges how one can make oneself that kind of person, and from all of this there proceeds an existential choice through which, insofar as one is able here and now to do so, one makes oneself to be that kind of person." In fact, not only is the expression "judgment of value" not employed here; the judgment that is spoken of is in fact *not* a judgment of value but a practical judgment: one "judges how one can make oneself that kind of person," not that it would be good for one to be that kind of person. In other words, the appearance of a judgment of value in the processions of act from act that constitute the analogy is fleeting in the early Trinitarian work. Lonergan is not yet quite "there" in his position on judgments of value and their distinctness vis-à-vis judgments of concrete fact, judgments on speculative understanding, and practical judgments. However, since he does employ the expression once in this context, in the definition of "spirans," we will refer to the human inner word that is the analogue for the divine Word even in Lonergan's earlier analogy as a judgment of value.

1   *Per Modum Operati* and Theological Understanding

> **Thesis 54:** *The movement from the church's confession of faith, "God from God," to the hypothetical understanding of the processions by analogy with human autonomous spiritual procession is mediated by the theological conclusion that divine processions must be according to the mode of* processio operati. *The analogical understanding affirmed in thesis 53 thus provides a hypothetical explanation of how this theological conclusion can be true.*

Here begins the difficult discussion that I referred to. What is difficult is Lonergan's mode of argumentation. Some readers may want to follow Lonergan in taking a long run at the determination of the meaning of *per modum operati*. Others may find this part of the presentation tedious. While they are right, I don't think it can be omitted.

Some background will be helpful. As we have already seen, act is implicitly defined in relation to potency and form, as follows. Act : form : potency :: To see : sight : eye :: To hear : hearing : ear :: To understand : intelligible species : possible intellect :: To will : volitional habit : will :: To be : substantial form : prime matter. Moreover, act is either central (existence) or conjugate (occurrence). In the present context, Lonergan draws his analogy from conjugate acts within human intellectual or spiritual consciousness.

Real acts are acts of which it reasonably can be affirmed, They are, they occur, they happen. The relevant acts, in the psychological analogy, are all intentional acts, but they are considered here not in their intending of an object but simply as occurring. Thus they are *natural,* where "natural" in Lonergan's definition means simply "they occur."

The acts are also *conscious* in that the presence of the subject to himself or herself is constitutive of them. The subject is present, not as what is intended but as what intends, where the act is present as that by which the object is intended. The presence of the subject to himself or herself is not a presence through reflection or introspection, where one is present as an object, as what is intended rather than as what intends. Such objective presence would not be possible unless the subject were first present as what intends, and it is the latter presence that constitutes consciousness.[10]

Next, the *emanation* itself that provides an analogy for Trinitarian procession is the emergence or procession of one such real, natural, conscious act from another such real, natural, conscious act, *within intellectual consciousness*. It is, then, a conscious psychological event constituted by intelligent and/or volitional acts and the conscious nexus between them, a *conscious procession* occurring by the dynamism of intellectual consciousness itself. But it is the procession of act from act, not of act from potency, as for instance the procession of insight from inquiry.

The conscious subject precisely as conscious is thus what is called the *principium quod* of the procession, ultimately responsible in his or her fidelity to the exigencies of conscious intentionality, whereas a conscious act qua conscious is its *principium quo*, whether that act be an act of direct or reflective understanding, from which there proceed inner words, or a judgment of value from which there proceeds an act of love.

Very important to emphasize is what we have already seen regarding the meaning of "intelligibilis" here, which cannot be lost even as we prefer to use other English words such as intelligent or spiritual: The proceeding act is consciously *because of* and *in proportion to* or in accord with (*secundum*) the act from which it proceeds. That is what makes the emanation "intelligible," what gives it its immanent intelligibility. But as we have seen, "because of" and "in proportion to" can happen in sensitive acts as well, "according to a particular law of nature" (143): "if one sees a large fierce-looking dog without a leash, one spontaneously feels fear." And that is not what Lonergan is talking about. This is the "mood" element of *Befindlichkeit,* which is not unrelated to the "conscious, transcendental exigencies of intellect itself," but which also is not "ordered to all that is intelligible, all that is true, all that is being, all that is good." To bring *Befindlichkeit* into that kind of ordering is a task. It does not happen spontaneously. It is perhaps the task of a lifetime. But processions within mood, disposition, state of mind, are not what Lonergan is talking about here. He is speaking of processions of operations.

Thus, the conscious mediation of the procession in question here occurs in virtue of the dynamism of intelligent consciousness, and so with the self-governing, autonomous, transcendental exigencies according to which our integrity or authenticity as human beings is a function of our ordered allegiance to complete intelligibility, truth, being, goodness, everything, the universe of being. The other "way of being conscious," the way that

Lonergan here calls sensibility and that I call psychic and that Heidegger calls *Befindlichkeit*, is lacking these characteristics of "self-governing, autonomous, transcendental." We have already related this difference to the distinction between spontaneity and autonomy.

Insofar as we are faithful to such exigencies, it is simply the case that one conscious act *will* arise or proceed from another conscious act through the mediation of intellectual consciousness itself: conception will arise from insight, judgment will emerge from grasp of the evidence, and decision will proceed from a judgment of value. Our mood or state of mind or disposition, our *Befindlichkeit*, may have a crucial role to play in determining whether such operations do indeed proceed, but the analogy is taken from the procession of operations, whether this be difficult (as it often is precisely for reasons having to do with dispositions) or easy.

But in addition to the distinction of emanation in sensitive consciousness and emanation in intelligent consciousness, there is a distinction to be drawn within intelligent consciousness itself. Such a procession is distinguished from other intellectual processions in that it is a procession of *act from act* and not of act from potency: *processio operati*, not *processio operationis*, such as the emergence of insight from questions. Again, "we define *because* we understand and *in accordance with* what we understand; again, we judge *because* we grasp evidence as sufficient and *in accordance with* the evidence we have grasped; we choose *because* we judge and *in accordance with* what we judge to be useful or proper or fitting or obligatory."[11]

The two questions that immediately come to mind on reading the first assertion are, What is meant by "per modum operati," "according to the mode of a *processio operati*"? And why does Lonergan proceed in this seemingly roundabout way? The answer to each question is complex.

The answer to the first is complex because there are different ways of speaking about the mode or kind of a procession, and some of these combine more limited ways of conceiving a procession. These must be sorted out if we are to determine the nature of the analogy that he is pursuing. In fact, the key to understanding the assertion lies in understanding the moves that Lonergan is making in the assertion with regard to the different manners of determining a procession. He completely rewrote this assertion for *De Deo Trino*, introducing all of this material, so he must have regarded it as important.

As for the second question, answering it will throw much light on Lonergan's understanding of what systematic theology is and on his methodological options for working in systematics. And while the questions are distinct, the response to the second will best be found as we work out the response to the first.

We proceed, then, to the complex response to the first question.

There are three steps. We begin with the confession of faith, "God from God, light from light, true God from true God." We move from there to a metaphysical transposition of that confession of faith: "according to the mode of a *processio operati.*" And third, we are enabled by that move to make another move: "on the basis of a likeness to intellectual emanation."

Thus, three statements are involved. The second is simply a metaphysical way of articulating what is contained in the first, the confession of faith. That metaphysical transposition is required, Lonergan argues, if we are to be able to meet the goal of systematic understanding. That goal is not yet reached in the metaphysical transposition, but is prepared for by it, for if we make that metaphysical transposition, then, and perhaps only then, will we be able to understand how it is that "God from God, light from light, true God from true God" can be understood on the basis of a likeness to intellectual emanation. That in a nutshell is the structure of the argument. But it is just the structure, the bare bones, and these must be given flesh before any understanding can emerge of precisely what he is up to here.

In the assertion itself Lonergan is moving from what he will call the *external and natural* determination employed in the confession of faith when it speaks of procession ("God from God"), to the *external and metaphysical* determination *per modum operati* that is an equivalent but technical way of saying the same thing as is said in the creed (along the lines of a procession of act from act), and then from that external and metaphysical determination to an *internal and natural* determination *secundum similitudinem emanationis intelligibilis* that enables us to *understand* analogically, imperfectly, and mediately how the processions that we confess in faith can be *processiones per modum operati.* Without the move to the technical determination *per modum operati,* there is not an adequate technical or systematic understanding by analogy with the intellectual emanations to be found in human intentional consciousness. One can best go from the external and natural determination of the confession of faith to the internal and natural determination of the psychological analogy by passing through the external and metaphysical determination of *per modum operati.*

In order to unpack this, we will examine the various ways in which Lonergan speaks about conceiving and determining procession. He mentions five ways of determining a procession by a single determination. *First,* there is *external* determination: conceive the procession in terms of the principle and what proceeds from it. *Second,* there is *internal* determination: conceive the manner in which it occurs. Is it violent or natural? conscious or unconscious? spontaneous or self-governed? *Third,* there is *metaphysical* determination: specify the procession in terms like "same and other," "potency and act," "absolute and relative." *Fourth,* there is *natural* determination: indicate the generic, specific, or individual *nature* of the procession: it is physical or chemical or biological or sensitive or intellectual or divine. *Fifth*, there is *analogical* determination: conceive the mode of procession of an unknown nature by a likeness with that of known nature.

The simple definition of "procession," the origination of one from another (*origo unius ex alio*),[12] is too abstract to be of much help. Concretely, there are different modes or kinds of procession, as the examples of processions *ad extra* and *ad intra*, sensitive procession, procession of an operation (from potency to act), and autonomous spiritual procession of act from act have already indicated.[13] More fully, the mode or kind of procession can be conceived, determined, and spoken of in a number of ways, and some of these combine different and more limited manners of conceiving procession. Some examples follow. It helps to get straight what Lonergan is doing in these examples, since they determine the nature of the analogy that he is pursuing. Especially if he is correct that this is the best or even the only kind of analogy that will satisfy the requirements of rigorous systematic theological reflection, then following him through what might seem to be a tedious list of distinctions could help prevent mistakes down the line. As Augustine reminds us, "nowhere else is a mistake more dangerous, or the search more laborious, or discovery more advantageous" than in seeking to understand "the unity of the three, of Father and Son and Holy Spirit."[14] It is with this caution in mind that I proceed with Lonergan's details, which appear precisely to guarantee against making such a mistake.

(1) If we conceive a procession in terms of the principle and what proceeds from it, we are giving it what Lonergan calls an *external* determination of the procession, where the use of the word "external" means "one from another." "External" does not here refer to a procession *ad extra*. It refers to a determination, a manner of speaking about any procession where the procession is described as "one from another," whether the procession be *ad extra* or *ad intra*. If what is emphasized is "one from another," then the determination is "external." Thus, "inner word from insight" is an external determination, even though the procession to which it refers is not *ad extra* but internal to intellectual consciousness.

(2) If we speak of the manner in which the procession occurs – it is forced or coerced, on the one hand, or natural, on the other; it is conscious or unconscious, *spontaneous or self-governed and so autonomous* (an important distinction, as we have seen), and so on – we are providing an *internal* determination of the procession. Here too, "internal" does not refer to a procession that occurs *ad intra*, but to a manner of speaking about any procession,

whether *ad extra* or *ad intra*, that emphasizes the immanent character of the procession itself: how does it occur? Thus, to say that certain processions are conscious is to provide an internal determination of these processions. To speak of a conscious procession of inner word from understanding is to provide both external and internal determinations of the same procession: external insofar as there is "one from another," and internal insofar as it is immanently characterized as conscious.

(3) If we specify the procession in such general metaphysical terms as "same" and "other," "potency" and "act," "absolute" and "relative," and so on, we are providing a *metaphysical* determination of the procession. We have already seen the distinction of processions of act from potency and processions of act from act. "Per modum operati" as a way of distinguishing the divine processions provides just such a metaphysical determination, as we will see.

(4) A *natural* determination would speak of the procession in terms of a generic, specific, or individual nature: it is a physical or a chemical or a biological or a sensitive or a spiritual or a divine procession.

(5) An *analogical* determination would conceive the mode of procession of an unknown nature (for example, the divine) by likeness with the mode of procession of a known nature (for example, procession in the spiritual dimension of human consciousness).

Obviously, some of these concrete ways of specifying a procession may be combined. We have already seen how speaking of a conscious procession of inner word from understanding provides both an external and an internal determination of the same procession. Lonergan gives the following five examples in which *external* and *metaphysical* determinations combine in the characterization of a procession:

(1) a procession *ad extra*, into another thing, that is, a procession of one thing from another thing – for example, producing something, creating, animal generation; here the mode of procession is determined in an external and metaphysical manner, since the principle and that which proceeds from it are named (external determination), and the metaphysical categories of "same" and "other" are employed in a particular manner (metaphysical determination);

(2) a procession *ad intra*, where the principle and what proceeds from it are within the same "thing," whether in the same

subsistent or in the same consciousness or in the same faculty or potency; here again the mode of procession is determined in an external and metaphysical manner, since the principle and that which proceeds from it are named (external determination), and the metaphysical categories of "same" and "other" are employed, but in a different manner, and "same" can mean "in the same substance," "in the same consciousness," or "within the same faculty or potency" (metaphysical determination);

(3) a *processio operationis,* a procession of an operation *ad intra,* in which the principle and what proceeds from it are related as potency and act; again, the determination of the mode is external and metaphysical: the principle and what proceeds from it are named, and the metaphysical categories of potency and act are employed to determine the mode of the procession; examples include the act of seeing proceeding from the potency of sight and from the eye; the act of understanding proceeding from what Scholastic philosophy called the "possible intellect" and the "intelligible species";[15]

(4) a *processio operati,* a procession of something "operated" *ad intra,* in which the principle is related to what proceeds from it as act to act; again the mode of determination is external and metaphysical, since the principle and what proceeds from it are named, the metaphysical category of act is employed in the determination of the mode of the procession, and the categories of "same" and "other" are at least implicitly appealed to; examples include the desire or fear that proceeds from an act of seeing, the hypothesis that proceeds from an act of understanding, the judgment that proceeds from an act of grasping sufficient evidence, the decision that proceeds from a practical judgment or judgment of value;

(5) a *processio per modum operati:* like a *processio operationis* and a *processio operati,* it is a *processio ad intra;* but unlike a *processio operationis* and like a *processio operati,* the *processio per modum operati* is one in which the principle and what proceeds are both act; but unlike even a *processio operati,* the *processio per modum operati* is one in which the act that is principle and the act that proceeds are really distinguished, not absolutely but relatively (*non ... secundum esse absolutum, sed secundum esse relativum*);[16] they are not really distinct entities, but really distinct relations within the same *esse absolutum;* the determination again is external and metaphysical; and the definition has been thought out with one thing in mind: precisely in order to conceive and speak about the divine

mystery. Thus, a procession that is "according to the mode of a *processio operati*" (*per modum operati*) is a procession *ad intra* of act from act, where the acts are distinguished, not by an absolute distinction in being, but by relational properties (later called "notional acts") within the same absolute act of existence. The determination of the procession is external (principle and what emanates from it) and metaphysical (act from act).

Lonergan then gives the following examples of other ways of determining the mode of procession than by external and metaphysical determination:

(6) when we use the expression *divine procession,* that is, when we speak of the procession of God from God, the mode of determination is still external, since it names the principle and what proceeds from the principle; but it is not a metaphysical determination but a natural one, since it specifies the procession in terms of the nature in which the procession occurs;

(7) the definition of *intelligent emanation* (or, in our terminology, autonomous spiritual procession) – a conscious procession of a real, natural, conscious act from a real, natural, conscious act, both within the spiritual dimension of consciousness and in virtue of that spiritual dimension of consciousness itself as such consciousness is determined by the prior act that is the principle of the emanation – employs a mode of determination that is both external (one from another) and, more importantly, internal, since it speaks of the procession as natural and conscious; and it employs a mode of determination that is natural (as well as metaphysical [act from act]), since it names the kind of nature ("intellectual consciousness" in Lonergan's terms, "the spiritual dimension of consciousness" in ours) in which such a procession occurs.

Now what makes the "psychological analogy" an analogy is that in us intelligent emanation or autonomous spiritual procession is the procession of one act from another act, where the acts (for example, the act of understanding and the inner word that proceeds from it) are really distinct in an absolute fashion: insight is not concept, but is rather the ground of concepts; reflective understanding is not a judgment of fact, but is rather the ground of such a judgment; existential-ethical insight is not a judgment of value, but is rather the ground of such a judgment; a judgment of value is not a decision, but is rather the ground of a decision; whereas the procession of God from God, divine procession, is the procession of act from act where the distinction is not one of absolutely different acts but of really distinct relations of origin *within* the one act that is God. So we move from the internal mode of procession that we experience in intelligent emanation or autonomous spiritual procession to an analogical understanding of the internal mode of the divine procession. When we name the latter procession "divine procession," we are not determining it in an internal but in an external manner ("God from God"); when we name it a procession *per modum operati*, we are determining it in an external and metaphysical manner; but when we say that it is understood on the basis of some likeness to what we experience as intellectual emanation or autonomous spiritual procession, we are giving a mediate, imperfect, and analogical *internal and natural determination* to a divine procession. No determination of a divine procession can ever be more than mediate, imperfect, and analogical, and this means that no matter how great the similarity may be with human intellectual procession, the dissimilarity is ever greater. The intricate distinctions that Lonergan has made here culminate in the reader's awareness of why this is the case. We do not know what God is, but what God is not: that is, we have no direct grasp of the internal processions natural to God; any faint grasp we may have must be mediate, imperfect, and analogical.

Lonergan's first assertion moves, then, (1) from an external and natural determination (divine procession, God from God) employed in the confession of faith, to an external and metaphysical determination (*per modum operati*) that is simply an equivalent way of talking about the same thing; and then, through the mediation of this external and metaphysical determination, (2) to an internal and natural determination (*secundum similitudinem emanationis intelligibilis*) that enables us to understand analogically, imperfectly, and mediately how it is possible that the divine processions that we confess in faith can be *processiones per modum operati*, processions entirely in the order of act but where the principle and what proceeds from it are not two absolutely distinct acts but relations of opposition within the same act. Again, (1) we first transpose the external and natural determination that we use in our confession of faith (divine procession, "God from God") to an external and metaphysical determination (*per modum operati*) that enables us to distinguish this procession from other types of procession already spoken of in the section in which intelligent emanation was defined (processions *ad extra, processio operationis,* and *processio operati*); and then (2) we try to *understand* what we have given this external and metaphysical determination by analogy with the internal and natural mode of determination that we employ when we speak of intelligent emanation (or, in our terminology, autonomous spiritual procession). The identification of "divine procession" with "*per modum operati*" is the first step. It simply transposes one way of talking about the reality in question (an external and natural way employed in the confession of faith) into another way of conceiving and determining the same reality (an external and metaphysical way employed in speaking of different kinds of procession). If there are divine processions (and we confess in faith that there are) they cannot be *ad extra* but must be *ad intra*; they cannot be *processiones operationis*, for in God there is no movement from potency to act; they cannot be *processiones operati*, for in God there is only one act; and so they must be *processiones per modum operati*, according to the mode of a *processio operati*, in that they are processions of act from act but also processions in which the act that is principle and the act that proceeds are really distinct, not in an absolute fashion but by relational properties; they are really distinct relations of origin (later to be called "notional acts") constitutive of the one real infinite and pure act that is the divine "actus totius entis."

Again, to speak of a divine procession is, as we said, to employ an *external* determination, but not a metaphysical determination; rather, the determination is natural: we are speaking of the procession of God from God, a procession proper to the divine nature, the procession characteristic of the generation of the Son from the Father or of the procession of the Holy Spirit from both. But the definition of an intelligent emanation – a conscious procession of a real, natural, conscious act from a real, natural, conscious act, both within intelligent consciousness and in virtue of that intelligent consciousness itself as such consciousness is determined by the prior act that is the principle of the procession – is primarily a natural but *internal* determination. The divine processions, which are *per modum operati*, are understood on the basis of the likeness of this internal, experienced character of intelligent emanation. And so we are involved in an *analogical*, mediate, and imperfect, not a natural, determination of their internal mode or character as processions. We are employing an internal and natural determination (intelligent emanation or autonomous spiritual procession) to understand analogically the internal mode of a procession that we name "divine procession" by external and natural determination (the generation of the Son from the Father and the procession of the Holy Spirit from both Father and Son). And supposing that there is in God intelligent emanation or autonomous spiritual procession conceived by remote analogy with the intelligent emanation or autonomous spiritual procession that we experience, we can understand how it can be true to speak of the divine processions with the external and metaphysical determination of *per modum operati*. This is the complicated structure of Lonergan's argument at this point.[17]

The two movements in the argument are quite distinct. The movement from "God from God" to "per modum operati" is a theological conclusion, a deduction. It shows the proper role of such conclusions in theology: to clarify the problem to be understood. The second movement is different.

In it we ask, What might be the condition of the possibility of the divine processions being *per modum operati?* How could this be? This is the question for systematic theology. The answer is that one possible source of such a conclusion is that they proceed by some likeness to intellectual emanation in our intellectual consciousness. Lonergan's issue here in general is with what he calls "conclusions theology," or with that type of Catholic theology that thought that systematics was a matter of drawing conclusions from the truths of faith or from reason and faith rather than understanding the mysteries of faith. There is a role for conclusions, and the procedure followed here is a perfect example of precisely what that role is. But such conclusions yield no understanding. They simply set up the possibility for systematic understanding to occur.

The assertion claims also that this gives us what seems to be the only possible analogy for conceiving systematically the divine processions, that is, for interiorly expressing that understanding that virtually suffices to resolve all the related questions in a treatise on the Trinity. The analogy that I will suggest is, of course, distinct from the one that Lonergan presents, but not in such a way as to negate the claim that *secundum emanationem intelligibilem* is the only likeness that will provide us with a remote analogy for the divine processions. As I argued earlier, both Lonergan's later analogy and the distinct analogy that I am suggesting have the same structure as the analogy we are studying now. The processions within the supernatural order created by the gift of God's love are processions of act from act in the spiritual dimension of consciousness, and this is precisely what is meant by the *emanatio intelligibilis* that establishes a suitable analogy. But as I have also stressed, it seems eminently sane and probably necessary to understand even our supernatural analogy by analogy with the natural analogy, and so we are dedicating ample space for the treatment of Lonergan's proposal in his earlier work on Trinitarian theology.

The church's confession is expressed as follows in the Athanasian Creed: "Pater a nullo est factus nec creatus nec genitus; Filius a Patre solo est, non factus nec creatus, sed genitus; Spiritus Sanctus a Patre et Filio, non factus nec creatus nec genitus, sed procedens" (DB 39, DS 75).[18] This is the doctrine that we are attempting to understand, the confession of divine processions, where the processions are named in an external ("one from another") and natural ("divine") fashion, and where one of them is generation and the other is not. The procedure, again, is to convert this confession into a statement where the processions are named in an external ("one from another") and metaphysical (*per modum operati*) fashion, and then to say that such a formulation could be understood in some obscure and remote fashion *if* we relied on an analogy with human processions of spiritual act from spiritual act.

The first part of the argument of the assertion, then, presents a technical formulation of the same doctrine, the doctrine that systematic theology is attempting to understand. This technical formulation shifts the determination of the procession to an external ("one from another") and metaphysical (in terms of "act") mode of speaking. From a technical point of view, given what we have already seen about the modes of procession understood metaphysically, what can we say in this mode about the divine processions? This formulation will also help, Lonergan says, to remove an apparent contradiction in the doctrine, precisely the same contradiction that seems to affect the "fundamental problem" that we saw earlier, namely, How is it that the Son and the Holy Spirit can be at once *a se* and not *a se*?[19]

In the second part of the argument a *hypothetical* systematic solution is proposed to the problem thus technically formulated. In other words, the question is raised, What is required in order that it be true that the divine processions be *per modum operati?* The answer is: The divine processions can be *per modum operati* if they can be understood analogically along the lines of intelligent emanation (or autonomous spiritual procession); this would be sufficient, and in fact is as far as we are able to go in understanding this mystery. So this hypothetical solution is offered in this second part. The systematic theological understanding is reached here. What is required for the processions to be *per modum operati?* We can *understand* how this can be so, if the processions can be understood analogically along the lines of intellectual or intelligent emanation.

And in the third part it is judged that this hypothetical solution seems to be the only way available to us of understanding the mystery that we confess. It is in this third part that very important specifications are given with regard to precisely *which* acts from *which* acts in human spiritual procession are most appropriate for an analogical understanding of Trinitarian processions. The core of the argument is found precisely here, that is, what distinguishes this analogy from most other attempts at a psychological analogy.

In order better to grasp Lonergan's procedure here, it is well to indicate that first he reviews various attempts to treat theologically (or to ignore) the mystery of the Trinity, and that he treats one of these at greater length in a number of places, whenever he criticizes what he calls "conclusions theology." It will help to grasp Lonergan's procedure and his view of the role of theological conclusions if we compare his approach with that of the so-called conclusions theology.

Conclusions theology is described as follows: "[T]here are those who believe the scriptures and embrace the dogmas and seek theological understanding. But they think the understanding should be a theological conclusion demonstrated from the truths of faith and from naturally known principles. It eludes their notice that, while science is concerned with conclusions, understanding is concerned with principles. So, because they aim at conclusions, they do not arrive at understanding."[20] In contrast is the procedure that Lonergan follows: "Then again, there are those who believe the scriptures, embrace the dogmas, and *deduce theological conclusions* [and this is as far as the theologians just discussed will go], but also proceed from those very conclusions to a technical formulation of a problem. They seek the solution to the problem not through deduction but through a hypothesis; and because they deny that we can attain any other understanding in this life, they think that the hypothetical understanding should be accepted."[21] This is precisely what Lonergan is doing: he *is* deducing a conclusion, namely, that the divine processions are *per modum operati*, but that deduction has not yet given him the *understanding* that is the goal of systematics. That understanding is achieved when, given that the processions are *per modum operati*, he asks how that could be so and answers that they can be *per modum operati* if they are conceived by analogy with the intellectual emanations or autonomous spiritual processions of word and love that can be discovered in human consciousness.

Part 1 of the elaboration of the assertion, then, sets forth the technical formulation of the problem, in fact the technical formulation of the doctrine itself that is to be submitted to systematic understanding. In this part of the assertion, Lonergan *does* use metaphysical principles to deduce a theological conclusion from the truth confessed in faith. But the conclusion does not give us understanding. It allows us to proceed to understanding, that is, to a hypothetical explanation of how the conclusion could be true. The conclusion itself differs from the doctrine of faith only verbally, and so it is theologically certain. This part of the assertion is a strict deduction from the truths of faith, using, as he says, metaphysical notions and principles available to everybody. Through these notions and principles, it offers nothing more than a technical formulation of the very same truth that we confess in faith.

The technical formulation states that a divine procession occurs *per modum operati*, according to the mode of a *processio operati*. Thus, it corresponds to the first part of the assertion itself: "Processiones divinae, quae sunt per modum operati ..." The deduction proceeds negatively at first, by way of eliminating other possibilities. Then it positively states its affirmation. And finally, it uncovers the roots of an apparent contradiction.

The negative portion proceeds through three steps. *First*, dogma, with a firm basis in scripture, denies that the Son and the Spirit are made or created, and so we know that divine procession is not a matter of making or creating; *second*, since in divine procession the same God is Father, Son, and Holy Spirit, a divine procession cannot be a *processio ad extra*; and *third*, while a divine procession is *ad intra*, it cannot be a *processio operationis*, for such a procession would be an origin of act from potency; nor can it be a *processio operati*, an origin even *ad intra* of one act from another act, where the distinction of the two acts is not only a real distinction but *secundum esse absolutum*: in God, who is simple, there can be only one act, and that an infinite act.[22] So much for the first, negative part of the argument.

The positive part of this portion of the assertion states that divine procession must be *per modum operati*, according to the mode of a *processio operati*, in that it is a procession in which the principle and what proceeds from it, *actus principians* and *actus principiatus*, while they are really distinct, are not two acts really distinct *secundum esse absolutum* – there is only one God, and the three divine persons are consubstantial – but are distinct *secundum esse relativum*, that is, as mutually opposed relations within one and the same infinite act. In the language of the Council of Florence, everything in God is one except where the opposition of relation dictates otherwise (DB 703, DS 1130).[23]

The apparent contradiction appears in the two statements that (1) God is from God, and (2) God is one. If there is a real procession of God from God, there would seem to be two gods. But if God is one, there would not seem to be any procession of God from God. Negatively, but only negatively, this contradiction is removed by distinguishing between a procession *ad extra* and a procession *ad intra*. In a procession *ad extra*, one thing, one complete reality, proceeds from another. If a divine procession were *ad extra*, there would be two gods or at least two complete realities. But a procession *ad intra* does not *necessarily* entail the existence of two distinct complete realities; it is not necessarily the case that if one thing proceeds from another it must do so *secundum esse absolutum*. To quote again what we have already seen in Aquinas, "id quod procedit ad intra processu intelligibili *non oportet* esse diversum; immo quantum perfectius procedit tanto magis est unum cum eo a quo procedit. Manifestum est enim quod quanto aliquid magis intelligitur tanto conceptio intellectualis est magis intima intelligenti et magis unum; nam intellectus secundum hoc quod actu intelligit, secundum hoc fit unum cum intellecto. Unde cum divinum intelligere sit in fine perfectionis …, necesse est quod verbum divinum sit perfecte unum cum eo a quo procedit absque omni diversitate."[24]

Now it is true that an internal procession *can* be and almost always is the procession of one act from another act within the same thing, where the two acts are distinct *secundum esse absolutum*. In human consciousness clear examples can be found in the procession of the first inner word (for example, an act of defining, or, more often, a hypothesis) from the act of understanding, and the procession of the second inner word, the judgment, the yes or no, from the act of grasping the sufficiency of evidence for the hypothesis. In either case, we are speaking of two acts that are really distinct *secundum esse absolutum.* And so Lonergan states that a solution to the apparent contradiction that proceeds by distinguishing *ad extra* and *ad intra* is merely negative, and that there is needed a positive solution that rests on a grasp of the difference between the divine nature and human nature. Generation *ad intra* does not occur in human beings. Only a positive doctrine about the divine nature can give us some understanding of why generation *ad intra* is not incompatible with the divine nature. That positive doctrine is given in the second part of the argument, where the hypothetical solution is offered. The positive resolution constitutes the second step in the argument of the assertion. The first step has deduced the conclusion that a divine procession is *per modum operati.* It has thus arrived, not yet at any *understanding* of divine processions, but at a *technical formulation* of the issue to be understood, that is, of the truth affirmed and confessed in faith. It has arrived at this technical formulation by deducing it from the truths of faith as a theological conclusion, using metaphysical principles to distinguish various modes of procession.

The second step seeks a hypothetical *understanding* of the truth thus technically formulated.[25] It proceeds through four steps: first, the divine processions can be *understood* to be *per modum operati* if we suppose that there is in God intelligent emanation or autonomous spiritual procession; second, such a deduction brings an increase, not of knowledge (*scientia,* in the technical sense of knowledge drawn from conclusions) but of understanding; third, it is determined in what this increase of understanding consists; and fourth, it is explained that this acquired understanding is mediate, imperfect, analogical, and obscure. The next, third step will argue why this hypothesis is to be accepted.

The hypothesis, then, is that there is in God intelligent emanation, that the *processio per modum operati* that constitutes a divine procession is to be understood by analogy with what we *experience* as intelligent emanation. The difference, of course, is that in our case one act arises from and is caused by another act and the two acts are distinct *secundum esse absolutum,* whereas in God there is no causality involved and there are really distinct relations within the one infinite act that is God. Generation *ad intra* is a procession whose terms are constitutive of *one* act because they are *identical* with the *relations* of generation and generated; and similarly for the procession of the Holy Spirit. The real distinction within the one act of two terms *only* by the mutually opposed relations that they *are* is not found in the creaturely realm, and *this is where we reach the point of mystery that cannot be gone beyond in our understanding. How can there be both relation and consubstantiality in God?*

There are three reasons for proceeding in this way. First, we cannot *demonstrate* that a procession *per modum operati* is an intelligent emanation, since from what is less determinate (*processio per modum operati*) we cannot demonstrate what is more determinate (*emanatio intelligibilis*). Moreover, demonstration is not to be sought of principles. There are principles that are per se known by reason; there are principles that are revealed by God and accepted in faith; and there are theological principles that are reached, not by faith alone nor by reason alone nor by deduction from faith and reason, but by the understanding that is the term of an inquiry undertaken by reason enlightened by faith. Such is the supposition of something in God analogous to intelligent emanation or autonomous spiritual procession in us. It is "worked out" by a thinking that takes place in order to understand.[26] Third, *the present inquiry bears precisely upon such a matter of principle, for a principle is what is first in some set of related matters, and we are here treating the first matter to be treated in a systematic exposition of an understanding of Trinitarian doctrine.* This principle is not naturally known, nor is it divinely revealed and believed in faith, nor is it concluded from what is divinely revealed and believed in faith (as was the assertion of *per modum operati*). Rather, what is being sought is an *understanding* of the faith, an understanding of what has been revealed by God, proposed by the church, and believed in faith.

2   The Hypothesis

We begin, then, with the *hypothetical supposition* – "Let us suppose" – that there is in God intelligent emanation, that is, dynamic spiritual consciousness, autonomous spiritual procession precisely in the sense of something like act from act. This is not an article of faith. It is not something that reason can know on its own resources. It is not a technical formulation of an article of faith. It is an intelligent hypothesis, and it will be employed to understand the articles of faith – the Son proceeds from the Father, and the Holy Spirit proceeds from the Father and the Son – that have already been technically formulated in metaphysical terms: namely, procession in God is not *ad extra*, nor is it *processio operationis*, nor is it *processio operati*, but it is *processio per modum operati*. Again, the hypothetical supposition proposes that the *processio per modum operati* that constitutes a divine procession is to be understood *by analogy* with what we experience in our own dynamic consciousness as an autonomous spiritual procession of act from act (*secundum similitudinem emanationis intelligibilis*). A divine procession can be, not simply affirmed through deduction from the articles of faith to be *per modum operati*, but also *understood* to be *per modum operati*, if (1) there is in God something like autonomous spiritual procession of act from act, and (2) this procession is distinct from what we experience, where one act arises from another act and the two acts are distinct *secundum esse absolutum*. In God the *one* infinite act is both *principians* and *principiatus*, and so, when we speak of *actus principians* and *actus principiatus*, we are not speaking of two acts really distinct *secundum esse absolutum,* but of *really distinct relations of origin constituting the one infinite act* that is God. Again, there occur in us internal processions, *processiones ad intra,* that are processions of act from act, *processiones operati;* but there does not occur in us an internal generation or begetting, a *generatio ad intra* whose *terms* are constitutive of *one* act because they are *identical with the relations* of generation and generated. In the triune God terms and relations are identical. This is true nowhere else.

Lonergan expresses the difference as follows in *Verbum:* "[T]he divine procession of the Word is not only real but also a natural generation. In us that does not hold. Our intellects are not our substance; our acts of understanding are not our existence; and so our definitions and affirmations [our inner words] are not the essence and existence of our children."[27] We rely on the notion of a procession of act from act, a *processio operati,* to understand the divine processions – this is precisely what is meant by *per modum operati* – but the *real* distinction within the one act of two terms *only* by the mutually opposed relations that they *are* is not something to be found in the creaturely realm. It is a notion that has been thought out precisely in order to provide some obscure understanding of Trinitarian life.

This formulation takes us beyond conceiving divine processions to affirming divine relations, however, and we have yet to examine Lonergan's explanation of how the divine processions can be *understood* to be *per modum operati* – that they are *per modum operati* has already been affirmed in the first part of the assertion – if they are conceived on an analogy with the autonomous spiritual processions of the inner word from understanding and of the act of love from that same understanding and that same inner word, where the word itself is a judgment of value (second step); we also must ask why he says this seems to be the only manner in which such an understanding is attainable (third step). How does the supposition or hypothesis of intelligent emanation help us to understand that the divine processions are according to the mode of a *processio operati,* and so that, as we profess in faith, God proceeds from God?

Again, what is going forward here is not a demonstration: the notion of *per modum operati* – which is already theologically certain when used as a formulation for the nature of divine procession – is of a lesser determination, is less specific, more generic, than that of *emanatio intelligibilis,* and so it cannot be concluded from *per modum operati* that divine procession is to be understood analogically *secundum similitudinem emanationis intelligibilis.* Thus, the way this second part of the assertion is formulated: *If* one supposes that there is in God something analogous to autonomous spiritual procession in us, it follows that there is a procession according to the mode of a *processio operati.*[28] We already know that divine procession is *per modum operati.* The question is, How can this be possible? It can be possible if divine procession can be understood *secundum similitudinem emanationis intelligibilis,* according to a likeness to human autonomous spiritual procession.

The effort, obviously, is to reach a hypothetical understanding of what already is accepted as a technical formulation of what is believed in faith. Moreover, principles cannot be demonstrated, and we are dealing here with a matter of principle, with the first issue in an ordered treatment of Trinitarian systematics. This principle is neither naturally known nor divinely revealed, but a matter of *intelligentia fidei,* of an understanding of what *is* divinely revealed and believed in faith: "Suppose this is the case; then it would follow that ..."

What, then, would an *emanatio intelligibilis et divina* be? As we have seen, an autonomous spiritual procession occurs in virtue of the dynamism of the spiritual dimension of consciousness itself as such consciousness is determined by some act. To suppose hypothetically that there is in God something like what we know as autonomous spiritual procession is to suppose hypothetically, then, (1) that there is consciousness in God and that this consciousness is intelligent, (2) that this intelligent consciousness is determined by some act, which in this case can be nothing other than infinite act, and (3) that this consciousness, so determined, is dynamic, that is, it consciously demands or requires an emanation.[29] All these points are contained in the supposition that there is in God autonomous spiritual procession, *emanatio intelligibilis.*

For Lonergan, six consequences follow from these hypothetical suppositions.

First, the act that is principle of the emanation is the infinite act that is God grasping the motive and appropriate proportion of the required emanation (*motivum propter quod et secundum quod exigatur emanatio*). For there cannot be in God any real distinction between infinite act and divine consciousness, and so we cannot conceive them in such a way that one is really determining (infinite act) and the other really determined (divine consciousness). Divine consciousness *is* infinite act. Thus, infinite act itself knows the "motive" that calls for an emanation and determines what it will be, and by this knowledge and conscious exigence infinite act is constituted as the act that is the principle (*actus principians*) of the emanation.[30]

Second, it follows that there truly and really proceeds within divine consciousness an act that is originated (*actum principiatum*). For it cannot be supposed that infinite act is limited by an inconsistency (*sibi non constare*), such that, while there is a conscious demand within it for an emanation, nonetheless the emanation does not exist, or that, while there is a demand that the emanation be within consciousness, nonetheless it is not within consciousness. By the very fact that there is posited an act that is principle, there necessarily also is posited a true and real emanation; and where there is a true and real emanation, there is also that which emanates, the act that proceeds (*actus principiatus*).[31]

Third, it follows that the *actus principiatus* is also infinite act: it is not nothing; and it cannot be finite, for (1) it is not created: everything created proceeds *ad extra*, but any act that proceeds within consciousness and in virtue of that consciousness itself proceeds *ad intra*; and (2) it is not contingent: whatever proceeds because of an exigence within divine consciousness proceeds by necessity.[32]

Fourth, then, it follows that God proceeds from God, for what is infinite is God.[33]

Fifth, it follows that the act that is principle and the act that proceeds are not really distinct *secundum esse absolutum*. For each is infinite, and the infinite is unique, and so there cannot be a real distinction *secundum esse absolutum* within infinite act.[34]

Sixth, it follows that they are really distinct *secundum esse relativum*. The real emanation that has been supposed gives rise necessarily to opposed relations of principle and proceeding. This is so even when the same infinite act is both principle and proceeding, for the emanation in question is not causal. A causal emanation demands that cause and effect be really distinct absolutes. But the emanation or procession in question *is* an intelligent emanation, an autonomous spiritual procession, one that, while not causal, involves *because* (*quia*) and so is *intelligibilis*: "to love the good is right *because* loving proceeds from the good truly affirmed, and affirming the good is true *because* affirming proceeds from a grasp of evidence."[35] Nor is there any reason why this truth and rightness are removed simply because the act of grasping, affirming, and loving is infinite act and infinite act is one.[36]

Lonergan makes the point in *Verbum* that it is precisely here that the difference between autonomous spiritual procession in us and in God shows up most clearly. The divine *dicere* is not a *producere verbum*, that is, it is not a causal relation, and there is not in God a *processio operati*, a procession of act from act.

> In us there are two acts, first, an act of understanding, secondly, a really distinct act of defining or judging. In God there is but one act. But not only did Aquinas advert to this rather obvious fact but also he assigned the reason for this difference: "id quod procedit ad intra processu intelligibili, non oportet esse diversum; imo, quanto perfectius procedit, tanto magis est unum cum eo a quo procedit" ...
>
> There are two aspects to the procession of an inner word in us. There is the productive aspect: intelligence in act is proportionate to producing the inner word. There is also the intelligible aspect: inner words do not proceed with mere natural spontaneity as any

effect does from any cause; they proceed with reflective rationality; they proceed not merely from a sufficient cause but from sufficient grounds known to be sufficient and because they are known to be sufficient.[37] I can imagine a circle, and I can define a circle. In both cases there is efficient causality. But in the second case there is something more. I define the circle because I grasp in imagined data that, if the radii are equal, then the plane curve must be uniformly round. The inner word of defining not only is *caused by* [productive aspect] but also is *because of* [intelligible aspect] the act of understanding. In the former aspect the procession is *processio operati*. In the latter aspect the procession is *processio intelligibilis*. Similarly, in us the act of judgment is caused by a reflective act of understanding, and so it is *processio operati*. But that is not all. The procession of judgment cannot be equated with procession from electromotive force or chemical action or biological process or even sensitive act. Judgment is judgment only if it proceeds from intellectual grasp of sufficient evidence as sufficient. Its procession also is *processio intelligibilis*.

What, then, does Aquinas mean when he writes: "id quod procedit ad intra processu intelligibili, non oportet esse diversum; imo, quanto perfectius procedit, tanto magis est unum cum eo a quo procedit?" He does not mean that there can be production, properly speaking, when principle and product are absolutely identical. He does mean that there can be *processio intelligibilis* without absolute diversity, indeed that the more perfect the *processio intelligibilis* is, the greater the approach to identity. In us inner word proceeds from act of understanding by a *processio intelligibilis* that also is a *processio operati*, for our inner word and act of understanding are two absolute entities really distinct. In God inner word proceeds from act of understanding as uttering by a *processio intelligibilis* that is not a *processio operati*, at least inasmuch as divine understanding and divine Word are not two absolute entities really distinct ...

Indeed, the divine procession of the Word is not only real but also a natural generation. In us that does not hold. Our intellects are not our substance; our acts of understanding are not our existence; and so our definitions and affirmations are not the essence and existence of our children. Our inner words are just thoughts, just *esse intentionale* of what we define and affirm, just *intentio intellecta* and not *res intellecta*. But in God intellect is substance, and act of understanding is act of existence; it follows that the Word that proceeds in him is of the same nature and substance as its principle, that his thought of himself is himself, that his *intentio intellecta* of himself is also the *res intellecta*. As there is an analogy of *ens* and *esse*, so also there is an analogy of the intelligibly proceeding *est*. In us *est* is just a thought, a judgment. But in God not only is *ipsum esse* the ocean of all perfection, comprehensively grasped by *ipsum intelligere*, in complete identity, but also perfectly expressed in a single Word. That Word is thought, definition, judgment, and yet of the same nature as God, whose substance is intellect. Hence it is not mere thought as opposed to thing, not mere definition as opposed to defined, not mere judgment as opposed to judged. No less than what it perfectly expresses, it too is the ocean of all perfection. Still, though infinite *esse* and infinite *est* are identical absolutely, nonetheless truly there is an intelligible procession. The divine Word is because of the divine understanding as uttering, yet "eo magis unum, quo perfectius procedit."[38]

Thus, Lonergan can claim that, if one supposes an intelligent emanation in God, there follow all the points that pertain to a divine procession and that have already been deduced from the truths of faith under the rubric of a *processio per modum operati*.[39] And a deduction yields some understanding, even when the premises are not anything more than supposition or hypothesis; therefore, if we suppose in God something analogous to autonomous spiritual procession in us, we arrive at some understanding of what we confess in faith.[40]

What the supposition of autonomous spiritual procession yields, then, is a hypothetical understanding of what we affirm in faith. More precisely, it yields a hypothetical understanding of how there can be processions *per modum operati* in God, where the first part of the assertion argued negatively that, if there are processions in God, they must be *per modum operati*. The supposition does not yield knowledge, for the conclusion follows from a principle that is not known but supposed: let us suppose there are in God processions analogous to autonomous spiritual processions in us. In this the reasoning is similar to that which occurs in scientific experimentation to test a hypothesis. If *A*, then *B*; but *B*; where *A* is the hypothesis and *B* the possible result of experimentation. The experiment does not prove *A*, as there could be many other explanations of *B*. But it does render *A* one possible explanation of *B*. In the case under consideration here, the conclusion is already known from other sources, namely, the first part of the assertion: divine processions are *per modum operati*; what this deduction does show is how it can be the case, how it might be possible. If there are in God processions analogous to autonomous spiritual processions in us, then these processions in God are *per modum operati*; but there are such processions in God; therefore … The argument proceeds by supposing a principle that would make it possible that the conclusion, already known, is true.

How can the doctrines be true? is the question for systematics. Wherever there is a deduction, the conclusion is known to the extent that the principle is known. But here the principle is not known but supposed, hypothetically posited, and so what is deduced is also not known from the force of the deduction, but supposed. While the conclusion – the divine processions are *per modum operati* – *is* known from the first part of the assertion, by being deduced from the truths of faith, the truth of this conclusion does not prove the principle from which it is derived: the same conclusion might be drawn equally well or better from another principle, as in every case of such a reasoning process: "If *A*, then *B*; but *B*; therefore, possibly *A*." "If *emanatio intelligibilis*, then *per modum operati*. But *per modum operati*. Therefore, possibly *emanatio intelligibilis*."

If the hypothesis does not yield knowledge, it does yield understanding, an understanding that is mediated by the deduction itself, that is imperfect, and that is analogous – and this is the only way we can understand an infinite act that is rationally and morally conscious. And so, in the present deduction, it is only mediately, imperfectly, and analogously that we understand a procession *per modum operati*. This is not negligible, however. It is precisely the kind of understanding approved by the First Vatican Council.[41]

The understanding thus yielded consists in reducing to one a number of elements that are both many and seemingly conflictual. Many elements are contained in the definition of a procession *per modum operati*, and they can be reconciled only in the infinity of God. More specifically, there are consequences that follow upon the fact that God is infinite act, and there are other consequences that follow from the supposition that God is dynamically conscious. From God's infinity it follows that what proceeds in God is infinite, and from the fact that the infinite is one and unique it follows that what proceeds and the principle from which it proceeds cannot be distinguished *quoad esse absolutum*. But from the conscious exigence in divine consciousness it follows that there is a principle, there is an emanation or proceeding, there is something that proceeds from the principle, and there is a real distinction *quoad esse relativum* between the principle and what proceeds.

As long as we consider each of these separately, there is no difficulty. But when they are considered together, there arise difficulties that manifest the depth of the mystery of the Trinity. Moreover, the argument of the assertion does not directly reconcile the reality of procession with the consubstantiality of what proceeds – it is precisely here that we are confronted with the *altitudo mysterii* – but indirectly and mediately it does reconcile them by reducing them to a common root, the act that is both infinite and dynamically conscious: from its infinity there follows consubstantiality, and from its dynamic consciousness there follows the reality of procession. But this is the best we can do; beyond this our understanding cannot penetrate.[42]

Therefore, the understanding thus yielded is imperfect. The one root to which everything is reduced is the infinite, rationally and morally conscious act that is God. A conclusion is understood only to the extent that the principle is understood, and a conclusion is not understood to the extent that the principle is not understood. Even if we can reduce to a common root everything pertinent to a procession *per modum operati* and to that extent reach some understanding, nonetheless the understanding reached is no better than our understanding of this one common root. But the root is the infinite, rationally and morally conscious act, and we do not understand the infinite in a positive way, but only in a negative way. Even our own rational and moral consciousness is something that we rather live than understand clearly and distinctly. While we suppose that this consciousness is an image of God, we also know that it is a very deficient image, through whose mediation we can conceive the divine consciousness only analogously and imperfectly. Moreover, we do not *know* there is dynamic consciousness in God; we reach this affirmation only on the basis that, if we presuppose it, those consequences follow which can also be concluded from the truths of faith (that is, that divine processions must be *per modum operati*). Nonetheless, such imperfection of understanding only confirms the intellectual divine emanation: "... never ... does [reason illumined by faith] become capable of understanding the mysteries the way it does truths which are its own proper object. For divine mysteries of their very nature so exceed the created intellect that even when they have been given in revelation and accepted by faith, that very faith still keeps them veiled in a sort of obscurity, as long as 'we are exiled from the Lord' in this mortal life."[43] We can say of Lonergan's treatment at this point what he says of Thomas's Trinitarian theology:

> [T]he procedure of the *Summa* ... reveals the measure of significance to be attached to the *imago Dei*. As we have seen, there is a twofold systematization: first, our concepts are *in fieri*; secondly, their order is reversed and they stand *in facto esse*. As long as our concepts are in development, the psychological analogy commands the situation. But once our concepts reach their term, the analogy is transcended and we are confronted with the mystery. In other words, the psychological analogy truly gives a deeper insight into what God is. Still, that insight stands upon analogy; it does not penetrate to the very core, the essence of God, in which alone trinitarian doctrine can be contemplated in its full intelligibility; grasping properly *quid sit Deus* is the beatific vision. Just as an experimental physicist may

not grasp most of quantum mathematics, but under the direction of a mathematician may very intelligently devise and perform experiments that advance the quantum theory, so also the theologian with no proper grasp of *quid sit Deus*, but under the direction of divine revelation really operates in virtue of and towards an understanding that he personally in this life cannot possess.

… do not think that Aquinas allows the psychological analogy to take the place of the divine essence as the one sufficient principle of explanation. The psychological analogy is just the side door through which we enter for an imperfect look.[44]

3   The Only Hypothesis?

Thesis 55: *The structure of the analogy from spiritual autonomy is the only viable structure for a Trinitarian analogy, and the most suitable instance from nature of such spiritual autonomy is the procession of the word of a judgment of value from existentially reflective understanding and the procession of a loving decision from the word of a judgment of value, precisely in the existential issues in which we inquire about ourselves, understand what we ought to be, judge how we can make ourselves be such, and proceed to the existential decisions through which we so constitute ourselves.*

Lonergan's third step consists in affirming that this particular analogy seems to be the only analogy we may employ for a systematic conception of the divine processions.[45] Thus, at this point Lonergan is arguing that the proposed solution ought to be accepted because no other solution seems viable.

He tries to order the various criteria by which one may judge the issue, and in doing so he further characterizes and qualifies the particular analogy that he is employing. These further qualifications will be of the utmost importance for us as we attempt to locate the processions in human consciousness that will form not only a set of analogies for understanding Trinitarian life but also our graced participation in that life as we play our part in determining the course of human history. Here is where the connections of religious and personal values are highlighted.

The first two qualifications have to do with the way we conceive the processions that will constitute the analogy. That way or mode must be concrete, and it must be analogical.

First, then, the mode of conception must be concrete. The abstract definition of a procession – the origin of one from another – yields only a minimal formality that prescinds from every concrete difference between modes. Thus, it yields no understanding at all. Concrete conceptions distinguish different modes of proceeding for different natures,[46] as we saw above in the discussion of the various determinations of modes of procession.

Second, the mode of conception must be analogical. There is no immediate knowledge of God in this life, and all mediated knowledge of God is necessarily imperfect and analogical, since every finite medium is deficient to the utmost in representing the infinite, and all knowledge reached through a deficient medium is necessarily imperfect and analogical.[47]

Third, the analogy must be systematic, that is, it must be one that is explicitly and thematically employed to resolve, not just one question but an entire series of questions. One does not proceed systematically if one uses analogies only implicitly and non-thematically; and if one employs different and ever new analogies in distinct questions or even in the same questions, then one achieves only a rhetorical heap of examples. A theologian should proceed systematically, and so much the more if one is investigating the mode of the divine processions, for the divine processions provide the key to the whole range of Trinitarian questions. We do not begin a Trinitarian systematics by treating immediately the divine persons, but rather we start from the processions, since the key to the entire problem is to be found in the notion of procession and the question of an appropriate mode of procession proper to the processions in God. Thus, the analogy proposed should be such as to resolve virtually every other theoretical question about the triune God.[48]

Fourth, the analogy should proceed from what is naturally known, as Vatican I taught. The reason is that all analogical knowledge is mediate, and all mediate knowledge is grounded in some immediate knowledge. Therefore, since we know the supernatural only analogically, we know it only mediately, and so should proceed from things naturally known.[49]

Fifth, the analogy should proceed from an immediately known *nature.* Common metaphysical notions – "ens, unum, verum, et bonum, idem et diversum, actus et potentia, absolutum et relativum, et eiusmodi"[50] – provide one way of knowing things immediately and naturally, namely, by the analogy of being. These notions have contributed to the present discussion in that they have yielded the conclusion that a divine procession is *per modum operati.* But things can be known immediately and naturally also in accord with their generic or specific natures, and only an analogy that proceeds from a specific nature immediately and naturally known to us enables us to conceive a divine procession by analogy with autonomous spiritual procession. Similarly, in natural theology we can proceed by common metaphysical notions to determine that God is *ipsum esse,* but only by moving from an analogy with a specific nature can we determine as well that God is *ipsum intelligere.*

Moreover, the very definite conclusions that we can arrive at by employing common metaphysical notions would not enable us to understand systematically two *distinct* divine processions, one of which is generation and the other of which is not. Nor would such conclusions provide the common root for treating systematically not only the processions but also the relations and the persons and all other related issues. So the analogy of being is not sufficient; we must seek an analogy that proceeds from a determinate nature immediately and naturally known to us.[51]

Sixth, this nature must be spiritual. God is immaterial, and so the Trinitarian analogy must proceed, not from minerals, plants, and animals, but from human beings, and indeed from what is proper to them as human. Now, of the elements that are proper to human beings, some are strictly spiritual, while others depend intrinsically on the body, on vegetative life, or on sensitive life. To understand, to judge, and to decide are not only proper to human beings but also depend on matter only extrinsically,[52] whereas speech, for example, while proper to human beings, nonetheless immediately and necessarily proceeds from mouth and tongue and throat. Since nothing in God depends intrinsically on matter, any similitude of nature that there may be between God and human beings can be found only in those elements that not only are proper to human beings but also strictly spiritual.[53]

Seventh, the analogy must be from a spiritual *procession*, for only there is found a *similitudo naturae* to a divine procession: the analogy has to be from a procession, and one whose mode will give a *similitudo naturae*, only a spiritual procession will do. Nor will those strictly spiritual processions suffice in which act proceeds from potency or habit. Nor is it sufficient to consider the strictly spiritual mode only in common metaphysical categories; specific determination is necessary. What is required is a created spiritual procession in which (1) a strictly spiritual act proceeds (2) from a strictly spiritual act (3) according to a strictly spiritual way of proceeding. Every strictly spiritual act is a real, natural, and conscious act; every conscious act is within consciousness; and where a conscious act proceeds from a conscious act within consciousness, the procession itself is conscious and occurs somehow in virtue of consciousness itself; such acts are not epiphenomena. Moreover, every strictly spiritual act that we know of occurs in the intellectual and volitional, cognitional and existential, dimensions of consciousness. So the analogy must be from the conscious procession of a real, natural, and conscious act from a real, natural, and conscious act, within intelligent consciousness and in virtue of that intelligent consciousness itself.[54]

Eighth, since we want a likeness of nature, we must attend to the internal mode of the procession. The phrase "in virtue of intelligent consciousness" or "in virtue of the spiritual dimension of consciousness" draws our attention to that internal mode, and helps us qualify the mode of procession internally as itself a spiritual mode of proceeding. Sensitive consciousness is governed by laws specific to its spontaneity, while intellectual consciousness is governed by laws commensurate with its transcendental aspirations, according to which we are equipped to give the law to ourselves. Thus, as we have already seen, in sensitive consciousness a conscious act proceeds from another conscious act by the spontaneity of sensitive nature itself; that spontaneity is perfected by acquired dispositions and habits, so that it quickly and easily and with delight does what is fitting for this determinate nature in proper circumstances. But the spontaneity of intelligent consciousness is regulated by laws that govern the self-possessed ordination of the person to the intelligible, to being, to the one, to the true, to the good. It is insofar as it is governed by this transcendental orientation that the human spirit is master of itself, self-determining, autonomous: ruled, yes, insofar as it is constituted by its own transcendental desire, but ruling itself insofar as, under the agency of God, it determines itself to its own acts according to the exigencies of its own nature as intelligent. In this sense it is legitimate to offer imperatives or precepts to this self-ruling unfolding of spiritual desire: Be attentive, Be intelligent, Be reasonable, Be responsible. Thus, whatever proceeds *vi conscientiae intellectualis* proceeds in virtue of a natural desire, an intellectual spontaneity, a tendency that is both conscious and transcendental. Such a tendency is displayed in questions, whether practical (What is to be done? Is it to be done?) or speculative (What is it? Is it so?) or existential (What am I to make of myself? Will I really make such of myself?). It is manifest in the precepts we direct to ourselves to inquire, reflect, deliberate. It is manifest in the reasons we offer for so proceeding: we must inquire so that we do not judge what we do not understand; we must reflect so that we do not mistake the false for the true; we must deliberate so that we do not blindly fall into perdition.[55]

Nonetheless, there are different ways of proceeding in virtue of intelligent consciousness. When intelligent consciousness is determined by some conscious act, from that determined consciousness as from a proximately proportionate principle there proceeds another act. Such is the autonomy of freedom when we choose *because* and *insofar as* we judge; such is the autonomy of rationality when we judge *because* and *insofar as* we grasp the evidence; such is the autonomy of intelligent clarity when we define *because* and *insofar as* we grasp the intelligible in the sensible. But when intelligent consciousness is not already determined by a conscious intellectual act, we are more spontaneous than autonomous. Thus it is that we proceed from questions to an act of understanding. And when we proceed to conscious acts from dispositions and habits that of themselves are not conscious, the procession is so far from being autonomous that it occurs unconsciously.

The type of procession that, however spiritual, is more spontaneous than autonomous, that is, a procession from potency to act, will not suffice for a Trinitarian analogy. What is needed is the procession of one act from another act, an autonomous rather than spontaneous procession; as when, by virtue of consciousness determined by an act of understanding, there proceeds an inner word, and by virtue of consciousness determined by a judgment of value, which itself is a complex inner word, there proceeds a decision.[56]

Ninth, the most suitable instance of such intelligent autonomy for a Trinitarian analogy is the procession of the word of a judgment of value from existentially reflective understanding and the procession of a decision from the word of a judgment of value, not in practical affairs and not in speculative matters, but *in the existential issues in which we inquire about ourselves, understand what we ought to be, judge how we can make ourselves be such, and proceed to the existential decisions through which we so constitute ourselves.* What is required is precisely the kind of autonomy that we argued for in our dialogue with Girard earlier in this work. For when we are inquiring about the triune God we are not considering God as creating or acting, and so we prescind from practical autonomy. Nor are we considering God insofar as God understands and affirms and loves all things, and so we prescind as well from speculative autonomy. Rather, we are considering God as God from eternity is constituted *in se* as triune, and therefore we take our analogy from the processions that exhibit an *existential autonomy* that bears some remote analogy to divine self-constitution.[57]

Thus, by a series of disjunctions Lonergan has argued that there is no *similitudo naturae* for understanding the divine processions other than the *emanatio intelligibilis* through which one conscious act proceeds from another conscious act in a manner that is both conscious and autonomous: the understanding can only be mediated, not immediate; the analogy should be explicit, thematic, and systematic, not implicit, unthematic, and rhetorical; the systematic analogy has to be grounded in a specific created nature and not just in metaphysical categories; the analogy from a likeness of nature has to be from a strictly spiritual nature, not a material nature; the mode of strictly spiritual procession has to be conscious and autonomous, not conscious but spontaneous nor unconscious; and the autonomy has to be represented in the sphere of the existential moment where one decides for oneself what one is going to make of oneself; nothing remains but the analogy suggested here, however much we will allow its structure to be embodied in different realizations.[58] The different realizations are variations on the single theme of human authenticity, and it is to authenticity that Lonergan appeals for the *imago Dei* that will yield some imperfect but fruitful understanding of the triune God whom we profess and adore in faith.

4   Two Processions

The first of Lonergan's three assertions on the divine processions establishes the generic notion of the kind of intellectual and intelligible or autonomous ("because and insofar as") spiritual procession that can serve as the basis for a psychological analogy for understanding the Trinitarian processions. But nothing specific has yet been said regarding the immanent constitution of the operations that would provide the appropriate analogy. The assertion offers one way of conceiving how there might be processions in God, but how many processions there are in God, and what precisely they are, has not yet been determined. The second and third assertions address these issues by specifying what up to now has been the generic notion of what I am calling autonomous spiritual procession. That generic notion is differentiated in the second assertion, which maintains that there are two and only two divine processions that can be conceived by analogy with human autonomous spiritual procession, namely, the procession of the word from the act of understanding that utters the word, and the procession of love both from the act of understanding that utters the word and from the uttered word itself.[59] It is partly in this way that the Catholic tradition understands the affirmation that we are made in the image and likeness of God. The process from reflective existential understanding to judgment of value and then from the two together to self-transcendent decision is an imitation of the divine processions, an imitation built into human nature in its authenticity. Then assertion 3 maintains that there is a difference between the two, such that the procession of word, but not that of love, can properly be called generation.[60] These assertions further support the theological viability for faith of the hypothetical construction, since they are in keeping with the articles of faith: two processions, one of which is generation or begetting.

I will attempt to state the assertions in Lonergan's own reformed Scholastic context and to interpret his articulation of their meaning. I will do the best I can to transpose them into categories derived from interiorly and religiously differentiated consciousness. From the beginning I will prefer the expression "autonomous spiritual procession" to "intelligible emanation." The transposition will be done against the background of a theology of history and with an eye to the appropriation of Girardian mimetic theory into a Trinitarian systematics that allows for a genuine meaning of the word "autonomous," although these elements will not be explicit for the moment.

While the notion of imitation is quite clear in the four-point hypothesis, the interpretation of "religious values" within the normative scale of values as entailing an imitation of the divine relations assumes for me a prominence that is less explicit in Lonergan's methodological statements. That background has also enabled me to transfer the insights gained by this interplay of related notions to the analogy that I am seeking to develop in the order of grace itself. The presentation here provides and interprets the basis for that analogy as this is presented in Lonergan's text. It aims at nothing more. We will treat also four questions with which Lonergan concludes the chapter on the divine processions. These will be taken up in our next chapter. These four questions are of utmost importance for our project, but they too must be transposed into the contemporary terms that will move this type of Trinitarian theology forward.

> **Thesis 56:** *Two and only two divine processions can be conceived by analogy with human autonomous spiritual procession, namely, the procession of the word as a judgment of value from the reflective act of existential self-understanding that utters the word, and the procession of love both from the act of understanding that utters the word of a judgment of value and from the uttered judgment of value itself. It is in this way that we are made in the image and likeness of God. This process from reflective existential understanding to judgment of value and then from the two together to love is a natural imitation of the divine processions.*

4.1 Terminology

Lonergan's treatment of the very important second assertion is brief. Regarding the terms employed in the assertion, what an intellectual emanation or autonomous spiritual procession is has already been established; what needs definition are the terms "speaker" or "the one who utters" (*dicens*), "word" (*verbum*), "love" (*amor*), and a term not employed in the wording of the assertion itself but in its elaboration, namely, "spirating" (*spirans*), a term that is very important for the four-point hypothesis and for the developments being suggested here.

First, then, *dicens* and *verbum.* The Father is *Dicens,* the One who utters, the One who speaks, and as such is the principle of the procession of the divine Word. But the Father is principle precisely because and insofar as the unrestricted act of understanding and love,[61] precisely as understanding and loving, utters a Word, a Word that receives the divine nature in the Father's utterance, a Word that receives the unrestricted act itself from the Father precisely as the Father utters the Word, a Word that exercises that unrestricted act precisely as Word, a Word that is to be understood on the analogy of a judgment of value, a Word thus constituted as *Verbum spirans Amorem*, the Word that breathes Love. The Father utters the eternal Word, in a manner remotely analogous to the way in which our act of insight is also *dicere*, grounding our inner word, whether that inner word be conceptual, as in a commonsense supposition or in a scientific hypothesis flowing from direct insight, or judgmental, as in an affirmation proceeding from reflective understanding, or existential, as in a judgment of value issuing from the equivalent in the order of value to the grasp of the virtually unconditioned in the order of fact.[62] While the structure of the autonomous spiritual procession is the same in each of these instances, Lonergan correctly insists that the analogy is best conceived in terms of the existential value judgment regarding self-constitution (word) and the decisions that flow from such a judgment regarding personal value (love). Such an analogy would obtain in either of the analyses of decision and the human good presented by Lonergan, that of *Insight* and that of *Method in Theology*.

Verbum is the immanent term of such an utterance. But as a judgment of value it is a *verbum spirans amorem*, a word from which our own loving decisions regarding our existential self-constitution proceed. In us it is the inner word grounded in and proceeding from deliberative insight insofar as such insight also utters the inner word of a judgment of value.[63] In us there is a twofold inner word, corresponding first to the twofold operation of human intellectual cognition as it operates in both the order of fact and the order of value: the word of definition or hypothesis or supposition that flows from an act of direct insight, and the word of affirmation or negation that flows from an act of reflective understanding in which we grasp evidence sufficient to enable us to pronounce judgment. In us that twofold process operates both in the order of the knowledge of fact and in the order of the knowledge of value, based on the knowledge of fact. But in God, whose essence it is to be, there is one infinite act of understanding, and so there is but one Word. That one Word is sufficient to express all that the Father is, all that the Father knows, that is, everything about everything, and all that the Father loves, again, everything about everything.[64] More precisely, the primary intelligible that the Father knows is the unrestricted act of understanding and loving itself, and the secondary intelligible is everything else that is contained in the idea of being that is the content of that unrestricted act. The one Word also understands and loves, of course, but precisely *as* the Word uttered, not as the Speaker who utters, nor as the Love that proceeds from the eternal exchange of the Speaker and the Word.

To help his readers understand the twofold inner word in us, Lonergan refers them to the second appendix of the book, "De actu intelligendi," section 2, "De obiecto intellectus ut fine et termino." A brief summary of what he says there may be helpful, since I find that no limit can be placed on the stress given these facts; a fuller discussion will be given below.[65] (The main source of data, of course, is Lonergan's *Verbum*, the study of which is essential for anyone who wishes to delve more deeply into the position that we are here summarizing from his work.)

If "object" means "end" or "objective," then the object of human intelligence is being in its entirety, everything that is, everything about everything. In Scholastic terms, *intellectus* is that by which we can do and become all things (*omnia*), where the term *omnia* is not limited to any genus.[66] In the transposed terms of *Insight*, being is the objective of the pure desire to know.[67] The desire to know, which in *Insight* is also the notion of being, is what Aristotle and Thomas called agent intellect. (It is quite likely that Lonergan did not yet have *Insight*'s conception of "the notion of being" when he wrote *Verbum*.) As God is unrestricted understanding, understanding of everything about everything, so we by spiritual nature are unrestricted desire, which includes the desire to know everything about everything.[68] "Everything about everything" is being. The objective of our intelligence is what God actually is and understands, that is, the knowing of everything about everything. Our intelligence is, first, our desire to know. While the desire to know is manifested in our questions for intelligence and for reflection, which head for being, that desire is not the verbal utterance of the questions, not the conceptual formulation of the questions, not any insight or thought, not any reflective grasp or judgment. Rather, it is "the prior [that is, preconceptual, preverbal] and enveloping drive that carries cognitional process from sense and imagination [and all presentations, including linguistic presentations of ordinary meaningfulness] to understanding [in the sense of original meaningfulness], from understanding to judgment, from judgment to the complete context of correct judgments that is named knowledge."[69] Obviously, that drive is not a concept of being nor an idea of being, but it can be called a notion of being, where "notion" has the precise meaning assigned to it by Lonergan in most of his employments of the term, that is, the conscious, heuristic, intelligent, and reasonable anticipation of an unrestricted objective of intelligence and reasonableness. In the terms of *Method in Theology* it is a transcendental notion.[70]

A similar structure obtains in the relation between the transcendental notion of value and its objective, the good. The good, or value, is "what is intended in questions for deliberation, just as the intelligible is what is intended in questions for intelligence, and just as truth and being are what are intended in questions for reflection."[71] As knowledge of being is gained incrementally in every true judgment of fact, so knowledge of the good is gained incrementally in every true judgment of value.

The judgment of fact and the judgment of value are both inner words, but the relevant inner word for the Trinitarian analogy will be found, as we have seen, in a particular type of judgment of value. This is true even in Lonergan's relatively early presentation of the analogy, at least as it appears in *De Deo Trino: Pars Systematica* (1964), even though the implications are not drawn clearly until later. Thus, the word "object," besides meaning "objective" or "end" and so referring to being and the good in their totality, can mean, in faculty-psychology terms, "a term produced within the intellect," or in intentionality-analysis terms, what is produced when the incremental steps in the cognitional and evaluative processes have come to "term." In this sense, the object of our unrestricted desire consists in the various inner words (*verbum cordis seu verbum interius*) that are uttered along the way to knowledge of being and the good. And since there are two operations constitutive of such knowledge, whether in the order of fact or in the order of value, there are two immanently produced terms in each order, that is, two terms in the order of the knowledge of fact and two terms in the order of the knowledge of value. There is the simple word of hypothesis, consideration, supposition, definition, or possible value (the latter often affectively mediated), and there is the compound or complex word of affirmation or negation, in which the synthesis constructed in the simple word is affirmed to be true. In straightforward language, we may say that the two inner words are (1) hypothetical conceptual interrelations or syntheses, which in the order of value are often highlighted affectively,[72] and (2) judgments, whether of fact or of value. These are treated in Thomist terms and with regard to the knowledge of fact in the first two chapters of *Verbum*, which are requisite reading for anyone who wishes to pursue these matters in greater detail. The material of those chapters is transposed into the contemporary context in the first ten chapters of *Insight*. The evaluative aspects are added in one context in chapter 18 of *Insight* and in another in chapter 2 of *Method in Theology*. As was mentioned above, I have related the two evaluative contexts to one another by drawing upon the Ignatian notion of the times of election and the Ignatian "rules" for discernment.[73] And as I have emphasized here, either of these contexts can be relied upon to work out the analogy, which remains structurally the same no matter what the context.

Inner words are not to be confused, then, with acts of understanding or for that matter even with *acts* of thinking, defining, supposing, considering, affirming, denying. Grasping the distinction is essential to understanding almost everything Lonergan wrote after the "verbum" articles. The inner word is *what is intended* through the latter acts, where "intended" is used in the phenomenological sense of "intentionality": by thinking, defining, supposing, considering, there becomes present what is thought about, defined, supposed, considered; and by affirming and denying, there becomes present what is affirmed or denied. What is considered and affirmed or denied, in its "natural" reality, is mediated by its "intentional" reality, that is, by the inner word that emanates from the act of understanding, whether direct or reflective. The inner word is what is intended, in its "intentional" being. This "intentional being" is the medium in which the thing itself is known: its formal intelligibility is expressed in the first inner word, and its actual intelligibility in the second. The inner word itself is not *noēsis* but *noēma*, not *la pensée pensante* but *la pensée pensée*, not *intentio intendens* but *intentio intenta*, not *intentio intelligentis* but *intentio intellecta*: not act but content. The acts of understanding, thinking, affirming, and so on, are *noēsis, la pensée pensante, intentio intendens, intentio intelligentis*.[74] But the respective inner words are the expression of what is known in these acts.

To get hold of insight, inner word, and the distinction between the two is a demanding chore. The scholarship manifest in Lonergan's articles on *verbum* is overwhelmingly convincing. Still, philosophers and theologians continue to go about their work paying little or no attention to what can only be called a permanent achievement in the understanding not only of Aquinas but also of ourselves. John Henry Newman's *Grammar of Assent* helped many (including Lonergan himself) to grasp what Lonergan calls reflective understanding, the grasp of sufficient evidence, as the ground of judgment, and so not only the act of reflective understanding and the judgment but also the distinction between them. If one wishes to root one's appropriation of these matters in the Christian and Catholic tradition, Lonergan's *Verbum* and Newman's *Grammar* are probably the best places to start. The matter is more obscure with direct insight and the conceptual inner words that follow upon it or emanate or proceed from it – hypotheses, hunches, suppositions regarding fact or value – than with reflective understanding and judgment. As I indicated above,[75] this is probably because in the transition from image through insight to formulation, we are working in both the preconceptual and the conceptual orders, whereas in the transition from reflective understanding to judgment, much has already been brought into the light that conceptual formulation throws on our questions and answers, and we are also aware of personal responsibility for judgment in a manner that simply does not obtain for direct insight. In either case, we are aware of the inner words, of course, but what easily escapes us in the move from insight to concept is how, when the inner words are original, they are grounded in acts of direct insight. In a number of lectures, Lonergan appeals to the example of the first proposition of the first book of Euclid's *Elements,* where the insight is clear but the conceptual justification took centuries for geometers to work out.[76]

If some variant on the relation between *dicere* and *verbum* in human conscious procession (namely, the relation between reflective existential insight and judgment of value) will provide the appropriate, though extremely remote, analogy for the procession of the Son, some variant on the relation between *spirans* and *amor* will give us a remote and obscure analogical understanding of the procession of the Holy Spirit. The remoteness in each case is based on the difference between unrestricted act in God and unrestricted desire, only incrementally satisfied, in us.

With *spirans* and *amor* we return to Lonergan's main text. The language of "spirating" and "spirated" emerged in the course of the tradition in an effort to express the procession of the Holy Spirit from the Father and the Son. The Father and the Son together are *Spirans*, the Ones who together "breathe," "spirate." As such, together they are, in their mutual recognition as Father and Son, paternity and filiation, *Dicens* and *Verbum*, the principle of a distinct procession that is also a relation of opposed terms and that can be conceived by analogy with human autonomous spiritual procession. The Father and the Son, *Spirans*, actively spirate proceeding Love. The originated reciprocal relation that proceeds from their mutual recognition, the Holy Spirit, *Spiratus*, is passive spiration. *Spirans* and *Spiratus* give another relation of opposed terms. In the analogy the term *spirans*, what "spirates," what breathes, means within us the act of reflective existential understanding and consequent inner word together that are the principle of an intelligent emanation or autonomous spiritual procession that is determined by both the act of understanding and the word spoken. What flows from that combined principle in us is a form of love, *amor*. In the language of the faculty psychology in which the analogy was expressed by Aquinas, *amor* is the fundamental act of the will. Just as an inner word is the immanent term of an autonomous spiritual procession from an act of understanding, so love is the immanent term of an autonomous spiritual procession from the combined principle of the act of understanding and its consequent inner word, when those latter principles function together in the existential order. This love, as "spirated" or breathed, is received in "the will"; it is a gift from understanding and word; as such it is the analogue for the divine relation that the tradition has called passive spiration, which is identical with the Holy Spirit, who is the Father's and the Son's Gift to one another, the first Gift. Active spiration is their giving to one another, while passive spiration is their mutual gift. Although in us the love that is the analogue for the Holy Spirit is received not in the intellect but in the will (to use the Scholastic categories that Lonergan still employs in his early work), still it occurs within intellectual consciousness, since the will is an intellectual appetite, that is, an appetite that follows upon intellect.[77] In the Trinitarian reality that we are attempting to understand through the analogy, "*Spirans*," Lonergan tells us in an important footnote, is the same as the "notionaliter diligere" of *Summa theologiae*, 1, q. 37, a. 1, c. ad fin., and what proceeds from it is the *amor procedens* of that same text. Aquinas's magnificent text, containing virtually the whole of a Trinitarian systematics, reads as follows: "… inquantum in amore vel dilectione non importatur nisi habitudo amantis ad rem amatam, amor et diligere essentialiter dicuntur, sicut intelligentia et intelligere; inquantum vero his vocabulis utimur ad exprimendam habitudinem eius rei quae procedit per modum amoris ad suum principium et e converso, ita quod per amorem intelligatur amor procedens et per diligere intelligatur spirare amorem procedentem, sic Amor est nomen personae et diligere vel amare est verbum notionale, sicut dicere vel generare."[78]

This, too, is a difficult matter to get hold of; it is no easier to grasp in our own consciousness the active loving that, proper to understanding and word, grounds proceeding acts of love, and the distinction between these, than it is to grasp the act of understanding that grounds the proceeding inner word, and the distinction between these; but as doing the latter provides the natural analogy for the procession of the Son, so doing the former will provide the natural analogy for the procession of the Holy Spirit. A good deal of the remaining material in the second chapter of *The Triune God: Systematics* is concerned with this analogy as Lonergan understood it at the time. And a good deal of our transposition of the analogy to the order of grace as reflected earlier in the book has been concerned with a new articulation of precisely that analogical structure, relying on the identification of the analogue for active spiration with the elevation of human central form that consists in the recollected gift of God's love without qualifications and with the judgments of value that proceed as inner word from that recollection, and the analogue for passive spiration with the conjugate form of charity, the dynamic state of being in love in return as proximate ground of habitual loving acts. Here we are attempting to grasp Lonergan's analogy in its own context, in order to assist us in understanding how to transpose it into the appropriate interior terms and relations that would provide an analogy in the order not of nature but of grace.

It is of the utmost importance to highlight that the relevant inner word that can function as contributing to the principle of the emanation of love is not a concept, not a judgment of fact, not even a practical judgment, but a judgment of value.[79] That statement represents a major development in Lonergan's own understanding, and a most important ingredient in his own developing Trinitarian analogy. A careful study is needed of the emergence in Lonergan's writings of the notion of judgment of value. The qualification of *spirans amorem* signals a development that occurred in Lonergan's own understanding after *Insight*. But despite the appearance of the term in *De Deo Trino: Pars Systematica*, the development was probably still inchoate at the time. As we have seen, in *Insight* judgments of value are spoken of only in chapter 20 (and so not in the generic discussion of decision in chapter 18). The development moves through *Divinarum personarum* (1957, 1959), where what spirates love is *iudicium practicum seu iudicium valoris*,[80] a practical judgment *or* judgment of value, and it concludes with the position on fourth-level structures where judgments of value are quite distinct from practical judgments. The fact that the expression occurs only once in the 1964 *De Deo Trino: Pars systematica* would seem to indicate that even then he was still very much in the process of thinking out the structure of judgments of value and their relation to other operations of intentional consciousness. Nonetheless, the characterization of the divine Word as remotely analogous to a judgment of value will be important in our considerations and, in my view, marks a turning point in the history of the psychological analogy for the Trinitarian processions. Perhaps – and I can say no more than "perhaps" – had this existential context been clear through the course of reflection on this analogy, the analogy itself would have been better understood through the ages and the contemporary resistance to it might be somewhat mitigated.

4.2 Lonergan's Argument for the Second Assertion

First, two divine processions can be conceived on the analogy of human autonomous spiritual procession. Second, only two processions can so be conceived.

First, then, at least two divine processions can be conceived on the analogy of human autonomous spiritual procession. Why? God is (1) being by essence and the very act of understanding (*ipsum intelligere*), (2) truth by essence and the very act of affirming (*ipsum affirmare*), and (3) goodness by essence and the very act of loving (*ipsum amare*). Now, every affirmation is true insofar as it emanates from an intelligent grasp of sufficient evidence, and all spiritual love is right and holy insofar as it proceeds from a true affirmation of the good.[81] Therefore, if anything analogous to human autonomous spiritual processions can be conceived in God, at least the emanation of the affirming word from intelligent grasp of sufficient evidence and the emanation of love from both intelligent grasp and affirming word can be conceived. Nor can these two be reduced to one, for love proceeds from the word, the *verbum spirans amorem*, while the word does not emanate from itself but from the reflective grasp that utters the word. To proceed from the word and not to proceed from the word are contradictories, and since no contradictions can be posited in God, the emanation of the word and the emanation of love cannot be posited as one and the same emanation. Therefore two divine processions can be conceived on the analogy of human autonomous spiritual procession.[82]

Second, *only* these two emanations can be conceived. Why is that so? Lonergan uses a syllogism to argue this second step.

When the argument is expressed in syllogistic form, the major states that in God there can be conceived only one act of understanding, one word, and one act of love, for (1) by reason of act, God is utterly simple and so in God there is only one act, and (2) by reason of object, by the infinite act of understanding there is attained all being, by the infinite act of affirming there is attained all truth, and by the infinite act of loving there is attained all good, and these are all one and the same act; and so there is no need for another act of understanding, or for another word, or for another act of love.[83]

The minor is to the effect that there is only one emanation of one love, and only one emanation of one word, and that the divine act of understanding cannot itself intelligibly proceed from some other principle. The first two points are obvious: the one divine act is eternal and immutable, and in that act there can be only one emanation of one word and one emanation of one love. The third point requires us to distinguish human from divine understanding. There is in us an intelligible procession of the act of understanding itself, since as intellectually conscious beings we inquire, investigate, and reason in order to arrive at an act of understanding. But this cannot be so in God, since God is not reduced from potency to the act of understanding.[84] *Ipsum esse subsistens* is *ipsum intelligere subsistens*.

4.3 Generation and Spiration

As we have seen, Lonergan's third and final assertion on divine processions maintains that the procession of the Word, but not that of Love, can properly be named generation. The Word, then, is properly named "Son," and the One who utters the Word "Father."

The core intelligibility of generation must be grasped first, and then the notion of what would constitute generation in the spiritual order. The latter step requires that the divine nature be acknowledged precisely as intellectual or spiritual, and that the difference be grasped between the emanation of the word and the emanation of love precisely in such a nature.

4.3.1 Generation

Generation, strictly so called, is the origin of something alive from a conjoined living principle, with a resulting likeness in nature (*origo viventis a principio vivente coniuncto in similitudinem naturae*).[85] While each and every element in this definition must be verified if we are to speak of something as generation, special attention has to be paid to the phrase "with a resulting likeness of nature," which does not mean only that what emanates or proceeds must be like in nature but also that *this likeness in nature must arise in virtue of the emanation or procession itself* (*haec in natura similitudo oriri debet vi ipsius emanationis*).[86] The likeness in nature is communicated to what proceeds, precisely by reason of the procession itself. In the instance of divine procession, the Father communicates the divine nature to the Son precisely in and through the eternal procession itself.

4.3.2 The Divine Nature as Intellectual

If the likeness of nature, thus understood and communicated, is so important, then attention must be paid to the divine nature and how we conceive it. What precisely is this divine nature that is communicated to the Son in the eternal generation from the Father?

"Nature" can be understood to mean either (1) an immanent principle of movement and rest[87] or (2) essence. But in either case there is a difficulty in conceiving the *divine* nature. As to (1), the notion of nature as an immanent principle of movement and rest would seem to have no place in God, for God is entirely simple, and so there can be in God no real distinction between a principle of movement or operation and the movement or operation itself, so that "nature" in this sense has no place in God. As to (2), if "nature" is taken to mean "essence," then while we can acknowledge nature in God in this sense, the divine nature cannot be known to us, for in this life we do not know what God is; while we use the word "God" to mean the divine nature, this word is not taken from a known nature; the most proper name of God, says Aquinas, is *Qui est*, precisely because this name is taken from the *esse* of God, omitting every determining form, so that it signifies an infinite ocean of substance.[88]

Lonergan responds to the second point first. Aquinas says that God's act of understanding *is* God's substance (*Summa theologiae*, 1, q. 14, a. 4), or conversely that the nature of God *is* God's act of understanding (*Summa theologiae*, 1, q. 18, a. 3 c. ad fin.), and that intellectual creatures are in the image of God because they possess a specific likeness precisely in their intellectuality (*Summa theologiae*, 1, q. 93, aa. 2–4). How is it possible for him to say this, if we cannot know what God is?

We cannot know the divine nature in this life, for we do not understand God through an intelligible species proportionate to the divine essence (*Summa theologiae*, 1, q. 12, aa. 2, 4, 5, 11). But this does not mean that we cannot have some analogical knowledge of God in this life, and so order the analogically known realities as to place something first in the order of our conceptions. In this sense, then, for Lonergan the nature of God is the unrestricted act of understanding, of which we have only a heuristic notion:

the understanding of everything about everything. On this there follow, in the order of our conceptions, God's infinity, aseity, simplicity, and whatever else there is in God that is not known to us. The "following" here is not in the order of causality but in that of intelligibility. There can be an order of "reasons" in our affirmations about God, even though there is no order of causes in God.

As we have seen,[89] this ordering of divine attributes is Lonergan's, not Aquinas's; Thomas, it seems, at least in the first part of the *Summa theologiae*, places divine simplicity first, not divine infinity. This difference is related to the fact that for Lonergan the affirmation of God as the unrestricted act of understanding, as *ipsum intelligere*, precedes, in the order of "reasons," the affirmation of God as *ipsum esse subsistens*. Given that priority, Lonergan's argument for his own ordering makes eminent sense. That argument is as follows.[90]

(1) *Infinity* belongs to the nature of intellect in such a way that intellect in act with respect to the totality of its object is itself infinite, the unrestricted act of understanding. For (a) intellect is *quo est omnia fieri*, and (b) the term "*omnia*" admits no generic or specific limitation, so that (c) the object of intellect is all of being, *ens totum* (*Summa theologiae*, 1, q. 79, a. 7). For this reason (d) human intellect tends toward its object in such a way that it does not rest until it sees God *per essentiam* (ibid. q. 12, a. 1; 1-2, q. 3, a. 8; q. 5, a. 5; *Summa contra Gentiles*, 3, cc. 25–63). For this reason, too, (e) every created intellect is a passive potency (*Summa theologiae*, 1, q. 79, a. 2) and (f) every created act of understanding is other than the substance of the creature, other than the creature's act of existing, and other than the creature's operative potency (ibid. q. 54, aa. 1–3). On the same grounds, (g) an intellect that is in act with respect to its complete object is itself infinite being (ibid. 1, q. 79, a. 2). The whole of Lonergan's position on the natural desire to see God is relevant at this point in a fully elaborated systematic theology.[91]

(2) Infinite being cannot be from another, and so an intellect in act with respect to its entire object is *a se*, from itself.

(3) The infinite excludes potency, for what is in potency to a further perfection *eo ipso* falls short of infinity.

(4) Intellect in act is the intelligible in act, so that intellect differs from the intelligible only insofar as both are in potency (ibid. 1, q. 14, a. 2); but the infinite excludes potency, and so (a) the act of understanding that is in act with respect to its total object is not distinct from the intellect that understands, in that there is

no intellect in potency to the act of understanding, (b) the infinite qua intelligible is not distinguished from the act of understanding by which it is understood (ibid. 1, q. 14, a. 4), and (c) the infinite act of understanding is true with respect to itself, not according to a likeness, as though knowing and known were two things, but according to the absence of any unlikeness (ibid. q. 16, a. 5, ad 2m).

(5) The *esse naturale* of the infinite is not something different from its *esse intentionale*, for the *esse naturale* of something is the *esse* by which it is, the *esse intentionale* is the medium by which it is known, and in the infinite the act of understanding by which it is known is the same as the intelligible that is known; and so its *esse naturale* is the same as its *esse intentionale* (ibid. q. 34, a. 2, ad 1m; see q. 27, a. 2 c. and ad 2m). In the terms of *Insight*, the unrestricted act of understanding understands itself and so is the primary intelligible, but besides the primary intelligible there are the secondary intelligibles, since the unrestricted act of understanding grasps everything about everything precisely inasmuch as it understands itself.[92] Both the primary intelligible and the secondary intelligibles are spoken in the eternal divine Word and loved in the eternal divine proceeding Love.

(6) The infinite is completely simple, for one act of understanding is simple, the infinite act of understanding is one act, and this one act is the same as everything that the infinite knows about the infinite.

(7) Although we can conceive the infinite only analogically insofar as we ascend from our own finite act of understanding, nonetheless the infinite act of understanding perfectly understands itself. And it does not understand itself as other than the act of understanding itself but as the same in all respects.

Thus, if the nature of God is conceived as intellect in act with respect to the whole of its object, there follow the infinity of God, the aseity of God, the simplicity of God, and whatever else there is in God that is not known to us. This much we can say, analogically of course, regarding the nature of God, where "nature" means "essence," and so the objection is answered that we cannot answer the question of what the divine nature is that is communicated in the divine processions since we cannot know the essence of God.

As for "nature" understood, not as the essence from which all the rest follows, but as an intrinsic principle of operation, we arrive again at the conclusion that the divine nature is intellectual. For while it is true that our natural knowledge of God yields no real distinctions in God, faith and theology do tell us of real distinctions, namely, the distinctions of persons constituted by relations of origin. But modes of origin are different in different things, according to the nature of each thing, and the distinction of the divine persons corresponds to the divine nature, where the Trinity is distinguished in accord with the procession of the Word from the one who utters it, and Love from the speaker and the Word (ibid. q. 93, aa. 5 and 6), that is, according to emanations of intellectual consciousness.[93] Thus the response to the first objection above moves beyond the range of the philosophy of God into the understanding of faith that is proper to systematic theology. But the move shows how congruent philosophy of God and strictly systematic theology are in the hands of a deft master of both.

The point of this entire second step, then, is that we are to conceive of the divine nature, whether as essence or as immanent principle of operation, as intellectual. It is thus that we can affirm with St Thomas that (1) *intelligere Dei est eius substantia*, (2) *Dei natura est ipsum eius intelligere*, and (3) *creaturae intellectuales sunt ad imaginem Dei quia similitudinem specificam habent*.[94] It is such a divine nature that is communicated to the Word and to proceeding Love in the emanations that are the Trinitarian processions. Each of the three divine persons is subject of the infinite intellectual consciousness of God in a distinct manner.

4.3.3 Emanation of Word and Emanation of Love

Third, however, if we turn to the analogue of intellectual nature that our own cognitional and evaluative processes provide, we find that there is a difference between the procession of the inner word and the procession of love. And so, while the divine nature is communicated both to the Son and to the Holy Spirit by virtue of the very processions by which they proceed (the Son from the Father, the Holy Spirit from the Father and the Son), still that communication of the divine nature to the Son is distinct from the communication to the Holy Spirit, so that the Son is subject of the one divine intelligent and loving consciousness in a manner distinct from that in which the Holy Spirit is subject of that same divine consciousness.

Lonergan is here working on the analogy "from below upward," according to which we first understand something, then from the understanding speak a true word about the thing understood, then from understanding and word spirate a love of the thing, and finally are carried by love toward the loved thing.[95]

Now, the emanation of the word heads toward the formation of an intentional likeness of what has been understood; a true word about the thing is had insofar as there is formed within the intellect a perfect likeness of the thing.[96] But love is had only insofar as the lover is inclined, borne, impelled to what is loved, is united with it, and adheres to it; and so the emanation by which love proceeds heads toward constituting an inclination, impulse, adherence.[97] These two attitudes or orientations are not only distinct but at least in human consciousness to some extent opposed. The object of intellect is the true, and the true is found within intellect itself, so that one who is intellectually committed to the interior formation of a true likeness of what is understood can sometimes seem to others to be rather cold, little inclined or drawn toward realities in themselves. On the other hand, the object of the will is the good, and the good exists not within the will but in realities themselves, so that the lover can be so preoccupied with the beloved that people who cultivate the affections rather than true knowledge are said to be blind. A complete circle of consciousness, of course, would see to it that one is intelligent enough to avoid the blindness of the lover and committed enough to reality itself to avoid the coldness of the intellectual. Such a complete circle of consciousness begins with the intellect's grasp, moves to the representation in a true word of what has been grasped, and proceeds to a love of what is so represented that heads one toward the loved reality as it is in itself and in its own right.[98] Each element in this process shares in the knowledge and love constitutive of the entire process, but each does so in its own way. Analogously, each divine person understands and loves with the understanding and love that are the infinite divine consciousness, but each of them in the manner proper to that person: the Father as unoriginate understanding and love, the Word as born of, spoken from, that understanding and love, and the Holy Spirit as the proceeding Gift of the two to one another, the seal, as it were, of the divine perfection. The "complete circle" of autonomous human consciousness that Lonergan is speaking of at this point in his treatment is very remotely analogous to the circumincession of the Trinitarian persons. (The analogy is less remote when the circle appears in the order of grace, as in the analogy suggested earlier in this work. But more on circumincession will appear in our work on missions and persons in the next volume.)

The emanation of the word and the emanation of love differ, then, in that true and false are in the mind, while good and evil are in things. It is because the intellect tends toward an interiorly held truth that the intrinsic intelligibility of the emanation of the word is to head toward the interior formation of a true likeness of what is understood. And it is because the will tends toward a good external to itself that the intrinsic intelligibility of the emanation of love is to head toward actuating an inclination toward the thing itself.[99]

The transposition of these faculty-psychology statements into intentionality analysis is easy. The operations of intelligent and reasonable consciousness head to the affirmation in which being is known, the interiorly held truth which Lonergan states is the objective of "the intellect," while the operations of deliberative, existential consciousness head beyond the judgment of value to the decision and action that implement that judgment, and so to the "good external to the will" of which a faculty psychology would speak. Consequently, there is very little effort involved in transposing Lonergan's analogy into intentionality analysis.

A very important reference is given to Thomas Aquinas, *De veritate*, q. 4, a. 2, ad 7m: "Haec autem est differentia inter intellectum et voluntatem: quod operatio voluntatis terminatur ad res, in quibus est bonum et malum; sed operatio intellectus terminatur in mente, in qua est verum et falsum ... Et ideo *voluntas non habet aliquid progrediens a seipsa, quod in ea sit nisi per modum operationis; sed intellectus habet in seipso aliquid progrediens ab eo, non solum per modum operationis, sed etiam per modum rei operatae.*"[100] The last sentence is crucial: whatever proceeds in the will itself proceeds only *per modum operationis*, whereas in the intellect there are not only *processiones per modum operationis* but also *processiones per modum operati*. The procession of the act of love is, of course, a *processio operati*, but it is not a procession *in* the will; rather, it is a procession *from* the intellect *into* the will. This, Lonergan will argue, is a point missed by most commentators on Aquinas. We will see its importance in the next chapter when we come to the last of the four questions that Lonergan adds to his assertions in the first chapter of *The Triune God: Systematics.* That question will be for us a springboard into the complexity of Lonergan's various treatments of the relationships between knowledge and love. At this stage in his thinking, love still flows from knowledge, but even in this strictly Thomist context, as we will see, there are grounds for conceiving a quite different relationship.

Again, in the terms of intentionality analysis rather than those of faculty psychology: (1) In the cognitive order represented by the successive "levels" that Lonergan presents in shorthand as experience, understanding, and judgment, there are processions of act from potency that remain immanent in the successive levels. In the strictly intellectual levels of understanding and reflection, these processions are represented principally by the emergence of direct insight from questions for intelligence and of reflective insight from questions for reflection. In the same order, there are also processions of act from act that remain immanent in their respective levels: the procession of the inner word of concept from the act of understanding, and the procession of the inner word of judgment from reflective understanding. But at the level of deliberation, evaluation, and decision, there are only processions of act from potency immanent in the existential consciousness itself; fourth-level activity reaches fulfillment only beyond itself in action commensurate with the decision. If the decision proceeds from the judgment of value, it does so as the procession of act from act, of course, but that procession is a procession from the cognitive order to the existential order, not a procession of act within the existential order itself.

4.3.4 The Argument

The three points on which Lonergan's argument depends have now been exposed. The argument consists in showing that all the elements of the definition of generation are verified in what can be said analogically about the procession of the divine Word, but not in what can be said about the procession of divine Love.

The procession of the divine Word, then, is a procession (*origo*) of what is living (God is living, and the divine Word is God) from a living principle (the Speaker is also the living God) that is conjoined with what proceeds from it (the two are, respectively, principle and term within the same consciousness) into a likeness (it is of the nature of the procession of the true word that it proceed to the formation of a true likeness) where the likeness is a likeness of nature (the intentional *esse* of God is identical with God's natural *esse*, so that, while other inner words are "like" only according to their intentional *esse*, the Word of God, by being like according to intentional *esse*, is necessarily also like according to natural *esse*).[101]

But not all of these elements are verified in the divine procession of love. It *is* an *origo viventis e principio vivente coniuncto*, and through it God does proceed from God *secundum esse Dei naturale*. But the analogy reveals that the procession of love is not a procession that heads toward the interior formation of a similitude of the thing loved but rather a procession that, proceeding from speaker and word and so possessing their full knowledge, heads beyond the lover in the constitution of an impulse or adherence to what is thus known and uttered. While there does arise from this procession what is similar in nature, the intelligibility (*ratio*) of the procession is not such that the procession is headed immanently to the constitution of a likeness but is headed beyond itself to cooperation with God in the ongoing constitution of the world itself.[102] Thus, from the analogy one gains a remote understanding of the distinction between the two processions and of how it is that the manner in which the Son is both *a se* and not *a se* is different from the manner in which the Holy Spirit is both *a se* and not *a se*.

4.3.5 Resolving a Problem

In an article in *Theological Studies* on "The Starting Point of Systematic Theology," I pointed to an internal inconsistency in Lonergan's presentation at this point in the analogy. This problem is stated again above.[103] It has to do with the character of the analogue for the divine Word as a judgment not of fact but of value. Let me quote the original posing of the problem, which was also used in summary fashion above:

> Even in his trinitarian treatises of the 1950s and 1960s, the word that provides an analogue for the divine Word is not a concept, not even a judgment of fact, but a judgment of value; and yet his unpacking of the processions is still in terms of the emanation of a purely cognitional judgment, a judgment in which there is formed (in Thomas's words) a likeness (*similitudo*) of what is known to be. The truth of a judgment of value cannot be expressed in this way, for a true judgment of value may disapprove of what is and approve of what is not. And so the work of elaborating what the truth of a judgment of value consists in, even when that judgment is generated in a movement from below, remains to be done. An overhauling even of the early analogy "from below" is required before we can proceed any further. What makes for the truth, not of a judgment of fact, but of a judgment of value? The appropriation of the emanation of a word that is a judgment of value is by no means as clear in Lonergan's work as is the appropriation of the procession of a true judgment of fact. We must try to shore up what is still inchoate in his writings, even in the later writings where a new notion of value emerges.[104]

What can we say in response to this problem? While the language of "judgment of value" (*iudicium valoris*) does appear once in the text, namely, when Lonergan presents the meaning of the term "spirans," still it may be argued that the later notion of judgments of value had not yet emerged. The *iudicium valoris* is still conceived on the lines of a judgment of fact. Still, the lines of a solution may be suggested.

The question that leads to the reflective act of understanding grounding a judgment of fact, namely, Is it so? and the question leading to a reflective act of understanding grounding a judgment of value, namely, Is it really worthwhile? are both headed toward self-transcendence, and self-transcendence is the sole criterion of the objectivity of the judgment in which the respective questions are answered. It is the meaning of the respective judgments, not their criterion, that is different. The meaning of the judgment of fact is what is so or what is not so. The meaning of the judgment of value is what is or is not truly good or really better. And even in the new context provided by Lonergan's later analysis of decision, the fact remains that the objective of the purely cognitional process is reached as an immanent term of the process itself, whereas the objective of the deliberative process is not immanent to that process but beyond it. The argument for the distinction of word and love that Lonergan makes in a faculty-psychology context in *The Triune God: Systematics* remains valid once one has transposed that context to intentionality analysis. The analogue for the eternally proceeding divine Word is a judgment of value, a *verbum spirans amorem*, and such a judgment in human consciousness, as opposed to a judgment of fact, does not bring a process to an end. The divine Word, the divine judgment of value, in a matter remotely analogous to the human judgment of value, heads beyond itself to love. Even the early analogy, for all its intellectualist overtones and context, represents divine self-transcendence in agapic terms, however disguised they may appear in contrast to the explicit emphases of the later analogy.

Perhaps to this I might add that Lonergan's notion of "judgment of value" perhaps needs further differentiation in terms of Frederick Crowe's distinction of complacency and concern. If the judgment of value that is perceived to be the analogue for the procession of the divine Word proceeds from "complacentia," the objection probably disappears.[105]

12

Enriching the Context

1   The Rule of the Kingdom and the Emergence of Genuine Autonomy

> **Thesis 57:** *Analogies based on the genuine autonomy of the human subject, analogies of act from act in the spiritual dimension of consciousness, are available to us only inasmuch as we have been not only freed from the illusions of false autonomy but also freed into a genuine autonomy through the grace that operates us beyond the deviated transcendence of mimetic rivalry.*

I wish now to introduce some considerations that will relate the previous chapter to a number of the points made in the two preceding chapters. These considerations will include the four questions that Lonergan adds to the three assertions of chapter 2 of *The Triune God: Systematics.*

I begin by recalling the intriguing suggestion of Jean-Michel Oughourlian that "the real human *subject* can only come out of the rule of the Kingdom; apart from this rule, there is never anything but mimetism and the 'interdividual.' Until this happens, the only subject is the mimetic structure."[1]

The significance of this remark in our present context is, of course, that on the interpretation being offered here not only of Lonergan but through Lonergan of ourselves, the "real human subject" in his or her autonomous spiritual dynamism is precisely what is providing the analogies, natural and supernatural, on which we are relying. On this reading and in this context, an appropriation of what Oughourlian and Girard are saying would insist that such analogies are available to us only inasmuch as we have been not only freed *from* the illusions of autonomy that we discussed earlier but also freed *into* a genuine autonomy through transcending the mimetic interdividuality in which all are caught, short of divine grace. We can proceed no further in constructing a Trinitarian analogy on the basis of such genuine human autonomy until we have explored this rich and fertile suggestion at least a bit, and unpacked at least some of its profound theological significance.

Clearly, then, I would identify the "real human subject" to which Oughourlian refers with the authentic subject in Lonergan's sense: in the intentional order, attentive, intelligent, reasonable, responsible, loving; in the psychic dimension, with symbolic structures that precede, feelings that accompany, and interpersonal relations that overarch the intentional operations. That is to say, intentionality analysis and psychic conversion teach us what is meant by the "real human subject." Such a subject is characterized by the *processiones operationis* and *processiones operati* that characterize intelligent, reasonable, responsible performance: the spontaneous emergence of act from potency in the order of inquiry, and the autonomous emergence of act from act in the order of actual understanding, judging, and deciding. This "real human subject" arises out of the interdividual situation of mimetic rivalry and violence, or, more fully, out of Lonergan's "primordial intersubjectivity" in both its positive and deeply dark and sinister aspects. Lonergan, as usual, has emphasized the positive aspects of the prior "We" out of which the individual emerges in his or her individuation; Girard has caught the dark side in much of its intrepid destructiveness; and Heidegger may very well have succumbed to that dark side throughout much of his philosophical career. The real human subject emerges into genuine autonomy only through the grace of the rule of God, which is not so much an interdividual or intersubjective reality as an interpersonal one. The course of human development may be described as a movement out of primordial intersubjectivity and interdividuality, both positive and negative, through individuation (which can be reinterpreted in contrast to Jungian psychology as the emergence of genuine autonomy) into the interpersonal situation of loving commitment, under the influence of the ultimate set of interpersonal relations, namely, the Trinitarian relations, as these relations-as-persons invite us into a participation in their own life. Even then, one remains the always precariously genuine subject of operations that proceed in accord with the transcendental laws of human integrity, the precepts of watchful attentiveness, creative intelligent inquiry, careful reasonable reflection, demanding existential self-constitutive and world-constitutive and effective deliberation and decision. Some, and only some, of these operations are genuinely autonomous, where autonomy has to do with the procession of act from act and is contrasted with the spontaneity that characterizes the emergence of act from potency, as in the emergence of insight from inquiry. A complete Christian anthropology can be assembled on the basis of this heuristic structure of the emergence of the authentic subject in communion with others through participation in the Trinitarian relations. That anthropology will include, of course, what I have spoken of as psychic conversion, which will be an aid to the movement out of interdividuality through individuation and into real love.

What Oughourlian calls the "rule of the Kingdom," because of which there emerges the "real human subject," is progressively revealed, differentiated, in the course of biblical literature, and it has to do with liberation from the interdividual mimetic structure that for Girard characterizes all religion except that which undergoes this liberation. For Girard, most religion is primitive and even dark intersubjectivity. While Lonergan's reading is more generous, he too rejects sacralizing relations based solely on primordial intersubjectivity, and would agree with Girard that the religion that emerges from the "rule of the Kingdom" is not intersubjective in this sense but interpersonal in the deepest sense of that term, where the three founding persons are the persons of the Trinity. In between the interdividuality of origins and the interpersonal love at the end of the process stands the individuation of the "real human subject" becoming attentive, intelligent, reasonable, and responsible through the processions of act from act at the levels of intelligence, reasonableness, and existential responsibility. This is a permanent developmental structure. I do not intend to present it as necessarily sequential. The nature that makes for progress, the sin that makes for decline, and the grace that makes for redemption are simultaneously operative in the emergence of the real human subject just as they are in the unfolding of cultural and social institutions.

Girard is not, of course, maintaining that such liberation is found only in biblical religions. He *is* claiming, however, and rightly so, that the Bible *reveals* the mimetic situation, the mechanisms of mimetic conflict and violence, and the key to moving beyond it into genuine human autonomy and freedom. And he is insisting that such revelation of what God is always doing in the world is not a secondary matter. In Lonergan's terms, the revelatory text on which Girard relies is the word of God precisely as true, and as true it is the source of all doctrinal and systematic theology faithful to the revealed word. The revelation of the mimetic situation and of its overcoming is not the only true word spoken in the Bible, but it may well be the most overlooked of those true words, and to the extent that it is overlooked, a dimension of doctrinal and systematic theology has been neglected. The neglect, perhaps, has meant a truncation of the possibilities of these theological functional specialties; and if that is the case, perhaps it is time to address the situation in such a way as to do something about it. Doing something about it will lead right back into our earlier insistence on transforming systematic theology into a theology of history. The mediated object of Doctrines becomes redemption in history, and the mediated object of Systematics becomes history itself, *Geschichte*, the history that is lived and written about, the ongoing and developing interchange of divine and human freedom in the establishment of the reign of God on earth.

I will, then, cut right to the chase and speak about the revelation of the rule of the Kingdom that takes place in the public life, crucifixion, and resurrection of the incarnate Word proceeding from and sent by the One who utters that Word. I assume here the best exegesis currently available on the preaching of the Kingdom by Jesus and on the events that led to his death. For this one can do no better at present, in my view, than N.T. Wright's *Jesus and the Victory of God.* Girard's much less technical understanding of the public ministry of Jesus is in keeping with Wright's magisterial treatment, except perhaps on the exegesis of several passages. The early preaching of the Kingdom by Jesus gave away the secret of the Kingdom, which lies fundamentally in the substitution of love for the prohibitions and rituals of the remnants of the darkly sacrificial religion that still contaminated Jewish practice in Jesus's day. The love that Jesus preached was one that completely and definitively eliminated vengeance and reprisal, retribution, forms of conduct that depend on violent initiative. Only an unconditional renunciation of violence will bring about the end of violence – and Jesus was addressing a small and vulnerable nation caught in a violent situation and tempted to use violence to overcome violence. It is in the context of a discussion of Jesus's own preaching of the Kingdom that Oughourlian makes his comment about the emergence of the "real human subject."

Most people rejected the message of the Kingdom in Jesus's preaching. Even the disciples did not understand it, as is manifest from their vying for the best positions in what they thought was another political movement. It is then that Jesus's more apocalyptic message takes center stage. This message has frequently been misunderstood. It meant precisely and only that if the people to whom the message was addressed were to turn down the peace that Jesus offers, a sacrificial and cultural crisis would eventuate whose radical effect would be the destruction of the nation. Girard insists that precisely that message, while delivered to the people of Israel and their rulers at a specific time under specific circumstances, is universal. The society born of violence and kept alive by violence will succumb to violence.

Jesus's passion and death occur for reasons intimately connected with the consequences of rejecting the Kingdom. The reasons for his passion and death are purely historical and have nothing to do with sacrifice *as sacrifice is understood either in the Jewish religion of his day or in other, more archaic forms of deviated transcendence.* The Word that earlier we have tried to understand as generated from the Father's all-embracing and all-loving understanding and wisdom is now revealed, in large part, as the Father's Word about violence and love. Jesus as the incarnation of the Word of the

Father suffers the destiny of that divine Word in history. As Girard says, he has revealed violence in the most apparently holy of institutions in his own Jewish religion, namely, in the temple, the last stronghold of sacrificial religion, and the violence turned against him is in direct response to that revelation. That violence also shows the truth of his word. Indeed, it shows that he is indeed the very Word of God itself. His death is not a sacrifice that resulted from a pact between himself and the Father. Such a view, so influential in Christian history and yet so terribly wrong, is put forth by Christians who do not want to admit that human beings alone do these sorts of things, that God has nothing to do with causing them, and who thus must invent an irrational requirement of sacrifice that absolves them and all the rest of us of any responsibility for violence in the world. Such a view misses entirely the revelation of the Father that Jesus himself is. As we have seen, Lonergan speaks of the created relation of Jesus's assumed humanity to the divine Word as the created participation in divine paternity that enables the Word spoken by the Father actually to speak. As Girard insists, what that Father, divine paternity, really is, was disclosed, revealed, in Jesus's preaching of the rule of the Kingdom: "You have heard that it was said, 'You shall love your neighbor and hate your enemy.' But I say to you, Love your enemies and pray for those who persecute you, so that you may be children of your Father who is in heaven. For he makes his sun rise on the evil and on the good, and sends rain on the just and on the unjust alike" (Matthew 5. 43–45). This is not a Father who insists on the sacrifice of his incarnate Son for the sake of vindicating his honor. While that may be a caricature of some more sophisticated theological understandings, still anything that smacks of such a reading must be discredited. The revelation of the Father takes place in Jesus precisely because of their common divine nature. This is why those who have seen Jesus have seen the Father. He does not die as a sacrifice, but so that there may be no more sacrifices in human history.[2]

Girard offers a very interesting and convincing exegesis of the New Testament passage that, more than any other, has influenced the Christian notion of the incarnate Word, namely, the prologue to the Gospel of John. The Johannine Logos is specified in the prologue in a way that includes what Girard calls the scapegoat mechanism in the very definition of the revelation of the divine Logos. "In him was life; and the life was the light of men. And the light shineth in darkness, *and the darkness comprehended it not. He was in the world, and the world was made through him, *yet the world knew him not.* He came to his own home, *and his own people received him not.*"[3] The Johannine Logos, the Word of God, is forever expelled, Girard says, forever an absent Logos that has no direct, determining influence over human cultures. It discloses the truth of violence precisely by being expelled. Expulsion is part of its definition. The specificity of the Johannine Logos is to be an outcast. It will always be expelled from a world built on violence. The Logos of Love always allows itself to be expelled by the Logos of violence, which for Girard is the Logos of Heraclitus that lies behind most of Western philosophy.[4] Again, for Girard, the expulsion of the Logos of Love is revealed in a more and more obvious fashion through the whole of the Bible, and by the same process the Logos of violence is revealed as what can secure its existence only by expelling the true Logos and feeding upon it in one way or another.[5]

These emphases should be included in what we say about the procession and mission of both the divine Word and divine Love. God is eternally constituted in the Trinitarian relations, and the relations include the missions as identical with the processions joined to an additional created external term. The existential judgment of value that provides us with the analogue for the proceeding divine Word sets up the possibility of such a theology of divine generation. We make an eternal difference to God's Trinitarian self-constitution, and the difference is precisely what is revealed in the incarnation of the eternal Word in Jesus. That revelation not only includes, but also is centered in, the disclosure of the truth about violence and love that Girard brings to the heart of any theological understanding of human history. The Word incarnate reveals an element of the structure of history itself, which includes the permanent tendency to exclude the divine Word and every true human word as well, precisely through the false sacralization that is identical with secularism. We will have further comments on these matters when we come to the question about the Father's speaking all things in the Word and so about the Word's proceeding from the Father's understanding not only of the Father but also of all creation. For now, I wish simply to suggest the enrichment that this perspective brings to the entire structure of Lonergan's "normative source of meaning in history," to that tidal movement that begins before consciousness, that emerges first into the primordial intersubjectivity or interdividuality that with little persuasion becomes darkly mimetic, but that proceeds to individuation as one learns attentiveness, genuine inquiry and intelligent response, critical reflection and reasonable judgment, responsible deliberation and self-transcending decision, and that finds its rest beyond these in the threefold interpersonal love of intimacy, human community, and supernatural participation in the intimate relations of the indwelling Trinity. That very emergence on the scale of universal human community is the meaning and purpose, the objective, of the participation in the divine relations that we are seeking, so haltingly, to understand.

2   Returning to Lonergan's Text: Four Questions

2.1 Understanding and Word

> **Thesis 58:** *The context is further enriched by the insistence that Loner-gan's distinction of insight and word, which occurs in the Scholastic context in which insight grasps intelligibilities resident in corporeal matter, can and must be extended to the fuller hermeneutic epistemology that acknowledges ordinary meaningfulness even at the level of presentations. This distinction in interiorly differentiated consciousness also permits a transposition of the Scholastic notions of active and passive potency into the context of an intentionality analysis heading to self-appropriation.*

Lonergan concludes his chapter on the divine processions by asking and answering four questions that are related not only to one another but also to the processions and to the analogy employed to understand them. I propose to review each of these questions and Lonergan's answers and to relate the thrust of his answers to the broader context that I have been attempting to set from the beginning of this book. With this effort, we conclude this first volume, hoping that this review will strengthen the points we are trying to make regarding the relation of religious and personal values in the normative scale of values.

The first question addresses the very possibility of the analogy that Lonergan is proposing in *The Triune God: Systematics.* Is it true that in us understanding and inner word are really distinct?[6] If they are not, then the analogy that Lonergan is proposing will not succeed in providing some remote hypothetical understanding of the procession of the divine Word. The same may be said *mutatis mutandis* regarding the analogies that his later work suggests and of the analogy that I am proposing, in that each of them presupposes a real distinction and relation between an inner word and the principle in consciousness from which that word proceeds, whether that principle be understanding or the dynamic state of being in love or the recollection in *memoria* of being on the receiving end of unqualified love, serving as evidence grasped in a reflective existential insight that would ground a judgment of value.

The argument proposed in *The Triune God: Systematics* is metaphysical rather than psychological, but in commenting on it I will introduce psychological considerations, and will emphasize those points that affect the movement from the existential equivalent of the grasp of the virtually unconditioned to judgments of value, since that is where the relevant analogy from nature is to be developed.

Lonergan treats two cases of understanding and inner word, and both of them are in the cognitional rather than the existential order. That is, they are both heading to judgments of fact rather than to judgments of value. The first treats the direct act of understanding and the inner word of concept or definition or hypothesis or supposition that proceeds from it, and the second has to do with the reflective act of understanding and the proceeding inner word of a judgment of fact. Despite his use of the expression "iudicium valoris" for the relevant inner word that provides an analogy for the divine Word proceeding from the Father, his treatment in *The Triune God: Systematics* of the relation between insight and the word that proceeds from it does not really advance to that level. It is probably still the case that what he says for judgments of fact is meant to apply also to judgments of value. It is likely that, as in *Insight*, considerations of value remained for him at this point an extension of intellectual activity, even if by 1964, when *De Deo Trino: Pars Systematica* was published, he has explicitly acknowledged a fourth level of consciousness, something which had not yet occurred in so many words in *Insight*.[7] Furthermore, as I said earlier, by 1968 not only had a clear distinction of a fourth level been made – that had probably happened at least a decade earlier – but also a new dynamic process had been acknowledged at this level. Still, the structure of judgments of value remains the same for him as that of judgments of fact. In any event, it is not a structural problem that we are confronting here, so much as an issue of the contents of the relevant insights and proceeding inner words. Lonergan makes it clear in the following passage from *Method in Theology* that the structure of judgments of fact and of judgments of value is the same, and as I have indicated that structure pervades every valid psychological analogy that has been proposed to help us understand the divine processions.

> Judgments of value differ in content but not in structure from judgments of fact. They differ in content, for one can approve of what does not exist, and one can disapprove of what does. They do not differ in structure, inasmuch as in both there is the distinction between criterion and meaning. In both, the criterion is the self-transcendence of the subject, which, however, is only cognitive in judgments of fact but is heading towards moral self-transcendence in judgments of value. In both, the meaning is or claims to be independent of the subject; judgments of fact state or purport to state what is or is not so; judgments of value state or purport to state what is or is not truly good or really better.[8]

What remains a matter of dispute in the interpretation of Lonergan's later account, however, has to do not with the structure of judgments of value but with the dynamics of their conscious procession. With the help of St Ignatius Loyola's comments on various times for making decisions, I have concluded that the account in *Method in Theology* corresponds to Ignatius's "second time," when one is experiencing affective pulls and counterpulls toward and away from possible value and disvalues. "Intermediate between judgments of fact and judgments of value," Lonergan writes, "lie apprehensions of value. Such apprehensions are given in feelings."[9] These apprehensions have to be connected to insights, and in fact identified with affect-laden insights, from which there proceed judgments of possible or real value. Lonergan has not clarified this particular step in the process. To clarify it would require, I believe, some detailed analysis of self-transcendent feelings, such as I have tried to begin presenting in my various accounts of psychic conversion.[10] My present point, however, is that if feelings are intermediate between judgments of fact and judgments of value, and if it is from such feelings that judgments of value proceed, the feelings have to be the feelings that accompany insights into possible values or, if there really are no further questions, into real values. I suspect most readers have had the experience of judgments of value issuing from affective grasp of possible values and disvalues. But what is required still among Lonergan students is some phenomenology of that procession.

At any rate, the metaphysical basis of Lonergan's argument is the familiar Aristotelian-Thomist principle that acts are distinguished in accord with different specific objects.[11] Despite the faculty-psychology context in which these considerations are raised, the points that are being made are important and in my view must be carried over and transposed as one moves to the context of intentionality analysis. Otherwise, two risks are run that would subvert most of Lonergan's project. The first is that the turn to interiority will cease to be explanatory and rather revert to common sense. There is nothing objectionable about commonsense interiority, but it is not sufficient to provide theological foundations. It is not what Lonergan is talking about when he speaks of interiorly and religiously differentiated consciousness. These are as much a matter of explanatory understanding as is chapter 11 of *Insight*, the self-affirmation of the knower. The second risk is that the correlation of operations and objects found in Husserl's meaning of "transcendental," which Lonergan increasingly adopted, is sacrificed to an exclusive emphasis on the subject and his or her operations. This risk entails the continuation of the mistaken assumption that Lonergan has not entirely transcended Kantian presuppositions. Adopting the Husserlian correlation of operations and objects into a critical realism missed by Husserl allows Lonergan's cognitional theory, epistemology, and metaphysics both to enrich and to be enriched by the basically positional reflections on these matters expressed by von Balthasar in his *Theo-logic*.

Five meanings of "object" are disengaged in the discussion of intellectual activity, and four of these name really distinct objects. Some of this we have seen already,[12] but a fuller treatment is worth pursuing at this point.

First, there is the object as end of all cognitional activity, that is, being. Being is the end or objective of intellectual and rational activity. "Being is the objective of the pure desire to know."[13] Second, there is the object as term of the second operation, that is, of judgment; here the object is the true. Third, there is the object that moves one to judgment, that is, sufficient evidence. Fourth, there is the object as term of the first operation, of understanding; here the object is the definition or hypothesis or supposition that represents the inner word conceptualizing what has been grasped in insight. And fifth, there is the object that moves us to understanding or insight itself, namely, the formal intelligibility grasped in the presentations of sense and of consciousness. I will expand in a moment on Lonergan's formulation of this last-mentioned object. But first, let me complete my report on Lonergan's statement. Being and the true are not really specifically distinct, since being is attained in the very act in which truth is reached. Truth is the medium in which being is known. So there are four specifically distinct objects of intellectual operation: evidence and the true (third level), and formal intelligibility and the simple inner word that proceeds from grasping it (second level).[14]

Lonergan reverts to specifically Scholastic language on the meaning of "object" as the quiddity or nature residing in corporeal matter. In fact, that is a remote specification of the object of human intelligence. It can get us started, as it got Lonergan started, but to leave it there invites the naive realism of so much thought that claims to take its inspiration from Aquinas but that fails to move that inspiration forward into historical consciousness and an account of the real world as mediated and constituted by meaning; that is to say, it invites cognitional theory to remain in the world of immediacy (corporeal matter) and it inclines cognitional theory to assume the criteria of knowledge in the world of immediacy as the criteria of knowledge in full human knowing. If Thomists would accept with Heidegger the universality of hermeneutic structure (however much they need to purge Heidegger's account of possible political motivation), the residual naive realism that continues to distort the interpretation of Aquinas's thought would perhaps be more easily advanced to the critical realism of Lonergan's thought. The presentations of sense and of consciousness are not raw data but are already patterned and in most instances already informed by human acts of meaning. To grasp their formal intelligibility is to grasp a form already provided by other human beings in this world mediated and constituted by meaning, an intelligibility passed on in the sedimentations of ordinary language or public discourse. As we have seen, Lonergan provides the basis of this affirmation in his diagram of the levels of consciousness in *Insight*, where he includes free images and utterances at the level of data, and states that these "commonly are under the influence of the higher levels before they provide a basis for inquiry and reflection."[15] This statement should, I believe, be made central to all presentations of Lonergan's cognitional theory, thereby removing once and for all the truncated view of the so-called first level of consciousness that continues to be found in some presentations of that theory. It may be argued that the fact that he began his presentation of cognitional theory with mathematics and science is what accounts for the very thin notion of "experience" in much literature on that theory. But even that is not sufficient warrant, since hermeneutic structures have been diagnosed in science itself.[16]

Sufficient evidence and the true are really distinct, and so, exercising the metaphysical principle that an act receives its specification from its object, we may say that it is in one act that we grasp the sufficiency of the evidence and that it is in another that we affirm what is true or deny what is false. The two acts are related by an intellectual and intelligible emanation or what I am calling an autonomous procession of the second from the first, since we are able to affirm the true *because* and only because we have grasped the sufficiency of the evidence. The "because" names the element that makes the emanation not only intelligent but also intelligible. It names the element of authentic autonomy in the procession. Consequently, in the matter of what in Scholastic language is called the second operation of the intellect and of what in Lonergan's language is the third level of consciousness, the one in which we answer the question, Is it so? it is necessary to distinguish between the act of understanding by which the sufficiency of the evidence is grasped and the affirmation of the true, which is the word (yes, no, maybe, possibly, probably, etc.) interiorly spoken.[17] Newman, more than Aquinas, was Lonergan's principal inspiration on the matter of what Lonergan called reflective understanding. In fact, it is a legitimate question whether the second *Verbum* article (now chapter 2 in the book *Verbum: Word and Idea in Aquinas*) could have been as clear as it is about the distinction of judgment from understanding had Lonergan not previously been schooled in Newman's *Grammar of Assent*. As Lonergan points out, even Aristotle and Aquinas are not entirely satisfactory on judgment, despite the fact that judgment is correlated with Aquinas's addition of the act of existence to Aristotle's account of the metaphysical elements.[18]

Regarding what in Scholastic language is called the "first act of the intellect" and what Lonergan conceives as the second level of consciousness, the level of understanding and conceptualization, the object that moves us to the act of understanding is the intelligibility immanent in the data of sense and of consciousness. In Scholastic terms this is spoken of as the quiddity or nature existing in bodily matter. On that analysis, first the corporeal and individual matter is disclosed to the senses; then from agent intellect there arises wonder, so that we ask what it is or why it is so; third, there is formed an image, so that the intelligible to be grasped in the sensible might be more clearly brought to light in the sensible itself; fourth, the possible intellect, turned to the image, grasps the intelligible in the image; and fifth, the same possible intellect, now actually understanding the intelligibility, speaks a simple inner word, the definition or the hypothesis.[19]

Essentially the same analysis can be applied to the broader base for which I have been arguing, and in fact must be so applied if we are to accept seriously Lonergan's insistence that the real world in which we live is the world that is mediated and constituted by meaning and that it is in *that* world that God's revelatory Word has become incarnate and to *that* world that the Holy Spirit is sent. The conception of the first, or empirical, level of consciousness as limited to the experience of "corporeal matter" is far too narrow, and is responsible, as I have said, for much of the naive realism that has infected the Thomist tradition. If the real world is mediated and constituted by meaning, then the level of presentations in human consciousness is itself "meaningful." It is not a level on which we experience only sheer raw sense data. We hardly ever experience sheer raw sense data. The notion that we do is intrinsically connected, I believe, with the notion of the real as the already out there now, to be known by taking a good look. Such a conception defines precisely what is meant by naive realism. As we have seen, I include far more in the objects of empirical presentations than "corporeal matter."

Whether we are dealing with the more elementary notion of empirical consciousness or the more complex notion that I am suggesting, the intelligible grasped in the presentations of sense and consciousness and the intelligible spoken in the word that proceeds from original insight are the same intelligible, but the object when it is grasped and the object when it is spoken are different.

When it is grasped in the more elementary type of empirical consciousness, what Scholastics call corporeal matter is made known through the senses but the intelligibility is made known by the intellect. But in the hypothesis or definition, what before were made known in distinct acts are joined into one. The matter that is posited in a definition or hypothesis is not the individual matter in which form was grasped by insight but the common matter involved in all such expressions of intelligibility, and what is defined or understood hypothetically is not just the quiddity, nature, or cause itself grasped by insight, but the "thing" in its intelligibility, that is, according to its quiddity, nature, or cause. Thus, because the objects are distinct, so too are the acts.[20]

What are we to say when we are considering the more complex notion of empirical consciousness, where devaluated formal and actual intelligibilities are included at the level of presentations? The situation is more complex, in that we have three rather than two instances of the same intelligibility. There is an intelligibility in the empirical presentations precisely as empirical presentations when, for instance, I hear the spoken utterances of another person. This is a devalued formal intelligibility at the level of presentations, of empirical consciousness. It is an instance of what in *Insight* Lonergan called presentations that are already under the influence of the higher levels before ever providing a basis for my own inquiry and reflection. Next, there is an intelligibility that proceeds from my own inquiry into what has been said to me, as I attempt to understand the meaning of the other who has spoken to me or to understand the "thing," the "matter," the *Sache,* about which she has spoken. Finally, there is an intelligibility that I utter in manifesting both to myself and to my interlocutor what I have understood as I continue the conversation. It is an intelligibility that I speak in a word that not merely repeats the utterance of the other like a parrot but that issues from my own insight into the meaning of that utterance and that manifests that insight. These three intelligibilities are the same, just as are the intelligibility grasped in the raw data of sense that Lonergan, following Aquinas, calls "corporeal matter" and the intelligibility uttered in my word proceeding from such a grasp. But again the object in each instance is different. When I am presented with the devalued formal intelligibility of someone else's meaning, that meaning resides in the sensible appearances of that other person's utterances, and is intelligently received at the level of presentations, in something like, I believe, at least one of Heidegger's uses of the word *Verstehen.* Our very empirical consciousness is, if you will, incipiently hermeneutical. When I grasp that meaning in an original insight of my own, I detach it from those sensible appearances and give it something of a generalized significance. When I express it to myself and to my interlocutor I have invested it with my own linguistic and perhaps more elemental carriers of meaning. Thus, when the intelligibility is grasped in the more complex and more usual form of empirical consciousness, presentations invested with ordinary meaningfulness are made known in receiving them; but an original meaningfulness emerges in the insight that follows upon inquiry; and again, the hypothesis that proceeds from original insight joins into one act what before were made known in distinct acts. In these more complex instances, the potential meaning presented in utterances is converted by insight into the original meaningfulness that moves a conversation or interpretation forward, while what is understood hypothetically in this original meaningfulness is the set of connections constitutive of the situation, language, text, or whatever that is being submitted to original investigation, and that is expressed in such a way as to make further authentic dialogue possible. Obviously, further phenomenological analyses of such conversational or dialogical encounters are desirable, but the heuristics of the analysis are provided by a simple extension of Lonergan's account of cognitional process so as to include instances in which the presentations are already under the control of higher levels.

Lonergan refers the reader to appendix 2 of the entire volume for further discussion of the relation between the act of understanding and the inner word. We have already seen one item from this appendix, but now we will treat it more fully. Appendix 2 is entitled "De actu intelligendi," "The act of understanding."

Understanding is required for, and grounds, the emanation or procession of a word or concept. The object that is term of this prior act of understanding from which an inner word proceeds cannot be the inner word itself that will proceed, and so it must be the case that "our intellect grasps not only conceptual objects but preconceptual objects as well. Otherwise we would not form conceptions because we understand, but rather, as the Scotists teach, we [would be] able to understand because in some unconscious manner conceptions have been formed."[21] The issue is crucial not only for our self-understanding and self-constitution through self-appropriation but also for Trinitarian theology. "[T]he unconscious formation of the word would destroy that intellectual emanation which we have considered to be the psychological analogy of the Holy Trinity."[22] There would be no psychological analogy for the divine processions if, in acts of original meaningfulness, inner words do not consciously proceed from acts of understanding.

As we have seen, in Scholastic thought correctly understood (and it has often been misunderstood, as in theories of vital act according to which every potency moves itself to its own act), "object" can mean any one of three things. It can refer to something that moves a potency to act. It can refer to a term produced by an act. And it can refer to the end to which a potency tends through acts, its "objective." It is because "object" has a causal relation both to potency and to act that "an object may be either a mover that brings about an act in a potency, or a term produced by an act, or the end to which a potency tends through acts."[23] "[A]n object is to the act of a passive potency as principle and moving cause; for color is the principle of vision insofar as it moves the faculty of sight. But an object is to the act of an active potency as term and end …"[24] What makes the difference is whether the potency in question is active or passive. The object is to the act of a passive potency as principle and moving cause, but an object is to the act of an active potency as term or end. "Object" is not a primitive notion, then, but is reducible to the notions of potency, act, mover, end, and term.

These Scholastic distinctions have not lost their importance with the move to intentionality analysis, the transition from theory to interiority. Their meaning must be preserved in any such transition, if "interiority" is to mean, not commonsense familiarity with one's various operations and states but explanatory interiorly differentiated consciousness, and if intentionality analysis is not to slip into an exclusive emphasis on the subject and his or her operations. The issue grows in complexity as we consider the transposition of the notions of active and passive potency in Lonergan's later work: "[T]he active potencies are the transcendental notions revealed in questions for intelligence, questions for reflection, questions for deliberation. The passive potencies are the lower levels as presupposed and complemented by the higher."[25] The transposition of the language of object vis-à-vis active potencies seems fairly straightforward in such a move, but the relation of object and passive potencies is problematic in this new formulation unless some careful elucidation is done.

The new formulation makes sense with regard to the passive potencies within the context of the vertical finality of the lower "levels" as presupposed, complemented, and sublated by the higher, but the horizontal finality of each "level" also exhibits its own character of passivity that is the key to the Aristotelian-Thomist analysis as well as to Lonergan's correct interpretation of that analysis in opposition to the distorted Scholastic metaphysics of vital act. But that horizontal passivity must be preserved in any transposition to interiority, for reasons that are not only cognitional-theoretic but also existential. Not preserving the proper receptivity of consciousness for both sense and intelligence creates an exaggerated autonomy, which, if it becomes one's self-understanding as one undertakes self-appropriation, will lead to a serious misunderstanding of the subject that one is. As we have already seen, the notion of "autonomy" has a limited validity. As did "vital act" theories in late Scholasticism, so exaggerated notions of autonomy in modernity miss the point that "object" is not a primitive notion. Lonergan himself can be read as tending in this direction, if the pre-*Insight* context of *Verbum* is neglected in interpreting him. The fact that "intelligere est quoddam pati" is not as clearly conveyed in *Insight* as in *Verbum*, and needs to be transposed from *Verbum* into Lonergan's own cognitional theory.

We will see in a moment, though, that the problem regarding the new meaning attached to the terms "active potency" and "passive potency" can be solved.

As we have just seen, the notion of object as end reflects *Insight*'s second-order definition of being as the objective of the pure desire to know. But the notion of object as term is far more modest: the term produced within the intellect is always the inner word of conception or judgment, the *verbum cordis*, which always represents but a minuscule increment in our advance toward the objective of being. There are two such inner words: the definition or hypothesis and the proposition affirming the true or negating the false. The existence of the inner word is proven from the use of outer words, for when we speak we mean something by what we say, and what we mean proximately is the inner word, which itself means the "thing" intended in the inner word. As Lonergan put it earlier in *Verbum*:

> [T]he inner word is what can be meant (*significabile*) or what is meant (*significatum*) by outer words, and inversely, ... the outer word is what can mean (*significativum*) or what does mean (*significans*) the inner word ... [C]ommonly [Thomas] asked what outer words meant and answered that, in the first instance, they meant inner words. The proof was quite simple. We discourse on "man" and on the "triangle." What are we talking about? Certainly, we are not talking about real things directly, else we should all be Platonists. Directly, we are talking about objects of thought, inner words, and only indirectly, only insofar as our inner words have an objective reference, are we talking of real things. The same point might be made in another fashion. Logical positivists to the contrary, false propositions are not meaningless; they mean something; what they mean is an inner word, and only because that inner word is false, does the false proposition lack objective reference.[26]

The conclusion is drawn succinctly in *The Triune God: Systematics*: "Hence primarily and *per se* outer words, whether spoken or written or present in the imagination, signify and are not signified. Things, on the other hand, are signified, but primarily and *per se* do not signify. Inner words, however, both signify and are signified: they are signified by outer words, and signify things themselves."[27] This is an early expression of what later would be affirmed in Lonergan's statement that the real world in which we live is mediated and constituted by meaning.

But do such inner words really exist? The question is real, as anyone who has so much as begun to read Wittgenstein's *Philosophical Investigations* will know all too well. It makes the matter more difficult in the context of linguistic philosophy that Lonergan in *Verbum* demonstrates the existence of inner words from the presence and functioning of outer words, which mean the inner words. The same demonstration is presented in *The Triune God: Systematics*.

> The existence of these inner words is proven from the meaning of outer words. We speak of "man" or "triangle," and we surely mean something by these words. Unless, therefore, you believe that universals subsist as real entities, you will necessarily conclude that universals are conceived in the mind and signified directly and immediately by external words. Again, human speech states what is true and what is false. What, then, is signified directly and immediately by

a false statement? Unless along with the neo-positivists you maintain that false statements signify nothing, you will necessarily acknowledge a compound word formed inwardly in the mind and signified directly and immediately in an external statement. Finally, we all hold that human speech also signifies things, and yet we do not accept anything unless it is true. But the true and the false are in the mind; truth, in fact, is formally only in a judgment. Again, therefore, one must conclude that outer words signify things, not immediately, of course, but through the medium of inner words that are true.

Hence, primarily and *per se* outer words, whether spoken or written or present in the imagination, signify and are not signified. Things, on the other hand, are signified, but primarily and *per se* do not signify. Inner words, however, both signify and are signified: they are signified by outer words, and signify things themselves.[28]

Again, as we have seen, this inner word is not to be confused with the act of understanding or with the acts of thinking, defining, supposing, considering, affirming, or denying. The inner word is "that which is understood, is thought, is defined, is supposed, is considered, is affirmed, is denied – not, of course, according to its natural existence but according to its intentional existence. Intentional existence [*esse intentionale*] is the medium in which a thing is known."[29]

Now, in the Scholastic context the intellect is a passive potency, and so there must be an object that moves it to its act, to the act of understanding. Since the intellect has two operations, it requires two moving objects. In the case of the second operation, the moving object is the sufficient evidence that moves the intellect to the grasp of its sufficiency in a reflective act of understanding. From the reflective act of understanding there is spoken the word of judgment, in an autonomous procession of act from act. In the case of the first operation, the moving object is "the actually intelligible as luminous in the phantasm and directly discerned by the intellect." This moves the intellect to the act of direct understanding, in a relation of potency to act, and from the direct act of understanding there is spoken, in an autonomous relation of act to act, the interior utterance of definition, hypothesis, supposition, or what have you. What is known through the entire process is the *quod quid est*, the "what something is."

Again, all of this has to be re-imagined and reformulated in the context of the hermeneutical turn to the world mediated and constituted by meaning, in terms of Lonergan's later appropriation of the notion of historical consciousness through the significance of the *esse intentionale*, intentional existence. But that can be done without violence to the genuine Aristotelian-Thomist analysis. It requires little more than an extension of "quod quid est" to something like "what's up." The appropriation of *esse intentionale* is what interiorly differentiated consciousness is all about, and history itself is a function of *esse intentionale*. Thus, historical consciousness emerges from what Lonergan calls "the transition from substance to subject." Once that step from substance to subject has been taken, the *esse intentionale* assumes a far greater importance in any attempts at philosophical or theological synthesis than classical Scholastic philosophy and theology was able to acknowledge. While it presupposes the *esse naturale* of human beings, still, as soon as one asks what kind of a subject one is or is to be, one enters into the order of what we understand, what we think, what we utter, what we consider true, what we choose, what we propose, what our intentions are, what our goals in life are. All of this is within the psychological-intentional order, and it is that order, the *esse intentionale* of our acts of knowing and willing, not our *esse naturale*, that settles our eternal destiny. It is in that order that the various carriers, functions, realms, and stages of meaning take on their significance for human life. That order is not only formally constitutive of human living. It develops. History itself is the history of the development of meanings and of orders that are constituted by meaning. Divine revelation is the explicit entrance of God's meaning, including God's incarnate meaning, God's incarnate Logos, into history. The exploration, then, of the realm in which a psychological analogy for the Trinitarian processions can be elaborated has profound significance for the theological articulation of the meaning of human history.

Within the context of historical consciousness, we can effect a transposition of the notions of active and passive potency that Lonergan had in his earlier work employed to articulate his cognitional theory in Scholastic language. Those notions had reference to faculties, which were thought of as sensitive, intellectual, apprehensive, and appetitive potencies. A good deal of Scholastic psychology was engaged in the questions about the mutual interactions of the faculties. But Lonergan has replaced the Scholastic faculty psychology with an intentionality analysis that distinguishes four levels of intentional consciousness: presentations of sense and of consciousness, understanding, judgment, and decision. The lower levels, as it were, are presupposed and complemented by the higher, while the higher sublate the lower into their more comprehensive concerns. In that context, the transcendental notions themselves assume the role of the active potencies, as these notions are manifest in questions for intelligence, questions for reflection, questions for deliberation, in the operators that, in *Insight*'s language, are relentless in transforming any temporary integrations that our interior development, the development of our *esse intentionale*, may have achieved. And the role of "passive potency" now characterizes each successive lower level of consciousness and all the operations and correlative objects at those levels, as the lower levels are presupposed, complemented, and sublated by the higher. This transposition of the notions of active and passive potency in no way detracts from the analysis of objects and operations that Lonergan provides in a more Scholastic context in *The Triune God: Systematics.* Insight remains insight into phantasm, where the intelligibility in the data of sense and of consciousness moves us to understand under the force of the questions for intelligence that are raised by the transcendental notion of the intelligible (which, after all, is partly constitutive, along with the other transcendental notions, of what Scholastic philosophy called "agent intellect"). Again, in the context of intentionality analysis, it remains true that the reflective grasp of sufficient evidence moves one to the inner word of judgment. In all these instances of transposition, then, nothing of permanent significance is abandoned. What are abandoned are the fruitless questions to which the older conceptuality was prone, in this case the questions concerning the relative priority of the various faculties with respect to one another.[30]

2.2 *Can We Demonstrate That There Is a Word in God?*

Thesis 59: *The understanding of why we are not able to demonstrate the existence of a divine Word further enriches the natural analogue for the Trinitarian processions. Inner words are required for the integrity, progress, explanatory power, and transcendental reach of human cognitional process. The argument to this effect can be extended to and enriched by the hermeneutical context of the world mediated and constituted by meaning. The enrichment of our understanding regarding the necessity of human inner words contributes to our appropriation of the indemonstrable mystery of the procession of the divine Word, in whose invisible mission our inner words share.*

The second question following Lonergan's assertions regarding the divine processions concerns the inability of reason unaided by faith to demonstrate the existence of the divine Word. The First Vatican Council repudiated the semirationalists, who maintained that such a demonstration was possible (DB 1816, DS 3041), but Lonergan's efforts are directed to understanding *why* we are not able to demonstrate this. Such efforts are bound to lead to yet further material for interior appropriation and differentiation of those human spiritual processions that provide the natural analogue for Trinitarian life.

Lonergan proceeds to investigate first why we not only utter but need to utter inner words, so as then to argue that there is no similar or analogous reason why there is a demonstrable need for a word in God.

The issue does not have to do with the ontological necessity of the divine Word; everything in God is necessary. The issue is rather whether *we* can demonstrate that there must be a divine Word. As Lonergan puts it in *Verbum*, "We are not concerned with the necessity *quoad se* of the Word in God; whatever is in God is necessary ... [W]e are concerned with the necessity *quoad nos* of an inner word in divine self-knowledge and in divine knowledge of the other. Why cannot we establish by the light of natural reason that there is a Word in God?"[31]

Why, then, are inner words required for the integrity of human cognitional process? Four reasons are provided in *The Triune God: Systematics*.

The *first* reason is expressed there in very limited Scholastic terms, but it can be expanded to the hermeneutical context that more accurately reflects his cognitional theory for a world mediated and constituted by meaning and motivated by values. What he says is that we need the first inner word, the word of conception, hypothesis, definition, in order to proceed from the grasped cause or quiddity to a conception of the "thing." That is, we are moved to the act of understanding by the causes or quiddities of things, but these causes and quiddities are not the things themselves but parts of things or perhaps relations. So the first reason a word is necessary is so that we might move from the understood quiddity to a quidditative definition of the "thing."

What on earth does this mean? Let's broaden the discussion from Scholastic talk about the quiddity of a "thing," "res," to speaking about, say, the formal intelligibilities of phenomena studied in science, or perhaps about the subtle combination of factors that enables one to be on top of a complicated human situation and to know just how to proceed in that situation, or even about the meaning of a divine mystery that must be approached only through the analogical understanding of a systematic theologian. Let's broaden "res," "thing," to *Sache* as the latter term is used in hermeneutical literature to refer to the object intended in a text or in another form of expression. Insight is involved in each of these instances. It is through a combination of insights that we will grasp a possible response to the question for understanding. But we never stop there, or at least we can agree that we should not stop there. We experience an inner exigency for a formulated hypothesis that expresses an ordered conception of whatever it is that we have understood through a series of insights. Only with that conception can we proceed to an ever more refined grasp and further articulation of what it is that we are after. We may be moved to our own acts of understanding by intelligibilities in the presentations of sense and consciousness, but these particular intelligibilities are not the phenomena or the affair or the situation or the divine mystery, or whatever, that we are after, but parts of them, aspects of them, relations within them, and so on. We need the help of inner words to proceed from the particular grasped intelligibilities to the intelligible whole, to the intelligent conception, hypothesis, definition, supposition, surmise, consideration of the affair, matter, situation, mystery, or whatever it is that we desire to know.[32] Late Scholastic philosophy expressed this distinction in terms of the "species impressa" and the "species expressa." The "species impressa" is given with the insight. It is Thomas's "species intelligibilis." The "species expressa," however, is the concept, the inner word of definition, hypothesis, surmise, supposition, from which alone we can proceed really to know whatever it is we desire to know. We need the inner word in order to proceed further, if our questions are to be answered to our satisfaction.

Second, we also require an inner word of judgment, a yes or no, if we are to proceed from conception, hypothesis, definition, supposition, surmise, consideration, and even grasp of evidence to the thing *as existing* or, more fully, to the affirmation that we have correctly understood the affair, matter, situation, mystery, or whatever, that we have been trying to figure out. This happens only if from the grasp of evidence there proceeds a true judgment, the intentional medium in which what is, being, is known.[33]

Third, we need certain kinds of inner words to develop scientific or theoretical knowledge, or more generally to move from description to explanation. Without the formation of technical concepts, our knowledge would be limited to commonsense description of things in their relations to us. Even this knowledge, of course, is dependent on the formation of inner words of supposition, surmise, etc. But a different kind of first inner word is required if we are to know the realities in this world in their relations to one another. Without the formation of exactly defined terms, a formation that is not given with scientific insight itself but that must be worked out on the basis of such insight – and this is the key issue, the place where the distinction becomes clear – we would risk being carried along by a flow of images as in mythic consciousness, never knowing clearly and distinctly what it is we are dealing with.[34]

And *fourth*, inner words both of conception and judgment are required if we are to move by analogy and by the way of eminence to some knowledge of what lies beyond the limits of this world, that is, if we are to move from knowledge of proportionate being to knowledge of transcendent being, whether in natural knowledge of God or in theological understanding of divine mysteries.[35]

Now the common root of these four requirements is the fact that the object that moves us to understanding is distinct from the object toward which we are tending as an objective or end. What moves our intellect in this life is the intelligibility in the data of sense and consciousness, and what we are tending toward is all of being.[36] The inner words of conception and limited judgment are necessary incremental steps along the way to the objective of human cognitional activity, which is everything about everything. Lonergan's Scholastic way of expressing this, which does not capture the richness of these considerations once the explicit move is made to historical consciousness operating in the world mediated and constituted by meaning, is the following: "[B]ecause we begin from the quiddity, the word is required, first, so that the thing may be defined through its quiddity; second, so that we may judge whether what we have defined exists; third, so that we may be directed away from sensibly perceived particulars toward the entirety of the visible universe; and fourth, so that we may be able to reach beyond the material world to God."[37]

In *Verbum* the first two of these reasons for our inability to demonstrate the existence of the divine Word are expressed as follows:

> [T]o ask about the essential necessity of inner words in us is to ask about the essential necessity of our complementing acts of understanding with inner words to obtain knowledge of external things. The answer will be had by comparing the object of understanding with the external things. Now the first and proper object of understanding, the "what is known inasmuch as one understands," must be simply intelligible; accordingly, the proportionate object of our intellects is the *quidditas rei materialis*. This quiddity prescinds from individual matter, for individual matter is not intelligible in itself but only in its relation to the per se universality of forms which it individuates. Again the quiddity prescinds from contingent existence, for contingent existence is not intelligible in itself but only in its relation to the necessarily Existent which is final, exemplary, and efficient cause of contingent beings. The essential necessity of inner words in our intellects is the necessity of effecting the transition from the preconceptual *quidditas rei materialis*, first, to the *res*, secondly, to the *res particularis*, thirdly, to the *res particularis existens*. The transition from *quidditas rei* to *res*, say, from *humanitas* to *homo*, occurs in conception in which there emerges intellect's natural knowledge of *ens*. In virtue of this step understanding moves from identity with its preconceptual object to confrontation with its conceived object; but as yet the object is only object of thought. The second step is a reflection on phantasm that enables one to mean, though not understand nor explanatorily define, the material singular. In this step intellect moves from a universal to a particular object of thought. Finally, by a reflective act of understanding that sweeps through all relevant data, sensible and intelligible, present and remembered, and grasps

understanding's proportion to the universe as well, there is uttered the existential judgment through which one knows concrete reality.[38]

The point of the section in *The Triune God: Systematics* that we are studying is that such a necessity cannot be said to exist in God. The divine intellect is not moved to understanding by something other than itself, nor does it tend toward something else as toward an end. Infinite in perfection, it exists eternally, both comprehending itself and perfectly understanding and knowing all other things in itself.[39]

Lonergan then proceeds to respond to arguments that claim to demonstrate a divine Word. In doing so, he hammers home, as it were, various important points regarding his cognitional theory.

A first objection argues that understanding needs to be expressed in words if it is to be clear and distinct, and that, since God's knowledge is completely clear and distinct, it cannot be without its verbal expression. Lonergan responds that it is true that an understanding that occurs from the coalescence of many acts is not clear and distinct without words, but this is not the case with the understanding of a single infinite act. Moreover, since the word is merely the expression of what is made known through the act of understanding, it is not per se that the word adds clarity and distinctness to our understanding; rather, it is *per accidens*, that is, when there are many diverse and imperfect acts of understanding, that words are needed for clarity and distinctness. Thus, did we not utter inner words, we would hardly be able to know what we have already grasped and what remains to be investigated.[40]

A second objection would argue that the duality of subject and object is of the very essence of knowledge, and so a divine subject would have to speak a word to know himself; and since God knows himself, God speaks a word. Lonergan responds, of course, by denying the principle of this argument, which for him is grounded in an image of the person looking and the thing looked at. The principle is found in the Platonic positing of the eternal subsistent simple Ideas in a first order or place, and at a second level the gods who contemplate the Ideas. It is found in Scotus's *distinctio formalis a parte rei*, which Lonergan will return to later. It is found in Günther's and Rosmini's attempts to demonstrate the necessity of the divine Word. It is found in Jean-Paul Sartre's distinction of *en soi* and *pour soi*, and so in his insistence that a God conscious of himself and at the same time simple is an intrinsic contradiction. It is found in conceptions of consciousness as perception of oneself, a notion that leads to insoluble difficulties concerning the consciousness of Christ. On Aristotelian and Thomist grounds, the intelligible in act is the intellect in act, and in that which is without matter the intellect and the understood are the same. The intellect differs from the intelligible to the extent that each is in potency.[41] A further distinction in the cognitional order emerges precisely with the construction of the first inner word on the basis of original insight or understanding.

A third objection would affirm that a dynamic intellectual consciousness, that is, one in which there is something analogous to the procession of act from act, is a pure perfection, and so that it must be posited in the infinite perfection of God. Lonergan responds that, of course, the procession of Word in God *is* completely necessary and completely perfect; but in what *we* naturally know of God, there occurs no demonstration that *dynamic* intellectual consciousness is a pure perfection (since, I believe, in our experience of dynamic intellectual consciousness there are movements from potency to act);[42] and so there is no demonstration of the fact that a dynamic intellectual consciousness, one in which there are processions, must be posited in God. Moreover, even with the help of inner words, we cannot arrive at a perfect understanding of what we believe in faith concerning divine procession, for the reality of procession and the consubstantiality of the one who proceeds with the one from whom he proceeds seem to be at variance with each other. Only with difficulty can we consider them simultaneously and reconcile them.[43] It is precisely here that the real mystery resides. It cannot be arrived at or demonstrated from the natural use of our cognitive powers.

The matter is treated in somewhat greater detail in *Verbum*. Two questions are faced, having to do respectively with the primary and secondary objects of divine knowledge: (1) "Why cannot natural reason demonstrate the existence of the divine Word from the premise of divine self-knowledge?"[44] and (2) Does not divine knowledge of the other seem to require an inner word?

The first question is handled with dispatch.

> First, the demonstration cannot be effected by contrasting the proper object of understanding with the divine essence. God is simply intelligible. He is pure form identical with existence. There is no distinction between his essence or his existence or his intellect or his understanding. There is not even a distinction between his *esse naturale* and his *esse intelligibile.* Secondly, the demonstration cannot be effected by arguing that without an inner word there would be no confrontation between subject and object. For one cannot demonstrate that such confrontation is essential to knowledge. Primarily and essentially, knowing is by identity. The natural light of reason will never get beyond that identity in demonstrating the nature of self-knowledge in the infinite simplicity of God.[45]

The second of these arguments matches the second objection and response in *De Deo trino*, but the first is an additional argument, drawing on what has immediately preceded it in *Verbum* itself. What does it mean?

We require inner words because there *is* a contrast between the proper object of understanding, which must be simply intelligible, for us (in Scholastic language) the *quidditas* of the material thing, and any *thing* that we come to know as *res,* as *res particularis,* and as *res particularis existens;* the Scholastic language can be generalized into the expressions we have employed in attempting to move this consideration into a more existential, hermeneutical, and historical context. But when God knows Godself there is no contrast between the proper object of understanding, the intelligible, and the divine essence that God knows. And so that particular ground of the necessity of the inner word in us does not obtain for God's self-knowledge.

What, then, about the divine knowledge of the other? Does it not seem to require an inner word? After all, "the other is not simply intelligible, nor always in act, nor identical with the knower. Further, in confirmation of this argument, there is the fact that Aquinas wrote some of his finest passages on *verbum* in the context of divine knowledge of the other. In additional confirmation there is the familiar doctrine that secondary elements in the beatific vision are known *in Verbo.*"[46]

Lonergan treats the two confirming arguments first. They are based, he says, on a traditional association that Aquinas was heir to, namely, the connection between the divine Word and the divine Ideas, a connection that is to be found in the entire Christian Platonist tradition and can be traced back to Philo's conception of the Logos as containing the ideas. More than likely, there was no "intrinsic exigence of his own thought" that led Aquinas to treat *verbum* in the context of the divine ideas.[47] Where he differs from the Platonist tradition is not in this association but on the basic assumption regarding knowledge. "The Platonist assumption that knowledge involves confrontation led later Scholastics to attribute to the ideas an *esse obiectivum.* Certainly Aquinas was free from that error, and so he can be expected to apply the Aristotelian theorem of knowledge by identity to reconcile divine simplicity with divine knowledge of the other."[48]

Regarding the issue itself, then, there are two steps that Lonergan takes in *Verbum.* First, he draws distinctions regarding our knowledge. Second, he takes steps to move from this finite model to God.

Regarding our knowledge, Lonergan distinguishes "(1) the thing with its virtualities, (2) the act of understanding with its primary and its secondary objects, (3) the expression of both primary and secondary objects in inner words." An example is given in *Verbum* that probably is not very helpful to someone who has made the transition from "soul" to "subject,"[49] and so after quoting the example I will suggest what might be a better one.

> [T]he human soul formally is an intellective soul, subsistent, immortal; it is not formally a sensitive soul nor a vegetative soul; but

virtually it does possess the perfection without the imperfection of sensitive and vegetative souls. When, however, we understand the human soul, we understand as primary object an intellective soul and as secondary object the sensitive soul and the vegetative soul; both objects are understood formally and actually, but the secondary object is understood in the primary and in virtue of understanding the primary. Further, once understanding of the human soul has developed, there are not two acts of understanding but one, which primarily is of intellective soul and secondarily, in the perfection of intellective soul, is of the sensitive and vegetative souls. Finally, our one act of understanding expresses itself in many inner words in which are defined intellective, sensitive, and vegetative souls and the relations between them; further, these inner words are the *esse intelligibile* or the *esse intentionale* of soul as distinct both from the *esse naturale* of soul itself and from the *esse intellectum* which is an extrinsic denomination from an *intelligere* of soul whether real or intentional.[50]

A clearer example, in my view, would be the relation between primary and secondary objects expressed in Lonergan's famous statement toward the end of the introduction to *Insight*: "Thoroughly understand what it is to understand, and not only will you understand the broad lines of all there is to be understood but also you will possess a fixed base, an invariant pattern, opening upon all further developments of understanding."[51]

At any rate, what happens when one moves from the model suggested in *Verbum* to God?

[T]he divine essence formally is itself but eminently it contains all perfection. The divine act of understanding primarily is of the divine essence but secondarily of its virtualities. The divine Word that is uttered is one, but what is uttered in the one Word is all that God knows. Moreover, the divine essence, the divine act of understanding, and the divine Word considered absolutely are one and the same reality; hence there can be no real distinction between "contained eminently in the essence" and "secondary object of the understanding" or between either of these and "uttered in the one Word." Further, utterance in the one Word does not confer on the ideas an *esse intelligibile* that otherwise they would not possess; for in God *esse naturale* and *esse intelligibile* are identical. It remains, then, that divine knowledge of the other provides no premise whence the procession of the divine Word could be established by natural reason. The plurality of divine ideas within divine simplicity is accounted for by an infinite act of understanding grasping as secondary objects the perfections eminently contained in the divine essence and virtually in divine omnipotence. As we can understand *multa per unum*, all the more so can God.

Hence, though our *intelligere* is always a *dicere*, this cannot be demonstrated of God's. Though we can demonstrate that God understands, for understanding is pure perfection, still we can no more than conjecture the mode of divine understanding and so cannot prove that there is a divine Word. Psychological trinitarian theory is not a conclusion that can be demonstrated but a hypothesis that squares with divine revelation without excluding the possibility of alternative hypotheses. Finally, Aquinas regularly writes as a theologian and not as a philosopher; hence regularly he simply states what simply is true, that in all intellects there is a procession of inner word.[52]

2.3 Does the Word Proceed from the Father's Understanding of Creatures?

The third question is related to what we have just seen from *Verbum*. It asks whether the divine Word proceeds from (and so contains in its "being uttered," its *dici*) the Father's understanding of the Father alone or whether the divine Word proceeds also from the Father's understanding of creatures (including, of course, ourselves and all of human history, which is the aspect we are most concerned with in this volume).

Initially (and, it must be said, on a very superficial view), it would seem that the latter could not be the case, since the Word of God is necessary and eternal, while creatures are contingent and temporal. But Aquinas taught that the Father understands himself and creatures in one act of understanding and speaks himself and creatures in one Word, and also that, as the divine act of understanding knows itself, and both knows and creates creatures, so the Word of God expresses God and both expresses and is operative of creatures.[53] Thus, it is Thomas's teaching that the Word of God proceeds from the Father's eternal understanding of everything about everything and is actively creative of everything that is not God.

Lonergan's later articulation of the first step in the analogy, where the Father is conceived not in terms of understanding but as *Agapē*, only deepens our awe and wonder at the claim that Thomas and Lonergan are making. The divine act of understanding knows itself and both knows and creates creatures. But also divine *Agapē* knows and loves itself and knows, loves, and creates the proportionate universe, including the dimensions of that universe that have evolved into human history and that continue to unfold precisely as *Geschichte*. In this realm "the higher system of intellectual development is primarily the higher integration, not of the man in whom the development occurs, but of the universe that he inspects."[54] Here, evolving proportionate being becomes the very notion of being and value aiming at and heading toward a knowledge and love of everything about everything. In fidelity to those transcendental notions lies the integrity of that dimension of the universe that has become human history. Into that dimension, and for the sake of redeeming it from the implications of infidelity, stepped the incarnate Word, the one in whom the entire universe, including the history into which the Word was born in creaturely flesh, has been uttered from eternity. He is the Utterance itself, and through the created relation of his assumed human nature to the Father and so his created participation in divine paternity, he utters the Father's Word which he himself is.

One could spend a lifetime meditating on the profound significance of this claim, for our understanding both of God and of ourselves. Do we make a difference to God? In one sense, no, we do not, that is, in the sense that, as Lonergan says, there are no divine afterthoughts.[55] In another, more profound sense, we make an eternal difference to God. God is eternally what God is because the unrestricted act of understanding, affirming, and loving knows, creates, and loves the entire order of the universe and everything in it, and utters the eternal decree that the Word becomes flesh in human history, born of the Virgin Mary, and discloses to us the secrets of God's reign: secrets intimately connected with the mystery of violence and evil from which the eternal Word become flesh would suffer and because of which he would die; and utters too the eternal decree regarding the universal mission of the Holy Spirit, sent in time even before the Word but requiring the Word to articulate the message that the Spirit writes in our hearts regarding God's love for us, the commandment that we love God and neighbor, and the precept regarding nonviolent response to evil. In the light of the subsequent mission of the Word, the mission of the Holy Spirit has the further task of continually reminding us of all that was revealed in the visible mission of the Word.

Let us return to Lonergan's text. The problem mentioned at the beginning of this section, namely, that the Word of God cannot proceed from the Father's understanding of creatures because the Word is necessary and eternal while creatures are contingent and temporal, is resolved, Lonergan says, by correctly grasping the nature of the psychological analogy. Our inner words do not proceed from objects. Nobody who conceives the emanation of the inner word as proceeding from an object, as the act of seeing proceeds from colors, will ever be able to admit that the divine Word proceeds from the understanding of creatures. One will have less difficulty admitting this if one conceives the inner word as proceeding from knowledge of the object, since the object then is not the cause *simpliciter* but a kind of co-cause. But one will have no difficulty whatsoever if one grasps the nature of intellectual consciousness itself, or of what I am calling spiritual autonomy. The proper principle of an autonomous spiritual procession is not the object but the subject. The emanation of the inner word is possible only to the extent that the subject is intellectually conscious in act. How much more is this the case with God, who is the first principle of all things.[56]

Moreover, the necessity of the emanation of the word and of the emanation of love, or better, the *exigency for these autonomous spiritual processions*, arises not from the object understood and loved but from the conscious spirituality of the subject: because intelligent consciousness is bound, owes it to itself (*sibi debet*), truly to express its understanding to itself, what is understood must be truly expressed; because intelligent consciousness is bound to bestow its love in a morally good way, what is truly judged to be good must also be loved. We are bound to judge on the basis of evidence and to choose on the basis of sound judgment, even to the extent that, should our understanding be deficient or our judgment in error, an unknown obligation does not hold us to act contrary to conscience; rather, the known obligation binds us to judge on the basis of evidence and to choose on the basis of judgment.[57]

This brings us back to the notion of spiritual autonomy. Lest it be thought that this is to exaggerate the autonomy of intellectual consciousness, Lonergan is quick to add, first of all, that divine autonomy (which is really what we are considering here) is absolute and so cannot be exaggerated; and second, even the autonomy of human consciousness, which supplies the analogy for the divine processions, is subordinate *not to any object*, and, we might add in the context of our considerations from Girard, not to any mediator of objects, but *only to the infinite subject* in whose image it is made and which it is bound to imitate.[58] Its autonomy resides precisely in the image in which it is made, the image of divine autonomy understanding, affirming, and loving; its authenticity resides in its fidelity to that image. Lonergan's intentionality analysis discloses in what that fidelity lies in the realm of nature, and the Gospel reveals the further component: "You must be perfect as your heavenly Father is perfect," where being perfect means mercy and forgiveness in the face of evil.

The concluding part of Lonergan's discussion may seem more remote and less pertinent to the kind of theology we are seeking to develop, but I hope to show in the final paragraph of this section that it does not detract at all from the emphases I have been highlighting. I include this material for the sake of completeness, since I wish to be as thorough as possible in presenting Lonergan's Trinitarian theology and transposing it into the context of a theology of history. Lonergan is here addressing himself to Scholastic disputes and questions. Again, while he addresses the issue in terms of divine understanding, his later starting point is divine *Agapē*, and so I will include both understanding and love in my exposure of his position.

Different objects enter, he argues, in different ways both into the act of understanding whence there proceeds the divine Word, and into the act of understanding and Word whence there proceeds divine Love. The primary object of divine understanding is the divine Trinitarian act of existence itself. All other objects are secondary objects. Moreover, these secondary objects are connected with the primary object in different ways. They may be "possibles under the formality of being," "possibles under the formality of possibility," or past, present, and future actual realities.[59]

"Possibles under the formality of being" are identical with God's active power, the power that can create them. Thus, the Father understands and speaks the "possibles" insofar as he understands and speaks his own power, which is one with his own essence and act of understanding.

"Possibles under the formality of possibility" are in the Father's understanding and speaking in the manner of what Lonergan calls an implicit being of reason: a being of reason, because the entire reality of the "possibles" is the divine active power itself; an *implicit* being of reason, because God does not speak as many distinct words as there are distinct "possibles," but only one Word, and so the "possibles as possibles" are spoken in the one Word. Nonetheless, they are all and each distinctly in God insofar as the Father, by understanding God's own power, clearly and distinctly understands each and every possible being, and by speaking God's own power, clearly and distinctly speaks in one infinite Word each and every possible being.

Finally, all past, present, and future actual beings God intuits by understanding and speaks by the Word and loves with the Love that proceeds from Understanding and Word. If another world existed, God would intuit and speak and love those other beings as actual, not because God can be now this and now that, and not because divine processions can be now this and now that, but because the knowledge and affirmation and love of actual beings add only a relation of reason to the infinite act of understanding and affirming and loving.[60]

Thus, the procession of the divine Word depends on the divine intellectual consciousness and on the infinite act of understanding. Because these are one not only with one another but also with the divine act of existence, the divine essence, and the divine power, the divine emanation of the Word depends as well on the divine essence and power. Furthermore, because divine understanding includes the possibles as possibles in the mode of an implicit being of reason, the divine emanation of the Word has an exigency to speak the possibles as possibles in the mode of an implicit being of reason. Again, because the divine understanding, due to the addition of a relation of reason over and above the infinite act, understands all actual beings as they are, the emanation of the divine Word has an exigency that, with this addition of a relation of reason, all these actual beings be spoken in the Word, and the divine emanation of Love has an exigency that, again with the addition of a relation of reason, all actual beings be loved with the Love that proceeds from understanding and Word. Finally, because the divine understanding clearly grasps that the divine Word and the divine Love do not depend on a relation of reason, because it clearly perceives that all actual and possible beings depend on divine understanding, on the divine Word, on divine Love, the divine Word proceeds from an understanding of creatures in such a way that creatures are spoken as truly and eternally dependent on the Word, and the divine Love proceeds from the divine understanding and affirmation of creatures in such a way that the creatures are truly and eternally loved as dependent upon this divine love.[61]

None of this affects the truth of the statement that we made earlier, that in a very definite sense we do make an eternal difference to God. For while the divine Word and the divine Love do not depend on, are not changed by, relations of reason, while all actual and possible creaturely realities depend rather on divine understanding, on the divine Word, and on divine Love, still among the creaturely realities included in this dependence are the *esse secundarium incarnationis* and the gift of sanctifying grace, both decreed from eternity as created participations in and imitations of divine life itself.

2.4   The Presence of the Beloved within the Lover: Is It Constituted or Produced by Love?

Thesis 60: *A still further enrichment occurs when Lonergan's question whether the presence of the beloved within the lover is constituted or produced by love is transformed by the shift of the basic starting point of the analogy from understanding to being in love and from being in love to being on the receiving end of a love that is unqualified and absolute.*

2.4.1   The Treatment in *De Deo Trino*

The fourth question to which Lonergan devotes special attention in his chapter on the divine processions has to do with the analogical conception of the procession of the Holy Spirit as the procession of love, and principally with the analogy itself, with the procession of love in human dynamic intellectual consciousness. The question is raised in the context of an intramural debate among Thomists, namely, a debate regarding the theory of John of St Thomas regarding vital act. According to this position every vital act is produced by that potency in which it is received, and so love must be produced by the will itself in which it is received. This is not the position of St Thomas, but it has been held by many Thomists. Lonergan's treatment of the issue in *De Deo trino* is an extensive refutation of this position, drawing both on the authority of Aquinas and on Lonergan's own arguments from our experience of the procession of love in human consciousness.

My concern will be quite different from the context of the Thomist debate. Lonergan's position on the relation of knowledge and love, which is at the heart of his position as expressed in *De Deo trino*, changed in the course of his career, and this is the issue that will occupy us here. This is the point, then, at which the issue of Lonergan's early and later analogies for the procession of the Holy Spirit must be raised. Again, the question is most relevant to the discussion of the so-called fifth level of consciousness, or better of that level that is beyond, and a higher integration of, the four levels of presentations, understanding, judgment, and decision. The fifth level, the level of love, is itself interpersonal. It is the level of total self-transcendence to another, whether in the love of intimacy or in love in the community or in the love of God, or in some combination of these. It is a level of consciousness effected by the gift of another's love and the challenge and decision to love in return.

The intramural Thomist context demanded that Lonergan ask the question in the following form: Is the presence of the beloved in the lover *constituted* by love, or is it *produced* by love? That is, is it really the same as love, as the act of loving (and so constituted by love), or is it really distinct from love and something that proceeds from love and so something that is produced by love in the mode of a *processio operati*? Does love "operate" something, namely, the presence of the beloved in the lover, or is that presence constituted by the very procession of love from the grasp of sufficient conditions and the judgment of value that follows upon that grasp? This later becomes for Lonergan the question of a fifth level of consciousness, where personal consciousness is itself interpersonal. In other words, there is a continuous line, from the affirmation that Lonergan provides in this section that the presence of the beloved in the lover is constituted by love and so is not distinct from love, to the late acknowledgment of an interpersonal core of personal identity conceived at times by the post-*Method* Lonergan in terms of a fifth level of consciousness.

The first question we might ask is, What difference does it make? If the presence of the beloved in the lover is constituted by love, then the beloved is in the lover through the procession of love, and the issue is to understand that procession itself. The beloved would be in the lover through the procession, just as the "thing," the situation or state of affairs spoken, is in the one who understands through the conception of the word. If the presence of the beloved in the lover is constituted by love, then the beloved is in the lover through the procession of love; the presence of the beloved in the lover is the same as love itself, the same as the act of loving itself. Then, within the context of the faculty psychology that Lonergan is employing at this point, the Trinitarian analogy is based on a first procession within the intellect, the procession of act from act manifest in the emergence of the word from understanding, and a second procession *from the intellect into the will,* a procession of act from act manifest in the emergence of love from the grasp of sufficient evidence and the consequent judgment of value. We judge *because and to the extent that* we have grasped sufficient evidence (procession of the word), and we choose or love *because and to the extent that* we have judged (procession of love). The "thing spoken or understood" is constituted in the one who understands through the word itself; the "beloved" is constituted in the lover through the proceeding love itself.

If, on the other hand, the presence of the beloved in the lover is produced by love, then the presence of the beloved in the lover is something distinct from the act of loving, and then the Trinitarian analogy is based on a *processio operati* within the intellect and a distinct *processio operati* not from the intellect into the will but within the will itself. From the act of understanding there comes forth a conception of the understood presentations in the one who understands, and similarly from one's love there comes forth a distinct impression of the beloved reality in the affections of the lover. The word is produced through the act of understanding, and the presence of the beloved in the lover is produced through the act of loving. This second position is in accord with John of St Thomas's theory of vital act, which Lonergan maintains, correctly, is not found in Aquinas's works.

The immediate relevance of the question for Lonergan has to do with the psychological analogy for the procession of the Holy Spirit. If the second of these ways of thinking about the presence of the beloved in the lover is the correct way of thinking about it, then the analogy that Lonergan has set up breaks down. For that analogy states that the procession of the Holy Spirit from the Father and the Son is analogous to the procession of the presence of the beloved in the lover as flowing from understanding and word. Thus, the analogy is drawn from the first of these ways of thinking rather than from the second.

We have already seen in passing, in our discussion of Lonergan's treatment of the previous question as to whether the Word proceeds from the understanding of creatures, the general approach that he will take to the procession of Love within God. All past, present, and future actual beings God intuits by understanding and speaks by the Word and *loves with the Love that proceeds from understanding and Word.* Thus, the analogy has Lonergan opting for the view that the presence of the beloved in the lover is *constituted by a love that proceeds from understanding and word, and so not by a love that is produced by a distinct act in the will.* He views this as the position of St Thomas, and in so doing he differs from John of St Thomas and Thomists in general.

Two different theoretical systems are represented in the question. The position that Lonergan rejects bases its conception on the assumption that there are in our dynamic intellectual consciousness two processions, one within the intellect and the other within the will; in the first, the act of understanding produces the word, and in the second the act of loving produces the presence of the beloved in the lover. This is the position of John of St Thomas and of most Thomists. Lonergan's own position is based on the *experience* of two processions, of which the first is within the intellect and the second is *from* the intellect *into* the will. By reason of the first procession we judge because and to the extent that we grasp sufficient evidence, and by reason of the second procession we choose because and to the extent that we judge. Lonergan's own articulation of this position precisely in terms of experience, and so of self-appropriation, occurs most sharply, I believe, in chapter 18 of *Insight*, and so the model that he is working from is what I have identified as the general form of one of three possible "times" of making decisions, St Ignatius's third time.

Actually, Lonergan begins by quoting two texts from St Thomas, one of which seems to favor Lonergan's position, and the other the opposed position.

In the first text (*Summa theologiae*, 1, q. 27, a. 3 c.) the beloved is said to be in the lover *by the procession of love* (*processio amoris, secundum quam amatum est in amante*), just as the thing spoken or understood is in the one who understands through the conception of the word (*sicut per conceptionem verbi res dicta vel intellecta est in intelligente*). As the thing spoken or understood is in the one understanding through the word, so the beloved is in the lover through the love that proceeds.[62]

But in the second text (*Summa theologiae*, 1, q. 37, a. 1 c.), from the fact that someone understands there emerges in the one who understands the conception of the thing understood, and similarly from the fact that someone loves there emerges a certain impression of the beloved in the affections of the lover. For the word is produced through the act of understanding, and in parallel fashion the presence of the beloved in the lover is produced, it seems, through the act of loving.[63]

Which of these positions is correct? Are there in us two processions, one of which is in the intellect and the other of which is in the will, so that according to the first the act of understanding produces the word and according to the second the act of loving produces the presence of the beloved in the lover? Or is it rather our *experience* that there are in us two processions of which the first is in the intellect – we judge because we grasp sufficient evidence and in accord with the evidence grasped – and the second is from the intellect into the will – we choose and love because we judge and in accord with the judgment of value that we have made? Clearly, Lonergan's position favors the latter option. And his analogy for the procession of the Holy Spirit depends upon it. My own suggestion is that, given the proximity of the two texts of Aquinas to each other, the question itself was not an explicit one for Aquinas at the time of the composition of the Trinitarian portion of the first part of the *Summa theologiae.* Lonergan is certainly right in his interpretation of Thomas's position regarding vital act, and that alone would lend strong support to his position on Aquinas's meaning on this particular question. But the issue for Lonergan is really one of experience and self-appropriation.

If the issue is one of experience, it has to do precisely with experience in that domain of interiority in which we have located whatever genuine autonomy the human subject can achieve. In treating the option that he prefers, Lonergan uses the words "in nobis experimur." Similarly, he says that he rejects the mainline Thomist view "tum quia *ab experientia nostra interna* praescindit in concipienda analogia trinitaria et psychologica, tum quia *ab experientia nostra interna* praescindit in interpretandis textibus S. Thomae de re psychologica."[64]

Lonergan proceeds to cite other passages from St Thomas that show that for St Thomas the beloved is present in the lover because love is present, not because anything is produced in the will through the act of love. I will not repeat these here, as they can easily be found in *The Triune God: Systematics.* Lonergan concludes, correctly it seems, that St Thomas explicitly taught: (1) the second procession is one of love from the word; (2) the Holy Spirit is both "amatum in amante" and proceeding love; (3) there is not a procession in the will except *per modum operationis*; and (4) the beloved is present in the lover because the beloved is loved (*secundum quod amatur*).

2.4.2 "Nihil Amatum Nisi Praecognitum": Is This True?

One of the more surprising developments in Lonergan's later years was his calling into question the basic order of operations on which the analogy for the divine processions is based. More specifically, what Lonergan questions is the assertion that we do not love anything except inasmuch as we apprehend it in a mental conception. The shift, however, affects not the procession of the Holy Spirit as such but rather the starting point of the entire analogy. While the shift occurred before the publication of *Method in Theology*, it punctuates that book, and I will present here the principal instances of the shift in *Method in Theology*, locating each of the instances in its proper context.

The shift in question is introduced in the discussion of faith in the chapter on religion. Faith is distinguished from beliefs, and is defined as "the knowledge born of religious love." Lonergan explains:

> [T]here is a knowledge born of love. Of it Pascal spoke when he remarked that the heart has reasons which reason does not know. Here by reason I would understand the compound of the activities on the first three levels of cognitional activity, namely, of experiencing, of understanding, and of judging. By the heart's reasons I would understand feelings that are intentional responses to values; and I would recall the two aspects of such responses, the absolute aspect that is a recognition of value, and the relative aspect that is a preference of one value over another. Finally, by the heart I understand the subject on the fourth, existential level of intentional consciousness and in the dynamic state of being in love. The meaning, then, of Pascal's remark would be that, besides the factual knowledge reached by experiencing, understanding, and verifying, there is another kind of knowledge reached through the discernment of value and the judgments of value of a person in love.[65]

That further knowledge will be of different kinds, depending on the love from which it is born. Faith is that further knowledge when the love is God's love flooding our hearts.

The theme is picked up several pages later in the concluding section of the chapter on religion, where Lonergan is explaining the consequences of the shift from a theology that acknowledges only the two realms of common sense and theory to one that distinguishes four realms of meaning, namely, common sense, theory, interiority, and transcendence.

> [T]he older theology, when it spoke of inner experience or of God, either did so within the realm of common sense – and then its speech was shot through with figure and symbol – or else it did so in the realm of theory – and then its speech was basically metaphysical. One consequence of this difference has already been noted. The older theology conceived sanctifying grace as an entitative habit, absolutely supernatural, infused into the essence of the soul. On the other hand, because we acknowledge interiority as a distinct realm of meaning, we can begin with a description of religious experience, acknowledge a dynamic state of being in love without restrictions, and later identify this state with the state of sanctifying grace.
>
> … It used to be said, *Nihil amatum nisi praecognitum*, Knowledge precedes love. The truth of this tag is the fact that ordinarily

operations on the fourth level of intentional consciousness presuppose and complement corresponding operations on the other three. There is a minor exception to this rule inasmuch as people do fall in love, and that falling in love is something disproportionate to its causes, conditions, occasions, antecedents. For falling in love is a new beginning, an exercise of vertical liberty in which one's world undergoes a new organization. But the major exception to the Latin tag is God's gift of his love flooding our hearts. Then we are in the dynamic state of being in love. But who it is we love, is neither given nor as yet understood. Our capacity for moral self-transcendence has found a fulfilment that brings deep joy and profound peace. Our love reveals to us values we had not appreciated, values of prayer and worship, or repentance and belief. But if we would know what is going on within us, if we would learn to integrate it with the rest of our living, we have to inquire, investigate, seek counsel. So it is that in religious matters love precedes knowledge and, as that love is God's gift, the very beginning of faith is due to God's grace.[66]

Again, we have the following on religiously differentiated consciousness, introduced in a section whose main purpose is to discuss the "more benign yet still puzzling variety" of pluralism that "has its root in the differentiation of human consciousness."[67]

> [L]et us consider religiously differentiated consciousness. It can be content with the negations of an apophatic theology. For it is in love. On its love there are not any restrictions or conditions or qualifications. By such love it is oriented positively to what is transcendent in lovableness. Such a positive orientation and the consequent self-surrender, as long as they are operative, enable one to dispense with any intellectually apprehended object. And when they cease to be operative, the memory of them enables one to be content with enumerations of what God is not.
>
> It may be objected that *nihil amatum nisi praecognitum*. But while that is true of other human love, it need not be true of the love with which God floods our hearts through the Holy Spirit he has given us (Rom. 5, 5). That grace could be the finding that grounds our seeking God through natural reason and through positive religion. It could be the touchstone by which we judge whether it is really God that natural reason reaches or positive religion preaches. It could be the grace that God offers all men, that underpins what is good in the religions of mankind, that explains how those that never heard

the gospel can be saved. It could be what enables the simple faithful to pray to their heavenly Father in secret even though their religious apprehensions are faulty. Finally, it is in such grace that can be found the theological justification of Catholic dialogue with all Christians, with non-Christians, and even with atheists who may love God in their hearts while not knowing him with their heads.[68]

The transcultural aspect of the shift is highlighted in the following passage.

> … God's give of his love … has a transcultural aspect. For if this gift is offered to all men, if it is manifested more or less authentically in the many and diverse religions of mankind, if it is apprehended in as many different manners as there are different cultures, still the gift itself as distinct from its manifestations is transcultural. For of other love it is true enough that it presupposes knowledge – *nihil amatum nisi praecognitum*. But God's gift of his love is free. It is not conditioned by human knowledge; rather it is the cause that leads man to seek knowledge of God. It is not restricted to any stage or section of human culture but rather is the principle that introduces a dimension of other-worldliness into any culture. All the same, it remains true, of course, that God's gift of his love has its proper counterpart in the revelation events in which God discloses to a particular people or to all mankind the completeness of his love for them. For being-in-love is properly itself, not in the isolated individual, but only in a plurality of persons that disclose their love to one another.[69]

Finally, we have the following, in a section on the consequences of moving beyond faculty psychology to intentionality analysis.

> [T]here arises the possibility of an exception to the old adage, *Nihil amatum nisi praecognitum*. Specifically, it would seem that God's gift of his love … is not something that results from or is conditioned by man's knowledge of God. Far more plausibly it would seem that the gift may precede our knowledge of God and, indeed, may be the cause of our seeking knowledge of God. In that case the gift by itself would be an orientation towards an unknown. Still, the orientation reveals its goal by its absoluteness; it is with all one's heart and all one's soul and with all one's mind and all one's strength. It is, then, an orientation to what is transcendent in lovableness and, when that is unknown, it is an orientation to transcendent mystery.[70]

The significance of the shift for the Trinitarian analogy is, in one sense, enormous. And yet the only real change in the analogy itself is in the starting point.

> The psychological analogy ... has its starting point in that higher synthesis of intellectual, rational, and moral consciousness that is the dynamic state of being in love. Such love manifests itself in its judgments of value. And the judgments are carried out in decisions that are acts of loving. Such is the analogy found in the creature.[71]

It has been objected to my use of this passage that I was too facile in interpreting Lonergan's reference in this passage to "the dynamic state of being in love" as denoting religious love.[72] While I have conceded that the psychological analogy presented in Lonergan's later work may properly begin from any of the three kinds of love that Lonergan emphasizes – the love of intimacy in the family, love in the community, and the love of God – still I have argued that it is legitimate to conceive an analogy that begins with religious love. I must add, though, that there are also serious exegetical grounds for the position that I have taken. In the quotation just given, there is mention of "the dynamic state of being in love," and in one of the quotations from *Method in Theology* that I have cited, that expression is reserved for "God's gift of his love flooding our hearts. *Then* we are in the dynamic state of being in love."[73] At any rate, in response to the objections, I have presented my argument for continuing to develop an analogy in the order of grace, and I take my stand on that argument[74] and continue to attempt to mine the riches of the hypothesis that such an analogy allows. As I have argued elsewhere, there are definitely two distinct but structurally isomorphic analogies in Lonergan's work for understanding the divine processions, the first being the analogy presented in *The Triune God: Systematics*, which we presented in chapter 11, and the second being the analogy suggested in his later work. I am suggesting something beyond even the latter analogy, but recognizing that the development both of Lonergan's later analogy and of the analogy that I am proposing depends on first grasping the earlier analogy from nature. If I am correct that a valid analogy proceeds within the supernatural order, then understanding it depends on working out the earlier analogy in the order of nature and making the necessary transpositions to the order of grace. This is precisely what I have attempted to do here.

I have indicated how the analogy that I wish to develop would proceed. I think it is sufficient in the present context to indicate that the shift in the relation between knowledge and love that is so prominent in Lonergan's later work does not affect so much the analogical understanding of the procession of the Holy Spirit as it does the very starting point of the analogy that

I am suggesting. The procession of the Holy Spirit is still conceived on the analogy of love, charity, proceeding from knowledge, including the *verbum spirans amorem* of the judgments of value of someone in the dynamic state of being in love; charity proceeds from faith as the knowledge born of the gift of God's love, a knowledge that is a participation in the invisible mission of the divine Word. And the gift itself proceeds from the divine knowledge and love from which the Holy Spirit proceeds in the life immanent to God.

It remains to extend a number of our considerations beyond the realms of religious and personal values to discuss more fully the social manifestations of grace at the other levels in the scale of values constitutive of historical integrity, and to integrate that understanding with the mission of the incarnate Word. These tasks involve relating Lonergan's theology of the divine missions to his theology of the divine relations and the divine persons. To this point we have been content with some understanding of the relation of the missions and the processions. We will proceed in a second volume to the missions and the relations, and then to the missions and the persons, with an eye to the influence of the missions, as constitutive of "religious values," on the cultural and social levels of value in the normative scale of values. With that, a reasonably coherent set of heuristic proposals regarding the presence and operation of the Trinity in history will be complete. Our leitmotif hypothesis already expresses grace as primarily participation in the divine relations. Moreover, I have suggested that graced participation in the divine relations of active and passive spiration provides the "special basic relations" of systematic theology in its entirety, in a transposition of the notions of sanctifying grace and charity, which are respectively the created participations in active and passive spiration, into the language of intentionality analysis and religious self-appropriation. Whether this participation be *vécu* (as it almost always is) or *thématique* (which perhaps is one of the great theological and ecclesial challenges of our age), it is constitutive of "religious values" in the normative scale of values. In this volume, where our focus has been on the relation of mission and procession, we have studied in abundance the relation between religious values and personal development and integrity. As we move to a fuller and more explicit treatment of the connection between the divine relations and the divine missions, we will move as well to a consideration of the relation of religious values to cultural and social values. That relation is mediated through the personal values that have come to the fore in this volume. For these personal values can be understood largely in terms of the autonomous spiritual processions that form the natural analogue for the divine processions. In fact, no specifically theological theme is more appropriate for considering cultural and social values than that of the divine relations and our created participation in them through grace. For that participation will itself be relational, and personal relations are at the heart of the social mediation of the human good. In fact, the state of grace is for Lonergan itself an interpersonal situation, where the founding persons are the divine Three, and where we are all invited to allow ourselves to be caught up in the circumincession of divine life. Our participation in the divine relations through grace is an elevation also of our relatedness to our fellow men and women, and in fact to all creation. That elevation will be mediated historically through cultural and social values. That is the next part of our theological vision to be established and communicated.

Notes

Introduction

1 Robert M. Doran, *Theology and the Dialectics of History* (Toronto: University of Toronto Press, 1990, 2001).

2 Robert M. Doran, "Consciousness and Grace," METHOD: *Journal of Lonergan Studies* 11:1 (1993) 51–75.

3 Robert M. Doran, "Revisiting 'Consciousness and Grace,'" METHOD: *Journal of Lonergan Studies* 13:2 (1995) 151–59.

4 Bernard Lonergan, *The Triune God: Systematics*, vol. 12 in Collected Works of Bernard Lonergan, trans. Michael G. Shields, ed. Robert M. Doran and H. Daniel Monsour (Toronto: University of Toronto Press, 2007).

5 Bernard Lonergan, *Divinarum Personarum Conceptionem Analogicam Evolvit B. Lonergan* (Rome: Gregorian University Press, 1957, 1959).

6 Bernard Lonergan, *Early Latin Theology*, vol. 19 in Collected Works of Bernard Lonergan, trans. Michael G. Shields, ed. Robert M. Doran and H. Daniel Monsour (Toronto: University of Toronto Press, 2011). The notes in question constitute the seventh part of this volume.

7 Frederick E. Crowe, "Son of God, Holy Spirit, and World Religions," in *Appropriating the Lonergan Idea*, ed. Michael Vertin (Toronto: University of Toronto Press, 2006) 324–43.

8 The doctrinal portion of Lonergan's trinitarian theology may be found in *The Triune God: Doctrines*, vol. 11 in Collected Works of Bernard Lonergan, trans. Michael G. Shields, ed. Robert M. Doran and H. Daniel Monsour (Toronto: University of Toronto Press, 2009).

Chapter 1

1   This chapter and the other chapters in this first part draw on and integrate previous papers: my 2007 Emmett Doerr Lecture at Marquette University, which has the same title as is here given part 1, and which was subsequently published in *Philosophy and Theology* in 2009; lectures delivered at the 2009 West Coast Methods Institute, held at Loyola Marymount University, and at the 2009 Lonergan Workshop, held at Boston College, entitled respectively "The Four *Entia Supernaturalia*: Expanding the 1957 Hypothesis with Earlier Course Notes" and "Sanctifying Grace, Charity, and Divine Indwelling: A Key to the *Nexus Mysteriorum Fidei*"; the latter is to be published in the proceedings of the 2009 workshop, and both can now be found on www. lonerganresource.com, under Scholarly Works – Books; my 2009 Emmett Doerr Lecture at Marquette, "What Is the Gift of the Holy Spirit?" now available on www.lonerganresource.com, under "Events – Conferences – Doing Catholic Theology in a Multi-religious World"; a paper entitled "Social Grace" delivered at the 2010 West Coast Methods Institute, and now published in *Method: Journal of Lonergan Studies* new series 2:2 (2011) 131–42, and also currently available on the previously mentioned website; a paper entitled "Functional Specialties for a World Theology," prepared for the 2010 Lonergan Workshop and to be published in the proceedings of that workshop, again available on the website; and my 2010 Doerr Lecture, "Social Grace and the Mission of the Word," again available under "Events – Conferences" on the same site.

2   Bernard Lonergan, *Method in Theology* (Toronto: University of Toronto Press, 1990) 271–76.

3   Robert M. Doran, *Theology and the Dialectics of History* (Toronto: University of Toronto Press, 1990, 2001) and *What Is Systematic Theology?* (Toronto: University of Toronto Press, 2005). The present part 1 traces developments in my thinking since the publication of *What Is Systematic Theology?*

4   Bernard Lonergan, *Insight: A Study of Human Understanding*, vol. 3 in Collected Works of Bernard Lonergan, ed. Frederick E. Crowe and Robert M. Doran (Toronto: University of Toronto Press, 1992).

5   See Bernard Lonergan, *Method in Theology* (Toronto: University of Toronto Press, 2003) 321, referring to DS 3016.

6   Karl Rahner, "The Human Question of Meaning in Face of the Absolute Mystery of God," *Theological Investigations* 18 (New York: Crossroad, 1983) 97.

7   The last forty years have witnessed to Lonergan's prescience in the following remark at the end of his pivotal paper "Dimensions of Meaning": "There is bound to be formed a solid right that is determined to live in a world that no longer exists. There is bound to be formed a scattered left,

captivated by now this, now that new development, exploring now this and now that new possibility. But what will count is a perhaps not numerous center, big enough to be at home in both the old and the new, painstaking enough to work out one by one the transitions to be made, strong enough to refuse half measures and insist on complete solutions even though it has to wait." Bernard Lonergan, "Dimensions of Meaning," in *Collection*, vol. 4 in Collected Works of Bernard Lonergan, ed. Frederick E. Crowe and Robert M. Doran (Toronto: University of Toronto Press, 1988) 245. The scattered left that determined much of church life in the wake of the Council has given way to the solid right that has gained ascendancy in our time and seems determined to renounce the genuine advances of the Council. Lonergan is ignored by both of these extremes in Catholic theology, by the right for being original and for despoiling modernity of its genuine gains, and by the left for being faithful to the dogmatic tradition. Neither extreme, in my view, will prove ultimately to be even orthodox, let alone effective. The not too numerous center will hold the course, in season and out, whether acknowledged widely or not.

8 Lonergan, *Method in Theology* 347, with reference to DS 3020.

9 See Robert M. Doran, *What Is Systematic Theology?* 39, 78–79, 89, 92, 144–46, 203.

10 This is emphasized in notes for Lonergan's 1959 course at the Gregorian University, "De intellectu et methodo." These notes will be published in Bernard Lonergan, *Early Works on Theological Method 2*, vol. 23 in Collected Works of Bernard Lonergan, trans. Michael G. Shields, ed. Robert M. Doran and H. Daniel Monsour (forthcoming from University of Toronto Press, 2013). Lonergan is drawing at least loosely on Gödel's theorem in mathematics. For his understanding of this theorem in its own context, see Bernard Lonergan, *Phenomenology and Logic*, vol. 18 in Collected Works of Bernard Lonergan, ed. Philip J. McShane (Toronto: University of Toronto Press, 2001) 49–67. For his application of it to his own cognitional theory, see Lonergan, *Insight* 19–20.

11 See Lonergan, *Method in Theology*, the chapters on Dialectic and Foundations.

12 See, among other places, Bernard Lonergan, "Reality, Myth, Symbol," in *Philosophical and Theological Papers 1965–1980*, vol. 17 in Collected Works of Bernard Lonergan, ed. Robert C. Croken and Robert M. Doran (Toronto: University of Toronto Press, 2005) 384–90, at 390. For Lonergan's use of the expression "tidal movement," see "Natural Right and Historical Mindedness," in *A Third Collection*, ed. Frederick E. Crowe (Mahwah, NJ: Paulist, 1985) 175; and for "the passionateness of being," see "Mission and the Spirit," ibid. 29–30. In both instances, the reality referred to by these expressions, which is ultimately the vertical finality of proportionate being

as this becomes humanly conscious, is related to the levels of intentional consciousness.

It has long been my contention that precision with regard to the way in which the two equiprimordial constitutive ways of being *Dasein* are related to each other is a crucial question. It is the question I have attempted in many ways to answer in my writings on psychic conversion. Answering it may prove to be the key to the complex relations between Lonergan's thought and Heidegger's. See my paper "Two Ways of Being Conscious: The Notion of Psychic Conversion," to be published in *METHOD: Journal of Lonergan Studies*.

13 Warrant for such an expression may be found in Bernard Lonergan, *Early Works in Theological Method 1*, vol. 22 in Collected Works of Bernard Lonergan, ed. Robert M. Doran and Robert C. Croken (Toronto: University of Toronto Press, 2010) 400.

14 The four biases are discussed in chapters 6 and 7 of *Insight*. While the structure and dynamics of psychic conversion are presented in *Theology and the Dialectics of History*, especially in chapters 2 and 6–10, I have since come to think of the dramatic bias that psychic conversion meets at its roots as related intimately (though not exclusively) to Max Scheler's notion of *ressentiment* and to René Girard's theory of mimetic rivalry and envy. See Max Scheler, *Ressentiment*, trans. William W. Holdheim, ed. Lewis A. Coser (New York: The Free Press of Glencoe, 1961). References to Girard's works will be given as they become relevant; Girard in particular will be a very important interlocutor as we attempt to suggest the parameters of a contemporary systematic theology. In my view the theories of *ressentiment* and mimetic rivalry contribute enormously to articulating general categories for a theology of original sin and an understanding of redemption.

15 See Ben F. Meyer, *Critical Realism and the New Testament* (Eugene, OR: Pickwick, 1989); *The Aims of Jesus* (Eugene, OR: Pickwick, 2002); *Reality and Illusion in New Testament Scholarship: A Primer in Critical Realist Hermeneutics* (Collegeville, MN: Michael Glazier, 1994). For a succinct statement of Meyer's appropriation of Lonergan's interpretation theory, see his "The Primacy of the Intended Sense of Texts," in *Lonergan's Hermeneutics: Its Development and Application*, ed. Sean E. McEvenue and Ben F. Meyer (Washington, DC: Catholic University of America Press, 1989) 81–131. For Meyer's influence on N.T. Wright, who in turn has influenced much of my appropriation of New Testament Christology, see Wright's preface to *The Aims of Jesus*.

16 This is most clear in notes that Lonergan wrote at the time of his breakthrough to functional specialization. I have appealed to these notes in *What Is Systematic Theology?* 153–56. They may be found online at www.lonerganresource.com, beginning at 47200D0E060.

17 Part 1 of volume 22 of Collected Works of Bernard Lonergan, *Early Works on Theological Method 1*, ed. Robert M. Doran and Robert C. Croken (Toronto: University of Toronto Press, 2010) contains a transcript of recordings of these lectures. The recordings are available on the website www.lonerganresource.com beginning at 30100A0DE060; the audio restoration is the work of Greg Lauzon.

18 See ibid. 340–41.

19 It is interesting to note that on Lonergan's reading, while the church's dogmatic-theological development moved from Trinitarian dogma (the "consubstantial") to Christological development ("one and the same" person in two natures) and then to firm parameters for understanding the doctrine of grace with the medieval breakthrough to the theorem of the supernatural, Aquinas's *Summa theologiae* treats the doctrine of grace before it presents a systematic treatment of Christological doctrine. The Trinitarian and Pneumatological context of a contemporary systematic theology would do well to retrieve this order.

20 I am doing a bit of an *Umdeutung*, a shift in meaning, on Lonergan's notion of the dogmatic-theological context, since for him it seems to have been something of an integral of Christian doctrine to the present point in history. My use of the term adapts its meaning to suit the notion of a unified field structure for systematic theology introduced in *What Is Systematic Theology?* For me, the dogmatic-theological context would be identical with the specifically theological portion of that unified field structure, the other portion of which is the heuristic notion of history contained in *Theology and the Dialectics of History*. Thus the Trinitarian, Pneumatological, and Christological integration, such as is represented in what I call the four-point hypothesis that links the dogmas in these areas with one another, constitutes for me the dogmatic-theological context of everything else.

21 Perhaps the most complete account of the distinction of the two orders can be found in Bernard Lonergan, *The Triune God: Systematics*, vol. 12 of Collected Works of Bernard Lonergan, trans. Michael G. Shields, ed. Robert M. Doran and H. Daniel Monsour (Toronto: University of Toronto Press, 2007) 58–77.

22 1 Corinthians 15.3–4: "I taught you what I had been taught myself, namely that Christ died for our sins, in accordance with the scriptures; that he was buried; and that he was raised to life on the third day, in accordance with the scriptures." For Lonergan this passage expresses "the original message." See Lonergan, *Method in Theology* 295.

23 I say "*even* Pneumatological" because much remains to be done in the very articulation of the doctrine of the Holy Spirit. I dare say this may prove to be the principal dogmatic task of the twenty-first century.

24 For the Thomist synthesis regarding grace, see especially Bernard Lonergan, *Grace and Freedom: Operative Grace in the Thought of St Thomas Aquinas*, vol. 1 in Collected Works of Bernard Lonergan, ed. Frederick E. Crowe and Robert M. Doran (Toronto: University of Toronto Press, 2000).

25 See above, note 19.

26 See for example www.bernardlonergan.com, at 47200DOE060, the basic breakthrough page to functional specialization, and 47400DTE060, p. 11.

Chapter 2

1 These statements are explained in intricate detail in Lonergan, *The Triune God: Systematics* 230–305.

2 See Doran, *What Is Systematic Theology?* 61–77.

3 Bernard Lonergan, *Divinarum personarum conceptionem analogicam evolvit Bernardus Lonergan* (Rome: Gregorian University Press, 1957, 1959) 214; *De Deo Trino: Pars systematica* (Rome: Gregorian University Press, 1964) 234–35.

4 The editors of the Collected Works volume on the systematics of the Trinity appeal in a footnote to a passage in Lonergan's "De ente supernaturali," Thesis 3, in an effort to explain what is meant by "never found uninformed." That passage occurs in volume 19 of Lonergan's Collected Works, *Early Latin Theology*, and it now reads in English translation a bit differently from the translation that was given in *The Triune God: Systematics* (though the meaning is the same):

> "Only charity is meritorious per se; the other virtues or their acts can be informed or uninformed. They are informed by sanctifying grace and charity, and when sanctifying grace departs they become uninformed and cease to be meritorious.
>
> "For this reason it seems worthwhile to distinguish between absolutely supernatural acts that are formally supernatural and absolutely supernatural acts that are virtually supernatural. The former attain God as he is in himself, while the latter do not attain God as he is in himself but only in some respect, as in the case of faith and hope."

An earlier translation is given in *The Triune God: Systematics* at 471. The editors comment that the point of Lonergan's phrase "never found unformed" is that the four absolutely supernatural created realities are formally supernatural, and necessarily so. For the created correlate of divine communication or divine self-giving is that the creature should attain God as God is *in se*. For that to happen, there must be a created external term that functions as a consequent condition of the truth of the proposition that affirms the divine self-communication. (We will see more about this requirement shortly.)

In Lonergan's explanation of the hypothesis he names these created external terms "consequent conditions." The hypothesis itself states precisely what they are. (The translation of "De ente supernaturali" is by Michael Shields, and is published in *Early Latin Theology*, Collected Works of Bernard Lonergan 19, ed. Robert M. Doran and H. Daniel Monsour [Toronto: University of Toronto Press, 2011] 125.)

5 Lonergan, *The Triune God: Systematics* 470–73.

6 These notes have the archival designation A205 in the Lonergan archives at the Lonergan Research Institute in Toronto, and can be found on the website www.bernardlonergan.com at 20500DTL040. As is there explained in the descriptive note, one important page of these notes was mistakenly relocated in the archives as the first page of A160 (16000DTL040 on the website). The notes are now published as chapter 7 in Lonergan, *Early Latin Theology*.

7 Bernard Lonergan, *Early Latin Theology* 581. "1" is placed in brackets since it does not appear in the text of Lonergan's notes found in the archives. "Justified" here replaces "just" in that translation.

8 On the stages of meaning, see Lonergan, *Method in Theology* 85–99.

9 See Robert M. Doran, "Preserving Lonergan's Understanding of Thomist Metaphysics: A Proposal and an Example," *Lonergan Workshop* 21, ed. Fred Lawrence (Boston College, 2009) 85–101.

10 Lonergan, *Method in Theology* 343, emphasis added.

11 See Charles Hefling, "On the (Economic) Trinity: An Argument in Conversation with Robert Doran," *Theological Studies* 68 (2007) 642–60, and my response in the same issue at 674–82, "Addressing the Four-point Hypothesis." The conversation was prompted by my earlier article in *Theological Studies* 67 (2006) 750–76, "The Starting Point of Systematic Theology."

12 Lonergan says in "De ente supernaturali," "… the disputed question whether sanctifying grace and the habit of charity are really distinct does not affect the substance of our treatment but only the way in which the matter is presented. It does not affect the substance of the doctrine, for all Catholic schools of thought admit a created communication of the divine nature; but it does influence the manner of presentation, inasmuch as different authors arrange the matter differently in order to expound it in an intelligible way." Lonergan, *Early Latin Theology* 73. In other words, the distinction is not a matter of doctrine but of systematic understanding of doctrine.

13 See Lonergan, *Early Works on Theological Method 1* 484 note 4. I adopted this position explicitly in a 1993 article entitled "Consciousness and Grace." See p. 359, note 32.

14 This remark was made in the fifth question-and-answer session at the 1974 Boston College Lonergan Workshop. The recording of this session may be found at 81500A0E070 on the website www.bernardlonergan.com, with a corresponding transcription at 81500DTE070.

15 The Jerusalem Bible translates verse 23 differently: "With me in them and you in me, may they be so completely one that the world will realize that it was you who sent me and that *I have loved them* as much as you loved me." The specific Trinitarian meaning that Lonergan develops is lost in the Jerusalem translation. While the Greek ηγάπησας supports Lonergan's reading, Raymond E. Brown's translation and notes in the Anchor Bible (New York: Doubleday, 1970, 768–69) acknowledge textual evidence for each reading; but Brown prefers the reading on which Lonergan is basing his argument.

16 "These divine attributes are called 'notional,' not as if they were conceptual beings, but because they cause the divine persons to be known as distinct from one another." Bernard Lonergan, *The Triune God: Doctrines*, trans. Michael G. Shields, ed. Robert M. Doran and H. Daniel Monsour (Toronto: University of Toronto Press, 2009) 413.

17 We will see in the next volume that relations are distinguished as relations, not by the multiplication of terms but by the multiplication of orderings. The immanent constitution of life in God has two orderings: from sanctifying grace to the Holy Spirit, and from charity to the Father and the Son. There are three terms, but two relations.

18 Karl Rahner, "Some Implications of the Scholastic Concept of Uncreated Grace," *Theological Investigations*, vol. 1, trans. Cornelius Ernst (London: Darton, Longman & Todd, 1961) 325. For Lonergan's position, see www.bernardlonergan.com, at 16000DTE040.

19 Rahner, "Some Implications ..." 334.

20 Possibly relevant here is a recent doctoral dissertation by Jorge Antonio Zurek Lequerica, "Delving into Mystical Creativity: A Dialogue on Mystical Transformation between Bernard Lonergan and Teresa of Avila," Regis College, Toronto School of Theology, University of Toronto, 2010.

21 For the language of "consequent condition," see Lonergan, *The Triune God: Systematics* 439. See also the treatment in the next chapter of contingent predication regarding God.

22 See Lonergan, *Early Latin Theology* 65.

23 Thomas Aquinas, *Summa theologiae*, 1, q. 38, a. 1, emphasis added.

24 Ibid. The sharing in the divine Word that Aquinas mentions will be developed momentarily into a participation in the invisible mission of the Son.

25 Thomas Aquinas, *Summa theologiae*, 1, q. 43, a. 3.

26 Ibid. a. 6, emphasis added.

27 See Lonergan, *The Triune God: Systematics* 218–29.

28 Charles Hefling, 'Revelation and/as Insight,' in *The Importance of Insight*, ed. John J. Liptay, Jr, and David S. Liptay (Toronto: University of Toronto Press, 2007) 112.

29 See, for example, Robert M. Doran, "Being in Love with God: A Source of Analogies for Theological Understanding," *Irish Theological Quarterly* 73 (2008) 227–42.

30 Bernard Lonergan, "Christology Today: Methodological Reflection," *A Third Collection* 93–94.

31 This quotation is taken from the third question-and-answer session at the 1974 Boston College Lonergan Workshop. The recording of this session may be found as item 812A0A0E070 on the website www.bernardlonergan. com, with a corresponding transcription at 812A0DTE070.

32 Robert M. Doran, "Consciousness and Grace," *Method: Journal of Lonergan Studies* 11:1 (Spring 1993) 51–75. An updated version may be found on the website www.lonerganresource.com under "Scholarly Works/Books/Essays in Systematic Theology," where it is the first essay.

33 See Lonergan, *Method Theology* 289.

34 The misinterpretation is shown when the passage is taken to refer to *our* love for God rather than *God's* own love. The meaning is clearly the second, and Lonergan recognized that; but even Lonergan's own reading of Romans 5.5 has been misunderstood.

35 Lonergan, *Method in Theology* 343.

Chapter 3

1 Lonergan, *The Triune God: Systematics* 439.
2 Ibid.
3 Ibid. 441.
4 Ibid.
5 Ibid. The bracketed materials are meant to help clarify the meaning of the word "term."
6 Ibid. 443.
7 Ibid.
8 Ibid. 443, 445.
9 Ibid. 455.
10 Ibid. 447.
11 Ibid. 449.
12 Ibid. 451, translation mine.
13 Ibid. 453.
14 Ibid. 447.
15 Ibid. 447, 449.
16 Ibid. 449, 451.
17 Ibid. 451.
18 Ibid. 451.

19 Thomas Aquinas, *Summa theologiae*, 1, q. 43, a. 1.

20 Lonergan, *The Triune God: Systematics* 451.

21 Ibid. 453.

22 Ibid.

23 For more on the notion of "ontological constitution," see Bernard Lonergan, *The Ontological and Pyschological Constitution of Christ*, vol. 7 in Collected Works of Bernard Lonergan, trans. Michael G. Shields, ed. Frederick E. Crowe and Robert M. Doran (Toronto: University of Toronto Press, 2002) 46–75, 98–105.

24 Ibid. 457. For the contrast with other positions, see ibid. 457, 459. The first of the contrary positions that Lonergan discusses is the position that he himself had propounded in the original draft of his 1946 course on grace and that Rahner had criticized as the predominant Scholastic position. See above, p. 25–26. The second contrary position is identified most prominently with the name of Maurice de la Taille, though he is not mentioned in the text. The main difference between the second position and Lonergan's is in the analogy employed; the second position argues by analogy with the union of potency and act, whereas Lonergan's analogy is with the common contingents discussed already: 'just as proper contingents are predicated of one or other of the divine persons, so common contingents are predicated of the three divine persons; and just as the latter are constituted by infinite act with the addition of a conceptual relation, so also the former are similarly constituted by an infinite relation of origin with the addition of a conceptual relation." Ibid. 463. The first position, that is, the position Lonergan had briefly held himself, is later said to be further removed from Lonergan's own position than the second. According to the first position, a mission follows a term; according to Lonergan's position, a term follows a mission. See ibid. 461 and 463. A position that Lonergan does not mention here is that of Karl Rahner, who understands the mission of the Holy Spirit in terms of quasi-formal causality.

25 Ibid. 459.

26 Ibid. 461.

27 Ibid. 465.

28 Ibid.

29 At this point, perhaps there should be raised the question of whether anything is added by production in the passive sense; and on this point perhaps Rahner can be helpful: The Son of God cannot change, suffer, etc., except in the "other" that is the assumed humanity; it remains to theology to fashion an analogous statement applicable to the Holy Spirit. Obviously, there are differences in that the Holy Spirit is not incarnate in any assumed human nature; but perhaps there can be devised an ontological explanation

for the sentiment expressed in the biblical injunction not to sadden the
Holy Spirit (Ephesians 4.30).

30 Note that "material external term'" is Lonergan's expression, and that it
means precisely "the external term considered in abstraction from the formality that makes it precisely the external term of a mission." The expression has nothing to do with materiality.

31 Ibid. 471. See also 447–51.

32 Ibid. 469, 471.

33 The basic statement is Aquinas's position on the divine missions as given
in *Summa theologiae*, 1, q. 43. For von Balthasar, see his *Theodrama: Theological Dramatic Theory*, vol. 3: *Dramatis Personae: Persons in Christ*, trans. Graham
Harrison (San Francisco: Ignatius Press, 1992) 157. For Lonergan, see chapter 6 in *The Triune God: Systematics* passim. The latter is by far the fullest account of the matter.

34 Lonergan, *The Ontological and Psychological Constitution of Christ* 152–55.

35 See ibid. part 4 passim.

36 See Lonergan, *The Triune God: Systematics* 470–73.

37 See ibid. 473, 475.

38 Ibid. 481.

39. Ibid. 471.

40 See Lonergan, *Method in Theology* 289.

41 See Lonergan, *The Triune God: Systematics* 473, 475.

42 On the distinction between the habit of grace and the state of grace, see
Lonergan, *The Triune God: Systematics* 512–21. We will see more of this as we
proceed.

43 See Lonergan, *Insight* 721–22.

44 Neil Ormerod, "Contingent Predication and the Four-point Hypothesis,"
unpublished paper delivered at the Melbourne conference on Lonergan's
Insight, September 2007.

45 For some elements in the heuristic structure of such an ecclesiology, see
chapter 5 in my book *Theology and the Dialectics of History* (Toronto: University of Toronto Press, 1990), entitled "The Community of the Servant of
God." Social grace will ultimately be understood in terms of the scale of values articulated in that book. But fidelity to the scale of values entails participation in the Law of the Cross.

Chapter 4

1 Lonergan, *Method in Theology* xi.

2 Robley Edward Whitson, *The Coming Convergence of World Religions* (New
York: Newman, 1971). For Lonergan's views of Whitson's book, see

Lonergan, "Prolegomena to the Study of the Emerging Religious Consciousness of Our Time," in *A Third Collection* 65–71.

3 Frederick E. Crowe, "Son of God, Holy Spirit, and World Religions," in Crowe, *Appropriating the Lonergan Idea,* ed. Michael Vertin (Toronto: University of Toronto Press, 2006) 324–43.

4 Lonergan, *The Triune God: Systematics* 479, 481.

5 Ibid. 481.

6 In quoting Lonergan, here, I include the footnotes found in the English translation in *The Triune God: Systematics.* Those footnotes without brackets are Lonergan's own, while the bracketed note 10 is editorial. The emphasis in the second paragraph of the following citation is my own.

7 Thomas Aquinas, *Summa theologiae,* 3, q. 26, a. 2.

8 Matthew 3.16–17.

9 John 17.23; see 17.26. See St Thomas Aquinas, *Ad Ephesios,* c. 1, lect. 1 and 2, §§ 9 and 16 in the Marietti edition.

10 [That is, the order is supernatural because the love in which we are caught up is the divine love that is really proper to the divine persons.]

11 Lonergan, *The Triune God: Systematics* 483.

12 Ibid. 485.

13 Ephesians 1.10.

14 Colossians 1.20.

15 1 Corinthians 15.28.

16 Lonergan, *The Triune God: Systematics* 485. The three previous footnotes (13–15) are Lonergan's.

17 Ibid.

18 Ibid.

19 John 15.9–10.

20 1 Corinthians 6.19. As the just are not their own but the Spirit's ("you are not your own"), so the Spirit himself is the Spirit of the just, since he has been given to them. See Romans 5.5.

21 Ephesians 4.30. Notes 19–21 are Lonergan's.

22 Romans 5.10.

23 Ephesians 1.14.

24 Titus 3.5–7. Notes 22–24 are Lonergan's.

25 Footnotes in the citation are Lonergan's, with editorial notes added in brackets.

26 Since a mission is to a subsistent, whereas the nature to be assumed is not subsistent except in the Nestorian heresy, the Son is not said to be sent to the nature that he assumed. Billot, *De Deo Uno et Trino* (Rome: Gregorian University Press, 1935) 652. [A mission is of a person, from a person, to a person or to persons.]

27 Hebrews 5.9.

28 John 20.21, 17.18.

29 Matthew 10.40; see 18.18.

30 Luke 10.16.

31 Acts 9.4.

32 John 10.10. Whatever is being done by Christ as man whether on earth through his historical influence or from his place in heaven is part of the visible mission of the Son.

33 1 Corinthians 15.24.

34 Galatians 4.6–7.

35 1 Corinthians 3.16.

36 Romans 5.5.

37 Romans 8.8–9.

38 Romans 8.11.

39 Lonergan, *The Triune God: Systematics* 487–91.

40 Crowe, "Son of God, Holy Spirit, and World Religions" 325–26.

41 Ibid. 326.

42 Ibid. 328.

43 Ibid. 329.

44 Ibid.

45 Lonergan, *Method in Theology* 112–13.

46 Crowe, "Son of God, Holy Spirit, and World Religions" 330.

47 Ibid. 333.

48 Ibid. 334.

49 Ibid.

50 See Lonergan, "Prolegomena to the Study of the Emerging Religious Consciousness of Our Time" 70–71.

51 Lonergan, *Method in Theology* 341.

52 Ibid. 106.

53 Ibid. 113.

54 Ibid.

55 Lonergan, *Insight* 716.

56 See Doran, *Theology and the Dialectics of History*, chapter 17, §1, "Subject and Culture."

57 Lonergan, *Insight* 721–22.

58 See Raymund Schwager, *Jesus in the Drama of Salvation: Toward a Biblical Doctrine of Redemption*, trans. James G. Williams and Paul Haddon (New York: Crossroad, 1999). The five acts are: (1) Jesus's preaching of the reign of God, (2) the conflict with the religious authorities because of his preaching of the reign of God, (3) the crucifixion and death of Jesus, (4) the resurrection of Jesus from the dead, and (5) the gift of the Holy Spirit at Pentecost. The latter I am conceiving not as the first and original gift of the Holy Spirit to humankind, which is a universal reality, but as the special confirmation

by the Holy Spirit that the mission of the Word was indeed the revelation of what God has been doing and will continue to do, namely, pour out divine love on humankind.

59 The use of "inner word" here is Lonergan's. See *Method in Theology* 119: "Then not only the inner word that is God's gift of his love but also the outer word of the religious tradition comes from God."

60 On the categories and their respective bases, see Lonergan, *Method in Theology* 281–93.

61 Lonergan, *Method in Theology* 115. For Lonergan's understanding of this universalist faith and its distinction from the religious beliefs of particular traditions, see ibid. 115–19.

Chapter 5

1 Lonergan, *Method in Theology* 31–32.

2 Bernard Lonergan, "*Insight* Revisited," in *A Second Collection*, ed. Bernard J. Tyrrell and William F.J. Ryan (Toronto: University of Toronto Press, 1996) 272.

3 Lonergan, *Method in Theology* 184.

4 Charles Hefling, "Revelation and/as Insight," in *The Importance of Insight*, ed. John J. Liptay, Jr., and David S. Liptay (Toronto: University of Toronto Press, 2007) 112.

5 Ibid.

6 I rely for much of what I am saying here on Hefling's paper cited in note 4.

7 See Hefling, "Revelation and/as Insight" 99.

8 Ibid. 103.

9 See ibid.

10 Ibid. 104.

11 Ibid.

12 Ibid.

13 Ibid. 105.

14 Ibid. 107.

15 See ibid. Lonergan, *The Ontological and Psychological Constitution of Christ*, 205 (emphasis added).

16 Ibid. 108.

17 René Girard, *Things Hidden since the Foundation of the World*, trans. Stephen Bann and Michael Metteer (Stanford: Stanford University Press) 275.

18 Bernard Lonergan, "Natural Right and Historical Mindedness," *A Third Collection* 176.

19 Ibid. 169.

20 Ibid. 176.

21 Ibid.

22 The plateaus of "Natural Right and Historical Mindedness" are the stages of

meaning in *Method in Theology*, but their function as objectifications of the "single object that can gain collective attention" is much clearer in "Natural Right." See Bernard Lonergan, *Method in Theology* 85–99.

23 See Lonergan, *Insight* 689–91.

24 I say "part of the nature" because, embracing and including the transcendental notions that constitute the levels of intentional consciousness is the "tidal movement" that begins before intentional consciousness, permeates it as it moves through its various questions and answers, and reaches beyond it in being in love. That vertical finality is the primary meaning of "nature" in "Natural Right and Historical Mindedness," and to the extent that the love is God's own love, that nature is obediential potency for grace.

25 The disclaimer, I think, is only partially correct: there *is* a second presentation of those dynamics, one that achieves inchoate expression in chapter 2 of *Method in Theology*. But, as I have argued in several places, each presentation has its limited validity, and neither is to be discarded. See www.lonerganresource.com under "Books": *Essays in Systematic Theology*, items 18 and 19.

26 See Lonergan, *Grace and Freedom* and "The Supernatural Order" (see below, p. 395, note 91).

27 Lonergan, "Natural Right and Historical Mindedness" 175.

28 See Bernard Lonergan, *The Triune God: Systematics*, trans. Michael G. Shields, ed. Robert M. Doran and H. Daniel Monsour (Toronto: University of Toronto Press, 2007) 218–29.

29 See John D. Dadosky, "Midwiving the Fourth Stage of Meaning: Lonergan and Doran," in *Meaning and History in Systematic Theology*, ed. John D. Dadosky (Milwaukee: Marquette University Press, 2009) 71–92; also in the same book, at 331–43, Philip McShane, "The Fourth Stage of Meaning: Essay 44 of the Series Field Nocturnes Cantower."

30 See Lonergan, *Early Works on Theological Method 1* 400.

31 See Eric Voegelin, "The Gospel and Culture," in *Jesus and Man's Hope*, ed. D.G. Miller and D.Y. Hadidian (Pittsburgh: Pittsburgh Theological Seminary, 1971) 63.

32 Why has it taken us so long to recognize the hermeneutic significance of *Insight*'s placing on the level of empirical consciousness the "free images" and "utterances" that "commonly are under the influence of the higher levels before they provide a basis for inquiry and reflection"? Lonergan, *Insight* 299.

33 See, e.g., Eugene Gendlin, *Let Your Body Interpret Your Dreams* (Wilmette, IL: Chiron Publications, 1986). Gendlin's more theoretical *Experiencing and the Creation of Meaning* (Toronto: Free Press of Glencoe, 1962) was helpful to me in my early statements on psychic conversion. See Robert M. Doran, *Subject and Psyche*, rev. ed. (Milwaukee: Marquette University Press, 1994) 115–17, 169–72.

34 Lonergan, *The Triune God: Systematics* 139.
35 Bernard Lonergan, 'Questionnaire on Philosophy: Response," *Philosophical and Theological Papers 1965–1980*, vol. 17 in Collected Works of Bernard Lonergan, ed. Robert C. Croken and Robert M. Doran (Toronto: University of Toronto Press, 2004) 355.
36 "In *understanding* and *state-of-mind*, we shall see the two constitutive ways of being the 'there.'" Martin Heidegger, *Being and Time*, trans. John Macquarrie and Edward Robinson (New York: Harper & Row, 1962) 171–72. 'Understanding' translates *Verstehen*, and 'state-of-mind' *Befindlichkeit*.
37 This session (16 June 1980) appears on www.bernardlonergan.com as 97300A0E080, with a transcription at 97300DTE080. Lonergan's comments on limitation appear at the very beginning.
38 See Lonergan, *The Triune God: Systematics* 512–21.

Chapter 6

1 See Bernard Lonergan, "Understanding and Method," in Lonergan, *Early Works on Theological Method 2*, trans. Michael G. Shields, ed. Robert M. Doran and H. Daniel Monsour (Toronto: University of Toronto Press, forthcoming 2013).
2 Lonergan, *Method in Theology* 290.
3 See the website www.bernardlonergan.com at 47200D0E060.
4 Lonergan, *Method in Theology* 267.
5 The term "interdividuality" is taken from René Girard, as we will see in detail later.
6 See www.bernardlonergan.com at 98700DTE080, from the 1981 Lonergan Workshop at Boston College.
7 See Lonergan, "Questionnaire on Philosophy: A Response," in *Philosophical and Theological Papers 1965–1980* 355–57.
8 Lonergan, *Method in Theology* xi.
9 Thus, for example, Yves Congar's *A History of Theology* belongs to this first phase, in that it is an account of what was going forward in the discipline of theology (3). Jaroslav Pelikan's several-volume history of Christian dogma also belongs to this first phase, but it does so not only as an account of the past history of the discipline but also as an account of the past history of the community struggling to articulate correctly its constitutive meaning (2). And finally, a book like N.T. Wright's *Jesus and the Victory of God* belongs to this first phase, but here the issue is strictly the account of what was going forward in the encounter between the grace of God active in the life, preaching, death, and resurrection of Jesus and the cultural matrix in which these events unfolded (1). This latter book is an account, not primarily of what was going forward in theology (3), nor primarily of what was going forward in the community's strivings to articulate its constitutive meaning (2),

but of what was going forward in what theology itself is all about, namely, the mutual self-mediation between the action of God in history and the cultural matrix in which God is acting (1).

10 Lonergan, *Method in Theology* 142.

11 On functional specialization as a complication of the basic structure of the normative subject, see Lonergan, *Early Works on Theological Method 1* 478–79. The occasion was the set of lectures that Lonergan delivered at Boston College in 1968, where he first went public with the notion of functional specialization.

12 As I have already indicated, the scale of values represents another complication of the structure of intentional consciousness elevated by divine grace.

13 See Bernard Lonergan, "The Ongoing Genesis of Methods," in *A Third Collection* 146–65.

14 The clarifications would regard primarily the first and the fourth "levels" in the structure. For my own suggestions, see, regarding the first "level," Robert M. Doran, "Reception and Elemental Meaning," *Toronto Journal of Theology* 20:2 (2004) 133–57, and, regarding the fourth, Robert M. Doran, "Ignatian Themes in the Thought of Bernard Lonergan: Revisiting a Topic That Deserves Further Reflection," *Lonergan Workshop* 19, ed. Fred Lawrence (Boston College, 2006) 83–106. These two papers are available on the website www.lonerganresource.com, "Scholarly Works – Books – *Essays in Systematic Theology.*"

15 Bernard Lonergan, *Method in Theology* 150.

16 Robert M. Doran, "Consciousness and Grace," *METHOD: Journal of Lonergan Studies* 11:1 (Spring 1993) 75. The paper has been uploaded to the website www.lonerganresource.com, in the *Essays in Systematic Theology* that can be found under "Scholarly Works – Books." New notes have been added.

17 See Robert M. Doran, "Preserving Lonergan's Understanding of Thomist Metaphysics: A Proposal and an Example," *Lonergan Workshop 21*, ed. Fred Lawrence (Boston: Boston College, 2009) 85–101. This too has been uploaded to www.lonerganresource.com, as part of the e-book *Essays in Systematic Theology.*

18 Christian Jacobs-Vandegeer, "Sanctifying Grace in a Methodical Theology, *Theological Studies* 68 (2007) 52–76.

19 See Bernard Lonergan, "Openness and Religious Experience," in *Collection*, vol. 4 in Collected Works of Bernard Lonergan, ed. Frederick E. Crowe and Robert M. Doran (Toronto: University of Toronto Press, 1988) 185–87.

20 See Robert M. Doran, "Ignatian Themes in the Thought of Bernard Lonergan: Revisiting a Topic That Deserves Further Reflection" (see above, note 14). More will be made of the Ignatian material in the next chapter.

21 See Bernard Lonergan, "The Natural Desire to See God," in *Collection* 81–91.

22 "Analysis Fidei" is now available with English translation as part 4 in Lonergan, *Early Latin Theology*.

23 See Bernard Lonergan, *The Triune God: Systematics* 218–29. See also pp. 341–43 in the present text.

24 Compare Adrienne von Speyr, in *The Farewell Discourses: Meditations on John 13–17*, trans. E.A. Nelson (San Francisco: Ignatius Press, 1948) 137: "He should stop desiring to be the subject himself, should let the Lord be the subject and entrust himself to him as object. Or let the Lord be the subject of his own subject."

25 The expression "unconscious desire" is unfortunate, but it is Lonergan's, not Blackwood's. At times Lonergan will use the word "unconscious" where he really means "conscious but unobjectified."

26 Bernard Lonergan, "Mission and the Spirit," in *A Third Collection* 23–34. I think especially of the discussion of the passionateness of being that "has a dimension of its own: it underpins and accompanies and reaches beyond the subject as experientially, intelligently, rationally, morally conscious." See ibid. 29–30.

27 Bernard Lonergan, "Natural Right and Historical Mindedness," in *A Third Collection* 169–83. Here the relevant material speaks of the "tidal movement that begins before consciousness, unfolds through sensitivity, intelligence, rational reflection, responsible deliberation, only to find its rest beyond all of these" in love. Ibid. 175.

28 Bernard Lonergan, "Philosophy and the Religious Phenomenon," in *Philosophical and Theological Papers 1965–1980*. The quote that Blackwood cites is on p. 400.

29 I have found distinct confirmation in one of the question-and-answer sessions from the 1975 Lonergan Workshop, on the website www.bernardlonergan.com at 85200DTE070:

> "QUESTION: *Recently you have spoken of a fifth level of human intentional consciousness, whereby a plurality of self-transcending individuals achieve a higher integration in a community of love. Please expand on this.*

> "LONERGAN: *There is very little to expand on this. Everyone knows what it means* [emphasis added]. Getting there is another thing. But the constitution of the subject is a matter of self-transcendence. You are unconscious when you are in a coma or a deep sleep, a dreamless sleep. When you start to dream, consciousness emerges, but it is fragmentary; it is symbolic. You wake up, and you are in the real world. But if you are merely gaping and understanding nothing, you are not very far in. And so you have another level of asking questions and coming to understand. There is the understanding that people can have from

myth and magic and so on, but arriving at the truth is a further step of being reasonable, liberating oneself from astrology, alchemy, legend, and so on and so forth. And responsible. And this is all a matter of immanent development of the subject. But even before you're born you are not all by yourself, and all during your life. Robinson Crusoe is a real abstraction. And if he really is all alone, his history does not go beyond himself. There is living with others and being with others. The whole development of humanity is in terms of common meaning. Not just my meaning, attention to my experience, development of my understanding, and so on. Common meaning is the fruit of a common field of experience, and if you are not in that common field of experience you get out of touch. There's common understanding, and if you have not got that common understanding, well, you are a stranger, or worse a foreigner, you have a different style of common sense, and so on. Common judgments: if what one man thinks is true another man thinks is false, well, they are not going to be able to do very much about anything, insofar as those judgments are relevant to what they do. Common values, common projects, and you can have a common enterprise, and if you don't [have common values], you will be working at cross-purposes. The highest form of this is love as opposed to hate. It is a hard saying, 'Love your enemies, do good to them that hate you, love them that persecute you,' and so on. There are all kinds of things in the New Testament expanding on this."

The links with René Girard are obvious: "[T]he real human *subject* can only come out of the rule of the Kingdom; apart from this rule, there is never anything but mimetism and the 'interdividual.' Until this happens, the only subject is the mimetic structure." Jean-Michel Oughourlian, in René Girard, *Things Hidden since the Foundation of the World* (Stanford, CA: Stanford University Press, 1987) 199, emphasis in the text. Girard's response (ibid.): "That is quite right." (We will return to this citation later. See pp. 310–12.)

30 Needless to say, many issues of distorted or deviated transcendence to the other will need to be sorted out in future discussions of this level of consciousness. Again, the relevance of Girard to this discussion is clear.

31 John D. Dadosky, "Is There a Fourth Stage of Meaning?" *Heythrop Journal* 51:5 (2010) 768–80; "Midwiving the Fourth Stage of Meaning: Lonergan and Doran," in *Meaning and History in Systematic Theology: Essays in Honor of Robert M. Doran, SJ*, ed. John D. Dadosky (Milwaukee: Marquette University Press, 2009) 71–92.

32 See Doran, *What Is Systematic Theology?* 112–16.

33 While I wish to stress this agreement with Balthasar's insistence on a theological aesthetics, the vast expansion of the Christian theological field that I

am suggesting will decisively move theological aesthetics beyond the residual classicism that confines Balthasar to a limited (even if quite extensive) field of data, namely, European Christianity.

Chapter 7

1 While the four-point hypothesis is the same in both texts, there are significant differences in other places in the texts. On the significance of some of the differences between the two texts, see my three articles: "The First Chapter of *De Deo Trino: Pars Systematica*: The Issues"; "*Intelligentia Fidei* in *De Deo Trino, Pars Systematica*"; and "The Truth of Theological Understanding in *Divinarum Personarum* and *De Deo Trino, Pars Systematica*," Method: *Journal of Lonergan Studies* 18 (2000) 27–48; 19 (2001) 35–83; and 20 (2002) 33–75. These are now available on the website www.lonerganresource.com under the heading "Essays in Systematic Theology."

2 The notion of transposition appears repeatedly in *Method in Theology*, but the dynamics entailed are not spelled out. See also Lonergan's 1979 paper "Horizons and Transpositions," in *Philosophical and Theological Papers 1965–1980*, ed. Robert C. Croken and Robert M. Doran, Collected Works of Bernard Lonergan 17 (Toronto: University of Toronto Press, 2004) at 426–31. Something of the dynamics involved in transposition can be found in Matthew L. Lamb, "Lonergan's Transposition of Augustine and Aquinas," unpublished paper delivered at a meeting of the Lonergan Philosophical Society, 2004. A contribution is also made by Christiaan Jacobs-Vandegeer, "Sanctifying Grace in a Methodical Theology" (see above, p. 367, note 18) and "The Hermeneutics of Interiority: Transpositions in the Third Stage of Meaning," in *Meaning and History in Systematic Theology* 191–215.

3 Special categories are the categories peculiar to theology, while general categories are those that theology shares with other disciplines. On general and special theological categories, see Lonergan, *Method in Theology* 285–91. The issue of the categories, general and special, and of their sources and interrelations, remains the most significant methodological question in theology, as it has been ever since the Augustinian-Aristotelian conflicts in the late Middle Ages. In terms that really are too general, and so that can easily be misunderstood, the issue of just how important the general categories are for theology determines the difference between Platonic and Aristotelian, Bonaventurian and Thomist, and perhaps Balthasarian and Lonerganian emphases in theology. But the present concern is with the special categories and, as I have already indicated, especially with *special basic relations*, which were never specified as such by Lonergan.

4 Lonergan, *The Triune God: Systematics* 470–73.

5 On the base and the term of relations, see above, pp. 24–25, 31–32.

6 See Lonergan, *Insight* 646–48, 720–22, 747, 762.

7 "Divina paternitas ... est divinus intellectus qua dicens Verbum suum et ita intellectualiter Filium suum generans. Quam generationem quodammodo imitatur eiusdem Filii Incarnatio; Incarnatio enim regeneratio quaedam est in qua non oritur nova persona sed personae exsistenti advenit nova natura." As indicated above, these notes have been published in vol. 19 of Collected Works of Bernard Lonergan, *Early Latin Theology*. The passage quoted here may be found on pp. 634, 636, with a corresponding English translation on pp. 635, 637.

8 Doran, *What Is Systematic Theology?* 62.

9 The complication of the structure is offered in a compendious form in chapter 10 of *What Is Systematic Theology?* It can also be found in a paper that I offered to the Boston College Lonergan Workshop in 2004 and that has been uploaded on www.lonerganresource.com in *Essays in Systematic Theology*. The title of the paper is "'Complicate the Structure': Notes on a Forgotten Precept." In its fuller details, the complication is offered in my book *Theology and the Dialectics of History*. The cognitional theory, epistemology, metaphysics, and fundamental existential ethics presupposed there are all Lonergan's work. The basic heuristic of history (progress-decline-redemption) is also his, but the amplification and development of the structure in terms of an analogy of dialectics of subject, culture, and community and in terms of the scale of values is my own responsibility. These are rooted in my suggestions of a psychic conversion to complement Lonergan's religious, moral, and intellectual conversions, and in the consequent affirmation of aesthetic-dramatic as well as intellectual, rational, and deliberative operators of human development: symbols, feelings, interpersonal relations, and love – in Heideggerian terms, *Befindlichkeit* as well as *Verstehen* (though both *Befindlichkeit* and *Verstehen* are understood far more fulsomely in a Lonerganian context). None of this, of course, is in the least bit foreign to Lonergan. I have been drawing out materials for which the room is already provided in his work.

10 Bernard Lonergan, "Questionnaire on Philosophy: Response," in *Philosophical and Theological Papers 1965–1980* 355–57.

11 This systematic position, of course, can and should be checked against the results of the best New Testament exegesis in our time. I will not repeat this exegesis here, but I rely heavily on the work of Ben F. Meyer, N.T. Wright, and Raymund Schwager. Correlating *Theology and the Dialectics of History* with the results of such scholarship regarding the reign of God will be a major task in validating the position here offered. Help for that task is provided by the thorough list of relevant biblical references to "kingdom" at the end of Wright's *Jesus and the Victory of God*.

12 My colleague in editing Lonergan's Collected Works, Daniel Monsour, is responsible for the expression "unified field structure," though the conception of this structure offered in *What Is Systematic Theology?* as well as here, the conception that includes the addition of the theory of history, is my own.

See also my paper "The Unified Field Structure for Systematic Theology: A Proposal." The paper was delivered several times in 2002–2003 in different forms; the final version is contained in "Essays in Systematic Theology" on www.lonerganresource.com; a record of the history of the proposal in its various versions may be found on the same site under "Events, Lectures."

13   Conversely, of course, Aquinas can benefit from Bonaventure, and Lonergan from von Balthasar. It is not a question of either/or, but of the appropriate integration of general and special categories in theology. As Aquinas and Lonergan excelled in the use of the general categories within their respective contexts, while not neglecting the special categories, so Bonaventure and von Balthasar have made major contributions to the development of theology's special categories in their respective contexts. But they are weak on the general categories. As I stated above, the appropriate integration of the realities named by general and special categories is the major methodological problem for systematic theology. It plagued the late Middle Ages in the Aristotelian-Augustinian conflict. The extremes to which it is prone can be found in relatively contemporary theology in some variants of the method of correlation, on the one hand, where special categories are collapsed into general categories, and at the other extreme in John Milbank's "radical orthodoxy," with its rejection of the significance of the general categories. See Milbank, *Theology and Social Theory: Beyond Secular Reason* (Oxford: Blackwell, 1990).

14   Lonergan speaks in *Method in Theology* (pp. 290–91) of five sets of special theological categories. It is clear from his 1968 lectures at Boston College, where he introduced publicly for the first time the functional specialization of *Method in Theology*, that he had been thinking that the five sets would be derived, respectively, from (1) complicating the structure of conscious intentionality, (2) turning to concrete instances of it, (3) filling it out, (4) differentiating it, and (5) setting it in motion. But what eventually became the third set is not accounted for by filling out the basic structure. If anything, it is the first set of special categories in *Method in Theology*, the set having to do with religious experience, that is a function of filling out the basic structure. For the third set, it seems, Lonergan came to see that he had to appeal not to the subject in his or her interiorly and religiously differentiated consciousness, and so not to the basic structure, but to the other dimension of foundations (see *Method in Theology* 267), namely, the tradition as mediated by the functional specialties of research, interpretation, history, and dialectic. Thus the third set, the one that is pertinent to the present discussion, is expressed in *Method in Theology* (291) as follows: "The third set of special categories moves from our loving to the loving source of our love. The *Christian tradition* makes explicit our implicit intending of God in all our intending by speaking of the Spirit that is given to us, of the Son who redeemed us, of the Father who sent

the Son and with the Son sends the Spirit, and of our future destiny when we shall know, not as in a glass darkly, but face to face" (emphasis added). This set, thus outlined, incorporates each of the elements contained in the four-point hypothesis. Work remains to be done on the movement in Lonergan's own thought from the 1968 directives for deriving the special categories to the actual sets that are proposed in *Method in Theology*. There are some overlaps among the sets suggested in the two presentations, but there is also a development whose progression is not yet clear in all its details. (The 1968 lectures here referred to are available on audio compact disc in Lonergan's own voice, produced by Greg Lauzon: "Transcendental Philosophy and the Study of Religion." These are now available on the Lonergan Archive website www.bernardlonergan.com, starting at 48100A0E060. A transcription appears as part 3 in Lonergan, *Early Works on Theological Method 1*.)

15 Lonergan, *Method in Theology* 83. See ibid. 239 for the references to empiricism, idealism, and realism.

16 Ibid. 343.

17 See above, p. 22.

18 Lonergan, *The Ontological and Psychological Constitution of Christ* 106–55.

19 For supportive evidence, see Neil Ormerod, "The Psychological Analogy for the Trinity – at Odds with Modernity," *Pacifica* 14 (2001) 281–94.

20 See www.bernardlonergan.com at 43200DTE060 (audio at 43200A0E060).

21 The problem is revisited, and lines of a solution suggested, at pp. 308–309.

22 For an effort at balance see Robert M. Doran, "Reception and Elemental Meaning: An Expansion of the Notion of Psychic Conversion"; "Insight and Language: Steps towards the Resolution of a Problem," *Divyadaan* 15:3 (2004) 405–26; "Empirical Consciousness in *Insight*: Is Our Conception Too Narrow?" in *The Importance of Insight*, ed. David Liptay and John Liptay (Toronto: University of Toronto Press, 2007) 49–63. The first two of these papers have been uploaded to www.lonerganresource.com. See also Doran, *What Is Systematic Theology?* 124–45.

23 For Lonergan's succinct statement of the problem and of the essential elements of a response, see *Method in Theology* 253–57.

24 Bernard Lonergan, "Theology and Understanding," in *Collection* 114–32.

25 Lonergan, *Method in Theology* 336.

26 Lonergan, *Method in Theology* 289.

27 On genuineness, see *Insight* 499–504.

28 See above, p. 357, note 9.

29 Lonergan, *Method in Theology* 289.

30 Lonergan, *Method in Theology* 37–38.

31 See Bernard Lonergan, "*Insight* Revisited," in *A Second Collection*, ed. William F.J. Ryan, s.j., and Bernard J. Tyrrell, s.j. (Toronto: University of Toronto Press, 1996) 277.

32 See Robert M. Doran, "Ignatian Themes in the Thought of Bernard Lonergan," *Toronto Journal of Theology* 22:1 (2006) 39–54. This paper was revised and expanded for presentation at the 2006 Lonergan Workshop at Boston College, and the revised and expanded version has been published in the proceedings of the workshop, *Lonergan Workshop 19*, ed. Fred Lawrence (Boston College, 2006) 83–106 with the title "Ignatian Themes in the Thought of Bernard Lonergan: Revisiting a Topic That Deserves Further Reflection." Both of these are available on the website www.lonerganresource. com. The present account draws heavily on these articles.

33 *The Text of the Spiritual Exercises of Saint Ignatius*, trans. Henry Keane, s.j. (London: Burns, Oates and Washbourne, 1952) §§175–78.

34 See Lonergan, *Insight* 629–30.

35 To be precise, I should indicate that, while Lonergan does not use the expression "judgment of value" in this context in *Insight* (completed for all practical purposes in 1953), in *Divinarum Personarum* (1957) he says "iudicium practicum seu iudicium valoris," "a practical judgment or judgment of value," and in *De Deo Trino: Pars systematica* (1964) "iudicium practicum" is dropped to leave only "iudicium valoris." Judgments of value are spoken of in *Insight* only in chapter 20, in the analysis of belief. There is needed a study of the development of Lonergan's language on this matter. Moreover, the "iudicium valoris" of 1964 is not exactly the same as the judgment of value in *Method in Theology*, for the second account of the process of decision had not yet found articulation. "Iudicium valoris" in the 1964 text is rather a slightly nuanced expression for the "judgment" referred to in *Insight*'s account of the process of making a decision.

36 See Lonergan, *The Triune God: Systematics* 512–19.

37 Lonergan, "Natural Right and Historical Mindedness," in *A Third Collection* 169–83.

38 See the two volumes in Lonergan's Collected Works devoted to macroeconomic theory: *Macroeconomic Dynamics: An Essay in Circulation Analysis*, vol. 15, ed. Frederick G. Lawrence, Patrick H. Byrne, and Charles C. Hefling, Jr. (Toronto: University of Toronto Press, 1999) and *For a New Political Economy*, vol. 21, ed. Philip J. McShane (Toronto: University of Toronto Press, 1998).

39 A summary and development of the understanding of the scale of values is presented in chapter 10 of *What Is Systematic Theology?* (sections 3.3–3.5).

40 The expression "focal meanings" is David Tracy's. See *The Analogical Imagination: Christian Theology and the Culture of Pluralism* (New York: Crossroad, 1981) passim.

41 For Lonergan's recommendations in these directions, see Doran, *What Is Systematic Theology?* 152. See also Robert M. Doran, "System Seeking *Method*: Reconciling System and History," in *Il Teologo e la Storia: Lonergan's Centenary (1904–2004)*, ed. Paul Gilbert and Natalino Spaccapelo (Rome: Gregorian

University Press 2006) 278–79. The latter paper can be found also on www.lonerganresource.com, under the rubric "Essays in Systematic Theology."

42 See Bernard Lonergan, "Healing and Creating in History," in *A Third Collection* 99–109.

43 Thus the explicit theological significance of the general theorem from my analysis of the scale of values in *Theology and the Dialectics of History*, to the effect that religious values condition the possibility of functioning schemes of recurrence in the sphere of personal value.

44 Thus the significance of the theorem that personal value conditions the possibility of functioning schemes of recurrence in the spheres of cultural, social, and vital values.

45 Lonergan, "Natural Right and Historical Mindedness," 174–75.

46 Lonergan, "Mission and the Spirit," 29–30.

47 There are explicit links to be drawn here with the mimetic theory of René Girard. I will begin to develop these in chapter 9.

48 See Doran, *What Is Systematic Theology?* 39, 78–79, 92, 144–46, 203.

49 Bernard Lonergan, *De Deo trino: Pars dogmatica* (Rome: Gregorian University Press, 1964), now presented with English translation as *The Triune God: Doctrines.*

50 Lonergan, *The Triune God: Systematics* 125. The "conceiving" to which Lonergan is referring is the *systematic* conceiving of divine relations and persons.

51 The twofold order of theological ideas is treated in some detail in Lonergan, ibid. 58–77.

52 Lonergan, *Method in Theology* 130–31.

Chapter 8

1 Lonergan, *The Triune God: Systematics* 471, 473.

2 See above, p. 39.

3 The italicized sentence is my own addition to the rest of the statement, which is found in Lonergan, *Method in Theology* 343.

4 Thus, the first sentence in Lonergan's chapter on the Trinitarian relations reads, "Now that we have conceived the two specifically distinct divine processions, we must ask what reality is to be attributed to them." Lonergan, *The Triune God: Systematics* 231. Emphasis added.

5 Ibid. 125.

6 See ibid. 127.

7 Nicene Creed (DB 54, DS 125).

8 Nicene-Constantinopolitan Creed (DB 86, DS 150).

9 Council of Florence, 1439 (DB 691, DS 1300).

10 DB 54, DS 125.

11 Athanasian Creed (Quicumque), Council of Toledo, 400 (DB 39, DS 75).
12 On the latter, Council of Florence (DB 691, DS 1300).
13 Lonergan, *The Triune God: Systematics* 129.
14 See ibid.
15 See Lonergan, *Insight* 682–83.
16 Lonergan, "Christology Today: Methodological Reflections" 94.
17 Further treatment of Lonergan's ordering of our analogical understanding of the divine essence is provided in Robert M. Doran, "The Triune God: Systematics on Divine Processions as Intelligent Emanations: A Commentary on pp. 124–229," on the website www.loneganresource.com, under "Scholarly Works/Articles," beginning at p. 51.
18 Karl Rahner, "Oneness and Threefoldness of God in Discussion with Islam," in *Theological Investigations* 18 (New York: Crossroad, 1983) 114.
19 May I add in fairness to Rahner that all of the references to Rahner in the work that Lonergan himself published are positive and affirming. In particular, Lonergan is at pains to tell us that he takes from Rahner the meaning of "sublation," and that he has been greatly aided by Rahner's understanding of the Ignatian consolation without preceding cause. See Lonergan, *Method in Theology* 241 (on sublation) and 106 (on consolation). These are two very important elements of Lonergan's own thought. He did speak of differences in the understanding of cognitional process in one of the lectures that he gave on *Method in Theology*, in response to a question from the audience and in an atmosphere of deep respect for Rahner. It also explains precisely the difference in their Trinitarian theologies: "Kant does not know about insight, and neither does Maréchal … Rahner asks what does this mean, this emanatio intelligibilis? It is the action of an intelligence. A person, insofar as he is acting intelligently, rationally, responsibly, is a principle of something else that occurs because this is intelligent, or because this is rational, or because this is the responsible thing to do. So you have causality in the material order and you have "be-causality" in the order of the mind, the order of the spirit. And because is because. So don't be discouraged if you don't get in there right away; but it is worth the effort, the labor of getting in." Taken from the recording of the first question session in the Regis College (Toronto) 1969 lectures on what then was the still uncompleted book *Method in Theology*. The recording itself can be found on www.bernardlonergan.com, at 535ROAOEO6o, and the transcription at 51600ATE06o. The quotation opens on the issue of "autonomous spiritual processions," which is our principal topic in this chapter. The relation to which Lonergan refers is that between insight and inner word, which is one of the key instances of what Aquinas called *emanatio intelligibilis* and of what I am calling autonomous spiritual procession.
20 Lonergan, *Insight* 539.

21 Lonergan, *Verbum: Word and Idea in Aquinas*, vol. 2 in Collected Works of Bernard Lonergan, ed. Frederick E. Crowe and Robert M. Doran (Toronto: University of Toronto Press, 1997) 207, emphasis Lonergan's. As we will see later, something similar may be said regarding the autonomous procession of decision and of acts of love.

22 Lonergan, *Insight* 539. It is these relationships of act from act, where the act that is principle is understanding or insight, whether direct or reflective, that Lonergan found lacking in Kant, Maréchal, and Rahner. See note 19 above.

23 Lonergan, "The Mediation of Christ in Prayer" 171.

24 See pp. 197–211.

25 "... anima humana intelligit se ipsam per suum intelligere, quod est actus proprius eius, perfecte demonstrans virtutem eius et naturam." Thomas Aquinas, *Summa theologiae*, 1, q. 88, a. 2, ad 3m, emphasis added. Lonergan translates this passage as follows: "the human soul understands itself by its understanding, which is its proper act, perfectly demonstrating its power and its nature." Bernard Lonergan, "Insight: Preface to a Discussion," *Collection* 143. Lonergan's enormously detailed and richly nuanced exegesis of the relevant texts in Aquinas can be found in *Verbum*. We will be appealing frequently to *Verbum* as we treat the various steps in Lonergan's argument. On *intelligere* as understanding, see *Verbum* 48–50, where Lonergan is nuanced enough to admit that Aquinas "does not employ the term *intelligere* exclusively in the sense of understanding." Still, "[i]t remains that the principal meaning of *intelligere* is understanding."

26 *Verbum* 39, note 126: "... there is needed an explanation of Scotist influence." It is well, I think, to refer to the complementary and extremely harsh judgment of Hans Urs von Balthasar: "On the circle of accessibility achieved between God and man rests both the culture of Antiquity and of the Middle Ages and ... the beginning of the modern age can ... be placed where its obviousness is first lost sight of (Duns Scotus)." In effect, von Balthasar is rooting modern atheism in the (now beatified!) John Duns Scotus. See von Balthasar, *The Glory of the Lord: A Theological Aesthetics*, vol. 4: *The Realm of Metaphysics in Antiquity*, trans. Oliver Davies et al. (San Francisco: Ignatius Press, 1989) 330. Further comments may be found in vol. 5, *The Realm of Metaphysics in the Modern Age* (see the index, Duns Scotus), where von Balthasar is especially critical of Scotus's concept of being. Lonergan roots the metaphysical mistake in a blunder in cognitional theory. The critiques complement one another perfectly. Let me add that if a study of Scotist influence was needed when Lonergan wrote *Verbum*, such a study is even more urgently required today. The entire series of empiricist and rationalist mistakes in philosophy that constitute in effect the history of modern European philosophy down to Hegel are rooted in Scotist counterpositions

on knowing and being. Scholastic philosophy and theology until Lonergan failed to address these issues because it too was infected by Scotist terminology and misconception. I hope that a beginning of the study that is required may be found in the work of Matthew Peters. See Peters, "Scotus: An Initial Lonergan Treatment," on www.lonerganresource.com under "Scholarly Works/Articles."

27 Lonergan, *The Triune God: Systematics* 133.

28 Ibid. More extensive treatments of Scotism and of conceptualism in general may be found in *Verbum* (see Conceptualism, and Scotus, in the index) and in Bernard Lonergan, *Topics in Education*, vol. 10 in Collected Works of Bernard Lonergan, ed. Robert M. Doran and Frederick E. Crowe (Toronto: University of Toronto Press, 1993) 108–10, where Thomist and Scotist theories of intellect are compared and contrasted. Also helpful is chapter 4 of Lonergan, *Early Works on Theological Method 1*, in chapter "1962–6," §1.2, "Thomist and Scotist Analysis." The upshot of Scotist analysis is expressed bluntly in the latter text: "There can be no psychological analogy for the Trinity." Ibid. 131.

29 Lonergan, *Verbum* 39, note 126, emphasis added.

30 George A. Lindbeck, *The Nature of Doctrine: Religion and Theology in a Postliberal Age* (Philadelphia: Westminster, 1984).

31 See Barth, *Church Dogmatics*, 1/1, ed. G.W. Bromiley and T.F. Torrance (Edinburgh: T. & T. Clark, 1975) 295. For Barth's explicit opposition to systematic procedures in theology, see *Church Dogmatics*, 1/2, trans. G.T. Thomson and Harold Knight (Edinburgh: T. & T. Clark, 1980) 861–62.

32 Barth, *Church Dogmatics*, 1/1 304, emphasis added.

33 See ibid. 308.

34 Ibid. 312; see also 333, 379, 414–15. Von Balthasar has presented a subtle analysis of Barth's hidden tendency to a theologically idealist (and definitely conceptualist) system, in *The Theology of Karl Barth*, trans. Edward T. Oakes, s.j. (San Francisco: Ignatius Press, 1992) 220–47.

35 See Doran, *What Is Systematic Theology?* 127–33; see also "Reception and Elemental Meaning: An Expansion of the Notion of Psychic Conversion," "Insight and Language: Steps toward the Resolution of a Problem," and "Empirical Consciousness in Insight: Is Our Conception Too Narrow?" (see above, p. 373, note 22).

36 Lonergan, *Method in Theology* 255–56.

37 See the schematic representation of "the three levels of cognitional process" on p. 299 of *Insight*, where "free images" and "utterances" are placed on the level of experiential data and yet acknowledged to be "under the influence of the higher levels before they provide a basis for inquiry and reflection." Development of this point is made by Lonergan almost every time he contrasts the data of the human sciences with the data of the natural sciences.

And yet it is quite common among students of Lonergan's work to regard the data of the first level, whether data of sense or data of consciousness, as not informed by meaning. This is a real gap, I believe, in the common reception of Lonergan's work by many of his own students.

38 "Quicumque enim intelligit, ex hoc ipso quod intelligit, procedit aliquid intra ipsum quod est conceptio rei intellectae, ex vi intellectiva proveniens et ex eius notitia procedens." Thomas Aquinas, *Summa theologiae*, 1, q. 27, a. 1. The translation is that of Michael G. Shields, in Lonergan, *The Triune God: Systematics* 133, with emphasis added here. Lonergan notes in a footnote at this point that the key phrase "ex vi intellectiva proveniens" (issuing from our intellective power) is omitted from the edition of questions 27–32 of the *Prima pars* prepared by B. Geyer in Florilegium Patristicum XXXVII (1934) 6. It is also omitted from the Blackfriars edition, being mentioned there only in a note as an alternative reading. See vol. 6 of the Blackfriars edition of the *Summa theologiae* (London: Eyre & Spottiswoode, and New York: McGraw-Hill, 1965) 4. If the phrase is left out, Aquinas's meaning is changed: the antecedent of the Latin "eius" becomes "rei intellectae" rather than "vi intellectiva." And so the translation is not "which is the conception of the thing understood, issuing from our intellective power and proceeding from its knowledge," but "which is the conception of the thing understood, proceeding from knowledge of it." The dynamic character of intelligence itself in its original meaningfulness and autonomy is not as prominent in the second rendition. The variations significantly change the meaning: in the variant that Lonergan accepts, the inner word proceeds from (and so is distinct from) knowledge; act proceeds from act. This is key to his entire cognitional theory, and in particular to the Trinitarian analogy he finds in cognitional process.

39 "… de ratione amoris est quod non procedit nisi a conceptione intellectus." Thomas Aquinas, *Summa theologiae*, 1, q. 27, a. 3, ad 3m, as translated by Michael G. Shields in Lonergan, *The Triune God: Systematics* 135. Lonergan does not devote the same attention to love in Aquinas as he does to understanding and the inner word that proceeds from understanding. Furthermore, in his later works he adopts a different position on the relation of love and knowledge from that expressed here by Aquinas, a position that, as we have already begun to see, allows another (though not contradictory but, rather, complementary and ultimately more satisfactory) conception of the psychological analogy for the Trinity; but it is an analogy, for in God *ipsum intelligere* and *ipsum amare* are *ipsum esse subsistens*. Further nuances are to be drawn here, I believe, than even Lonergan states explicitly. We have already introduced some of these further nuances, and they will be developed later.

40 "… id quod procedit ad intra processu intelligibili non oportet esse diversum; imo quanto perfectius procedit, tanto magis est unum cum eo a quo

procedit." Thomas Aquinas, *Summa theologiae*, 1, q. 27, a. 1, ad 2m; translation by Michael Shields, in Lonergan, *The Triune God: Systematics* 135. Aquinas adds: "Manifestum est enim quod quanto aliquid magis intelligitur tanto conceptio intellectualis est magis intima intelligenti et magis unum; nam intellectus secundum hoc quod actu intelligit, secundum hoc fit unum cum intellecto. Unde cum divinum intelligere sit in fine perfectionis ..., necesse est quod verbum divinum sit perfecte unum cum eo a quo procedit absque omni diversitate." ("It is clear that the better something is understood the more intimate is the intellectual conception to the one who understands and the more one with him or her; for by the very fact that the intellect understands in act, it becomes one with what is understood. Thus, since divine understanding is at the pinnacle of perfection ..., the divine Word is necessarily perfectly one with that from which it proceeds, without any diversity.") *Summa theologiae*, 1, q. 27, a. 1, ad 2m.

41   Ibid., corpus of article, emphasis added. My translation, incorporating that of Shields: "And this is especially clear in the case of the intellect, whose activity, namely, to understand, remains in the one who understands. For whenever we understand, by the mere fact that we do understand, something proceeds within us, which is the conception of the thing understood, issuing from our intellective power and proceeding from its knowledge. The spoken word means this conception, which is called the word of the heart, signified as it is by the spoken word ... [a procession] not as there is a procession in corporeal things or through local motion or through the action of a cause on an effect distinct from it, ... but according to intelligible emanation, such as is that of the intelligible word that remains in the intellect."

42   I suspect he may mention it first here because in fact it is easier for us to recognize. Direct insight as grounding conceptualization is not as clear in consciousness as grasp of evidence grounding judgment, probably because the integrity of the subject is far more at stake in the second set of operations than in the first.

43   Lonergan, *Insight* 356.

44   See Lonergan, *The Triune God: Systematics* 135, 137. The dynamics of judgment of fact are studied in detail in *Insight*, chapters 9 and 10, and with reference to the texts of Aquinas in *Verbum*, chapter 2. What would later be called the dynamics of judgments of value are studied (in less detail) in chapter 18 of *Insight* (where the expression "judgment of value" does not occur), and, as we have seen, it is on these dynamics as understood in *Insight* that Lonergan relies in his early systematics of the Trinity for his analogy regarding the procession of the divine Word. This reliance will cause a problem in interpreting Lonergan that we will attempt to resolve. I called attention to the problem above. See p. 148. For an attempt to resolve the issue, see pp. 308–309.

45 "Omnes enim experiendo novimus ..." Lonergan, *The Triune God: Systematics* 134, 136, emphasis added.

46 Ibid. 137.

47 Ibid. Lonergan adds a further comment, to be qualified in his later work where the psychological analogy is somewhat differently conceived: "Therefore, since by its very nature the will is a rational appetite, and since this appetite cannot be actually rational unless it actually follows upon reason, we must say that 'it is of the nature of love to proceed only from a conception of the intellect.'" Ibid., quoting Aquinas. Lonergan's entire presentation of decision here follows the presentation of *Insight*, which was later complemented by other considerations. The matter is treated in *What Is Systematic Theology?* chapter 9, §4.2; it has been further qualified in the present book, and these further nuances will be developed in greater detail later.

48 See Lonergan, *The Triune God: Systematics* 141. The words "and also by virtue of intellectual consciousness itself as determined by the prior act" reflect the reading of *Summa theologiae*, 1, q. 27, a. 1, discussed in note 38 above: "ex vi intellectiva proveniens et ex eius notitia procedens."

49 Lonergan, *The Triune God: Systematics* 139.

50 Ibid. 139.

Chapter 9

1 Lonergan, *The Triune God: Systematics* 139.

2 See the section "The Duality of Consciousness" in *Theology and the Dialectics of History* 46–47.

3 See Lonergan, *Verbum* 107–33, and especially 130–33.

4 I am grateful to Neil Ormerod for pointing out the relevance of this distinction to interpreting and evaluating the work of Girard.

5 Lonergan, *The Triune God: Systematics* 213, 215.

6 See Doran, "Reception and Elemental Meaning: An Expansion of the Notion of Psychic Conversion."

7 We will see more on the meaning of "per modum operati," pp. 261, 263–78.

8 Lonergan, *The Triune God: Systematics* 139.

9 Lonergan, "Natural Right and Historical Mindedness" 174–75.

10 Lonergan, "Mission and the Spirit" 29–30. Note the insistence on "it is natural ... to love." Possibly it is this natural love that Lonergan was thinking of when he offered his later psychological analogy. But clearly the analogy is open to the supernatural instancing of it that I have adopted here, the instancing that "lies not in what is possible to nature but in what is effected by the grace of Christ." I believe it is antecedently probable that Lonergan was thinking of the latter instance.

11 Ernest Becker, *The Denial of Death* (New York: The Free Press, 1973) passim.
12 See http://www.archive.org/details/MartinHeidegger-
     TheSelfAssertionOfTheGermanUniversity1933.
13 Lonergan, *Method in Theology* 110. An earlier presentation of some of these
     ideas can be found in METHOD: *Journal of Lonergan Studies* 23 (2005, pub-
     lished in 2009) 149–86, under the title "Imitating the Divine Relations: A
     Theological Contribution to Mimetic Theory." This paper appears as well in
     the e-book *Essays in Systematic Theology* on the website www.lonerganresource.
     com.
14 Lonergan, *Method in Theology* 110: "Our advance in understanding is also
     the elimination of oversights and misunderstandings. Our advance in truth
     is also the correction of mistakes and errors. Our moral development is
     through repentance for our sins. Genuine religion is discovered and real-
     ized by redemption from the many traps of religious aberration."
15 See Bernard Lonergan, "The Ongoing Genesis of Methods," in *A Third Col-
     lection* 156–57.
16 For an extended argument to this effect, see Robert M. Doran, "The Non-
     violent Cross: Lonergan and Girard on Redemption," *Theological Studies* 71
     (2010) 46–61.
17 René Girard, *Deceit, Desire, and the Novel: Self and Other in Literary Structure*,
     trans. Yvonne Freccero (Baltimore: Johns Hopkins University Press, 1966) 9.
18 Ibid.
19 Ibid. 10.
20 Note Girard's way of conjoining the words "spontaneous" and "autono-
     mous," whereas we are distinguishing them. It is only the *processions of act
     from act in the spiritual realm* that Lonergan calls autonomous, since these
     processions are governed *not* by the interdividual field that constitutes the
     first way of being conscious and that can infect the second way as well, nor
     by the emergence of answers from questions, of act from potency, that con-
     stitutes the spontaneity even of the second way of being conscious, but by
     the transcendental laws of the human spirit as, in its movement from expe-
     rience through understanding and judgment to right decision, it manifests
     along the way not only spontaneous emergences of act from potency but
     careful, self-possessed, assured originations of new acts from previous acts: of
     inner words of hypothetical conceptualization from insightful grasp of intel-
     ligibility, of judgments of fact from the reflective grasp of the sufficiency of
     evidence, of judgments of value from loving grasp of the evidence of good-
     ness, and of loving acts from the collaboration of loving grasp and the word
     of value that it has uttered. In the emergence of act from potency, the prin-
     ciple is the object; in the emergence of act from act, the principle is the
     subject.
21 Girard, *Desire, Deceit, and the Novel* 1–2.

22 Ibid. 3.
23 Ibid. 4.
24 Ibid.
25 Ibid. 7.
26 Ibid.
27 Ibid. 8.
28 See Chris Fleming, *René Girard: Violence and Mimesis* (Cambridge, UK: Polity Press, 2004) 24.
29 Ibid.
30 Ibid. 25–26.
31 Ibid. 28. One thinks also of Hegel's master–slave relationship.
32 For material in this and the next paragraph, see Richard Golsan, *René Girard and Myth* (New York: Routledge, 2002) 13–16. Golsan's book is an excellent introduction to Girard's work. Also recommended are Fleming, *René Girard: Violence and Mimesis* and Michael Kirwan, *Discovering Girard* (Cambridge MA: Cowley, 2005).
33 Golsan, *René Girard and Myth* 21.
34 Ibid.
35 See ibid. 21–22.
36 John Ranieri, "Individual Bias and Group Bias: A Girardian Reading," unpublished paper delivered at the Boston College Lonergan Workshop, June 2003; "Girard, Lonergan, and the Limits of Common Sense," unpublished paper delivered at the Second International Lonergan Workshop, Toronto, August 2004.
37 Golsan, *René Girard and Myth* 1.
38 For a more extended argument to this effect, see Doran, "The Non-violent Cross."
39 See Bernard Lonergan, "The Mediation of Christ in Prayer," in *Philosophical and Theological Papers 1958–1964*, vol. 6 of Collected Works of Bernard Lonergan, ed. Robert C. Croken and Robert M. Doran (Toronto: University of Toronto Press, 1996) 174–76. I am indebted to conversations with Gilles Mongeau of Regis College, Toronto, for these connections.
40 To speak of "mutual self-mediation" vis-à-vis the Trinity is not to posit a process notion of God. As Lonergan is reported to have responded once to the question, Do we make a difference to God? "We make an eternal difference to God."
41 See Wright's book *Jesus and the Victory of God* (Minneapolis: Fortress Press, 1996), and especially chapter 12.
42 See Raymund Schwager, *Jesus and the Drama of Salvation*, trans. James G. Williams and Paul Haddon (New York: Crossroad, 1999). See also Schwager, *Must There Be Scapegoats? Violence and Redemption in the Bible*, trans. Maria L. Assad (New York: Crossroad, 1987). For Meyer, see above, p. 354, note 15.

43 See Lonergan, *Method in Theology* 33.

44 See James Alison, *The Joy of Being Wrong: Original Sin through Easter Eyes* (New York: Crossroad, 1998).

45 See Girard, *Deceit, Desire, and the Novel* 14.

46 *A Pilgrim's Journey: The Autobiography of Ignatius of Loyola*, trans. and ed. Joseph N. Tylenda, s.J. (Wilmington, Delaware: Michael Glazier, 1985) 14.

47 Ignatius Loyola, *The Text of the Spiritual Exercises of Saint Ignatius*, trans. with a preface by Henry Keane, s.J. (London: Burns Oates and Washbourne, 1952) §98.

48 Girard, *Things Hidden since the Foundation of the World* 7.

49 Ibid. 18.

50 René Girard, *Violence and the Sacred*, trans. Patrick Gregory (Baltimore: Johns Hopkins University Press, 1977).

51 Girard, *Things Hidden* 18.

52 Girard, *Violence and the Sacred* 91.

53 Lonergan, *Insight* 721–22.

54 Matthew 5.43–48.

55 See above, pp. 191, 379 note 38.

56 Thomas Aquinas, *Summa theologiae*, 1, q. 27, a. 1.

57 Lonergan, *The Triune God: Systematics* 139, emphasis added.

58 Ibid. 141. On potency, form, and act as metaphysical elements isomorphic with the experience-understanding-judgment structure of human cognitional process, see Lonergan, *Insight* 456–63.

59 "[T]here are two aspects to psychological acts; for the same psychological act is intentional insofar as it refers to some other, and natural insofar as it is considered in itself." Lonergan, *The Triune God: Systematics* 141. See note 16 to chapter 5 in *Philosophical and Theological Papers 1958–1964* (CWL 6) 105.

60 "In every sensitive and intellectual act, whether apprehensive or appetitive, there are three things that occur *simultaneously*: (1) the object is intended; (2) the intending subject himself is rendered present to himself; (3) the act of the subject is rendered present to the subject. Distinguish sharply between the presence of the subject to himself and the presence of the object to the subject: the object is present as *that which is intended*, the act is present as *that by which the object is intended*, the subject is present as *that which intends*. In a similar way, distinguish this presence of the subject through consciousness and the presence of the same subject through reflection or introspection: reflection or introspection renders the subject present as an object, as that which is intended; but this could not be were not the subject already present to himself through consciousness, as subject, as that which intends." Lonergan, *The Triune God: Systematics* 141. On consciousness, see Lonergan, *Insight* 344–52. See also Lonergan, *The Ontological and Psychological Constitution of Christ* 157–89.

61 Lonergan, *Method in Theology* 243.
62 See Lonergan, *The Triune God: Systematics* 143. Lonergan adds, "Therefore, the phenomenalism of consciousness that would deny causality, or the mode of causality proper to consciousness, is excluded." There is causality, of course in the *imago* or *imitatio*, not in the original, not in divine processions.
63 Ibid.
64 I will leave Lonergan's expression *processio operati* untranslated. It should become a precise technical term in systematics, and it is more likely to do so if it is left in its Latin form rather than translated into very stilted English. We will see more on this issue shortly. See below, pp. 263–78. For an array of details on the matter, see Lonergan, *Verbum*, chapter 3.
65 See Bernard Lonergan, "Natural Right and Historical Mindedness" 172.
66 Lonergan, "Christology Today: Methodological Reflections" 93.

Chapter 10

1 Bernard Lonergan, "Sacralization and Secularization," in *Philosophical and Theological Papers 1965–1980* 264. I wish to call attention to the applications of these categories made by John D. Dadosky in two papers, "Sacralization, Secularization, and Religious Fundamentalism," *Studies in Religion/Sciences religieuses* 36 (2007) 513–29, and "The Church and the Other: Mediation and Friendship in Post–Vatican II Roman Catholic Ecclesiology," *Pacifica*, October (2005) 302–22. I hope that the sources that I will identify for discriminating each of these processes can ground Dadosky's applications.

  The present chapter is a development on my paper "Lonergan and Girard on Sacralization and Desacralization," in *Revista Portuguesa de Filosofia* 63 (2007) 1171–1201. This paper can now be found on the website www.loneganresource.com.

2 See Mohandas K. Gandhi, *An Autobiography: The Story of My Experiments with Truth*, trans. Mahadev Desai (Boston: Beacon Press, 1993) 35.
3 Here I have learned from my former student Ravi Michael Louis, who has argued that the basic "mood" that Heidegger identifies with "care" should really be identified with discernment. This argument appears, for instance, in Louis's paper "The Christian Imagination: Some Operative Symbols" (unpublished). In terms that I borrowed many years ago from Eric Voegelin, that same "mood" may be described as the search for direction in the movement of life. See Voegelin, "The Gospel and Culture," in *Jesus and Man's Hope*, ed. Donald G. Miller and Dikran Y. Hadidian, vol. 2 (Pittsburgh: Pittsburgh Theological Seminary, 1971) passim.
4 A more complete treatment of the question, drawing on material that we have already spoken of here, may be found in Robert M. Doran, "The Nonviolent Cross: Lonergan and Girard on Redemption."

5 Bernard Lonergan, *De Verbo incarnato* (Rome: Gregorian University Press, 1964) thesis 17, as translated by Charles C. Hefling. All quotations of this work are from Hefling's translation.

6 Girard, *I See Satan Fall Like Lightning*, trans. James G. Williams (Maryknoll, NY: Orbis, 2002) 151.

7 Lonergan, *Insight* 720.

8 As we have seen, in the four-point hypothesis the consequent conditions required in order that it be true that the gift has been given are twofold, namely, sanctifying grace as the elevation of central form and the habit of charity as a supernatural conjugate form "spirated" from sanctifying grace in a manner analogous to the passive spiration of the Holy Spirit by the Father and the Son together. Thus the "fourfold" character of the divine self-communication: hypostatic union, sanctifying grace, charity, and the beatific vision.

9 Charles C. Hefling, Jr., "A Perhaps Permanently Valid Achievement: Lonergan on Christ's Satisfaction," METHOD: *Journal of Lonergan Studies* 10 (1992) 51–76.

10 See Neil Ormerod, "The Eucharist as Sacrifice," in *The Eucharist: Faith and Worship*, ed. M. Press (Homebush, NSW: St Pauls, 2001) 42–55, and "The Dual Language of Sacrifice in Christian Tradition," *Pacifica* 17 (2004) 159–69.

11 Doran, *Theology and the Dialectics of History* 121–22.

12 Bernard Lonergan, "The Redemption," in *Philosophical and Theological Papers 1958–1964*, ed. Robert C. Croken and Robert M. Doran (Toronto: University of Toronto Press, 1996) 28.

13 Charles Hefling, "About What Might a 'Girard–Lonergan' 'Conversation' Be?" *Lonergan Workshop* 17, ed. Fred Lawrence (Boston College, 2002) 122–23.

14 "Sacralization and Secularization" 270, 274–75.

15 Ibid. 271.

16 See Robert M. Doran, *Theology and the Dialectics of History*, index, "Soteriological constitutive meaning," "differentiation."

17 See above, p. 383, note 36.

18 See Girard, *I See Satan Fall Like Lightning*, index, "Powers and principalities." See also Girard, *Things Hidden since the Foundation of the World* 199–205.

19 Alfred North Whitehead, *Religion in the Making* (New York: Meridian, 1960) 16.

20 See Doran, *Theology and the Dialectics of History*, chapter 4 passim.

21 See Lonergan, "Sacralization and Secularization" 274–75.

22 Doran, *Theology and the Dialectics of History*, chapters 4 and 5.

23 Lonergan, "Sacralization and Secularization" 262.

24 Ibid. 263. Girard, of course, provides similar assistance, and on firmer grounds, even firmer psychological grounds, than those of Freud. It could

be said that Girard pushes what Ricoeur calls the hermeneutics of suspicion so far that it turns into a hermeneutics of recovery.

25 Lonergan, *Method in Theology* 79–80.
26 See Lonergan, "Religious Knowledge," in *A Third Collection* 144.
27 Lonergan, "Sacralization and Secularization" 263.
28 Ibid. 265–66.
29 Quoted ibid. 265.
30 Quoted ibid. 264. The quotations in this and the preceding note appear in a summary by Claude Geffré, o.p., in "Desacralization and the Spiritual Life," *Concilium* 19 (1966) 111–31. Geffré's paper is the source of Lonergan's information on the debate.
31 Lonergan, "Sacralization and Desacralization" 280.
32 Ibid.
33 Ibid. One thinks of clericalism in the Catholic church, for instance.
34 Ibid. 280.
35 Collective responsibility sets the context for one of Lonergan's most important papers, "Natural Right and Historical Mindedness." But it must be understood theologically in the context of social grace. I tried to provide such a context in part 1, arguing in effect that both social grace and collective responsibility are a matter of the objectification, the "being writ large," of the normative subject under grace that is the key to all the problems with which we are attempting to come to grips in the present work.
36 These considerations are linked to my earlier work on cosmological as contrasted with anthropological and soteriological constitutive meanings and the manner in which they inform cultures. See Doran, *Theology and the Dialectics of History*, part 4.
37 Lonergan, "Sacralization and Secularization" 269.
38 See, for example, Girard, *Things Hidden since the Foundation of the World*, book II, "The Judaeo-Christian Scriptures." This entire section begins with the quotation from John 1.1, "In principio erat Verbum."
39 Ibid. 269. It must of course be said that this notion of God was only progressively revealed in Hebrew religion itself. And Lonergan's brief account of the progressive revelation does not contain explicitly the anthropological precision that Girard finds in the exposure of the victim mechanism. The latter, I wager, is part of the divine revelation, as I think Girard would insist. Religions of the superstructure, that is, of the explicit word, are authentic only to the extent that their word is a progressive revelation of the genuine, nonviolent, sacred. The religion of the word, of the book, can itself be as violent as any religion of the infrastructure, as contemporary history renders all too obvious, whether the book be the Koran or the bible.
40 Charles Hefling, "Revelation and/as Insight."
41 See Matthew 5.43–48.

42 One might think here of the film *Atanarjuat: The Fast Runner*, which portrays an ancient Inuit story in which the principal protagonist comes to a realization that nonviolent and unequivocally expressed forgiveness of injury alone will heal his community.

43 Lonergan, "Sacralization and Secularization" 269–70.

44 Ibid. 270.

45 See Matthew 12.22–32.

46 Girard, *I See Satan Fall Like Lightning* 180.

47 Lonergan, "Sacralization and Secularization" 275.

48 Bernard Lonergan, "Dimensions of Meaning," *Collection* 245.

Chapter 11

1 Lonergan, *The Triune God: Systematics* 145. An earlier version of the first assertion appeared in *Divinarum personarum* in 1957 and 1959. See *The Triune God: Systematics* 764–81. I have studied the difference between the two assertions. This difference is of great interest. See "The Triune God: Systematics *on Divine Processions as Intelligent Emanations*," on the website www.lonerganresource.com, under Scholarly Works: "Articles," §8, "Comparison of Chapter Two with *Divinarum personarum*."

2 Bernard Lonergan, "A Post-Hegelian Philosophy of Religion," in *A Third Collection* 213. See also *Method in Theology* 240: "So we move to the existential moment when we discover for ourselves that our choosing affects ourselves no less than the chosen or rejected objects, and that it is up to each of us to decide for himself what he is to make of himself."

3 Lonergan, "A Post-Hegelian Philosophy of Religion" 208.

4 See Lonergan, *The Triune God: Systematics* 176–79.

5 I called attention to Lonergan's development on this issue above, p. 373, note 21, and p. 380, note 44. I must add that in fact Lonergan uses the phrase "judgment of value" twice in *Verbum* (at pp. 152 and 209) in relation to the Word that breathes proceeding Love. I am grateful to Neil Ormerod for calling this to my attention.

6 "The third act, then, is a judgment on the value of deciding to believe with certitude or with probability that some proposition certainly or probably is true or false. As any judgment, it proceeds with rational necessity from one's own grasp of the virtually unconditioned, and it posits precisely what is grasped as unconditioned. As any judgment, it may be true or false, for the investigation leading up to the judgment may or may not have been free from the undue influence of desires other than the pure desire to know, and again, one may or may not be insufficiently or excessively exigent in determining the presence of the virtually unconditioned. However, it differs from judgments of fact and from theoretical judgments, for it settles a question of

value; and it differs from other judgments of value, for it is concerned not
with the good of the senses nor with the good of the will nor with the good
of the whole man nor with the good of society but simply and solely with the
good of intellect. Moreover, it is concerned not with the good of intellect
in general but with a particular belief. Accordingly, it presupposes that it is
good for intellect to reach the unconditioned through its own inquiry and
reflection, that it is good for intellect to communicate to others the unconditioned that it has reached, and that it is good for intellect to accept from
others the unconditioned that they have reached. But the judgment of value
now under discussion goes beyond these generalities to pronounce upon
the value of accepting from others in a determinate instance what they communicate as unconditioned." Lonergan, *Insight* 730.

7 Ibid. 635.
8 See Lonergan, *The Triune God: Systematics* 180–81. For the reference in *Divinarum personarum*, see ibid. note 24.
9 Ibid., emphasis added.
10 For Lonergan on consciousness, see *Insight*, chapter 11, and *The Ontological
   and Psychological Constitution of Christ*, part 5.
11 Lonergan, *The Triune God: Systematics* 143.
12 Lonergan, *The Triune God: Systematics* 144–45.
13 See above, pp. 267–72.
14 Augustine, *The Trinity*, trans. Edmund Hill, o.p. (Brooklyn: New City Press,
   1991) 66.
15 While the language here is both Scholastic and metaphysical, the point can
   be clarified in experiential terms: the act of understanding proceeds from
   the spirit of inquiry raising and answering questions.
16 Lonergan, *The Triune God: Systematics* 148–49.
17 For the above distinctions, see ibid. 144–51.
18 "The Father is not made by anyone, not created by anyone, not begotten by
   anyone. The Son is from the Father alone, and is not made, not created, but
   begotten. The Holy Spirit is from the Father and the Son, and is not made,
   not created, not begotten, but proceeds." See ibid. 150–51.
19 See Lonergan, *Method in Theology* 132: "It [systematics] is concerned to work
   out appropriate systems of conceptualization, *to remove apparent inconsisten-
   cies*, to move towards some grasp of spiritual matters both from their own
   inner coherence and from the analogies offered by more familiar human
   experience." Emphasis added.
20 Lonergan, *The Triune God: Systematics* 153.
21 Ibid. 153, 155, emphasis added.
22 Ibid. 157.
23 Perhaps it would be well to give this item in its entirety: "Sacrosancta Ro-
   mana Ecclesia, Domini et Salvatoris nostri voce fundata, firmiter credit,

profitetur et praedicat, unum verum Deum omnipotentem, incommutabilem et aeternum, Patrem et Filium et Spiritum Sanctum, unum in essentia, trinum in personis: Patrem ingenitum, Filium ex Patre genitum, Spiritum Sanctum ex Patre et Filio procedentem. Patrem non esse Filium aut Spiritum Sanctum; Filium non esse Patrem aut Spiritum Sanctum; Spiritum Sanctum non esse Patrem aut Filium: sed Pater tantum Pater est, Filius tantum Filius est, Spiritus Sanctus tantum Spiritus Sanctus est. Solus Pater de substantia sua genuit Filium, solus Filius de solo Patre est genitus, solus Spiritus Sanctus simul de Patre procedit et Filio. Hae tres personae sunt unus Deus, et non tres dii: quia trium est una substantia, una essentia, una natura, una divinitas, una immensitas, una aeternitas, omniaque sunt unum, ubi not obviat relationis oppositio."

24 Thomas Aquinas, *Summa theologiae*, 1, q. 27, a. 1, ad 2m; emphasis added. For a translation, see above, p. 191, at note 40.

25 See Lonergan, *The Triune God: Systematics* 153.

26 See *Verbum* 18, "a thinking out, an *excogitare*" and 22–23, 51, for the notion of thinking in order to understand.

27 Lonergan, *Verbum* 208.

28 "Supposita in divinis emanatione intelligibili, sequitur processio per modum operati." Lonergan, *The Triune God: Systematics* 160–61.

29 Ibid. 163.

30 Ibid.

31 Ibid.

32 Ibid.

33 Ibid.

34 Ibid. 163, 165.

35 Ibid. 165, emphasis added.

36 Ibid.

37 That is, they are autonomous in the sense in which, borrowing from Lonergan, we are using this term.

38 Lonergan, *Verbum* 206–208.

39 "Supposita ergo emanatione intelligibili et divina, sequuntur omnia quae ad processionem divinam pertinent, quaeque sub nomine processionis per modum operati ex veritatibus fidei iam probavimus." Lonergan, *The Triune God: Systematics* 164.

40 Ibid. 165.

41 Ibid. 164–67.

42 Ibid. 167.

43 Ibid. 169, quoting DB 1796 (DS 3016).

44 Lonergan, *Verbum* 208–209.

45 "Praeter similitudinem emanationis intelligibilis non alia esse videtur analogia ad systematicam conceptionem divinae processionis efformandam." Lonergan, *The Triune God: Systematics* 168.

46 Ibid. 169.

47 Ibid. 169, 171.

48 Ibid. 171. Just how much Lonergan's approach in *The Triune God: Systematics* meets this systematic criterion or qualification can be seen in its fruitfulness for establishing further analogies that have the same structure.

49 Ibid. I have already indicated that Lonergan's later suggestion of an analogy may be interpreted as at least opening on the possibility of an analogy that proceeds from the supernatural gift of grace. But even this, as well as the analogy that I am proposing, which is a development on the possibilities latent in Lonergan's later analogy, will be understood by analogy with precisely the natural realities to which we are currently appealing. That is one of my reasons for going into so much detail on the analogy from nature, even if I wish to promote an analogy from supernatural participation in divine life. The other reason, of course, is to establish the relations from above between the realm of religious values and the personal value of the subject in his or her self-transcendence.

50 Ibid. 170.

51 Ibid. 171, 173.

52 See Lonergan, *Insight* 540–41. "Matter" is characterized as that whose functioning could not occur apart from the empirical residue, that is, "apart from manifolds of instances in a space-time continuum, and apart from actual frequencies that nonsystematically diverge from ideal frequencies," and so matter is defined as "whatever is constituted by the empirical residue or is conditioned intrinsically by that residue." The spiritual, then, or the immaterial is what is neither constituted by, nor conditioned intrinsically by, the empirical residue. Not constituted: "inasmuch as we are understanding, we are abstracting from that residue; and inasmuch as we are grasping the unconditioned, we are attaining the lucid, fully rational factualness that contrasts so violently with the brute factualness with which instances similar in all respects still are different instances, with which the multiplicity of the continuum is noncountable because nonordinable, with which actual frequencies diverge from ideal frequencies in any manner provided it is nonsystematic. But if insight and grasp of the unconditioned are constituted quite differently from the empirical residue, so also are the inquiry and critical reflection that lead to them and the conception and judgment that result from them and express them." Not conditioned intrinsically: "Quite obviously, there is some conditioning. Our inquiry and insight demand something apart from themselves into which we inquire and attain insight; initially and commonly that other is sensible experience, and in it is found the empirical residue. But if sensible experience and so the empirical residue condition inquiry and insight, it is no less plain that that conditioning is extrinsic. Seeing is seeing color, and color is spatial, so that seeing is conditioned intrinsically by the spatial continuum. But insight is an act of understanding,

and so far from being conditioned intrinsically by the empirical residue, understanding abstracts from it. Again, to grasp the unconditioned there is a prerequisite of a known fulfilment of conditions; commonly this fulfilment lies in sensible experience; still, the fulfilment is anything but unconditioned; and it is the unconditioned that intrinsically conditions a grasp of the unconditioned."

53 Ibid. 173.

54 Ibid. 173, 175.

55 See ibid. 174–77.

56 Ibid. 175, 177.

57 This point is so important that we will cite Lonergan's Latin. "*Autonomia existentialis.* Tripliciter in homine exercetur illa autonomia secundum quam ex intelligentia oritur verbum et ex verbo oritur electio. Primo modo, in practicis quatenus homo intelligit, iudicat, eligit agenda et facienda. Altero modo in speculativis quatenus homo de universo quaerit, illudque quantum potest intelligit, unde et quale sit iudicat, ut denique in amorem quendam contemplativum universi prorumpat. Tertio denique modo in existentialibus quatenus homo de se ipso quaerit, et qualis esse debeat intelligit, et quemadmodum ipse se talem facere possit iudicat, unde procedit electio existentialis per quam, quatenus hic et nunc in se est, ipse se talem facit.

"Proinde, analogia trinitaria ex exercitio autonomiae existentialis sumenda esse videtur. Qui enim de Deo trino quaerit, non Deum considerat ut creantem vel agentem, et ideo ab autonomia practica praescindit; neque Deum considerat quatenus omnia intelligit et iudicat et diligit, et ideo a speculativis praescindit; sed Deum considerat prout ipse Deus ab aeterno in se ipso constituitur ut trinus, et ideo analogiam ex processionibus secundum autonomiam existentialem sumit." Ibid. 176, 178.

58 Ibid. 179, 181.

59 "Per similitudinem emanationis intelligibilis duae et tantummodo duae processiones divinae concipi possunt, nempe verbi a dicente, et amoris ab utroque." Lonergan, *The Triune God: Systematics* 180.

60 "Divinam verbi emanationem, non autem emanationem amoris, consequitur ratio generationis proprie dictae." Ibid. 188.

61 In the earlier treatment, the Father is understood on the analogy of the act of understanding, and in the later treatment the Father is understood as *Agapē.* This is the only real difference in Lonergan's two presentations of the Trinitarian analogy, and the two can be put together as I am doing here.

62 "*dicens:* principium emanationis intelligibilis quatenus per actum intelligendi determinatur." Ibid. 180.

63 "*verbum:* immanens terminus emanationis intelligibilis ex dicente." Ibid. I am adding to this definition the existential context that Lonergan specifies as the best context within which to develop the analogy.

64 Ibid. note 23.

65 See below, pp. 323–28.

66 We are referred here to Thomas Aquinas, *Summa theologiae*, 1, q. 79, a. 7 c.: "Intellectus … respicit suum obiectum secundum communem rationem entis; eo quod intellectus possibilis est *quo est omnia fieri.*"

67 Lonergan, *Insight* 372.

68 As we have seen in dialogue with Girard, human desire is far more complicated than this, giving rise to a plethora of existential and ultimately theological problems that will feature heavily in a systematic theology of history.

69 Ibid. For my qualifications in terms of linguistic presentations and ordinary and original meaningfulness, see above, p. 373, note 22, and p. 378, note 35. Note that the opening pages of Wittgenstein's *Philosophical Investigations* contain a severe critique of the Augustinian position, which is the basic or grounding position on this matter in the tradition in which Lonergan stands. Lonergan's response in *Method* is typical: he advances the position in Wittgenstein before reversing the counterposition.

70 See Lonergan, *Method in Theology* 11–12.

71 Ibid. 34.

72 "Intermediate between judgments of fact and judgments of value lie apprehensions of value. Such apprehensions are given in feelings." Lonergan, *Method in Theology* 37. I would emphasize that the apprehensions are given in predeliberative and deliberative *insights* that are laden with feeling (*Befindlichkeit*), where the feeling itself is a response to the apprehended possible value.

73 For the references see above, p. 367, note 14.

74 Lonergan, *The Triune God: Systematics* 565. I am reminded here of the wonderful passage from *Insight*: "Besides the *noēma* or *intentio intenta* or *pensée pensée* illustrated by the lower contexts *P, Q, R,* … and by the upper context that is Gödel's theorem, there also is the *noēsis* or *intentio intendens* or *pensée pensante* that is constituted by the very activity of inquiring and reflecting, understanding and affirming, asking further questions and reaching further answers. Let us say that this noetic activity is engaged in a lower context when it is doing mathematics or following scientific method or exercising common sense. Then it will be moving towards an upper context when it scrutinizes mathematics or science or common sense in order to grasp the nature of noetic activity. And if it comes to understand and affirm what understanding is and what affirming is, then it has reached an upper context that logically is independent of the scaffolding of mathematics, science, and common sense. Moreover, if it can be shown that the upper context is invariant, that any attempt to revise it can be legitimate only if the hypothetical reviser refutes his own attempt by invoking experience, understanding, and reflection in an already prescribed manner, then it will appear that, while

the *noēma* or *intentio intenta* or *pensée pensée* may always be expressed with greater accuracy and completeness, still the immanent and recurrently operative structure of the *noēsis* or *intentio intendens* or *pensée pensante* must always be one and the same." Lonergan, *Insight* 19–20. However, this passage from *Insight* emphasizes the subjective pole, while the texts we are studying now stress the objective pole. Interestingly enough, Lonergan came late in his discussion of the meaning of "transcendental" to prefer Husserl's acknowledgment of the correlative status of subject and object to Kant's exclusive emphasis on the subject. For a hint in this direction, see note 8 in "Religious Knowledge" in *A Third Collection*. It is in this territory that Lonergan's cognitional theory and von Balthasar's ruminations on truth in the *Theologic* can be mediated with each other. See Hans Urs von Balthasar, *Theo-logic: Theological Logical Theory*, 3 vols., trans. Adrian Walker (San Francisco: Ignatius Press, 2000).

75 See above, p. 294.

76 See, for example, Bernard Lonergan, *Understanding and Being*, vol. 5 in Collected Works of Bernard Lonergan, ed. Elizabeth A. Morelli and Mark D. Morelli (Toronto: University of Toronto Press, 1990) 23–24. The example is not as clear to everyone as Lonergan perhaps had hoped it might be.

77 "*amor*: fundamentalis actus voluntatis: cf. *Sum. theol.*, I, q. 20; I-II, qq. 26–28; II-II, qq. 23–33. Qui quidem amor, quamvis non in intellectu sed in voluntate recipiatur, sane est intra ipsam conscientiam intellectualem, cum voluntas sit appetitus intellectum sequens seu intellectualis. Quare sicut verbum est immanens terminus emanationis intelligibilis ex dicente, ita amor est immanens terminus emanationis intelligibilis ex spirante." Lonergan, *The Triune God: Systematics* 180.

78 See ibid., note 24, where Lonergan indicates that "spirare" is the "notionaliter diligere" of this passage. The passage may be translated as follows: "where the love intended in the terms 'love' or 'dilection' is simply the relationship of lover to loved, then they are essential terms, as are 'intelligence' and 'understanding' [that is, they refer to the love common to all three divine persons, not to the notional acts]. But where we use these terms to express the relation of what proceeds in love to its principle and the converse relation of the principle to what proceeds, so that through 'love' is meant the love that proceeds and through 'to love' is meant to spirate the love that proceeds, then 'Love' is the name for a person, and 'to love' is a term for a notional act, even as are 'to speak' or 'to beget.'" The notional act in question is active spiration.

79 "*spirans*: principium emanationis intelligibilis quatenus determinatur tum per actum intelligendi tum etiam per consequens verbum *quod est iudicium valoris*." Lonergan, *The Triune God: Systematics* 180, emphasis added.

80 See Lonergan, *Divinarum personarum* 69.

81 "A true affirmation of the good" is the equivalent at this point in Lonergan's development of what is meant by "judgment of value."

82 See Lonergan, *The Triune God: Systematics* 186–89.

83 See ibid. 188–89.

84 See ibid. Actually, there is not found in us an *intelligible emanation* of the act of understanding, *if* intelligible emanation is defined as the *autonomous* procession of act from act. It would have been more accurate for Lonergan to have said "*In nobis autem aliqualiter invenitur processio actus intelligendi.*" It can be said, however, that in the definition of terms for this thesis he uses the word *emanatio* more broadly than he did earlier in his discussion of *emanatio intelligibilis*, defining it here simply as *quaecumque origo.*

85 Ibid. 190–91.

86 Ibid. 192–93.

87 The definition is Aristotle's; more fully, "principium motus et quietis in eo in quo est primo et per se et non secundum accidens." Ibid. 192–93, with a reference to Aristotle, *Physics*, II, 1, 192b 23.

88 See Lonergan, *The Triune God: Systematics* 192–95, with reference to Thomas Aquinas, *Summa theologiae*, 1, q. 13, a. 8 c. and ad 2m; a. 11 c. and ad 1m.

89 See above, p. 182.

90 All of this should be complemented by reading chapter 19 of *Insight*. Lonergan writes elsewhere that he wishes philosophy of God to be included in systematics rather than taught separately in philosophy departments with no link to the systematic-theological questions. The present context would certainly be one place where a full treatment of Lonergan's philosophy of God would be appropriate. For Lonergan's comments in this regard, see *Philosophical and Theological Papers 1965–1980* 159–218, and *Method in Theology* 335–40. The most relevant secondary source remains Bernard J. Tyrrell's *Bernard Lonergan's Philosophy of God* (Notre Dame, IN: University of Notre Dame Press, 1974).

91 See Bernard Lonergan, "The Natural Desire to See God," *Collection* 81–91, and more fully Lonergan's early systematic treatise "De ente supernaturali," now translated as "The Supernatural Order" in Bernard Lonergan, *Early Latin Theology* 78–255.

92 Lonergan, *Insight* 681, 683.

93 See Lonergan, *The Triune God: Systematics* 196, 198.

94 (1) God's act of understanding is God's substance, (2) God's nature is God's act of understanding, and (3) intellectual creatures are in the image of God because they have a specific likeness to God.

95 See ibid. 198.

96 Ibid.

97 Ibid.

98 Ibid. 198, 200. As Lonergan's solution readily suggests, the problem that he is talking about is much less acute theoretically in an intentionality analysis

than in a faculty psychology, and much less acute existentially in a person who has appropriated the full range of the dynamics of intentionality (both from below and from above, I might add) than in one who has not.

99   Ibid. 200.

100   "This is the difference between intellect and will, that the will's operation terminates at things, where good and evil are found, while that of intellect terminates in the mind, where we find the true and the false … Therefore, the will does not have anything proceeding in itself from itself except by way of a procession of an operation, whereas the intellect has in itself something proceeding from itself not only by way of a procession of an operation but also by way of the procession of something operated."

101   This suggests the magnificent argument of Aquinas in *Summa contra Gentiles,* 4, c. 11.

102   See ibid. 200–203.

103   See above, p. 148.

104   Robert M. Doran, "The Starting Point of Systematic Theology," *Theological Studies* 67 (2006) 759.

105   See Frederick E. Crowe, *Three Thomist Studies,* ed. Michael Vertin (Boston: Boston College Lonergan Workshop supplement to vol. 16) 71–203.

Chapter 12

1   Quoted from René Girard, *Things Hidden since the Foundation of the World* 199.

2   Raymund Schwager convinced Girard that there is a legitimate Christian meaning of the term "sacrifice." In my view, however, we capture that meaning better if we soft-pedal the use of sacrificial language and learn the language of love. The genuine meaning of "sacrifice" is the meaning that Lonergan intends in speaking of self-sacrificing love; and that is the sole genuine meaning of "sacrifice." Girard reserves the word "sacred" for the religions of the hidden scapegoat, and the word "sacrifice" for participation in such false religion. I tried above to fill out in chapter 10 Lonergan's notion of a sacralization to be fostered, but it has to do entirely with the nonviolent message of the Kingdom in history.

3   Girard's translation, translated again into English in *Things Hidden since the Foundation of the World* 271.

4   I do not think Girard is aware of the extent to which Thomas Aquinas not only appropriated Aristotle but transformed Aristotelian philosophy. But perhaps this has escaped many Christian and Catholic philosophers and theologians as well. The major transformation, of course, is the introduction of *esse,* the act of existence, as a metaphysical element, the element that

Lonergan calls central act. This allows a philosophical theology that includes creation of all contingent reality by a God of love, and a strictly systematic theology that understands that creation as occurring through the very Word that became incarnate in Jesus. What has Jerusalem to do with Athens? Fundamentally, Jerusalem transforms Athens. The same is true of Aquinas's massive theological contribution to an understanding of nature, where "nature" is understood precisely in the Aristotelian sense of an immanent principle of movement and rest. Lonergan has transposed this contribution into a contemporary context through his intentionality analysis. For perhaps the clearest statement of the transposition, see Lonergan, "Natural Right and Historical Mindedness." This emphasis supports the notion of a secularization to be fostered, something with which Girard's sin-grace dialectic, without nature, might not be sympathetic.

5 See Girard, *Things Hidden Since the Foundation of the World* 270–80.

6 "Utrum aliud in nobis sit intelligere et aliud verbum." Lonergan, *The Triune God: Systematics* 202.

7 See Lonergan, *Insight* 619: "… the extension of intellectual activity that we name deliberation and decision, choice and will."

8 Lonergan, *Method in Theology* 37.

9 Ibid.

10 See, for example, chapter 2 in Doran, *Theology and the Dialectics of History.*

11 "Cum actus ex obiecto sumat speciem, ubi aliud et aliud inveniuntur obiecta specifica, alius et alius actus distingui debent." Lonergan, *The Triune God: Systematics* 202.

12 See above, p. 294.

13 Lonergan, *Insight* 372.

14 See Lonergan, *The Triune God: Systematics* 202–205.

15 Lonergan, Insight 299.

16 See Patrick Heelan, "Hermeneutical Phenomenology and the Natural Sciences," *Journal of the Interdisciplinary Crossroads* 1 (2004) 71–88. Heelan can hardly be said to be unaware of Lonergan's cognitional theory, and he is filling out some very important elements in that theory in much of his own work.

17 Lonergan, *The Triune God: Systematics* 202–205.

18 See, for example, Lonergan, *Method in Theology* 335: "For Kant understanding (*Verstand*) was the faculty of judgment. It is a view with antecedents in Plato and Scotus and, to a less extent, in Aristotle and Aquinas." The meaning of "to a less extent' is then explained, indicating where Aristotle and Aquinas are to be preferred: "For in the latter pair there is emphasized a distinction between two operations of intellect," giving in effect the distinction of understanding and judgment. Still, they did not emphasize sufficiently that the second operation is more than a conceptual synthesis. It is, as

Lonergan stresses in *Verbum,* the positing of synthesis. See Lonergan, *Verbum* 71: "The act of judgment is not merely synthesis but also positing of synthesis ... [T]he pure synthetic element in judgment arises on the level of direct understanding and consists in the development of insights into higher unities ... [Judgment] is characterized by the fact that in it there emerges knowledge of truth ... knowledge of the correspondence between the mental and the real *compositio.*"

19 Lonergan, *The Triune God: Systematics* 204–205.

20 For examples, see *The Triune God: Systematics* 204–207.

21 Ibid. 558–61.

22 Ibid. 560–61.

23 Ibid.

24 Thomas Aquinas, *Summa theologiae,* 1, a. 3 c.

25 Lonergan, *Method in Theology* 120.

26 Lonergan, *Verbum* 14–15.

27 Lonergan, *The Triune God: Systematics* 563.

28 The *Triune God: Systematics* 563.

29 Ibid. 562–65.

30 For further details on this transposition, see the section called "A Technical Note" in Lonergan, *Method in Theology* 120–24.

31 Lonergan, *Verbum* 192.

32 This is an attempt at a contemporary transposition of the following very Scholastic (and very limited) articulation of the issue: "Prima ergo necessitas verbi in nobis est ut ex perspecta causa seu quidditate in rem concipiendam procedere possimus. Nam ad actum intelligendi movemur per rerum causas seu quidditates; quae tamen causae seu quidditates non sunt res ipsae sed rerum partes vel relationes; et ideo prima necessitas verbi est ut ex perspecta quidditate in rem quidditative definitam procedatur." Lonergan, *The Triune God: Systematics* 206, 208.

33 Transposing the following: "Altera autem verbi necessitas est ut ex definitionibus et ex perspecta evidentia in res qua existentes procedamus, quod tamen non fit nisi ex perspecta evidentia procedat verum affirmatum in quo tamquam in medio ens cognoscatur." Ibid. 208. In the case of the analogical understanding of divine mysteries, a separate argument for the need of an inner word is made when Lonergan presents his fourth reason. There is always a qualification to be made regarding the truth of such understanding. This is treated probably more fully than anywhere else in theological literature in chapter 1 of *The Triune God: Systematics,* §4, "The Truth of Theological Understanding," pp. 30–59. See also Doran, *What Is Systematic Theology?* 28–41.

34 "Tertia autem verborum necessitas est ut scientias excolere possimus. Nisi enim verba universalia formarentur, totum mundum aspectabilem

numquam scire possemus, sed ad particularia experta vel imaginata relig-
aremur. Item, nisi verba exacte definita formarentur, fluxu quodam imagi-
num ad modum mentalitatis mythicae ferremur, cum numquam clare et
distincte constaret de quanam re ageretur." Ibid.

35 "Quarta denique verborum necessitas est ut ultra limites mundi aspectabilis
per analogias et viam eminentiae procedamus. Quod sane numquam fieri
posset, nisi verba interiora tum definitiva tum iudicativa formarentur." Ibid.

36 Ibid.

37 "Quia enim ex quidditate incipimus, primo requiritur verbum ut res per
quidditatem definiatur, deinde requiritur verbum ut res definita utrum
existat iudicetur, tertio requiruntur verba ut ex sensibilibus in universum
aspectabile convertamur, et quarto requiruntur verba ut ultra mundum ma-
terialem in Deum ascendere possimus." Ibid., with the translation on 209.

38 Lonergan, *Verbum* 193.

39 Lonergan, *The Triune God: Systematics* 208–209.

40 Ibid. 211.

41 Ibid. 210–11. A footnote at this point mentions *Summa theologiae*, 1, q. 14,
aa. 2 and 4.

42 It is not entirely clear just how Lonergan understands the notion of "pure
perfection." In a discussion session in 1962 he seems to show some agreement with Emerich Coreth's position that pure perfections are perfections
that admit infinity. See Bernard Lonergan, *Early Works on Theological Method
1*, vol. 22 in Collected Works of Bernard Lonergan, ed. Robert M. Doran
and Robert C. Croken (Toronto: University of Toronto Press, 2010) 279.

43 Lonergan, *The Triune God: Systematics* 211, 213.

44 Lonergan, *Verbum* 201.

45 Ibid.

46 Ibid. 202. The passages from Aquinas that Lonergan mentions are *De veritate*, q. 3, a. 2; *Summa contra Gentiles*, 1, c. 53; *Summa theologiae*, 1, a. 15, a. 2.

47 Lonergan does not argue this point. The connection seems quite appropriate to me, and so I would not be surprised if there is a greater "exigence"
in Aquinas's thought on this point than Lonergan seems ready to grant. But
this does not affect Lonergan's argument in the least.

48 Ibid.

49 See Lonergan, "The Future of Thomism," in *A Second Collection*, at 50–51.
Lonergan is quick to clarify what he means and does not mean: "I do not
mean that the metaphysical notion of the soul and of its properties is to be
dropped … But I urge the necessity of a self-appropriation of the subject,
of coming to know at first hand oneself and one's own operations both as
a believer and as a theologian. It is there that one will find the foundations
of method, there that one will find the invariants that enable one to steer
a steady course, though theological theories and opinions are subject to

revision and change. Without such a basis systematic theology will remain what it has been too often in the past, a morass of questions disputed endlessly and fruitlessly." Ibid. 51.

50 Ibid. 195. "Extrinsic denomination" is explained in Lonergan's supplement "De scientia atque voluntate Dei." "God knows that this world exists" is an extrinsic denomination from the existence of this world; for it to be true requires the existence of this world. Two simultaneous truths are posited in this one judgment: "This world exists" and "God knows that this world exists." So too, the proposition "The soul, whether in its *esse naturale* or its *esse intentionale* has been understood (*esse intellectum*)" is an extrinsic denomination from the act of understanding. It requires the existence of "an *intelligere* of soul whether real or intentional" for it to be true. Two simultaneous truths are posited in this one judgment: "An act of understanding has occurred in which either the *esse naturale* or the *esse intentionale* of soul has been understood" and "The soul, whether in its *esse naturale* or its *esse intentionale* has been understood." The matter is identical with what we saw above concerning contingent predication regarding God. See above, chapter 3.

51 Lonergan, *Insight* 22.

52 Lonergan, *Verbum* 203–204.

53 Lonergan *The Triune God: Systematics* 213. The reference is to *Summa theologiae*, 1, q. 34, a. 3 (utrum in nomine Verbi importetur respectus ad creaturam): "... in Verbo importatur respectus ad creaturam. Deus enim cognoscendo se, cognoscit omnem creaturam. Verbum autem in mente conceptum est repraesentativum omnis eius quod actu intelligitur; unde in nobis sunt diversa verba secundum diversa quae intelligimus. Sed quia Deus uno actu et se et omnia intelligit, unicum verbum eius est expressivum non solum Patris, sed etiam creaturarum. Et sicut Dei scientia Dei quidem est cognoscitiva tantum, creaturarum autem cognoscitiva et factiva, ita verbum Dei eius quod in Deo Patre est est expressivum tantum, creaturarum vero est expressivum et operativum."

54 Lonergan, *Insight* 494.

55 Ibid. 717–18.

56 Lonergan, *The Triune God: Systematics* 212.

57 Ibid. 214.

58 Ibid.

59 The discussion on possible being should, I think, be understood as having to do not simply with "possible beings" but also and primarily with possible total world orders. Again, I thank Neil Ormerod for this caution.

60 See ibid. 214–17.

61 Ibid. 217.

62 "[I]n divinis non est processio nisi secundum actionem quae non tendit in aliquid extrinsecum, sed manet in ipso agente. Huiusmodi autem actio in

intellectuali natura est actio intellectus et actio voluntatis. Processio autem verbi attenditur secundum actionem intelligibilem. Secundum autem operationem voluntatis invenitur in nobis quaedam alia processio, scilicet processio amoris, secundum quam amatum est in amante sicut per conceptionem verbi res dicta vel intellecta est in intelligente. Unde et praeter processionem verbi, ponitur alia processio in divinis, quae est processio amoris." ("[I]n God there is procession only according to action that does not tend toward something extrinsic but remains within the agent itself. But such action in an intellectual nature is that of the intellect and that of the will. The procession of the word is considered in connection with the action of the intellect. However, another procession is found in us in connection with the operation of the will, namely, the procession of love, whereby the beloved is in the one who loves, just as the reality spoken or understood is in the one who understands through the conception of the word. Hence, in addition to the procession of the Word, another procession is to be posited in God, namely, the procession of Love.") See Lonergan, *The Triune God: Systematics* 219.

63　"Sicut enim ex hoc quod aliquis rem aliquam intelligit, provenit quaedam intellectualis conceptio rei intellectae in intelligente, quae dicitur verbum; ita ex hoc quod aliquis rem aliquam amat, provenit quaedam impressio, ut ita loquar, rei amatae in affectu amantis, secundum quam amatum dicitur esse in amante, sicut et intellectum in intelligente. Ita quod, cum aliquis seipsum intelligit et amat, est in seipso non solum per identitatem rei, sed etiam ut intellectum in intelligente, et amatum in amante." ("Just as from the fact that someone understands something, there comes forth in the one who understands some intellectual conception of the reality understood, which is called the word; so from the fact that someone loves something, there comes forth in the affection of the lover some impression, so to speak, of the reality loved, whereby the beloved is said to be in the one who loves, just as what is understood is in the one who understands. So it is that, when one understands and loves oneself, one is in oneself not only by an entitative identity, but also as what is understood is in the one who understands, and as the beloved is in the one who loves.") Ibid.

64　"We take the trinitarian analogy from the fact that we experience in ourselves two processions, the first of which is within intellect, while the second is from intellect toward will ... Thus, we do not follow the opinion of Thomists in this matter, both because it prescinds from our internal experience in its conception of the psychological trinitarian analogy, and because it prescinds from our internal experience in its interpretation of the texts of St Thomas on psychological reality." Ibid. 221.

65　Lonergan, *Method in Theology* 115.

66　Ibid. 120–23.

67 Ibid. 276.
68 Ibid. 278.
69 Ibid. 282–83.
70 Ibid. 340–41.
71 Lonergan, "Christology Today: Methodological Reflections" 93.
72 Charles Hefling, "On the (Economic) Trinity: An Argument in Conversation with Robert Doran," *Theological Studies* 68 (2007) 653.
73 Lonergan, *Method in Theology* 122.
74 Robert M. Doran, "Addressing the Four-point Hypothesis," *Theological Studies* 68 (2007) 674–82.

Index

Act: central or conjugate a., 279; conscious a., 279; in God, see God: act in; implicitly defined, 222, 279; infinite a. and divine consciousness, 36, 158, 276–81, 284, 293, 300, 303, 332, 336, 339, 340, 360 n. 24; natural a., 279; real a., 279

Act from act: and autonomous spiritual processions, 183, 186, 194, 198, 203, 205, 260, 267, 278, 310; contrasted with act from potency, 186, 194, 196, 198, 204, 264, 265, 268, 311; and image of God, 199, 202, 219, 220, 226; and mimetic theory, 207, 310, 311, 312, 382 n. 20; natural and supernatural processions of, 202, 203, 220, 260, 273; and procession of concept/hypothesis from direct understanding, 193, 221, 260, 306, 342; and procession of decision from ethical insight and judgment of value, 193, 221, 260, 306–307, 342; and procession of judgment of fact from reflective understanding, 192, 221, 260, 306, 326, 342; and procession of judgment of value from existential ethical insight, 260, 263; and psychological analogy, 158, 191, 198, 260, 261, 270, 272, 278–79, 281. *See also Processio operati; Processio per modum operati*

Active spiration: identical with paternity and filiation together, 18, 28, 29, 31, 162, 171, 176; and imitating God, 219, 251, 254; and lovableness, 36–37, 55, 60, 80, 161, 167, 346, 347; and *memoria*-judgment of value (faith), x–xi, 17, 32–35, 81, 82, 176, 225–26; and non-violence, 56, 219; and *notionaliter diligere*, 18, 24, 28, 32, 34, 60 (*see also Notionaliter diligere*); and passive spiration, xi, 17, 60, 176, 177, 297; and sanctifying grace, x–xi, 17, 19, 25, 31, 32, 36–38, 40, 54, 56, 59, 60, 61, 62, 63, 64, 79, 127, 136, 137, 152, 153, 159, 167, 171, 172, 174, 219, 239, 254, 298; as uncreated relation to Holy Spirit, 31; and Word spirating Love, 25, 31, 33, 35, 54, 55, 61, 63, 152. *See also* Father: and active spiration; *Gratia gratum faciens*; Sanctifying grace

Alison, J., 214, 384 n. 44

Anthropology, Christian, 311

Aristotle/Aristotelian, xii–xiii, 21, 22, 37, 122, 123, 127, 139, 142, 195, 216, 220,

225, 246, 250, 294, 318, 320, 324, 326, 332, 334, 370 n. 3, 372 n. 13, 395 n. 87, 396–97 n. 4, 397 n. 18

Arius, 192

Aseity, 180, 181, 302, 303

Athanasian creed, 273

Athanasius, 12, 189

Augustine/Augustinian, x, 21, 33, 34, 36, 37, 72, 73, 126, 146, 161, 163, 164, 169, 171, 211, 250, 267, 352, 370 n. 3, 372 n. 13, 393 n. 69

Authenticity: affective a., 109, 151–52; and basic terms and relations, 142; and being made like God, 90; conditioned by grace/religious values, 173, 243, 245; and conversion, 203; and criterion of judgments of value, 155; and criterion of transition to genuine sacred and secular, 242–43; and dialectic of culture, 105, 244; and *imago Dei*, 290–91, 338; major and minor a., 99–100, 246–47; objectification of, 101; and personal values, 259; a. precarious, 201, 203, 236; and realm of sacred, 218, 242; and religions of infrastructure, 254; and religions of suprastructure, 255; and religious conviction, 247; and self-transcendence, 154, 203, 242, 243, 247; and transcendentals, 264

Autonomous spiritual procession: as "act from act," see Act from act: and autonomous spiritual procession; and "because"/"because of," 185, 186, 223, 264, 282, 283, 289, 320; contrasted with spontaneous processions, 185, 186, 194, 198, 204, 207, 223, 224–25, 264, 265, 267, 289, 290, 311, 382 n. 20; defined, 190–91, 194, 221, 270; and divine–human collaboration, 164; and *emanatio intelligibilis*, 183, 185, 187, 191, 192, 193, 221, 376 n. 19; exigency for,

338; generic notion differentiated, 291; in God, 280, 281; in God and in us, 281; and imitating God, 202; and love, 147; and original meaningfulness, 187, 189; and participation in active and passive spiration, 202, 219, 260; and personal values, 349; proper principle of a.s.p. is subject, 338; and psychological analogy, 149, 194, 263, 270–71, 272, 274, 275, 277, 278, 279–80, 283, 287, 291, 292, 293, 297, 299 (*see also Processio per modum operati*; Psychological analogy); and resolution of problems of mimesis, 205, 211, 218; and vocation, 217

Autonomy: divine and human, 338; exaggerated a., 324; existential a., 259; existential a. and psychological analogy from nature, 259, 261–62, 286, 290; false and genuine a., 310–11, 344; and Girard, 203–204, 206, 224, 290, 310–12; and giving the law to oneself, 114; and individuation, 114, 311, 312 (*see also* Individuation); and spiritual processions, *see* Autonomous spiritual procession; subordinate to infinite subject, 198. *See also* Act from act; Autonomous spiritual processions

Barth, K., 119, 188–89, 378 nn. 31–34

Beauty, as a transcendental, 130–31, 229

"Because": and autonomous spiritual procession, *see* Autonomous spiritual procession: and "because"/"because of"

Becker, E., 201, 382 n. 11

Befindlichkeit, x–xi, 8, 9, 37, 104, 189, 201, 229, 244, 264–65, 366 n. 36, 371 n. 9, 393 n. 72

Being: analogy of, 287–88; becomes notion of b., 337; and consciousness,

95, 223; as everything about everything, 224, 264, 294; goodness of,
167; idea of, 293, 300; intelligibility
of, 184–85; intention of, 96, 199, 224,
264, 289, 294, 330–31; knowledge of,
294, 306, 319, 330; notion of, 196,
294; as object of intellect, 302; as objective of pure desire to know, 196,
294, 295, 319, 324; passionateness of,
7, 131, 199–200, 353 n. 12, 368 n. 26;
possible b., 400 n. 59; proportionate b. and transcendent b., 330; and
time, for Heidegger and Lonergan,
9; vertical finality of, 353–54 n. 12
Being in love: 73, 91, 101, 130, 153, 163,
340; as affective self-transcendence,
151–52; and Agapē, 36, 158; and charity, 137, 138, 152, 160, 172, 298; dynamic state of, 8, 23, 35, 36, 125, 150,
152, 159, 160, 174, 225, 298, 316, 345,
346, 348, 349; unrestricted, 129, 137,
138, 152, 155, 172, 345; with God, 38,
125, 151, 155, 159
Being on the receiving end of love/
Being loved, 34, 38, 39, 75, 80, 81,
103, 125, 127, 150, 151, 153, 159, 160,
166, 170, 172, 316, 340
Bias(es): and decline, 85, 212, 250; dra-
matic/psychic b., 8, 86–87, 103, 204,
211, 212, 354 n. 14; four b., 8, 86–87,
214, 234, 242, 248, 354 n. 14; and
moral evil, 235; and social sin, 88;
and total source of meaning, 102
Billot, L., 362 n. 26
Blackwood, J., 127, 128, 129, 130, 368 nn.
25 and 28
Bonaventure, 140, 372 n. 13

Categories: as functional specialty,
110–16, 121, 125; general c., 8, 9, 15,
122–23, 139–40, 142, 149, 162, 175,
188, 354 n. 14; general and special c.,

xii–xiii, 78, 113, 114, 116, 135, 139, 140,
162, 163, 175, 364 n. 60, 370 n. 3, 372
n. 13; Heidegger and theological c.,
9; metaphysical c., 268–69, 288, 290;
methodological c., ix, xi, 18, 21, 108,
110, 111, 142, 291; special c., 35, 38,
112, 127, 135, 140, 141, 150, 161, 163,
175, 372–73 n. 14
Chalcedon, Council of, xii, 32, 94
Charity: as accident in will, 22; as analogue for Holy Spirit, 81, 167, 168,
173, 287, 386 n. 8; and antecedent
universal willingness, 35, 81, 137, 152,
153; and assent to gift of God's love,
25; as dynamic state of being in love
without restrictions, 36, 137, 152, 159,
160, 172, 298; and faith (judgment
of value), 25, 33, 34, 76, 80, 81, 136,
138, 150, 153, 159, 171–72, 176, 202,
349; and fifth level of consciousness,
114, 125–26; and four-point hypothesis, 19, 58, 59, 137, 164, 168, 251; and
methodological transposition, 22, 23,
127, 349; and mission of church, 57,
86; and non-violence, 56, 57, 75, 76,
86, 90, 159, 160, 202, 214; as participation in Holy Spirit, xi, 17, 18, 25,
32, 35, 37, 38, 40, 54, 57, 63, 80, 86,
152, 159, 172; and passive spiration,
x–xi, 17, 18, 19, 32, 34, 54, 57, 59,
60, 63, 80, 127, 136, 152, 159, 161–62,
167, 239, 251, 254, 386 n. 8; proceeds
from *memoria*-faith, xi, 18, 35, 81, 160,
176; and psychological analogy, *see*
Psychological analogy: new form of;
and relation to Father and Son, x–xi,
18, 19, 25, 32, 35, 37, 38, 40, 80, 202,
358 n. 17 (*see also* Father: and charity); and sanctifying grace, x, 17, 18,
22, 23, 25, 27, 32, 35, 37, 38, 54–55,
60, 84, 96–97, 126–27, 136, 145, 150,
151, 167, 172, 214, 233, 356 n. 4, 357 n.

12 (*see also* Religiously differentiated consciousness); and solution to problem of evil, 76; and special basic relations, 35, 39, 172; and state of grace, 56; universalist c., 81

Chasm, as methodological problem, 109

Chenu, M.-D., 249–50

Christology: and divine and human consciousnesses and knowledge of Jesus, see Jesus; and dogmatic-theological context, see Dogmatic-theological context; and historical causality of Jesus, 13, 16; Logos-C. and Spirit-C., 170; and Pneumatology, 170; and redemption, 13; and structure of systematic theology, 12; updating of, 16

Church: mission of, 40, 57, 106 (*see also* Mission(s)); as mission, 63, 212; and mutual self-mediation, 66; and secularization, 249–50; as servant on mission, 106–107, 212; and structure of systematic theology, xii, xiii, 11, 12, 13, 14–15, 16, 57, 163, 175

Circumincession, 305, 350

Collective responsibility: 98; and fourth stage of meaning, 130; and invisible mission of Word, 249, 251; and scale of values, 86; and social grace, 99, 387 n. 35. *See also* Community

Communications, as functional specialty, 111, 113, 114, 116, 120, 121, 122, 125, 127

Community: and collective responsibility, 86, 130; defined, 78; dialectic of, 84, 86, 87, 102, 103, 105, 106, 162, 173, 243, 371 n. 9; divine c., 106; and divine missions, 69; and fifth level, 125, 130, 368 n. 29; and mediation of divine love, 103; as mission of church, 57; new c., 231–37, 239–40; of

religions, 74, 78, 80–81, 123, 124, 125; and social values, 83–84, 88–89, 106, 141, 173, 259

Conclusions: role of in theological argumentation, 272, 273, 274–75; and *scientia*, 277; c. theology, 273, 274–75

Conflict resolution, three steps in, 213–14

Congar, Y., 366 n. 9

Consciousness: and active and passive potencies, 327; and being, 95, 223; of Christ, *see* Jesus; complete circle of, 305; conceived as perception, 332; contraction of and basic sin, 235; data of, 319, 320, 328, 329, 330; divine c., 28, 66, 153, 233, 278, 280–81, 284, 285, 304, 305, 307, 339; dynamism of intellectual/spiritual c., 195, 198, 221–24, 264–65, 270, 278, 280, 288–90, 338, 343; emerging religious c., 66, 74–75; exigencies of, 196, 264–65; and grace, 17, 34, 98, 106, 125, 127, 128, 129, 153, 171, 172, 260, 310; and grounding of terms and relations, 21–22, 143, 144; heightening of, 143; as intentionality and psyche, 8, 9, 102–105, 131, 140, 145, 165, 194, 196, 197, 200–202, 204, 224, 315, 354 n. 13, 365 n. 24; interpersonal level of, 101, 112, 125–31, 341, 368 n. 29, 369 n. 30; levels of, 11, 91, 101, 112, 114, 125–31, 324; normativity of, 91; not knowledge, 95, 126; and obediential potency, *see* Obediential potency; and psychological analogy, 35–36, 145, 146, 149, 159, 173, 174, 180, 189, 195, 205, 225, 260, 261, 264, 266, 268, 270, 273, 275, 278, 286, 297, 305, 310, 316, 348; receptivity of, 324; and scale of values, 91–92, 98, 101, 106, 128; as self-presence, 94, 222, 264, 384 n. 60; soteriological differentiation of,

75, 240, 241; structure of invariant, 123; theoretically differentiated c., 151; two vectors in, 102; unity of, 128. *See also* Autonomous spiritual processions; Historical c.; Interiorly differentiated c.; Mythic c.; Religiously differentiated c.

Consequent conditions, 6, 27, 31, 40, 41, 42, 43, 47, 50, 51, 55, 57, 79, 97, 164, 168, 169, 239, 356–57 n. 4, 358 n. 21, 386 n. 8

Constitution: in active sense, 48, 55; of contingent truths about God, 41, 42, 46; divine self-c., 290, 315, 323; existential self-c., 157, 158, 173, 186, 219, 260, 261, 293; c. by meaning, *see* Meaning: constitutive; of missions, *see* Mission(s), divine: constitution of; ontological c. of Christ, 94, 95; in passive sense, 48, 56

Consubstantiality: and emanation, 158; and procession, 284, 333; and relation, 277

Contingent predication: 11, 30, 40–64 passim. *See also* Consequent conditions; Extrinsic denomination

Conversion: and authenticity, 203; and bias, 8, 102; Christian c., 25; four dimensions of, 6–7; and the functional specialty Horizons, 113; intellectual c., *see* Intellectual c.; moral c., *see* Moral c.; psychic c., *see* Psychic c.; religious c., *see* Religious c.; and self-transcendence, *see* Self-transcendence

Conviction, religious, 246–48

Coreth, E., 399 n. 42

Correlation, method of, 188, 372 n. 13

Critical realism: and correlation of operations and objects, 318; and duality of consciousness, 105; and intellectual conversion, 9; and naive realism, 142, 319

Crowe, F., xi, 67, 71–77, 124, 125, 309, 351 n. 7, 362 n. 3, 396 n. 105

Cultural values: and dialectic of culture, 105–106; and invisible mission of Word, 85, 89; and scale of values, 84, 173, 259; and social grace, 89–92, 97, 105, 106, 168; and social values/dialectic of community, 84, 86, 87

Dadosky, J., 101, 130, 365 n. 29, 369 n. 31, 385 n. 1

Daniélou, J., 249–51, 252, 257

Decision: and analogue for Holy Spirit, 35, 157, 158, 161, 171, 174, 176, 186, 191, 193, 194, 201, 225, 259, 260, 261, 269, 286, 290, 291, 293, 306, 348; Lonergan's account of, 100, 154, 155, 156, 157, 158, 161, 308, 327, 374 n. 35, 381 n. 47; and personal value in scale of values, 91. *See also* Ignatius Loyola

De la Taille, M., 360 n. 24

Desacralization, 230, 231, 240, 241, 244, 255

Desire: autonomous d., 201; dialectic of, 196–226 passim; and discernment, 196; elicited d., 198, 388 n. 6; interference of d., 196, 197; d. to know, 22, 184, 195, 196, 201, 216–17, 220, 294–95, 297, 319, 324, 330, 388 n. 6; mediated d., 205–206, 208–209, 210, 212; natural d., 201; natural d. for vision of God, 77, 129, 215, 302; radical ontological d., 209, 213, 215; transcendental d., 197, 201, 216–17, 224, 289; and two dimensions of consciousness, 103, 194, 199, 201, 202, 204, 211, 212. *See also* Girard, R.; Mimetic: desire

Development: of doctrine/dogma, 10, 11–13, 15, 16, 116, 355 n. 19;

operational d., 103; psychic/affective d., 8, 102, 104, 114, 204–205, 206, 242, 311; religious d., 38, 90, 112, 151, 233, 243, 248, 250; and retardation, 243, 245–47, 249; of theology, 11–13, 15, 16, 139, 168–75, 355 n. 19

Diadochus of Photice, 38

Dialectic: analogy of, 162, 371 n. 9; and bias and healing, 102; of community, *see* Community: dialectic of; of contraries and of contradictories, 104–105, 162–63; of culture, 105, 162, 173, 244; of desire, 196–226 passim; as functional specialty, 110, 111, 113, 116, 117, 121, 125, 372 n. 14; of history, 99, 101, 102, 162, 163, 164, 165, 169, 191, 194; for Lonergan, 104; of progress and decline, 252; of psyche and intentionality, 164; and returning good for evil, 57, 219; and scale of values, *see* Scale of values; and dialectic, 104, 105–106; and source of meaning, 98; of subject, 102, 105, 162, 243; three processes of d., 9, 15, 16, 105–106, 162, 173, 371 n. 9; and two dimensions of consciousness, 9, 197

Dicens, and *verbum*, 42, 137, 292, 297, 392 n. 61

Dicere: divine d. not *producere verbum*, 281; and four-point hypothesis, 302; *intelligere* as d., 37, 293, 336; and *verbum*, 297

Dici, and divine Word, 53, 85, 97, 326

Discernment: and charity, 86; communal d., 86; and desire, 196; and feelings, 154–55, 156, 229, 244; and Heidegger's *Sorge*, 385 n. 3; for Ignatius, 156, 295; and secularization, 252; and two ways of being conscious, 201; of value, 345

Discovery, way of, 12, 166, 169

Doctrines: and four-point hypothesis, xii, 141, 165; as functional specialty, 15, 108, 109, 111, 113, 114, 116, 119, 120, 121, 124, 125, 140, 163; mediated object of, 15, 116, 121, 140, 163, 312; revealed d., 93; and salvation history, 117, 118; and systematics, 16, 109, 120, 175, 188, 284; theological d., 11, 14–15, 50, 87, 163, 180, 183; theological d. regarding divine missions, 77–82; and theory of history, 16; understanding d., 16. *See also* Dogmatic-theological context

Dogmatic-theological context: as expanding, xii, 15–16, 170, 213; and four-point hypothesis, xi, xii, 18, 135, 139, 140, 141, 168, 212; in general, 11–14; for Lonergan, 355 n. 20; as Trinitarian, Christological, and Pneumatological, 11, 12, 13, 14, 15, 17, 18, 57, 355 n. 20; and unified field structure, xii, 15, 16, 139, 140, 141, 355 n. 20

Doran, R., 351 nn. 1–3, 352 n. 3, 353 n. 9, 356 n. 2, 357 n. 9, 359 nn. 29 and 32, 363 n. 56, 365 n. 33, 367 nn. 14 and 16–17 and 20, 369 n. 32, 371 n. 8, 373 n. 22, 374 nn. 32 and 41, 375 n. 48, 376 n. 17, 378 n. 35, 381 n. 6, 382 n. 16, 383 n. 38, 385 n. 4, 386 nn. 11 and 16 and 20 and 22, 387 n. 36, 396 n. 104, 397 n. 10, 398 n. 33, 399 n. 42, 402 n. 74

Dulles, A., 91

Ecclesiology: and church as mission, 63, 212; and dogmatic-theological context, 12, 13, 15, 16. *See also* Church

Efficient causality: and essential divine love, 24–25, 26, 27, 28, 42, 58, 62; and external term, 48, 58; and immanent constitution, 24–27, 42; and intelligibility of contingent existence, 331; and procession, 186, 282

Election, times of and Lonergan's psychological analogies, 129, 153–62, 295. *See also* Ignatius Loyola

Elevation: of central form, 32, 128, 129, 152, 167, 172, 298, 386 n. 8; and fifth level, 130; of knowing, 129; and levels of consciousness, 98, 106, 128, 129; and return of good for evil, 100; and sanctifying grace, 21, 24, 31, 32, 79, 202, 350; and scale of values, 98, 106

Emanation/*Emanatio intelligibilis*: and act of understanding, 187; Aquinas on, 191–93, 221; Aquinas compared to Lonergan on, 146, 183; and autonomous spiritual procession, *see* Autonomous spiritual procession: and *emanatio intelligibilis*; and "because," 185, 264, 320 (*see also* Autonomous spiritual procession: and "because"/"because of"); and consubstantiality, 158 (*see also* Consubstantiality); defined, 190, 270, 272; distinct meanings of, 180; divine and human e. collaborating, 164; in God, 280–83, 339–40; and judgment of value, 146–47, 148, 202, 308; natural and supernatural, 171, 173, 180, 202, 219; only two in God, 181, 186, 299–300, 304–307; and philosophy of language, 148; in sensitive consciousness, 223, 264, 265; and spiritual intelligibility, 184, 185; subject as principle of, 198, 338. *See also* Act from act; Autonomous spiritual procession; Procession(s)

Empirical consciousness, and reception/received meaning, 102, 190, 198, 319–20, 321–22, 365 n. 32, 379 n. 39

Esse intentionale. and *esse naturale* in God, 303; and history, 326–27; and inner words, 282, 335

Esse secundarium. See Secondary act of existence

Euclid, 296

Evaluative insight, and judgment of value, xi

Evangelization: and problem of evil, 75, 76; and soteriological differentiation, 75

Evidence: for judgment of value, 34, 36, 81, 157–58, 160, 167, 171–74, 176, 190–91, 202, 203, 219, 225, 259, 260, 261, 265, 281, 316, 342; and truth/judgment of fact, 185, 186, 192, 195, 201, 219, 222, 225, 265, 276, 282, 289, 293, 296, 299, 319, 320, 326, 328, 330, 338, 343

Evil: and deviated transcendence, 76; and evangelization, 75; and Girard, 10, 238, 240; and Law of Cross/nonviolence, 40, 56–57, 66, 75, 76, 84, 86, 90, 100, 138, 152, 153, 160, 202, 215–16, 218–20, 228, 229, 231–32, 233, 234, 236, 237, 239, 240, 255, 337, 338; moral, 100, 193, 228, 234–35, 237, 242; natural, 228; physical, 228; supernatural solution to, 220, 233

Exemplary causality, and four-point hypothesis, 59

Existential moment, and psychological analogy, 261, 290, 388 n. 2

Experience, developing Lonergan's notion of. *See* Empirical consciousness

Extrinsic denomination, 31, 335, 400 n. 50. *See also* Contingent predication

Faith: and active spiration, *see* Active spiration; and beliefs, 35, 75–76, 91, 93, 345, 364 n. 61; and charity, *see* Charity: and faith; f. ineffable, 33,

90–91; and invisible mission of Word, xi, 18, 25, 32–33, 61, 80, 87, 89, 92, 93, 136, 258; and judgment of value, xi, 17, 32–33, 34, 81, 152, 159, 160, 345, 349; as knowledge born of love, xi, 61, 63, 25, 76, 80, 89, 90, 92, 93, 94, 160, 202; and *memoria*-judgment of value (faith), reason illumined by, 6, 149, 278; and social grace, 87; universalist f., 25, 32–33, 35, 75, 80, 81, 87, 89–90, 92, 93, 94, 152, 364 n. 61

Father: and active spiration, x, 18, 31, 32, 40, 54, 55–56, 62, 79, 80, 81, 89, 137, 152, 153, 158, 159, 167, 172, 176, 177, 251, 254, 297; and *agapē*, 153, 158, 159, 181, 182, 336; and charity, x, 17, 19, 25, 32, 33, 38, 40, 54–55, 80, 81, 86, 136, 137, 138, 152, 167; as *Dicens*, 42, 292; and generation, 179, 272, 301, 313; and God in New Testament, 36; and hope, xi, 25, 32, 35, 72, 81, 203, 245; and humanity of Jesus, 53, 62, 85, 97, 137, 166, 314, 337 (*see also* Secondary act of existence); and Law of Cross, 237; love of, and gift of Holy Spirit, 20, 23, 24, 28, 29, 40, 50, 53, 56, 59, 62, 68, 72, 79; love of for eternal and incarnate Son, 20, 23, 24, 28, 59, 62, 67, 72, 77, 80; and mission of Son, 71; and non-violence, 56, 159, 161, 213–16, 219–20, 251, 254, 313–14, 338; as originating love, 36, 153, 158, 159, 181, 182; and processions, 261, 272, 278, 292–93, 297, 301, 304, 315, 317, 336; and sanctifying grace, x, 20, 23, 24, 31–32, 54–55, 79, 81, 137, 152, 159, 167, 172, 254; as sending, 43–48, 50, 53–54, 57, 63–64, 77, 78. *See also* Memory (*memoria*)

Feelings: and levels of consciousness, 128, 311; and psychic conversion, 318;

self-transcendent f., 318; and values, 154, 155, 161, 318, 345

Felt sense, 159, 160, 166, 170, 172

Fifth level of consciousness, 92, 102, 112, 114, 125, 126, 127, 128, 129, 130, 131, 341, 368 n. 29

Filiation, 18, 31, 36, 40, 57, 59, 61, 136, 137, 153, 162, 167, 171, 172, 173, 174, 176, 177, 239, 297

Finality, vertical, 8–9, 104, 130, 131, 199–201, 324, 353 n. 12, 365 n. 24

First Council of Constantinople, 12

First Vatican Council, 6, 7, 18, 149, 158, 284, 287, 328

Fleming, Chris, 383 nn. 28–32

Formal effects, 11, 20, 21, 27, 28, 36, 57–64, 238

Foundations, ix, 9, 112, 113, 114, 143–44, 204, 318

Four-point hypothesis: at beginning of systematics, ix, xi, 138, 146, 165, 168, 171; and dogmatic-theological context, *see* Dogmatic-theological context; and focal meanings, 163; and four-point hypothesis; and history, 180–81; and immanent and economic Trinity, 180, 183; integrates processions and missions, 180; in Lonergan's work, 50, 51, 58, 169, 370 n. 1; and mimetic theory, 204, 251, 254; and relations, *see* Relations: and four-point hypothesis; and scale of values, 163, 292; and special categories, 161, 167, 175, 202; stated, 18, 19, 136; as systematic, xii; and Trinity in history, 19, 42, 180; and unified field structure, xiii, 19, 135, 138–41

Fourth Lateran Council, 158, 160

Fourth stage of meaning, 101, 130, 131

Freud, S., 206, 210, 245, 246, 247, 248, 249, 258, 386 n. 24

Functional specialty/specialties: ninth f.s., 8, 113, 114, 115; as objectification of normative subject, 108; schema of, 111; and world theology, x, 10, 11, 108–33

Gandhi, M., 216, 229, 385 n. 2
Gendlin, E., 103, 365 n. 33
Generation: defined, 300; and likeness of nature, 300–1; and procession, 179, 181, 186, 272, 273, 277, 279, 282, 288, 291, 300, 307; and relations, 177, 181, 182, 279
Genuineness, law of, 151, 373 n. 27. *See also* Authenticity; Limitation and transcendence
Gift: and analogy in order of grace, 81, 153, 159, 202, 260, 273, 297, 298, 391 n. 49 (*see also* Grace, analogy of; Psychological analogy: as natural and supernatural); created g., 6, 24–25, 31, 35, 49, 52, 55, 79 (*see also* Grace: created g.); differentiation of, 38; and distinction of sanctifying grace and charity, *see* Charity: and sanctifying grace; of divine person, 29; and fifth level, 92, 341; of God's love, xi, 17, 25, 33, 34, 39, 41, 57, 76, 77, 79, 123, 143, 144, 152; of Holy Spirit, xi, 20, 23, 28, 29, 30, 49, 56, 57, 74, 75, 76, 77, 78, 79, 164; and image of God, 219; and Law of Cross, 66, 86; and mission, xi, 30, 31, 55, 77, 85, 136; of participation in active and passive spiration, 60, 84, 172; of participation in Word, 79, 86, 89–91; properly said of Holy Spirit, 29–30, 36, 49, 54, 62, 63, 73, 77, 127, 297; and scale of values, 86; and social grace, 88–89, 92, 168; and special basic terms and relations, 39, 150, 177; and transcendental

imperatives, 215, 220, 242, 243, 247; transcultural, 347; uncreated g., 6, 20, 23, 26, 28, 29, 31, 49, 52, 63, 79, 97, 125, 233 (*see also* Grace: uncreated); universal, 77, 78, 125, 347
Girard, R., x, 8–10, 97, 98, 198, 203–15, 217–20, 224, 227, 230–42, 244–48, 251–57, 290, 291, 310–15, 338, 354 n. 14, 364 n. 17, 366 n. 5, 369 nn. 29–30, 375 n. 47, 381 n. 4, 382 nn. 17–21, 383 nn. 22–27 and 32–35, 384 nn. 45 and 48 and 50–52, 386 nn. 6 and 18 and 24, 387 nn. 38–39, 388 n. 46, 393 n. 68, 396 nn. 1–4, 397 n. 5
God: act in, 158, 195, 271–72, 276, 277, 279, 280, 281, 284, 293, 303; as *agens per intellectum*, 47–48; attributes of, 47–48, 182, 301–302; and basic sin, 228, 314; contingent predication about, *see* Contingent predication; as *ens per intellectum*, 47–48; as *ipsum amare*, 299; as *ipsum esse*, 287, 299, 300, 302; as *ipsum intelligere*, 287, 299, 300, 302; is necessary being, 51, 329, 333; love of, *see* Love; nature of, 301–304; primary and fundamental meaning of name "God," 74; as *Qui est*, 301; as simply intelligible, 333; as unrestricted act of understanding, 294, 297; utterly simple, 177, 181–82, 300, 301, 333; works of *ad extra*, 46
Gödel, K., 353 n. 10, 393 n. 74
Golsan, R., 383 nn. 32–35 and 37
Good: human g., 121, 293; in *Insight*, 154; in *Method in Theology*, 154; objective of transcendental notion of value, 77, 85, 146, 196, 199, 200, 204, 215, 217, 224, 229, 264, 289, 294; object of will, 305; g. of order, 83, 86, 88, 89, 163, 173, 232, 233, 244, 259; social mediation of human g., 86,

100, 350; supreme g. in redemption, 228, 231–34, 237, 255. *See also* Scale of values

Good for evil, 56, 57, 75, 76, 84, 86, 90, 100, 138, 152, 202, 218, 219, 229, 231, 232, 233, 236, 239. *See also* Law of the Cross

Grace: analogy of, 33–39, 150, 153, 166, 260, 292, 298, 305, 348; created g., 24, 25–27, 30–32, 33, 51, 56, 79, 125, 166; created g. has Trinitarian form, 33, 81; as healing, 13; offer of g. universal, 346; operative and cooperative g., 100; phenomenology of, 169, 170; sanctifying g., *see* Sanctifying grace; and scale of values, 84, 106, 173; and secularization, 245–51; and self-transcendence, 84, 100, 168, 249, 258, 260, 311; social g., *see* Social grace; state of as interpersonal, 56, 106, 160, 173, 233, 235–36, 350; and supernatural, *see* Supernatural; uncreated g., 25, 30–32, 56, 125. *See also* Gift

Grace of union, 51, 52, 58–59, 97. *See also* Secondary act of existence

Gratia gratum faciens, *see* Sanctifying grace

Grund- und Gesamtwissenschaft, for Lonergan, xiii, 115, 123, 139

Günther, A. 332

Habermas, J., 248

Heelan, P., 397 n. 16

Hefling, C., 33, 90, 94, 237, 239, 254, 357 n. 11, 358 n. 28, 364 nn. 4–14, 386 nn. 9 and 13, 387 n. 40, 402 n. 72

Hegel, G.W.F., 91, 98, 115, 223, 377 n. 26, 383 n. 31

Heidegger, M., x, 8, 9, 37, 97, 98, 104, 148, 189, 190, 201, 265, 311, 319, 322, 354 n. 12, 366 n. 36, 371 n. 9, 382 n. 12, 385 n. 3

Heraclitus, 315

Hermeneutics: of recovery 246, 248, 387 n. 24; of suspicion, 224, 246, 387 n. 24

Hermeneutic structure: in science, 320; universality of, 319

Historical consciousness, 319, 326–27, 331

History: and autobiography/biography, 88–89; dialectic(s) of, *see* Dialectic: of history; as functional specialty, 108–11, 113–14, 116–17, 118, 124–25; and general categories, xiii, 8, 15, 123, 135, 139, 140, 175; meaning of and Law of Cross, 98, 245; as mediated object of systematics (*Geschichte*), 15, 116, 312; mediating object of, 116, 121; normative source of meaning in, 100, 102, 104, 131, 164, 315; peculiarity of as field of investigation, 88–89; redemption in h. as mediated object of Doctrines, 15, 121, 140, 163, 312; and religious studies, 124; sacred in h., 227–58; salvation h., 117, 118; and scale of values, 140, 163, 173, 245; sin and grace in h., 211–12; structure of, 85, 168, 245, 315; systematic theology a theory of h./theology of h., 6, 8, 10, 11, 14–16, 19, 56, 123, 141, 142, 162–65, 167, 169, 178, 180, 214, 312, 338; total source of meaning in, 98, 102, 104; and unified field structure, xiii, 19, 83, 135, 139, 141, 146, 162–65, 171

Holy Spirit: as *a se* and not *a se*, 178–82, 191, 261, 274, 307; and charity, *see* Charity: as participation in Holy Spirit; and gift, *see* Gift; and homoousion, 12; indwelling, 17, 24, 25, 32, 74, 78, 141; mission of, *see* Mission(s); as proceeding Love, 17, 24, 30, 32, 35, 36, 42, 54, 55, 80, 81, 125, 153, 172,

344; and sanctifying grace, x, 19, 24, 25, 28, 31, 32, 34, 37, 40, 49, 60, 61, 63, 79, 136, 137, 153, 159, 167, 251. *See also* Passive spiration; Procession(s)

Homoousion, and dogmatic-theological context, 12, 13

Hope: and light of glory, 41, 57, 61, 63, 164; and relation to Father, ix, 25, 32, 35, 72, 81, 203, 245; and sanctifying grace, 20, 32, 62

Horizon, and theological operations, 108, 109

Horizons: and base of categories, 110; as functional specialty, 110–16, 121, 125; as mediation of mediating subject, 116

Husserl, E., 247, 318, 394 n. 74

Ignatius Loyola, 38, 81, 129, 143, 144, 153, 156, 157, 158, 161, 216, 317, 318, 343

Imago Dei/Image of God, 158, 199, 202, 203, 218–26, 285, 291, 301, 338, 395 n. 94

Imitation of God, 90, 136, 166, 214, 218, 219, 220, 222, 225, 251, 254

Incarnation: and Christian uniqueness, 66; and consciousness and knowledge of Christ, 95; constitution of, 49; doctrinal status of, xii, 14; and dogmatic-theological context, 16; and mission of Son, *see* Mission(s); and order of teaching, xii, 77; and paternity, *see* Father: and humanity of Jesus; as personal introduction of God's Meaning in history, 135; production of, 48; and revelation, 21, 95, 241, 315; and secondary act of existence, *see* Secondary act of existence

Individuation, 8, 114, 200, 205, 206, 215, 311, 312, 315

Indwelling. *See* Holy Spirit: indwelling

Infinity. *See* God: attributes of

Infrastructure and superstructure, and religion, 250, 252, 253, 254, 255, 387 n. 399

Intellectual conversion, 6, 7, 8, 9, 87, 113, 203, 371 n. 9

Intelligere est pati, 197, 324

Intelligibilis, 184, 264, 281

Interdividuation/Interdividuality, 8, 114, 204–207, 210, 212, 214, 224, 233, 234, 236, 252, 255, 310, 311, 312, 315, 366 n. 5, 369 n. 29, 382 n. 20. *See also* Intersubjectivity

Interiority: and categories/parameters of systematics, 6–11, 13, 14, 15, 17, 18, 169, 242; commonsense i., 21, 23, 127, 142, 318, 323; as ground, 7, 11; and metaphysics, 21, 22, 127, 151; and normative subject, 8; as realm of meaning, 345; and third stage of meaning, 21, 127; twofold constitution of, 8, 9, 145

Interiorly differentiated consciousness: and categories, *see* Categories: methodological; and *esse intentionale*, 327; and four-point hypothesis, 17; and ground, 6, 21, 142–62, 171; includes intentionality and psyche, 145; as post-theoretical, 151; and psychological analogy, *see* Psychological analogy. *See also* Interiority

Interpretation, as functional specialty, 110, 111, 113, 114, 116, 117, 120, 121, 124, 372 n. 14

Interreligious: context of theology, 6, 10, 11, 13, 14, 15, 18, 65, 71–82, 110; dialogue, x, 65, 66, 78, 80, 93. *See also* Religions

Intersubjectivity, 7, 84, 85, 105, 114, 200, 218, 250, 252, 311, 312, 315. *See also* Interdividuation/Interdividuality

Isomorphism, 22, 33, 91, 98, 117, 121, 128, 142, 169, 348, 384 n. 58

Jacobs-Vandegeer, C., 128, 130, 367 n. 18, 370 n. 2
Jesus: being of is divine Son, 52; companionship with and charity, xi, 25, 32, 35, 81, 202; constitution of mission of, *see* Mission(s): constitution of; Father's love for, *see* Father: love of for eternal and incarnate Son; historical causality of, 13, 16; human consciousness of, 13, 14, 93, 96, 251, 254; human knowledge of, 13, 93, 95, 251, 254; human knowledge of beatific and ineffable, 94, 98; human knowledge of and revelation, 87, 93, 97, 98, 251, 254, 256 (*see also* Revelation: and visible mission of Word); and Law of Cross, 236–40, 256; and mission of Spirit, 10, 12, 75, 78; and preaching of reign of God, 83, 86, 87, 313, 314, 363 n. 58; resurrection of., 15, 16, 66, 236; as revelation of divine love, *see* Revelation: and visible mission of Word (*see also* Incarnation: and revelation); and secondary act of existence, *see* Secondary act of existence; and social grace, 87
John: First Letter of, 35, 36, 38, 43, 44, 45, 60, 144; Gospel of, 24, 29, 43, 44, 45, 53, 63, 73, 166, 213, 254, 314; prologue to Gospel of, 314
John of St Thomas, 340, 342, 343
Judgment: and actual intelligibility, 184; and community, 78; and elevation, 129; as intelligible emanation/autonomous procession, 184, 192–93, 201; and objectivity, 91; and reflective understanding, 184, 186, 190–91, 194, 201, 225, 260, 269, 270, 282, 296, 317, 326, 328, 330, 380 n. 42

Judgment of value: and active spiration, *see* Active spiration: and *memoria*-judgment of value; as analogue for Son/Word, 153, 202, 262, 315; and charity, 33, 37, 80–81, 152, 153 (*see also* Charity); and community, 78; and faith, *see* Faith: and judgment of value; and inner word in analogy, 145; and judgments of fact, 130, 147, 308–309, 317; Lonergan's accounts of, 148, 153–62, 374 n. 35; and Lonergan's psychological analogies, 35–36, 54, 259–309 passim
Jung, C.G., 8, 9, 104, 200, 205, 206, 215, 311

Kant, I., 318, 376 n. 19, 377 n. 22, 394 n. 74, 397 n. 18
Kierkegaard, S., 246
King, M.L., 216
Kingdom of God. *See* Reign (kingdom) of God
Kirwan, M., 383 n. 32
Knowledge, and love *See* Love: and knowledge
Komonchak, J., 126

Lamb, M., 370 n. 2
Language: corrupting l., 247; l. house of Being (Heidegger), 97; and ineffable knowledge, 93, 96, 97; insight and l., 187–90, 373 n. 22, 378 n. 35; new l. and interreligious context, 74; philosophy of l. and psychological analogy, 148; technical l., 109. *See also* Meaningfulness
Lauzon, G., 355 n. 17, 373 n. 15
Law of the Cross: and bias, 248; and church's mission, 57; as developmental process, 232; and mimetic theory, 205; and new community, 231–37, 239–40; pattern of universal, 66, 75,

86; and revelation, 98, 255; and sacralization-secularization, 227, 228, 229, 231–40, 242, 244, 256, 257; and scale of values, 245, 361 n. 45; and solution to problem of evil, 75, 90, 229, 231–40, 255; structure of, 236–40

Light of glory: as created external term and consequent condition, 40, 52, 57, 59; as created participation in and imitation of filiation, *see* Filiation; has special relation to Father, 19, 61, 136, 138, 162, 173, 239; and hope, 41, 57, 61, 63, 164

Limitation and transcendence, 105, 145, 366 n. 37. *See also* Genuineness

Lindbeck, G., 188, 378 n. 30

Lonergan, B.: works referred to: "Analysis fidei," 129, 368 n. 22; "Christology Today," 35, 152, 153, 359 n. 30, 376 n. 16, 385 n. 66, 402 n. 71; *De Deo trino: Pars dogmatica*, 169, 375 n. 49; *De Deo trino: Pars systematica*, ix, 19, 135, 147, 149, 233, 261, 262, 295, 298, 299, 317, 356 n. 3, 370 n. 1; "De ente supernaturali" ("The Supernatural Order"), 28, 356–57 n. 4, 357 n. 12, 365 n. 26, 395 n. 91; "De scientia atque voluntate Dei" ("God's Knowledge and Will"), 400 n. 50; "Dimensions of Meaning," 148, 258, 352–53 n. 7, 388 n. 48; *De Verbo incarnato*, 231, 233, 234, 386 n. 5; *Divinarum personarum*, 19, 135, 147, 149, 262, 299, 351 n. 5, 356 n. 3, 370 n. 1, 374 n. 35, 388 n. 1, 389 n. 8, 394 n. 80; *Early Latin Theology*, x, 351 n. 6, 356–57 n. 4, 357 nn. 6–7 and 12, 358 n. 22, 368 n. 22, 371 n. 7, 395 n. 91; *Early Works on Theological Method 1*, 354 n. 13, 355 nn. 17–18, 357 n. 13, 365 n. 30, 367 n. 11, 373 n. 14, 378 n. 28, 399 n. 42; *Early Works on Theological Method 2*, 353 n. 10, 366 n. 1; *For a New Political Economy*, 374 n. 38; "The Future of Thomism," 399 n. 49; *Grace and Freedom*, 356 n. 24, 365 n. 26; "Horizons and Transpositions," 370 n. 2; *Insight*, 6, 9, 75, 76, 98, 99, 100, 104, 105, 113, 114, 124, 128, 137, 139, 146, 148, 149, 151, 153–58, 161, 182, 184–87, 191, 192, 197, 201, 211, 216, 233, 234, 248, 250, 261, 262, 293, 294, 295, 298, 299, 303, 317, 318, 319, 322, 324, 327, 335, 343, 352 n. 4, 353 n. 10, 354 n. 14, 361 nn. 43–44, 363 n. 55, 365 nn. 23 and 32, 370 n. 6, 373 n. 27, 374 nn. 34–35, 376 nn. 15 and 20, 377 n. 22, 378 n. 37, 380 nn. 43–44, 381 n. 47, 384 nn. 53 and 58 and 60, 386 n. 7, 389 nn. 6–7 and 10, 391 n. 52, 393 nn. 67 and 69 and 72 and 74, 395 nn. 90 and 92, 397 nn. 7 and 11 and 15, 400 nn. 51 and 54–55; "*Insight*: Preface to a Discussion," 377 n. 25; "*Insight* Revisited, 364 n. 2, 373 n. 31; *Macroeconomic Dynamics*, 374 n. 38; "The Mediation of Christ in Prayer," 377 n. 23, 383 n. 39; *Method in Theology*, xiv, 9, 20, 23, 35, 39, 71, 83, 89, 101, 103, 109, 112, 113, 117, 124, 139, 150, 154–58, 161, 175, 184, 293, 294, 317, 318, 344, 348, 352 nn. 2 and 5, 353 nn. 8 and 11, 355 n. 22, 357 nn. 8 and 10, 359 n. 35, 361 n. 40, 361 n. 1, 363 nn. 45 and 51–54, 364 nn. 59–61, 364 nn. 1 and 3, 365 nn. 22 and 25, 366 nn. 2 and 4 and 8, 367 nn. 10 and 15, 370 nn. 2–3, 372 n. 14, 373 nn. 15–16 and 23 and 25–26 and 29–30, 374 n. 35, 375 n. 52, 375 n. 3, 376 n. 19, 378 n. 36, 382 nn. 13–14, 384 n. 43, 385, n. 61, 387 n. 25, 388 n. 2, 389 n. 19, 393 nn. 70–72, 95 n. 90, 398 nn. 8 and 18, 398 nn. 25 and 30, 401 nn. 65–66, 402 n. 73; "Mission and the Spirit," 130, 353 n. 12, 368 n. 26, 375 n. 46, 381 n. 10; "The Natural Desire to See God," 129, 367 n. 21, 395 n. 91; "Natural Right and Historical Mindedness," 98, 99, 100, 102, 130, 162, 164, 353 n. 12, 364 n. 18, 365 nn. 22 and 24 and 27, 368 n. 27, 374 n. 37, 375 n. 45, 381 n. 9, 385 n. 65, 387 n. 35, 397 n. 4; Notes on sanctifying grace, x, 19–32, 36, 57, 126; "The Ongoing Genesis of Methods," 367 n. 13, 382 n. 15; *The Ontological and Psychological Constitution of Christ*, 51, 361 n. 34, 364 n. 15, 373 n. 18, 384 n. 60, 389 n. 10; "Openness and Religious Experience," 129, 367 n. 19; *Phenomenology and Logic*, 353 n. 10; *Philosophical and Theological Papers 1958–1964*, 384 n. 59; *Philosophical and Theological Papers 1965–1980*, 395 n. 90; "Philosophy and the Religious Phenomenon," 130, 368 n. 28; "A Post-Hegelian Philosophy of Religion," 388 and nn. 2–3; "Prolegomena to the Study of the Emerging Religious Consciousness of Our Time," 74, 362 n. 2, 363 n. 50; "Questionnaire on Philosophy," 366 n. 35, 366 n. 7, 371 n. 10; "Reality, Myth, Symbol," 353 n. 12; "The Redemption," 386 n. 12; Regis College 1969 lectures on method, 11, 376 n. 19; "Religious Knowledge," 387 n. 26, 394 n. 74; "Sacralization and Secularization," 227, 240, 249, 250, 385 n. 1, 386 nn. 14–15 and 22 and 23, 387 n. 27, 388 n. 43 and 47; *Topics in Education*, 378 n. 28; *The Triune God: Doctrines*, 351 n. 8, 368 n. 16, 375 n. 49; *The Triune God: Systematics*, ix, 19, 41, 51, 55, 57, 65, 67, 103, 130, 138, 146, 157, 170, 179, 260, 298, 306, 309, 310, 316, 317, 325, 328, 329, 332, 344, 348, 351 n. 4, 355 n. 21, 356 nn. 1 and 4, 357 n. 5, 358 nn. 21 and 27, 359 n. 1, 360 n. 20, 361 nn. 33 and 36 and 41–42, 362 nn. 4–6 and 11–12 and 16, 363 nn. 39–44, 365 n. 28, 366 nn. 34 and 38, 368 n. 23, 370 n. 4, 374 n. 36, 375 n. 50, 375 nn. 1 and 4–6, 376 nn. 13–14, 378 n. 27, 379 nn. 38–39, 380 nn. 40 and 44, 381 nn. 45–50, 381 nn. 1 and 5 and 8, 384 nn. 57 and 59–60, 385 nn. 62–63, 388 nn. 1 and 4, 389 nn. 8–9 and 11–12 and 16–18 and 20–22, 390 nn. 25 and 28–36 and 39–43 and 45, 391 nn. 46–51, 392 nn. 53–60 and 62–63, 393 nn. 64 and 74, 394 nn. 77–79, 395 nn. 82–88 and 93 and 95–98, 396 nn. 99 and 102, 397 nn. 6 and 11–12 and 14 and 17, 398 nn. 19–23 and 27–29 and 32–33, 399 nn. 34–37 and 39–41 and 43, 400 nn. 53 and 56–58 and 60–61, 401 nn. 62–64; *Understanding and Being*, 394 n. 76; *Verbum*, 146, 184, 185–86, 188, 191, 192, 197, 279, 281, 294, 295, 296, 320, 324, 325, 329, 331, 333, 334, 335, 336, 377 nn. 21 and 25–26, 378 nn. 28–29, 380 n. 44, 381 n. 3, 385 n. 64, 388 n. 5, 390 nn. 26–27 and 38 and 41, 398 nn. 18 and 26 and 31, 399 n. 38 and 44–46, 400 n. 52

Louis, R.M., 385 n. 3

Lovableness, and active spiration, 36–37, 55, 60, 80, 161, 167, 346, 347

Love: avowal of, 73, 91, 93; being in love, *see* Being in love; as charity, *see* Charity; of enemies, 56, 76, 86, 100, 161, 212–16, 219–20, 228, 239, 251, 254, 313–14, 369 n. 29 (*see also* Law of the Cross); essential divine l., 24, 26–28, 42, 55, 56, 58, 62, 64, 79; and faith, *see* Faith: as knowledge born

of love; of Father, and gift of Holy
Spirit, *see* Father: love of, and gift
of Holy Spirit; of Father for Son, *see*
Father: love of for eternal and incarnate Son; and fifth level, *see* Charity:
and fifth level of consciousness; as
first gift, 30, 73; gift of God's l., *see*
Gift: of God's love; and hope, 41, 57,
61; and judgment of value, 33, 35 (*see
also* Judgment of value); and knowledge, 147, 160, 305–307, 345–47, 379
n. 39; notional divine l., 24, 26–28,
32, 42, 54, 55, 56, 58, 62, 64, 67, 79;
passively spirated l. in God, *see* Holy
Spirit; and presence of beloved in
lover, 101, 130, 340–50, 401 n. 62;
Proceeding Love, *see* Holy Spirit; and
sanctifying grace, xi, 33–34, 38, 40,
55, 60, 61, 62, 75, 79–80, 81, 90, 103,
125–27, 137, 144, 151, 153, 159, 160,
172, 174, 202, 239, 260, 298, 316; and
special basic terms, 39, 177; three
forms of (intimacy, community, love
of God), 8, 114, 125, 151–53, 200–201,
315, 341, 348

Macroeconomics, and general categories, 162, 374 n. 38
Matthew 5.43–45, 56, 159, 214, 215, 216,
314, 384 n. 54, 387 n. 41
Maturity, religious, 245
McShane, P., 365 n. 29
Meaning: carriers of, 96, 97, 109, 121,
137, 322, 327; common m., 78, 89,
369 n. 29; constitutive m., 105, 122,
189; constitutive m. of church, xii,
6, 8, 9, 11, 119, 122, 139, 175; and cultural values, 84, 86, 88, 89–90, 92;
divine m., 1, 87, 97, 106, 136, 137, 327;
elemental m., 93, 189, 237; focal m.,
163, 374 n. 40; fourth stage of, 101,
130, 131; functions of, 327; incarnate
m., 78, 93, 99, 136, 249, 251, 327; and
interpretation as functional specialty,
116, 121; linguistic m., 78, 93, 96, 97,
99, 136; metaphysics and control of,
21, 127, 151; normative source of, 100,
102, 104, 131, 164, 315; and phases of
theology, 116–17, 119–22; potential
m., 322; praxis of, 121; realms of, 327,
345; received m., 102, 103, 190, 198,
221, 322, 378–79 n. 38; and revelation, *see* Revelation; and social grace,
see Social grace; soteriological m.,
107 (*see also* Law of the Cross); stages
of, 21, 127, 151, 357 n. 8, 365 n. 22; as
term of operation, 117; total and dialectical source of, 98, 102, 104; world
mediated by, 105, 319, 321, 325, 326,
327, 328, 329, 331
Meaningfulness, ordinary and original,
187, 189, 190, 198–99, 255, 294, 316,
322, 323, 379 n. 38, 393 n. 69
Mediation: of cultural matrices and religion, xiii, 65; of desire, 205, 206,
208, 210; of general and special categories, 163; m. of mediating subject, 116; and mission, 44; mutual
self-m., 65, 66, 122, 123, 213, 215, 367
n. 9; from past into present, 115–16;
from present into future, 115–16; m.
of procession by consciousness, 223,
224, 254; self-m., 66; social m. of
good, 86, 100, 350
Memory (*memoria*): and charity, *see*
Charity: proceeding from *memoria*;
and conscious representation of *gratia gratum faciens*, 37; m. and faith as
participation in active spiration, *see*
Active spiration: and *memoria*; and
four-point hypothesis, *see* Four-point
hypothesis; and lovableness, *see* Lovableness; and paternity, 18, 37, 81;
and psychological analogy, x, 163,

316; as retrospective appropriation of being loved, 33–34

Metaphysics: Aristotle's m. and Aquinas's categories, xii, 122, 139; and control of meaning, *see* Meaning: metaphysics and control of; and total and basic science, xiii, 115, 123, 139. *See also* Interiority: and metaphysics

Meyer, B., 9, 214, 354 n. 15, 371 n. 11, 383 n. 42

Milbank, J., 372 n. 13

Mimesis: acquisitive, 205, 210, 211, 212, 214, 217, 224; and bible, 213, 312; conflictual, 205, 213, 215; and contagion, 207, 213, 242, 245; and cultural integration, 217; distorted, 218; false m., 203; of God, 160, 166, 214, 234, 251, 254; infected m., 212, 234; and kingdom of God, 251, 254; and Law of Cross, 236, 237; and original sin, 213; positive m., 204, 216; and sin, 238

Mimetic: cycle, 234–37, 239, 240, 245; desire, 198, 202, 204–206, 209–13, 215, 217, 224; relations, 218, 242, 310; rivalry, 213, 214, 236, 245, 248, 255, 310, 311, 354 n. 14 (*see also* Mimesis: conflictual); structure, 310, 312; theory, 8, 10, 198, 199, 204, 212, 214, 218, 220, 224, 242, 291, 354 n. 14, 375 n. 47 (*see also* Act from act: and mimetic theory); violence, 211, 212–13, 215, 239, 248, 257, 311, 312

Mission(s), divine: analogy with human m., 68–69; and m. of church, 40, 44, 57, 63, 100, 106, 212; constitution of, 40, 43, 46, 47, 50, 51, 53, 55, 56, 67, 70, 169, 315; end of, 70; external terms of, 40, 41, 43, 46–51, 53–55, 63, 67, 71, 164, 168–69, 361 n. 30; and faith, xi, 25, 32–33, 61, 63, 76, 80, 87, 89, 90, 92, 93, 100, 136, 258; formality of, 71; invisible m. of Word: and culture, 83–107 passim, 248–49, 251, 328; invisible m. of Word and faith, *see* Faith: and invisible m. of Word; m. of Holy Spirit as inner word of God's meaning, 135–36; m. of Holy Spirit universal, x, xiii, 13, 65, 66, 123, 125, 244, 337; order of, 11, 65–82 passim; and processions ("who from another," relation of origin), 45, 46, 47, 50, 53, 55, 67, 77, 164, 168–69, 171, 173, 177, 178, 180, 183, 251, 254, 315; technical meaning of, 46; and theology, xiii; and universal m. of Spirit, 10, 80; visible m. of Holy Spirit, 78; visible m. of Word: xi; — and reign of God, 96–98; — and revelation, 77–78, 93–96, 218–19, 337; — and social objectification of m. of Spirit, 77; — and universal m. of Spirit, 10, 77; m. of Son/Word universal, 80; m. of Word and social grace, 83–107 passim

Mitsein, 8, 114

Mongeau, G., 383 n. 39

Monsour, H.D., xii, 371 n. 12

Moral conversion, 6, 7, 8, 87, 113, 156–57, 158, 203, 317, 371 n. 9

Moral impotence, 100, 105, 242

Murray, J.C., 120

Mystery/mysteries: and meaning of name "God," 74; and systematic theology, 6, 7, 9, 10, 18, 65, 139, 141, 149, 150, 159, 163, 166, 197, 273, 285, 329, 330, 398 n. 33; m. in Trinitarian theology, 158, 179, 260, 277, 284, 285, 333

Mythic consciousness, 231, 330

Naive realism, 142, 319, 321

Nature: analogy from, *see* Psychological analogy: as natural; divine n. communicated, 20, 23, 28, 32, 34, 50, 64, 77, 126, 301, 304, 357 n. 12; divine n. intellectual, 300, 301–304, 395 n. 94;

as essence, 301; human n. in Christ,
49–52, 59, 67, 69, 70, 71, 85, 94, 95,
137, 337, 355 n. 19, 360 n. 29, 362 n.
26; as immanent principle of movement and rest, 100, 200, 225, 301,
397 n. 4; and obediential potency, *see*
Obediential potency; as principle of
operations, 303–304; and vertical finality, 365 n. 24
Newman, J.H., 21, 296, 320
Nicea, Council of, xii, 12, 189
Nihil amatum nisi praecognitum, 35, 344–50
Non-violence. *See* Active spiration: and
non-violence; Charity: and non-violence; Father: and non-violence;
Good from evil; Law of the Cross;
Matthew 5.43–45
Notional acts, 24, 79, 170, 177, 270, 272,
394 n. 78. See also *Notionaliter dil-
igere*; Relations: and notional acts
Notionaliter diligere, 19, 24, 28, 34, 35, 55,
60, 167, 171, 172, 298, 394 n. 78

Obediential potency, 49, 51, 52, 78, 100,
101, 123, 129, 196, 215, 230, 365 n. 24
Object(s): and active and passive potencies, 323; and categories, 142; common sense as o., 98–99; of desire,
198, 205–10, 212, 213; o. of divine understanding, 333, 339–40; as end/
objective, 294, 319, 323, 324, 330,
331; fifth-level o., 130; of intellect,
302–303, 305; mediated o., xiii, 15,
115, 116, 121, 125, 140, 163, 312; mediating o., 115, 116, 121; o. moving to
operation, 319–23, 326, 330; and operations as correlatives, 109, 115, 116,
222, 318, 327; primary and secondary
o., 335–36; not a primitive notion,
323, 324; proportionate o., 331; supernatural o., 129–30; as term of operation, 294, 319–24; of will, 305

Objectivity, 91, 308
"One and the same," and Chalcedon,
xii, 12, 355 n. 19
Operations: and objects, *see* Object(s):
and operations. *See also* Functional
specialties; Horizon
Operator: aesthetic-dramatic o., 104,
131, 165, 371 n. 10; affective o., 165;
communitarian o., 165; moral o., 130;
quasi-o., 200; question as o., 327, 371
n. 10; symbolic o., 165
Order of teaching: xi–xii, 12, 138, 169,
171, 178, 189
Original sin, and mimetic desire, 213,
214, 235, 354 n. 14
Ormerod, N., 57, 237, 361 n. 44, 373 n.
19, 381 n. 4, 386 n. 10, 388 n. 5, 400
n. 59
Oughourlian, J.-M., 310–13

Participation, understood analogously
in four-point hypothesis, 136–38
Pascal, B., 21, 345
Passive spiration: and active spiration,
see Active spiration: and passive spiration; and Amor procedens, *see* Holy
Spirit: as Proceeding love; and charity, *see* Charity: and passive spiration;
and decisions, 226; as Holy Spirit, x,
34, 47, 54, 57, 62, 172, 177; and religious values, 259. *See also* Four-point
hypothesis; Holy Spirit; Procession(s)
Paternity: and active spiration, *see* Active spiration: identical with paternity and filiation together; and *esse
secundarium*, *see* Secondary act of existence. *See also* Father; Four-point
hypothesis; Relations, divine
Patterned experience, 102. *See also* Empirical consciousness: and recep-
tion/received meaning
Paul, 24, 29, 45, 73, 74, 239

Pelikan, J., 366 n. 9

Pentecost, 65, 78, 87, 363 n. 58

Personal values: and authenticity, 259; and autonomous spiritual processions, 349; and decision, 91; and dialectic of subject, 105; and religious values, *see* Religious values: and personal values. *See also* Authenticity; Scale of values

Peters, M., 378 n. 26

Phases, and functional specialties, 112–22, 124–25, 366 n. 9

Philip the Chancellor, xii, 139

Pius xii, 26, 42

Plato, 206, 325, 332, 334, 370 n. 3, 397 n. 18

Pluralism, 5, 346

Pneumatology, 10–18, 57, 141, 170, 355 nn. 19–20 and 23

Potency/potencies: active and passive, 302, 316, 323–24, 326–28

Praxis: and genuine religious word, 229; and interdisciplinary collaboration, xii, xiii; p. of meaning, 121; and reorientation of commonsense living, xii, xiii; as theological topic, 163, 175

Procession(s): analogy for, 146, 161, 166, 171, 173, 174, 185, 186, 197, 203–4, 259 (*see also* Psychological analogy); and consubstantiality, 158, 294, 333; defined, 267; intelligible p., 186; and missions, *see* Missions: and processions; and relations, 171, 176, 177, 178, 180, 195; and starting point, 166, 168, 169, 170, 171, 178, 181, 183; two and only two, 36, 291–309; ways of determining, 266–70. *See also* Act from act; Autonomous spiritual procession; Generation; *Processio operati*; *Processio operationis*; *Processio per modum operati*; Understanding: and procession of inner word

Processio operati, 186, 198, 199, 225, 260–61, 263, 265–66, 269–72, 275–79, 281–82, 306, 341–42, 385 n. 64

Processio operationis, 197, 225, 265, 269, 271, 275, 278

Processio per modum operati, 199, 261, 263, 265–66, 268, 269–79, 283–85, 287, 306

Production, in active and passive sense, 48

Progress-decline-redemption, 15, 16, 85, 101, 250, 252, 312, 371 n. 9

Psychic conversion, 6, 7, 8, 9, 113, 131, 139, 175, 194, 197, 203, 204, 211, 224, 311, 312, 318, 354 nn. 12 and 14, 365 n. 33, 371 n. 9

Psychological analogy: Aquinas's, 33, 146, 163, 191, 286; Augustine's, 33–34, 146, 163, 169; and autonomous spiritual processions, see Autonomous spiritual procession: and psychological analogy; and beloved in lover, 342; and created grace, 33; Lonergan's early p.a., 33, 145–46, 163, 191, 259, 291; Lonergan's early and later p.a. and Ignatian election, 148–49, 153–62; Lonergan's later p.a., 35–36, 147, 150, 174, 225, 348; as natural, 270; as natural and supernatural, 166, 250; new form of, x, 11, 145, 160; and original meaningfulness, 189 (*see also* Act from act: and psychological analogy); structure of, 317; as supernatural, 33, 175, 202. *See also* Act from act: and psychological analogy; Consciousness: and psychological analogy

Quiddity: as object and naive realism, 319, 320, 321, 329, 331

Rahner, K., 5, 25–26, 30, 31, 92, 119, 144, 146, 183, 223, 352 n. 6, 358 nn. 18–19,

360 nn. 24 and 29, 376 nn. 18–19, 377
n. 22

Ranieri, J., 212, 214, 242, 383 n. 36

Received meaning. *See* Empirical consciousness: and reception/received
meaning

Reflective understanding. *See* Judgment: and reflective understanding

Reign (kingdom) of God: and communications, 121; and divine meaning
and value, 97; for Girard and Lonergan, 238–39, 242; as mimesis of Abba,
251, 254; and scale of values, 83–86;
and social grace, 87, 99; and unified
field structure, 140–41, 161, 175; and
visible mission of Word, 96–98. *See
also* Jesus: and preaching of reign of
God

Relations: base of, 52; basic terms and,
11, 103, 140, 143, 144, 146, 150; derived terms and r., 39, 144; distinguished by orders and not terms, 358
n. 17; and divine indwelling, 39; r. to
each of three divine persons, 23, 24,
25, 26, 27, 29, 39, 42; general basic r.,
39, 177; and Girard's theory, 218, 235;
metaphysical terms and r., 21, 142; as
objective of missions, 69–71; special
basic r., 34, 35, 39, 140, 150, 172, 177,
370 n. 3; and state of grace, 56–57,
235; and supreme good (new community), 232–40, 255; term of, 58, 62,
79, 80, 81, 136; terms and r. identical
in God, 279. *See also* Relations, divine

Relations, divine: and consubstantiality, 277; and four-point hypothesis, ix,
x, 17, 18, 19, 27, 50–54, 58–63, 79, 85,
97, 126, 136–38, 166–67, 170–73, 176–
77, 181, 202; and missions, *see* Missions: and processions ("who from
another," relation of origin); and
notional acts, 24, 55, 62, 79, 177, 270,
272; and *per modum operati*, see *Processio per modum operati*; and processions, *see* Processions: and relations;
three really distinct divine r., 18, 176,
182. *See also* Generation

Religion: authentic r., 76, 81, 115, 217;
and culture/cultural matrix, 65–66,
118, 121, 242; false r. (inauthentic r.,
deviated transcendence), 56, 76, 160,
217, 396 n. 2; and genuine secularization, 244; redemptive role of, 250;
sacrificial r., 257, 313, 314, 396 n. 2;
theology's concern with, 117–18; and
violence, 204, 230; Whitehead's definition of, 243

Religions: Christian approach to, 72, 74,
78, 124; and contemporary context,
13, 18, 76; convergence of, 16, 66,
80; of infrastructure and suprastructure, 250, 252–55, 387 n. 39. *See also*
Interreligious

Religious conversion, 6, 7, 8, 87, 113,
203, 371 n. 9

Religious development, 38, 243, 245,
247, 250

Religiously differentiated consciousness, 6, 17, 21, 23, 40, 85, 113, 115, 127,
142, 145, 150–53, 161, 162, 163, 169,
171, 291, 318, 346, 372 n. 14

Religious studies: and theology, 117, 123,
124–25

Religious values: 10, 173; and personal
values (authenticity), xiii, 79, 106,
163, 259, 286, 316, 349, 375 n. 43, 391
n. 49; and scale of values, xiii, 83–84,
85, 86, 87, 91–92, 97, 140–41, 163,
167, 229, 243–44, 292, 349

Research, as functional specialty, 109,
110, 111, 113, 116, 117, 121, 124, 372 n. 14

Ressentiment, 214, 354 n. 14

Resurrection: and confession of faith,
12; and eschatology, 15, 16; and Law

of Cross, 213, 229, 236–40; and mission of Holy Spirit, 75; and original message, xii; and revelation, 241, 313; and sacralization, 256; and uniqueness of Christian, 66

Revelation: and beliefs, 35, 93, 140; and God's meaning in history, 135, 136, 327; and human consciousness and knowledge of Jesus, *see* Jesus; and Law of Cross, 66, 75, 98, 237, 239; and mimetic mechanisms/situation, 213, 220, 232, 312; progressive r., 73, 213, 241, 251–57, 387 n. 39; and sacred, 253–57; as theological topic, xii, xiii, 11, 13, 14, 15, 16, 163, 175; r. about violence, 213, 220, 256, 314, 315; and visible mission of Word, xi, 78, 87, 93–96, 99, 313, 364 n. 58

Ricoeur, P., 245–49, 258, 387 n. 24

Rosmini, A., 332

Sabellius, 192

Sacralization: false s., 230, 256, 257, 315; legitimate domain of, 248–49, 250, 256; to be dropped, 227, 228, 230, 240, 241, 244, 251, 252; to be fostered, 227, 228, 230, 240, 241, 244, 245, 251, 252, 255, 256, 257, 396 n. 2

Sacred: false s., 248, 250, 252; genuine s., 218, 229, 231, 240, 241, 242, 243, 248–49, 250–54, 387 n. 39; for Girard, 218, 396 n. 2; primitive s., 254

Sacrifice: animal s., 253; human s., 252, 253, 257; legitimate meaning of, 231, 396 n. 2; and passion of Jesus, 313–14; and sacrificial crisis, 218

Sacrificial: crisis, 218, 313; notion of Passion/redemption, 234, 237; religion, 257, 313, 314

Sanctifying grace: and active spiration, *see* Active spiration: and s.g. (*see also* Father: and sanctifying grace); biblical basis for notion of, 20–24, 57–59, 67; and charity, *see* Charity: and sanctifying grace; in Christ, 62; as created base of relation to Holy Spirit, *see* Holy Spirit: and sanctifying grace; as created communication of divine nature, 28, 34; as created external term and consequent condition, *see* Consequent conditions; as effect and as term of divine love, 24–25, 27–28, 62; and elevation of central form, 172, 386 n. 8 (*see also* Elevation: and sanctifying grace); as entitative habit rooted in essence of soul, 21, 22, 58, 126, 152, 345; and lovableness, *see* Lovableness; and *memoria*-judgment of value, *see* Active spiration: and *memoria*; as supernatural, 49; transcendental formal effects of, *see* Formal effects. *See also* Love: and sanctifying grace

Sartre, J.-P., 332

Scale of values: and categories, 175; and collective responsibility, 86; and consciousness, 91–92, 98, 101, 106, 108, 128, 367 n. 12; and cultural values, 84, 89, 92, 173, 259; and dialectic, 104, 105–106, 163, 173, 371 n. 9; and elevation, 98, 106; and four-point hypothesis, 163, 292; and grace, 84, 106, 173; and history, xiii, 15–16, 19, 140, 163, 173, 245; and invisible mission of Word, 85–86; and Law of Cross, 245, 361 n. 45; Lonergan's statement of, 83; and praxis, xii; and reign of God, 83–86; relations among levels of, 243; and religious authenticity, 99–100; and religious values, xiii, 19, 83–84, 85, 86, 87, 91–92, 97, 140–41, 162, 163, 167, 229, 243–44, 259, 292, 316, 349 (*see also* religious values: and personal values); and self-transcendence, 83; and social grace, 83, 87, 89, 92, 349

Scapegoat, 205, 213, 217, 218, 227, 228, 230, 256, 257, 314, 396 n. 2

Scheler, M., 214, 354 n. 14

Schwager, R., 78, 214, 363 n. 58, 371 n. 11, 383 n. 42, 396 n. 2

Scotus, John Duns, 20, 23, 148, 187, 188, 332, 377 n. 26, 378 n. 28, 397 n. 18

Secondary act of existence: base of real relation of human nature of Jesus to eternal Word, 19, 40, 51, 52, 53, 136, 166, 168; as category in methodical theology, 22, 144, 162, 169–70; as created external term and consequent condition, *see* Consequent conditions; as created participation in and imitation of paternity, 19, 40, 97, 136, 166, 171, 239 (*see also* Father: and humanity of Jesus). *See also* Grace of union

Second Vatican Council, 7, 13

Secularism, 230, 257–58, 315

Secularization: legitimate domain of, 249, 250, 379, 381–82; to be resisted, 227, 230, 240, 241, 252, 255, 256, 257; to be welcomed, 227, 229, 240, 241, 243–44, 252, 258, 397 n. 4

Self-appropriation: and fifth level, 128; and Girard, 224; as explanatory, 151; includes psychic dimension, 104, 139, 140, 204; and psychological analogy, 146, 163; required for categories, 9

Self-transcendence: affective s.-t., 150, 151–52; and authenticity, 154, 203, 242, 243, 247; and being in love with God, 150, 153; and conversion, 7; as criterion, 154, 308; and cultural values, 84, 92; and fifth level, 130, 341; and scale of values, 83

Semi-rationalism, 328

Simplicity: divine s. for Aquinas and Lonergan, 181, 182, 302, 303, 333, 334, 335

Sin: basic s., 100, 228, 234, 235, 236, 237, 239, 242, 314; s. and grace in history, 211–12; original s., xii, 11, 13, 14, 15, 16, 163, 175, 213, 214, 233, 234, 235, 242, 354 n. 14; social s., 57, 86, 87, 88, 101

Social grace, xiii, 10, 11, 33, 40, 57, 61, 83–107 passim, 168, 173, 259, 361 n. 45, 387 n. 35

Social sin. *See* Sin: social sin

Social values, xii, 9, 15, 16, 83, 84, 86, 87, 91, 100, 106, 141, 173, 259, 349, 350

Son: as *a se* and not *a se*, 178–82, 191, 261, 274, 307; and judgment of value, *see* Judgment of value. *See also* Filiation; Jesus; Mission(s); Word

Soteriological differentiation, 75, 241

Spiritual, determination of, 391 n. 52

Spiritual Exercises, 38, 81, 156, 215, 374 n. 33, 384 n. 47

State of grace, as social, 56, 106, 160, 173, 233, 235–26, 350, 361 n. 42

Subject: autonomous s., 186, 198, 203, 310; in Christ, 14, 94, 95, 101; as conscious, 222, 263–64, 384 n. 60; and conversion, 7; as criterion, 242, 317; dialectic of, 102, 105, 162, 173; elevated, 79, 128, 129; existential s., 156, 259, 261; and fifth level, 130; in God, 28, 36, 66, 181, 182, 304; and intelligible emanation, 184; in intentional and psychic orders, 203; mediating s., 113, 115, 116, 121; and mimetic interdividuality, 310; normative s., 8, 11, 91, 108, 110, 112, 113, 114, 115, 125, 243, 367 n. 11, 387 n. 35; as principle of procession, 198, 223, 264, 338, 382 n. 20; real s. and Kingdom/grace, 310–13, 369 n. 30; self-actualizing s., 200; self-transcendent s., 260; turn to, 191

Sublation, 10, 21, 105, 125, 127, 128, 130, 138, 151, 168, 201, 223, 240, 324, 327, 328, 376 n. 19

Suffering servant, 114, 229, 241, 242, 244, 251, 254

Supernatural: absolutely s. realities, xii, 19, 23, 52, 68, 81, 100, 129, 130, 136, 345, 356 n. 4; s. analogy, 33, 37, 148–50, 153, 159, 160, 162, 165–67, 169, 170, 172, 174, 202, 203, 226, 230, 260, 273, 310, 348, 381 n. 10, 391 n. 49; and consciousness, 192–95; created s. relations, 32, 35, 49, 52, 79, 81, 212; and distinction of charity and sanctifying grace, 23, 32, 36, 54; and dogmatic-theological context, 19; and elevation, 32, 130; s. end, 6, 77; s. evaluative insight, xi; s. existential, 92; formally s. acts, 356 n. 4; and four-point hypothesis, x, xii, 19, 40, 49, 50, 51, 52, 57, 136, 140, 163, 202, 76–77; s. fulfilment, 74, 77, 123, 213, 215, 230, 242 (*see also* Obediential potency); and good for evil, 159; and grace, 64, 19, 52–60; and history, 164; and Holy Spirit, 77; s. hope, 203; s. imitation, 220, 228; in *Insight*, 6; s. judgment of value, 31, 32, 33, 37, 80; s. knowledge of Christ, 96; materially s. acts, 356 n. 4; and mysteries of faith, 5; and natural, 114, 118, 120; s. order and psychological analogy, 52–60; and Philip the Chancellor, vi; s. processions, 202, 273; and sanctifying grace, 31, 34, 49, 54, 61, 68, 160; and scale of values, 163; and secondary act of existence, 76; s. solution, 220; and special categories, xiii; and theology, 6; theorem of, xii–xiii, 6, 12, 139, 355 n. 19

System: methodological meaning of, 108–11; theological meaning of, 108–10

Systematic theology/Systematics: as collaborative, 5; as functional specialty, 108–31 passim, 149; genetic sequence of, 7, 168, 175; goal of, 9; grounds of, 7, 142–61; hypothetical, 37, 53; interreligious context of, 10; mediated object of, *see* Object(s): mediated; and order of teaching, 178, 189; principal function of, 7; starting point of, xi, 11, 12, 14, 138, 141, 146, 165, 169, 173, 175; as theological theory of history, 10, 15, 16, 135, 140, 152–75; and understanding of mysteries of faith, 6

Teresa of Avila, 26

Terms, created external. *See* Consequent conditions

Thomas Aquinas, x, xii, xiii, xiv, 10, 12, 13, 21, 23, 24, 27–30, 33, 49, 50, 52, 72, 73, 77, 79, 95, 97, 100, 119, 122, 123, 139, 140, 144, 146, 147, 149, 152, 154, 163–65, 167, 168–71, 173, 174, 177, 178, 182–84, 186–89, 191, 192, 197, 203, 217, 220, 221, 225, 250, 276, 281, 282, 285, 286, 294, 296–98, 301, 302, 304, 306, 308, 319, 320, 322, 325, 330, 334, 336, 340–44, 358 nn. 23–26, 360 n. 19, 362 nn. 7 and 9, 377 n. 25, 379 nn. 38–39, 380 nn. 40–41, 384 n. 56, 390 n. 24, 393 n. 66, 395 n. 88, 396 n. 4, 398 n. 24, 401 n. 64

Tracy, D., 374 n. 40

Transcendence: deviated t., 18, 76, 203, 214, 218, 229, 310, 313; false t., 245, 257; and fifth level, 369 n. 30; and grace-nature, 250; in Old Testament, 253; as realm of meaning, 345; and revelation, 254; and vertical finality, 8. *See also* Limitation and transcendence; Self-transcendence

Transcendental: exigencies, 201, 220, 224, 227, 264, 289; imperatives/ precepts, 91, 100–1, 114, 194, 215, 218, 221, 229, 244, 258, 311, 382; notions, 146, 157, 196, 197, 199, 201, 215,

216–17, 220–21, 294, 324, 327, 328, 337, 365 n. 24

Transcendentals/transcendental objectives, 77, 130, 197, 199, 229; and beauty, 130–31

Transposition, methodical, 22–23, 27, 38, 163, 177, 291, 298, 305, 316, 324, 327–28, 348, 349, 370 n. 2

Trinity: and dogmatic-theological context, *see* Dogmatic-theological context; immanent and economic, 177, 180, 183; and unified field-structure, *see* Unified field structure

Truth, and evidence. *See* Judgment: and reflective understanding

Two ways of being conscious. *See* Consciousness: as intentionality and psyche

Tutu, D., 233

Tyrrell, B., 395 n. 90

Understanding: and procession of inner word, 95, 146–47, 185–86, 193, 197, 221, 225, 264, 267, 268, 270, 276, 279, 281–82, 290, 293, 295, 296, 297, 298, 306, 316–40; theological u., 149, 150, 163, 263–78

Unified field structure: xi, xii, xiii, 16, 19, 83, 135, 138–42, 145, 146, 161, 162, 165, 167, 171, 175, 183, 355 n. 20, 371 n. 12

Value, notion of. *See* Transcendental notions. *See also* Judgment of value

Values, and feelings. *See* Feelings: and values. *See also* Cultural values; Personal values; Religious values; Scale of values; Social values

Verbum: and *Dicens*, 42, 281, 292, 293, 297; *v. spirans amorem* (word breathing love), 25, 31, 33, 34, 35, 36, 37, 54, 55, 56, 61, 63, 67, 80, 81, 89, 118, 145,

152, 159, 160, 219, 293, 299, 309, 349 (*see also* Active spiration)

Verstehen: for Heidegger, 8, 9, 37, 104, 189, 198, 201, 322, 366 n. 36, 370 n. 9

Vertical finality, 8, 9, 104, 130, 131, 199, 200, 201, 324, 353 n. 12, 365 n. 24

Vital act, 323, 324, 340, 342, 344

Voegelin, E., 102, 254, 365 n. 31, 385 n. 3

Von Balthasar, H.U., 10, 50, 131, 140, 146, 318, 361 n. 33, 369 n. 33, 370 n. 3, 372 n. 13, 377 n. 26, 378 n. 34, 394 n. 74

Von Speyr, A., 368 n. 24

Whitson, R.E., 65, 66, 74, 361 n. 2

Wittgenstein, L., 189, 190, 325, 393 n. 69

Word, divine: and *dicere/dici*, 53, 85, 97, 137, 292; and Father, 28, 35, 36, 40, 51, 85, 97, 137, 158, 159; and graced analogue, xi, 54, 153, 172 (*see also* Psychological analogy); mission of, *see* Mission(s); sharing in, 29–30. *See also* Secondary act of existence; *Verbum*: *v. spirans amorem*

Word, inner: and faith, xi, 33, 34, 35, 36, 37, 61, 63, 80, 81, 90; and judgment of value, *see* Judgment of value. *See also* Faith; Social grace; Understanding: and procession of inner word

Word, outer: and avowal of love, 73; and beliefs, 89, 91; and inner word, 95; and visible mission of Son, *see* Mission(s). *See also* Revelation

Wright, N.T., 214, 313, 354 n. 15, 366 n. 9, 371 n. 11, 383 n. 41

Zurek Lequerica, J.A., 358 n. 20

www.ingramcontent.com/pod-product-compliance
Lightning Source LLC
Chambersburg PA
CBHW031940120326
40992CB00008B/124/J